Supervision and Leadership in a Changing World

Supervision and Leadership in a
Changing World

Gary Dessler
Florida International University

Prentice Hall

Boston   Columbus   Indianapolis   New York   San Francisco   Upper Saddle River
Amsterdam   Cape Town   Dubai   London   Madrid   Milan   Munich   Paris   Montreal   Toronto
Delhi   Mexico City   Sao Paulo   Sydney   Hong Kong   Seoul   Singapore   Taipei   Tokyo

Editorial Director: *Vernon Anthony*
Executive Editor: *Gary Bauer*
Development Editor: *Linda Cupp*
Editorial Assistant: *Tanika Henderson*
Director of Marketing: *David Gessel*
Senior Marketing Manager: *Stacey Martinez*
Marketing Assistant: *Les Roberts*
Senior Managing Editor: *JoEllen Gohr*
Project Manager: *Christina Taylor*

Senior Operations Specialist: *Pat Tonneman*
Senior Art Director: *Diane Ernsberger*
Cover Art: *[To come]*
Full-Service Project Management: *Peggy Kellar*
Composition: *Aptara®, Inc.*
Printer/Binder: *Edwards Brothers*
Cover Printer: *Lehigh-Phoenix Color Corp./Hagerstown*
Text Font: *Minion*

Credits and acknowledgments borrowed from other sources and reproduced, with permission, in this textbook appear on appropriate page within text (or on page 561).

Microsoft® and Windows® are registered trademarks of the Microsoft Corporation in the U.S.A. and other countries. Screen shots and icons reprinted with permission from the Microsoft Corporation. This book is not sponsored or endorsed by or affiliated with the Microsoft Corporation.

Library of Congress Cataloging-in-Publication Data

Dessler, Gary
  Supervision and leadership in a changing world/Gary Dessler.—1st ed.
    p. cm.
  ISBN-13: 978-0-13-505865-7
  ISBN-10: 0-13-505865-1
  1. Self-directed work teams.   2. Leadership.   3. Strategic planning.   4. Employee motivation.   I. Title.

  HD66.D467 2012
  658.4′092—dc22

2010054162

10 9 8 7 6 5 4 3 2 1

Prentice Hall
is an imprint of

www.pearsonhighered.com

ISBN 10:   0-13-505865-1
ISBN 13: 978-0-13-505865-7

Brief Contents

Contents

Preface

"Everything's changing. No matter what field you work in, the earth is shifting. Any supervisors or managers who lead tomorrow like they lead today should have quit leading yesterday. Those supervisors, who intend to lead and succeed in the years ahead, need to prepare to become tomorrow's leader today." Robert Ramsey, "Preparing to Be Tomorrow's Leader Today,"

Supervision 71, no. 1 (January 2010): 7–9

A while ago I was on an overnight fast train from Shanghai to Beijing. I was in China for discussions with prospective sales representatives and joint venture partners on behalf of an engineering company on whose board I serve, and to discuss management and human resource management with students, professors, and managers who use some of my other books in China. Although the people I met with reflected a range of backgrounds and responsibilities, one thing they agreed on is that the traditional notion that China's workforce is docile and obedient was out of date. A combination of things—a new China labor law, a younger, more tech-savvy workforce, and a noticeable tightening in the labor supply—had combined to make dealing with and supervising even these traditionally "obedient" employees much more challenging than it had ever been before. Supervisors there can't just rely on "command and control": They need well-honed leadership skills, too.

As we'll see in Chapter 1, that's not unique to supervising employees in China. Most workers in the United States today tend to be technologically savvy "knowledge workers." This puts a big premium on building and supervising human capital, often in self-managing teams. *Human capital* means the knowledge, education, training, skills, and expertise of a firm's workers.

But supervising teams of self-managing workers requires supervisors who are leaders, not just order-givers. Ordering around people who should be self-managing obviously doesn't make much sense. Leading in situations like these requires extraordinary levels of patience, leadership, and coaching skills. Today, as management guru Peter Drucker once said, "You have to learn to manage in situations where you don't have command authority, where you are neither controlled nor controlling."[1] *Leadership* means influencing someone to work willingly toward a predetermined objective. Your supervision students will need to be leaders. They'll need to get their employees to want to follow the path they've laid out for them, while relying less on the fact that the company says "you're the boss." Not everyone is cut out for this kind of leadership. But, as the introductory quote says, "Any supervisors or managers who lead tomorrow like they lead today should have quit leading yesterday." Supervisors and prospective supervisors need a supervision book that recognizes that. I wrote *Supervision and Leadership in a Changing World* to fill that need. This book has three distinguishing themes:

1. **Integrating Supervision and Leadership**
2. **Supervising Culturally Diverse Employees**
3. **Building Practical Basic Supervisory Skills**

[1]T. George Harris, "The Post-Capitalist Executive: An Interview with Peter F. Drucker," *Harvard Business Review* (May–June 1993).

1. Integrating Supervision and Leadership

First, *Supervision and Leadership in a Changing World* fully integrates the *leadership and supervision bodies of knowledge*. As I explain in Chapter 1, effective supervision today requires effective leadership more than at any time before because both the workers and the work they do are changing. Supervisors need to know how to earn personal respect and how to sharpen and apply their leadership and coaching skills to influence and motivate employees. You'll therefore find, in *Supervision and Leadership in a Changing World,* two chapters (Chapter 2: Leading a Diverse Workforce and Chapter 11: Leading the Team Effort) devoted largely to building your students' leadership knowledge and skills, as well as explicit and practical research-based coverage of the full range of leadership topics in every chapter, as summarized in the following table:

Leadership Concepts and Applications	Chapter
Initiating structure, central role leadership plays in supervision	Chapter 1 The Supervisor's Role in a Changing World
Leadership approaches including **great man/trait, behavioral styles, transformational, leadership continuum, contingency,** and **integrative; Ohio State and Michigan** studies	Chapter 2 Leading Today's Diverse Workforce
Importance of decisiveness in leadership; role of decisiveness in **Heroic Leadership theory** and **Trait Leadership** Theory	Chapter 3 Solving Problems and Making Decisions
Participative vs. Autocratic Goal Setting	Chapter 4 Planning and Setting Goals
Hersey's Situational Leadership® **Model;** the **leadership continuum, Close vs. General Leadership**	Chapter 5 Understanding How to Control Work Processes
Initiating structure; instrumental leadership and **Path Goal theory; Substitutes for Leadership** theory	Chapter 6 Organizing Jobs and Work
Pygmalion leadership effect	Chapter 7 The Supervisor's Role in Equal Employment
Leadership traits and testing and selecting leaders	Chapter 8 How to Interview and Select Employees
Building **transformational leadership skills**	Chapter 9 Training and Developing Employees
Charismatic leadership	Chapter 10 Using Motivation and Incentives
Dyadic leadership theory, **LMX leadership** theory, **distributed leadership**	Chapter 11 Leading the Team Effort
Servant/Follower–based leadership	Chapter 12 Coaching and Communicating Skills for Leaders
LMX theory; dyadic leadership	Chapter 13 Appraising and Managing Performance
Autocratic leadership	Chapter 14 Supervising Ethics, Fair Treatment, and Discipline at Work
Leadership consideration and **interpersonal skills**	Chapter 15 Supervising Grievances and Labor Relations
Leadership and culture	Chapter 16 Protecting Your Employees' Safety and Health

2. Supervising Culturally Diverse Employees

Second, students will be supervising the most culturally diverse workforce in U.S. history. For example, we'll see in Chapter 1 that the Hispanic and Asian workforce segments will grow much faster than will the white, Millennials are entering the workforce and the average age of the U.S. workforce is rising. Tomorrow's supervisors must be skilled at managing diversity—maximizing diversity's potential advantages while minimizing the potential barriers, such as prejudices and bias. Managing diversity isn't easy. For one thing, we'll see that even supervisors who view themselves as unprejudiced often jump to conclusions about people based on little more than how they look or the groups to which they belong. Studying this book should better position your students to supervise in this new environment.

3. Building Practical Basic Supervisory Skills

Finally, students need the basic supervisory skills required for doing supervisory work. Unlike top managers, there's not much theoretical about what supervisors do. They're always on the front line, actually making work assignments, sizing up employees, and interviewing prospective team members. That's why every chapter in *Supervision and Leadership in a Changing World* develops tested and practical supervisory skills that your students can apply starting the first day they're on their jobs, from how to interview job applicants (Chapter 8: Selection and Interviewing), to how to reduce unsafe accident-causing conditions (Chapter 16: Employee Safety). For example, supervisors get things done through others, and so knowing how to delegate is a crucial supervisory skill. So Chapter 6 (Organizing) lists and illustrates Principles of Effective Delegation, including Clarify the Assignment, Delegate, Don't Abdicate, Know What to Delegate, Specify the Subordinate's Range of Discretion, Authority Should Equal Responsibility, Make the Person Accountable for Results, and Beware of Backward Delegation. *Supervision and Leadership in a Changing World* focuses on these skills in Chapters 3–16.

Organization of the Book

There are many ways to organize a book such as this. None is perfect. I tend to think sequentially. I therefore organized it (after Part 1) to start with the supervisory tasks involved with planning and organizing the work (Part 2), then to get employees up to speed on their jobs (Part 3), then to lead and motivate them to do the jobs they're on (Part 4), and finally to appraise and supervise their work-related issues (Part 5).

Important Features of the Book

I've used two boxed features to illustrate and emphasize the book's two main themes, namely, *integrating supervision and leadership* and *supervising a diverse workforce*.

Leadership Applications for Supervisors Features

Each chapter's **Leadership Applications for Supervisors** feature illustrates chapter-relevant leadership concepts and skills. Each presents explicit, practical, and research-based leadership applications that supervisors can use every day with employees. For example, Applying Hersey's Situational Leadership® Model and Taking Corrective Action with the Right Leadership Style in Chapter 5 (control) describes a football coach who saw his big game evaporate when his young kicker flubbed a 10-yard kick. How should the coach act now? Autocratically tell the young kicker he's off the team? Try participative management? The coach could apply the Hersey model here. For example, *delegating* works best when followers are willing to do the job and are able to (know how to) go about doing it. *Participating* works best when followers are able to do the job, but are unwilling and so require emotional support.

Supervising the New Workforce Features

Each chapter's **Supervising the New Workforce** feature presents practical insights to help supervisors do a better job of understanding and dealing with the challenges of supervising a diverse workforce. Illustrative feature topics here include the Gender Gap in Appraisals in Chapter 13 (appraising), and Protecting Vulnerable Workers in Chapter 16 (safety). The Leading Diverse Work Teams feature in Chapter 11 (teams) notes that with the workforce increasingly diverse, eventually "you'll find yourself supervising a team comprised of people of diverse ages, nationalities, and backgrounds." What sorts of problems can you expect? How should you address those problems? We'll see how a study answers these questions. The researchers looked at 55 diverse teams. This feature shows how successful supervisors dealt with the "diversity faultlines" that were causing the problems for the teams.

Resources for Students

MYBIZSKILLSKIT for Supervision

MyBizSkillsKit contains a wealth of study aids, illustrated case simulations, and access to the Golden Personality Type Profiler Assessment. An access code to MyBizSkillsKit can be value packaged with the textbook or purchased online at www.pearsonhighered .com. It includes:

- **BizSkills Illustrated Business Simulation Cases** present students with workplace situations where they have to make the call. These illustrated case applications contain built-in feedback and scoring and can feed a gradebook, if desired.

- **The Golden Personality Type Profiler.** This popular personality assessment, similar to the full Myers-Briggs assessment program, but oriented toward workplace behavioral assessment, provides students with information about fundamental personality dimensions. It takes about 15–20 minutes to complete and students receive an easy-to-use and practical feedback report based on their results. This tool helps students improve their self-knowledge and ability to work effectively with others by providing students with feedback on their leadership and organizational strengths, communication and teamwork preferences, motivation and learning style, and opportunities for personal growth.

- **Test-prep Quizzes** for each chapter, including true/false, multiple-choice, and short essay questions; all questions include immediate feedback.

- **Web Exercises** for each chapter

- **Web Links** to useful online resources

- **MySearchlab** gives students access to EBSCO's ContentSelect Research Database. MySearchLab also includes a plagiarism tutorial, citation tutorial, and tools to help improve student writing, including the Longman Online Handbook of Writing. Preview at www.mysearchlab.com.

Also available separately:

Prentice Hall's Self-Assessment Library (SAL)

SAL is a print with CD-ROM product developed by Steve Robbins that contains 51 research-based self-assessments that provide students with insights into their skills, abilities, and interests. It is easy to use, self-scoring, and can be packaged with this text at a discounted price. Please contact your Prentice Hall representative to obtain a review copy.

Resources for Instructors

To access supplementary materials online, instructors need to request an instructor access code. Go to **www.pearsonhighered.com/irc**, where you can register for an instructor access code. Within 48 hours of registering you will receive a confirming e-mail including an instructor access code. Once you have received your code, locate your text in the online catalog and click on the Instructor Resources button on the left side of the catalog product page. Select a supplement and a log in page will appear. Once you have logged in, you can access instructor material for all Prentice Hall textbooks.

- **Instructor's Manual with Test Item File**—The Instructor's Manual for this text is available as a downloadable Word document at http://www.pearsonhighered.com under Instructor Resources. It contains multiple-choice and true/false test questions, chapter outlines and lecture notes, answers to case problems, and comments about the exercises.

- **Pearson MyTest Electonic Testing Program**—Pearson MyTest is a powerful assessment generation program that helps instructors easily create and print quizzes and exams. Questions and tests can be authored online, allowing instructors ultimate flexibility and the ability to efficiently manage assessments anytime, anywhere. Educator access to MyTest is already included in Pearson's Instructor Resource Center (IRC) Educator suite. Simply go to www.pearsonmytest.com and log in with your existing IRC login name and password.

- **Powerpoint Lecture Presentation Package**—The package contains lecture presentation screens for each chapter.

- **CourseConnect Supervision Online Course: Convenience, Simplicity, Success**—Looking for robust online course content to reinforce and enhance student learning? Course Connect courses contain customizable modules of content mapped to major learning outcomes. Each learning object contains interactive tutorials, rich media, discussion questions, MP3 downloadable lectures, assessments, and interactive activities that address different learning styles. CourseConnect courses can be delivered in any commercial platform, such as WebCT, BlackBoard, Angel, Moodle, or eCollege. For more information, call 800-635-1579.

Acknowledgments

I am very grateful for the support and advice that I received from reviewers, and from the professionals at Pearson Education and my family. In the proposal stage and as the book progressed we received many insightful, conscientious, and useful reviews. The reviewers and their affiliations include:

George Kelly, *Erie Community College, City Campus*

Daniel Montez, *South Texas College*

Tim Allwine, *Lake Community College*

Vondra Armstrong, *Pulaski Technical College*

Charles Blalack, *Kilgore University*

Joan Hartley, *Portland Community College*

David Bodkin, *Cumberland University*

Mitchell Lautenslager, *Fox Valley Technical College*

Sharon Lundeen, *Johnson County Community College*

Zack McNeil, *Metropolitan Community College of Kansas City*

Debra Walsh, *Western Technical College*

John Watt, *University of Central Arkansas*

Special thanks go to David Bodkin for his contributions to the end of the chapter material and the instructor's manual, and to Joan Hartley and Sharon Lundeen for their work, respectively, on the test item file and the companion website.

No book like this sees the light of day without the support and dedication of a competent and dedicated publishing team. At Pearson Education, I want to first thank Gary Bauer, Executive Editor for Prentice Hall, whose market knowledge and clear vision of what this book should be were extraordinarily valuable for creating this book and for keeping it on track. Without the dedicated efforts of Pearson's sales professionals, books like these often just languish on prospective adopters' shelves, and I am very grateful for the sales professionals' hard work, diligence, and efforts on the book's behalf. At home, I want to thank my wife, Claudia, for all her support and for supervising our household so that I could concentrate on my writing, and my son Derek, who is still the best supervisor I know.

To Claudia

About the Author

Gary Dessler has degrees from New York University, Rensselaer Polytechnic Institute, and the Baruch School of Business of the City University of New York, where he studied and conducted leadership research for his doctorate with Professor Robert J. House. A prolific author, Dr. Dessler's best-selling *Human Resource Management*, 12th edition (Prentice Hall, 2011) is also available in more than 10 languages, including Russian and Chinese. Dessler's other books include *Framework for Human Resource Management*, 6th edition (Prentice Hall, 2011), *Fundamentals of Human Resource Management*, 2nd edition (Prentice Hall, 2012), *Managing Now* (Houghton Mifflin, 2008), *Management: Modern Principles and Practices for Tomorrow's Leaders*, revised 3rd edition (Cengage, 2007), and *Winning Commitment: How to Build and Keep a Competitive Workforce* (McGraw-Hill, 1993). He has published articles on employee commitment, leadership, supervision, and quality improvement in journals including the *Academy of Management Executive, SAM Advanced Management Journal, Supervision, Personnel Journal*, and *International Journal of Service Management*. With the title Founding Professor at Florida International University, Dessler served for many years in FIU's College of Business as a professor, Associate Dean, and Chairman of the Management and International Business department, teaching courses in human resource management, strategic management, and management. For the past few years, Dessler has focused on his research and textbook writing, and on giving lectures, seminars, and courses at venues in Asia and around the world on topics including strategic management, modern human resource management, evidence-based human resource management, and talent management. Dessler also serves on the board of directors of a closely held corporation that designs and manufactures chemical engineering–based pollution control devices for manufacturers worldwide.

1 The Supervisor's Role in a Changing World

CHAPTER OBJECTIVES

After studying this chapter, you should be able to answer these questions:

1. What Do Supervisors Do?
2. Do I Have What It Takes to Be a Supervisor?
3. Is Supervising for Me?
4. How Have the Responsibilities of Supervisors Evolved?
5. What Does the Change in These Responsibilities Mean for Supervisors?

OPENING SNAPSHOT

Doris Turns Things Around

Jennifer Carter graduated from State University in June 2009, and after considering several jobs, decided to do what she always planned to do—go into business with her father, Jack Carter. Jack opened his first combined coin laundry and dry cleaning store, Carter Cleaning Center, in 1995 and his second store three years later. He was pleased enough with their performance to open four more stores over the next five years. Each store had about seven employees and annual revenues of about $800,000. An on-site supervisor managed each store. Jennifer's aim was to learn the business and bring to it modern management techniques. Her first assignment was to straighten out their Pompano, Florida, store.

The store was in crisis. A "boil-over" occurred last week when Ron, the store's supervisor, added water to the super-hot perchloroethylene used to clean clothes, severely burning the store's cleaner-spotter. Revenues, which should be about ten times a store's rent, were barely half that. Ten customers called Jack last week to complain of lost or damaged clothes.

Jennifer's solution, with which her father concurred, was swift: He fired Ron. He replaced him with Doris, a long-term counter person at Carter's first store in nearby Lauderdale Lakes.

Doris took charge. On day one she called an employee meeting, shared the store's financial data, and got their suggestions and commitment to improve. For a week, each night after closing, supervisors from different Carter stores met with her cleaners, pressers, and counter people to retrain them. Doris proved to be no-nonsense. She checked the quality of each employee's work, made the store spotless, and ensured each employee followed procedures. She let go Rosa, one of two pressers, when she ignored Doris's insistence on meeting Carter's 25 pants-per-hour pressing standards.

The results were quick and dramatic. Customer complaints evaporated. Drop-offs of clothes the second week after Doris took over were 50% higher than they'd been any week since Jack opened the store. "It's like night and day," Jack said to Jennifer.

1. What Do Supervisors Do?

The effects of good supervision are amazing.[1] Take an underperforming—even chaotic—situation and install a skilled supervisor, and he or she can soon get the enterprise humming. Right now, supervisors at thousands of businesses—diners, dry cleaners, motels, as well as those on assembly lines at giants like GE—are running their units with courteous, prompt, first-class service, high-morale employees, and a minimum of problems such as "You didn't press my pants." What do you think would happen if we took the competent supervisors away and dropped in ones without training or skills? You know the answer, because you've probably experienced the effects yourself—untrained or unprepared staff, orders not prepared on time, lost reservations, dirty rooms. About 90% of the new businesses started this year will fail within five years, and Dun & Bradstreet says the reason is usually poor management.

Yet the flip side can also be true. Take a successful enterprise that's been managed well for years—say, a neighborhood stationery store—and watch as a new, less-competent supervisor takes over. Shelves are suddenly in disarray, products out of stock, bills unpaid. Studies over time confirm these commonsense observations. Companies with better supervisors have lower turnover rates, and higher profits and sales per employee.[2] It's hard to overstate how important good supervisors are to American industry.

Organization Defined

All the enterprises with which you're familiar—your college, Sony, the dry cleaner, Apple Computer—are *organizations*. An **organization** consists of people with formally assigned roles who work together to achieve stated goals. Organizations need not just be business firms. *Organization* applies equally well to colleges, local governments, and nonprofits like the American Red Cross. The U.S. government is an organization—certainly a not-for-profit one—and its head manager, or chief executive officer, is the president. And the term "organization" similarly applies to the units within these enterprises, units such as the work teams, assembly lines, sales units, and even the advisory groups that help politicians run their offices. All organizations, big or small, have several things in common.

First, organizations are (or should be) *goal-directed*. Thirty strangers on a bus from New York to Maine are not an organization, because they're not working together to accomplish some singular aim.

Organizations are also (hopefully) "organized" in that everyone has a job to do, and people know who does what. For example, even the local dry cleaner has an *organizational structure*. Employees know who does what (pressers press, for instance, and cleaners clean) and how the work (in this case, the incoming clothes) will flow through the store and get done.

Whether organizations achieve their goals depends on how they are *supervised*. This is because organizations, by their nature, cannot simply run themselves. Who would ensure that each of the people actually knew what to do? Who would ensure that they worked together more or less harmoniously? Who would decide what the goals should be? The answer, of course, is "the supervisor," people like Doris at Carter's Pompano store.

Management Defined

We'll see that *supervision* is a special type of management, so let's start by defining management. Business guru Peter Drucker once said that management is "the responsibility for contribution."[3] In other words, all managers at every level are responsible for making sure that their units achieve their goals. Specifically, a **manager** is someone who is responsible for accomplishing an organization's goals, and who does so by planning, organizing, staffing, leading, and controlling the efforts of the organization's people. **Management** most often refers to the group of people—the managers—who are responsible for accomplishing an organization's goals, through planning, organizing, leading, and controlling the efforts of the organization's people. However, *management* also refers to the totality of managerial actions, people, systems, procedures, and processes in place in an organization (such as when someone says, "The management of that crisis was totally inept"). And supervisors, again, are special types of managers.

Types of Managers

In practice, there are three ways to classify managers. We can classify them based on their *organization level* (top, middle, first-line), their *organizational position or rank* (supervisor, manager, director, or vice president, for instance), and their *business function title* (such as "sales supervisor" or "vice president for finance").

Figure 1.1 illustrates this. The managers at the top *level*, of course, are the firm's top management. These are the company's **executives**. Typical *positions* here are president, senior vice president, and executive vice president. *Functional titles* here include "senior vice president *for sales*" and "chief *financial* officer" (CFO).

Beneath the top management level (and reporting to it) may be one or more levels of middle managers. The positions here usually include the words *manager* or *director* in the titles. (In larger companies such as IBM, managers report to directors, who in turn report to top managers such as vice presidents.) Examples of functional titles here include "production manager," "sales director," "human resource (HR) manager," and "finance manager." Finally, **first-line supervisors** are at the first rung of the management ladder. *Organizational positions* here include supervisor or assistant manager.

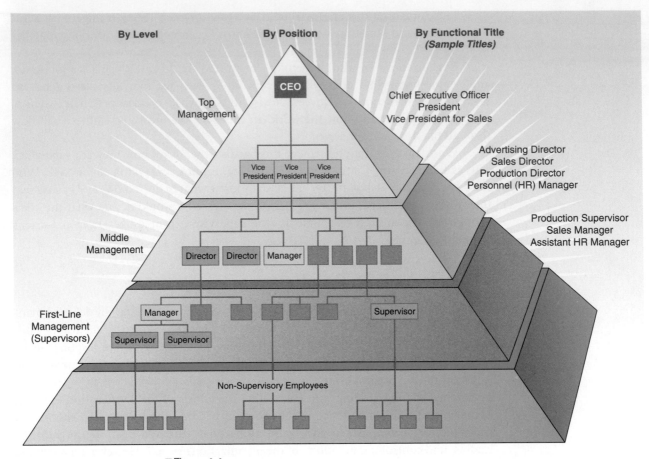

By Level / By Position / By Functional Title *(Sample Titles)*

- **CEO** — Top Management
- Chief Executive Officer / President / Vice President for Sales
- Vice President / Vice President / Vice President
- Advertising Director / Sales Director / Production Director / Personnel (HR) Manager
- Director / Director / Manager — Middle Management
- Production Supervisor / Sales Manager / Assistant HR Manager
- Manager / Supervisor — First-Line Management (Supervisors)
- Supervisor / Supervisor
- Non-Supervisory Employees

■ Figure **1.1**

Types of Managers

Functional titles might include "production supervisor," "store manager," and "assistant marketing supervisor."

Three Aspects of Supervisory Work

What Do Supervisors Do?

Whether it's a president, director, or first-line supervisor, there are always three essential aspects of supervisory work. First, a supervisor is always *responsible for contribution*—on his or her shoulders lies the responsibility for accomplishing the unit's goals. Therefore, supervising is never just theoretical. Supervisors such as Doris are responsible for getting things done. That is why former Honeywell CEO (and successful manager) Lawrence Bossidy named his book *Execution: The Discipline of Getting Things Done.*

Second, supervisors always get things done *through other people*. The owner/entrepreneur running a small florist shop without the aid of employees is not supervising. It is only when she starts hiring people and trying to get things done through them that she can call herself a supervisor. She'll have to train and motivate her new employees, and put controls in place so that the person who closes the store won't borrow any of her day's receipts.

Some entrepreneurs—the people who provide the sparks that get new businesses off the ground—never make it to supervisor. When it comes to hiring people, putting systems in place, or giving orders, they just can't cut it. The same happens in big companies, too. You will often hear the phrase, "They took a great salesperson (or engineer, mechanic, accountant—or whatever) and turned the person into an awful sales (or some other) supervisor." Bernard Baker, founder of Fuel Cell Energy Inc. in Danbury, Connecticut, handed over the CEO job several years ago. He said, "My first love was research and development. . . . I wasn't a businessman and I knew I wasn't a businessman."[4]

The third aspect of supervisory work refers to what supervisors actually do (and why some people turn out to be better at supervising than others). That third aspect is this: Supervisors *must be skilled at planning, organizing, staffing, leading, and controlling* if they are to accomplish the organization's goals through other people. Management writers traditionally refer to the supervisor's five basic functions—planning, organizing, staffing, leading, and controlling—as the **management process**. They include the following:

- **Planning.** Planning means setting goals and deciding on courses of action, developing rules and procedures, developing plans (both for the organization and for those who work in it), and forecasting (predicting or projecting what the future holds for the firm).

- **Organizing.** Organizing is identifying jobs to be done, hiring people to do them, establishing departments, delegating or pushing authority down to subordinates, establishing a chain of command (in other words, channels of authority and communication), and coordinating the work of subordinates.

- **Staffing.** Staffing is finding good candidates for jobs and then selecting, training, appraising, compensating, and overseeing the health and labor relations of the unit's employees.

- **Leading.** Leading means influencing other people to get the job done, maintaining morale, molding company culture, and managing conflicts and communication.

- **Controlling.** Controlling is setting standards (such as sales quotas or quality standards), comparing actual performance with these standards, and then taking corrective action as required.

Some people think that supervising is easy and that anyone with half a brain can do it. After all, you will find no exotic mathematical formulas in this book. But, if it is so easy, why do 90% of new businesses fail within five years due to poor management? Why did Ron fail so miserably with only six employees to supervise at Carter's Pompano store? The words in this book are easy to read. But don't let that lull you into thinking that anyone can be a supervisor or that supervising is easy.

What Else Do Supervisors Do?

"Planning, organizing, staffing, leading, and controlling" are the heart of what supervisors do, but there is more to the supervisor's job. For example, when Apple CEO Steve Jobs presented the latest iPhone to the world, he was acting as Apple's *spokesperson,* a duty his board of directors would expect him to perform as CEO.

SUPERVISORY ROLES   Some time ago, Professor Henry Mintzberg studied what those supervising others actually do. Mintzberg found that in a typical day, supervisors didn't just plan, organize, staff, lead, and control. Instead, they filled various roles, including the following:

- **The figurehead role.** Every supervisor spends some time performing ceremonial duties, such as giving team members attendance awards.[5]
- **The leader role.** Every supervisor must function as a leader, motivating and encouraging employees.
- **The liaison role.** Supervisors spend a lot of time in contact with people outside their own departments, essentially acting as the liaison between their departments and other people within and outside the organization.
- **The spokesperson role.** The supervisor is often the spokesperson for his or her organization.
- **The negotiator role.** Supervisors spend a lot of time negotiating; the head of a sales team might try to negotiate better raises for his or her team, for instance.

All managers (from CEO down to first-line supervisor) have a lot in common. They all plan, organize, staff, lead, and control. And all managers at all levels and with every functional title spend most of their time with people—talking, listening, influencing, motivating, and attending meetings.[6] In fact, even chief executives (whom you might expect to be somewhat insulated from other people, up there in their executive suites) spend about three-fourths of their time dealing directly with other people.[7] All managers (including supervisors) are also *accountable* to those at the next level up. Thus if your own boss assigns you a task, you are accountable (answerable) to him or her for the effective execution of that task.

However, two main things set the position of first-line supervisors like Doris apart:

- *First*, top and middle managers both have managers for subordinates. In other words, they are in charge of other managers. *First-line supervisors have workers— nonmanagers—as subordinates.*
- *Second*, top, middle, and first-line managers use their time differently. Top managers tend to spend more time planning and setting goals (like "double sales in the next two years"). Middle managers then translate these goals into specific projects (like "hire two new salespeople and introduce three new products") for their subordinates to execute. *First-line supervisors then concentrate on directing and controlling the employees who actually do the work on these projects day to day.* Actually selling the product is one example.

A CLOSER LOOK AT THE SUPERVISOR   The word "supervisor" conjures up several meanings for most of us. The supervisor is the boss, the overseer, and the superior. He or she "supervises," or directs and controls, the work of his or her workers. So in some respects, every manager, including the CEOs of giant firms like GE and IBM, "supervises" and is a supervisor.

However, this is a book for current and future supervisors, so we need a more precise definition. In this book, by **supervisors** we mean *managers who have workers— nonmanagers—as subordinates, and who direct and control the employees who actually do* *the work* (selling the products, pressing the clothes, helping the patients, or painting the cars, for instance) *day to day*.

Supervisors play a crucial role in any company, large or small. Steve Jobs can make grand plans to launch new iPads. But, at some point it is Apple's first-line supervisors—the men and women running the assembly lines and supervising the sales reps—who actually get the work out. Jack is lost without supervisors like Doris, who got her cleaners, pressers, and counter people to turn their Pompano store around.

In this book, we're going to focus on the supervisor. Here in Chapter 1 we look at who they are, what makes them tick, and the challenges they face. In Chapters 2–16, we'll focus on the leadership concepts and tools you'll need to be a better first-line supervisor. But let's look first at what it takes to be a supervisor.

2. Do You Have What It Takes to Be a Supervisor?

Do I Have What It Takes to Be a Supervisor?

Whether you're starting your first supervisory job or just thinking of joining the supervisory ranks, there's a wealth of research to help you to decide whether supervising is the occupation for you.[8] It suggests that supervisors have certain traits, competencies, and skills.

What Traits Should Supervisors Have?

Career counseling expert John Holland says that personality (including values, motives, and needs) is an important determinant of career choice. Specifically, he says that six basic "personal orientations" determine the sorts of careers to which people are drawn. Research with his Vocational Preference Test (VPT) suggests that almost all successful supervisors need at least one of two of these personality types or orientations:

- **Social orientation.** "Social" people are attracted to careers that involve working with others in a helpful or facilitative way. (So, supervisors as well as others such as clinical psychologists and social workers would exhibit this orientation.) Socially oriented people usually find it easy to talk with all kinds of people; are good at helping people who are upset or troubled; are skilled at explaining things to others; and enjoy doing social things such as helping others with their personal problems, teaching, and meeting new people.[9] It's hard to be a supervisor if you're not comfortable dealing with people.

- **Enterprising orientation.** "Enterprising" people tend to like working with people in a supervisory or persuasive way. They especially enjoy influencing others (lawyers and public relations executives would also exhibit this orientation). Enterprising people often characterize themselves as being good public speakers, as having reputations for being able to deal with difficult people, as successfully organizing the work of others, and as being ambitious and assertive. They enjoy influencing others, selling things, serving as officers of groups, and supervising the work of others. Supervisors need to be comfortable influencing others.

What Competencies Should Supervisors Have?

Edgar Schein says career planning is a process of discovery. He says that as each of us works at various tasks, we slowly develop a clearer occupational self-concept, in terms of what our talents, abilities, motives, and values really are. He says people in different occupations have different competencies. We can infer from his studies that supervisors have what he calls **managerial competence**.[10] These people show a strong motivation to manage others. They are motivated to seek positions that let them use their managerial competence.

Specifically, these people see themselves as competent in three areas. One is *analytical competence*. This is the ability to identify, analyze, and solve problems under stressful conditions. A second is *interpersonal competence* (the ability to influence, supervise, lead, manipulate, and control people at all levels). The third is *emotional competence*. They are stimulated, not exhausted, by emotional and interpersonal crises. They have intestinal fortitude.

What Skills Should Supervisors Have?

Successful supervisors don't just have the right traits and competencies. They also have the right skills. Supervisors need three sets of skills, technical, interpersonal, and conceptual skills.[11] *Building supervisory skills* is a basic theme of this book. The book should help to provide you with many of the hands-on technical, interpersonal, and conceptual skills all supervisors need to succeed.

TECHNICAL SKILLS   First, supervisors have to be *technically competent*. They must know how to plan, organize, staff, lead, and control. For example, they should know how to develop a plan, write a job description, and discipline an employee. Chapters 2–16 focus on providing these technical skills, such as how to set goals, interview job candidates, and discipline employees.

INTERPERSONAL SKILLS   Researchers at The Center for Creative Leadership in North Carolina studied why supervisors fail. They came to some useful conclusions. Some supervisors simply didn't do their jobs. They often thought more about their next promotion than about excelling in their jobs.[12] However, most of the failures were interpersonal. These supervisors failed because they had abusive or insensitive styles, disagreed with their own management about how the business should be run, left a trail of bruised feelings, failed to adapt to the management culture, or didn't resolve conflicts among subordinates.

The implication is that supervisors must have good interpersonal skills. Interpersonal skills "include knowledge about human behavior and group processes, ability to understand the feelings, attitudes, and motives of others, and ability to communicate clearly and persuasively."[13] These skills include tact and diplomacy, empathy, persuasiveness, and oral communications ability. Supervisors with these skills have relationships that are more cooperative. They can do things such as listening attentively and sympathetically when a subordinate has a problem. Chapters 10–12 will help you learn many of these skills.

CONCEPTUAL SKILLS   Third, studies also show that effective supervisors tend to have more *cognitive ability*. In other words, they make good decisions.[14] Conceptual (or "cognitive") skills "include analytical ability, logical thinking, concept formation, and inductive reasoning."[15] Conceptual skills manifest themselves in things such as good judgment, creativity, and the ability to see the "big picture" when confronted with information. Of course, intelligence is one thing, good judgment another. Many high-IQ people have wobbly judgment, and many less-than-stellar IQ people have great judgment. As Lawrence Bossidy puts it, "If you have to choose between someone with a staggering IQ and elite education who is gliding along, and someone with a lower IQ but who is absolutely determined to succeed, you'll always do better with the second person."[16] Chapter 3 will help you hone your conceptual skills.

3. Is Supervising for You?

Now, let's turn to the details of what supervisors do and whether supervising is the best career for you. What do they actually do? A short, formal job description for a supervisor would state that he or she *directly supervises and coordinates activities of workers; may perform duties such as budgeting, accounting, and personnel work, in addition to supervisory duties.* Some illustrative supervisory job titles would include the following:

- Production Supervisor
- Sales Supervisor
- Assembly Supervisor
- Sales Manager
- Shift Supervisor

- Branch Manager
- Retail Store Manager
- Manufacturing Supervisor
- Department Manager
- Team Leader

But in fact, job titles like these just scratch the surface, because supervising is something we're often called upon to do every day. In business, for instance, even a nonsupervisory employee may have to supervise occasionally. The person in charge of marketing might ask a marketing analyst to head (supervise) a small team to analyze a new product's potential. Everyone who works should therefore know something about how to supervise. The accompanying Application Example illustrates this.

■ **Application Example:**

You Too Are a Supervisor

In fact, you don't have to be in business to need supervisory skills. For example, let's suppose you and some relatives or friends decide to spend two weeks abroad in France. None of you knows much about hotels or traveling in France, so they've asked you to supervise the trip. Where would you start? (Resist the urge to call a travel agent, please.) You might start with *planning*. Among other things, you'll need to plan the dates your group is leaving and returning, the cities and towns in France you'll visit, the airline you'll take there and back, how the group will get around in France, and where you'll stay when you're there.

Of course, you will need help. You might divide the work and create and *staff* an *organization*. For example, you might put Rosa in charge of checking airline schedules and prices, Ned in charge of checking hotels, and Ruth in charge of checking the sites to see in various cities as well as the means of transportation between them. However, the job won't get done with Rosa, Ned, and Ruth simply working by themselves. Rosa obviously can't make any decisions on airline schedules unless she knows what city you're starting and ending with. Ned can't schedule hotels unless he knows from Ruth what sites you'll be seeing and when. You'll either have to schedule weekly supervisors' meetings or coordinate the work of these three people yourself.

Leadership could be a challenge, too. Ned and Ruth don't get along too well, so you'll have to make sure conflicts don't get out of hand. Rosa is a genius with numbers, but tends to get discouraged. You'll have to make sure she stays motivated and focused.

Finally, you will have to ensure that the whole project stays "in *control*." At a minimum, you'll want to make sure that all those airline tickets, hotel reservations, and itineraries are checked and checked again so there are no mistakes.

Is Supervising for Me?

A Closer Look at the Supervisor's Tasks, Activities, Skills, and Traits

For many years, experts from the United States Department of Labor (DOL) have studied what employees in thousands of different jobs actually do. For most of that time, they published their results in a massive *Dictionary of Occupational Titles*. Today, a government Web site makes that wealth of information available online (from http://www.onetcenter.org, see Figure 1.2 as an example). Their information on supervisors probably presents the most comprehensive and authoritative picture available of what supervisors do.

Figure 1.3 brings together a bird's-eye view of what the DOL discovered about supervisors' tasks, work activities, skills, and traits. The figure is a synthesis of several

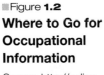

■Figure **1.2**

Where to Go for Occupational Information

Source: http://online. onetcenter.org/find/ (accessed May 2010).

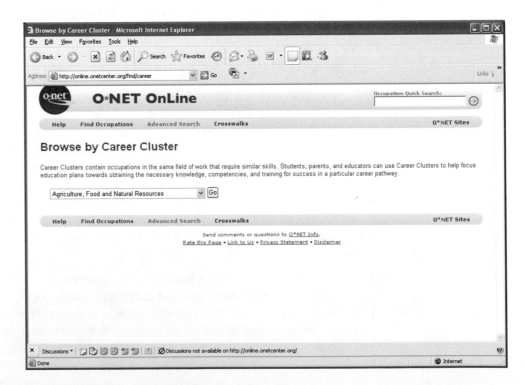

Is Supervision For You? Here's What Supervisors Do, and Need to Be Good at *

*(Source: Compiled and adapted from several supervisory positions at online.onet.gov Accessed May 2010)

TASKS—IN TERMS OF HOW YOU'LL SPEND A TYPICAL DAY AS A SUPERVISOR, EXPECT TO HAVE TO DO THINGS SUCH AS:

Listen to and resolve complaints regarding services, production, products, or personnel.

Monitor staff performance to ensure that goals are met.

Hire, train, and evaluate your employees.

Confer with company officials to develop methods and procedures to increase sales, expand markets, and promote business.

Direct and supervise employees engaged in sales, production, inventory-taking, reconciling cash receipts, or performing specific services such as pumping gasoline for customers.

Provide staff with assistance in performing difficult or complicated duties.

Plan and prepare work schedules, and assign employees to specific duties.

Attend company meetings to exchange product information and coordinate work activities with other departments.

Enforce safety and sanitation regulations.

Prepare sales, production, and/or inventory reports for management and budget departments.

Read and analyze charts, work orders, production schedules, and other records and reports, in order to determine production requirements and to evaluate current production estimates and outputs.

Confer with other supervisors to coordinate operations and activities within or between departments.

Recommend and/or implement measures to *motivate employees* and to improve production methods, equipment performance, product quality, or efficiency.

Confer with management or subordinates to resolve worker problems, complaints, or grievances.

WORK ACTIVITIES—TO SUCCESSFULLY CARRY OUT THESE TASKS, YOU'LL HAVE TO BE GOOD AT:

Interacting With Computers—Using computers and computer systems (including hardware and software) to program, write software, set up functions, enter data, or process information.

Establishing and Maintaining Interpersonal Relationships—Developing constructive and cooperative working relationships with others, and maintaining them over time.

Organizing, Planning, and Prioritizing Work—Developing specific goals and plans to prioritize, organize, and accomplish your work.

- plan or organize work

Communicating with Supervisors, Peers, or Subordinates—Providing information to supervisors, co-workers, and subordinates by telephone, in written form, e-mail, or in person.

- such as, conduct or attend staff meetings
- consult with managerial or supervisory personnel
- dictate correspondence

Getting Information—Observing, receiving, and otherwise obtaining information from all relevant sources.

Coaching and Developing Others—Identifying the developmental needs of others and coaching, mentoring, or otherwise helping others to improve their knowledge or skills.

Coordinating the Work and Activities of Others—Getting members of a group to work together to accomplish tasks.

Guiding, Directing, and Motivating Subordinates—Providing guidance and direction to subordinates, including setting performance standards and monitoring performance.

- such as, assign work to staff or employees
- evaluate performance of employees or contract personnel
- monitor worker performance

Making Decisions and Solving Problems—Analyzing information and evaluating results to choose the best solution and solve problems.

- such as, select software for clerical activities

(Continued)

Communicating with Persons Outside Organization—Communicating with people outside the organization, representing the organization to customers, the public, government, and other external sources. This information can be exchanged in person, in writing, or by telephone or e-mail.

- such as, make presentations

Developing and Building Teams—Encouraging and building mutual trust, respect, and cooperation among team members.

Processing Information—Compiling, coding, categorizing, calculating, tabulating, auditing, or verifying information or data.

- such as, investigate customer complaints

Scheduling Work and Activities—Scheduling events, programs, and activities, as well as the work of others.

- such as, develop maintenance schedules
- schedule activities, classes, or events
- schedule employee work hours

Analyzing Data or Information—Identifying the underlying principles, reasons, or facts of information by breaking down information or data into separate parts.

- such as, analyze sales activities or trends

Updating and Using Relevant Knowledge—Keeping up-to-date technically and applying new knowledge to your job.

- such as, use knowledge of written communication in sales work

Monitoring and Controlling Resources—Monitoring and controlling resources and overseeing the spending of money.

- such as, develop budgets
- order or purchase supplies, materials, or equipment
- purchase office equipment or furniture
- requisition stock, materials, supplies or equipment

Documenting/Recording Information—Entering, transcribing, recording, storing, or maintaining information in written or electronic/magnetic form.

- such as, inventory stock to ensure adequate supplies
- maintain production or work records

Performing Administrative Activities — Performing day-to-day administrative tasks such as maintaining information files and processing paperwork.

- such as, prepare rental or lease agreement
- prepare reports

Providing Consultation and Advice to Others—Providing guidance and expert advice to management or other groups on technical, systems-, or process-related topics.

- such as, recommend improvements to work methods or procedures
- recommend purchase or repair of furnishings or equipment

Interpreting the Meaning of Information for Others—Translating or explaining what information means and how it can be used.

- such as, explain rules, policies or regulations

Staffing Organizational Units—Recruiting, interviewing, selecting, hiring, and promoting employees in an organization.

- such as, evaluate information from employment interviews
- hire, discharge, transfer, or promote workers
- publicize job openings
- recommend personnel actions, such as promotions, transfers, and dismissals

Thinking Creatively—Developing, designing, or creating new applications, ideas, relationships, systems, or products, including artistic contributions.

- such as, write advertising copy

Resolving Conflicts and Negotiating with Others—Handling complaints, settling disputes, and resolving grievances and conflicts, or otherwise negotiating with others.

- such as, resolve customer or public complaints
- resolve or assist workers to resolve work problems

Training and Teaching Others—Identifying the educational needs of others, developing formal educational or training programs or classes, and teaching or instructing others.

- such as, demonstrate or explain assembly or use of equipment

Coaching and Developing Others—Identifying the developmental needs of others and coaching, mentoring, or otherwise helping others to improve their knowledge or skills.

SKILLS—TO DO THESE THINGS, YOU'LL NEED THESE SKILLS:

Speaking—Talking to others to convey information effectively.

Time Management—Managing one's own time and the time of others.

Active Listening—Giving full attention to what other people are saying, taking time to understand the points being made, asking questions as appropriate, and not interrupting at inappropriate times.

Reading Comprehension—Understanding written sentences and paragraphs in work related documents.

Social Perceptiveness—Being aware of others' reactions and understanding why they react as they do.

Active Learning—Understanding the implications of new information for both current and future problem-solving and decision-making.

Critical Thinking—Using logic and reasoning to identify the strengths and weaknesses of alternative solutions, conclusions or approaches to problems.

Judgment and Decision Making—Considering the relative costs and benefits of potential actions to choose the most appropriate one.

Management of Personnel Resources—Motivating, developing, and directing people as they work, identifying the best people for the job.

Instructing—Teaching others how to do something.

Mathematics—Using mathematics to solve problems.

Negotiation—Bringing others together and trying to reconcile differences.

Persuasion—Persuading others to change their minds or behavior.

Monitoring—Monitoring/Assessing performance of yourself, other individuals, or organizations to make improvements or take corrective action.

Service Orientation—Actively looking for ways to help people.

Writing—Communicating effectively in writing as appropriate for the needs of the audience.

Coordination—Adjusting actions in relation to others' actions.

Learning Strategies—Selecting and using training/instructional methods and procedures appropriate for the situation when learning or teaching new things.

TRAITS—AND YOU'LL NEED THESE PERSONAL TRAITS:

Integrity—Job requires being honest and ethical.

Initiative—Job requires a willingness to take on responsibilities and challenges.

Leadership Ability—Job requires a willingness to lead, take charge, and offer opinions and direction.

Concern for Others—Job requires being sensitive to others' needs and feelings and being understanding and helpful on the job.

(*Continued*)

Stress Tolerance—Job requires accepting criticism and dealing calmly and effectively with high stress situations.

Achievement/Effort—Job requires establishing and maintaining personally challenging achievement goals and exerting effort toward mastering tasks.

Persistence—Job requires persistence in the face of obstacles.

Self Control—Job requires maintaining composure, keeping emotions in check, controlling anger, and avoiding aggressive behavior, even in very difficult situations.

Dependability—Job requires being reliable, responsible, and dependable, and fulfilling obligations.

Social Orientation—Job requires preferring to work with others rather than alone, and being personally connected with others on the job.

Cooperation—Job requires being pleasant with others on the job and displaying a good-natured, cooperative attitude.

Independence—Job requires developing one's own ways of doing things, guiding oneself with little or no supervision, and depending on oneself to get things done.

Analytical Thinking—Job requires analyzing information and using logic to address work-related issues and problems.

Adaptability/Flexibility—Job requires being open to change (positive or negative) and to considerable variety in the workplace.

Attention to Detail—Job requires being careful about detail and thorough in completing work tasks.

Innovation—Job requires creativity and alternative thinking to develop new ideas for and answers to work-related problems.

O*NET supervisory jobs (for example, for retail and nonretail supervisory positions, and for production and sales supervisory positions). As you go through each line in the figure, you may want to place a check mark next to the supervisory tasks, work activities, skills, and traits that seem to appeal and/or apply to you. This may give you a better feel for what supervisors do and whether supervising is for you. Let's look at each.

THE SUPERVISOR'S TASKS   What does Figure 1.3 tell you about the supervisor's day-to-day tasks? (These tasks include, for instance, *listen* to and resolve complaints regarding services, *monitor* staff performance, *hire, train, and evaluate* employees, *confer* with company officials, and *provide staff with assistance* in performing difficult duties). Perusing the list of tasks leads to several conclusions. For example, like all managers, supervisors spend almost all their time interacting with people—listening to, training, and helping them. Are these the sorts of tasks on which you'd like to spend your days?

THE SUPERVISOR'S WORK ACTIVITIES   Figure 1.3 also shows that to successfully carry out these tasks, you'll have to be good at a fairly long list of work activities. For example, you'll have to be good at *maintaining* interpersonal relationships, *communicating* with subordinates, *coaching and developing* others, and *making* good decisions. Are these the sorts of activities at which you think you do well?

THE SUPERVISOR'S SKILLS   And of course to do these sorts of things, you'll need a toolkit of personal skills. Not surprisingly (again see Figure 1.3), these skills include things such as *speaking, persuading, negotiating, critical thinking*, and *active listening*. There are no absolutes, but, looking at the big picture, supervisors need better than average interpersonal skills, communications skills, and conceptual/decision-making skills. Are those among your strong suits?

THE SUPERVISOR'S TRAITS   Finally, effective supervisors need certain personal characteristics or traits. Figure 1.3 again lists these. They include *integrity, initiative, leadership ability, stress tolerance,* and *cooperativeness.* Such characteristics or traits tend to be more a part of our personalities. So, they're not quite so easy to change as are skills such as active listening.

Do you possess traits like initiative and integrity? It may not be easy to answer that. For one thing, few people (even in private) rate themselves as dishonest, undependable, and lazy! However, it's still useful to ask yourself whether, if your career depended on it, traits like those toward the end of Figure 1.3 reflect your strong points. The Leadership Applications for Supervisors feature illustrates why one of these characteristics—leadership ability—is essential for supervisors.

What Are the Supervisor's Job Prospects?

Of course, it's not just whether you like some occupation and would be good at it that's important. It is also useful to know what the occupation's employment prospects are. The Bureau of Labor Statistics (BLS) does not split out forecasts specifically for first-line supervisors (just for managers in general). However, their latest forecasts show that the demand in the United States for managers and supervisors should remain buoyant for the foreseeable future.[17] They even have a special icon to show this; it is "Bright Outlook", with a sun icon like this: ☼.[18] But (and this is a big but) the prospects for supervisors will be much better in some industries than in others. Here are some specific examples.

SUPERVISORY OCCUPATIONS THAT WILL GROW ABOUT AVERAGE   The demand for supervisors in most industries will grow about as fast as the rest of the U.S. economy—about average, in other words. This includes industries like advertising and marketing, education, engineering, farming, finance, lodging, and purchasing.

SUPERVISORY OCCUPATIONS THAT WILL GROW FASTER THAN AVERAGE   Demand for supervisors in some industries will grow faster than average. This includes computer systems supervisors, construction supervisors, human resource and training supervisors, medical/health services supervisors, and (with more people moving into apartments) property supervisors.

SUPERVISORY OCCUPATIONS THAT WILL GROW SLOWER THAN AVERAGE   In some industries, increasing productivity and (perhaps) offshoring should translate into lower than average growth in demand for supervisors. These industries include food services (especially fast food), and production.

One last point: Education will be the key. For all these supervisory jobs—but especially for those where growth may taper off—"Opportunities should be best for college graduates," the BLS says. So if you're reading this book, you're already on the right track.

4. The Supervisor's Changing World

Skilled machinist Chad Toulouse exemplifies today's supervisor.[19] After an 18-week training course, this former college student now works as a team leader in a plant where about 40% of the machines are automated. In older plants, machinists manually controlled the machines that cut chunks of metal into things such as engine parts. Supervisors like Chad spent their time passing down management's daily directives and enforcing management's rules.

Today, Chad and his team spend much of their time typing commands into computerized machines that produce precision parts for water pumps. His multiethnic employees are correspondingly better educated and more savvy and professional than yesterday's worker, as well as much more diverse demographically. Team decisions on things such as how to correct problems tend to be made collegially, not unilaterally by Chad.

That means Chad and his supervisory colleagues can't just rely on being "the boss" to get things done. Today they need the leadership and interpersonal skills to build team consensus. And they need the cross-cultural sensitivity to shape diverse employees into cooperative, mutually respectful teams.

How Have the Responsibilities of Supervisors Evolved?

Changes in the supervisor's responsibilities didn't occur overnight. Instead they evolved slowly, in response to changing conditions in businesses' workforce, competitive, and technological environments.

Workforce Trends

For the first-line supervisor, the first and perhaps most obvious changes are in the demographic makeup of the workforce itself.

DEMOGRAPHIC TRENDS   Most important, the U.S. workforce is fast becoming older and more multiethnic.[20] Table 1.1, from the U.S. Department of Labor's Bureau of Labor Statistics, provides a bird's-eye view. For example, between 1998 and 2018, the percentage of the workforce that it classifies as "white, non-Hispanic" will drop from 83.8% to 79.4%. At the same time, the percentage of the workforce that is black will rise from 11.6% to 12.1%, those classified Asian will rise from 4.6% to 5.6%, and those of Hispanic origin will rise from 10.4% to 17.6%. The percentages of younger workers will fall, while those over 55 years of age will leap from 12.4% of the workforce in 1998 to 23.0% in 2018.

At the same time, demographic trends are making finding, hiring, and supervising employees more challenging. In the United States, long-term labor force

■ Table **1.1**

Demographic Groups as a Percentage of the Workforce, 1998–2018			
Age, Race, Ethnicity	1998	2008	2018
Age: 16–24	15.9%	14.3%	12.7%
25–54	71.7	67.7	63.5
55+	12.4	18.1	23.9
White, non-Hispanic	83.8	81.4	79.4
Black	11.6	11.5	12.1
Asian	4.6	4.7	5.6
Hispanic Origin	10.4	14.3	17.6

Source: Adapted from http://www.bls.gov/news.release/ecopro.t01.htm (accessed May 10, 2010).

growth is not expected to keep pace with job growth, with an estimated shortfall of about 14 million college-educated workers by 2020.[21] One study of 35 large global companies' senior HR officers said "talent management"—in particular, the acquisition, development, and retention of talent to fill the companies' employment needs—ranked as their top concern.[22]

"GENERATION Y"   Also called "Millennials," Generation Y employees are roughly those born from 1977 to 2002. They take the place of the labor force's previous new entrants, Generation X, who were born roughly from 1965 to 1976. Gen X'rs were the children of the Baby Boomers, who were born just after the Second World War, from roughly 1944 to 1950.

Although every generation obviously has its own new generation of labor force entrants, Generation Y employees are different in several ways. For one thing, says one expert, they have "been pampered, nurtured and programmed with a slew of activities since they were toddlers, meaning they are both high-performance and high-maintenance."[23] As a result:

1. They want fair and forthright supervisors who are highly engaged in their employees' professional development.

2. They seek out creative challenges and view colleagues as resources from whom to gain knowledge.

3. They want to make an important impact from Day 1.

4. They want small goals with tight deadlines so they can build up ownership of tasks.

5. They aim to work faster and better than other workers do.[24]

Fortune magazine says that today's Generation Y employees will bring challenges and strengths. It says that they may be "the most high maintenance workforce in the history of the world." Referring to them as "the most praised generation," *The Wall Street Journal* explains how Lands' End and Bank of America are teaching their supervisors to compliment these new employees with prize packages and public appreciation.[25] But, as the first generation raised on iPads and e-mail, their capacity for using information technology will also make them the most high-performing.

Adding to the challenge is the fact that Generation Y is entering the labor force just as employers face an aging workforce (remember, the percentage of those aged

55 and up will almost double, from 12.4% of the labor force in 1998 to 23.9% in 2018). That fact has all sorts of implications. Sixty-year-old supervisors will be supervising 20-year-olds whose values may seem exasperating. Twenty-year-olds will be supervising people old enough to be their parents (similarly exasperating.) So whether you're older or younger, supervising will be a challenge. To quote one observer,

> Generation Y is much less likely to respond to the traditional command-and-control type of management still popular in much of today's workforce. . . . They've grown up questioning their parents, and now they're questioning their employers. They don't know how to shut up, which is great, but that's aggravating to the 50-year-old supervisor who says, "Do it and do it now."[26]

RETIREES   Many human resource professionals call "the aging workforce" the biggest demographic trend affecting employers. The basic problem is that there aren't enough younger workers to replace the projected number of older-worker retirees.[27]

Employers are dealing with this challenge in many ways. One survey found that 41% of surveyed employers are bringing retirees back into the workforce; 34% are conducting studies to determine projected retirement rates in the organization; and 31% are offering employment options designed to attract and retain semiretired workers.[28]

NONTRADITIONAL WORKERS   At the same time, there has been a shift to nontraditional workers. Nontraditional workers include those who hold multiple jobs, or who are "contingent" or part-time workers, or people working in alternative work arrangements (such as a mother–daughter team sharing one clerical job). Today, almost 10% of American workers—13 million people—fit this nontraditional workforce category. Of these, about 8 million are independent contractors who work on specific projects and move on once the projects are done.

Globalization and Competitive Trends

Globalization refers to the tendency of firms to extend their sales, ownership, and/or manufacturing to new markets abroad. Examples abound. Toyota produces the Camry in Kentucky, while Dell produces PCs in China. Free trade areas—agreements that reduce tariffs and barriers among trading partners—further encourage international trade. The North American Free Trade Area (born out of NAFTA, the North American Free Trade Agreement) and the European Union (EU) are examples.

More globalization means more competition, and more competition means more pressure to be "world-class"—to lower costs, to make employees more productive, and to do things better and less expensively. When Spanish retailer Zara opens a new store in Manhattan, this pressures local employers like the Gap to improve their products, service, and performance.

ECONOMIC TRENDS   These trends are occurring in a context of challenge and upheaval. In the United States, the gross national product (GNP)—a measure of the United States of America's total output—boomed between 2001 and 2007. During this period, home prices leaped as much as 20% per year. Unemployment remained docile at about 4.7%. Then, around 2007/2008, all these measures seemed to fall off a cliff. GNP fell. Home prices dropped by 10% or more (depending on the city). Unemployment nationwide rose to more than 10% in 2010.

Why did all this happen? That is a complicated question, but for one thing, many years of accumulating debt ran their course. Banks and other financial institutions (such as hedge funds) found themselves owning trillions of dollars of worthless loans. Governments stepped in to try to prevent their collapse. Lending dried up. Many businesses and consumers stopped buying. The economy tanked.

Economic trends will undoubtedly turn positive again, perhaps even as you read these pages. However, they have certainly grabbed employers' attention. After what the world went through starting in 2007–2008, it's doubtful that the deregulation, debt accumulation, and globalization that drove economic growth for the previous 50 years will continue unabated. That may mean slower growth for many countries, perhaps for years. Companies will need to be supercompetitive to survive. They'll therefore need a new breed of highly skilled supervisors.

OFFSHORING   The search for greater efficiencies is prompting employers to export or offshore more jobs to lower-cost locations abroad. *Offshoring* means transferring to lower-wage workers abroad jobs that another country's workers used to do. For example, customers with questions about Dell PCs (or thousands of other firms' products and services) are likely to reach a call center abroad when they call. Between 2005 and 2015, about 3 million U.S. jobs, ranging from office support and computer jobs to management, sales, and even legal jobs, will likely move offshore.[29]

Workforce Diversity

Given these relentless workforce, demographics, and other trends, just about every supervisor in America faces the most diverse workforce in this country's history.

Diversity means being diverse or varied, and diversity at work means *having a workforce composed of two or more groups of employees with various racial, ethnic, gender, cultural, national origin, handicap, age, and religious backgrounds.*[30] Today, you'll find yourself supervising members of many such groups, most notably the following:

- **Racial and ethnic groups.** African Americans, Pacific Islanders, Asian Americans, Native Americans, and other people of color comprise about 25% of the U.S. population.
- **Gender.** Women represent about half of the U.S. workforce. Many of these are single mothers (and there are increasing numbers of single fathers as well).
- **Older and younger workers.** About 24% of the workforce will be over 55 years of age in 2018. People are retiring later (or not at all), which effects the gradual aging of the workforce, as does the larger number of older people remaining at work.
- **People with disabilities.** The Americans with Disabilities Act makes it illegal to discriminate against people with disabilities who are otherwise qualified to do a job.
- **Religion.** Domestic and world events are underscoring differences, similarities, and tensions relating to the diversity of religions among employees.

WHY IS TODAY'S WORKFORCE DIVERSE?   America's workforce diversity reflects the interplay of numerous demographic, globalization, competitive, and political trends. In particular:

- Globalization ratcheted up the competition for U.S. employers, forcing local companies to compete with those from abroad if they wanted to grow.

- In turn, economic growth ultimately depends on both population growth and rising productivity.
- However, demographic trends (including declining U.S. birthrates and an aging workforce) would have meant a moderating population growth.
- This, combined with an evolving pro-diversity climate in the 1960s, prompted Congress to modify immigration laws to encourage immigration.
- Furthermore, birthrates vary among demographic groups, with that of minorities somewhat higher.
- Improved educational and other opportunities for women (and the need for more family income) prompted more women, including minority women, to join the workforce.
- International inequities in wages and opportunities encouraged more foreign workers to enter the United States.
- Globalization encourages employers to hire more people with the cultural and language skills to deal with the employers' global vendors and customers. The net result is a more diverse workforce.

In summary, there's not one, but several interrelated reasons for the trend toward workforce diversity in America.

Technological Trends

Technology is changing the nature of almost everything supervisors do. Technology (in the form of Internet-based communications) enabled Dell and those thousands of other employers to send call-center jobs offshore to India. Zara doesn't need the expensive inventories that burden the Gap. Zara operates its own Internet-based worldwide distribution network, linked to the checkout registers at its stores around the world. When its headquarters in Spain sees a garment "flying" out of a store, Zara's computerized manufacturing system dyes the required fabric, cuts and manufactures the item, and speeds it to that store within days.[31]

Trends in the Nature of Work

Technology is also changing the nature of work, even factory work. Most important, in plants throughout the world, knowledge-intensive high-tech manufacturing jobs are replacing traditional factory jobs, as it did for Chad Toulouse and his team.

The implication is that supervisors—not just the workers—need to be technologically savvy. For example, Chad and his colleagues are more likely to use Web-based appraisal systems like Employee Appraiser, rather than traditional paper and pencil forms, to assess their employees online. They take their supervisory management courses in their spare time from online sites such as SkillSoft (http://www.skillsoft.com).

SERVICES   Technology is not the only trend driving this change from "brawn to brains." Today over two-thirds of the U.S. workforce produces and delivers services, not products.

Between 2004 and 2014, almost all the 19 million new jobs in the United States will be in **services**, not in goods-producing industries.[32]

Teams Workers today are also much more likely to get their work done through teams. Toyota's Lexington, Kentucky, subsidiary is one famous example. Work here is organized around work teams of 10 to 12 employees. Each team is responsible for a complete task, such as installing dashboard units or maintaining automated machines. Highly trained workers largely do their own hiring, control their own budgets, monitor the quality of their own work, and generally manage themselves. Supervisors here spend more time supporting the team, for instance, interacting with plant management to ensure their teams have the sources they need.

5. What These Changes Mean for Supervisors

What Does the Change in These Responsibilities Mean for Supervisors?

Reading about economic, demographic, and technological trends is fine. The question is, what does this all mean for what supervisors must know to be successful today? These trends have three implications for supervisors:

- *You'll need strong leadership skills.*
- *You'll need to supervise in a diverse, multicultural workplace.*
- *You'll need world-class basic supervisory skills.*

Let's look at each one.

1. With More Professional, Self-Directed Workers, You'll Need Outstanding Leadership Skills

First, most workers today tend to be technologically savvy "knowledge workers." This puts a big premium on building and supervising human capital. *Human capital* means the knowledge, education, training, skills, and expertise of a firm's workers. These workers are more likely to manage themselves in small, self-managing teams.

Supervising teams of self-managing workers means that supervisors must be leaders, not just order-givers. Ordering around people who should be self-managing obviously doesn't make too much sense. Leading in situations like these requires extraordinary levels of patience, leadership, and coaching skills. Today, as management guru Peter Drucker once said, "You have to learn to manage in situations where you don't have command authority, where you are neither controlled nor controlling."[33] *Leadership* means influencing someone to work willingly toward a predetermined objective. You'll need to be a leader and get your employees to want to willingly follow the path you've laid out for them, while relying less on the fact that the company says you're the boss. Not everyone is cut out for this kind of leadership. You'll need to earn personal respect and hone your leadership and coaching skills to influence and motivate your employees. We'll see how throughout this book.

2. You'll Need to Supervise in a Diverse, Multicultural, Multiage Workplace

Second, we saw that you'll be supervising the most culturally and generationally diverse workforce in U.S. history. You'll therefore have to be skilled at managing diversity. *Managing diversity* means maximizing diversity's potential advantages while minimizing the potential barriers—such as prejudices and bias—that can undermine the functioning of a diverse team.

DIVERSITY'S POTENTIAL PROS AND CONS   Why "manage diversity"? The answer is that diversity can produce problems that undermine collegiality and cooperation. Potential problems include the following:

- **Stereotyping** is a process in which someone ascribes specific behavioral traits to individuals based on their apparent membership in a group.[34] For example, "Older people can't work hard." **Prejudice** is a bias that results from prejudging someone based on some trait. For example, "We won't hire him because he's old."

- **Discrimination** is prejudice in action. **Discrimination** means taking specific actions toward or against the person based on the person's group.[35]

  In many countries, including the United States, it's generally illegal to discriminate at work based on a person's age, race, gender, disability, or country of national origin. But in practice, discrimination is often subtle. For example, many argue that an invisible "glass ceiling," enforced by an "old boys' network" (friendships built in places like exclusive clubs), effectively prevents women from reaching the top ranks. Equal-opportunity laws aim to prohibit and eliminate such discrimination.

- **Tokenism** occurs when a company appoints a small group of women or minorities to high-profile positions, rather than more aggressively seeking full representation for that group. Tokenism is a diversity barrier when it slows the process of hiring or promoting more members of the minority group. Token employees face obstacles to full participation, success, and acceptance in a company.[36]

- **Ethnocentrism** is the tendency to view members of other social groups less favorably than one's own. For example, one study found that supervisors attributed the performance of some minorities less to their abilities and effort and more to help they received from others. Conversely, the same supervisors attributed the performance of *non*-minorities to their own abilities and efforts.[37]

- Discrimination against women goes beyond glass ceilings. Working women also confront **gender-role stereotypes**, the tendency to associate women with certain (frequently nonsupervisory) jobs. In one study, attractiveness was advantageous for female interviewees when the job was nonsupervisory. When the job was supervisory, there was a tendency for a woman's attractiveness to reduce her chances of being hired.[38]

SOME DIVERSITY BENEFITS   Yet it is clear that diversity, properly managed, does produce many benefits. For one thing, as *The Wall Street Journal* said, "As companies do more and more business around the world, diversity isn't simply a matter of doing what is fair, or good public relations. It's a business imperative."[39]

Furthermore, effectively managing diversity should create "a workplace where differences can be learned from and leveraged."[40] For example, IBM created task forces focused on customer groups such as women and Native Americans.[41] These task forces helped drive up IBM's sales and profits. One task force decided to focus on expanding IBM's market among multicultural and women-owned businesses. They did this in part by providing "much-needed sales and service support to small and midsize businesses, a niche well populated with minority and female buyers."[42] As a result, this market grew from $10 million to more than $300 million in revenue in just three years. After PepsiCo employed a similar program, new "diversity" products (such as wasabi-flavored snacks) soon accounted for about one percentage point of PepsiCo's 8% revenue growth."[43]

MANAGING DIVERSITY   Smart employers therefore take formal steps to manage diversity. **Managing diversity** means maximizing diversity's potential advantages while minimizing the potential barriers—such as bias—that can undermine the functioning of a diverse workforce.

Diversity management programs generally start at the top. One expert says these five activities form the basis of any diversity management program.

1. **Provide strong leadership.**   CEOs of companies with exemplary reputations in managing diversity typically champion diversity. "Leadership" here means, for instance, being a role model for the behaviors required for the change.

2. **Assess the situation.**   Common tools for measuring a company's diversity include equal employment hiring and retention metrics, employee attitude surveys, management and employee evaluations, and focus groups.[44]

3. **Provide diversity training and education.**   The most common starting point for a diversity management effort is usually some type of employee education program.

4. **Change culture and management systems.**   Combine education programs with other concrete steps aimed at changing the organization's culture. For example, change the performance appraisal procedure to appraise supervisors based partly on their success in reducing intergroup conflicts.

5. **Evaluate the diversity management program.**   For example, do employee attitude surveys now indicate any improvement in employees' attitudes toward diversity?

But in practice, the diversity management rubber hits the road with the daily interactions among the supervisor and his or her subordinates, and here managing diversity isn't easy. For one thing, even supervisors who view themselves as unprejudiced often jump to conclusions about people based on little more than how they look or the groups to which they belong. The accompanying Supervising the New Workforce feature explains.

3. You'll Need World-Class Basic Supervisory Skills

Finally, you'll need the basic supervisory skills required for doing supervisory work. (Recall that this work includes things such as *hire, train, and evaluate* employees, *monitor* employee performance, and *confer* with company officials). The basic required supervisory skills therefore include things such as planning and setting goals, organizing jobs and work, interviewing and screening employees, and appraising and managing performance.

Understanding Stereotypes

We all tend to take shortcuts when meeting people and to jump to conclusions based on little more than how they look, dress, or smile. Similarly, we all tend to jump to conclusions based on *stereotypes*. **Stereotypes** are generalizations that we ascribe to people based on the groups to which they belong. These stereotypes may or may not accurately apply to specific individuals in that group. For example, on discovering that the company just hired a 75-year-old worker to join her team, the supervisor might immediately assume that the worker will tire quickly and not be able to remember things very well. *What's your first reaction when you think of people from the groups in the accompanying table?*

As a supervisor, you need to be very aware of the power of stereotypes. Stereotyping affects how you react to people, how you treat them, and perhaps even how you supervise them. Like the public school teacher who erroneously assumes that all students from particular socioeconomic groups aren't as smart as the other kids in her class, you might mistakenly give some employees less challenging assignments (and even less credit for what they do), simply because of the erroneous stereotypes that you ascribe to them.

Category	What's your first reaction when you think of people from this group?
African-American Female	
Russian Male	
Japanese Female	
Person with AIDS	
Working Mother	
Cigar Smoker	

What's Ahead

The basic aim of *Supervision and Leadership in a Changing World* is to provide you with the knowledge and tools you'll need to supervise today's knowledge-based and multicultural workers. We saw in this first chapter that supervising and leading in a changing world requires, first, sharpening your leadership and multicultural skills. We'll therefore focus on leadership and diversity in Chapter 2. Then, Chapters 3–16 each focus on basic supervisory skills. Part 2 focuses on the knowledge and skills you'll need for *setting up the work*. Then we move on to *getting your employees started* (Part 3), to *leading and motivating* them (Part 4), and finally to *appraising and (if necessary) disciplining* them, and supervising their safety and union relations (Part 5). Here is the outline:

Part 1 Understanding supervision and leadership in a changing world
      Chapter 1 The supervisor's role in a changing world
      Chapter 2 Leading a diverse workforce

Part 2 Setting up the work
      Chapter 3 How to make better decisions
      Chapter 4 Planning and setting goals
      Chapter 5 Understanding budgets and how to control work processes
      Chapter 6 Organizing jobs and work

Part 3 Getting employees started
      Chapter 7 The supervisor and equal employment
      Chapter 8 Interviewing and screening employees
      Chapter 9 Orienting and training employees

Part 4 Leading and motivating employees
    Chapter 10   Using motivation and incentives
    Chapter 11   Leading the team effort
    Chapter 12   Coaching and communicating at work

Part 5 Appraising and supervising employees
    Chapter 13   Appraising and managing performance
    Chapter 14   Supervising discipline, ethics, and fair treatment at work
    Chapter 15   Handling grievances and labor relations
    Chapter 16   Supervising health and safety at work

KEY FEATURES   Because sharpening one's leadership and multicultural skills is so important, we use two boxed features in each chapter to highlight and illustrate the leadership and cultural diversity aspects of what supervisors do:

- **Leadership Applications for Supervisors** shows how supervisory tasks like planning and disciplining employees require strong leadership skills.
- **Supervising the New Workforce** emphasizes why supervisors need strong multicultural skills to do their jobs.

Chapter 1 Concept Review and Reinforcement

Key Terms

Discrimination, p. 22

Diversity, p. 19

Ethnocentrism, p. 22

Executives, p. 3

First-Line Supervisors, p. 3

Gender-role
Stereotypes, p. 22

Management, p. 3

Management Process, p. 5

Manager, p. 3

Managerial
Competence, p. 8

Managing Diversity, p. 23

Organization, p. 2

Prejudice, p. 22

Services, p. 21

Stereotypes, p. 24

Stereotyping, p. 23

Supervisors, p. 6

Tokenism, p. 22

Review of Key Concepts

Supervision	**Supervision** is the first rung of the management ladder. Supervisors are responsible for accomplishing an organization's goals by planning, organizing, staffing, leading, and controlling the efforts of the organization's people. **Supervisors** are managers who have workers—nonmanagers—as subordinates, and who direct and control the employees who actually do the work (selling the products, pressing the clothes, helping the patients, or painting the cars, for instance) day to day.
Organization	An **organization** consists of people with formally assigned roles who work together to achieve stated goals.
Types of Managers	**Types of managers** can be classified by organization level (top, middle, first-line), organizational position or rank (supervisor, manager, director), and business function title (president, sales director, CEO).
Management Process	The **management process** is made up of the supervisor's five basic functions: planning, organizing, staffing, leading, and controlling.
Supervisory Roles	**Supervisory roles** include figurehead, leader, liaison, spokesperson, and negotiator. Each role has the responsibility to reach or exceed organization goals through the management process.
Supervisory Traits	**Supervisory traits** are certain personal characteristics including integrity, initiative, leadership ability, stress tolerance, and cooperativeness, which are difficult to change and tell us much about the individual's ability to manage.
Supervisory Skills	**Supervisory skills** include technical, interpersonal, and conceptual skills. *Building supervisory skills* is a basic theme of this book. These skills are necessary if the supervisor is going to succeed.
Typical Day	A **typical day** in the life of a supervisor includes the tasks, activities, skills, and traits necessary to get the job done.

Globalization	**Globalization** refers to the tendency of firms to extend their sales, ownership, and/or manufacturing to new markets abroad. It means more competition, which in turn means more pressure to be "world class." Free trade, extended sales, new manufacturing, and global ownership will open additional supervisory and management opportunities worldwide.
Diverse Workforce	A **diverse workforce** means having a workforce composed of two or more groups of employees with various racial, ethnic, gender, cultural, national origin, handicap, age, and religious backgrounds. These trends will continue to challenge tomorrow's supervisors.

Review and Discussion Questions

1. What is supervision?
2. Given that organizations are goal directed, give some examples of how decisions to allocate resources (supplies, machines, etc.) that are made by middle managers affect how first-line supervisors do their jobs?
3. How much influence and input do you think a first line supervisor should have when the CFO (chief financial officer) changes a department budget item affecting that supervisor? Why?
4. Briefly outline the five functions of the management process.
5. Within the management process, which of the supervisory roles is most critical? Explain.
6. Why is leadership ability a key personal characteristic when identifying supervisory traits?
7. What steps would you take to build technical skills for a new supervisor? Interpersonal skills? Conceptual skills?
8. Given a typical day in the life of a supervisor, give examples of how the ability to listen and communicate are critical tasks that, if not executed properly, could deter the supervisor from reaching his or her goals.
9. How can today's supervisors better prepare for tomorrow's supervisory challenges?
10. Why is it so important that supervisors learn how to manage in a diverse workplace?

Application and Skill Building

Case Study One

"This Is My Life"—Job of a Supervisor

Anyone who has ever met Kyle Thompson comes away liking the way he looks at life. He's optimistic, likes people, and works hard. He really likes working with, helping, and talking to people. Kyle's company is located in a medium-size midwestern city. The firm distributes wholesale food and tobacco products to small convenience stores in a three-state area. Kyle got into the wholesale distribution business after working for his father in the family business during high school and two years of college. He regrets not finishing his college degree, but he has learned his business well while on the job. In the type of wholesale business that his company is in, clients come and go to competitors without much reason, so getting and keeping customers is a big part of Kyle's job.

Kyle has the title of Sales Supervisor. In that role he supervises a total of 10 drivers, sales reps, and merchandisers serving over 200 client stores. A large part of his job involves looking for new accounts. Kyle has a philosophy of leading by example—he never expects his people to do anything that he would not do himself. His strong work ethic reflects credibility, honesty, self-esteem, and good communications. His relationship with his boss is one of "best friends" and he receives 100% support for his decisions. Although his company supplies many incentives and benefits, such as new account bonuses, full benefits, and a company car, balancing personal and work lives isn't easy. An average day in this supervisor's life begins at 6 a.m. and ends with the final deliveries at 5 p.m. And anyone in this position still has to be available by telephone or e-mail seven days a week and up to 24 hours a day.

Kyle started in his present sales supervisor position 11 years ago. Although there is a formal job description for his position, he has not looked at it for a while. He feels that as long as he keeps doing his job well, he has nothing to worry about. Over the years he has completed some diversity training and short supervisory management courses through his current employer. However, he feels that the best education has been real-life experience. Kyle has determined that business success must be based on putting the customer first, being honest, and always instilling in his people a focus on trying to exceed expectations and raising the bar of performance. It hasn't always been easy, but Kyle will tell you, "I would do it all over again. This is my life."

Discussion Questions:

1. What specific indications are there that Kyle Thompson is performing the five basic functions of management: planning, organizing, staffing, leading, and controlling?
2. In his position as a sales supervisor, how is Kyle filling the various supervisory roles outlined in this chapter?
3. What recommendations would you make to Kyle that would help him to be a better supervisor ?
4. Does Kyle exhibit the managerial competence that supervisors should have?

Case Study Two

Angelo's Pizza

Angelo Camero was raised in the Bronx, New York, and always wanted to be in the pizza store business. As a youngster, he would sometimes spend hours at the local pizza store, watching the owner knead the pizza dough, flatten it into a large circular crust, fling it up, and then spread on tomato sauce in larger and larger loops. After graduating from college as a marketing major, he made a beeline back to the Bronx, where he opened Angelo's Pizza Store, emphasizing all-natural, fresh ingredients.

As an entrepreneur/supervisor, he knew he had the distinct advantage of being able to run the whole operation himself. With just one store and a handful of employees, he could make every decision and watch the cash register, check in the new supplies, oversee the takeout, and personally supervise the service. Unfortunately, that was proving more difficult than he thought it would be.

There were several issues that particularly concerned Angelo. Finding and hiring good employees was number one. He'd read the new National Small Business Poll from the National Federation of Independent Business Education Foundation. It found that 71% of small-business owners believed that finding qualified employees was "hard." Small firms were particularly in jeopardy. Giant firms can outsource many (particularly entry-level) jobs abroad, and larger companies can also afford to pay better benefits and to train their employees. Small firms rarely have the resources to do that.

While finding enough employees was his biggest problem, finding enough honest ones scared him even more. Angelo recalled from one of his business school courses that companies in the United States are losing about $9 per employee per day or about $12,000 a year for a typical company. Furthermore, small companies like Angelo's are particularly prone to employee theft. Small firms are more likely to have a single person doing several jobs, such as ordering supplies and paying the delivery person. This undercuts the checks and balances managers often strive for to control theft. Furthermore, the risk of stealing goes up dramatically when the business is based largely on cash. In a pizza store, many people come in and just buy one or two slices and a cola for lunch, and almost all pay with cash, not credit cards.

That he was having trouble hiring good employees, there was no doubt. The restaurant business is particularly brutal when it comes to turnover. Many restaurants turn over their employees at a rate of 200% to 300% per year—so every year, each position might have a series of two to three employees filling it. As Angelo said, "I was losing two to three employees a month."

The problem was bad at the hourly employee level: "We were churning a lot at the hourly level," said Angelo. "Applicants would come in, and (being desperate) I'd just hire them and not do much training.

Angelo knew he should have a more formal screening process. As he said, "If there's been a lesson learned, it's much better to spend time up-front screening out candidates that don't fit than to hire them and have to put up with their ineffectiveness." He also knew that he could identify many of the traits that his employees needed. For example, he knew that not everyone has the temperament to be a server (he has a small pizza/Italian restaurant in the back of his store). As Angelo said, "I've seen personalities that were off the charts in assertiveness or overly introverted, traits that obviously don't make a good fit for a waiter a waitress." "I should know better," but he hired people based almost exclusively on a single interview (he occasionally made a feeble attempt to check references).

What was he looking for? Mostly for service-oriented courteous people. For example, he'd hired one employee who used profanity several times, including once in front of a customer. On that employee's third day, Angelo had to tell her, "I think Angelo's isn't the right place for you," and he fired her. As Angelo said, "I felt bad, but also knew that everything I have is on the line for this business, so I wasn't going to let anyone run this business down." Angelo wants reliable people (who'll show up on time), honest people, and people who are flexible about switching jobs and hours as required.

Angelo's Pizza business has only the most rudimentary human resource management system. Training is entirely on-the-job. Angelo personally trained each of his employees. If you asked Angelo what his reputation is as an employer/supervisor, Angelo, being a candid and forthright person, would probably tell you that he is a supportive but hard-nosed supervisor who treats people fairly, but whose business reputation may suffer from disorganization stemming from inadequate organization and training. He approaches you to ask you several questions.

Questions

1. For what you can tell, how am I doing overall as a supervisor? Do I have the necessary skills? Am I fulfilling all the core supervisory responsibilities? Please explain your answer to me.
2. Identify and briefly discuss five specific human resource management-type errors that I seem to be making.
3. Based on what you know about Angelo's, and what you know from having visited pizza restaurants, write a one-page outline showing specifically how you think Angelo's should go about selecting employees.
5. Why do you think Angelo is "at a distinct advantage" being able to personally keep an eye on everything happening in his store? Do you agree with him? Why?

Experiential Activities

Activity 1. Jennifer Carter, after graduating from college, decided to go into business with her father. Since 1995, Jack Carter opened six combined coin laundry and dry cleaning centers. Each store had about seven employees and an on-site supervisor. Jennifer's aim was to learn the business and bring to it modern management techniques.

We saw in the opening snapshot that Carter's Pompano, Florida, store was in crisis. A "boil-over" severely burned the stores cleaner-spotter. Doris, a long-term counter person, took charge. She helped retrain all of the store's employees and made some personnel changes; the results were quick and dramatic. Drop-offs of clothes were 50% higher the second week after Doris took over.

The bottom line is that the effects of good supervision are amazing. Install a skilled supervisor, and he or she can soon get the enterprise humming. About 90% of new businesses started this year will fail within five years. Companies with better supervisors perform better. It is hard to overstate how important good supervisors are to American industry.

Doris As Supervisor

Purpose: The purpose of this exercise is to give you practice applying what you learned in this chapter about the supervisor's job.

Required understanding: You are going to evaluate Doris' effectiveness as a supervisor. You should therefore be fully familiar with this chapter's explanation of what supervisors do, and what makes a supervisor effective.

How to Set Up the exercise/Instructions: Divide the class into groups of 4–5 students.

1. Answer the question: Based on the opening snapshot, list the supervisory traits, skills, and competencies that Doris seems to bring to her job as supervisor. What do you base your answer on?
2. Next, your group should list the work activities that Doris, as store supervisor, can be expected to engage in.
3. Based on what you know, how would you rate Doris' supervisory effectiveness. Why? What would you suggest she do to improve her effectiveness (assuming it requires some improvement.)

Activity 2. On your computer, go to an Internet search provider and type in "supervisor job openings." Choose three job openings that list required skills. Create a one-page summary listing the job title, job location, and the required skills for each of the job openings. Bring this summary to class and compare it to those of the other students.

Activity 3. Contact and interview two individuals who are supervisors (according to this text's definition). Ask each interviewee to indicate to you what activities/tasks, (such as interviewing, disciplining, and coaching) he or she performs in an average workday. Also, ask each interviewee to estimate the percentage of time spent performing the functions of management, planning, organizing, staffing, leading and controlling. Bring a summary of these interviews to class for discussion. How do these supervisors' activities compare to those in Figure 1.3?

Role-Playing Exercise

Hiring of a Supervisor: The Situation

The HR department at your university has decided to search for, interview, and hire a highly qualified candidate for a supervisory position in the maintenance department. They know that you have closely studied the material in this chapter and are qualified to put together a list of questions to ask a candidate for this position.

Instructions

All students should read the situation above and should have studied Chapter 1 closely. Each team will be assigned 4–5 members and will choose one member who will play the job candidate while the other members will make up an interviewing panel to interview the job candidate. The "interviewers" should make up a list of questions that the interview panel would like to ask the candidate. The questions should focus on discovering whether the "candidate" has the competencies, skills, and traits that effective supervisors need. Then, spend several minutes having one interviewer ask the candidate the questions.

A Class Discussion Will Follow the Role-Playing Presentation

Each team should type or neatly write their questions and the candidate's answers and hand them in with a cover sheet at the end of the class presentation. If time permits the teams should compare their questions and their results from the interviews.

2 Leading Today's Diverse Workforce

CHAPTER OBJECTIVES

After studying this chapter, you should be able to answer these questions:

1. What Is Leadership?
2. What Are the Basic Theories of Leadership?
3. How Can a Supervisor Put Leadership Theory into Practice?
4. How Can a Supervisor Strengthen Leadership Skills?
5. What Guidelines Help a Supervisor Lead a Diverse Workforce?

OPENING SNAPSHOT
Where Did Rudy Go Wrong?

On his first day supervising the new-claims unit at Alpha Insurance Group, Rudy, the newly appointed supervisor, gathered his team to give them their assignments for the day. Having never done anything quite like this before, he haltingly told each person what to do. "Uh, Domingo, I'd like you, uh, to please make a list of the new claims we received yesterday evening, and, uh, Bianca, would you please help, uh, Domingo?" Still staring at his notes, Rudy heard some chuckling from the back. He was disheartened to find at the end of the day that his team had accomplished nothing. The whole distasteful experience that day left Rudy wondering if he was cut out for supervising. What (if anything) did he do wrong, and what should he do now to solve the problem?

1. What Is Leadership?

At the end of the day, supervision comes down to execution. It matters not if you know everything about the job's technical aspects, or about how to plan, organize, staff, and control. Your team must accomplish its goals, and (since it is people who do the work) execution requires effective leadership.

Defining Leadership

What Is Leadership?

Leadership means *influencing someone to work willingly toward a predetermined objective.* Leadership is the distinctly motivational and interpersonal facet of what supervisors do.

Leadership is a difficult subject to learn. You can excel at tasks like planning just by learning technical things such as how to budget. The tricky thing about leadership (as you probably know from your own experience) is that leadership isn't just technical. Effective leaders seem to have a talent for getting other people to follow them willingly. There is always a bit of magic in what makes great leaders great.

Studying Leadership

The question of what makes some leaders more effective than others has therefore long fascinated experts. Machiavelli, a shrewd advisor to kings and princes, addressed the question 400 years ago, and the Bible often refers to actions leaders should take to be more effective (as in Exodus, "Therefore now go, lead the people unto the place which I have spoken unto thee: behold, Mine Angel shall go before thee.") Certainly, medieval kings, pharaohs, and even the earliest "team leaders" who led bands of cave dwellers across the plains must have asked themselves, "What makes some people more effective as leaders than others?"[1]

The current thinking, in brief, is this: Effective supervisory leadership reflects a balance of (1) your traits and skills, and (2) how you act (your leadership behaviors), all combined in a way that is (3) right for the situation. Leadership, in other words, reflects who we "are" (in terms of traits and skills) and how we "behave" (our leadership style) in particular situations.

2. Basic Theories of Leadership

What Are the Basic Theories of Leadership?

The three main scientific approaches to studying leadership therefore focus on the leader's *traits and skills*, on his or her *behavior*, and on how the *situation* influences what type of leader is best.[2] We start with leadership traits and skills.

It's Who You Are: The Leader's Traits

The idea that great leaders have particular personality traits that make them great resonates with most people. Who hasn't had a classmate whose charisma and decisiveness made him or her stand out as the most likely to succeed? It's therefore not surprising that the earliest leadership researchers thought that if they studied great leaders' personalities, they would stumble on the traits that made these people great. These "Great Man Theory" experts' assumption (often unstated) was that great leaders are born, not made. In other words, if you don't have these in-bred traits, nothing will make you a leader. But most experts today would probably disagree. They'd say that there is a lot we can all do to build up the traits that we're born with and so develop our leadership potential.[3]

WHAT TRAITS DO LEADERS NEED? Research suggests that successful leaders are not like other people. For example, after reviewing 163 studies of leadership traits some years ago, Professor Ralph Stogdill put it this way:

> The leader is characterized by a strong drive for responsibility and task completion, vigor and persistence in pursuit of goals, venturesomeness and originality in problem solving, drive to exercise initiative in social situations, self-confidence and sense of personal identity, willingness to accept consequences of decision and action, readiness to absorb interpersonal stress, willingness to tolerate frustration and delay, ability to influence other persons' behavior, and capacity to structure social interaction systems to the purpose at hand.[4]

Table 2.1 summarizes the leadership traits that Stogdill concluded were important.

More recent research supports Stogdill's findings. For example, "The evidence indicates that there are certain core traits which significantly contribute to business leaders' success."[5] These include drive, the desire to lead, honesty, self-confidence, cognitive ability, and knowledge of the business. Let's look at these traits.

LEADERS HAVE DRIVE Great leaders are action-oriented people who want to achieve. They derive satisfaction from challenging tasks. Leaders are more ambitious than non leaders. They need high energy because "working long, intense work weeks requires an

■ Table **2.1**

Traits and Skills That Distinguish Leaders from Nonleaders	
Leadership Traits	**Leadership Skills**
Adaptable to situations	Clever (intelligent)
Alert to social environment	Conceptually skilled
Ambitious, achievement oriented	Creative
Assertive	Diplomatic and tactful
Cooperative	Fluent in speaking
Decisive	Knowledgeable about the work
Dependable	Organized (administrative ability)
Dominant (power motivation)	Persuasive
Energetic (high activity level)	Socially skilled
Persistent	
Self-confident	
Tolerate of stress	
Willing to assume responsibility	

Source: Based on Ralph Stogdill, *Handbook of Leadership: A Survey of the Literature* (New York: Free Press, 1974), p. 237.

individual to have physical, mental, and emotional vitality."[6] Leaders are also tenacious. They're better at overcoming obstacles than are nonleaders.[7]

LEADERS ARE MOTIVATED TO LEAD   Leaders prefer to be in leadership rather than subordinate roles. They willingly accept the mantle of authority.[8]

LEADERS ARE HONEST   If people can't trust you, why should they follow you? Studies find that people tend to rate leaders as more trustworthy and reliable than followers.[9] One sure way to undermine your leadership prospects is to give people reason to mistrust you.

LEADERS HAVE SELF-CONFIDENCE   The first mistake Rudy probably made with his new-claims team was in coming across as insecure. Two experts put it this way: "Obviously, if the leader is not sure of what decision to make, or expresses a high degree of doubt, then the followers are less likely to trust the leader and be committed to the vision."[10]

LEADERS HAVE COGNITIVE ABILITY   Would you keep following someone who keeps making mistakes? Probably not. "Cognitive ability" means the ability to make good decisions. It's the leader who must pick the right direction and then put mechanisms in place to get there. The leader's intelligence and judgment are, therefore, crucial leadership traits.[11] We'll explain how to improve your decision-making skills in Chapter 3.

LEADERS KNOW THE BUSINESS   The more you know about the problem at hand, the better your decisions should be. That's why effective leaders work hard to be knowledgeable about the tasks they're supervising. Their knowledge helps them anticipate their decisions' implications and thus make better decisions.[12] For example, when he moved from president of Boeing Aircraft to CEO of Ford Motor Company a few years ago, Alan Mullaly immersed himself in the details of Ford's businesses for six months, so he could then make informed decisions. But this isn't true for CEOs. Whether you're supervising an auto repair shop or a team of insurance adjusters, make sure you know how to actually do the work.

Do You Have the Clout? Power and Leadership

Power is another important leadership trait. Perhaps you've had the unfortunate experience of being in charge of something—only to find that your subordinates ignore your instructions. This underscores a fact of supervisory leadership: *A leader without power is really not a leader at all, since he or she has no chance of influencing anyone to do anything.* Knowing how to enhance your authority at work is therefore crucial.

SOURCES OF POWER   The first thing to know is that supervisors derive their power from several sources. For example, some positions in the company (such as CEO) have more *position* power than do others (such as plant manager). You also have power based on your authority to *reward* employees who do well, or to *coerce* or *punish* those who don't. You may have *expert* power. Here you are such an authority on a subject that people do what you ask because they respect your expertise. And perhaps you possess *referent* power based on your personal magnetism and charisma.

Control over *information* is another source of power. Some people in a **gatekeeper** position (such as the president's assistant) control access to information, and thereby exercise power over others.

Whatever your source of power at work, it must be *legitimate*. After all, leading means influencing people to work *willingly* toward achieving the objective. That is not to say that a little fear can't be a good thing for leaders. Here is how Machiavelli summed this up in his book *The Prince*:

> One ought to be both feared and loved, but as it is difficult for the two to go together, it is much safer to be feared than loved, for love is held by a chain of obligation which, men being selfish, is broken whenever it serves their purpose; but fear is maintained by a dread of punishment which never fails.[13]

The point is, do not leave your authority to chance. Skillful supervisors work to bulk up their authority from all sources. The accompanying checklist shows some ways to do this.

DON'T IGNORE YOUR FOLLOWERS' INFLUENCE   Years ago management expert Chester Barnard wrote that supervisors only have as much power *as their followers grant them.*[14] This may seem counterintuitive: After all, aren't you the boss? Here is what Barnard would say. You may be in charge of Alpha Insurance's new-claims unit. However, if your subordinates don't respect you or take you seriously, your orders may not be obeyed.

Checklist » Don't Leave Your Authority to Chance

You have more
Reward power if you can:

Increase pay levels and specific benefits.

Control or influence getting a raise or a promotion.

Coercive power if you can:

Give undesirable work assignments and make the job difficult or unpleasant.

Discipline and/or dismiss employees.

Legitimate position power if you have:

A clear position in the chain of command, with authority to issue orders.

Clear and visible support of your superiors.

Clear and visible support from your peers.

Expert power if you can:

Provide needed technical knowledge.

Share considerable experience and/or training.

Provide sound job-related advice.

Information power if you can:

Control access to important information, people, or schedules.

Referent power if you can:

Exhibit charisma through the power of your personality.

Use the right leadership style for the situation.

Thus you must always be thinking through how to convince (or entice) your followers to *accept* your orders.

COMMAND AND CONTROL? This acceptance issue is especially important today. Generation Y employees are averse to blindly following orders. Furthermore, companies today often organize around self-managing teams. Trying to lead people like these by relying too much on formal (position) authority is a dubious tactic. After all, does it make sense to be constantly telling a self-managing team how to do things? Therefore, the command and control ("I'm the boss, so you must do what I say") approach to leadership is giving way to a more coaching-based system. But coaching and convincing subordinates is more tricky than simply telling them what to do. That's why it is important today for supervisors to have strong leadership skills.

It's How You Behave: Leader Behaviors

"I wouldn't work for him again if he were the last person on earth" sums up how some people feel about a particularly disagreeable former supervisor. At the other extreme are those gifted supervisors whose employees say, "I'd follow her through a burning building if she asked." What is it about how a leader behaves that triggers such emotions?

Having power and the right built-in traits won't guarantee successful leadership—they are only a foundation, a precondition. For example, we all know brilliant people whom we'd rather not work for because their actions are so abominable.[15] As two experts said, "Traits only endow people with the potential for leadership."[16] The leader must then engage in the *behaviors* required to get his or her people to move in the desired direction. In other words, your subordinates want to see how you act and how you treat them. Wouldn't you?

Researchers have spent decades trying to explain how a leader's style or behavior relates to his or her effectiveness. The assumption underlying this line of research is generally that leaders are there to perform two main functions—*accomplishing the task* and *satisfying followers' needs*. The leader's *task*-oriented behaviors include clarifying for subordinates what they must do, and then making sure they do it. The leader's social or *people-oriented* behaviors include reducing tension and boosting morale. As in Figure 2.1, we'll see next that various experts approached these task and people dimensions in several ways.[17]

THE OHIO STATE STUDIES Research aimed at studying leadership styles began years ago at The Ohio State University. Ralph Stogdill and his team developed a survey called the Leader Behavior Description Questionnaire (LBDQ).[18] It measures two leadership styles which they called consideration and initiating structure:[19]

- **Consideration.** Leader behavior indicative of mutual trust, friendship, support, respect, and warmth. (Example: "The leader is friendly and approachable.")
- **Initiating structure.** Leader behavior by which the person organizes the work to be done and defines relationships or roles, the channels of communication, and

■Figure **2.1**

**How Different
Research Centers
Define People and
Task Leadership
Styles**

Research Center	What They Called the *People-Oriented* Style	What They Called the *Task-Oriented* Style
Ohio State	Consideration	Initiating structure
University of Michigan	Employee-oriented	Job-centered
University of Michigan	General	Close

ways of getting jobs done. (Example: "The leader lets group members know what is expected of them.")

Stogdill's basic question was, "Which of these styles (being task-oriented, or being considerate) makes a leader more effective?" That subordinates were usually more *satisfied* with considerate, supportive leaders is not in doubt.[20] The problem is that many considerate leaders actually had *lower* performing groups! Conversely, task leadership didn't always work either. These hard-nosed leaders tended to produce higher performance, but also more grievances. However, digging deeper into the Ohio State line of research, perceptive supervisors can draw at least two useful conclusions:

1. *First*, it's usually not one style or the other but a balance that works best.[21] For example, beware of becoming what some experts call the "country club" leader: all consideration and no focus on the work.[22] Great leaders balance supportiveness with an insistence that employees get their jobs done. As one said, "I've tried to create a culture of caring for people in the totality of their lives, not just at work. . . . How you treat them determines how they treat people on the outside."[23] However, this former Southwest Airlines CEO also kept all his employees focused on the company's cost-cutting goals. Southwest still remains a leader in airline efficiency

2. *Second*, the leadership style (considerate or task) that's right for one situation might be wrong for another. We'll see that effective supervisors have a knack for adapting their style to the situation.

THE UNIVERSITY OF MICHIGAN STUDIES   While the Ohio State researchers were working with their LBDQ, Professor Rensis Likert and his University of Michigan team were conducting a parallel series of leadership style studies. Likert's **employee-oriented leaders** focus on the individuality and personality needs of their employees and emphasize building good interpersonal relationships. His **job-centered leaders** focus on production and the job's technical aspects. Based on his review of the research results, Likert recommended a balanced approach. He said that,

> Supervisors with the best record of performance focus on the human aspects of their subordinates' problems and on endeavoring to build effective work groups with high performance goals.[24]

Other University of Michigan researchers have yet another twist on the basic people and task leadership styles. They studied what they called close and general leadership styles. **Close supervision** is at "one end of a continuum that describes the degree to which a supervisor specifies the roles of subordinates and checks up to see that they comply with these specifications."[25] The **laissez-faire leader** who follows a hands-off policy with subordinates is at the other extreme. A **general leader** is toward the middle of the continuum. He or she sets guidelines, but lets employees use their discretion within those guidelines.

Not surprisingly, they found that most people don't like being closely supervised. Close supervision was usually associated with lower employee morale. Yet, in practice, knowing when to put your foot down and when to back off is a dilemma. In many situations, employees do need to have close, specific guidelines, if the work is to get done right, and in such situations, laissez-faire leadership can be a disaster (would you want a laissez-faire captain if your sailboat were sinking?). Findings such as these further underscored the idea that leaders probably have to adjust their styles to fit the task.

■ Figure **2.2**

How Level 5 Leaders Behave

Source: Adapted from Jim Collins, "Level 5 Leadership," *Harvard Business Review*, January 2001, p. 73.

Personal Humility Behaviors	Professional Will Behaviors
Demonstrates a compelling modesty, shunning public adulation, never boastful.	Creates superb results, a clear catalyst in the transition from good to great.
Acts with quiet, calm determination, not charisma, to motivate.	Demonstrates an unwavering resolve to do whatever must be done to produce the best long-term results, no matter how difficult.
Channels ambition into the company, not him- or herself.	Sets the standard of building an enduring, great company; will settle for nothing less.
Looks in the mirror, not out the window, to apportion responsibility for poor results, never blaming other people, external factors, or bad luck.	Looks out the window, not in the mirror, to apportion credit for the success of the company—to other people, external factors, and good luck.

THE LEVEL 5 LEADERSHIP STYLE   Is there one style of leadership that can make a good company great? That is a question researchers Jim Collins and Jerry Porras pursue in their book *Built to Last: Successful Habits of Visionary Companies.*[26] Collins and Porras studied 11 companies that had started out as "good" (competent, but nothing spectacular) and then ended up as "great." The "great" firms' market values grew eight to nine times faster than average.

Collins and Porras found that most good-to-great companies had leaders who exhibited what Collins calls the Level 5 Leadership Style. Figure 2.2 summarizes the two main sets of behaviors associated with this style. Level 5 leadership is a blend of *personal humility* and *professional will.* In terms of humility, Level 5 leaders are modest, calm. They are willing to take the blame when things go wrong. But they also exhibit professional will. They have an unwavering resolve to do what's necessary to produce the best results.

LEADERSHIP STYLE AND EMOTIONAL INTELLIGENCE   A supervisor's leadership style also depends partly on his or her level of "emotional intelligence." People who score high on emotional intelligence act self-confident, trustworthy, achievement-oriented, culturally sensitive, and persuasive. Those scoring low behave quite the opposite.

As an example, researchers studied 3,810 executives. They concluded that these executives typically used one or more of six leadership styles (see Figure 2.3). They called these leadership styles coercive, authoritative, affiliative, democratic, pacesetting, and coaching.

They concluded that each style reflected and depended upon different aspects of emotional intelligence. For example (see Figure 2.3), consider the coercive, do-what-I-tell-you leader. His or her style reflects facets of his or her emotional intelligence, such as the drive to control. Democratic leadership reflects emotional intelligence facets such as collaboration and communication.

The researchers came to two useful conclusions for supervisors. First, "[l]eaders with the best results do not rely on only one leadership style; they use most of them in any given week—seamlessly and in different measure—depending on the business situation."[27] The second conclusion stems from the first: The best style for one situation might not work in another situation. The leader must fit the leadership style to the situation.[28]

Transformational Leadership

In his book *Leadership,* James McGregor Burns puts a different spin on the question of leadership style.[29] Burns argued that a leader's behavior is either *transactional* or *trans-*

For each style, the Leader's	Coercive Style	Authoritative Style	Affiliative Style
Distinctive behavior>>>>>	Demands immediate compliance	Mobilizes people toward a vision	Creates harmony and builds emotional bonds
The style in a nutshell>>>>	"Do what I tell you."	"Come with me."	"People come first."
Underlying **emotional intelligence** traits this style reflects >>>>>>	Drive to achieve, initiative, self-control	Self-confidence, empathy, change catalyst	Empathy, building relationships, communication
When this leadership style works best >>>>>>	In a crisis, kick-start a turnaround, or with problem employees	When changes require a new vision, or when a clear direction is needed	To heal rifts in a team or to motivate people during stressful circumstances
Overall impact on employees' morale >>>>>	Negative	Strongly positive	Positive

For each style, the Leader's	Democratic Style	Pacesetting Style	Coaching Style
Distinctive behavior>>>>>	Forges consensus through participation	Sets high standards for performance	Develops people for the future
The style in a nutshell>>>>	"What do you think?"	"Do as I do, now."	"Try this."
Underlying **emotional intelligence** traits this style reflects >>>>>>	Collaboration, team leadership, communication	Conscientiousness, drive to achieve, initiative	Developing others, empathy, self-awareness
When this leadership style works best >>>>>>	To build buy-in or consensus, or to get input from valuable employees	To get quick results from a highly motivated and competent team	To help an employee improve performance or develop long-term strengths
Overall impact on employees' morale >>>>>	Positive	Negative	Positive

■Figure **2.3**

Emotional Intelligence and Six Leadership Styles at a Glance

Source: Daniel Goleman, "Leadership That Gets Results," *Harvard Business Review*, March–April 2000, pp. 82–83.

formational.[30] He says leader behaviors such as initiating structure and consideration, or close and general, all just reflect "quid pro quo" transactions. In other words, "You do something for me, and I'll do something for you." ("You do this, and you'll get a raise," for instance.) So (says McGregor) the "people" and "task"-type leader styles are both **transactional behaviors.** They are "largely oriented toward accomplishing the tasks at hand and at maintaining good relations with those working with the leader [exchanging promises of rewards for performance]."[31] Burns says that transactional leadership is okay for many everyday situations. However, he says, transactional leadership won't work when the task requires inspiring people to make a big change. Motivating major change requires more than just a "you do this and I'll give you a raise" approach.

WHAT TRANSFORMATIONAL LEADERS DO   That's where transformational leadership comes in. **Transformational leaders** are those who bring about "change, innovation, and entrepreneurship."[32] Whether it's a new work procedure, or moving to new offices, or reorganizing how the work is done, they're the supervisors who are capable of providing their followers with a new vision and of revitalizing and institutionalizing the change.[33] What specific behaviors do transformational leaders use to work such magic? They are the following:

- **Charismatic.** Employees often develop strong emotional attachments to them. A typical comment is, "I am ready to trust him or her to overcome any obstacle."[34]

- **Inspirational.** "The [transformational] leader passionately communicates a future idealistic organization that can be shared. The leader uses visionary explanations to depict what the employee work group can accomplish."[35]
- **Considerate.** The transformational leader treats employees as individuals, and stresses developing them in a way that encourages the employees to become all they can be.
- **Stimulating.** The transformational leader encourages "employees to approach old and familiar problems in new ways."[36] He or she "shows me how to think about problems in new ways."

So, to summarize, in most day-to-day situations you'll face as supervisor, knowing how to balance just how participative/people-oriented and directive/task-oriented you behave is probably sufficient. But there will be times when some big change is in order. For that, you'd better know how to be transformational.

HOW SUPERVISORS USE TRANSFORMATIONAL LEADERSHIP DAY TO DAY   Of course, when a manager like Alan Mullaly comes into a struggling Ford to turn it around, it's obvious that the leader must be transformational. But transformational leadership is *not* just for turning around entire companies. Even pushing through small changes (such as leading the introduction of a new product) requires transformational leadership, for instance.[37] So the bottom line is that even first-line supervisors can benefit from being transformational (inspirational, charismatic, stimulating, and considerate) when the situation arises. To be a transformational supervisor:[38]

Supervising the New Workforce

Gender Differences in Leadership Styles

Although the number of women in supervisory jobs has risen to almost 40%, women hold barely 2% of top leadership posts.[39] The question is, why?

The evidence suggests that it's not due to some inherent inability of women to lead. That's hardly a surprising conclusion given business leaders such as Avon CEO Andrea Jung and Kraft CEO Irene Rosenfeld. But then, what is the reason?

Institutional biases (a "glass ceiling") explain part of the problem. Women often simply don't get access to the same old boy network their male colleagues so easily draw on.

Persistent, *inaccurate stereotypes* are another reason. For example, people tend to identify masculine (competitive) characteristics as managerial. They identify (cooperative and communicative) characteristics as nonmanagerial.[40] Another inaccurate stereotype is that women managers fail under pressure, respond impulsively, and have difficulty managing their emotions.[41]

Such stereotypes don't hold up. Studies suggest few measurable differences in the leader behaviors women and men use on the job. Women supervisors were somewhat more achievement-oriented; men were more candid with coworkers.[42] In another study, the only gender differences were that women were more understanding than men.[43] Women and men who score high on the need for power (the need to influence other people) tend to behave more like each other than like people with lower power needs.[44]

How do women supervisors rate when compared with men? In actual work settings, "Women and men in similar positions receive similar ratings."[45] In an assessment center, in which supervisors had to perform realistic leadership tasks (such as leading problem-solving groups), men and women supervisors performed similarly. Only in several off-the-job laboratory studies did men score higher in performance.[46]

There was one difference. Women often score higher on measures of patience, relationship development, social sensitivity, and communication. And these may be precisely the leadership skills supervisors need to manage diversity and self-managing teams.[47]

- Articulate a clear and appealing vision.
- Explain how the vision can be attained.
- Act confident and optimistic.
- Express confidence in followers.
- Provide opportunities for early successes.
- Celebrate successes.
- Use dramatic, symbolic actions to emphasize key values.
- Lead by example.
- Empower people to achieve the vision.

Do women and men have different approaches to leadership styles? The accompanying Supervising the New Workforce feature addresses this question.

Adapting Your Style to the Situation: Situational Leadership Theories

By this point, you've probably noticed two things from our discussion on leadership traits and styles:

[handwritten: is situational based on this]

1. First, the leadership traits and styles that might be right for one situation may backfire in another. For example, considerate leaders sometimes have low-performing teams.

2. Second, leaders can exhibit more than one style—they can be considerate but still directive, for instance.

The question is, When and under what conditions should a supervisor use one style (or styles) or another? When should you let your subordinates participate, and when should you clamp down? Researchers have studied and put forth several models to help supervisors decide how to answer this. We'll look at three of these models next.

FIEDLER'S CONTINGENCY THEORY OF LEADERSHIP   Researcher Fred E. Fiedler and his team created the first and perhaps best-known situational (or "contingency") theory of leadership. They started out to study whether a leader who was lenient in evaluating associates was more likely or less likely to have a high-producing group than a leader who was more demanding.[48]

Fiedler measured leadership style with what he named his Least Preferred Co-worker (LPC) scale. Leaders who describe their least preferred coworker *favorably* (pleasant, smart, and so on) are "high LPC" and more people-oriented. (Fiedler reasonably assumed that you must be a "people person" if you described even people you don't like favorably.) "Low LPCs" describe least preferred coworkers *unfavorably*. Fiedler viewed these people as more task-oriented. Figure 2.4 presents the Fiedler LPC scale. Those scoring high (4.9 or above) on it are high LPCs. Those scoring low (1.8 or below) are low LPCs.

According to Fiedler's theory, three aspects of the situation determine whether the high-LPC (people-oriented) or the low-LPC (task-oriented) style is best for the situation:

1. **Leader position power.**   The degree to which the leader's status and rank enable him or her to get group members to follow orders. In other words, how much clout do you have?

■Figure **2.4**

Fiedler's LPC Leadership Scale

Source: Fred E. Fiedler, *A Theory of Leadership Effectiveness* (New York McGraw-Hill, 1967), p. 41.

Look at the words at both ends of the line before you put in your "X." Please remember that there is *no right or wrong answer*. Work rapidly; your first answer is likely to be the best. Please do not omit any items, and mark each item only once.

LPC

Think of the person *with whom you can work least well*. He or she may be someone you work with now, or he may be someone you knew in the past.

He or she does not have to be the person you like least well, but he or she should be the person with whom you had the most difficulty in getting a job done. Describe this person as he or she appears to you.

Pleasant	:___	:___	:___	:___	:___	:___	:___	:___:	Unpleasant
	8	7	6	5	4	3	2	1	
Friendly	:___	:___	:___	:___	:___	:___	:___	:___:	Unfriendly
	8	7	6	5	4	3	2	1	
Rejecting	:___	:___	:___	:___	:___	:___	:___	:___:	Accepting
	1	2	3	4	5	6	7	8	
Helpful	:___	:___	:___	:___	:___	:___	:___	:___:	Frustrating
	8	7	6	5	4	3	2	1	
Unenthusiastic	:___	:___	:___	:___	:___	:___	:___	:___:	Enthusiastic
	1	2	3	4	5	6	7	8	
Tense	:___	:___	:___	:___	:___	:___	:___	:___:	Relaxed
	1	2	3	4	5	6	7	8	
Distant	:___	:___	:___	:___	:___	:___	:___	:___:	Close
	1	2	3	4	5	6	7	8	
Cold	:___	:___	:___	:___	:___	:___	:___	:___:	Warm
	1	2	3	4	5	6	7	8	
Cooperative	:___	:___	:___	:___	:___	:___	:___	:___:	Uncooperative
	8	7	6	5	4	3	2	1	
Supportive	:___	:___	:___	:___	:___	:___	:___	:___:	Hostile
	8	7	6	5	4	3	2	1	
Boring	:___	:___	:___	:___	:___	:___	:___	:___:	Interesting
	1	2	3	4	5	6	7	8	
Quarrelsome	:___	:___	:___	:___	:___	:___	:___	:___:	Harmonious
	1	2	3	4	5	6	7	8	
Self-assured	:___	:___	:___	:___	:___	:___	:___	:___:	Hesitant
	8	7	6	5	4	3	2	1	
Efficient	:___	:___	:___	:___	:___	:___	:___	:___:	Inefficient
	8	7	6	5	4	3	2	1	
Gloomy	:___	:___	:___	:___	:___	:___	:___	:___:	Cheerful
	1	2	3	4	5	6	7	8	
Open	:___	:___	:___	:___	:___	:___	:___	:___:	Guarded
	8	7	6	5	4	3	2	1	

2. **Task structure.**   How structured and predictable the work group's task is.
3. **Leader-member relations.**   The extent to which the leader gets along with workers and the extent to which they have confidence in and are loyal to him or her.

Of the three situational factors, Fiedler wrote that leader–member relations seem to be the key: "A leader who is liked, accepted, and trusted by his members will find it easy to make his [or her] influence felt."[49]

Fiedler concluded that the appropriateness of the leadership style depends on how "favorable" the situation is for the leader. He said that where the situation is either favorable or unfavorable for the leader (*where leader–member relationships, task structure, and leader position power all are either very high or very low*), a more task-oriented, low-LPC leader is best. Why? In favorable situations, the leader can get away with just focusing on the task. In unfavorable situations, the leader essentially has no choice but to focus on the task.

In the middle range, where the three factors are more mixed and the task is not as clear-cut, a more people-oriented, high-LPC leader is appropriate.

Figure 2.5 summarizes both the relationships involved and how to apply Fiedler's model. Many subsequent research findings produced mixed results. The usefulness of Fiedler's theory, including its more recent variants, remains in dispute.[50]

PATH–GOAL LEADERSHIP THEORY   Path–goal leadership theory says leaders have two basic tasks. One is to increase the personal rewards subordinates receive for achieving their goals. The other is to make the path to these goals easier to follow by reducing roadblocks—such as by explaining what needs to be done and organizing the work. Stripped to its essentials, path–goal theory says this: If the job is ambiguous, structure it. If it is demoralizing, be supportive. If it's not clear how the employees will be rewarded, clarify it.

Path–goal leadership theory is based on the *expectancy theory of motivation*. Expectancy theory says that whether a person will be motivated depends on whether the person believes he or she *can accomplish* a task, and on whether he or she *desires* to

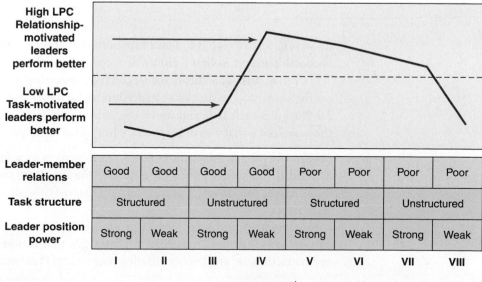

■Figure **2.5**

How Style of Effective Leadership Varies with Situation

Source: Adapted and reprinted by permission of the *Harvard Business Review*. "How the Style of Effective Leadership Varies with the Situation" from "Engineer the Job to Fit the Manager" by Fred E. Fiedler, September–October 1965. Copyright © 1965 by the President and Fellows of Harvard College; all rights reserved.

Leader-member relations	Good	Good	Good	Good	Poor	Poor	Poor	Poor
Task structure	Structured		Unstructured		Structured		Unstructured	
Leader position power	Strong	Weak	Strong	Weak	Strong	Weak	Strong	Weak
	I	II	III	IV	V	VI	VII	VIII

Fitting the Style to the Situation Using Path–Goal Theory

Leadership Style	What Does This Leader Do?	Best For What Situation?	Motivational Effects of This Leader Behavior
Directive	Lets subordinates know what is expected of them, gives specific guidance as to what should be done and how it should be done, and schedules the work	Ambiguous, unstructured	Reduces ambiguity; increases follower beliefs that effort will result in good performance, and that performance will be rewarded.
Supportive	Friendly and approachable, and shows concern for followers' status and well-being	Frustrating, stressful, or dissatisfying tasks. Employees may lack self-confidence.	Increases self-confidence; increases the personal value of job-related effort.
Participative	Consults with subordinates, solicits their suggestions, and may even let the employees themselves make the decisions	Ambiguous, nonrepetitive, challenging	Reduces ambiguity, clarifies expectations, increases involvement with and commitment to organizational goals.
Achievement-oriented	Sets challenging goals, expects subordinates to perform at their highest levels, continuously seeks improvement in performance, and shows a high degree of confidence in subordinates	Ambiguous, nonrepetitive, challenging	Increases subordinate confidence and the perceived value of goal-directed effort.

Source: Adapted and modified from Jon Howell and Dan Costley, *Understanding Behavior for Effective Leadership* (Upper Saddle River, NJ: Prentice Hall, 2001), p. 43.

do so. The leader's job is to make sure both the "ability" and "desire" answers are "yes." Leadership expert Robert J. House developed path–goal leadership theory.[51]

Today, path–goal theory focuses on four leadership styles: directive leadership, supportive leadership, participative leadership, and achievement-oriented leadership.[80] Table 2.2 illustrates each style and shows the situations in which it's most appropriate. Again, the basic idea is that you've got to adapt how directive or participative you are to the task.

SUBSTITUTES FOR LEADERSHIP THEORY Path–goal theory implies that the leader's job is to substitute somehow for the nature of the situation. For example, ambiguous situations call for directive leadership.[52] Dissatisfying situations call for supportive leadership.

Steve Kerr and J. M. Jermier propose a "Substitutes for Leadership" theory that sort of turns that idea on its head.[53] They argue that various characteristics of the subordinates, the task, and the organization may either (1) *substitute for* (render unnecessary)

■ Table 2.3

Substitutes for Leadership: Substitutes and Neutralizers for Supportive and Instrumental Leadership		
Characteristics of the Subordinates, Task, or Organization That May Substitute for (Render Unnecessary) or Neutralize These Leader Behaviors>>>>>	**Effect of Characteristics from column one on need for *Supportive* Leadership**	**Effect of Characteristics from column one on need for *Instrumental* Leadership**
SUBORDINATE CHARACTERISTICS		
1. Experience, ability, training		Substitute
2. Professional orientation	Substitute	Substitute
3. Indifference toward rewards	Neutralizer	Neutralizer
TASK CHARACTERISTICS		
1. Structured, routine task		Substitute
2. Feedback provided by task		Substitute
3. Intrinsically satisfying task	Substitute	
ORGANIZATION CHARACTERISTICS		
1. Cohesive work group	Substitute	Substitute
2. Low position power	Neutralizer	Neutralizer
3. Formalization (roles, procedures)		Substitute
4. Inflexibility (rules, policies)		Neutralizer
5. Dispersed subordinate work sites	Neutralizer	Neutralizer

Source: Based on Steve Kerr and J. M. Jermier, "Substitutes for Leadership: Their Meaning and Measurement," *Organizational Behavior and Human Performance* 22 (1978); as printed in Gary Yukl, *Leadership in Organizations* (Upper Saddle River, N.J.: Prentice Hall, 1998), p. 274.

leadership action, or (2) *neutralize* (prevent) the leader's best efforts. Path goal theory says the leader's behavior compensates for what's missing in the situation. Substitutes for leadership theory says that some situations make leadership more or less unnecessary.

Table 2.3 lists the leadership substitutes and leadership neutralizers. For example, if your subordinates are highly professional, their professionalism should substitute for (reduce the need for) either supportive or instrumental leadership.

One big implication of substitutes for leadership theory is that a leader can "set the stage" to make his or her job easier.[54] Here are two examples.

- **Choose the Right Followers.** If you select and train your followers well, there may be less need to exercise leadership on a daily basis. The greater your subordinates' ability, the more their experience, the better their training, and the more professional their behavior, the less direct supervision they will need. Similarly, choose followers who are cooperative, flexible, and trustworthy, who have initiative, and who are good at solving problems.[55]

- **Organize the Task.** You may also be able to adjust organizational factors to reduce the need for day-to-day leadership. For example, jobs for which the performance standards are clear require less leadership.[56] Similarly, employees engaged in work that is intrinsically satisfying (work they love to do) require less leadership.[57]

3. Translating Leadership Theory into Practice

How Can a Manager Put Leadership Theory into Practice?

In the pressure of the moment, most supervisors want (and need) a quick way to cut through all the theorizing and to help them decide what type of leadership style the situation calls for. Two famous "Integrative Leadership Theories" for doing so are the Vroom-Jago-Yetton and Hersey–Blanchard models. They're called integrative because they help tie together the trait, behavioral, and contingency approaches in a practical way.

The Vroom-Jago-Yetton Model

In many situations, you'll need to decide how participative you should be. Should you make the decision yourself? Or should you let your employees participate?

Leadership experts Victor Vroom, Arthur Jago, and Philip Yetton argue that being participative is not an either/or decision. Instead, these are different degrees of participation. They developed a leadership model. It lets you assess a situation and decide how participative to be. Their technique consists of three components: (1) a set of *management decision styles*; (2) a set of *diagnostic questions*; and (3) a *decision tree* for identifying how much participation the situation calls for.

THE MANAGEMENT DECISION STYLES   We've seen that there are degrees of participation. As shown in Figure 2.6, Vroom and his associates propose five decision styles. At one extreme is style AI—no participation. Here, the leader solves the problem and makes the decision alone. GII, total participation, is at the other extreme. Here, the leader shares the problem with subordinates, and they reach an agreement together. You can see in Figure 2.6 that between these two extremes are styles AII, CI, and CII, each with more participation.

THE DIAGNOSTIC QUESTIONS   In the Vroom-Jago-Yetton model, the appropriate degree of participation depends on several attributes of the situation. The situational attributes include the importance of the quality of the decision, as well as the extent to which the leader has enough information to make a good decision alone. The supervisor can

■Figure **2.6**
Types of Management Decision Styles

AI. You solve the problem or make the decision yourself, using information available to you at that time.

AII. You obtain the necessary information from your subordinates, then decide on the solution to the problem yourself. You may or may not tell your subordinates what the problem is when getting the information from them. The role played by your subordinates in making the decision is clearly one of providing the necessary information to you, rather than generating or evaluating alternative solutions.

CI. You share the problem with relevant subordinates individually, getting their ideas and suggestions without bringing them together as a group. Then you make the decision, which may or may not reflect your subordinates' influence.

CII. You share the problem with your subordinates as a group, collectively obtaining their ideas and suggestions. Then you make the decision, which may or may not reflect your subordinates' influence.

GII. You share a problem with your subordinates as a group. Together, you generate and evaluate alternatives and attempt to reach agreement (consensus) on a solution. Your role is much like that of a chairperson. You do not try to influence the group to adopt "your" solution, and you are willing to accept and implement any solution that has the support of the entire group.

Vroom and Yetton Decision Process Flowchart

Source: Adapted from *Leadership and Decisionmaking* by Victor H. Vroom and Philip W. Yetton, by permission of the University of Pittsburgh Press. Copyright © 1973 by University of Pittsburgh Press.

Note: The letters A, B, C, etc. refer to each of the 6 diagnostic questions.

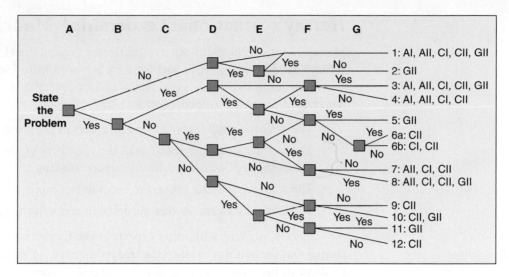

assess the presence of these attributes by asking the following sequence of diagnostic questions (see Figure 2.7):

- A. Is there a quality requirement such that one solution is likely to be more rational than another?
- B. Do I have sufficient information to make a high-quality decision?
- C. Is the problem structured?
- D. Is acceptance of the decision by subordinates critical to effective implementation?
- E. If you were to make the decision by yourself, is it reasonably certain that it would be accepted by your subordinates?
- F. Do subordinates share the organizational goals to be obtained in solving this problem?
- G. Is conflict among subordinates likely over preferred solutions?

THE DECISION TREE   The decision tree in Figure 2.7 puts this all together. This chart enables the leader to choose quickly the appropriate degree of participation. By starting on the left side of a chart and answering each sequential diagnostic question (A through G) with a yes or no, you can work your way across the decision tree and determine which leadership style is best. For example (follow Figure 2.7's top line), when the problem (A) does not possess a quality requirement (in other words, when the decision is not exceptionally important) and (D) when acceptance of the decision by subordinates is not important for effective implementation, then any of the styles (including the most directive style) would be appropriate. On the other hand, even if there is no particular quality requirement (Question A) but if acceptance of the decision by subordinates *is* important for implementation (Question D) *and* it's likely your decision won't be accepted if you make it yourself (Question E), then style GII—sharing the problem with your subordinates as a group—is the way to go. Studies generally support this model or variations of it.[58]

Hersey's Situational Leadership® Model

Management development expert Paul Hersey created the Hersey's Situational Leadership® Model. Stemming in part from earlier work he did with Kenneth Blanchard, this model aims to provide a practical way for a leader to decide how to adapt his or her style to the task.[59] It focuses on four leadership styles:

- The *delegating style* leader lets the members of the group decide what to do.
- The *participating style* leader asks the members of the group what to do, but makes the final decisions (shared decision making.)
- The *selling style* leader makes the decision but explains the reasons.
- The *telling style* leader makes the decision and tells the group what to do.

Hersey, working with other experts at the Center for Leadership Studies, concluded that the best way to assess the leadership needs of an individual or group could be distilled into what Hersey called 'Readiness'. Readiness is the amount of willingness and ability the follower or group demonstrates while performing a specific task. Willingness is a combination of confidence, commitment, and motivation. Figure 2.8 graphically summarizes how each style is appropriate in a specific situation.

- *Delegating* works best when followers are willing to do the job and are able to (know how to) go about doing it. Delegating leaders encourage autonomy, provide support and resources, and delegate activities.

- *Participating* works best when followers are able to do the job, but are unwilling and so require emotional support. Participating leaders "share ideas and facilitate the decision making."

■ Figure **2.8**

Applying the Situational Leadership Model

Source: Adapted from Paul Hersey, *Situational Selling* (Escondido, CA: Center for Leadership Studies, 1985), p. 19. Reprinted with permission.

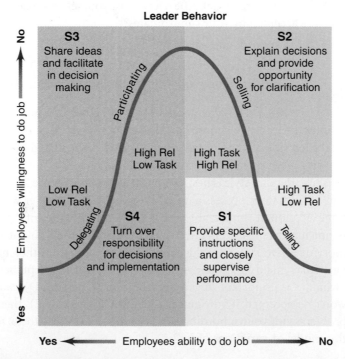

- *Selling* works best when followers are neither willing nor able to do the job. The selling leader "explains decisions and provides opportunity for clarification."
- *Telling* works best when followers are willing to do the job, but don't know how to do it. The telling leader "provides specific instructions and closely supervises performance."

How to Improve Your Leadership Skills

How Can a Manager Strengthen Leadership Skills?

No formula can guarantee that someone can be a leader. However, based on the research in this chapter, you certainly can improve the chances that, in a supervisory leadership situation, you will be effective. Doing so requires strengthening six leadership skills, as follows.

SKILL 1: DECIDE IF YOU ARE READY TO BE A LEADER   We saw that some people are more ready and inclined to be leaders than are others. For example, leadership is very interpersonal. It therefore helps if the prospective leader enjoys working with and helping other people. The quiz in Figure 2.9 may provide some insights on a supervisor's readiness to assume leadership responsibilities. Scoring somewhat lower does *not* preclude leadership. It means the person should carefully read each of the statements in the quiz to see what (if anything) might need to be done to change one's attitudes or behaviors.[60]

SKILL 2: FIT YOUR STYLE TO THE SITUATION   Most people probably have one prevailing leadership style. However, effective leaders fit their style to the situation.

In picking the right style, there are several situational leadership models to choose from and apply. Review Tables 2.2 (page 46) and 2.3 (page 47) to get a sense (from the path–goal and substitutes theories) of whether the situation is already so structured and/or satisfying that it doesn't warrant additional structure and/or support. If the leadership question you face is, "To what extent should I let my subordinates participate in making the decision?" apply the Vroom-Jago-Yetton model (Figure 2.7, page 49). If the situation seems to call for a more varied range of leader styles, apply the Hersey model (Figure 2.8, page 50).

SKILL 3: PICK THE RIGHT LEADERSHIP SITUATION   Suppose that (while most people seem to be somewhat flexible) your leadership style is your style and can't be changed?

One solution is to gravitate toward supervisory situations that *do* fit your leadership style. To do this, use the situational leadership models to *choose the right situation for your style* (rather than to find a style to fit the situation). For example, suppose you're a more authoritarian, "telling"-type leader. Hersey-Blanchard would say that a tough turnaround situation in which your employees are willing but cannot do their jobs may be right for you. If you tend to be participatory and to prefer delegating most decisions, then unstructured situations with professional employees who tend to have the right answers may be best for you, say Vroom, Jago, and Yetton. Fiedler suggests recruiting and hiring supervisors based on the types of situations in which they're expected to lead. He says, "The organization must . . . be aware of the type of leadership situations into which the individual should be successively guided."[61]

SKILL 4: BUILD YOUR POWER BASE   Remember that a powerless leader is not a leader at all. Therefore, bolster your reward, coercive, and other leadership power by enhancing your authority. Use this chapter's checklist on page 37.

■Figure **2.9**

Are You Ready to Be a Leader?

Source: Andrew DuBrin, *Leadership: Research Findings, Priorities, and Skills* (Houghton Mifflin, 1995).

The following self-assessment exercise can give you a feel for your readiness and inclination to assume a leadership role.

INSTRUCTIONS: Indicate the extent to which you agree with each of the following statements, using the following scale: (1) disagree strongly; (2) disagree; (3) neutral; (4) agree; (5) agree strongly.

1. It is enjoyable having people count on me for ideas and suggestions.	1	2	3	4	(5)
2. It would be accurate to say that I have inspired other people.	1	2	3	4	(5)
3. It's a good practice to ask people provocative questions about their work.	1	2	3	4	(5)
4. It's easy for me to compliment others.	1	2	3	4	(5)
5. I like to cheer people up even when my own spirits are down.	1	2	3	4	(5)
6. What my team accomplishes is more important than my personal glory.	1	2	3	4	(5)
7. Many people imitate my ideas.	1	2	3	4	(5)
8. Building team spirit is important to me.	1	2	3	4	(5)
9. I would enjoy coaching other members of the team.	1	2	3	4	(5)
10. It is important to me to recognize others for their accomplishments.	1	2	3	4	(5)
11. I would enjoy entertaining visitors to my firm even if it interfered with my completing a report.	1	2	3	4	(5)
12. It would be fun for me to represent my team at gatherings outside our department.	1	2	3	4	(5)
13. The problems of my teammates are my problems too.	1	2	3	4	(5)
14. Resolving conflict is an activity I enjoy.	1	2	3	4	(5)
15. I would cooperate with another unit in the organization even if I disagreed with the position taken by its members.	1	2	3	(4)	5
16. I am an idea generator on the job.	1	2	3	4	(5)
17. It's fun for me to bargain whenever I have the opportunity.	1	2	3	4	(5)
18. Team members listen to me when I speak.	1	2	3	4	(5)
19. People have asked me to assume the leadership of an activity several times in my life.	1	2	3	4	(5)
20. I've always been a convincing person.	1	2	3	(4)	5

Total score:

SCORING AND INTERPRETATION Calculate your total score by adding the numbers circled.

A tentative interpretation of the scoring is as follows:

90–100 High readiness for the leadership role
60–89 Moderate readiness for the leadership role
40–59 Some uneasiness with the leadership role
39 or less Low readiness for the leadership role

If you are already a successful leader and you scored low on this questionnaire, ignore your score. If you scored surprisingly low and you are not yet a leader or are currently performing poorly as a leader, study the statements carefully. Consider changing your attitude or your behavior so that you can legitimately answer more of the statements with a 4 or a 5.

SKILL 5: EXERCISE BETTER JUDGMENT   Decisiveness and good judgment (cognitive ability) are essential leadership traits. Knowledge and good judgment just about always trump high IQ. We'll address decision making in Chapter 3. But for now, decision-making guidelines supervisors can use include the following:

- **Increase your knowledge.** The more you know about the problem and the more facts you can marshal, the better the decision.

- **Free your judgment of bias.** Biases can distort a supervisor's judgment. Reducing or eliminating biases such as prejudice and stereotyping is therefore a crucial step toward making better decisions.

- **Be creative.** The ability to develop novel responses—creativity—is essential for developing new alternatives and correctly defining the problem.

- **Use your intuition.** A preoccupation with analyzing problems rationally and logically can sometimes backfire by blocking someone from using his or her intuition. What does your "gut" tell you?
- **Don't overstress the finality of your decision.** Very few decisions are forever; there is more give in more decisions than we realize.
- **Make sure the timing is right.** Passing moods affect decisions. Therefore, consider your state of mind and emotions before making important decisions.

SKILL 6: IMPROVE YOUR OTHER LEADERSHIP TRAITS AND SKILLS   We saw that leaders have traits that distinguish them from nonleaders. These traits are not set in stone. Just as you can improve your judgment, supervisors can cultivate these other leadership traits

For example, leaders exhibit *self-confidence.* Developing self-confidence is a lifelong process, but you can enhance yours. For example, gravitate toward situations that make you confident, such as those in which you are an expert. *Act like a leader*: Make decisions and stick with them—and act somewhat reserved. Display *honesty and integrity*; apply high ethical standards to everything you do. Your *knowledge of the business* is among the easiest traits to modify. Immerse yourself in the details of your new job.

4. Special Leadership Skills for Leading a Diverse Workforce

In Chapter 1 we saw that smart employers institute programs for managing diversity. **Managing diversity** means maximizing diversity's potential advantages while minimizing the potential barriers—such as bias—that can undermine the functioning of a diverse workforce. Managing diversity is basically a leadership issue.

Such programs typically start at the top, with an edict from HR and the CEO. However, the critical interactions will take place between you and your subordinates. In other words, *at the end of the day, it's not some formal companywide program that determines if your diverse employees work together cooperatively; instead, it's the steps you take to influence them and how you behave.* For supervisors, diversity management is therefore basically a leadership issue. Leadership means influencing your team to move in some desired direction. Turning a diverse group of employees into a cohesive team in the face of potential barriers such as bias is a leadership challenge. Do you have what it takes to influence your subordinates to manage diversity? The following are important guidelines for leading a diverse workforce.

Ask: Are You Adjusting to Individual Differences?

What Guidelines Help a Manager Lead a Diverse Workforce?

Travel books are filled with examples of the cultural pitfalls lying in wait for people traveling abroad. The traveler might be told, for instance, not to criticize an Asian person publicly, because, "saving face" is so important there. In Mexico, remember that Mexican employees may put a high emphasis on respecting one's status.

The first important thing to remember about supervising a diverse team is therefore this: *Never forget that your supervisory actions (such as disciplining an employee or giving an order) may trigger different reactions, depending on the subordinate's ethnic, cultural, or other background.* This may seem obvious. However, it's easy to forget that not everyone thinks the same. As an example, one study compared the motives of workers in China and the United States. The American workers put a big emphasis on "self-actualizing"—on driving yourself to become the person you think you're capable of becoming. In China, the motives were less individualistic. There, helping and furthering one's group was often paramount. (That's why even today, there's more emphasis on individual incentives in America and on team incentives in Asia.) Remember that approaches that may work well with people from one culture can backfire with those from another. You'll need to fine-tune your supervisory actions and leadership style to these individual differences.

Develop Your "Multicultural Consciousness"

In July 2009, after a heated exchange on his Cambridge, Massachusetts doorstep, Professor Henry Louis Gates Jr., a nationally known African American Harvard professor, was arrested for disorderly conduct. Professor Gates initially accused the police of racially profiling him. The arresting officer (whom the department had appointed as a trainer to show fellow officers how to avoid racial profiling) denied any racial motives. President Obama, at a news conference, accused the Cambridge police of using less than good judgment. Whatever else one can say about the episode, it seems clear that three people who should know quite a bit about multicultural consciousness differed dramatically about how culturally sensitive the other person had been.

One moral of this story is that being "sensitive to and adapting to individual cultural differences" is easier said than done. We all tend to view the world through the prism of our own experiences. Sometimes it's not easy for even the most well-meaning of us to really appreciate how people who are different from us may be feeling. That certainly doesn't mean we should give up trying. It does mean that we all need to be continually alert to the possibility that we're not appreciating the other person's point of view. And it means that we all have to take steps to keep moving toward the goal of developing a diversity consciousness. Here are steps one expert suggests for improving one's diversity consciousness.[62]

1. **Take an active role in educating yourself.** For example, develop diverse relationships and widen your circle of friends. Read the sorts of articles and personal narratives (such as about the history of people from different cultures) that can help give you a better perspective on where people from other cultures are "coming from."

2. **Put yourself in a learning mode in any multicultural setting.** For example, try to "wipe the slate clean" when it comes to the sorts of stereotypes we all grew up with. Instead, view the person you're dealing with just as an individual and in terms of the experiences you've actually had with him or her.

3. **Move beyond your personal comfort zone.** For example, put yourself in more situations where you are an "outsider."

4. **Don't be too hard on yourself if misunderstandings arise.** As this expert says, "The important thing is to acknowledge our mistakes and learn from them."[63]

5. **Realize that you are not alone.** Remember that there are other people including colleagues, friends, and mentors at work to whom you can turn for advice as you deal with diversity issues.

Ask: Are You Really Treating Everyone Equally?

Human nature being what it is, most leaders don't treat all their subordinates the same. *You need to understand that you probably treat the people who are more similar to you better than you treat the others.* That fact has particular implications for anyone leading a diverse team.

LEADERSHIP RESEARCH INSIGHT   Here's what the leadership research shows. The **leader-member exchange (LMX) theory** says that leaders tend to adapt their styles to the *quality of the relationship (the "exchange") between the leader and the subordinate.*[64]

Specifically, LMX theory says leaders tend to divide their subordinates into an in-group and an out-group (and you can guess who gets the better treatment!). What determines whether someone becomes part of the leader's "in" or "out" group? It's usually an instinctive, not a calculated, decision on the leader's part. But perceived leader-member similarities—gender, age, or attitudes, for instance—are usually very important.[65]

Here is an example. Researchers received completed attitude surveys from 84 registered nurses and their 12 supervisors in a large hospital.[66]

It turned out that the supervisors' perceptions of two things—how similar were leader and follower, and the follower's extroversion—seemed to determine the quality of leader–member relations. Supervisors sized up the *similarity* between themselves and their nurses in terms of six things: family, money, career strategies, goals, education, and overall perspective. And of course, they acted better toward followers with whom they shared similarities. Nurses also completed questionnaires that enabled the researchers to label them as introverted or extroverted. The extroverted nurses were more likely to have good leader–member relationships (exchanges) than were the introverts. This was presumably because they were more outgoing.

There are two practical implications for supervisors:

1. First (particularly insofar as you may tend to view people from different backgrounds as belonging to the out-group), make sure you *work doubly hard to make your in-groups more inclusive.* (See how to "Encourage Inclusiveness", below).
2. Second (assuming you want good relations with your own boss), the research suggests, don't go out of your way to emphasize differences. Instead, try to emphasize honest similarities in things such as politics and endeavor to be sociable.

Encourage Inclusiveness

The supervisor is in a perfect position to help overcome the barriers (such as prejudice) that hamper some employees from being fully included in the team. What can the supervisor do? Figure 2.10 helps to answer this. For example, on a *personal level*, be aware of any prejudices or other barriers you yourself may have. On an *interpersonal level*, work hard to facilitate communication and participation among your employees. And at the *organizational level*, make sure your employees have access to the company's minority networks and focus groups.

Actively Integrate Immigrants into Your Team[67]

When it comes to being inclusive, one of your greatest challenges will be in integrating immigrant employees into your team. *Immigrants* are people who come to a country

■Figure **2.10**

What the Supervisor Can Do to Overcome Barriers to Inclusion

Source: Norma Carr-Ruffino, *Making Diversity Work* (Upper Saddle River, NJ: Pearson Education, 2005), p. 104.

INCLUSIVE STRATEGIES THAT OVERCOME BARRIERS TO INCLUSION

Inclusive Strategies	Barriers to Inclusion
Personal Level	
Become aware of prejudice and other barriers to valuing diversity	Stereotypes, prejudices
Learn about other cultures and groups	Past experiences and influences
Serve as an example, walk the talk	Stereotyped expectations and perceptions
Participate in managing diversity	Feelings that tend to separate, divide
Interpersonal Level	
Facilitate communication and interactions in ways that value diversity	Cultural differences
Encourage participation	Group differences
Share your perspective	Myths
Facilitate unique contributions	Relationship patterns based on exclusion
Resolve conflicts in ways that value diversity	
Accept responsibility for developing common ground	
Organizational Level	
All employees have access to networks and focus groups	Individuals who get away with discriminating and excluding
All employees take a proactive role in managing diversity and creating a more diverse workplace culture	A culture that values or allows exclusion
All employees are included in the inner circle that contributes to the bottom-line success of the company	Work structures, policies, and practices that discriminate and exclude
All employees give feedback to teams and management	
All employees are encouraged to contribute to change	

usually to take up permanent residence. Immigrants play a big role in America. Recently, there were about 33.5 million foreign-born people residing in America, or about 12% of the U.S. population. Of these, about half came from Latin America, 25% from Asia, 14% from Europe, and the rest from other regions.[68]

There are many good reasons for working diligently to welcome immigrants to your team. For one thing, you have little choice. As we said, immigration plays a central role in ensuring that America has the population growth it needs to support a growing economy. As a matter of national policy, you therefore can expect more, not fewer future applicants to come from abroad. Similarly, most employers actively seek the skills, work ethic, and ambition that immigrants can bring to their jobs. In some technical areas, the shortage of skills is so acute that it's almost impossible to fill positions without immigrants. The bottom line is that your employer will expect and need you to integrate these people into your team. Let's look at how.

THE CHALLENGES   First, expect to confront several challenges when integrating a new immigrant employee into your team. *Language barriers* may make the simplest communications difficult and add to the immigrant's sense of *isolation*. Immigrants will bring *differences in culture* (including things such as manners, religion, holidays, and modes of dress). These differences may fan the flames of *prejudice* that some employees may already feel toward "outsiders." Differences regarding *political issues* such as immigration quotas further intensify emotions. The differences may even subliminally cause you to treat these people as members of the "out" group (remember leader-member exchange theory?).

SPECIAL SOLUTIONS FOR INTEGRATING IMMIGRANTS INTO YOUR TEAM   Actions such as encouraging inclusiveness, being multiculturally sensitive, and valuing each person as an individual will certainly make it easier to integrate these employees. But beyond that, you can take several practical steps to overcome challenges such as language barriers and prejudice, and to integrate your new employee into the team.

- **Make sure all immigrants you employ are legal.** Be aware of and follow all the legal requirements (we'll cover these in detail in Chapters 7 and 8). For example, carefully review the applicant's identification and working documents. Your employer will want to make sure there is an accurate I-9 form for every employee (not just immigrants).

- **Make doubly sure that the employee gets off on the right track.** Employee orientation is always important, but particularly so with someone who may feel less than secure about his or her language skills and "fitting in." Your employer may not have thought to take simple steps such as translating job descriptions, workplace signage, and work rules. If not, at least make sure that the new employee understands the job and the work rules, and has a cordial relationship with the other team members. Be vigilant for signs of isolation.

- **Watch for any warning signs of prejudice.** If you sense any, remember Figure 2.10 about encouraging inclusiveness. Your leadership role here is to influence your subordinates to do the right thing. For example, share your perspective with the other people on the team, and take steps to facilitate communication and interactions. If necessary, suggest to your human resources department that diversity training may be useful for the team.

- **Walk the talk.** Finally, as one expert writes, "ultimately, the supervisor is the key to transforming diversity into unity. Your attitude and actions toward immigrant workers will spell the difference between harmony and discord on the job."[69]

Chapter 2 Concept Review and Reinforcement

Key Terms

Close Supervision, p. 39
Employee-Oriented
   Leaders, p. 39
Gatekeeper, p. 36

General Leader, p. 39
Job-Centered
   Leaders, p. 39
Laissez-Faire Leader, p. 39

Leader-Member Exchange
   (LMX) Theory, p. 55
Leadership, p. 34
Managing Diversity, p. 53

Transactional
   Behaviors, p. 41
Transformational
   Leaders, p. 41

Review of Key Concepts

Leadership	Leadership means influencing someone to work willingly toward a predetermined objective. Leadership is the distinctly motivational and interpersonal facet of what supervisors do.
Basic Theories of Leadership	
Traits and Skills of Leadership	Core traits that significantly contribute to business leaders' success include: Drive Desire to Lead Honesty Self-Confidence Cognitive Ability Knowledge of the Business
Power	A leader without power is really not a leader at all, since he or she has no chance of influencing anyone to do anything. Power can emanate from position, ability to reward or punish, being an expert, having referent power, or having control over information.
Behaviors	A leader must engage in the behaviors required to get his or her people to move in the desired direction. Most studies assume that leaders perform two main functions: accomplishing the task and satisfying followers' needs.
Ohio State Studies	Measures two leadership styles: consideration and initiating structure. A balance of the two styles works best, and the leadership style that's right for one situation might be wrong for another.
University of Michigan Studies	Measures two leadership styles: employee-oriented leaders and job-centered leaders. These styles focus on the individuality and personality needs of employees and focus on production and the job's technical aspects.
Transformational Leadership	Transformational leaders bring about change, innovation, and entrepreneurship. They recognize the need for revitalization, creating a new vision and institutionalizing change. Behaviors exhibited include charismatic, inspirational, considerate, and stimulating.

Situational Leadership	This type of leadership is based on the premise that leadership traits and styles that might be right for one situation may backfire in another. Leaders can exhibit more than one style in the same situation.
Fielder's Contingency Theory of Leadership	Fiedler's theory identified three aspects of the situation that determine which style, people-oriented or task-oriented, is best for a given situation.
Path–Goal Leadership Theory	Path–goal theory focuses on four leadership styles: directive leadership. supportive leadership, participative leadership, and achievement-oriented leadership.
Leadership Theory into Practice	Applying the situational leadership model involves: Delegating—when followers are willing to do the job. Participating—when followers are able to do the job but require emotional support. Selling—when followers are neither willing nor able to do the job. Telling—when followers are willing to do the job but do not know how to do it.
Supervising a Diverse Workforce	Fundamental guidelines to keep in mind when supervising a diverse workforce: Are you adapting to individual differences? Are you developing your multicultural consciousness? Are you really treating everyone the same? Are you encouraging inclusiveness?

Review and Discussion Questions

1. What is leadership?
2. Rank (6) high to (1) low the leadership traits discussed in Chapter 2 in order of their importance. Discuss why you ranked them as you did, by illustrating how specific public figures exhibit such traits or could benefit from having more of such traits.
3. How effective can a leader (supervisor) be without a power base to influence people? Why?
4. Using your knowledge of the studies of leadership behavior, give examples of how leaders such as George W. Bush or Barak Obama seem to use various styles in order to move people in the desired direction?
5. Name and briefly describe the effects of five individuals who have demonstrated transformational leadership.
6. Give an example to show how you could apply situational leadership theories at work or when engaged in some non-work activity with friends.
7. Why do you think delegating such an important part of the situational leadership model?
8. List and briefly discuss the four fundamental guidelines to keep in mind when supervising a diverse workforce.

Application and Skill Building

Case Study One

Just Promoted—Born to Lead?

In the Beginning

Joe Smith, a native of Glasgow, Kentucky, jumped at the opportunity to work as a production supervisor in Glasgow for the electronics division of a large midwestern company headquartered in Indianapolis, Indiana. This division manufactures electrolytic capacitors for the television and small motor industries. Joe has been with this company for almost six years directly out of high school. Although Joe had no college or formal training in electronics, he demonstrated very soon after coming to work a strong work ethic and a personal motivation to learn a new technology. After only two years on the line, Joe was promoted to a position in machine setup and was made the assistant to the supervisor. Although Joe was involved in following through on many of the decisions he made he did not have any formal authority. In the view of his supervisor, Joe was considered to be a model employee.

Company Decision

A long-standing policy of this company is to promote from within. Candidates for promotion are expected to have a positive attitude, a knowledge of the jobs and work processes, and the ability to communicate and get along with other employees. Joe met or exceeded all of these expectations in the eyes of the company management. Joe was offered and accepted the position of production supervisor in the Glasgow assembly department effective May 1.

The Dilemma

Joe was placed in his new position with only limited orientation. He was given a copy of his job description, which he realized later did not do a good job of describing his duties. He was presented with two volumes of company policies, which he read and then promptly forgot. Joe knew the jobs, knew the people, and now he was expected to learn how to make leadership decisions on the job.

Very quickly, Joe found that leading other people was a lot more difficult than it looked. When a production team got in trouble meeting production schedules, Joe would sit down at the machine and complete the job himself while the workers watched. If one of Joe's workers had a personal problem, Joe would not take it too seriously—production had to come first. When an employee made a mistake, Joe did not always stand up for him or her. Joe could not figure out how to motivate his workers when he left the work area. Upon returning, he would find his workers standing around waiting for additional instructions. Yesterday Joe received a call from the human resources department. One of his workers filed a discrimination charge claiming inequality based on ethnic background. Joe believes that he is in trouble and needs some help in his new job. This job just is not working out as he expected it would.

Discussion Questions

1. How well does Joe exhibit the traits that can contribute to a leader's success?
2. If leadership is the distinctly motivational and interpersonal facet of what supervisors do, how would you evaluate the job that Joe is doing?
3. When a company uses a policy of promotion from within, what are some of the potential pitfalls?
4. List what you believe are Joe's strong points and weak points as a new supervisor.
5. What recommendations would you make to Joe that would enable him to better lead?

Case Study Two

Turning Around the U.S.S. *Benfold*

While "leadership" may seem a little theoretical in some situations, that's certainly not the case when it comes to the U.S. Navy. When you're the captain of the ship, the lives of all the people on that ship are in your hands. Leadership style can have a corrosive effect on sailors' morale and on their—and the ship's—performance. *

For several years, in fact, the U.S. military was in what one officer calls "deep trouble." Commander Mike Abrashoff says, "People aren't joining. More people are leaving. The attrition rates are going through the roof. In the navy, 33% of those who join never complete their first tour of duty. Combat readiness is declining." Given those trends, Commander Abrashoff's experience in instituting a new leadership initiative when he took over as captain of the U.S.S. *Benfold* is all the more remarkable. In the two years he was leading the ship, the *Benfold* retention rate went from about 25% to 100% in most of the ship's top job categories. Attrition went from more than 18% to less than 1%, and mission-degrading casualties dropped from 75 to 24. During his final 12 months in command, the ship even ran on 75% of its operating budget, and returned millions of dollars to the navy.

To a large extent, this turnaround in attitudes was a consequence of a remarkably simple initiative on Abrashoff's part: He brought a new leadership style to the U.S.S. *Benfold* when he took command. Abrashoff says that when he took over, he decided right away that before he could fix the problems on the ship, he had to find out what those problems were. He started his command by interviewing every crew member individually. He'd start each interview with several questions, such as "Where are you from?" "Why did you join the navy?" "What are your goals in the navy?" "What are your

---

Adapted from, Polly T LaBarre The Agenda—Grassroots Leadership, Fast Company, March 31, 1999, http://www.fastcompany.com/magazine/23/grassroots. html accessed December 5, 2010.

goals in life?" Then he asked three more questions: "What do you like most about the Benfold?" "What do you like least?" "What things would you change if you could?"

As Abrashoff puts it, "The minute I started these interviews, our performance took off like a rocket. Whenever I got an outstanding idea from a sailor—and about 70% of the ideas that I got were, in fact, outstanding—I would implement that idea right on the spot." He used the public address system to tell the rest of the crew what the new idea was, which sailor the idea came from, and that he was implementing it immediately and needed their support in doing so.

Mike Abrashoff says that whenever he needed a reminder about what leadership was all about, he took out an index card he kept in his wallet. On the card were the eight leadership traits he always used as personal guidelines: A leader is trusted. A leader takes the initiative. A leader uses good judgment. A leader speaks with authority. A leader strengthens others. A leader is optimistic and enthusiastic. A leader never compromises his absolutes. A leader leads by example.

Questions

1. How would you describe Commander Abrashoff's leadership style?
2. Abrashoff's index card contains eight leadership traits. How do these eight traits compare with the foundation traits of leadership covered in this chapter? In what ways are they similar? Different'
3. Which situational leadership theories would you have applied in Abrashoff's situation? Apply one of those theories, and explain why you believe his leadership style is (or is not) right for the situation.
4. In addressing the problems on the U.S.S. *Benfold*, did Abrashoff what influence do you think the interviews with his sailors had?
5. As ship's captain, Abrashoff has about as much authority as any leader anywhere. With all that power, why (if at all) does he even have to be concerned with his leadership style? Can't he just count on giving orders and having them obeyed? Why?

Experiential Activities

Activity 1. Rudy, the newly appointed supervisor, had a rough first day supervising the new-claims unit at Alpha Insurance. Having never given orders before, he was shy and wavering as he told each person what to do. Still staring at his notes, Rudy heard some chuckling from the back of the room. He was disheartened to find that at the end of the day his team had accomplished nothing. What went wrong, and what should he do now? See the following, Execution Requires Leadership.

Execution Requires Leadership

Purpose: The purpose of this exercise is to help you to apply what you've learned about how to be a more effective leader.

Required Understanding: You are going to develop an outline on what leadership is, what traits leaders need, and where the sources of power emanate from. You are expected to be thoroughly familiar with the discussion and theories of leadership found in this chapter.

How to Set Up the Exercise/Instructions: Divide the class into groups of 4–5 students.

1. Answer the question: "Why, at the end of the day, had Rudy's team accomplished nothing?"
2. Next, your group should develop a Leadership Primer that Rudy could use to exercise the power and leadership necessary to accomplish his goals.
3. Have a spokesperson from each group share their recommendations for Rudy with the class. What could management have done to give Rudy a better start on his first day as a new supervisor?

Activity 2. Based on what you have studied in this chapter, meet with a team of three or four of your fellow students; then write a one-page checklist to be used by new supervisors who have been assigned to supervise a diverse workforce. Be prepared to discuss this in class with other teams.

Activity 3. Transformational leaders are said to be those who bring about "change." Meet with a team of 4–5 fellow students and collectively choose three American leaders who have met the definition of a transformational leader. Make a list of the behaviors each of these chosen leaders have exhibited that qualify them to be termed a transformational leader. Be prepared to discuss your lists in class.

Role-Playing Exercise

Interviewing a Leader: The Situation

Leadership has been deemed the distinctly motivational and interpersonal facet of what supervisors do. Leadership has been defined as influencing someone to work toward a predetermined objective. Although we go to great lengths in determining what leadership is and how it can be learned and practiced by supervisors in today's workplace, many practicing and successful supervisors have not had the opportunity to formally use the available resources. These practicing supervisors are not aware of the theories of traits, behaviors, and situations, and yet they exhibit many of these traits and behaviors on a daily basis.

Instructions

All students should read the materials on leadership included in this chapter. One student will play the role of a reporter writing an article for a business column in a local newspaper. This article will address leadership and supervision today. The student reporter will interview another student "supervisor" from the team, preferably one who has had some experience supervising others.

Role of Student Reporter

This student reporter will prepare ahead for this interview by using the materials and concepts presented in Chapter 2. A list of questions will be gleaned from the input of fellow team members and used in the interview. After the interview (in class) the reporter will summarize the responses and share them with his or her class members. The reporter should make sure that questions cover the basic concepts, including the following, but pease do not share the questions with the "supervisor" until the actual interview:

- Leadership defined
- Leadership theories including traits, skills, behaviors, and situations
- The use of power by supervisors
- Change leadership (transformational)
- Attitudes toward the use of guidelines for leading a diverse workforce

Role of the Practicing Supervisor

You have been a supervisor in the Gap store at the local mall for about 3 years. You enjoy the job, but a few of the employees are troublesome. One is always 10 minutes late getting to work, another spends 15 minutes every two hours standing outside the store on cigarette breaks, and two won't do anything unless you're standing over them all the time. Now you've just heard that the Gap is planning a new campaign that will involve switching to a new technology for monitoring inventory and sales, and you've got to think of a way to get your already troublesome employees on board with the new way of doing things. You go to school all day and then work nights and weekends at the Gap, and the last thing you need is a bunch of college students telling you how to supervise your employees, but you agreed to be interviewed by some students as a favor to your professor.

Questions for Discussion

1. How well did the student reporter do in covering the major concepts in this chapter?
2. If you had the opportunity to interview this supervisor, how differently would you have done it? What other questions would you have asked?
3. What differences do you detect between the text review of leadership theories and the actual practice of leadership by a supervisor in daily practice?
4. What leadership suggestions would you make to this supervisor?

3

Solving Problems and Making Decisions

....

CHAPTER OBJECTIVES

After studying this chapter, you should be able to answer these questions:

1. Sound Decision Making: Why Is It Important for Supervisors?
2. Programmed or Nonprogrammed Decisions: Which Is Needed?
3. Decision Making in Practice: How Rational Are Decision Makers?
4. What Steps Can a Supervisor Follow to Develop Sound Decision Making Skills?

5. What Can You Do to Improve the Quality of Decisions?
6. How Can Information Technology Tools Help a Supervisor Make Decisions?
7. How Can You Avoid Psychological Traps When Making a Decision?

OPENING SNAPSHOT

Roz's Decision

Roz had been in turmoil all month because of complaints about one of her employees, Geraldo. Several other supervisors as well as the firm's HR supervisor told Roz that Geraldo wasn't doing his job. He frequently left the premises for unexplained 30-minute breaks, took overly long lunch hours (without recording this on his time cards), and spent most of his workday wandering from office to office chatting with other clerks. Both the president of the company and the head of HR had discussed all this with Roz. However, both felt that, as Geraldo's direct supervisor, this was a matter for Roz to deal with. Yet Roz dragged her heels on making a decision.

1. The Basics of Decisions and Decision Making

Sound Decision
Making: Why Is It
Important for
Managers?

Everyone constantly faces the need to choose—the route to school, the job to accept, or the disciplinary action that's appropriate. A **decision** is a choice from among the available alternatives. **Decision making** is the process of developing and analyzing alternatives and making a choice.

Why Make Decisions?

Problems (like what to do with Geraldo) prompt most decisions. A **problem** is a discrepancy between a desirable and an actual situation. If you need $50 to see a show but can only afford to spend $10, you have a problem. Should you borrow money from a friend? Skip the show? Wait to see if ticket prices fall? You must decide. However, decisions don't always involve problems. Having two job offers to choose from is not a problem, but just having a choice requires you to decide.

The *problem-solving process* (the steps one goes through to solve a problem) is the same as the process for making decisions. It is "the process of developing and analyzing alternatives and making a choice." Most people, therefore, use the terms *decision making* and *problem solving* interchangeably.

The quality of a decision usually depends more on good judgment than on raw IQ. Some brilliant people have poor judgment. Some less brilliant people have great judgment. *Judgment* refers to the cognitive, or "thinking," aspects of the decision-making process.[1] We'll see in this chapter that poor decision-making habits and biases can influence one's judgment and decisions.

Supervisors are always making decisions. The accounting supervisor decides whether to extend credit to a customer. The sales supervisor decides which sales representatives to use in each region. The production supervisor decides which employees to assign to the new shift. And Roz needs to decide what to do about Geraldo. No supervisor can avoid making decisions. The accompanying leadership application feature expands on this.

Types of Decisions

Some decisions are obviously easier to make than are others. For example, some decisions are more difficult because they're bigger and harder to change (more "strategic"). Buying a house is more strategic than leasing a car. Some decisions are also more obvious than others—they are "no-brainers." If your car is out of gas, you have to fill it. The bigger, strategic decisions usually take more thought, as we will see.

Whatever the decision, supervisors don't want to have to keep addressing the same problem time and again. Doing so is a waste of time. The supervisor of a Macy's shoe department doesn't want clerks to have to check with her every time customers want to make returns. She wants to focus on the big decisions, such as what to purchase for the fall line. Supervisors therefore endeavor to premake (or "program") as many decisions as they can. That way, their employees can make these decisions more or less automatically.

Programmed or
Nonprogrammed
Decisions. Which Is
Needed?

PROGRAMMED AND NONPROGRAMMED DECISIONS   Knowing when and how to program (routinize) decisions is an important supervisory skill. Thankfully, many (or most)

Heroic Leadership and the Importance of Leadership Decisiveness

In May 2010, Europe was in economic chaos. Greece had run up a huge budget deficit, and those debts were threatening to topple Greece's banks, and then, like dominos, the banks in other European countries that held Greek bonds. Faced with calls to use German funds to bail out Greece as well as strong resistance to doing so from her constituents, Angela Merkel, Germany's chancellor, hesitated. It took her weeks to make a decision. During those weeks she tried unsuccessfully to navigate a middle road. By the end of May, The Wall Street Journal reported that "Recent poll data suggest that a majority of Germans have lost confidence in Ms. Merkel's leadership ability. . . . More than 60% of Germans believe Ms. Merkel has shown poor leadership during Europe's debt crisis."[2]

Decision crises such as this one are common for all leaders. Several years ago, the calls for President Obama to make a decision about Afghanistan troop levels reached a crescendo. He had already spent about four months meeting with his war council reviewing his options. One magazine, referring to the long decision-making process, noted that some critics were (unfairly) using the word "ditherer" to explain the president's alleged lack of leadership. John McCain, the president's former rival for the presidency, called Mr. Obama's decision process too "leisurely."[3]

It's always easy for politicians such as Ms. Merkel and Mr. Obama to have detractors, but these recent situations underscore a leadership fact. As we mentioned first in Chapter 2, making good decisions is so central to what leaders (and supervisors) do that it's basically impossible to separate decision making from leadership. Leaders lead, and they do so by deciding where to go and then showing their followers the way. If the supervisor's decisions are wrong (or aren't forthcoming at all), then fewer and fewer people will follow that leader.

Decisiveness is therefore part of many leadership theories. In his trait theory of leadership, Professor Ralph Stogdill lists "decisiveness" as a trait that distinguishes leaders from nonleaders. He also says that leaders must be willing to "accept consequences of decision and action." Some leadership experts even refer to what they call the "Heroic Leader." They say that people want their leaders to be heroic figures "who are capable of determining the fate of their organizations." There is even, they say, "a mystical, romantic quality associated with leadership."[4] Like Ms. Merkel's constituents, people expect their leaders to exercise leadership, and that means deciding on a course and showing the way. Followers always expect a bit of hero (and thus decisiveness) in their leaders. Any supervisor ignores that fact at his or her peril.

That's not to say that leaders (like any heros) can't occasionally make mistakes. For example, two researchers studied what caused 83 major bad decisions. They found that many supervisors jumped to erroneous conclusions by assuming that the situation they faced was pretty much identical to one they'd experienced before, when it wasn't. That can be a big mistake. Just because Max did a good job fixing the coffee maker doesn't mean he'll be able to fix the company car.[5]

The bottom line is that you can't be an effective supervisor or leader without making good decisions, and decision making isn't easy. Many psychological traps can trip you up. We'll see later in this chapter how to avoid them.

---

supervisory decisions are programmable. **Programmed decisions** (really, *programmable* decisions) are decisions you can set up to be made in advance. These decisions address recurring issues or problems. The company usually creates policy, procedure, and rule manuals to help employees make routine (programmed) decisions on their own. "If the shoes were bought less than two weeks ago and are unworn, refund the full purchase price" is an example.

In contrast, supervisors usually *cannot* set up employees to make nonprogrammed decisions in advance. **Nonprogrammed decisions** (really, *nonprogrammable* decisions) address problems that are unique and novel, and that involve matters of great importance. Nonprogrammed decisions are usually the most important decisions that people make, such as getting married, changing a career, or starting a new business.

Decisions like these (for example, "Should we expand overseas?") usually can't be made in advance. When the issue arises, the supervisor needs to analyze the decision carefully and weigh the options and pros and cons. These decisions tend to require intuition, creativity, and judgment. We'll present decision-making skills in this chapter to improve your ability to make such decisions.

Supervisors distinguish between programmed and nonprogrammed decisions because the supervisor's time is precious. The more decisions you can program or make routine, the less time you need to devote to them. The supervisor's employees or systems can make these decisions more or less automatically. The *Principle of Exception* then says, "Only bring exceptions to the way things should be to the supervisor's attention. Handle routine matters (decisions) yourself."

Tools for Making Programmed and Nonprogrammed Decisions As we said, making *programmed* decisions usually involves establishing and then following rules. For example, to expedite its refund process, a department store may use this rule: "If the customer returns a jacket, you may give that person a refund if the tag is not removed, if the jacket is not damaged, and if the purchase was made within the past two weeks." Figure 3.1 presents another example.

Nonprogrammed decisions generally require a very different decision-making approach, since it's hard to preplan (program) how to respond to unexpected problems. Deciding what career to pursue, which job to take, whether to move across the country,

■Figure **3.1**

Employee Conduct and Work Rules

Source: Adapted from *Policies Now!* Knowledgepoint, 1129 Industrial Avenue, Petaluma, CA 94952.

RELSEDCO—Employee Conduct Policy and Work Rules
Effective Date: 4/18/10

Policy: To ensure orderly operations and to provide the best possible work environment, Relsedco expects employees to follow rules of conduct that will protect the interests and safety of all employees and the organization.

Rules: It is not possible to list all the forms of behavior that are considered unacceptable in the workplace. The following are examples of infractions of rules of conduct that may result in disciplinary action, up to and including termination of employment:

- Theft or inappropriate removal or possession of property
- Falsification of timekeeping records
- Working under the influence of alcohol or illegal drugs
- Possession, distribution, sale, transfer, or use of alcohol or illegal drugs in the workplace, while on duty, or while operating employer-owned vehicles or equipment
- Fighting or threatening violence in the workplace
- Boisterous or disruptive activity in the workplace
- Negligence or improper conduct leading to damage or employer-owned or customer-owned property
- Insubordination or other disrespectful conduct
- Violation of safety or health rules
- Smoking in prohibited areas
- Sexual or other unlawful or unwelcome harassment
- Possession of dangerous or unauthorized materials, such as explosives or firearms, in the workplace
- Excessive absenteeism or any absence without notice
- Unauthorized absence from workstation during the workday
- Unauthorized use of telephones, mail system, or other employer-owned equipment
- Unauthorized disclosure of business "secrets" or confidential information
- Violation of personnel policies
- Unsatisfactory performance or conduct

Employment with Relsedco is at the mutual consent of Relsedco and the employee, and either party may terminate that relationship at any time, with or without cause, and with or without advance notice.

Programmed and Nonprogrammed Decisions Compared		
	Programmable	**Nonprogrammable**
Nature of Decision	Predictable; precise information and decision criteria (late request by customer for a refund)	Unpredictable; ambiguous information and decision criteria (each employee accuses the other of damaging the machine)
Decision-Making Strategy	Reliance on rules and computation	Reliance on principles; judgment; creative problem-solving processes
Decision-Making Tools	Management science; capital budgeting; computerized solutions; rules	Judgment; intuition; creativity

and whom to marry are personal nonprogrammed decisions. These decisions rely heavily on judgment. Table 3.1 compares programmed and nonprogrammed decisions.

Decision-Making in Practice: How Rational Are Decision Makers?

Decision Making in Practice: How Rational Are Decision Makers?

Before turning to a detailed discussion of the decision making process, we should pose an important question: just how rational are you when it comes to making decisions? For example, suppose you run a retail store and must decide which of several trucks to buy for deliveries. If you are like most people, you probably assume that you would be quite rational in deciding. For example, would you not size up all your options and carefully weigh the pros and cons of each one? Perhaps, and perhaps not. There are two main schools of thought (or "models") regarding how people make decisions: the classical approach and the administrative approach. We'll see that it's a mistake to assume that anyone is entirely rational when they're making decisions.

THE CLASSICAL APPROACH   The idea that supervisors (and most people) are totally rational has a long and honorable tradition in economic and management theory. Early classical economists needed a simplified way to explain economic phenomena, such as how demand affects prices. Their solution was to accept some simplifying assumptions about how supervisors made decisions. Specifically, they assumed that the rational supervisor:

1. Had complete or "perfect" information about the situation, including the full range of goods and services available on the market and their exact prices.
2. Could distinguish perfectly between the problem and its symptoms.
3. Could identify all the criteria that he or she wanted the decision to satisfy, and accurately weigh all the criteria according to his or her preferences.
4. Knew all alternatives and could assess each one against each criterion.
5. Could accurately calculate and choose the alternative with the highest perceived value.
6. Could, therefore, be expected to make an "optimal" choice, without being confused by "irrational" thought processes.

THE ADMINISTRATIVE APPROACH   You probably sense from your own experiences that these assumptions leave something to be desired. For example, does anyone really (even with the Internet) ever have perfect knowledge of all the options? Does anyone really, unemotionally, analyze every single option?

Herbert Simon and his associates proposed a decision-making model they believe better reflects these realities. They agree that decision makers try to be rational. However, they point out that such rationality is, in practice, subject to many constraints: "The number of alternatives [the decision-maker] must explore is so great, the information he would need to evaluate them so vast that even an approximation to objective rationality is hard to conceive."[6]

We're all familiar with situations like these. For example, most people probably wouldn't check every local store before buying an iPad. Experiments support this commonsense notion. In one study, participants had to make decisions based on information the researchers transmitted on a screen. Most participants did okay at first. But as more information hit the screen faster, participants soon suffered "information overload" and began adjusting in several ways. For example, some omitted or ignored some of the information, while others began giving approximate answers (such as "about 25" instead of "24.6").[7]

Based on decision-making realities like these, Simon uses the term "bounded rationality" to explain how supervisors actually make decisions. **Bounded rationality** means that in reality a supervisor's decisions are only as rational as his or her values, abilities, and limited capacity for processing information permit them to be.

There are two main take-aways from Simon's administrative approach. One is to remember that *most people don't keep searching till they find the perfect solution—they don't optimize*. He says most people **satisfice**. They look for solutions until they find a satisfactory one. They look for the optimal solution only in exceptional cases. Spending too much time looking may mean the supervisor is overanalyzing the problem.

The second thing supervisors can learn from Simon is that *many cognitive biases and traps lie in wait* for unsuspecting supervisors. We'll see that wise supervisors take their own values, biases, abilities, and various other psychological traps into account before blundering into decisions.

2. How to Make Decisions

What Steps Can a Manager Follow to Develop Sound Decision-Making Skills?

Some people assume that good judgment is like good singing—either you have it or you don't. However, that's not true. Even with lots of training, most people will never be great singers. But a conscientious effort at improving decision-making skills can turn almost any supervisor into a better decision maker. In this section, we look at each step in the decision-making process and at how to improve one's decision-making skills. The steps are:

- Define the problem.
- Clarify your objectives.
- Identify alternatives.
- Analyze the consequences.
- Make a choice.

Step 1. Define the Problem[8]

Identifying or "defining" a problem is trickier than it may appear. Supervisors commonly emphasize the obvious and get misled by symptoms.[9] Here is a classic example. Office workers in a large office building were upset because they had to wait so long for the elevators, and many tenants were threatening to move out. The owners called in a consulting team and told them the problem was "that the elevators were running too slow."

If you agree with defining the problem as "slow-moving elevators," then the potential solutions are all quite expensive. The elevators were running about as fast as they could, so speeding them up was not an option. You could ask the tenants to stagger their work hours, but that could cause more anger than the slow-moving elevators. Adding more elevators would be too expensive.

So here is the point: *The alternatives you identify and the decisions you make depend on how you define the problem.* What the consultants actually did here was define the problem as, "The tenants are upset because they have to wait for an elevator." Then, the solution they chose was to have full-length mirrors installed by each bank of elevators so the tenants could admire themselves while waiting! The solution was both inexpensive and satisfactory: The complaints virtually disappeared. The moral of the story? *Never* take the statement of the problem for granted. (Recently, a new China-based company began installing slow-changing video ads beside elevators, based on much the same thinking.)

HOW TO DEFINE THE PROBLEM   The consultants' clever solution illustrates the first (and most important) step in defining problems: *Always ask, "What triggered this problem?"* Doing so will help you more accurately define the problem. Luckily for the owners, the consultants did not jump to any conclusions. They asked themselves, "What triggered the problem (as stated by the owners)?" The answer, of course, was the tenant's complaints, complaints triggered by frustration at having to wait. The problem then became: How do we reduce or eliminate frustration with having to wait?

There are some useful hints to keep in mind here.[10] *Start by writing down your initial assessment of the problem.* Then, dissect it. Ask, "What triggered this problem? Why am I even thinking about solving this problem? What is the connection between the trigger and the problem?" That's how the consultants approached defining the problem—and how you should, too. The application further illustrates this.

■ Application Example

Let's see how this might work in practice. Harold has had his job as marketing supervisor for Universal Widgets, Inc., for about five years. He has been happy with his job and with the company. However, the recent widget downturn wreaked havoc with the company's business, and it had to cut about 10% of the staff. Harold's boss gave him the bad news: "We like the work you've been doing here, but we're closing the New York office. We want you to stay with Universal, though, so we found you a similar position with our plant in Pittsburgh." Harold is thrilled. As he tells his parents, "I have to move to Pittsburgh, but at least I still have a job. The problem is, where should I live?" He immediately starts investigating housing possibilities in Pittsburgh. His father thinks Harold may be jumping the gun. What do you think? What would you do?

Harold's father is right. Harold jumped to the conclusion that his problem now is finding a place to live in Pittsburgh. Is that really the main decision he has to make? Why is Harold even thinking about solving this problem? What triggered this problem? What is the connection between the trigger and the problem? The trigger was his boss's comment that Universal no longer needed his services in New York and that it was, therefore, transferring him to Pittsburgh. What's the real problem Harold must face here? Let us assume that the issue—and the decision Harold really must make—is this: Should I move to Pittsburgh with Universal Widgets? Or should I try to get the best marketing supervisor job I can, and if so, where?[11]

Step 2. Clarify Your Objectives

Most people are looking to achieve several aims when making a decision. For example, in choosing a location for a new plant, the employer typically wants to do several things: minimize distance from the company's customers; get close to raw materials; have available transportation; have access to a good labor supply; and perhaps satisfy a few personal preference issues, such as be able to fish on weekends.

HAVE MORE THAN ONE OBJECTIVE   Therefore, few supervisors would make a decision with just a single objective in mind. (There are exceptions. The great football coach Vince Lombardi once reportedly summed this up by saying, "Winning isn't everything. It's the only thing.") However, for most decisions, most people haven't the luxury of focusing like a laser on just a single objective. When deciding on a new laptop computer, you may want to get the most memory, portability, and reliability you can for the price. You'd buy the one that, on balance, best satisfied all these objectives (or, to put this another way, satisfied all these criteria). Hopefully, you wouldn't make your decision on the assumption that your main aim, such as minimizing price, was your only aim.

HOW TO CLARIFY OBJECTIVES   Your objectives should provide an explicit expression of what you really want. If you don't have clear objectives, you will not be able to evaluate your alternatives. For example, if Harold isn't clear about whether he wants to stay close to New York, wants at least a 10% raise, or wants to stay in the widget industry, how could he possibly decide whether to stay with Universal Widgets or leave—or which of several job offers were best? The answer is, he could not.

How do you decide what your main aims are—what you want the decision to accomplish for you? Here, from an expert, is a useful five-step procedure.[12]

1. **Write down all the concerns you hope to address through your decision.**   Don't worry about repetition. There are several big concerns Harold wants his decision to address. These include the impact of his decision on his long-term career; enjoying what he's doing; living close to a large urban center; and earning more money than he earns now.

2. **Convert your concerns into specific objectives.**   Make your objectives measurable. Harold's concerns translate into these objectives: getting a job that puts him in a position to be marketing director within two years; a job with a consumer products company, preferably in the widgets industry; being within a one-hour

drive of a city with a population of at least one million people; and earning at least $1,200 per week.

3. **Separate ends from means to establish your fundamental objectives.** This step helps you zero in on what you really want. One way to do this is to ask, several times, "Why?" For example, Harold asks himself, "Why do I want to live within a one-hour drive of a city with a population of at least one million people?" Because he wants to make sure he can meet many other people who are his own age, and because he enjoys what he sees as big city benefits such as museums, theater, and opera. This helps clarify what Harold really wants. For example, a smaller town might do if the town has the right demographics and cultural attractions.

4. **Clarify what you mean by each objective.** You must banish fuzzy thinking. For example, "getting a raise" would be a fuzzy objective. Harold has already clarified what he means by his financial objective. He wants to "earn at least $1,200 per week."

5. **Test your objectives to see if they capture your interests.** This is your reality check. Harold carefully reviews his full list of final objectives to make sure they completely capture what he wants to accomplish by his decision. In summary:

   How to Clarify Your Objectives

   - Write down all the concerns you hope to address through your decision.
   - Convert your concerns into specific, succinct objectives.
   - Separate ends from means to establish your fundamental objectives.
   - Clarify what you mean by each objective.
   - Test your objectives to see if they capture your interests.

Step 3. Identify Alternatives

You must have a choice (in other words, two or more options) if you are going to make an effective decision. If Harold's only option is Pittsburgh, there really isn't a decision to make—except perhaps to "take it or leave it."

Wise supervisors, therefore, usually ask, "What are my options? What are my alternatives?" Decision-making experts call alternatives "the raw material of decision-making." They say alternatives represent "the range of potential choices you'll have for pursuing your objectives."[13]

How to Identify Alternatives   There are several keys to generating good alternatives.

- Be *creative*; start by trying to generate as many alternatives as you can yourself. (We'll address creativity below.)
- Then *expand your search for options* by checking with other people, including experts.
- Another useful technique is to look at each of your objectives and ask, "How?" For example, Harold might ask, "How could I get a position that would lead to a marketing director's job within two years?" One alternative is certainly to take a senior marketing manager's job. Another might be to go after the senior director's job right away.
- One caveat is this: *Know when to stop.* Remember that most supervisors "satisfice." It's rarely practical to spend the time and energy required to find the optimal solution.

Through this approach, Harold generates several good alternatives. He can take the Pittsburgh Universal Widget job, or he can leave. If he leaves, his search for alternatives turns up four other possible alternatives: a job with a dot-com as senior manager in New York; a marketing director's job with Ford in Detroit; and two other marketing manager jobs, one with a pet food company in Newark, and one with Nokia in Washington, DC.   .

Step 4. Analyze the Consequences

There is a big danger in making decisions, and it is this: You make them today, but you feel them tomorrow. You buy an iPad today, and tomorrow you discover it doesn't really satisfy your needs, because your word processing requirements are now greater. Harold decides today to stay with Universal. Then he finds out next year that his prospects of promotion are almost nil because the company already has two Pittsburgh marketing directors, who have no plans to leave. "If only I'd thought of that," Harold says. As a supervisor, you never want to say, "If only I'd thought of that."

Therefore, the next decision-making step is to analyze what the consequences would be of choosing each alternative. One expert says, "This is often the most difficult part of the decision-making process, because this is the stage that typically requires forecasting future events."[14] Harold needs a practical way to determine what the consequences of each of his alternatives are. Only then can he start to decide which option is best.

HOW TO ANALYZE THE CONSEQUENCES   Your job here is to think through, for each alternative, what the consequences of choosing that alternative will be *for each of your objectives.* Your aim is to make sure you never have to say, "Why didn't I think of that?" Here is a useful three-step process for thinking through how each alternative might rate in terms of your objectives:[15]

1. Mentally put yourself in the future.

2. Eliminate clearly inferior alternatives.

3. Organize your remaining alternatives in a consequences table.

First, mentally put yourself into the future. For example, imagine that you bought that new computer, and that you're actually using it now, six months later. How do you like it? Has anything changed in your life that should have influenced your decision six months ago? Looking into the future is a crucial analytical skill. One way to improve this skill is by using *process analysis.* **Process analysis** means analyzing a problem by thinking through the process involved from beginning to end, imagining, at each step, what actually would happen.[16]

Consider this example A frugal person named Joe can make one whole cigar from every five cigar butts he finds. How many cigars can he make if he finds 25 cigar butts? Before you answer "five," think through Joe's cigar-making process, step by step. There he sits on his park bench, making (and smoking!) each of his five cigars. As he smokes each cigar, he ends up with one new cigar butt. Putting yourself in Joe's place (figuratively speaking) and actually "experiencing"—thinking through—each step in the process and its outcomes, you can see something you may not have noticed before. In smoking his five handmade cigars, Joe ends up with five new butts, which he in turn combines into a sixth whole new cigar.[17] In this case, process analysis meant envisioning Joe sitting on his park bench and then thinking through each of the steps he would take as if you were there.

Second, eliminate any clearly inferior alternatives. For example, if Harold does his homework and thinks through the consequences of each of his alternatives, it should be obvious that his prospects for promotion to marketing director are virtually nil if he goes to Pittsburg with Universal Widgets. Therefore, why even continue considering this alternative? He crosses it off his list.

Third, organize your remaining alternatives into a consequences table. A consequences matrix (or table) lists your objectives down the left side of the page and your alternatives along the top. In each box of the matrix, put a brief description that shows the consequences of that alternative for that objective. This provides a concise, bird's-eye view of the consequences of pursuing each alternative.

◼ Application Example

Harold's Consequences Table

Harold started with five alternatives and four basic objectives. Here they are in consequences table form, along with what he sees as the consequences for each one:

Alternative	Objective			
	Marketing director in two years	**Consumer products company**	**One-hour drive from major city**	**Earn at least $1,200 per week**
Marketing supervisor, Universal Widgets, Pittsburgh	Little or no possibility— *eliminate this option*	NA (Eliminated)	NA (Eliminated)	NA (Eliminated)
Senior manager, dot-com, NY	High probability— if company survives that long	Consumer-oriented, but does not really sell products	Yes, excellent	$1,250 plus stock options
Marketing supervisor, Ford, Detroit	Moderate possibility— bigger company, longer climb	Yes, but not as interesting as selling widgets; I may get bored	Yes	$1,100 plus great benefits (discount on new T-Bird)
Marketing supervisor, pet foods, Newark	High probability— small, growing company with little marketing expertise now	Yes, but not quite as interesting as selling widgets	Yes	$1,200
Marketing supervisor, Nokia, Washington, DC	Fairly high probability—fast-growing company	Yes—exciting industry	Yes—exceptional cultural attractions and demographics	$1,200

Step 5. Make a Choice

Your analyses are useless unless you make the right choice. Under perfect conditions, doing so should be straightforward. Simply review the consequences of each alternative and choose the alternative that achieves your objectives. But in practice, making a decision—even a relatively simple one like choosing a computer—usually can't be done so accurately or rationally. However, several techniques can help anyone make a better decision.

3. How to Make Even Better Decisions

What Can You Do to Improve the Quality of Decisions?

Let's look at some techniques to help you improve the quality of your decisions. We begin with an important one: Increase your knowledge.

Increase Your Knowledge

"Knowledge is power," someone once said, and that's particularly true in making decisions. Even the simplest decisions—like mapping your route to work each morning—become difficult without basic information, such as the traffic report. And complex decisions rely on information even more. *To increase your knowledge:*

ASK QUESTIONS   Always use the six main question words—Who? What? Where? When? Why? How?—to probe and to boost your knowledge. In buying a used car, for instance, ask "*Who* is selling the car, and *who* previously owned it?" "*What* do similar cars sell for?" "*What* is wrong with this car?" "*Where* did the owner service it?" "*When* did the owner buy it?" "*Why* does the owner want to sell?" "*How* much do you think you could buy it for?" Most people could save themselves a lot of aggravation by arming themselves with some good questions.

GET EXPERIENCE   For many endeavors, there's simply no substitute for experience. That's certainly true on a personal level. Many students find that interning in a job similar to the occupation they plan to pursue can help enormously in clarifying if that's the right occupation for them.[18]

USE CONSULTANTS   Supervisors use consultants' experience (such as in personnel testing or workforce planning) to supplement their own lack of experience in particular areas.

These needn't be management consultants, of course. Sometimes, just talking the problem over with an expert from the HR department can help, particularly if he or she has had experience solving similar problems.

USE YOUR EMPLOYEES   More to the point, remember to get your employees' opinions, perhaps by calling a team meeting toward the end of the day. Few people (including high-priced consultants) are as familiar with the issues as are the front-line employees themselves. Figure 3.2 (on page 78) presents several simple problem-solving tools employees can use to analyze problems in their work area. Figure 3.3 (on page 79) contains a more detailed example of how to use one of these tools, the fish-bone diagram. The leadership applications feature further explains how to get your employees' input when making decisions.

DO YOUR RESEARCH   Whatever the decision, there's usually a wealth of information you can tap. For example, thinking of moving from New York to D.C.? How do salaries

Leadership Applications for Supervisors

Should You Let Your Employees Participate, or Not?

In practice, one of the most important leadership decisions you'll have to make is whether and to what extent you should make the decision yourself, or let your subordinates help you to decide. In other words, you'll have a decision to make ("Is this a good person to join our team?" "What's the best way to implement this new work procedure?" "What should we do to correct this quality problem?") and you'll have to decide whether to make the decision yourself, or to hand it over to your subordinates.

Of course, it's usually not an either/or situation. Most leadership experts tend to view employee participation in decisions as falling along a *continuum*. At one end is autocratic *decision-making, which means you make the decision yourself without asking for opinions or suggestions*. At the opposite end is delegation, *which means you give the group the authority to make the decision (perhaps retaining the right of ultimate approval)*. In between these two extremes, you could try consultation, *which means getting your subordinates' opinions and suggestions and then making the decision yourself*. And there's joint decision making, *which means that you and your team jointly sit down to make the decision, with no one (including you) having a black ball*. Autocratic decisions, of course, implies that your subordinates don't participate in making the decision at all, while consultation, joint decision making, and delegation imply increasing levels of employee participation.

There is a lot to be said about participative leadership (whether it's of the consultative, joint decision making, or delegating variety). The bottom line is that the quality of a participatively arrived at decision is often better, because more points of view and levels of expertise are brought to bear. (Indeed, we've seen that getting your employees' input can be as or more useful than bringing in some high-powered consultant!) Furthermore, employees tend to be more accepting of and committed to decisions in which they participated.

Of course, the rubber hits the road when you need to decide how much participation to allow, and here, as we've seen in Chapter 2, various leadership experts have made good suggestions. For example, Vroom and Yetton suggest asking questions like these before deciding how participative to be:

- Is there a quality requirement such that one solution is likely to be more rational than another?

- Do I have sufficient information to make a high-quality decision?
- Is the problem structured?
- Is acceptance of the decision by subordinates critical to effective implementation?
- If you were to make the decision by yourself, is it reasonably certain that it would be accepted by your subordinates?
- Do subordinates share the organizational goals to be obtained in solving this problem?
- Is conflict among subordinates likely over preferred solutions?

And we saw that Paul Hersey suggests the following:

- Delegating *works best when followers are willing to do the job and are able to (know how to) go about doing it. Delegating leaders encourage autonomy, provide support and resources, and delegate activities.*
- Participating *works best when followers are able to do the job, but are unwilling and so require emotional support. Participating leaders "share ideas and facilitate the decision making."*
- Selling *works best when followers are neither willing nor able to do the job. The selling leader "explains decisions and provides opportunity for clarification."*
- Telling *works best when followers are willing to do the job, but don't know how to do it. The telling leader "provides specific instructions and closely supervises performance."*

Assuming you do decide that some participation is appropriate, here's what one leadership expert suggests about how to encourage participation:[33]

Encourage employees to express their concerns.

Describe a proposal as tentative.

Record ideas and suggestions.

Look for ways to build on ideas and suggestions.

Be tactful in expressing concerns about a suggestion.

Listen to dissenting views without getting defensive.

Try to utilize suggestions and deal with concerns.

Show appreciation for suggestions.

Source: Gary Yukl, *Leadership in Organizations* (Upper Saddle River, NJ: Prentice Hall, 1998), p. 133.

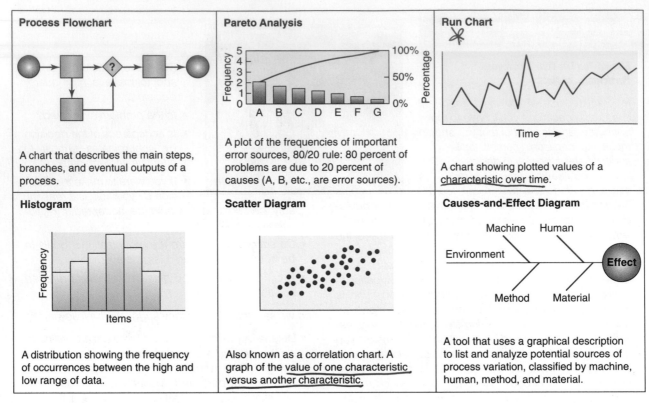

Process Flowchart

A chart that describes the main steps, branches, and eventual outputs of a process.

Pareto Analysis

A plot of the frequencies of important error sources, 80/20 rule: 80 percent of problems are due to 20 percent of causes (A, B, etc., are error sources).

Run Chart

Time →

A chart showing plotted values of a characteristic over time.

Histogram

Frequency

Items

A distribution showing the frequency of occurrences between the high and low range of data.

Scatter Diagram

Also known as a correlation chart. A graph of the value of one characteristic versus another characteristic.

Causes-and-Effect Diagram

Machine   Human

Environment

Effect

Method   Material

A tool that uses a graphical description to list and analyze potential sources of process variation, classified by machine, human, method, and material.

■Figure **3.2**

Commonly Used Tools for Problem Solving and Continuous Improvement

Source: Adapted from Richard Chase and Nicholas Aquilero, *Production and Operations Management*, 6th ed. (Homewood, IL: Irwin, 1992), p. 197.

in Washington compare with those in New York? Web sites like http://salary.com can answer that question.

FORCE YOURSELF TO RECOGNIZE THE FACTS WHEN YOU SEE THEM Don't let what you want to do blind you to the facts. For example, it's easy to make the financials of a vacation look better when you want to take that vacation. Therefore, endeavor to maintain your objectivity. Base your decision on an objective review of the facts as they really are.

Use Your Intuition

Several years ago Malcolm Gladwell published a popular book named *Blink: The Power of Thinking Without Thinking*. Hs basic point was that people tend to make quick, snap decisions based on intuition. The psychiatrist Sigmund Freud made this similar observation on making decisions:

> When making a decision of minor importance, I have always found it advantageous to consider all the pros and cons. In vital matters, however, such as the choice of a mate or a profession, the decision should come from the unconscious, from somewhere within ourselves. In the important decisions of our personal life, we should be governed, I think, by the deep inner needs of our nature.[19]

■Figure **3.3**

Using the Fish-Bone (Causes and Effect) Diagram

Source: Jay Heizor and Barry Render, *Operations Management*, 6th ed. (Upper Saddle River, NJ: Prentice Hall, 2001), p. 182, example 1.

Note: A team of airline employees might use a diagram like this to think of and analyze the possible causes of dissatisfied customers.

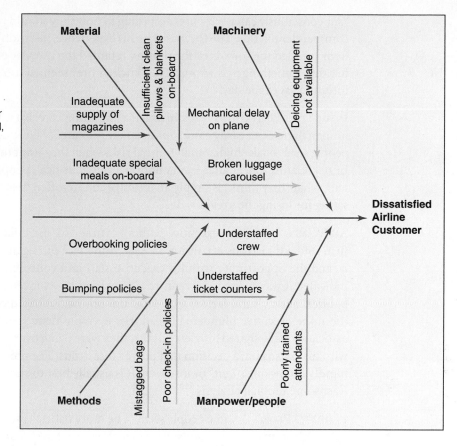

Another expert explains intuition this way: He says you can usually tell when a decision fits with your inner nature, because it brings an enormous sense of relief. Good decisions, he says, are the best tranquilizers ever invented; bad ones often increase your anxiety.[20]

These experts are talking about intuition. **Intuition** is a cognitive process whereby a person instinctively makes a decision based on his or her accumulated knowledge and experience.

Psychologist Gary Klein tells this story to illustrate intuitive decision making. A fire commander and his crew encounter a fire at the back of a house. The commander leads his team into the building. Standing in the living room, they blast water onto the smoke and flames, which appear to be consuming the kitchen, yet the fire roars back and continues to burn. The fire's persistence baffles the commander. His men douse the "kitchen fire" again, and the flames subside, but then they flare up with an even greater intensity. The firefighters retreat a few steps to regroup. Suddenly, an uneasy feeling grips the commander. His intuition (which he calls his "sixth sense") tells him to vacate the house. He orders everyone to leave. Just as the crew reaches the street, the living room floor caves in. The fire was in the basement, not the kitchen. Had they still been in the house, the men would have plunged into an inferno.[21]

As this story shows, we often reach intuitive decisions by quickly (and apparently unthinkingly) comparing our present situation to situations we've faced in the past. For example, in his study of firefighters, Klein found they accumulate experiences and "subconsciously categorize fires according to how they should react to them."[22] The fire commander did this. The fire, based on his experience, just didn't make sense. Why? The floor muffled the sounds of the fire and retarded the transfer of heat. The commander felt that something was wrong: The "kitchen fire" seemed too quiet and too cool. His intuition saved the day.

INTUITION'S LIMITATIONS   Yet, in practice, intuition can also mislead. "Various traits of human nature can easily cloud our decision-making."[23] For example, studies show that people tend to take higher than normal risks when they want to recover a previous loss. In negotiating a deal after losing out on a previous deal, people often "bet the ranch" with what (they think) is simply an intuitive counteroffer. In fact, they are overcompensating for losing the previous deal.[24]

AN EXAMPLE   A rising executive with a Fortune 100 manufacturing company led his firm into a disastrous expansion in Asia in the face of negative evidence. He first discussed the opportunity with his executive staff and consultants; this rational analysis indicated it was a very risky venture. The market data looked barely favorable, and the political and cultural factors were huge unknowns, yet based on little more than intuition, the executive blundered ahead. His overconfidence led him to assume that his associates really shared his view but that they were being overcautious.[25] He went ahead with his expansion, a decision that proved disastrous. The point is that it's dangerous to blindly follow one's "gut" or intuition. It is usually best to supplement intuition with at least some rational analysis.[26]

INTUITIVE PEOPLE   Some people seem to be more naturally inclined to take an intuitive approach to making decisions. Research shows that *systematic decision makers* take a more logical, step-by-step approach to solving a problem.[27] *Intuitive decision makers* use a more trial-and-error approach. They bounce from one alternative to another to get a feel for which seems to work best.

We can measure intuitiveness. The short test in Figure 3.4 provides an approximate reading on whether you are more systematic or intuitive in your decision making.[28]

■Figure **3.4**

Are You More Rational or More Intuitive?

Source: Adapted and reproduced by permission, from the Personal Style Inventory by William Taggart, Ph.D., Copyright 1991.

WHAT IS MY ORIENTATION?

You can get a rough idea of your relative preferences for the systematic and intuitive ways of dealing with situations by rating yourself on four items. For each statement, rank yourself on a six-point scale—from 1 (never), 2 (once in a while), 3 (sometimes), 4 (quite often), 5 (frequently but not always), to 6 (always)—and place your response in the box to the right of the item:

1. When I have a special job to do, I like to organize it carefully from the start. ☐
2. I feel that a prescribed, step-by-step method is best for solving problems. ☐
3. I prefer people who are imaginative to those who are not. ☐
4. I look at a problem as a whole, approaching it from all sides. ☐

Now add the values for the first two items for one total and for the last two items for another total. Subtract the second total from the first. If your total has a positive value, your preference is *Rational* by that amount, and if your total has a negative value, your preference is *Intuitive* by that amount. Ten represents the maximum possible rational or intuitive score from the equally preferred midpoint (0). Mark your position on the range of possible scores:

These items are taken from a 30-item Personal Style Inventory (PSI) assessment of preferences for Rational and Intuitive behavior created by William Taggart.

Don't Overstress the Finality of the Decision[29]

Knowing when to quit is important. The City of London government lost millions when its efforts to automate the London Stock Exchange collapsed due to technical difficulties. Experts subsequently said the venture might have been a victim of what psychologists call *escalation*. Escalation is the act of making a wrong decision and then losing even more through a continued devotion to that decision.[30] So, once the decision is made, stick with it if you believe you're on the right track. But know "when to fold" if the decision turns out to be a poor one.

In making the choice, remember that few decisions are forever. Some strategic decisions are hard to reverse. However, the supervisor can modify most decisions, even bad ones, with time.

Make Sure the Timing Is Right

"Timing is everything" someone once said, and the same applies to making decisions. With most people, their moods or the pressure they're under affects their decisions. Deliberately cut off by another driver while on the highway, even a placid driver might unwisely decide to retaliate. Psychologists know that when people feel "down," their actions tend to be aggressive and destructive. When they feel good, their behavior swings toward balance and tolerance. Similarly, people tend to be lenient when they're in good spirits and tough when they're grouchy.

Do a quick reality check prior to making a decision. Avoid making regrettable decisions when your moods are extreme, or when you are under duress. In summary:

In Making a Choice

- Increase your knowledge.
- Use your intuition.
- Weigh the pros and cons.
- Don't overstress the finality of your decision.
- Make sure the timing is right.

Encourage Creativity

To make good decisions, it also helps if the supervisor is creative—in how he or she defines the problem and generates alternatives, for instance. **Creativity** is the process of developing original, novel responses to a problem. It is an integral part of making good decisions. There are several simple things supervisors can do to foster creative solutions:

ENCOURAGE BRAINSTORMING   Meetings called to discuss problems often turn out to be useless. Employees may come to the meeting willing and even enthusiastic to define a problem and discuss solutions. However, if their suggestions are met with comments such as "that's ridiculous" or "that's impossible," people are unlikely to make risky, innovative suggestions.

Brainstorming is a technique aimed at banishing this problem. It involves requiring that all participants withhold any criticism and comments until all suggested alternatives are on the table. One important point here is that people should feel comfortable about making suggestions even if the suggestions seem strange. In an environment where everyone can build on everyone else's suggestions, it's often the most implausible idea that eventually produces the perfect solution.

SUSPEND JUDGMENT   Suspending judgment is the heart of brainstorming, but doing so works equally well when making creative decisions "solo." For example, people tend to approach situations by comparing them to similar experiences they've faced in the past. Doing so can hamper their creativity. "Unfortunately, . . . [no] two situations are identical. Many decision makers spot the similarities between situations very quickly but . . . ignore critical differences."[46] To get around this, Professor Michael Ray suggests suspending judgment. Don't automatically go with your first reaction. Think through the similarities and differences of the present and former situations.

GET MORE POINTS OF VIEW   When it comes to creativity, more points of view are usually better than fewer, and diverse points of view are better than homogeneous ones. "Creativity works better when you have a group of three or four than it does with one, because you have the synergistic effect where people are working with each other, building on others' ideas," says one creativity expert. Try to obtain different opinions. For example, rather than just having production people analyze a production problem, get input from other departments as well.

ENCOURAGE ANONYMOUS INPUT   Even in the most supportive environment, some employees may be too introverted to participate fully. Allowing for anonymous and/or written input can help encourage people like these to participate more.[31]

■ Application Exercise

Harold's Choice

So, which alternative should Harold choose? He first did some research. He learns that there are two marketing directors at the Pittsburgh plant. Because the prospects of a promotion are virtually nil, he discards that option. That leaves four options—the dot-com in New York, Ford in Detroit, pet food in Newark, and Nokia in D.C. How would you proceed if you were Harold?

He reviews his consequences matrix. For three of the jobs—the dot-com, Ford, and pet foods—his research and intuition suggest they probably lack the direct interaction with consumers and consumer products that he prefers. Promotion to senior director would probably take him more than two years at Ford, which is suffering big reversals. He asks himself where he'll be six months from now if he takes the dot-com job and is dissuaded by the high failure rate of dot-corns. Six months from now, he might well be out of a job!

Harold puts together a decision matrix (Figure 3.5) to summarize all this information. This shows how important each of his objectives is to Harold when it comes to choosing a job. He then uses this matrix to *rank each possible job* (in other words, each alternative) *on how well it fulfills each of his objectives.* The pet food and Nokia jobs look like the best bets. The pet food job is a possibility. In terms of senior director, it's a good career move. However, he's a little less enthusiastic about the pet food business, although it scores a bit higher than the Nokia job.

Harold's Objectives	How Harold Rates Relative Importance of Each Objective	How Harold Rates Senior Manager, Dot-com, NY*	How Harold Rates Marketing Supervisor, Ford, Detroit*	How Harold Rates Senior Marketing Manager, Pet Foods, Newark*	How Harold Rates Marketing Supervisor, Nokia, Washington, DC*
Marketing director in two years	0.50	2 (2 × 0.50 = 1)	2 (2 × 0.50 = 1)	5 (5 × 0.50 = 2.5)	4 (4 × 0.50 = 2)
Consumer products company	0.20	2 (2 × 0.20 = 0.4)	3 (3 × 0.20 = 0.6)	3 (3 × 0.20 = 0.6)	5 (5 × 0.20 = 1)
One-hour drive from major city	0.15	5 (5 × 0.15 = 0.75)	5 (5 × 0.15 = 0.75)	5 (5 × 0.15 = 0.75)	5 (5 × 0.15 = 0.75)
Earn at least $1,200 per week	0.15	4 (4 × 0.15 = 0.6)	3 (3 × 0.15 = 0.45)	4 (4 × 0.15 = 0.6)	4 (4 × 0.15 = 0.6)
Sum	1.00	2.75 (1 + .4 + .75 + .6)	2.80 (1 + .6 + .75 + .45)	4.45 (2.5 + .6 + .75 + .6)	4.35 (2 + 1 + .75 + .6)

◼ Figure **3.5**

Harold's Decision Matrix

Note: *The numbers (such as 2, 4, or 5) show Harold's ratings for how the alternative at the top of the column might satisfy the objective at left in the row. Then Harold multiplies his rating for the alternative by the importance (to him) weight he assigned to that particular objective.

Harold has a good feeling about the Nokia job. It satisfies his objectives, and his research suggests that living costs in D.C. are comparable to those in New York. He's excited about the cell phone business. Looking down the road, he sees this industry's fast growth opening many new options for him. He can definitely see himself living in Washington, DC. He takes the job.

Use Information Technology Tools

How Can Information Technology Tools Help a Manager Make Decisions?

For most supervisors today, gathering information and making decisions is unthinkable without information technology (or IT). We use computers, e-mail, software, smart phones, iPads, fax machines, flash drives, and scanners to assist with our daily chores. We search for travel options on Expedia and take online college courses. Computerized diagnostic tools analyze our autos' problems, point-of-sale computers process our credit-card purchases, and computerized traffic-flow systems control our trips to work.[32]

At work, *information systems* help supervisors handle much of their information processing and decision-making chores. The term **information system** refers to the interrelated components working together to collect, process, store, and disseminate information to support decision making, coordination, analysis, and visualization in an organization. We'll look at a few examples.

DECISION SUPPORT SYSTEMS A **decision support system (DSS)** is a set of computerized tools that help supervisors make decisions in two ways. It helps the person access the data he or she needs to make better decisions (for instance, on which products his or her team produced the most of last year). And it provides user-friendly software to analyze that data.

ENTERPRISE RESOURCE PLANNING SYSTEMS An **enterprise resource planning (ERP) system** is a companywide integrated computer system. It is comprised of compatible software modules for each of the company's separate departments (such as sales, accounting, finance, production, and human resources). Often Internet-based, the ERP modules are designed to communicate with each other and with the central system's database. That way, information from all the departments is readily shared by the ERP system and is available to employees in all the other departments. ERP strips away the barriers that typically exist among a company's stand-alone departmental computer systems. The name notwithstanding, enterprise resource planning systems are not primarily planning systems. We'll generally refer to them as *enterprise systems* in this book.

With an enterprise system, activities that formerly required human intervention (such as production telling accounting that it should bill a customer because an order just shipped) occur automatically. By integrating the separate departmental modules, enterprise systems can do things that the separate departmental systems (sales, production, finance, and human resources) could not do on their own. For example, when a customer buys a Dell computer online, Dell's ERP automatically records the sale, orders the necessary parts, schedules production, orders UPS to pick up and deliver the finished product, and has Dell's accounting department send the customer a bill.

KNOWLEDGE MANAGEMENT   In today's competitive business environment, it's usually the company with the best information that's the most successful. This is because its supervisors are best positioned to make good decisions. As a result, many supervisors today are using what they call *knowledge management*. **Knowledge management** refers to any efforts aimed at enabling the company's supervisors and employees to better utilize the information available anywhere in the company.

Much of the problem in managing knowledge is that most information isn't written down, but in employees' heads. For any company—and especially a large one—to capture such information and transform it into knowledge that others can use can be quite a challenge.

For example, Xerox has about 23,000 repair technicians around the world fixing copiers at clients' sites. In many cases, the repair solutions exist "only in the heads of experienced technicians, who can solve complex problems faster and more efficiently than less experienced ones."[28] The challenge for Xerox was to find a way to access all that brain-based knowledge and translate it into a usable form. What could Xerox do to give the company's entire 23,000-person worldwide repair force access to this knowledge?

Xerox's solution was to create an intranet-based communications system named Eureka, linked to a corporate database. The company encourages repair technicians around the world to share repair tips by inputting them into the database via Eureka. Xerox gave all technicians laptop computers to facilitate this. Soon, more than 5,000 tips were in the database. Now this experienced-based knowledge is easily accessible by other service reps and their supervisors around the world.

4. Avoiding Psychological Traps

How Can You Avoid Psychological Traps When Making a Decision?

In practice, sprinkled across the supervisor's decision-making terrain are various decision-making traps. If you're a supervisor who is "trapped" into making a poor decision, you may not even realize what hit you. Let's look at some of these psychological traps.

Decision-Making Shortcuts

People who make decisions tend to take shortcuts. They do this by using **heuristics**, also known as decision-making shortcuts, or "rules of thumb." For example, banks used to abide by the heuristic that "people shouldn't spend more than 28% of their gross monthly income on mortgage payments and other house-related expenses."[48] More recently they abandoned that rule of thumb, to their peril.

Heuristics manifest themselves in many ways. For example, supervisors often (unwisely) predict what a job candidate's performance will be, based on the supervisor's experience with others of the same ethnic or other background. Another shortcut involves basing decisions on what happened most recently. For example, supervisors tend to appraise employees based on the person's past few weeks' performance, because that's what's most easily recalled.

Based on 150 interviews with decision makers, one researcher concluded, "Relatively few decisions are made using analytical processes such as generating a variety of options and contrasting their strengths and weaknesses."[34] Instead, most people tend to use cognitive shortcuts, such as rules governing what to do in new situations that are similar to those addressed in the past. So the first trap to avoid is unknowingly making a choice based on some unstated shortcut.

Anchoring

Anchoring means unconsciously giving too much weight to the first information you hear. It can cause you to define the problem incorrectly.

Anchors pop up in the most unexpected ways. Assume you're selling your car, which you know is worth about $10,000. Joe has responded to your classified ad; when he arrives, he offhandedly remarks that the car is only worth about $5,000. What would you do? On the one hand, you know that Joe is probably just positioning himself to get a better deal, and you know that $5,000 is ridiculous. On the other hand, only one other person called, but never showed up. So you start bargaining with Joe. He says $5,000; you say $10,000; and before you know it, you've arrived at a price of $8,000 (for your $10,000 car), which Joe graciously points out is "better than splitting the difference" from your point of view.

What happened? You just got anchored (to put it mildly). Without realizing it, you gave disproportionate weight to his apparently offhand "$5,000" comment, and your decision making (and bargaining) from then on revolved around his price, not yours. What should you have done? One response might have been, "Five thousand dollars? Are you kidding? That's not even in the ballpark!" At least that might have loosened that subliminal anchor. Then the bargaining could take place on your terms, not his.

Psychological Set

Failing to "think out of the box" is another decision-making trap. The technical term for this is **psychological set**, which means the tendency to look at things with a rigid point of view when solving a problem.[35]

Doing so can severely limit your ability to create alternative solutions. Figure 3.6 presents a classic example. Your assignment is to connect all nine dots with no more

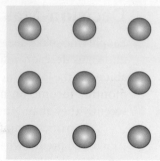

■Figure **3.6**

Looking at the Problem in Just One Way

Source: Lester A. Lefton and Laura Valvatine, *Mastering Psychology*, 4th ed. Copyright © 1992 by Allyn & Bacon. Reprinted by permission.

than four lines running through them, and to do so without lifting your pen from the paper. Hint: Don't take a rigid point of view.

To avoid this trap, always question your assumptions. Look again at the problem of the nine dots in Figure 3.6. Remember that your instructions were to connect all nine dots with no more than four lines running through them, and to do so without lifting your pen from the paper. How would you do it? Start by checking your assumptions.

Most people view the nine dots as a square—they're victims of psychological set. Viewing them as a square limits your solutions. There is actually no way to connect all the dots as long as you assume the dots represent a square. Figure 3.7 shows one creative solution. The key was checking your assumptions about how you could solve the problem. Now solve the problem in Figure 3.8.

The psychological-set trap helps explain why many decisions go bad. For example, the owners of the building with the "slow elevators" were victims of psychological set. They could only see the problem in one way, and they did not question their assumptions. Luckily, the consultants didn't fall into the same trap.

Perception

The fact that we don't always see things as they really are is another psychological trap. Specifically, **perception** is the selection and interpretation of information we receive through our senses, and the meaning we give to the information. The problem is that many things, such as our biases, needs, and fears influence how we see things. For example, a nervous person may agonize for days about being called to a meeting with the boss, although the boss only wanted to ask the employee for some advice.

Things like this happen every day. You might be less happy with a B in a course after finding out that your friend got an A with about the same test grades.[52] Similarly,

■Figure **3.7**

The Advantage of Not Just Looking at the Problem in One Way

Source: Max H. Bazerman, *Judgment in Managerial Decision Making.* Copyright © 1994 Wiley, p. 93. Reprinted by permission of Wiley.

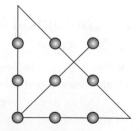

■Figure **3.8**

Using Creativity to Find a Solution

How many squares are in the box? Now, count again. Only 16? Take away your preconception of how many squares there are. Now, how many do you find? You should find 30!

Source: Applied Human Relations, 4th ed., by Benton/Halloran cW 1991. Reprinted by permission of Prentice Hall, Upper Saddle River, NJ.

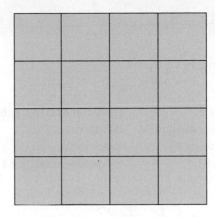

in organizations, prior experiences and position influence how a supervisor perceives a problem and reacts to it. Thus a sales supervisor may perceive a problem as a sales problem, while a production supervisor says it's a production problem. People tend to "see" things from their own points of view (as the accompanying Supervising the New Workforce further illustrates).

Supervising the New Workforce

Minority and Nonminority Differences in How We See Things

The hardest thing to appreciate about "perception" is that it's not just theoretical. Intellectually, most supervisors sense that different people react to things in different ways. But when they actually have to coach, or discipline, or give orders to employees, they tend to do so as if everyone has about the same point of view as they do. Let's look at some actual situations to appreciate better how people's backgrounds affect how they see things.

Decisions regarding equal employment issues are some of the trickiest that you'll have to tackle. Your employees will usually come to you first when they feel they've been the target of some improper racial, cultural, religious, age-related, or sexual harassment–type issue.

The problem is that what's harassment to one person may be innocent to another. Harassers sometimes don't perceive that their abominable behavior is offending others. For example, men don't view harassment the same way as do women.[36] Women perceive a broader range of behaviors (including derogatory attitudes toward women, dating pressure, or physical sexual contact) as harassing.[37] In studies in the U.S. military, for instance, women perceived higher occurrences of sexual harassment than men did; blacks perceived higher incidences of sexual harassment and racist/sexist behaviors than whites did; and officers in general, especially black officers as compared with black enlisted personnel, perceived higher incidences of sexual harassment and discriminatory command behaviors.[38] Even the courts will consider whether the employee subjectively *perceives* the work environment as abusive. For example, did he or she welcome the conduct or immediately show that it was unwelcome?[39]

In any case the thing to remember is that deciding what to do in a situation without considering your and the other person's points of view is dangerous.

Chapter 3 Concept Review and Reinforcement

Key Terms

Review of Key Concepts

The Basics of Decision Making	• A decision is a choice from among the available alternatives. Decision making is the process of developing and analyzing alternatives and making a choice. A problem is a discrepancy between a desirable and an actual situation. The *problem-solving process* is "the process of developing and analyzing alternatives and making a choice." Making good decisions is so central to what supervisor do that it's impossible to unscramble decision making from leadership. • Programmed decisions are decisions you can set up to be made in advance. In contrast, nonprogrammed decisions address problems that are unique and novel and that involve matters of great importance. The more decisions you can program or make routine, the less time you need devote to them. Making *programmed* decisions usually involves following rules. *Nonprogrammed* decisions generally require a very different decision-making approach, because it's hard to pre-plan (program) how to respond to unexpected problems.
The Classical Approach	This approach to decision making assumes that supervisors are totally rational and have complete knowledge of all options. Herbert Simon argues that "bounded rationality" more accurately represents how supervisors actually make decisions.
How to Make Decisions	The steps in decision making are: • Define the problem. • Clarify your objectives. • Identify alternatives. • Analyze the consequences. • Make a choice. In defining the problem, always ask, "What triggered this problem? Why am I even thinking about solving this problem?"
Clarify Your Objectives	To do this: (1) Write down all the concerns you hope to address through your decision. (2) Convert your concerns into specific objectives. (3) Separate ends from means to establish your fundamental objectives. (4) Clarify what you mean by each objective. (5) Test your objectives to see if they capture your interests. There are several keys to generating good alternatives. These include: Be *creative*; start by trying to generate as many alternatives as you can yourself. Then *expand your search for options* by checking with other people, including experts. One caveat is this: *Know when to stop.* Remember that most supervisors "satisfice."

Analyze the Consequences	A basic three-step process to use is: Mentally put yourself in the future; eliminate clearly inferior alternatives; and organize your remaining alternatives in a consequences table. Finally, your analyses are useless unless you make the right choice. We discussed several techniques that can help anyone make a better choice.
How to Make Even Better Decisions	• Increase your knowledge, for example, ask questions, get experience, use consultants, do your research, and force yourself to recognize the facts when you see them. • Use your intuition. • Don't overstress the finality of the decision. • Make sure the timing is right. • Encourage creativity, for example, through brainstorming. • Use information technology tools. *Information system* refers to the interrelated components working together to collect, process, store, and disseminate information to support decision making, coordination, analysis, and visualization in an organization. These include decision support systems and enterprise resource planning (ERP) systems. An ERP is a companywide integrated computer system. Knowledge management refers to any efforts aimed at enabling the company's supervisors and employees to better utilize the information available anywhere in their company.
Avoid Psychological Traps	People usually aren't as rational as they think they are when making decisions, because psychology plays a big role in how we see and do things. The traps include: • People making decisions tend to take shortcuts. They do this by using *heuristics*, which are decision-making shortcuts, or "rules of thumb." • Anchoring means unconsciously giving too much weight to the first information you hear. It can cause you to define the problem incorrectly. • Failing to "think out of the box" is another decision-making trap. The technical term for this is *psychological set*, which means the tendency to look at things with a rigid point of view when solving a problem. • The fact that we don't always see things as they really are is another psychological trap. *Perception* is the selection and interpretation of information we receive through our senses and the meaning we give to the information. Many things, including our individual needs, influence how we perceive things.

Review and Discussion Questions

1. List four programmed decisions and four nonprogrammed decisions you typically make.
2. For supervisors, what are some of the practical implications of Simon's administrative theory?
3. Explain the five steps in the decision process?
4. Give one original example of why it is important to define the problem correctly.
5. Explain how you would use a consequences matrix (table) to make a better decision.
6. Give an example of how you have used intuition to make a decision.
7. Explain what you would do to increase the creativity in a work group.

Application and Skill Building

Case Study One

Making the Right Decisions

Dave Thomas recently finished his business degree at the University of Illinois School of Business and was excited to have landed a position as a management trainee at the Central Foundry Division of General Motors. The plant is an iron foundry with over 4,000 employees. Located in central Illinois, it's less than 100 miles from where Dave grew up in Gary, Indiana. The management training program cycles new supervisors through all the departments from the foundry to finishing within a three-month period. After less than two months Dave was assigned to the crankshaft finishing department because of a shortage of supervisors. The crankshaft finishing department was organized to take malleable iron crankshafts from the annealing ovens and clean, straighten, grind, and drill them before sending them to a machining operation at another GM plant in Ohio. Dave's department was comprised of 18 workers performing in 6 different operations in 2 locations located 200 yards apart in the larger plant. All decisions made by Dave were to be focused on efficiency and productivity. Although Dave recognized the importance of efficiency, also on his mind were quality, safety, and customer service. His lack of knowledge and experience in the foundry industry made it difficult to make informed decisions. Dave wanted to do a good job, but he was not gaining the respect that he needed to succeed. Within this plant one labor union had a significant influence on how and when Dave and the other supervisors made a work-related decision. He was told by management to pretend to the workers in his department that he knew what he was doing until he could learn. This did not work.

Dave was overwhelmed by the number of decisions he had to make each shift.

On the other hand, John Camp had worked as a finishing department supervisor for over 12 years. He was knowledgeable, experienced, respected, and made the supervisor's job look easy. John did not have to tell each worker what to do, as they already knew. As a supervisor, John was considered tough and demanding but also fair. He was consistent, and when he identified a problem he would follow up until the problem was solved. Even when facing a problem with limited information, John made decisions that were not only timely but also looked ahead to what would be done if they did not work. GM management liked that forward-looking approach because they were very sensitive to nonproductive idle time. If something did not work the way John wanted, he was always prepared to go in a different direction.

Dave Thomas wonders how he can be more like John Camp.

Questions

1. How many John Camps versus Dave Thomas's do you think are out there in the business world supervising? Support your answer.
2. How should Dave resolve the discrepancy between his personal values of dealing with safety and quality versus focusing on efficiency?

3. What do you feel are John's strongest points as a supervisor and decision maker?
4. What do you feel are Dave's weakest points as a supervisor and decision maker?
5. Based on what you read in this chapter, what does Dave Thomas need to consider in order to acquire the success that John has enjoyed as a supervisor?

Case Study Two

The President's first pardons

In December 2010, as he was flying back to the U.S. from his announced holiday visit to Afghanistan, the White House announced that President Obama had pardoned 9 people who had been convicted many years earlier for crimes ranging from illegal possession of government property to adultery, drug use, and mutilating coins. They were the first pardons of his presidency. **

The White House declined to comment on why the president had chosen these particular people to pardon (the Associated Press noted that he had previously only pardoned Thanksgiving turkeys). None of those people he pardoned were well-known, and many of the crimes had been committed decades earlier and had often involved minor punishment in the first place—such as a few months probation. For example, one man had received probation in 1963 and a $20 fine for mutilating coins. Another was sentenced to two years of probation in 1960 for a liquor law violation. One got in 30 days in jail and three years of probation for in 1986 conspiracy to distribute cocaine.

Previous presidents sometimes made more controversial pardons. For example, President George W. Bush was criticized when he commuted the sentence of Vice President Dick Cheney's former chief of staff, in a case involving the leaking of a CIA operative's name. President Clinton's decision to pardon a fugitive financier was highly controversial.

Questions

1. Outline the decision making process that you think President Obama probably used to make his pardon decisions.
2. What do you think were the main criteria he used in arriving at his decisions?
3. Why do you think he chose those criteria?
4. Could the environment at the time—for instance, high unemployment, the recent loss of a Democratic majority in the House of Representatives—have influenced the pardons he decided to make? If so, how? What does that say about how people make decisions?

**Adapted from Erica Werner, "Obama pardons 9 people convicted of drug crimes, other offenses", http://channels.attbusiness.net/index.cfm?fuseAction=viewNewsArticle&nav_id=33&category_name=Washington&article_id=b2f7bbd285d0be914b76d39bdfbed2af accessed December 5, 2010.

Experiential Activities

Activity 1. Roz had been receiving complaints about one of her employees, Geraldo. Other supervisors and the HR supervisor were reporting that Geraldo was not doing his job. Both the president of the company and the HR director had discussed all this with Roz, who was dragging her heels. The president and the head of HR felt that Roz needed to deal with Geraldo. Now they were trying to decide what to do next.

Who Is Solving Problems and Making Decisions?

Purpose: The purpose of this exercise is to give you practice on how to define a problem and make a decision.

Required Understanding: You are going to develop a plan for Roz to follow for making effective decisions.

How to Set Up the Exercise/Instructions: Divide the class into groups of 4–5 students.

1. Your group should develop a detailed step-by-step plan Roz can use to analyze and solve the problem and to deal with Geraldo, using the resources available in this chapter.
2. Answer the questions: "What is the problem here? "How is Roz going to deal with Geraldo? What actions do you feel are going to be necessary?"
3. Make recommendations on how Roz should handle the questions from the company president and the head of HR.
4. Next, have a spokesperson from each group share with the class their answers to the questions above. Follow up with a class discussion.

Activity 2. Contact someone you know who is a supervisor. (This can be an individual in a family business or in the community.) Ask this person to write down, in a notebook, *every* supervisory decision, big or small, that he or she makes for one day (and that he or she is comfortable divulging of course). Then write a one-page report indicating what each decision is, dividing them into programmed and nonprogrammed decisions. What percentage of the decisions made by this supervisor were programmed? How many were nonprogrammed? Be prepared to discuss this in class.

Activity 3. It's interesting to ponder if one can ever find the "rational" supervisor. As a member of a team of 4–5 students, your job is to think of all the supervisors you've know (and perhaps read about) and to classify them according to how rational you think they are (or were). Did anyone in your team feel that they had found the more or less perfectly rational supervisor? If so, why? If not, why? Each team will put together a one-page report of their findings and bring them to class for discussion. Use Chapter 3 as a basis for your research please.

Role-Playing Exercise

Making Better Decisions: The Situation

Much has been written about how managers make decisions. Most writers agree that a conscientious effort at improving decision-making skills can turn almost anyone into a much better decision maker. Although most decisions that we make are programmed, usually just by following the rules, some decisions are one of a kind and require a very different decision-making approach.

How we make these difficult decisions is supported by a decision-making process. This process includes defining the problem, clarifying the objectives, identifying alternatives, analyzing the consequences, and then making a choice. As a supervisor who has held your position for less than one year, you are looking for advice on how to make even better decisions. You are asking your own supervisor, the department manager, to help you do a better job as a line manager.

Instructions

All students should read the situation above. One student will play the role of the first-line supervisor and the second student will play the role of the department manager. Each student should only read his or her assigned role below. Then both students, in front of the class, should engage in a 15-minute conversation.

A class discussion will follow the role-playing presentation.

Department Manager: This supervisor has come to you for help. He or she wants to do a better job of decision making. As supervisor, you feel that the person has done a satisfactory job of supervising with limited experience, knowledge, and skill set. Your assignment is to coach the person on ways to make even better decisions. You realize that supervision is a learning experience and you want to help. Some of the points that you will want to make should include:

- Increasing your knowledge
- Asking questions
- Getting more experience
- Asking others for their opinions
- Involving your employees
- Researching additional information
- Acquiring *all* of the facts you can prior to making a decision

Supervisor: As a supervisor, even if for a short time, you have always been a good listener. This short coaching session from your department manager is meant to help you do your job better. You realize that the better part of any supervisory position involves decision making. As your department manager shares several points with you on how to improve your decision-making ability, be prepared to foster two-way communication. Ask for examples and clarifications. Do not just listen. Participate!

Questions for Class Discussion

1. When discussing several techniques to help improve the quality of decisions made, how well did the department manager do in persuading the supervisor to use the techniques?
2. In your opinion, did the supervisor ask for enough examples and clarifications?
3. Can you name any additional techniques that might be used by the supervisor to improve his or her ability to make better decisions?

4 Planning and Setting Goals

CHAPTER OBJECTIVES

After studying this chapter, you should be able to answer these questions:

1. Is Planning a Silver Bullet?
2. What Are the Fundamentals of Business Planning?
3. Business Plans: What Are the Basic Elements?
4. How Can Charts Be Used to Illustrate and Clarify Plans?
5. How Can Setting Goals Benefit a Team?
6. What Forecasting Tools Are Available for Making Better Decisions?

OPENING SNAPSHOT

Can Ralph Set Effective Goals?

Ralph could not figure out what to do. He'd been one of Allied's star salespeople for five years, before moving up to sales supervisor about eight months ago. As such, he supervised the company's 14 salespeople. In addition to interviewing, training, and appraising them, Ralph was supposed to make sure they were reaching their quotas, and that's where his problems lie. For the past six months, not one salesperson has made his or her quota. In fact, not only are they missing their quotas, 12 of them hardly work at all. They spend hours around the office doing what they claim is paperwork, and the absence rate is so high that Allied almost never has even 10 salespeople show up for work on the same day. Ralph walked by one salesperson's cubicle yesterday, and the salesperson was fast asleep. Ralph's boss, Alice, has had enough: "Ralph, you either get these people cracking, or you're going to be Allied's ex-sales supervisor before you know it."

95

1. Is Planning the Silver Bullet?

There aren't many supervisory "silver bullets"—tools that almost always improve some-one's performance. But if there is a silver bullet, it's probably *planning and setting goals.* A **plan** is any method developed in advance that shows (1) what you want to accomplish (a goal) and (2) the course of action that you'll use to reach that goal.

Let's consider an actual situation. Only about a third of full-time U.S. college students graduate in four years, and about a fourth don't finish at all. That's a big problem, and one that cries out for a practical solution. Canadian researchers recently studied about 85 college students who were experiencing academic difficulties. Here's what they did.

The researchers randomly assigned about half the students to a group that received training in how to set career goals, while the other half received no training. Those that learned how to set goals went through a series of exercises. First they spent a few minutes describing "their ideal future" and listed things they could do better and habits they could improve. Then they set seven or eight goals that they thought would help them make these improvements. The students wrote down short, specific plans for pursuing each of these goals.[1]

The results were impressive. Compared with the students who did not set improvement goals and plans, those who did raised their grade point averages and were much more likely to maintain full course loads. The message of this study (the results of which are supported by hundreds of similar goal-setting studies) is this: There's probably no simpler way to improve one's performance than to set realistic goals and plans for achieving them.

Why are planning and setting goals so advantageous? For several reasons.

People Are Goal-Directed

Decades of research in what psychologists call "the goal-setting studies" leaves no doubt about one thing: People are highly *motivated and self-directed to accomplish goals* that are important to them. Similarly, very often, when employees are not doing their jobs, it's not because they don't want to do the job, but because they either don't know what they're supposed to be accomplishing, or think they are already accomplishing it.

A Sense of Purpose

Planning also provides *direction and a sense of purpose.* For example, those underachieving college students who learned to envision "their ideal future" and to list things they could do better and habits they could improve suddenly had a clear sense of purpose to guide them. Similarly, seeing where they were heading—whatever that "ideal future" was—provided a *unifying framework* (standards or criteria) against which they could assess all those day-to-day decisions they'd have to make (this course or that, for instance.)

Thinking Things Through Ahead of Time

The fact that planning entails deciding now what to do in the future underscores another great planning benefit. Planning lets you *make your decisions ahead of time*, with the luxury of having the time to weigh your options. Similarly, planning also helps *identify potential opportunities and threats* and reduce long-term risks. It also helps you *anticipate the consequences* of various courses of action and think through the practicality of each, without actually having to carry out that course of action. (That's why putting together a family budget for the year can help you anticipate whether your current family income will cover that new car you'd like to buy.)

A Means for Control

Last but not least, *planning facilitates control.* Control means ensuring that activities conform to plan. Your department's plan may specify that profits will double within five years. This goal becomes the standard against which to measure, compare, and control the supervisor's actual performance.

"Planning" and "control" are inseparable. You cannot control if you don't know what your standards are; and it's futile to have a plan if you don't control how you are doing. We'll turn to controlling in Chapter 5.

2. Fundamentals of Business Planning

What Are the Fundamentals of Business Planning?

After the tragic sinking of its Transocean Deepwater Horizon oil rig in the Gulf of Mexico in 2010, BP had to formulate and execute several plans. According to their Web site at the time, "We are attacking this spill on all fronts, bringing into play all and any resources and advanced technologies we believe can help," said Tony Hayward, BP Group's former chief executive. "Our action plan is safety-focused, multi-layered and has the full resources of the BP Group behind it."[2] And, "On the surface, BP continued to aggressively move forward with its oil spill plan." BP launched its comprehensive, pre-approved oil spill response plan following the April 22 sinking.[3]

Several months later, oil continued to gush from the undersea well and to creep toward the shore. Many critics asked why BP didn't have more effective plans in place for handling such a catastrophe, or, for that matter, better plans for building a more failsafe well in the first place. In any case, the tragedy quickly torpedoed several other BP plans. Their board of directors had to cancel a stockholder dividend BP was to pay. BP suddenly needed a new plan to raise money for the unplanned Gulf expenses. And the U.S. Congress wanted to know why BP didn't have better safety plans in place.

The Planning Process

Most businesses run on plans. Top management decides early in the year what their revenues and expenses are (hopefully) going to be, and what sorts of products and markets they're going to focus on. Then these broad plans trickle down as lower-level managers and supervisors create their own plans to support top management's plan. This basic planning process is as follows:

1. Tentatively *set an objective,* such as "Double sales revenue to $16 million in fiscal year 2011."

2. *Make forecasts,* for instance, of industry trends and of what your competitors are doing.

3. *Determine what your alternatives are for getting from where the company is now to where you want to be.* The aim here is to identify what courses of actions will get the firm to the "double sales revenue by 2011" goal best. (For example, should we buy a competitor or try to boost our own sales effort, or both?)

4. *Evaluate your alternatives.*

5. Finally, *implement the plan.*

The Hierarchy of Goals

In well-run companies, the goals from the very top of the company down to where you're working form a more or less unbroken chain (or "hierarchy") of goals.

The hierarchy of goals diagram in Figure 4.1 illustrates this. At the top of the company, the president and his or her staff set overall "strategic" goals (such as to "Double sales revenue to $16 million in fiscal year 2011"). Lower level managers (in this case, department managers) then set goals (such as to "Add one production line at plant"). These goals should flow from those at the next level up and make sense in terms of the higher-up goals. (In other words, "What must I as production manager do to help make sure that the company accomplishes its 'double sales' goal?") Then those managers' subordinates—in this case, the first-line supervisors—set their own goals, and so on down the line.

In this way, management creates a hierarchy or chain of departmental goals from the top down to the first-level supervisors, and even employees. Then if everyone does his or her job—if each salesperson sells his or her quota, and the sales supervisor hires enough good salespeople, and the HR manager creates the right incentive plan, and the purchasing head buys enough raw materials—the company and the president should also accomplish the overall, companywide goals. You could therefore say with great certainty that without a clear plan at the top, no one in the company (including you and the other supervisors) would have the foggiest notion of what to do. At best, you'd all be working at cross-purposes.

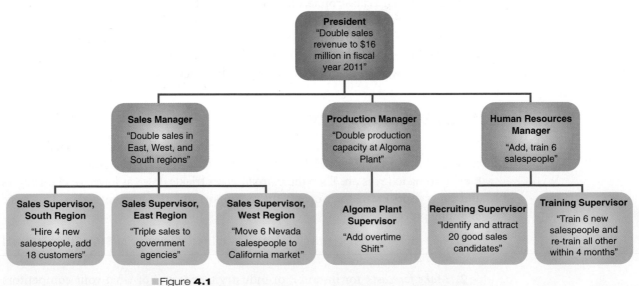

■Figure **4.1**
Sample Hierarchy of Goals Diagram for a Company

Strategic Planning in Brief

In most companies, planning begins by deciding what the company's overall strategic or longer-term direction will be. Each department and team then formulates plans that (hopefully) make sense in terms of this strategic plan. All supervisors, therefore, should know something about strategic planning.

THE LANGUAGE OF STRATEGIC PLANNING   Starbucks recently ran into trouble. After years of serving just coffee and croissants, it diversified into selling sandwiches too, and compounded that by overexpanding its number of stores. Soon waiting lines were getting longer, per-store sales were diminishing, and the *baristas'* friendly attitudes were starting to fray.

Every company needs a strategic plan. The company's **strategic plan** shows (1) the business or businesses the firm wants to be in, and (2) the goals it must achieve to get there, given (3) the company's opportunities, threats, strengths, and weaknesses. A **strategy** is a course of action. It shows how the company will move from the business it is in now to the business it wants to be in. **Strategic planning** is the process of identifying the firm's business today, its desired future business, and the courses of action it should pursue to get there, given its opportunities, threats, strengths, and weaknesses. **Strategic management** is the process of formulating *and executing* the organization's strategic plan. Strategic planning is pointless without effective execution.

WHAT BUSINESS ARE WE IN?   Strategic planning is largely about deciding what business the company wants to be in. Starbucks had been in the business of offering comfortable rest-stops for people who want high-quality coffee. Diversifying into sandwiches was a somewhat risky move. When managers change their strategies, they generally change one (or more) of four things:

- The company's **product scope**, which means (as at Starbucks) the range and diversity of products they sell.
- Whether to **vertically integrate**, in other words, produce our own raw materials, or distribute our own products. The preppy clothing company Ralph Lauren not only produces clothes, but sells them, in part through its own company-owned stores.
- The company's **geographic scope**. For example, Starbucks is everywhere now, from Brooklyn to Paris, to China's Great Wall.
- How the company will **compete**. Starbucks emphasizes its pleasant shop environment and special drinks, while Dunkin' Donuts focuses more on price.

TYPES OF STRATEGIES   In practice, managers use three types of strategies, one for each level of their companies. There is *corporatewide* strategic planning, business unit (or *competitive*) strategic planning, and *functional* (or departmental) strategic planning. Figure 4.2 helps to illustrate this. We'll look briefly at each type of strategy.

CORPORATE-LEVEL STRATEGY   Most (but not all) companies consist of a collection of several businesses. For instance, Disney includes movies, theme parks, and a television network. A company's *corporate-level strategy* identifies the portfolio of businesses that make up the corporation and the ways in which these businesses fit together.

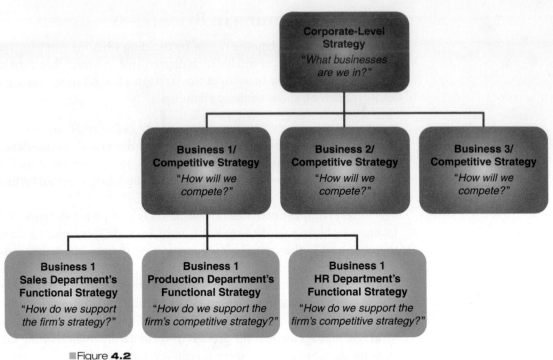

■Figure **4.2**

Three Levels of Strategy

COMPETITIVE/BUSINESS–LEVEL STRATEGY   At the next level down, the question becomes, "How will each of these businesses compete?" In other words, each business needs a business-level or *competitive strategy*. The competitive strategy specifies how the company will compete—for instance, based on *low cost* (Walmart), or perhaps some *differentiating feature* like high quality (Mercedes-Benz).

DEPARTMENTAL/FUNCTIONAL STRATEGIES   Finally, each business (such as PepsiCo) is made up of departments, such as production, marketing, and HR. The *departmental/ functional strategies* specify the basic actions and policies each department must follow in order for the company to succeed. For example, Walmart's competitive advantage is low cost. Each of its departments have functional (departmental) strategies that support Walmart's low cost strategy. For example, the purchasing department presses its vendors for ultra-low prices. The store-location department presses for low-cost leases. The HR department presses to keep employee costs low.

SWOT ANALYSIS   In strategic planning, the thousand-pound gorilla is SWOT analysis. SWOT stands for strengths, weaknesses, opportunities, and threats analysis. SWOT analysis is important because strategic planning means formulating a plan that will balance (1) the firm's strengths and weaknesses with (2) its external opportunities and threats. *Opportunities* might include the possibility of serving additional customers in China. *Threats* might include the likely entry of new, lower-cost foreign competitors. *Strengths* might include good financial resources and patented technology. *Weaknesses* might include obsolete facilities.

Companies use **SWOT analysis** (see Figure 4.3) to compile and summarize information that serves two purposes: (1) It shows illustrative opportunities, threats, strengths,

POTENTIAL STRENGTHS	POTENTIAL WEAKNESSES
• Market leadership • Strong research and development • High-quality products • Cost advantages • Patents	• Large inventories • Excess capacity for market • Management turnover • Weak market image • Lack of management depth
POTENTIAL OPPORTUNITIES	POTENTIAL THREATS
• New overseas markets • Failing trade barriers • Competitors failing • Diversification • Economy rebounding	• Market saturation • Threat of takeover • Low-cost foreign competition • Slower market growth • Growing government regulation

and weaknesses to guide the manager's analysis; and (2) it provides a standardized four-cell format for seeing the company's situational information at a glance.

THE SUPERVISOR'S ROLE IN STRATEGIC PLANNING   Strategic planning is one of the main things that companies pay top managers to do. Therefore, realistically, first-line supervisors usually aren't very involved in creating strategic plans. However, department and first-line supervisors are usually the ones who must translate the firm's strategic choices (such as, "We've got to cut costs to the bone") into departmental strategies. We saw that in each Walmart store, every store manager and every department supervisor (for women's wear, fishing tackle, or whatever) must keep its employee costs low. Executing on the plan is always the supervisor's bread and butter job. Except in the tiniest of companies, no top manager could ever expect to do everything that needs doing by him or herself. With careful oversight, they therefore rely on their supervisors to do the planning, organizing, staffing, leading, and controlling that are required to execute the company's and each department's plans and goals. That means, for instance, the day-to-day hiring, firing, scheduling, buying, and selling that executing the plan requires.

3. Types of Plans

Business Plans: What Are the Basic Elements?

Supervisors routinely deal with many types of plans, from business plans to policies to Gantt charts to contingency plans. We'll look at types of plans next.

The Business Plan

Business planning, of course, produces a business plan. The **business plan** provides a comprehensive view of the firm's companywide and departmental financial goals and plans for the next 3–5 years. There are no rigid rules regarding what such plans contain. However, they usually include, at a minimum, a (1) *marketing plan*, (2) the *financial plan*, (3) a *production plan*, and (4) the *management* and/or *personnel* (or *HR*) *plan*. Notice that the business plan translates the hierarchy of goals into specific descriptive and financial terms. It then guides every department in the firm, from the front-line sales and manufacturing teams up to the president.

THE MARKETING PLAN   Marketing gurus talk about the "5Ps" of marketing: product, people, place, price, and promotion. The marketing plan shows the *product(s)* or service(s) the company will offer. It also lays out what the company plans to do with respect to *pricing* and *promoting* the product or service, and getting it sold and *delivered* (place) to the customers (*people*).

THE PRODUCTION PLAN   Selling products often requires producing them (of course, many businesses, such as retail stores, simply buy and then sell products.) The production plan lays out how the business plans to produce the necessary products. For example, GM needs factories and machines to assemble cars. GM must therefore plan how it will meet its planned car sales projections. After the economic meltdown in 2008–2009, GM closed many factories as its sales forecasts dried up. In 2010, with sales apparently reviving, they began running more factories year-around again.

THE STAFFING PLAN   Selling and producing requires managers and other human resources/personnel, and therefore a staffing plan. For example, how many people will we have to hire in sales to double sales by 2011? In production? Where will they come from—internal promotions or external recruiting? How much will it cost to hire and train these extra people?

THE FINANCIAL PLAN   "What's the bottom line?" is the first question most managers and bankers ask. The question underscores a truism about business and management. At the end of the day, most managers' plans, goals, and accomplishments end up expressed in financial terms.

The financial plan (or budget) is the vehicle for doing so. For example, the budget will often show the revenue, cost, and profit (or loss) implications of the company's marketing, production, and staffing (business) plans. The budget says this: If your plans work out as you anticipate, these are the revenues, costs, and profits or losses you should produce each month (or quarter, or year). It shows you the bottom line. All supervisors usually have budgets to guide them. We'll discuss budgets in more detail in the following chapter.

Contingency Plans

Many companies create *contingency plans* to guide action in case some major unforeseen event occurs. The recent sinking of BP's oil rig in the Gulf of Mexico has quickly become a classic example of why business needs contingency plans. When significant emergencies develop—be it a sinking rig, a terrorist attack, an explosion, or a plane losing power—management won't have time to get together to discuss what to do next. Ideally, the contingency plan should kick in, and everyone immediately does the job he or she was trained to do. That's why airline companies' cabin attendants periodically practice what to do should an airliner problem arise. Some critics complained that BP didn't seem to have a contingency plan and spent much time trying to figure out what to do next. Supervisors should be very familiar with their area's contingency plans, because their workers will look to them for guidance on what to do.

Policies, Procedures, and Rules

We said earlier that a plan is any method developed in advance that shows what you want to accomplish (a goal) and the course of action that you will use to reach that goal. Policies, procedures, and rules are special types of plans (called "standing plans"). They show you and your employees what to do if a particular situation arises. **Policies** are

■Figure **4.4**

IBM's Purchasing Integrity and Ethical Standards Policies and Procedures

Source: http://www-03.ibm.com/procurement/proweb.nsf/contentdocsbytitle/United+States~Policies+and+procedures (accessed June 18, 2010).

(Note: Sample policies in red, procedures in green.)

It is IBM's policy to conduct itself ethically and fairly in relation to its suppliers and all others with whom IBM does business. If, at any time, this policy is perceived as being compromised in any way, please report your concern to the IBM Global Procurement Ombudsman (800-233-3073). Concerns will be addressed promptly with care, respect, and confidentiality.

Reciprocity:
IBM's goal is to buy goods and services which have the best prices, quality, delivery, and technology. IBM has a policy against reciprocal buying arrangements because those arrangements can interfere with this goal.

Confidentiality:
IBM considers its business relationships with each of its suppliers and potential suppliers to be a private matter between the two parties. IBM will treat information received from suppliers in a responsible fashion, and expects suppliers to treat information received from IBM in the same manner. Further, IBM does not wish to receive from a supplier any information which is considered to be confidential unless the supplier and IBM have entered into a confidential disclosure agreement which covers such information.

Patents:
IBM does not knowingly infringe the patent rights of others. Conversely IBM requires patent indemnification on all procured materials. IBM will discuss ideas or inventions with outside individuals and, where necessary, will contract for the development of special products. In all such cases, appropriate contractual arrangements must be made in advance.

Supplier diversity program:
IBM maintains a commitment to ensure a diverse supplier base. It is our policy to provide opportunities in all areas of IBM's procurement, marketing and contracting activities to people of different ethnic origins, women, people with disabilities, etc.

Gifts and gratuities:
IBM employees and members of their families may not solicit or accept gratuities from suppliers or prospective suppliers. Only gifts of $25 or less can be accepted by employees.

Business meals and entertainment:
IBM employees who deal with suppliers may accept customary business amenities such as meals and entertainment, provided the expenses involved are kept at a reasonable level and are not prohibited by law or known supplier business practices. IBM employees are expected to reciprocate and share these costs equally over time.

Appropriate conduct on IBM premises:
All individuals on IBM premises are expected to engage in appropriate conduct and behave in a business-like manner. Examples of inappropriate conduct are being under the influence of or affected by alcohol; use of illegal drugs; use of a controlled substance, except for approved medical purposes; possession of a weapon of any sort; and/or harassment threats or violent behavior.

broad guidelines. For example (see Figure 4.4), it might be IBM's purchasing policy "to conduct itself ethically and fairly in relation to its suppliers and all others with whom IBM does business." This is a plan insofar as it shows IBM's employees a method to adhere to in dealing with suppliers. **Procedures** spell out the steps to take if a specific situation arises (see Figure 4.4). For example, "If, at any time, this [IBM] policy is perceived as being compromised in any way, please report your concern to the IBM Global Procurement Ombudsman (800-233-3073)." A **rule** is like a specific law; one might be, for instance, "Anyone violating IBM's purchasing policy will be subject to discipline up to and including dismissal."

Scheduling and Planning Charts

How Can Charts Be Used to Illustrate and Clarify Plans?

One good way to present a plan is in the form of a chart or graph. Supervisors use various scheduling charts to graphically depict what operations are to be carried out and when.

This Gantt chart shows the steps and the timing of each step for each order.

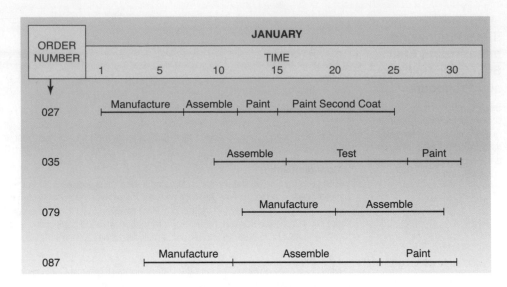

GANTT CHART The **Gantt chart** shown in Figure 4.5 is one example of a scheduling plan. It shows the activities required to complete a product or project, and the period in which the manager anticipates performing each activity.

Henry Gantt, a management pioneer, devised several versions of his chart. The example in Figure 4.5 shows time on the horizontal scale. For *each order*, it shows the start and stop times sequentially. Another type of Gantt chart lists *each operation* separately in the left column, one under the other, and time along the bottom. That way, the manager can monitor the start and stop times for all operations.

In practice, a supervisor scheduling production would work from the required delivery date backward. He or she would then determine how long each assembly will take, how long it will take to obtain raw materials, and so forth. The supervisor can then decide whether the firm can meet its required delivery date, and what bottlenecks to unclog.

The Gantt chart is adequate for planning simpler projects (with not too many subassemblies or activities). Complex projects usually require more advanced planning tools.

PERT CHARTS A *PERT chart* (for "program evaluation and review technique) is an example of an advanced planning tool. The PERT chart graphically shows the project's steps and the timing and linkages among those steps. A project is a series of interrelated activities aimed at producing a major, coordinated product or service. Examples include introducing the new Boeing 787 "Dreamliner", or building a house.

PERT charts map out the steps and related times for complicated projects. The basic purpose of a PERT chart is to show the sequence of activities required to complete a complex project, each in its proper chronological order. Events and activities are the two major components of PERT networks. As Figure 4.6 shows, **events**, depicted by circles, represent specific accomplishments, such as "foundation laid." Arrows represent **activities**, which are the time-consuming aspects of the project (such as laying the foundation). By studying the PERT chart, the person doing the scheduling can determine the **critical path**, the sequence of critical events that, in total, requires the most time to complete. We can summarize the steps in building a PERT chart as follows:

1. Identify each of the activities and events required to complete the project, each in its proper order. For building a house, *activities* might include buying supplies.

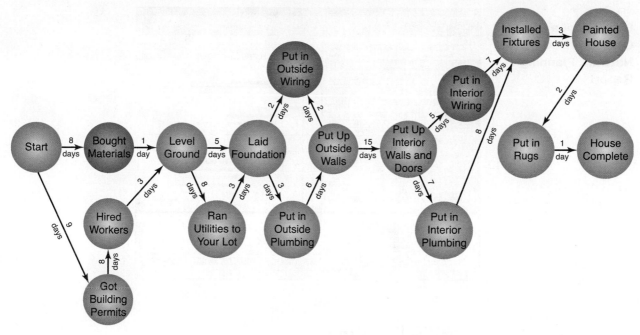

■ Figure **4.6**

PERT Chart for Building a House

In a PERT chart like this one, each event is shown in its proper relationship to the other events. The blue circles show the critical—or most time-consuming—path.

Events would include rugs installed. One of the keys to building a PERT chart (or PERT "network") is to lay out the activities and events in the proper chronological sequence. For example, laying the foundation would have to come before painting the house.

2. Using all this information on activities, events, and sequencing, you can actually lay out the project in the form of a PERT network diagram (a PERT chart is one type of network planning method). In Figure 4.6, this PERT network or chart graphically displays activities, events, and chronological sequencing.

3. Next you want to decide how much time it is going to take you to execute all the tasks required to build the house. You do this by estimating how much time you will probably have to devote to each activity (such as laying the foundation). Planners sometimes assign three time estimates: optimistic, most likely, and pessimistic.

4. As you can see in Figure 4.6, some chains of activities (such as the blue one in the figure) will take longer than the other routes, because the chain of activities for these "critical" routes collectively add up to more time than does any other alternative route you might take from beginning to end. Planners call this longest-time route the "critical path." Once you know the critical path, you know (hopefully) the maximum time it may take for you, starting today, to finish building the house, and therefore where you need to focus your energies in making sure that your time estimates do not slip. Many companies such as Smart Draw (http:// www.smartdraw.com/) provide software to facilitate drawing PERT network plans. Schedulers use computerized programs (see Figure 4.7) to create PERT networks for complex projects.

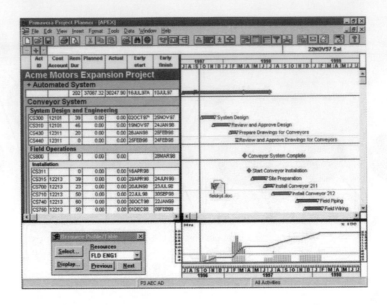

Work Scheduling

For supervisors, the rubber usually hits the road (with respect to planning) when it comes to workforce scheduling. Whether you are supervising salespeople, Starbucks baristas, or workers on an assembly line, you'll need to schedule who is working when.

Supervisors generally use spreadsheets such as that in Figure 4.8 to accomplish this. Various online tools are also available, such as those at http://shiftschedules.com/simplescheduler.htm.

S1-Simple Scheduler Scheduling Sheet

Schedule Start Date
January 1, 2006

Specify the month and the calendar template will change to show that month.

January 2006

Sunday		Monday		Tuesday		Wednesday		Thursday		Friday		Saturday	
1		**2**		**3**		**4**		**5**		**6**		**7**	
Marge Q	8A-4P	Marge Q	7A-3P	Larry S	7A-3P	Harry A	7A-3P	Ellen G	7A-3P	Larry D	7A-3P	Marge Q	8A-4P
Allen X	8A-4P	Larry S	7A-3P	Allen H	7A-3P	Larry S	7A-3P	Allen X	7A-3P	Sally V	7A-3P	Allen X	8A-4P
Carol I	8A-4P	Sally W	9A-5P	Harry R	9A-5P	Harry O	9A-5P	Carol I	9A-5P	Allen O	9A-5P	Geoff C	8A-4P
		Harry A	9A-5P	Carol A	9A-5P	Carol X	9A-5P	Sally W	9A-5P	Marge F	9A-5P		
		Allen O	9A-5P	Carol S	9A-5P	Harry K	9A-5P	Ellen D	9A-5P	Carol A	9A-5P		
		Chuck M	11A-7P	Allen O	11A-7P	Ziggy H	11A-7P	Carol A	11A-7P	Chuck M	11A-7P		
		Marge G	11A-7P	Harry M	11A-7P	Harry E	11A-7P	Irene D	11A-7P	Marge E	11A-7P		
8		**9**		**10**		**11**		**12**		**13**		**14**	
	8A-4P		7A-3P		7A-3P		7A-3P		7A-3P		7A-3P		8A-4P
	8A-4P		7A-3P		7A-3P		7A-3P		7A-3P		7A-3P		8A-4P
	8A-4P		9A-5P		9A-5P		9A-5P		9A-5P		9A-5P		8A-4P
			9A-5P		9A-5P		9A-5P		9A-5P		9A-5P		
			9A-5P		9A-5P		9A-5P		9A-5P		9A-5P		
			11A-7P		11A-7P		11A-7P		11A-7P		11A-7P		
			11A-7P		11A-7P		11A-7P		11A-7P		11A-7P		
15		**16**		**17**		**18**		**19**		**20**		**21**	

Use the drop-down menus to schedule employees and shifts on the simple scheduling calendar.

■Figure **4.8**
Worker Scheduling Spreadsheet

Source: http://shiftschedules.com/Software-Webpages/S1-Scheduling.pdf (accessed April 28, 2010).

4. How to Set Effective Goals

The supervisor may not be too involved in developing the company's plans. However, he or she will always be involved in meeting with his or her employees to set specific goals the team will use to help achieve the company's plan. Excelling at setting goals is therefore a crucial supervisory talent.

Using Management by Objectives

The basic reason for setting goals at work is usually to make sure that what your employees are doing makes sense in terms of what the company wants to accomplish. **Management by objectives (MBO)** is the classic way to do this. It means you and your subordinates jointly set goals to achieve what the company wants to do, and then periodically assess progress toward those goals. Of course, you can always do this informally. However, MBO usually refers to a formal companywide program. Here supervisors meet with employees to set goals that make sense in terms of each department's assigned goal(s). This MBO process typically includes using special goal-setting forms and assessing employees' progress frequently. The MBO process should translate the company's hierarchy of goals into reality, as follows:

1. Work out the company's overall strategic plan and the goals the company wants to achieve in pursuing that plan.

2. Each department head and supervisor down the chain of command then meets with employees to set supporting goals *for their departments*.

3. Next, each supervisor takes these departmental goals and, working with his or her employees, sets goals for each subordinate that make sense in terms of the department's goals.

4. The supervisor and subordinates meet periodically to review the latter's progress toward their goals.

Using the Management Objectives Grid

With or without MBO, every manager needs a system for organizing how his or her subordinates' goals dovetail with those of the company. The *management objectives grid* provides an easy way to do this. Figure 4.9 gives an example. This chart spells out each department manager's assigned goals in support of achieving the firm's overall goals. In this case one long-term top management goal is to "Double sales revenue to $16 million in fiscal year 2011." The grid in Figure 4.9 summarizes the goals each department needs to achieve if the firm is to meet its overall $16 million sales goal.

Managers use the management objectives grid for several things. Top managers use it to show each of their department supervisors what their goals are, in other words *to list their subordinate managers' supporting goals*. Then each of these department supervisors creates his or her own grid, to summarize for his or her employees *what their own goals are*, in light of the department's goal(s). And finally, each supervisor may use the grid's start and end dates as a quick way *to track their employees' progress*.

Companywide or Departmental Objective: *Double sales revenue to $16 million in fiscal year 2011*

Supervisor's or Subordinates' Objectives in Support of Above Objective	Supervisor or Subordinate Responsible	Start Date	End Date	Progress as of:
Double sales in East, West, and South regions	Sales supervisor	8/1/09	7/31/10	President checked 11/09, sales up 60%.
Add one new production line at plant	Production supervisor	8/1/09	10/31/09	President checked 9/09, work 80% done.
Add and train six new salespeople	Human resources manager	8/1/09	9/3/09	President checked 9/30/09, all hired, new people trained.

Emphasize the Team's Mission

A successful quality control team at an Acura car factory, the emergency room team at City Hospital, and the platoon in the old movie *Saving Private Ryan* all have one thing in common: they all have a mission to which they're dedicated. In business planning, the company's *mission* is the essential task, duty, or assignment that all its efforts aim to achieve. Experienced soldiers know that, on the battlefield, formal goal setting isn't nearly as important as is making sure that you and your comrades are all dedicated to helping each other achieve the platoon's mission. Employees just tend to be more motivated when they're not simply working but are dedicated or committed to achieving some mission that seems "bigger than ourselves." For example, Google's stated mission (see http://google.com) is to "organize the world's information and make it universally accessible and useful."

Companies put a great deal of thought into formulating both a mission to which its employees can be committed, and a vision. (The latter is a more hoped-for long-term dream that top management has for the business.) Figures 4.10 and 4.11 summarize the missions and visions for Coke and Pepsi.

Coke, for instance, has as its mission "To refresh the world . . . To inspire moments of optimism and happiness . . . To create value and make a difference." That probably sums up quite well what happens when someone thirsty drinks a Coke! Pepsi's vision is a lofty one: "Our vision is put into action through programs and a focus on environmental stewardship, activities to benefit society, and a commitment to build shareholder value by making PepsiCo a truly sustainable company"; they call that vision, "Performance with Purpose."

Missions work best when all your employees buy into it. Therefore, whether they're supervising a car quality team or an emergency response team, every supervisor has a responsibility to crystallize a mission or vision for his or her team. It's usually not enough to say "We're going to improve quality by 15% next year." People

At PepsiCo, we believe being a responsible corporate citizen is not only the right thing to do, but the right thing to do for our business.

Our Mission

Our mission is to be the world's premier consumer products company focused on convenient foods and beverages. We seek to produce financial rewards to investors as we provide opportunities for growth and enrichment to our employees, our business partners and the communities in which we operate. And in everything we do, we strive for honesty, fairness and integrity.

Our Vision

"PepsiCo's responsibility is to continually improve all aspects of the world in which we operate—environment, social, economic—creating a better tomorrow than today."

Our vision is put into action through programs and a focus on environmental stewardship, activities to benefit society, and a commitment to build shareholder value by making PepsiCo a truly sustainable company.

Performance with Purpose

At PepsiCo, we're committed to achieving business and financial success while leaving a positive imprint on society—delivering what we call *Performance with Purpose*.

Our approach to superior financial performance is straightforward—drive shareholder value. By addressing social and environmental issues, we also deliver on our purpose agenda, which consists of human, environmental, and talent sustainability.

The world is changing all around us. To continue to thrive as a business over the next ten years and beyond, we must look ahead, understand the trends and forces that will shape our business in the future and move swiftly to prepare for what's to come. We must get ready for tomorrow today. That's what our 2020 Vision is all about. It creates a long-term destination for our business and provides us with a "Roadmap" for winning together with our bottling partners.

Our Mission

Our Roadmap starts with our mission, which is enduring. It declares our purpose as a company and serves as the standard against which we weigh our actions and decisions.

- To refresh the world.
- To inspire moments of optimism and happiness.
- To create value and make a difference.

Our Vision

Our vision serves as the framework for our Roadmap and guides every aspect of our business by describing what we need to accomplish in order to continue achieving sustainable, quality growth.

- **People:** Be a great place to work where people are inspired to be the best they can be.
- **Portfolio:** Bring to the world a portfolio of quality beverage brands that anticipate and satisfy people's desires and needs.
- **Partners:** Nurture a winning network of customers and suppliers, together we create mutual, enduring value.
- **Planet:** Be a responsible citizen that makes a difference by helping build and support sustainable communities.
- **Profit:** Maximize long-term return to shareowners while being mindful of our overall responsibilities.
- **Productivity:** Be a highly effective, lean and fast-moving organization.

want a mission or vision that transcends themselves that they can be committed to. "Goal-setting" is therefore a sterile and relatively ineffectual process unless as supervisor you are able to translate what you want your team to do into a "saving Private Ryan"–type mission to which your employees can dedicate themselves. Thus an Acura work team might be committed to the mission that "we're here to build the world's greatest cars."

How to Set SMART goals

Yet employes still need goals, and experienced supervisors have a simple way to check if their goals are good—they use the acronym "SMART." They say good goals are *specific* (make clear what to achieve); *measurable*; *attainable*; *relevant* (in terms of what you're setting the goal for); and *timely* (they have deadlines and milestones).

For example, suppose you supervise an automobile salesperson who has been selling about half the cars he should be selling, and also selling too many easier-to-sell fuel-efficient cars, leaving the gas guzzlers in the back of the showroom. Here an *in*effective "un-smart" goal might be, "Rick, you've got to double the number of vehicles you sell next month." That goal ("double the number") is fairly specific (it would be better if he also knew what kinds if cars you wanted him to sell), and it is measurable. Whether it's attainable is debatable (given his performance to date). It's not relevant in terms of what you're setting the goal for (namely, also getting Rick to sell some gas guzzlers). It is timely in that you said he must sell them in the next month.

What would be a better way to formulate Rick's goal? Perhaps this: "Rick, by the end of June, two months from today, you've got to sell double the total number of vehicles you sold in the last two months, and three-quarters of those new vehicles must come from the gas guzzlers we have in inventory." This goal is specific, measurable, probably more attainable (given his shaky performance), relevant, and timely.

How to Set Motivational Goals

Goals are only useful if they motivate your employees to achieve them. Research known as the *goal-setting studies* provides useful insights into how to set motivational goals. Supervisors should do the following:[4]

- **Assign Specific Goals** Employees who have *specific goals* usually perform better than those who do not. The accumulation of years of behavioral research would say this: Setting specific goals with subordinates is the simplest, most effective way to motivate subordinates. Never just say "Do your best."
- **Assign Measurable Goals** Always try to express the goal in terms of numbers, and include target dates or deadlines.
- **Assign Challenging but Doable Goals** Goals should be challenging, but not so difficult that they appear impossible or unrealistic.[5]

The accompanying Leadership Applications for Supervisors feature shows another essential characteristic of motivational goals.

How to Set Participative Goals

Throughout your supervisory career, you'll be faced with this decision: Should I just *tell* my employees what their goals are, or should I let them participate *in setting their goals?* Sometimes, there is no choice. If your boss says, *"Boost sales by 10% next month,"* you and your team need to comply.

Often you will have a choice. For example, if you want to encourage your subordinate to improve his or her performance after a bad performance review, the goals you set for him or her needn't be yours alone.

Which leadership approach is best here—to let your subordinate participate, or not? Actually, in this case it's sort of a no-brainer. This is what the leadership research suggests:[6]

1. Employees who participate in setting their own goals perceive themselves as having had more impact *on setting those goals* than do employees who just get their goals from their managers.

2. Participatively set goals tend to be higher *than the goals the supervisor would normally have assigned.*

3. Even when participatively set goals are more difficult than those assigned, the employees don't perceive them as such.

4. Participatively set goals do not consistently result in higher performance than assigned goals, nor do assigned goals consistently result in higher performance than participatively set ones. It is only when the participatively set goals are more difficult than the assigned ones (as they often are) that the participatively set goals produce higher performance.

So (because participatively set goals do tend to be more challenging), participation does usually produce higher performance. It's therefore usually sensible to discuss goals with your employees before setting them. A more participative style also creates a sense of ownership in the goals that are set, and it can reduce employees' resistance to trying to achieve the goals. Just make sure, however, that the goals you two set are really challenging.

The Action Plan

We began this chapter with a description of how college students learned how to identify roadblocks that stood in the way of their success, and how to set specific goals for overcoming these impediments and reaching their ultimate goals. As in the case of the students, there are five logical steps in developing an action plan:

1. Identify your goal, such as "Reduce customer complaints by 90% by the end of this year".

2. Identify your obstacles, in other words, everything standing between you or your team and the goal. These obstacles might include, for instance, information that you need, or resources that must be acquired.

3. List tasks required to overcome each obstacle. For each obstacle, write one or two ways that you or your team could overcome that obstacle.

4. Assign deadlines to each task. They should include start and completion dates for each of the tasks that are necessary to overcome the obstacles and achieve your goal.

5. Establish periodic reminders or alerts so that you can monitor how you're doing on each task.[7]

The Importance of Feedback and Support

Motivation experts are fond of pointing out that "performance equals motivation times ability." In other words, being motivated won't get you very far if you haven't the ability to do the job. Similarly, as "motivating" as setting goals can be, supervisors must ensure that their subordinates have the resources, feedback, and skills they need to actually apply that motivation and to accomplish their goals. One supervisory training expert calls this having "the three success super-factors":

1. *Establish specific and measurable goals*; doing so involves applying the ideas we discussed earlier in this chapter. This expert also advocates doing a quick check to make sure all your employees are on the same page as far as what their goals are. He says, "Hold a morning huddle at the beginning of the shift. Give each person a pencil and paper. Request that there be no talking and that no names be put on the papers. Then ask everyone to list the three or four main goals of the work unit for the current year. . . . A quick tabulation will let the supervisor know how clearly the goals have been deployed."[8]

2. *Provide regular feedback on performance to achieve those goals.*

3. *Provide the support necessary to reach these goals.* Remember, as this expert says, that "supervisory leadership today is more about collaboration and facilitation than directing and controlling. And creating a climate where the supervisor is viewed as a coach is the catalyst that accelerates commitment to goal attainment."[9]

5. How to Make Better Forecasts

What Forecasting Tools are Available for Making Better Decisions?

As anyone who has ever planned a picnic without checking the weather forecast knows, forecasting is an important part of planning. After the BP well sank in the Gulf of Mexico, it turned out that BP had based some of its plans on a forecast by the Minerals Management Agency, a U.S. government agency. The agency had predicted that oil from a Gulf spill would not reach a U.S. shore. (It thought such oil would simply evaporate or break up and sink.) To the extent that that forecast was obviously wrong, so were BP's plans. We'll look at some important forecasting tools in this section.

A forecast is a prediction. To **forecast** means "to estimate or predict in advance." Even if they don't think about it, supervisors base their plans on forecasts. They hand in sales forecasts based on sales estimates, and they schedule production based on their predictions of what they think the future holds.

Sales Forecasting Techniques

All supervisors involved with sales—from sales supervisors to retail store supervisors to medical office supervisors—need a way to estimate what their future sales will be. The retail store supervisor might want to know, for instance, "The July 4th weekend is coming up; how has that holiday affected our sales the past few years?" The sales department supervisor will want to be able to give his or her boss an estimate of what the company's sales will be next year. Sales forecasts are very important. Most business activities—production, finance, and hiring employees, for instance—depend on the level of sales.

Supervisors can use quantitative or qualitative sales forecasting methods (or a combination of the two). **Quantitative forecasting** uses "numbers"—statistical methods and/or mathematical models—to examine data and find underlying patterns and relationships. **Qualitative forecasting** emphasizes human judgment.

QUANTITATIVE FORECASTING METHODS Quantitative methods look at numbers to identify trends. For example, a **time series** is a set of observations taken at specific times, usually at equal intervals. Examples of time series are a department store's total monthly sales receipts and the daily closing prices of a share of stock. Many retail store owners use a simple way to forecast sales: They keep a diary that shows actual sales for each day as well as anything special about that day, such as whether it rained, or if it was a holiday. Then each week the owner can look back to previous years to estimate what the next week's sales might be, based on what happened in similar weeks in the past.

Plotting time-series data on a graph may reveal a pattern. For example, plotting monthly sales of air conditioning units would probably reveal seasonal increases in late spring and early summer, and reduced sales in the winter. The basic purpose of time-series forecasting is to identify trends and patterns.

QUALITATIVE FORECASTING TOOLS **Qualitative forecasting tools** emphasize human judgment. They gather, in as logical, unbiased, and systematic a way as possible, all the information and human judgment that a manager can apply to a situation.[10]

Supervisors use such qualitative, subjective forecasting for several reasons. Planning is inherently a judgmental process. No one ever knows the future for sure. Even with time-series projections and trends, things change from year to year (such as the unexpected economic collapse a few years ago). Time-series methods also are not so useful for identifying unique, unexpected events—for example, Apple's introduction of the original iPhone blindsided firms like Motorola and Nokia.

Qualitative forecasts can usefully supplement quantitative tools. For example, the **jury of executive opinion** technique involves asking a "jury" of key people to forecast sales for, say, the next year. Generally, each person—purchasing managers at the company's main clients, for instance—might be asked for their estimates of what the future holds.

The **sales force estimation** method gathers the opinions of the company's own sales force regarding what they think sales will be in the forthcoming period. Each salesperson estimates his or her next year's sales, usually by product and customer. Sales supervisors review each estimate, compare it with the previous year's data, and discuss changes with each salesperson. The sales supervisor then combines the separate estimates into a sales forecast for the firm.

While generally useful, basing plans solely on subjective sales forecasts can be perilous. Several years ago, Nortel Networks Corp. planned to meet what they thought would be big demand by spending almost $2 billion to boost production. Throughout the year, Nortel executives questioned their customers to compile sales estimates. Unfortunately, those customer estimates turned out to be wildly optimistic.

Marketing Research

Sales forecasting tools can help supervisors think about the future and develop better plans. But there are times when you want to know, not just what may happen in the future, but also what customers are thinking today, say, about the features of your service that they like and don't like. **Marketing research** refers to developing and analyzing information from customers to help make better plans.

Marketing researchers depend on two main types of information. One is *secondary data*, or information collected or published already. For example, if you wanted to answer the question, "What do people think of the service in our restaurant?" there are numerous online Internet sites that provide such reviews (think of http://www.zagat.com and http://www.yelp.com, for instance.) Good sources of secondary data include the Internet, libraries, trade associations, company files and sales reports, and commercial data (for instance, from companies such as A. C. Nielsen). *Primary data* refers to information specifically collected to solve a current problem. Primary data sources include e-mail, mail and personal surveys, in-depth and focus-group interviews, and personal observation (watching the reactions of customers who walk into a store).[11] That's why you'll occasionally find mail-in cards at restaurants asking about the service.

Forecasting and Supply Chain Management

Companies today increasingly improve the quality of their forecasts by linking themselves more closely to their "supply chain" partners.

Every firm has a **supply chain**, "a collection of physical entities, such as manufacturing plants, distribution centers, conveyances, retail outlets, people, and information, which are linked together into processes supplying goods or services from sources through consumption."[12] The idea of *supply chain management* is to use information technology to integrate customer, supplier, and distributor into one boundaryless, continuously interactive process.

For example, at Walmart, each time a customer buys a pair of size 30 Levi's jeans, a message moves electronically from the point-of-sale cash register to Levi's. The replenishment process thus becomes virtually automatic.

Internet-based supply chain systems integrate—link together via the Internet—all components of the supply chain, such as the customer, supplier, manufacturer, and shipper. When you order a new PC from Dell, Dell's computer system automatically tells suppliers to replenish circuit boards at the plant, the plant to assemble your PC, the display vendor to get ready to have your display picked up, and UPS to pick up and deliver all the parts and your PC to you. Therefore, to a large extent, firms like Levi's, Walmart, and Dell do not have to depend on short-term sales forecasts. They make their supply and production decisions based on actual demand.[13]

Chapter 4 Concept Review and Reinforcement

Key Terms

Activities, p. 104
Business
  Plan, p. 101
Compete, p. 99
Critical Path, p. 104
Events, p. 104
Forecast, p. 112
Gantt Chart, p. 104
Geographic
  Scope, p. 99

Jury of Executive
  Opinion, p. 113
Management by
  Objectives
  (MBO), p. 107
Marketing
  Research, p. 114
Plan, p. 96
Policies, p. 102
Procedures, p. 103

Product Scope, p. 99
Qualitative
  Forecasting, p. 113
Qualitative Forecasting
  Tools, p. 113
Quantitative
  Forecasting, p. 113
Rule, p. 103
Sales Force
  Estimation, p. 113

Strategic
  Management, p. 99
Strategic Plan, p. 99
Strategic Planning, p. 99
Strategy, p. 99
Supply Chain, p. 114
SWOT Analysis, p. 100
Time Series, p. 113
Vertically Integrate, p. 99

Review of Key Concepts

Planning	Planning provides direction and a sense of purpose. Planning helps identify potential opportunities and threats while making your decisions ahead of time. Control means ensuring that activities conform to a plan, and planning facilitates control.
The Planning Process	The planning process entails setting an objective, making forecasts, determining alternatives for getting from point A to point B, evaluating your alternatives, and finally, implementing and evaluation your plan.
Business Plan	The business plan provides a comprehensive view of the firm's situation today and of its companywide departmental goals and plans for the next 3–5 years.
Operational Plans	First-line supervisors focus on short-term operation plans, which represent detailed, day-to-day planning.
SMART Goals	Effective supervisors have a simple way to check if their goals are good: Their goals are Specific, Measurable, Attainable, Relevant, and Timely.
Motivational Goals	Research has suggested that motivational goals assigned are specific, measurable, and challenging yet accomplishable.
Management by Objectives	Management by objectives (MBO) is a technique in which supervisors and subordinates jointly set goals and then periodically jointly assess progress toward said goals.

Strategic Planning	Strategic planning is the process of identifying the firm's business today, its desired future business, and the courses of action it should pursue to get there, given its opportunities, threats, strengths, and weaknesses.
SWOT Analysis	SWOT analysis consolidates information regarding the firm's internal strengths and weaknesses and external opportunities and threats.
Forecast	A forecast is a prediction that estimates or calculates the future in advance.
Quantitative Forecasting	Quantitative forecasting uses statistical methods and/or mathematical models to examine data and find underlying patters and relationships.
Qualitative Forecasting	Qualitative forecasting gathers, in as logical, unbiased, and systematic a way as possible, all information and human judgment that a manager can apply to a situation.
Marketing Research	Marketing research refers to developing and analyzing customer-related information to help managers make marketing decisions.
Competitive Intelligence	Competitive intelligence is a systematic way to obtain and analyze public information about competitors.
Supply Chain	The supply chain is the collection of physical entities (manufacturing plants, distribution centers, conveyances, retail outlets, people, and information) that are linked together into a process of supplying goods or services from sources through consumption.

Review and Discussion Questions

1. Explain why planning and problem-solving are similar.
2. List the steps in the planning process.
3. From a financial perspective, why is the business plan so important?
4. Why do business owners need a business plan?
5. What is meant by SMART goals?
6. Why do motivational goals need to be challenging but accomplishable?
7. In what ways can a supervisor use management by objectives (MBO) to motivate subordinates? What major advantage does MBO have?
8. Explain why SWOT analysis can represent a strong tool for forecasting the future direction of a company.
9. Describe two qualitative forecasting techniques.
10. What is the supply chain? What are its components?

Application and Skill Building

Case Study One

Opening the Hollywood Knitting Factory

You don't raise $5 million and run a successful, growing business for more than 10 years unless you know where you're going. But when it comes to making detailed business plans, managers at KnitMedia—a company that runs jazz clubs called the Knitting Factory in several cities—still have some doubts. For example, when asked if the company does much planning, Michael Dorf, the firm's CEO, replies,

> Sure, we actually are, you know, starting to use budgets—I can't even say it because it's so hard for me to adhere to them, but, you know, we are using budgets to some extent. [In fact], every so often, I put together the business plan and I talk with every team member and try and consolidate all our ideas and our plans. [However], it's difficult to be very fast-moving, especially at Internet speeds, if everything has to be constricted to a pure schedule and plan.

In fact, Dorf's dilemma is often the dilemma that all start-ups (and especially technology-oriented start-ups) face every day. As he says, KnitMedia's managers have to adapt very quickly to stay ahead of the competition, and it's not easy to do that if every step was decided several months or years ago.

Alan Fried, KnitMedia's chief operating officer, makes much the same point. As he says,

> I mean, we are very much a media company and as some of the cliches around go, Internet years happen much quicker than calendar years. And if you have to move so fast, you have to move fast because if you're thinking of it, somebody else's thinking of it and first player advantage means a lot. So, sometimes we don't have the good fortune to just sort of sit down and plan everything. [What we do, though], is have an idea, and we have some meetings about it and we just move where I think we have to.

That way, the company is always moving in the new direction even though it doesn't have a rigid, predetermined plan.

The problem is that Dorf and his team are not entirely convinced that this more or less seat-of-the-pants approach to planning is necessarily the best, although it's certainly worked so far. Furthermore, as more people invest money in the business, it's become increasingly important to develop formal plans so others will know where you're planning to go.

The management team has approached you to help it formalize KnitMedia's planning process. Working as a team, use what you learned in this chapter to answer the following questions.

Discussion Questions

1. At a minimum, what sorts of plans do you think management should develop and use at KnitMedia? Why?
2. Their immediate task is to open the new Hollywood, California, club. What forecasting tools do you suggest they use? Provide them with an outline of an executive assignment action plan that they can use to guide them in opening that location.
3. Is it possible for them to assign specific goals to department managers even though they don't have a formal planning process? If so, how?
4. Give me examples of how we can use descriptive plans, graphical plans, and financial plans.
5. List four forecasting tools you think we should apply and why.

Case Study Two

Getting JetBlue Up and Running

David Neeleman attributed much of JetBlue's initial success to the fact that he and his team stuck closely to his original concept and plan. As Neeleman says, "We're Southwest with seat assignments, leather seats, and television."[14] The foundations of his original plan called for strong financing, fleet homogeneity (so maintenance people, pilots, and flight service crews could easily switch from plane to plane), high fleet utilization, attractive pricing, and experienced management.

To a large extent, things are working out according to plan. JetBlue is flying about 80% full, versus an industry average of about 68%. JetBlue is also profitable, an impressive feat given the fact that virtually all its competitors are racking up losses. Although its fleet of brand-new Airbus A-320 jets meant higher purchase and/or leasing costs, they are also much less expensive to fly; they burn less fuel and require virtually no expenditures on heavy maintenance (since Airbus warranties them for the first few years). As Mr. Neeleman says, "The way to have low-cost is to buy brand-new airplanes."

However, any plan is only as good as the assumptions it's based on, and no manager is ever dealing with an entirely predictable future. On the one hand, some things have worked in JetBlue's favor. For example, right after JetBlue began flying out of JFK, LaGuardia was hit with months of record delays, making JFK a more attractive alternative. Furthermore, Neeleman's most basic assumption—that there was a huge, pent-up demand for flights from places like Fort Lauderdale to JFK on a low-cost airline with new planes and top-quality service—proved very accurate.

On the other hand, many other things were impossible to predict. No one, for instance, expected the 9/11 attacks or the decline in air travel that followed it. Furthermore, while competition was to be expected, even JetBlue's managers were surprised by the aggressiveness of some of their competitors. For example, in a letter to

Chris Kunze, the manager of Long Beach Airport, California, American Airlines pointed out that JetBlue was using few of its slots at the airport and that "it is important that American receive (4) slots so that another air carrier cannot deprive us of the right to operate at Long Beach." Under the terms of its agreement, JetBlue has several years before it must fully utilize its slots. However, American Airlines can file suit to try to win some of those slots and thereby compete head-to-head with JetBlue. Soaring oil prices and a slowing economy didn't help JetBlue. One problem small airlines can't hedge against is rising fuel costs, because they haven't the financial wherewithal to do so. The big carriers can. As someone who ran a company that developed and marketed airline scheduling and reservation forecasting systems, Neeleman was well positioned to understand how to develop sophisticated forecasting systems. However, those sophisticated scheduling and reservation systems require several years' experience on which to build their forecasts. Neeleman and his team, therefore, had to make decisions (such as how many planes to add to particular routes and what fares to charge) more on instinct than on quantitative techniques. As the firm's chief financial officer put it, "The peak last Christmas was far deeper, stronger, and longer than expected. This year there'll be fewer discounts. For now, we're heavily biased to working manually." Partly as a result of all this, JetBlue, which is still in strong financial condition, was soon quickly accumulating debt.

Assignment

You and your team are consultants to Mr. Neeleman, who is depending on your management expertise to help him navigate the launch and management of JetBlue. Here's what he wants to know from you now:

1. From what you know, how well did my team and I do in applying effective planning procedures? Please list what we did right and wrong.
2. Develop an outline of a business plan (just the main headings, please), including the component functional plans we will need for the company as a whole.
3. Give me examples of how JetBlue can use descriptive plans, graphical plans, and financial plans.
4. List four forecasting tools you think we should apply and why.

Experiential Activities

Activity 1. Ralph, one of Allied's star salespeople for five years, moved up to sales supervisor. Ralph was supposed to make sure that his 14 salespeople reached their quotas. But, for the past six months, not one salesperson has made his or her quota. Absentee rates are so high that most of the salespeople never show up on the same day. Ralph has been told by his boss that either he get his people cracking or he will be Allied's ex-sales supervisor.

Planning and Control Are Inseparable

Purpose: The purpose of this exercise is to give you practice in the fundamentals of the business planning process.

Required Understanding: You are going to develop a planning process in order to assure that your salespeople will make or exceed their sales quotas. Therefore, you should be thoroughly familiar with the discussion of planning and setting goals in this chapter.

How to Set Up the Exercise/Instructions: Divide the class into groups of 4–5 students.

1. First, do your best to answer the question of why Ralph, formally a star salesperson, had problems supervising a sales staff toward reaching their sales quotas.
2. Next, your group should develop an outline of a planning process that could be used by Ralph in order to reach his goals.
3. Then your group should set up standards for monitoring the progress of the sales staff in meeting their goals.
4. Have a spokesperson from each group share their outline of a planning process with the other groups. Follow up with a class discussion on how planning and control are inseparable.

Activity 2. It is probably safe to say that your career plan is one of the most important plans you'll ever create. Unfortunately, most people never lay out such a plan, or they don't realize they need one until it's too late. Using the concepts and techniques in this chapter, develop an outline of a career plan for yourself, one that is sufficiently detailed to provide direction for your career decisions over the next five years. Make sure to include an action plan and measurable goals and/or milestones.

Activity 3. You are the chancellor of the California State University system, which has 23 campuses. California has a population of about 37 million people, who represent a microcosm of the world's population. You know that with an increasing birthrate and continuing immigration into the state, your college system could be swamped by the year 2014. Many of the campuses are already filled to capacity. There have been limited funds allocated for introducing technology into every classroom. Some faculties are not as computer literate as their students. This situation may worsen as the years go by. The freshmen of 2014 are likely to be more sophisticated than the current freshmen. The world of technology seems to grow geometrically in terms of the knowledge you need to understand in order to effectively use computers. You have quite a planning challenge. Working as a 4–5 person team, outline how you would use the information provided in this chapter about planning and setting objectives to formulate a plan for the California State University system. Assume that there is increased funding, along with increased pressures to educate a larger percentage of the population as 2014 approaches.

Role-Playing Exercise

Using MBO to Set Goals: The Situation

With management by objectives (MBO), the supervisor and subordinate jointly set goals and periodically assess progress toward those goals. MBO has been referred to as a philosophy, not a rigid sequence of steps. Subordinate goals usually emanate from strategic and departmental goals already set by management. Although MBO is time-consuming, its benefit of employee participation usually outweighs its disadvantage of time consumption. The supervisor of a small machine shop has read and studied about MBO in a supervisory management text and has decided to use MBO to help motivate the company's employees. The owner has already shared with the supervisor the company-wide and department goals the owner expects to achieve. The supervisor has set up a meeting with one of the employees who is not sold on using MBO.

Instructions

All students should read the situation above. One student will play the role of supervisor of the machine shop and the second student will play the role of the subordinate. Each student should only read his or her assigned role below. Then both students should engage in a 15-minute conversation.

A class discussion will follow the role-playing presentation.

Supervisor: Your role is that of a salesperson. This subordinate seems to look for every way that MBO will not benefit the group. You must convince the person that the use of MBO will be to his or her advantage. You have used MBO before and know that it usually works. Specific points that you want to address in your conversation include the following:

- As employees reach their individual goals, they will be supporting organization and department goals set by the owner.
- You (the employee) will participate in setting your own goals.
- You will have the opportunity, periodically, to assess your own progress toward attaining said goals.
- If you are having a problem keeping to a time schedule, then your supervisor is there to guide and support you and obtain needed resources.
- MBO will help to document your success. Documenting start and end dates is a way to track your progress.

Subordinate: Someone must explain to you how this MBO program is going to work and benefit you. You have a number of clarifications that must be made to convince you that this is to your benefit. Specific points/questions you want to address in your conversation include the following:

- If the goals change in mid-year, how will I keep up with any changes?
- This program is going to take up a lot of my time. Is it worth it?

- How will you, as my supervisor, support me when I get into trouble reaching these goals on time?
- Are these time requirements going to be fair to me?
- How much input am I going to have in setting goals?

Questions for Class Discussion

1. Based on what you studied in this chapter, did the supervisor do a good job in convincing the subordinate to participate in MBO?
2. If you were the supervisor, would you have done anything differently in your approach to this subordinate?
3. Do you feel that the attitude of the subordinate is representative of that of most employees introduced to the MBO program?
4. Do you think that the subordinate did a good job in supporting the reasons why he or she did not want to participate in MBO?

5 Understanding How to Control Work Processes

CHAPTER OBJECTIVES

After studying this chapter, you should be able to answer these questions:

1. Why Is Control of Work Processes Important?
2. How Does Timing of Controls Affect Outcomes?
3. What Is the Basic 3-Step Control Process?
4. How Do Traditional and Commitment-Based Controls Compare?
5. What Are Traditional Control Systems and Their Components?
6. How Do People React to Control?
7. How Can Gaining Employee Commitment Encourage Self-Control?

OPENING SNAPSHOT

Benjy's Bad News

Benjy is the accounting supervisor at Apex Industrials, and his boss had been quite explicit: "I have a sales presentation with BigCo Inc. in two days at their offices in Kansas City. I need you to go down to our warehouse to get me the files I'll need to make the quote. I'm flying out at 3 p.m., so have the files on my desk by 1 p.m. tomorrow at the latest." Benjy lives in the opposite direction from the warehouse. So, on his way home that evening, Benjy left e-mail and voice mail messages for Sarah, one of Apex's sales clerks. He said, "Stop off at the warehouse on your way in tomorrow and get me the BigCo files, please." When tomorrow morning came and went, Benjy walked to Sarah's office to ask where the files were. Sarah had been out sick for two days and was still out. There was no way Benjy could get to the warehouse and back by 3 p.m., let alone by 1 p.m. He slowly walked to his boss's office to tell him the bad news.

123

1. The Building Blocks of Effective Control

Control means ensuring that activities are providing the desired results. **Control systems** monitor, collect and convey information on profits or other measures for the purpose of maintaining control. We'll see how supervisors use control systems in this chapter. Controlling some process requires that you set targets, standards, or goals. That is why you'll often see the word *planning* used with the word *control*. **Controlling** involves *setting a target*, *measuring performance*, and *taking corrective action*. Benjy's situation shows what happens when things go out of control. As one expert says, "The goal [of control] is to have no unpleasant surprises."[1]

Why Control Is Important to Supervisors

If you could be sure that every plan you made and every task you assigned would be perfectly executed, you wouldn't need control. Unfortunately, as Benjy just discovered, even simple things rarely go this smoothly. Sometimes, what you think is going to happen ("Sarah will get my message tonight") just doesn't happen. And even if things *do* go more or less as planned, your subordinates may not follow through. After all, people vary widely in their abilities, motivation, and ethics. So, not asking yourself, "How should I make sure things are under control?" (that things are going as expected) is a recipe for disaster—just ask Benjy.

Many supervisors equate "control" with things such as budgets, but budgets are just part of what control is about. Control actually means keeping an eye on *every* task—financial or nonfinancial—that you delegate. Some tasks may be so trivial that you don't need to bother. However, most supervisors (like Benjy) soon discover that such abandonment of one's responsibility is risky. As someone once said;

> A poor supervisor delegates nothing, and a mediocre supervisor delegates everything. An effective supervisor delegates all that he or she can to subordinates. At the same time, he or she sets up checkpoints so that he or she knows the work has been performed.

So for every task you delegate, you will need to ask, "How will I keep track of whether this job is done right?" We'll see how to do that in this chapter.

Making Sure Your Controls Are Timely: Steering, Concurrent, and Postaction Controls

Whether you use a budget or some other means of control, your control needs to be timely. It did Benjy no good to discover at noon that he couldn't get the files in time for his boss's 3 p.m. flight. He should have known that earlier in the morning (or, even better, last night!).

Some control tools are designed to be more timely than are others. We can distinguish among *steering*, *concurrent*, and *postaction* control tools. All the control tools we discuss in this chapter fall into one of these categories.

STEERING CONTROLS **Steering control** tools let you take corrective action *before* the activity or project is complete.[2] They are designed to be the most timely of controls, because they warn you ahead of time, before things go wrong. Steering controls are preventive. For example, after sending a flight to Mars, NASA doesn't want to find out after the fact that it missed its mark. Engineers therefore track the flight continuously. They adjust the trajectory before it's too far off track. Driving a car is the same. You're continually adjusting your speed and route, according to traffic conditions. (That's why supervisors call these "steering" controls.)

Supervisors often use steering control, usually by periodically checking progress long before the project is complete. (For example, Benjy should have confirmed with Sarah last night that she would pick up the files in the morning. He could have said, "Call me when you get this message"; or, "Call me by 8 a.m. when you pick up the files"). Similarly, supervisors use quality control charts to monitor quality trends. If the number of rejects starts trending up, you know you have a problem. You can then "steer" the quality back in the right direction, perhaps by fine-tuning the production machine. As another example, supervisors review daily budget reports to better identify trends. Twice a year, Siebel Systems collects data from about 20% of its customers to see how satisfied the customers are with specific Siebel departments and employees.[3] Siebel does not want to find at the end of the year that there's a problem.

Controlling on Internet Time. The Internet has vastly improved supervisors' abilities to make timely midcourse corrections. Boeing has an Internet-based network used by about 1,000 Boeing vendors and customers.

The network lets Boeing and its suppliers' supervisors maintain control. Access to the e-network lets suppliers continually get real-time updates regarding schedule changes. That helps them make course corrections if required. Customers can view the status of their orders at any time over the Web. That's supposed to minimize delivery surprises.

Alas, while Boeing's Web-based control system did keep customers informed, it didn't do much to keep its airplane assembly schedule on time. Boeing had to push back the first deliveries of its new "Dreamliner" plane by several years. The good news was that Boeing's control systems did notify supervisors that there were scheduling problems. The bad news was that the job of coordinating the far-flung suppliers was so vast that Boeing couldn't move fast enough to solve the problems. Sometimes, even timely feedback isn't enough to overcome problems.

CONCURRENT CONTROLS Supervisors apply **concurrent ("yes/no") control** tools *at the moment* the action to be controlled takes place, so they can instantly make yes-no decisions. Yes-no (or concurrent) controls often involve applying company policies and rules. When some situation that the rule applies to arises, the employee can say "yes" or "no." For example, a movie theater clerk makes on-the-spot decisions about whether someone is old enough to see a particular movie. Or the salesperson tells the customer, "I've got to check with my boss before giving you that discount." Yes-no controls aim to maintain control by preventing employees from doing things that management previously decided should be management's prerogative alone. Employees use the company's standing plans—its policies, procedures, and rules—as the criteria for deciding whether to say "yes" or "no" when a situation arises. If the employees follow those guidelines, then the activities should stay under control.

POSTACTION CONTROLS   Steering and concurrent control tools help you know ahead of time (or as the action is actually happening) if things are under control. *Postaction controls* always occur after the fact. With **postaction controls**, you compare results to the standard and take action *after* the project is complete. The final inspection on a car assembly line is an example. So are annual budgets and the end-of-term final grades students receive.

The problem with postaction controls, as with final grades, is that you can't do much to remedy the situation once the results are in. That's why professors (and supervisors) rarely rely just on postaction controls. They always try to inject some "steering control" (Mars landing) timeliness into how they keep track of things. Instead of just a final exam, they give a midterm, too. Instead of just an end-of-year budget, the supervisor gets weekly budget reports, too. Mid-term exams and weekly budgets are still postaction controls. But at least they give you more time to make corrections.

Using Technology to Stay in Control at UPS.   UPS uses technology to inject timeliness into their controls. UPS delivers about three billion parcels and documents each year in the United States and more than 185 other countries. Each UPS driver uses a handheld computer called a Delivery Information Acquisition Device. It captures customers' signatures, along with pickup, delivery, and time-card information, and lets the driver automatically transmit this information to headquarters via a cellular telephone network.

Through TotalTrack, its automated package-tracking system and its own global communication network, UPS controls packages throughout the delivery process. It electronically transmits documentation on each shipment directly to customs officials prior to arrival. Shipments are therefore either cleared for shipment or flagged for inspection when they arrive.

UPS uses the Internet to help it and its customers monitor and control the progress of all those millions and millions of packages. For example, the UPS Internet-based tracking system lets a customer store up to 25 tracking numbers and then monitor the progress of each package. That lets the customer (and UPS) keep on top of each package's progress.

The Basic Three-Step Control Process

What Is the Basic 3-Step Control Process?

Supervisors should know that "Control" does not just mean rectifying a problem. Control always involves setting targets, measuring performance, and taking corrective action. Let's look more closely at each step.

STEP 1: SET STANDARDS (OR "TARGETS" OR "GOALS")   Here, you pinpoint what the results *ought* to be. You can express standards in terms of money, time, quantity, or quality (or a combination of these). A salesperson might have a (money) quota of $8,000 per month. Benjy had till 1 p.m. (time) to get the files. Production supervisors must produce a specified number of units (quantity) of product per week. Lexus highlights its few defects per car (quality).

Setting effective standards is one hallmark of effective supervision. As in Figure 5.1, the usual procedure is to decide what *yardstick* to use, and then set a *standard*. For example, *units produced per shift* is a (quantity) yardstick.[4] *Fourteen units produced per shift* would then be one possible standard.

Always strive to set *measurable* standards, even when that may seem difficult. In Figure 5.1, each standard in the right column is measurable—14 units, 10 rejects, 90% reports on time, and exceeding expenses no more than 5%. Supervisors can and do

Area to Control	Possible *Yardstick*	Possible *Standard*
Quantity	Number of units produced per shift	Produce 14 units per shift
Quality	Number of rejects	No more than 10 rejects per day
Timeliness	Percentage of sales reports in on time	Return 90% of sales reports on time
Dollars	Percentage of deviation from budget	Do not exceed budgeted expenses by more than 5% during year

translate even subjective measures such as morale into measurable ones. For example, FedEx conducts annual attitude/morale surveys. They then quantify and track these results (percentage of employees satisfied with pay, and so on) from year to year, by department, for comparison purposes.

Part of the art of supervising is choosing strategic *control points*. **Strategic control points** are the selected list of standards you will use to control a particular situation. The supervisor needs to be judicious in what he or she tracks. For example, a sales supervisor who wants to control how his or her salespeople are performing could track dozens of results, such as attendance, customers visited, hours worked, sales per week, and customer complaints. However, realistically, given the time available, the supervisor needs to choose just a few "strategic" (important) standards on which to focus. For example, at the end of the day, the supervisor may decide that it doesn't really matter how many hours the salesperson works, or how many customers visited, and so on: The supervisor just wants to track two strategic results—sales per week and customer complaints.

STEP 2: MEASURE ACTUAL PERFORMANCE AGAINST STANDARDS   A mayor of New York would often ask citizens he met on the street, "How am I doing?" Like the mayor, once you set standards, you must compare actual performance to that standard. Thus if Benjy expected Sarah to call him by 8 a.m. with news, then at 8:01 he should have been asking, "Where's Sarah?"

We'll see in this chapter that supervisors use many tools to compare actual results to the standard. Benjy might have *personally monitored* how Sarah was doing (by following up by phone). That's also how the New York mayor got much of his feedback.

But in practice, all supervisors must also supplement such personal control with more impersonal tools, such as budgets and performance reports. After all, you can't be everywhere at once, personally following up on everything. That's why companies also use control techniques such as budgetary reports, quality control reports, inventory control reports and "digital dashboards" (the latter to continuously monitor on a computer screen how the team is doing).

STEP 3: TAKE CORRECTIVE ACTION   You've now compared results with your plans. How do they compare? Is there a big difference? If so, you should take corrective action.

Sometimes the action to take is obvious. For example, you've told your employee five times that she must wear her safety goggles, and in violation of company policy, she still refuses. It's time to discipline her.

Often, the corrective action isn't so obvious. For example, it wasn't Sarah's fault she didn't get Benjy's message. Effective supervisors know that things aren't always as they seem. Deciding what corrective action to take may thus require problem solving. Perhaps you set the sales target too high. Perhaps the salesperson isn't right for the job. Correcting the deviation may therefore require all your supervisory skills. For example,

The Hersey Model and Taking Corrective Action with the Right Leadership Style

The football coach, his team within 1 point of the state championship, saw the game evaporate when his young kicker nervously flubbed a 10-yard kick. For the supervisor, the rubber hits the road once you've discovered the performance discrepancy and its cause. How should you act now? Unilaterally tell the subordinate "You're off the team"? Try some participative management?

How you behave now is essentially a leadership issue. In Chapter 2 (Leadership), we saw that it's important for supervisors to adjust their leadership style to the situation. As the football coach knows, taking corrective

action certainly demands the right leadership style. For example, here's what the Hersey two-dimension situational leadership model (discussed in Chapter 2, page 50) might suggest for our football coach:

His young kicker certainly had the willingness to do the job. Unfortunately, his inexperience meant that he probably didn't have the ability to do it under pressure. Corrective action here would call for a high task–low relationship leadership style. The coach should provide his young kicker with specific instructions and then monitor his performance in the future.

are you doing a good job training your employees? Is their morale low? Taking corrective action requires you to apply all you know about planning, organizing, staffing, and leading—not just controlling. The accompanying Leadership Applications for Supervisors feature expands on this.

Comparing Traditional and Commitment-Based Controls

How Do Traditional and Commitment-Based Controls Compare?

Assume you just took over as volunteer editor of your professional association's monthly newsletter. What are some of the things you would want to control? A (very) short list would include article length and quality, advertising revenues, operating expenses, article deadlines, article topics, and the format for each issue. How will you make sure all these things "stay under control"? You have several options, but they all basically boil down to two: First, you can use *traditional control systems* such as budgets to control what's happening. Or, you could rely on your team's *self-control* by appealing to their sense of commitment. It's therefore useful to think of control tools in terms of traditional versus self-control.

Traditional Control Tools

Supervisors use three traditional types of control for keeping things under control—diagnostic controls, personal controls, and rules and policies.

- **Diagnostic controls** are formal systems, such as budgets, that help supervisors zero in on, compare, and *diagnose* gaps between what ought to be and what is. These tools include budgets, financial reports, and computerized information systems. Diagnostic control tools such as these usually spring to mind when most people think of "control." For example, departmental supervisors (and their bosses) typically get weekly budgets. But diagnostic control tools needn't be old-fashioned—for instance, modern computerized control systems fit under this umbrella.

- Supervisors also traditionally use ***personal, interactive control*** to personally compare "what should be and what is" and to influence activities.
- Third, supervisors use ***rules and policies*** to guide behavior and to set limits beyond which employees should not proceed (at least without first checking with the supervisor). The control question here would be, "Did this employee adhere to the policy or not?"

Commitment and Self-Control

The problem is that traditional controls like budgets, personal observation, and rules only get a supervisor so far. No control tools (like budgets or rules) can anticipate every possible crisis. Employees have many ingenious ways of getting around the system. And, in many situations (such as building high-quality cars), you want the employees to *want* to build in quality; you can't really force them to do so.

That is why shrewd supervisors and employers work hard to get employees to exercise self control—in other words, to get them to want to do the best job possible, even when they're not being watched. Starbucks, for instance, owns over 14,000 stores worldwide. How could supervisors at its U.S. headquarters possibly keep things under control in Miami, Shanghai, and Honolulu just through personal observation and budget reports? Experienced supervisors know that keeping things under control just by closely supervising all their subordinates is futile. It's much easier to keep things on track when your subordinates know what to do and want to do a great job. That's why, to help encourage self-control, Starbucks provides all its employees with (among other things) a "special blend" of one of the best benefits packages in industry, including stock options.

Summary: Basic Types of Control

The bottom line is that as a supervisor, you can take two basic approaches to making sure that things in your team stay under control. You'll find these two approaches summarized in Figure 5.2.[5] *Traditional controls* include budgets and financial reports; modern computerized systems like "digital dashboards"; rules and polices that set guidelines

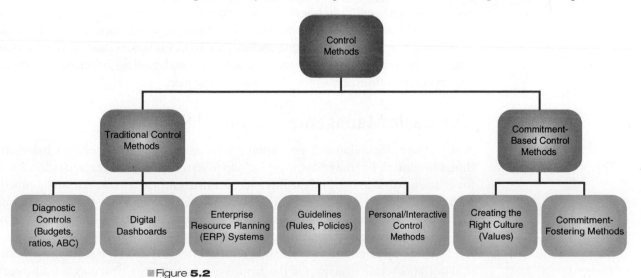

■Figure **5.2**

Examples of the Basic Types of Control Methods

for what employees can or cannot do; and personal/interactive control. *Commitment-based* approaches involve cultivating self-control.

One of the surprises new supervisors face is that the more they try to control things, the more out of control things seem to get. Sometimes, the more you try to supervise employees and check up on them, the more they find ways to gum up the works. The bottom line is that trying to control things without also encouraging self-control is a fool's errand. You need to be good at both. Let's look at traditional control methods first.

2. Understanding Traditional Control Systems

What Are Traditional Control Systems and Their Components?

Let us look first at five traditional control systems supervisors use: *diagnostic financial and budgetary control systems, digital dashboards, enterprise resource planning (ERP) systems, rules and policies for setting guidelines,* and *personal/interactive control systems.*

Diagnostic Controls and Budgetary Systems

Diagnostic controls is just a technical name for control tools that supervisors use to zero in on and diagnose gaps between what ought to be and what is. When most people think of controls, they think of diagnostic control systems. Budgets and production reports are examples. Semiannual performance reviews are another.

Diagnostic control tools such as monthly budget reports are invaluable. They reduce the need for supervisors to personally monitor everything for which they are responsible.[6] Once targets are set, the supervisor can (at least in theory) leave the employees to pursue the goals. Ideally (but, really just in theory), you can be secure in the knowledge that if the standards aren't met, the deviations will show up as red flags in the performance reports. This idea is at the heart of what supervisors call the principle of exception. The **principle of exception** (or "management by exception") holds that to conserve supervisors' time, only significant deviations or exceptions from the standard, "both the especially good and bad exceptions," should be brought to the supervisor's attention. Traditional diagnostic control tools include, the basic budgetary control system; ratio analysis; financial responsibility centers; activity-based costing; balanced scorecards; and enterprise resource planning. We look at these next.

The Basic Management Control System

A supervisor (including our professional association's newsletter editor) has many things to control. For the editor, these include advertising revenues, expenses, deadlines for articles, article length and quality, and the format for each issue. Yet from a practical point of view, it's usually the financial aspects—the bottom line—that is first among equals when it comes to control. Financial or *budgetary* controls thus form the heart of any company's basic management control system.

Setting up financial controls always starts with planning. Top management formulates an overall strategy for the firm. We saw that this provides a framework within which the rest of the planning process occurs. Next, management formulates, lower-level plans and a hierarchy of goals. At the top, the president sets strategic goals (such as "Have 50% of sales revenue from customized products by 2012"). As we discussed in Chapter 4, each of the president's direct reports—and, in turn, each of their subordinates—then receives goals to achieve.

The result is a chain or hierarchy of divisional and departmental goals. At each step in this hierarchical process, management translates the goals and plans into financial targets, and embodies them in budgets.

THE BUDGET PROCESS   Budgets therefore bring the company's plans to life. **Budgets** are formal financial expressions of a supervisor's plans. They show targets for things such as sales, cost of materials, production levels, and profit, expressed in dollars. These planned targets are the standards against which the supervisor compares and controls the unit's actual financial performance. The first step in budgeting is generally to develop a sales forecast and sales budget. The **sales budget** shows the planned sales activity for each period (usually in units per month) and the revenue expected from the sales.

The company can then produce various operating budgets. **Operating budgets** show the expected sales and/or expenses for each of the company's departments for the planning period in question. For example, the production and materials budget (or plan) shows what the company plans to spend for materials, labor, administration, and so forth in order to fulfill the requirements of the sales budget (see Figure 5.3).

The next step in budgeting is to combine all of these sales, production, and other departmental budgets into a *profit plan* for the coming year. The other name for a profit plan is the budgeted **income statement** (or "pro forma" income statement). By bringing together all the departmental sales and expense estimates, the income statement shows overall expected sales, expected expenses, and expected income or profit for the year.

In practice, cash from sales usually doesn't flow into the firm in such a way as to coincide precisely with cash disbursements. (Some customers may take 35 days to pay their bills, for instance, but employees expect paychecks every week.) The **cash budget** or plan shows, for each month, the amount of cash the company can expect to receive and the amount it can expect to disburse. The supervisor can use it to anticipate his or her cash needs and to arrange for short-term loans, if need be.

The company will also have a budgeted **balance sheet**. The budgeted balance sheet shows supervisors, owners, and creditors what the company's projected financial picture should be at the end of the year, in terms of what the company owns and what it owes. It shows *assets* (such as cash and equipment), *liabilities* (such as long-term debt), and *net worth* (the excess of assets over other liabilities).

Budgets of one kind or another are the most widely used control device. Each manager, from first-line supervisor to company president, gets a budget. Remember,

■Figure **5.3**

Example of a Budget

Operating Budget for Machinery Department, June 2011	
Budgeted Expenses	Budget
Direct Labor	$2,107
Supplies	$3,826
Repairs	$402
Overhead (electricity, etc.)	$500
TOTAL EXPENSES	$6,835

Performance Report for Machinery Department, June 2010				
	Budget	Actual	Variance	Explanation
Direct Labor	$2,107	$2,480	$373 over	Had to put workers on overtime.
Supplies	$3,826	$4,200	$374 over	Wasted two crates of material.
Repairs	$402	$150	$252 under	
Overhead (electricity, etc.)	$500	$500	0	
TOTAL	$6,835	$7,330	$495 over	

however, that the budget (as in Figure 5.3) just reflects the standard-setting step in the three-step control process. You must still compare the actual and the budgeted figures. And, if necessary, you'll need to diagnose the problem and take corrective action.

Your company's accountants compile the actual financial results and feed it back to the appropriate supervisors. As in Figure 5.4, this *performance report* shows budgeted or planned targets. Next to these numbers, it shows the department's actual performance numbers. **Variances** show the differences between budgeted and actual amounts. The report may provide a space for the supervisor to explain any variances. After reviewing (and diagnosing) the performance report, management can take corrective action.

The firm's accountants also periodically audit the firm's financial statements. An **audit** is a systematic process that involves three steps: (1) objectively obtain and evaluate evidence regarding important aspects of the firm's performance; (2) judge the accuracy and validity of the data; and (3) communicate the results to interested users, such as the board of directors and the company's banks.[7] The purpose of the audit is to certify that the firm's financial statements accurately reflect its performance.

Ratio Analysis and Return on Investment

Some supervisors also use financial ratio analysis to diagnose performance and maintain control. **Financial ratios** compare one financial measure on a financial statement to another. The rate of return on investment (ROI) is one ratio. ROI equals net profit divided by total investment; it is a gauge of overall company performance. Rather than measuring net profit as an absolute figure, it shows profit in relation to the total investment the owners have in the business. This is often a more informative figure. For example, a $1 million profit is more impressive with a $10 million investment than with a $100 million investment. Figure 5.5 lists some widely used financial ratios.

Analyzing financial ratios helps supervisors understand their performance. For example, too much investment may help account for a low ROI. In turn, too much investment might reflect too much inventory, too many accounts receivable, or too much cash.[8]

Financial Responsibility Centers

Supervisors are usually responsible for meeting specific financial targets. These targets show the supervisor how the firm will evaluate his or her performance. They also make it easier for the employer to evaluate each supervisor's performance. When the company assigns a supervisor an operating budget for his or her team that is tied to specific

Name of Ratio	Formula	Industry Norm (As Illustration)
1. Liquidity Ratios (measure the ability of the firm to meet its short-term obligations)		
Current ratio	$\dfrac{\text{Current assets}}{\text{Current liabilities}}$	2.6
Acid-test ratio	$\dfrac{\text{Cash and equivalent}}{\text{Current liabilities}}$	1.0
2. Leverage Ratios (measure the contributions of financing by owners compared with financing provided by creditors)		
Debt to equity	$\dfrac{\text{Total debt}}{\text{Net worth}}$	56%
Current liability to net worth	$\dfrac{\text{Current liability}}{\text{Net worth}}$	32%
3. Activities Ratios (measure the effectiveness of the employment of resources)		
Inventory turnover	$\dfrac{\text{Sales}}{\text{Inventory}}$	7 times
Average collection period	$\dfrac{\text{Receivables}}{\text{Average sales per day}}$	20 days
4. Profitability Ratios (indicate degree of success in achieving desired profit levels)		
Sales (profit) margin	$\dfrac{\text{Net profit after taxes}}{\text{Sales}}$	3.2%
Return on investment	$\dfrac{\text{Net profit after taxes}}{\text{Total investment}}$	7.5%

financial targets, then we say the supervisor is in charge of a *financial responsibility center*. **Financial responsibility centers** are organizational units that are responsible for and measured by a specific set of financial activities. These centers may include work teams, departments, divisions, or, indeed, the company as a whole.

There are several types of financial responsibility centers. For example, **profit centers** are responsibility centers that the company holds accountable for profit. (Profit is a measure of the difference between the revenues generated and the cost of generating those revenues.) **Revenue centers** are responsibility centers whose supervisors are accountable for generating specified levels of sales revenues. For example, firms generally measure sales supervisors in terms of the sales produced by their revenue centers/departments.

Activity-Based Costing (ABC)

Traditional budgeting systems often can't show what it actually costs to produce and sell a product or service. Consider a simplified example. Suppose an insurance company has a contract to provide insurance to a big client. The insurance firm's president wants to know, "What is this contract costing our company?" The traditional accounting system might show what the company pays out in claims, and perhaps what it paid the salesperson as a commission for getting the client. It might even show (as approximations) what share of the insurance firm's "overhead" expenses, for things like office lighting and heating, the accounting system is charging to this particular contract.

What the insurance firm's accounting system probably cannot show are all those actual costs of serving this big client that are scattered around the insurance company. For example, how much time do this client's employees spend on the phone with the insurance firm's customer service reps? How much time do the doctors that serve this client's employees spend getting approvals for medical procedures from the insurance company's gatekeepers?

The problem is that traditional accounting systems tend to isolate departments. The customer rep department knows what it's spending *overall* for customer reps. The gatekeeper department knows what it's spending *overall* for physician gatekeepers. But the president can't reach across the insurance company's various departments and determine what each of them is spending *on this particular client.*

Modern management information systems, called enterprise resource planning (ERP) systems (discussed below), change that. With these new computer systems, all departments use compatible software modules. All departments' systems communicate with the central database. By linking the information from compatible accounting modules in different departments together, ERP enables supervisors to use activity-based costing. **Activity-based costing (or ABC)** is a system for allocating costs to products or clients that takes all the product's or client's costs into account (including production, marketing, distribution, and sales and follow-up activities) in calculating the actual cost of each product or client.[9]

Activity-based costing is a powerful control tool. With ABC, the president can reach across departments and monitor all the costs associated with any "activity" he or she wants to control, such as by order, client, project, contract, or business process, rather than just by department or cost center. This enables the insurance company's president to determine how much time, effort, and money each department is expending on this client. Again, ERP systems enable the company to do this, by linking the information from compatible accounting modules in different departments together. This makes it easier for the president to get a bird's eye view of what's happening across his or her company.

Strategy Maps, Digital Dashboards, and the Balanced Scorecard Process

Many businesses today use the *balanced scorecard* approach to maintain control. The **balanced scorecard** is not a scorecard. It is a process for controlling employees' performance and for aligning employees' actions with the company's objectives. The balanced scorecard process involves three steps: assigning financial and nonfinancial goals, monitoring employees' performance, and quickly taking corrective action.[10] The "balanced" in balanced scorecard reflects the balance of financial and nonfinancial measures, and of short-term and long-term goals. "Profits" might be one financial goal, while "customer complaints" is a non-financial goal.

STRATEGY MAPS   Using the balanced scorecard approach usually starts with *strategy mapping.* A **strategy map** is a graph that summarizes the cause-and-effect chain of activities that contribute to a company's success.

For example, Southwest Airlines' aim is to keep costs and ticket prices to a minimum, while offering good service. Figure 5.6 presents a strategy map for Southwest Airlines. It

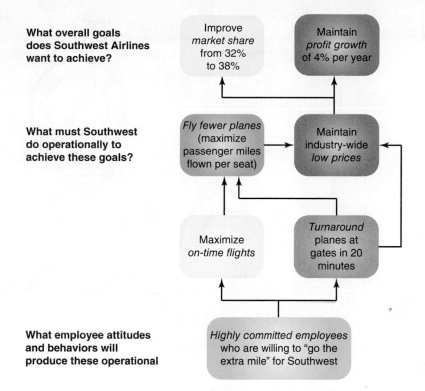

shows the chain of activities that contributes to Southwest's success. To boost revenues and profits, Southwest needs to *fly fewer planes (to keep costs down), attract and keep customers, maintain low prices, and maintain on-time flights.* What drives these activities? In turn, on-time flights and low prices require *fast airplane turnaround at the gate.* And, fast turnaround requires *motivated, committed ground and flight crews.* Each ground and flight crew member can see that by working hard to turn planes around fast, he or she is contributing to an ascending chain of activities that help make Southwest profitable.

DIGITAL DASHBOARDS   In turn, Southwest's ground crew supervisors use digital dashboard displays to monitor activities such as aircraft turnaround time.

The saying "a picture is worth a thousand words" explains the purpose of the digital dashboard. A **digital dashboard** (see Figure 5.7) presents the supervisor with desktop graphs and charts. That way he or she gets a picture of where his or her department has been and where it's going, in terms of each activity in the strategy map. For example, a top manager's dashboard for Southwest Airlines might display daily trends for activities such as fast turnaround, attracting and keeping customers, and on-time flights. This gives the manager time take to corrective action. For example, if ground crews are turning planes around slower today, financial results tomorrow may decline unless the crew's supervisor takes action. The ground crew's supervisor would look at his or her own digital dashboard and see how the team is doing relative to the team's standards.

Enterprise Resource Planning (ERP) Systems

Balanced scorecards, ABC control, and digital dashboards would be impossible without **enterprise resource planning** (ERP) systems. As explained in Chapter 3, ERP is a

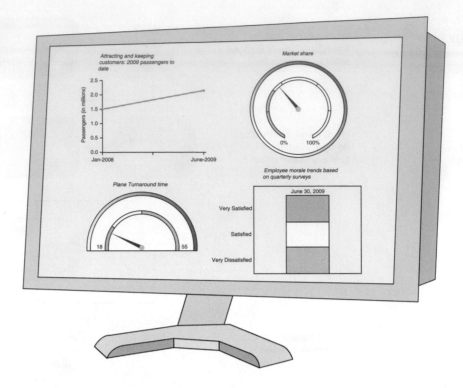

companywide integrated computer system that is composed of compatible software modules for each of the company's separate departments (such as sales, accounting, finance, warehousing, production, and HR).[11] Each department gets its own ERP module.[12] The ERP modules are designed to communicate with each other and with the central system's database. That way, information from all the departments is readily shared by the central ERP system and is available to all the other departments.[13] Activities that formerly required human intervention (such as production telling accounting that it should bill a customer because an order just shipped) occur automatically. ERP strips away the barriers that typically exist among a company's stand-alone (and often incompatible) departmental computer systems. It enables the computer systems to communicate with one another.

The check-printing company Deluxe Paper Payment Systems used its ERP system to "get a clearer picture of which of its customers were profitable and which were not."[14] For example, its enterprise system helped it discover that orders for checks from banks were much more profitable when they arrived via electronic ordering. Deluxe then launched a campaign to increase electronic ordering—particularly by its 18,000 bank and small-business customers. The number of checks ordered electronically jumped from 48% to 62% in just a few months. This dramatically improved profits.

Using Policies and Rules to Maintain Control

Control tools don't necessarily involve numbers, budgets, or even computer systems. One of the most familiar and time-honored ways to control employees is to set up policies and rules that set restrictions on their behavior. Rules like "Don't clock out more than two minutes before your shift ends" and "Do not accept for return any item that is not in its original sealed box" are examples. These rules help to keep things under

> **Our Credo**
>
> We believe our first responsibility is to the doctors, nurses and patients,
> to mothers and fathers and all others who use our products and services.
>
> In meeting their needs, everything we do must be of high quality.
>
> We must constantly strive to reduce our costs
> in order to maintain reasonable prices.
>
> Our suppliers and distributors must have an opportunity
> to make a fair profit.
>
> We are responsible to our employees,
> the men and women who work with us throughout the world.
>
> Everyone must be considered as an individual.
>
> We must provide competent management,
> and their actions must be just and ethical.
>
> We must be good citizens—support good works and charities
> and bear our fair share of taxes.
>
> When we operate according to these principles,
> the stockholders should realize a fair return.

control by identifying actions that employees must avoid.[15] Disciplinary rules are another example. They say, "Here's what you cannot do at work, and here's what happens to you if you do it." Breaching these guidelines (rules) should trigger disciplinary action.

Ethics codes are also examples of such controls. Asked if there's anything he loses sleep over, Jeffrey Immelt, GE's CEO, once said that he worries about an ethical lapse on the part of some employee: "Some employees just don't get it," he said. Johnson & Johnson's Credo (see Figure 5.8) is a famous ethics code example. It lays out the guidelines that all Johnson & Johnson employees should follow in policing themselves.

Unfortunately, Johnson & Johnson's ethics code also illustrates how controls can go astray. J&J's code famously starts with, "We believe our first responsibility is to the doctors, nurses and patients, to mothers and fathers and all others who use our products and services." Yet in 2010, the U.S. Justice Department charged the company with paying "tens of millions of dollars in kickbacks" to boost sales of its products to nursing home patients.[16] For its part, the company said what it did was "lawful and appropriate," and it may well turn out they are right. Still, the mere allegation suggests that even in the best of firms, you can't always rely on formal rules and controls to deliver the employee behavior that you desire. In September 2010 J&J replaced the head of its consumer products division.

Personal/Interactive Control Systems and Close Supervision

Tiny companies have one big control advantage over huge multinational ones like Johnson & Johnson or GE: "Mom and Pop" can talk face to face with everyone in the firm. They can thus monitor in real time how everything is going.

Maintaining control by personally monitoring how everyone is doing is **personal (or "interactive") control**. It is the oldest and most traditional way to stay in control. Even the Bible describes how leaders like Moses divided up their flocks into units small enough to be personally supervised by Moses' "assistants."

Personal control has a lot going for it. There's often no substitute for being able to personally monitor how things are going, in real time. That way, you can make adjustments almost instantaneously. Every supervisor uses personal control to some degree. One problem is that as your department gets bigger and bigger, there may simply be too many people to keep a personal eye on. This is why many companies are shrinking their units' sizes. For example, Intuit divided its business into smaller units. In this way, interactions in each unit remain more instantaneous and personal. Other companies emphasize "management by walking around" to get supervisors out to personally interact with employees.

The other potential drawback to personal control is that you may inadvertently slip into close supervision. Most employees don't like being closely supervised, and they may bristle at being closely monitored. The accompanying Leadership Applications for Supervisors feature addresses this.

Leadership Applications for Supervisors

Close versus General Leadership

Part of the art of good supervision is knowing when to closely supervise your subordinates, and when to back off. Robert Tannenbaum and Warren Schmidt created a simple model (Figure 5.9) to illustrate how leaders can adjust their styles to the task. In a famous Harvard Business Review *article called "How to Choose a Leadership Pattern" they introduced their "Continuum of Leadership."*

As you can see, the model shows that a supervisor can exhibit a range of leadership styles. These range from making the decision and announcing it, to asking for employee input, and finally to letting the employees make the decision themselves.

What determines which style you use? Tannenbaum and Schmidt say it depends—on the leader (for instance, on how confident you are), on the employees (for instance, on their ability to make a good decision in that situation), and on the situation itself (for instance, on the need to take quick action). Of course, at first glance, this might not seem very useful. For example, who walks around with a calculator for computing how the leader, employees, and situation add up to this leader style or that?

But the model does make two valuable points. First, most of us are capable of adjusting how we behave (at least within certain limits). You may be participatively inclined, but that does not mean you can't put your foot down on occasion. Second, it makes the point that (even without precisely computing your response), you need to use common sense in adjusting your style to the situation. You cannot (and should not) automatically be autocratic (or participative, or whatever) all the time, even if one style or the other is normally your default. For instance, if your employees know what they're doing and if you don't have all the facts, of course it may pay to back off and "give them more space." But if the ship is sinking, you'd better take charge and lead your people out—it's pretty safe to say that here, few people will object to being closely supervised!

Close supervision				Area of employee discretion
Area of supervisor authority				General **supervision**
You make decision and announce it	You make decision, then try to sell it to employees	You present your preliminary decision, subject to discussion and change	You present issue, ask for employees' opinions	Employees manage themselves, within limits

■Figure **5.9**

The Leadership Continuum: Close versus General Leadership

Source: Adapted from Robert Tannenbaum and Warren Schmidt, "How to Choose a Leadership Pattern," *HBR,* May–June 1973.

ELECTRONIC PERFORMANCE MONITORING AND CONTROL   When it comes to close supervision, the grand prize probably goes to electronic performance monitoring. Two researchers say, "As many as 26 million workers in the United States are subject to electronic performance monitoring (EPM)—such as having supervisors monitor through electronic means the amount of computerized data an employee is processing per day—on the job."[17] The supervisors can then take immediate action by speaking with or contacting the errant employee.

Do not assume that electronic performance monitoring applies only to subordinates and not to bosses. For example, the Japanese company that controls 7-Eleven is imposing an EPM system on its store supervisors in Japan and in the United States. Like all 7-Eleven stores, the ones belonging to Michiharu Endo use a point-of-sale computer to let headquarters know each time he makes a sale. In the case of 7-Eleven's new system, headquarters monitors both how much time Endo spends using the analytical tools built into the computerized cash register to track product sales and how effective he is at weeding out poor sellers. Headquarters then ranks stores by how often their operators use the computer as a measure of how efficient they are.

The system ran into particular resistance in the United States. Many 7-Eleven supervisors thought they had escaped the bureaucratic rat race by taking over their own stores. They were therefore surprised at the degree of control this new EPM system exposed them to.[18] The bottom line is, you never quite know how a subordinate may react to "being controlled."

3. How Do People React to Control?

How Do People React to Control?

In fact, if "controlling" employees' behavior were the only (or the best) way to ensure effective performance, we could disregard much of this book. For example, we wouldn't need to know much about what motivates people. As a supervisor, you could just set standards—and then personally control your employees' work.

But you probably already know that no supervisor could ever rely solely on control tools like budgets and close supervision for keeping employees in line. For one thing, it's not practical. For example, where do you find the time to watch, say, how the front-desk clerk is greeting guests every minute of every day?

The second reason you can't rely on formal control tools is that employees often short-circuit controls, often with ingenious tactics. The accompanying supervising the new workforce feature looks at one aspect of this.

Unintended Consequences of Controls

Your employees may use several tactics to evade controls. We can label these as tricky behavior, games, delays, and negative attitudes.[19]

TRICKY BEHAVIOR   Tricky behavior means that your controls encourage employees to ignore common sense and instead focus exclusively on what you're measuring. For example, a famous supervisory truism is, "You get what you measure." Setting performance targets (such as "Cut $500 in costs this month") will focus employees' efforts on those targets. The problem arises when the employees focus just on what you're measuring and disregard other, equally important goals.

Attitudes at Work

Not everyone reacts to controls in the same way. Supervisors endeavoring to exercise control should understand that minority employees might react more negatively than do their nonminority colleagues. For example, studies have found that white workers were more likely to view their employer as fair and inclusive than employees of color were. Another study found that black employees perceived "minor, pervasive mistreatment and unfairness" at work more often than white employees.[20] Another study found that visible minorities in Canada reported significantly greater discrimination and prejudice than whites. Unfortunately, studies also suggest that these attitudes aren't baseless. They suggest that minorities often do experience greater objective employment disadvantage.

The bottom line is that exercising control over minority employees sometimes may require some extra discretion. No two of your subordinates will ever react to your attempts to closely supervise them or to discipline them in precisely the same way. However, some minority employees may especially tend to view your attempts as less than fair.

The tricky behavior problem stems mostly from limiting what you measure to just one or two targets. For example, Nordstrom set up a policy of measuring employees in terms of sales per hour worked. Unfortunately, without other performance measures, the system didn't work. Some employees claimed their supervisors were pressuring them to underreport hours on the job to boost reported sales per hour. In 2010, several high school teachers in Georgia allegedly changed their students' test scores, supposedly because the teachers were being evaluated solely based on how well their students did on the tests.

GAMES "Games" means taking actions that improve performance in terms of the control system without producing any economic benefits for the firm. For example, one supervisor overshipped products to distributors at year-end. The aim was to ensure that he would meet his budgeted sales targets. He did, but then his company had to deal with excess returns the following year.

Other control tools lead to operating **delays**. For example, a "yes-no" control policy that prohibits signing agreements without your boss's approval can help keep the firm out of trouble. However, it may also mean losing a good project if a competitor can move faster to make agreements. Streamlining the approval process can solve this problem.

NEGATIVE ATTITUDES Most people are programmed from childhood to resist efforts to control them. It's therefore not surprising that traditional control tools often trigger negative employee attitudes. There's nothing new about this. The word *sabotage* derives from the French word for shoe. It refers to angry French workers' habit of throwing their shoes in the machine gears to slow production.

4. Encouraging Self-Control: Using Commitment-Based Control

The bottom line is that there are two reasons to be skeptical about relying on traditional controls like budgets, computers, close supervision, and ethics codes. First, we saw that employees will use tactics like games to look good in terms of the controls, but really do the company harm. The last thing you want as a supervisor is to have your employees throwing their shoes—actually or figuratively—into the gears.

Second, for most activities today, forcing employees to do things just won't work—you need the employees to *want* to do a great job. It's just about impossible to build great cars (or to design great computer programs, or to teach a great class, or whatever) if the employees doing the work aren't willing to exercise self-control.

Today's empowered, work team approach to running things makes encouraging self-control even more important. Imposing too much control on supposedly self-managing teams is obviously counterproductive. How can a team be self-managing if you're watching everything that they do? Smart supervisors therefore work hard to supplement traditional controls like budgets with efforts aimed at encouraging employees to control themselves.

How to Get Subordinates to Exercise Self-Control

How do you get your people to control themselves? You can use three basic methods.

1. You can use motivation. Obviously, *motivated employees* are more likely to exercise self-control and to do their jobs right. We will discuss motivation techniques in Chapter 10.

2. People's actions tend to reflect their *values* (such as "honesty is the best policy" or "always lend your teammates a hand"), so you can cultivate and guide your employees' *values and beliefs.*

3. Finally, *committed and engaged employees* tend to be more dedicated to doing what's right for the company, so you can take actions to improve employee commitment.

In this final section, we'll look at how supervisors foster the right employee values and build employee commitment.

The Supervisor as Leader: Using Culture and Values to Foster Self-Control

If you remember nothing else of what you read in this book, remember that every one of your subordinates is going to look to you, and to what you say and do, in determining what the right thing to do is. Leading by example is the essence of leadership. According to one report, for instance, "the level of misconduct at work dropped dramatically when employees said their supervisors exhibited ethical behavior." Only 25% of employees who agreed that their supervisors "set a good example of ethical business behavior" said they had observed misconduct in the last year. That compared with 72% of those who did not feel that their supervisors set good examples.[21] Do you want to lead subordinates astray? Then,

- Tell staffers to do whatever is necessary to achieve results.
- Overload top performers to ensure that the work gets done.
- Look the other way when wrongdoing occurs.[22]

SET THE RIGHT CULTURE   These examples illustrate an important aspect of the interplay between leadership and control. Your own behavior sends signals about the appropriate way to behave. Those signals then create the culture that guides your employees' behavior. We can define **organizational culture** as the "characteristic values, traditions, and behaviors a company's employees share." A *value* is a basic belief about what is right or wrong, or about what you should or shouldn't do. ("Honesty is the best policy" would be a value.) Values are important because they guide and channel behavior. Supervising people and shaping their behavior therefore depends to some extent on you shaping the values they use as behavioral guides. A vast array of "out of control" things that occur at work— ethical lapses, poor service, excessive tardiness, even abominable employee behavior— often have their roots in the signals workers pick up (or think they pick up) from the boss.

The point is that one way to make your control job easier is to make clear your expectations with respect to the values you think are critical. Then, walk the talk. Don't say, "Don't fudge the financials," or "don't be discriminatory" and then do so yourself.

How Supervisors Build Employee Commitment

When a music company recently sold a subsidiary to another company, the music firm's president thanked the subsidiary's employees for their past hard work and dedication. He also reminded them that during the transition, "It's more important than ever to ensure that our company performs at the highest levels."

His message underscores a supervisory dilemma. All supervisors need and want employee **commitment**. In other words, you want your subordinates to identify with and be engaged in the company and its mission. After all, if your subordinates believe in the company and are loyal to it, they're more likely to do their best for the company. The dilemma is this: In the recession years of 2008 through 2010 combined, employers carried out a total of over 51,000 mass layoffs, idling over 5 million workers in total.[23] What can a supervisor do to maintain commitment in the face of such employment turmoil?

How Can Gaining Employee Commitment Encourage Self-Control?

The answer is, not a lot, but still something. Much of the responsibility here lies higher up the chain of command. It's usually the CEO and board that set the policies for layoffs and companywide compensation. But still there are things you can do to help cultivate your subordinates' commitment. Let's look at them.[24]

FOSTER PEOPLE-FIRST VALUES   Supervisors who have high-commitment employees tend to embrace "people-first values." They trust their employees, believe in respecting their employees as individuals and in treating them fairly, and are committed to their employees' welfare.

BUILD A SENSE OF SHARED FATE AND COMMUNITY   Part of fostering commitment involves making employees feel that "we're all in this together." Harvard University's Rosabeth Moss Kanter found that leaders help do this by *minimizing status differences*.[25] At Toyota's Camry plant in Kentucky, for instance, supervisors and office employees share one large space, with movable cubicles, and supervisors shun status symbols such as executive washrooms. It also helps to encourage *joint effort*, for instance, by getting the team together to solve a production problem.

MAKE IT A CRUSADE   Have you watched films of great football coaches exhorting their teams to win? You'll almost always see them building their case in terms much bigger than the game: Win for our alma mater, or for our injured teammate, or because we've long been at "war" against this other team. They know that committed people need a grand mission to which to be committed, preferably a mission that they feel "is bigger than we are." Employees at organizations like Google thus become soldiers in a crusade. Through their employment, they redefine themselves and their goals in terms of the team's broader mission ("to organize the world's information"). The employee, says Kanter, "finds himself anew in something larger and greater [than himself]." Make your case by framing your appeal in grander terms.

Use Financial Rewards and Profit Sharing   You can't buy someone's commitment, but it's futile to try to get employee commitment with substandard pay. High-commitment firms generally provide above-average pay and incentives. Fight for pay raises and bonuses for your people. Even if your company doesn't have much of an incentive plan, don't miss an opportunity to recognize good efforts.

Encourage Employee Development and Self-Actualization   Even with today's mergers and layoffs, supervisors can show that they're committed to their employees' personal development. Personal development is a powerful need. Psychologist Abraham Maslow emphasized that people's highest need is to self-actualize, "to become . . . everything that one is capable of becoming."[26]

Supervisors can do this in many ways. For example, when appraising employees, ask what their career aspirations are; then try to support them getting the development opportunities (training, and so forth) they need to achieve those aspirations.

At FedEx, one supervisor described his experience as follows: "At Federal Express, the best I can be is what I can be here. I have been allowed to grow with Federal Express. For the people at Federal Express, it's not the money that draws us to the firm. The biggest benefit is that Federal Express made me a man. It gave me the confidence and self-esteem to become the person I had the potential to become."[27] That's how great companies build commitment.

Summary: How Do You Foster Employees' Self-Control?

It is unwise to rely just on traditional controls like close supervision and budgets to keep things "under control." Budgets, financial reports, close supervision—all those traditional control tools—only go so far. Ultimately, you need a balance of traditional and self-control.

You can accomplish this in three ways. *Applying motivation tools* such as those we present in Chapter 4 can help, since motivated employees should perform better. What people do reflects what they value, so *fostering the right values and culture* is another useful method, as we explained in this chapter. Finally, there is much you can do to *build employee commitment*. Committed employees identify with the team's mission. They exercise self-control because their team's missions and goals really are their own. In a sense, they do their jobs "as if they're owners, not just workers." Fostering employee commitment involves creating a workplace setting that,

- Fosters people-first values
- Builds a sense of shared fate and community
- Makes accomplishing the task part of a bigger crusade
- Supplies good rewards and recognition
- Encourages self-actualization

Chapter 5 Concept Review and Reinforcement

Key Terms

Activity-Based Costing (or ABC), p. 134
Audit, p. 132
Balance Sheet, p. 131
Budgets, p. 131
Cash Budget, p. 131
Commitment, p. 142

Concurrent ("yes/no") Control, p. 125
Control, p. 124
Control Systems, p. 124
Controlling, p. 124
Financial Ratios, p. 132
Financial Responsibility Centers, p. 133

Income Statement, p. 131
Operating Budgets, p. 131
Organizational Culture, p. 142
Postaction Controls, p. 126
Principle of Exception, p. 130

Profit Centers, p. 133
Revenue Centers, p. 133
Sales Budget, p. 131
Steering Control, p. 125
Strategic Control Points, p. 127
Variances, p. 132

Review of Key Concepts

Control	**Control** means ensuring that activities are proving the desired results. Basically, controlling means setting a target, measuring performance and comparing to the target, and taking corrective action if necessary.
Timely Controls	Experts distinguish between **steering** controls, **while** it's **happening** controls, and **postaction** controls.
Control Methods	**Traditional control systems** include budgets, performance reports, digital dashboards, ERP systems, policy guidelines, and personal/interactive control systems. **Commitment-based systems** focus on creating the right culture (walk the talk) and fostering employee commitment through your actions.
Budgets	**Budgets** are formal financial expressions of a supervisor's plan. Budgets represent both a control and planning tool.
Activity-Based Costing (or ABC)	**ABC** is a **system** for allocating costs to products or services that takes all of the product's or service's costs into account (including production, marketing, and distribution) in calculating the actual cost of each product or service.
Balanced Scorecard	The **balanced scorecard** is a process for managing employee performance and aligning all employees with key objectives.
Strategy Map	A **strategy map** is a graph that summarizes the cause-and-effect chain of activities that contribute to a company's success.

Digital Dashboard	A **digital dashboard** presents the supervisor with desktop graphs and charts that give a picture of where the department has been and where it is going in terms of each activity in the strategy map.
Enterprise Resource Planning (ERP) Systems	**ERP** is a companywide integrated computer system that is composed of compatible software modules for each of the company's separate departments.
Employee Empowerment	As companies expand worldwide and compete in fast-changing markets, there may be problems in relying on traditional control systems. **Employees** have become more responsive by being more **empowered**, but close controlling can detract from that.
Harmful Employee Reactions	Traditional controls can lead to **unintended**, undesirable, and often harmful employee **reactions** including behavioral displacement, gamesmanship, operating delays, and negative attitudes.
Self-Control	Achieving control today also relies on employees' **self-control**. Motivation techniques, building value systems and fostering commitment are three ways to tap such self-control.

Review and Discussion Questions

1. What is control?
2. Are midterm exams examples of steering, concurrent, or postaction controls? Explain your answer.
3. Explain why a department budget would be of great importance to a supervisor in that department.
4. What is the balanced scorecard, and how can supervisors use it for control?
5. What is the greatest benefit of using a commitment-based control system?
6. Name one advantage and one disadvantage of using a postaction control.
7. Give examples of unintended consequences of controls.
8. Outline a strategy map for a company with which you are familiar.
9. What is enterprise resource planning (ERP) and what important role does it play in control?
10. How does activity-based costing differ from budgeting?
11. Explain how employee commitment has enabled employees to be more responsive on the job. How does employee commitment affect supervisors?

Application and Skill Building

Case Study One

Controlling a Ritz-Carlton

Many consider business hotels as offering a generic service—a safe, clean, comfortable room in a city away from home. Ritz-Carlton Hotel Company views its business differently. Targeting business travelers, conferences, and affluent travelers, the Atlanta-based company manages 25 luxury hotels that pursue the goal of being the very best in each market. Ritz-Carlton succeeded with more than just its guests. For example, it received the U.S. government's Malcolm Baldrige National Quality Award. Given its mission of true excellence in service, what types of control systems did Ritz-Carlton need to achieve its goals?

In the presentation of the Baldrige award, the committee commended Ritz-Carlton for a management program that included participatory leadership, thorough information gathering, coordinated planning and execution, and a trained workforce empowered "to move heaven and earth" to satisfy customers. Of all the elements in the system, Ritz-Carlton management felt their most important control mechanism was committed employees.

The firm trains all employees in the company's "Gold Standards." These set out Ritz-Carlton's service credo and the basics of premium service. The company has translated key product and service requirements into a credo and 20 "Ritz-Carlton Basics." Each employee is to understand and adhere to these standards, which describe processes for solving any problem guests may have.

The corporate motto is "ladies and gentlemen serving ladies and gentlemen." Like many companies, Ritz-Carlton gives new employees an orientation followed by on-the-job training. Unlike other hotel firms, Ritz-Carlton then certifies employees. It reinforces its corporate values continuously by daily employee lineups, frequent recognition for extraordinary achievement, and a performance appraisal based on expectations explained during the orientation, training, and certification processes.

All workers are required to act at the first sign of a problem, regardless of the type of problem or customer complaint. Employees are empowered to do whatever it takes to provide "instant pacification." Other employees must assist if a coworker requests aid in responding to a guest's complaint or wish. There is never an excuse for not solving a customer problem.

Responsibility for ensuring high-quality guest services and accommodations rests largely with employees. All employees are surveyed annually to determine their understanding of quality standards and their personal satisfaction as a Ritz-Carlton employee. In one case, 96% of all employees surveyed singled out excellence in guest services as the key priority.

Discussion Questions

1. Why do you think Ritz-Carlton doesn't just try to control the quality of its service by having supervisors closely supervise employees?
2. Based on what you read in this chapter, list five things Ritz-Carlton does to foster its employees' commitment.

3. How do you think the company's value system fosters employee self-control?
4. List five control-type actions Ritz-Carlton supervisors can take to improve performance in specific areas such as room service, housecleaning, and valet service.

Case Study Two

Control at Carter Cleaning Company

Employee theft is an enormous problem for the Carter Cleaning Company dry cleaner, and one that is not just limited to employees who handle the cash. For example, the cleaner-spotter and/or the presser often open the store themselves, without a supervisor present, to get the day's work started, and it is not unusual to have one or more of these people steal supplies or "run a route." Running a route means that an employee canvasses his or her neighborhood to pick up people's clothes for cleaning and then secretly cleans and presses them in the Carter store, using the company's supplies, gas, and power. It would also not be unusual for an unsupervised person (or his or her supervisor, for that matter) to accept a one-hour rush order for cleaning or laundering, quickly clean and press the item, and return it to the customer for payment without making out a proper ticket for the item posting the sale. The money, of course, goes into the worker's pocket instead of into the cash register.

The more serious problem concerns the store supervisor and the counter workers who actually have to handle the cash. According to Jack Carter, the owner, "You would not believe the creativity employees use to get around the management controls we set up to cut down on employee theft." As one extreme example of this felonious creativity, Jack tells the following story: "To cut down on the amount of money my employees were stealing, I had a small sign painted and placed in front of all our cash registers. The sign said: YOUR ENTIRE ORDER FREE IF WE DON'T GIVE YOU A CASH REGISTER RECEIPT WHEN YOU PAY. CALL 552–0235. It was my intention with this sign to force all our cash-handling employees to place their receipts into the cash register where they would be recorded for my accountants. After all, if all the cash that comes in is recorded in the cash register, then we should have a much better handle on stealing in our stores. Well, one of our counter persons found a diabolical way around this. I came into the store one night and noticed that the cash register this particular person was using just didn't look right, although the sign was placed in front of it. It turned out that every afternoon at about 5:00 p.m. when the other employees left, this character would pull his own cash register out of a box that he hid underneath our supplies. Customers coming in would notice the sign and, of course, the fact that he was meticulous in ringing up every sale. But unknown to them and us, for about five months the sales that came in for about an hour every day went into his cash register, not mine. It took us that long to figure out where our cash for that store was going."

Questions

1. If you were supervising one of these cleaning stores, what controls would you put in place to stop employees from running a route?

2. Mr. Carter's method for controlling the cash register seems to be foolproof, but it obviously didn't work. Why did it fail as a control system, and what would you do to improve or replace his system?
3. Is there anything the store supervisor can do to reduce the incidence of theft, before the employees are formally hired? What would those methods be? Are they examples of steering controls? Why or why not?

Experiential Activities

Activity 1. When tomorrow morning came and went, Benjy walked to Sarah's office to ask where the files were. Sarah had been out sick for two days and was still out. There was no way Benjy could get to the warehouse and back by 1 p.m. He slowly walked to his boss's office to tell him the bad news.

Delegating without Losing Control

Purpose: The purpose of this exercise is to write a summary for a supervisor explaining how to make sure things get done when you delegate tasks to employees.

Required Understanding: You should be thoroughly familiar with the discussion of control tools in this chapter.

How to set up the exercise/Instructions: Divide the class into teams of 4–5 students. Then address these issues:

1. In terms of what we discussed in this chapter, make a list of at least 5 mistakes Benjy made when he lost control of the task he delegated to his assistant.
2. List 5 things that he should have done to make sure the problem did not arise.
3. If you were Benjy, how would you handle the situation with your own supervisor now?

Activity 2. College students deal with professors all the time, but may not realize how difficult it is for the college's administrators to control what their faculties are doing. The typical professor has a number of responsibilities, including teaching classes, writing research articles, and attending curriculum-development committee meetings. Furthermore, the dean also wants to make sure faculty members are conducting themselves professionally—for instance, in terms of how they interact with their students. Knowing that you are a supervisory expert, the dean has asked you to develop a control package for a college of business professors. The package is to include, at a minimum, a list of the things that you want to control and a corresponding list showing how you plan to control them. In teams of four or five students, develop a package for the dean.

Activity 3. Based on what you learned in this chapter, meet with a team of four or five of your fellow students; then write a one-page document listing what the U.S. Transportation Safety Administration should do to improve safety inspections at U.S. airports.

Activity 4. There is nothing quite like eating in a restaurant where things—from customer service to hygiene—are out of control. Before coming to class, visit one or two local restaurants and make a list of the things you see that might suggest that things are a bit out of control. Then meet in teams of 4–5 students, compare notes, and create a checklist for assessing the adequacy of a restaurant's control mechanisms. If time permits and if there is an on-campus cafeteria, use your checklist to evaluate the school eating place's controls.

Role-Playing Exercise

The Falsified Sales Reports: The Situation

The sales supervisor of the city furniture manufacturing company just completed a two-week trip of auditing customer accounts and prospective accounts in the south-eastern states. The supervisor's primary intention was to do follow-up work on prospective accounts contacted by the sales staff members during the past six months. Prospective clients were usually furniture dealers or large department stores with furniture departments.

To the supervisor's amazement, she discovered that almost all the so-called prospective accounts your people listed were fictitious. The salespeople had obviously turned in falsely documented field reports and expense statements. Company salespeople had actually called upon only three of the 22 reported furniture stores or department stores. The supervisor confirmed that not one salesperson had a clean record.

The supervisor decided that immediate action was mandatory. Angry as the supervisor is, this person would prefer firing them all. But the supervisor is responsible for sales and realizes that replacing the staff would seriously cripple the sales program for the coming year. The supervisor is about to walk into an appointment with the salesperson who falsified the most call reports.

Instructions

All students should read **the situation** above.

One student will play the role of sales supervisor, and a second student will play the role of the salesperson.

Each student should *only read his or her assigned role* below. Then the two students should engage in a 15-minute conversation.

After the 15-minute role play has ended, the class (including the two role-playing students) should read and address the **questions** at the end of this exercise.

Role for the Supervisor

You have had it. All your salespeople have been lying to you, and now your own manager is going to know that your department is out of control. One problem you face is what to do with the salespeople. Another is how to get sales up so you will meet your quota. You have to find out what happened, and you need to figure out a way to make sure it does not happen again.

Role for the Salesperson

You are a little embarrassed that your supervisor discovered the falsified reports, but after all, everyone has been doing the same thing for years, so what's the big fuss? Besides, you've hit your actual sales targets for the past two years, so what is the difference how many customers you actually get to meet? Frankly, if you had to spend the time the supervisor expects calling on all these prospective customers, you're not sure you'd have the time to call on the big stores that actually produce most of your sales.

Questions for Class Discussion

1. Based on what you read in this chapter, did the supervisor do a good job diagnosing what the issue is and taking corrective action? Why or why not?
2. In what way(s) was the salesperson's reactions in the role play typical of what you'd expect an employee to do in such a situation?
3. If you were the supervisor, what would you do now with this salesperson?
4. What would you do to improve your control system?

6 Organizing Jobs and Work

CHAPTER OBJECTIVES

After studying this chapter, you should be able to answer these questions:

1. What Is Organizing?
2. What Is Departmentalization?
3. How Do Supervisors Coordinate Work Activities?
4. How Do Authority, Delegation, and Other Factors Affect the Organization of Activities?
5. What Are the Steps in Developing Job Descriptions?

OPENING SNAPSHOT
You'd Better Get Your People Organized

Meg was delighted to finally be promoted to comptroller/accounting supervisor for Andean Research LLC, a 90-person company that solved pollution control problems for client companies. With a CPA degree and four years' experience as an accountant at Andean, she was well qualified for the job, and she looked forward to her first day as a supervisor. Andean's founder and owner had dismissed Meg's predecessor, the previous comptroller, allegedly due to an excessive number of errors emanating from that department. Meg was sure she'd do better. Four people reported to Meg in her new position: an accountant/internal auditor, and accounting clerks for accounts payable, for accounts receivable, and for payroll. About one month into her new job, she was astonished when the president entered her office to tell her that the payroll reports for the past two months were entirely wrong. Apparently, whoever was supposed to compare the IRS reports to the actual payroll data from ADP, the company's payroll vendor, wasn't doing his job. The issue had serious implications for a variety of matters, including the accuracy of the employment taxes that Andean had been withholding. Meg was mortified. How could the payroll clerk not know that he had to do this? "You'd better get your people organized," said the president as he stormed out.

1. What Is Organizing?

An *organization* consists of people with formally assigned roles who work together to achieve stated goals. *Organizing* means identifying the jobs to be done, establishing departments, delegating or pushing authority down to subordinates, establishing a chain of command (in other words, channels of authority and communication), and coordinating the work of subordinates. Organizing is something supervisors often overlook. Many people (like Meg) seem to think that clarifying who does what and who reports to whom is so elementary that it just takes care of itself. Nothing could be further from the truth. In this chapter we'll look at what supervisors must know about how to organize.

Job Descriptions

If you think your company's organization is something over which you don't have much control, you're partly right. Top management usually lays out the company's grand design. They work with middle managers to organize the company's main divisions and departments, and to decide who will report to whom.

With respect to organizing, the first-line supervisor's main aim is to make sure that each worker knows what to do. The traditional way to do this is with a job description. **Job descriptions** list exactly what each employee does, including duties, responsibilities, and working conditions. As we said, an organization consists of people with formally assigned roles who work together to achieve stated goals. The job description should show the employee what his or her role is. Ensuring that each subordinate knows what he or she is supposed to do is probably the single most fundamental duty a supervisor has.

Departmental Organization Charts

However, before ensuring that each subordinate knows what he or she is supposed to do, someone must lay out the big picture, showing (for the company) who reports to whom, and what everyone's job title is. The usual way of doing this is with an **organization chart**. This shows the "structure" of the organization—specifically, the *title* of each supervisor's position and, by means of connecting lines, *who is accountable to whom*, who has **authority** for each area, and which people are expected to routinely *communicate* with each other. (You'll find an example in Figure 6.1). The organization chart also shows the *chain of command* (sometimes called the scalar chain or the line of authority) between the top of the organization and the lowest positions in the chart. The **chain of command** represents the organization's hierarchy of authority. It shows the path an order should take in traveling from the president to first-line supervisors and employees at the bottom of the organization chart, or the path a comment should take in traveling from employees at the bottom to the president at the top.

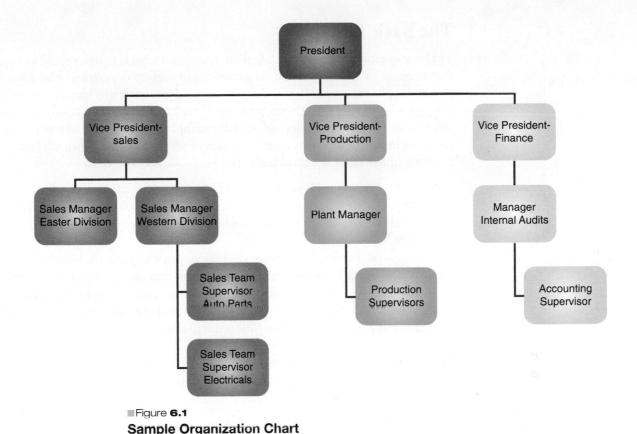

■Figure **6.1**

Sample Organization Chart

One thing the organization chart does not show is the **informal organization**. This is the informal, habitual contacts, communications, and ways of doing things employees develop. Thus, a salesperson might call the plant supervisor directly to check the status of an order. The formal route—asking her sales supervisor, who in turn asks the plant supervisor—may simply take too long.

Again, most first-line supervisors won't be too involved in drawing up organization charts for the company as a whole or for creating departments. However, you should know how it's done so you will better understand the context for your employees' jobs and be able to write job descriptions for them. We'll therefore address organizing basics next.

2. Creating Departments

What Is Departmentalization?

Every enterprise must engage in particular activities in order to accomplish its goals. In a company, these activities include manufacturing, sales, and accounting. In a hospital, they include nursing, medical services, and radiology. **Departmentalization** is the process through which managers group the enterprise's activities together and assign them to subordinates; it is the organizationwide division of work. (The groupings of activities go by names like department, division, unit, section, or some other similar term.)

The Basic Question

The basic question in departmentalization is, "Around what activities should we organize departments?" For example, should a travel agency set up departments for sales, ticket purchasing, finance, and HR? Or should it set up departments to handle trips to different places, such as Europe, Asia, and the United States? In a company, should you organize departments for sales and manufacturing? Or should there be separate departments for industrial and retail customers, each of which then has its own sales and manufacturing units? There are three basic choices.

THREE BASIC CHOICES   In the old Russell Crowe movie *Gladiator*, each Roman legion, consisting of about 6,000 soldiers, was managed by about 60 *centurions*, each of whom managed about 100 soldiers. Armies and some other enterprises still organize, as did the Roman legions, by *simple numbers*.

In general, however, supervisors use this approach sparingly. Most business tasks (such as sales or HR) require specialized efforts, so organizing a company just in terms of numbers wouldn't make much sense. Furthermore, using simple numbers to divide up the work usually makes sense only at the bottom of the chain of command (as when dividing up the soldiers). It makes little sense to organize departments just in terms of numbers. Supervisors therefore have two realistic choices when it comes to dividing up the company's work into departments. They can organize departments around *functions*. Or, they can organize departments around the end-user *products, customers, or geographic areas* the company serves.

- **Functional Organization** For example, the editor-in-chief of a newspaper can appoint *functional* department heads (editors) for editing, production, and sales. Working under the editor-in-chief, this team publishes all the paper's issues.

- **Product, Customer, or Geographic Organization** Or, the editor-in-chief can appoint editors to be in charge of *end-user units*. For instance, he or she could appoint editors for each of the paper's four editions—East, West, North, and South. Each edition's supervisor would then have, within his or her department, their own editorial, production, and sales editors. Each edition's department here would focus on its own (East, West, North, and South) end users. Each edition's supervisor would control most of the activities (editing, production, sales) for getting his or her edition out.

The decision on how to organize departments depends more on experience, logic, and common sense than on a scientific formula. However, we will explain some rules that supervisors use. Let's start with *functional organization*.

Creating Functional Departments

Functional departmentalization means grouping activities around functions such as manufacturing, sales, and finance. The supervisor puts subordinates in charge of each of these functions. Figure 6.2 shows the organizational chart for the ABC Car Company. At ABC, management organized each department around a different business function, in this case, sales, finance, and production. Here, the production director reports to the president and manages ABC's production plants. Other directors carry out the sales and finance functions.

Functional Departmentalization

This chart shows business *functional* organizations, with departments for basic functions such as finance, sales, and production.

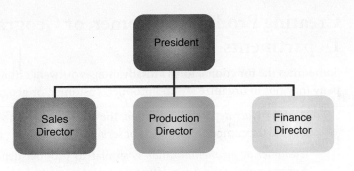

This is a simple and obvious way to organize. In fact, regardless of how the company organizes (by functions or by self-contained units), someone must perform these functions if the firm is to get its work done.

Companies organize departments around business and managerial functions. The *business functions* are those the enterprise must engage in to survive. A manufacturing company's business functions include production, sales, and finance. Banks have business function departments for operations, control, and loans. Starbucks needs business function supervisors for purchasing and sales.

Some companies organize by *managerial functions.* This means putting supervisors in charge of managerial functions such as planning, control, and administration.

ADVANTAGES   Organizing by functions has several advantages.

1. *It is simple and logical.* The enterprise must somehow carry out these functions to survive.

2. *It can promote efficiency.* For example, there is one production department for all the company's products, rather than separate ones for each product.

3. *It can simplify supervisory hiring and training.* The supervisors running these departments have specialized jobs (sales supervisor, for instance). It can be easier to find good specialist supervisors than supervisors with the breadth of experience to manage several functions at once.

DISADVANTAGES   Organizing by function also has disadvantages. For example,

1. *It increases the coordination workload for the top manager.* With separate departments for functions like sales and manufacturing, the CEO may be the only one in a position to coordinate the work of the functional departments. This may not be a problem in a small business. But as size and diversity of products increase, the job of coordinating production, sales, and finance decisions for many different products or markets may prove to be too much for one person.

2. *It may reduce the firm's sensitivity to and service to the customer.* For example, suppose JC Penney organized nationally around the functions of merchandising, purchasing, and personnel. Then all of its U.S. stores might tend to get the same merchandise to sell, even if customers' tastes in Chicago were different from those in El Paso.

Creating Product, Customer, or Geographic Departments

Sometimes the functional form's disadvantages outweigh its advantages. If so, the company may opt to organize around product, customer, or geographic departments.

- With *product departmentalization*, the company organizes the main departments around the company's products or services (such as Chevrolet, Buick, and Cadillac).
- *Customer departmentalization* is similar to product departmentalization, but the company organizes around its main customer sectors (such as retail and industrial).
- With *geographic (or territorial) departmentalization*, a company such as JC Penney sets up departments for each of the territories in which the company does business. Each territory gets its own management team, often with its own merchandising, sales, and personnel activities.

Figure 6.3 illustrates product departmentalization. Here, a pharmaceuticals company organized its top-level departments so that each contains all the activities required to develop, manufacture, and sell *a particular product* (skin care, vitamins, or drugs). The head of each division then has functional departments—for production, sales, and development—reporting to him or her. Kodak reorganized this way. Their structure consists of five product-business units. Each division focuses on a product line such as cameras.

Supervisors sometimes refer to product-based departments as **divisions** (as in "the Buick Division") and to companies organized around products as **divisional organizations**. *Divisionalization* means the firm's major departments are organized to serve end users in such a way that the heads of the divisions manage all (or most of) the activities needed to develop, manufacture, and sell a particular product or product line. Thus GM has divisions for Chevrolet, Buick, and Cadillac. Each division's general manager tends to have oversight over most of the sales, production, and development activities for his or her division. (Divisionalized companies are also usually *decentralized*, as we will see later in this chapter.)

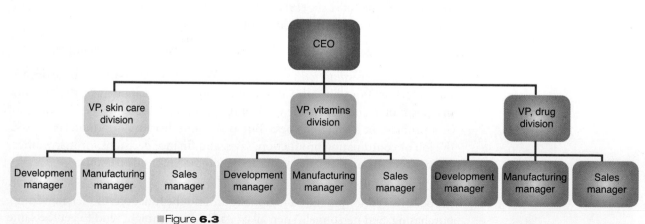

■Figure **6.3**

Product Departmentalization/Divisional Organization for Pharmaceuticals Company

What are some of the advantages and disadvantages of the product/customer/geographic division approach?

ADVANTAGES   Organizing around products, customers, or territories has several advantages.

1. *Each product (or customer, or geographic region) gets the undivided attention of its own general manager, and so its customers may get better, more responsive service.*

2. *It's easier to judge performance.* If a product (or customer or geographic) department is (or is not) doing well, it is clear who is responsible, because one general manager is managing the whole thing, including its sales, production, and HR functions.

DISADVANTAGES   The disadvantages include the following:

1. *It means duplication of effort.* For example, each product department (Chevrolet, Buick, Cadillac) may have its own production plants, sales force, and so on.

2. *It requires more managers with general management abilities.* Each department is, in a sense, a miniature company, with its own production plant, sales force, personnel department, and so forth. This means these firms must develop managers with general management potential.

Organizing in Action: Rosenbluth International

Sometimes, organizing doesn't follow obvious rules. For example, before being acquired by American Express, Rosenbluth International was a fast-growing, 1,000-office global travel agency. However, the way it's organized grew out of what CEO Hal Rosenbluth learned on a cattle farm.

Standing on a field in rural North Dakota one day, Rosenbluth made a discovery. "The family farm is the most efficient type of unit I've ever run across, because everybody on the farm has to be fully functional and multifaceted." He decided to create an organization structure that would get all his employees involved in helping to run the company.

How he ended up organizing also shows how managers usually combine several types of departments—functional and end user, for instance. In his case, Rosenbluth broke his company into more than 100 geographic units, (which he called "farms"), each serving clients in specific regions. Corporate headquarters then became what Rosenbluth calls "farm towns." Here central functional "stores" (departments) such as human resources and accounting are available for all the regional "farms" to use. The firm's computerized Global Distribution Network links each of its travel agents to the company's computers in Philadelphia. This helps to ensure that clients with offices in several different geographic regions get coordinated assistance from Rosenbluth travel agents.[1]

How Supervisors Coordinate Work Activities

It does a company little good to have a sales supervisor sell a big order that's to be delivered May 4, if the production department can't produce it until June 8. The moral is that, when work has been divided among employees or business units, it needs to be *coordinated*. **Coordination** is the process of achieving unity of action among interdependent activities. It is required whenever two or more interdependent individuals, groups, or departments (such as sales and production) must work together to achieve a common goal (such as getting the order to the customer by May 4). When America's president says that a potential terror attack almost occurred because the various security departments "didn't connect all the dots," he means that there was inadequate coordination.

HOW TO COORDINATE ACTIVITIES   All supervisors use several basic ways to make sure the work of their subordinates is coordinated.[2] _Direct supervision_ means that when questions arise, subordinates bring the problem to the supervisor. Thus the sales supervisor and production supervisor may take their scheduling problem up the chain of command to the president. _Interpersonal_ coordination means you achieve coordination by relying on face-to-face interpersonal interaction. In simple situations (such as two people lifting a log), you might achieve coordination by having one person count, "one, two, three, lift." (Similarly, our sales supervisor should have checked with production before signing the order for May 4.) Many supervisors appoint _committees_ to coordinate things. For example, interdepartmental committees meet periodically to discuss common problems and ensure interdepartmental coordination. You can also achieve coordination by setting _specific goals_. For example, tell Mike and Marie that the projects they are working on must be finished by, say, February 8. Then if they both achieve their goals, you can combine their projects into the final product on time.

Project Management

Particularly when big projects are involved, coordinating the work of dozens or hundreds of suppliers and contractors can be overwhelming.

That is why many companies use Web-based project coordination software. For example, such software helps construction companies that are managing jobs to coordinate all the hundreds or thousands of parties involved. By using the Internet and a laptop, everyone involved in the project—from owners and architects to contractors and subcontractors—receives instantaneous updates regarding design changes and construction status. That way, any of the parties in the project need only to click on their laptops to see the project's status and to know when their activity is scheduled to start and end. The _easyprojects_ project management tool at http://www.easyprojects.net/ provides one example. The accompanying screen-grab in Figure 6.4 illustrates the information such programs provide.

A Modern Look at the Principles of Organizing

The question of how to organize has long been associated with a management expert who lived and wrote more than 100 years ago. Henri Fayol, an executive of a French iron and steel firm, memorialized a lifetime of supervisory experience in his "14 Principles." To this day, when most people think of organizing, several of Fayol's principles invariably pop to mind (although most people probably don't associate them with a Frenchman from 100 years ago!).[3] For example, when someone tells you to "stick to the chain of command" the person is quoting (whether he or she knows it or not) Fayol's "Scalar Chain Principle." This basically says that authority, orders, and communication should follow a clear and unbroken chain from the top to the bottom of the organization.

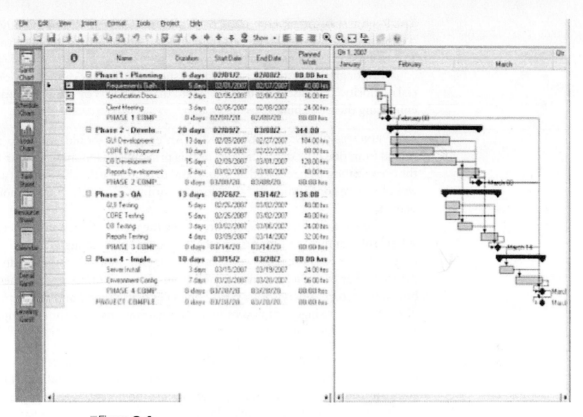

■Figure **6.4**

Sample Report from Project Management Software Program

Source: http://online-project-management-software-review.toptenreviews.com/48141-tenrox-project-managementsoftware1-screenshot.html, accessed April, 2010.

Fayol had worked his way up from supervisor to top executive, and so he was not some pie-in-the-sky theoretician. He knew there were exceptions to all his principles, and that, for instance, there might be times when (perhaps in an emergency) you should not stick to the chain of command. However, Fayol also believed that supervisors needed certain rules they could apply to situations they faced every day, and so his 14 principles were born. Today's supervisors need to apply Fayol's principles in light of the new challenges they face, but his principles—particularly the five pertaining to how to organize—still provide useful rules of thumb for today's supervisors.

THE PRINCIPLE OF DIVISION OF WORK   This principle capitalizes on the idea that practice makes perfect. It says to give each worker a specific task that he or she can specialize in, and let the person do it repeatedly. The assumption (often true at the time and still sometimes true today) is that a specialized division of work leads to more productivity per employee, and thus more efficiency.

Of course, as time went by, supervisors discovered the drawbacks of highly specialized jobs. For many workers, stripping out the variety and responsibility from a job leads to boredom and negativism. Increasingly today, supervisors need to be willing to sacrifice some of specialization's efficiency to gain more motivation and commitment.

THE PRINCIPLE OF AUTHORITY AND RESPONSIBILITY Supervisors need authority that is commensurate with their responsibilities, and the company should have safeguards against supervisors abusing their authority.

Although this is still very true today, supervisors today cannot rely on their official authority. They also need to supplement that authority by acting like leaders and by enhancing their coaching skills.

THE PRINCIPLE OF UNITY OF COMMAND An employee should report to and receive orders from one boss only. The idea of this principle was to make it clear throughout the organization who reported to whom, and to minimize the chances that an employee would receive conflicting (and therefore confusing) instructions from more than one person.

There is a wealth of research supporting the idea that many employees do indeed suffer "role conflict" and confusion when faced with conflicting orders from, say, their boss and their boss's boss. However, modern organizations increasingly do violate this principle. For example, in some organizations, it is not unusual for someone to have both a functional supervisor (say, from the sales department) and also a project supervisor. Not surprisingly, employees in such organizations sometimes complain of role conflict and confusion.

THE PRINCIPLE OF CENTRALIZATION The organization must balance the extent to which decisions are centralized versus decentralized. If they are too centralized, it may take the company too long to make a decision. If they are too decentralized, employees lower in the chain of command may make decisions that are at odds with what is best for the company as a whole.

The need for balancing centralization and decentralization is as important today as in Fayol's time. Overall, the trend has been toward flattening the chain of command (by eliminating levels of middle managers), and toward letting more decisions get made lower down. This has the advantage of letting people who are closer to the customer make quicker decisions, an important consideration in today's competitive business environment.

THE PRINCIPLE OF SCALAR CHAIN Authority, orders, and communication should follow a clear and unbroken vertical chain from the top to the bottom of the organization. Fayol believed that it should be clear who reports to whom, who is the boss of whom, and who has authority for what. However, having said that, Fayol also said that occasions would arise when an employee should not adhere to the chain of command—such as in an emergency. He even went so far as to propose a "bridge" that one supervisor could use (if need be) to violate the chain of command and reach a supervisor in another department.

In Fayol's day, such exceptions were probably rare. Today, with more work done by teams and more teams working on multiteam projects, it's not unusual to have more of a "network" approach with much cross-communication, rather than simple vertical communications. We'll look more closely at the issue of authority next.

One principle Fayol did not address is the fact that how you organize has a big influence on what supervisory leadership style is best. The accompanying Leadership Applications for Supervisors feature explains the important role that leadership plays in organizing.

Adapting Your Instrumental Leadership Style to the Task

One of the most persistent issues supervisors face concerns the degree to which they need to closely supervise what their subordinates are doing. Although "closely supervising" someone tends to conjure up negative connotations, the fact is that if employees don't know what they're doing or how to do it, there may be no alternative for the supervisor than to stand there, watching over their shoulders, giving them instructions.

As we explained in Chapter 2, leadership experts use the term initiating structure (or instrumental leadership) to describe the sorts of day-to-day structuring activities that supervisors use to ensure that their subordinates are doing their jobs correctly. Initiating structure leadership behaviors include activities such as defining and structuring your own and your subordinates' roles in terms of things such as criticizing poor work, emphasizing why it's important to meet deadlines, defining standards of performance, asking subordinates to follow standard procedures, offering new approaches to problems, and coordinating subordinates' activities.[4]

Yet we've also seen that there are tasks that as a rule render unnecessary leadership behaviors such as these (recall "substitutes for leadership theory" from Chapter 2). For example, the more specialized and repetitive task is—the more the subordinate does the same short-cycle job over and over many times a day—the more the leader can step back a bit, because the job itself provides the structure required to keep things going smoothly. Similarly, "when the task provides automatic feedback on how well the work is being performed, the leader does not need to provide much feedback."[5]

On the other hand, while very specialized jobs like these may not require as much leader initiating structure, that doesn't mean the leader can just go to lunch. Many employees find jobs like these particularly boring and unsatisfying, and so they particularly covet and benefit from considerate and supportive leadership behaviors. The point is, think of your actions as substitutes and supplements to the job: If the job is very routine, back off a bit, and if it's exceptionally boring, think about providing an extra pint of support.

3. Understanding Authority and the Chain of Command

So far we have skirted an important organizing issue. Assigning jobs to subordinates assumes you give them the authority to do their jobs. We should therefore look more closely at what authority means and how supervisors authorize subordinates to take action.

What Is Authority?

How Do Authority, Delegation, and Other Factors Affect the Organization of Activities?

Authority means a person's legal right or power to take action, to make decisions, and to direct the work of others. In a corporation, authority stems from the owner/stockholders of the company. They elect a board of directors and authorize the board to represent the owners' interests. The owners, through the board, are at the top of the chain of command. The board's main functions are to choose the top executives, to approve strategies and long-term plans, and to monitor performance to make sure management is protecting the owners' interests. The board and its chairperson then *delegates* or passes down to the CEO the authority to actually run the company—to develop plans, to hire subordinate supervisors, and to enter into agreements. The CEO in turn delegates to or authorizes his or her subordinates to do their jobs. This is how an organization chart and chain of command evolve.

Line and Staff Authority

Companies distinguish between "line authority" and "staff authority." Line and staff authority simply denote different types of relationships. **Line authority** gives the supervisor the right (or authority) to *issues orders* to other supervisors or employees. It creates a superior-subordinate relationship. **Staff authority** gives the supervisor the right (authority) to *advise* other supervisors or employees. It creates an advisory relationship. **Line managers** have line authority. **Staff managers** have staff authority. The latter generally cannot issue orders down the chain of command (except in their own departments).

In popular usage, people associate line managers with managing functions (such as sales or production) that are essential for the company to exist. Staff managers run functions that are generally advisory or supportive, such as purchasing, legal, human resource management, and quality control. This line-staff distinction makes sense as long as the "staff" department is in fact advisory. But in some companies, quality control, for instance, is so important that it is a line function, and it directs how other departments control the quality of their activities. So, strictly speaking, it is not the type of department the person is in charge or its name that determines if the manager in charge is line or staff. It is the nature of the relationship. The line manager can issue orders. The staff manager can advise.

There is one exception. A staff manager may also have functional authority. **Functional authority** means the person can issue orders down the chain of command within the very narrow limits of his or her functional authority. For example, to protect the company from discrimination claims, the president might order that no screening tests be administered without first getting the HR supervisor's approval. The HR supervisor then has functional authority over personnel testing. He or she might order the production supervisor to use (or not use) a particular test. (The HR supervisor would probably want to be diplomatic, however, lest line-staff conflict emerge).

Some small organizations use only line managers (they are line organizations), but most larger ones have staff managers too—these are thus *line and staff organizations*. Typical line positions include the CEO and the supervisors for sales and production. Typical staff positions include the supervisors for marketing research, accounting, security, quality control, legal affairs, and HR.

LINE-STAFF CONFLICT   In organizations, employees sometimes put their own aims above the company's. Time they could have used productively evaporates, as employees hide information and jockey for position. **Line-staff conflict** is a typical example. Such conflict might result when line supervisors feel staff supervisors are encroaching on their prerogatives, or when "staff" feels "line" is resisting its good advice. Diplomacy, courtesy, and common sense hopefully head off such conflict before it gets out of hand. Otherwise, someone higher in the chain of command may have to intercede.

What Are the Sources of a Supervisor's Authority?

In corporations, as we said, authority stems from the owner-stockholders. They pass down (or delegate) authority first to the board of directors and then to the CEO.

This is how the chain of command (or hierarchy of authority) evolves. Strictly speaking, authority therefore flows down from the top and depends on a person's **rank or position**. The president of software manufacturer Intuit has more authority based on rank than does one of his senior vice presidents, and so on down to each supervisor.

However, you probably already know that rank alone rarely determines how much authority a person really has. At worst, some supervisors can't scrape together even an ounce of the authority to issue orders that their positions would seem to merit. There are other sources of authority.

PERSONAL TRAITS   Some people also have authority because of *personal traits*, such as intelligence or charisma. People follow the instructions of such individuals because of the power of their personalities. Where such authority comes from is hard to say, since for many leaders it's just part of their psyches. However, there are some commonsense things a supervisor can do to enhance personal trait authority. Maintain a certain detachment. Act like a leader. Treat subordinates fairly and honestly. Use decision-making guidelines like those in Chapter 3 to exercise good judgment.

EXPERTS   Others have authority because they are *experts* in an area or have knowledge that requires others to depend on them.

REWARDS   A supervisor's ability to influence subordinates is generally proportionate to his or her ability to control their rewards and punishment. For most supervisors, their authority to appraise, assign, and recommend for a raise, promotion, demotion, or dismissal is a powerful source of their overall ability to influence their subordinates. Supervisors need to use this authority wisely. Unfair actions are often the first step in a supervisor's downfall.

ACCEPTANCE   Some astute management writers argue that, regardless of source, authority always depends on subordinates' *acceptance* of supervisors' orders. Theorist Chester Barnard was an early proponent of this view. He argued that for orders to be carried out, they must lie within a subordinate's "zone of acceptance"—in other words, they must be viewed as acceptable. Experts often argue that getting employees' acceptance is increasingly important today, given the emphasis on empowered workers and team-based organizations.

A supervisor's authority is not always what it seems. One executive began a speech with the following story:

> A young and enthusiastic lion, straight out of lion school, was hired by a circus. After his first day on the job, the trainer gave the lion, not a bowl of meat, but a bunch of bananas. The young lion stormed over to the ringmaster and said, "I'm the lion. What are you doing feeding me bananas?" "Well, the problem is," the ringmaster said, "our senior lion is still around, so you're down on the organization chart as a monkey."

The point is that one's authority isn't always what it appears to be, based on the company's organization chart. One thing the organization chart does not show is the real authority some people (or lions have), based on their experience, expertise, or acceptance.

Guidelines for Delegating Authority

We've seen that organizing would be impossible without delegation, which is the pushing down of authority from supervisor to subordinate. The assignment of responsibility for some department or job traditionally goes hand in hand with the delegation of authority to get the job done. It would be inappropriate, for example, to assign a subordinate the responsibility for designing a new product, and then deny him or her the authority to hire the necessary designers to get the job done.

A well-known management saying is, "You can delegate authority, but you cannot delegate responsibility." The president can delegate sales duties to the sales supervisor, but the president is still ultimately responsible for what occurs on his or her watch. Similarly, any supervisor is ultimately responsible for ensuring that the job he or she is in charge of gets done properly. Because the person doing the delegating always retains the ultimate responsibility, delegation of authority always entails the creation of *accountability*. Subordinates become accountable—or answerable—to the supervisor for the performance of the tasks assigned to them, particularly if things go wrong. The boss may fire or discipline the subordinate who fails to do the job. However, the boss is still responsible for all that goes wrong (or right) in the department.

Supervisors get things done through others, and so knowing how to delegate is a crucial supervisory skill. Principles for delegating include the following:[6]

CLARIFY THE ASSIGNMENT   Make it clear what you want the subordinate to accomplish, the results expected, and by when you want those results. Frequently, when employees don't perform up to par, it is not because they're not motivated, but because they're not sure what you expect of them.

DELEGATE, DON'T ABDICATE   Never delegate without thinking through how you are going to monitor the results. Just giving a person a job to do but not following up is abdication, not delegation.

KNOW WHAT TO DELEGATE   Larry Bossidy, the executive who turned AlliedSignal around and helped it merge with Honeywell, says there is "one job no CEO should delegate—finding and developing great leaders."[7]

In Bossidy's case, finding and developing great leaders was "the job no CEO should delegate." For a supervisor at a different level, there will be other tasks that he or she cannot (or should not) delegate to someone else. Knowing what you shouldn't delegate is an art, but there are some commonsense examples. As a supervisor, you shouldn't delegate the job of reviewing your team's daily or weekly performance reports, for instance. Nor would you want to delegate to someone else the job of disciplining one of your direct reports.

SPECIFY THE SUBORDINATE'S RANGE OF DISCRETION   When you delegate authority to someone, he or she should understand what the limits of his or her authority are. You don't want the employee overstepping his or her authority, for instance, by obligating your team to incur an excessive expense.

A supervisor can use two guidelines here. *First*, give the employee enough authority to do the task successfully, but not so much that the person's actions can have adverse effects outside the areas for which you have made the person responsible. For example, delegate the authority to spend what's necessary to get the job done, but not so much that he or she could exceed your departmental budget.

Second, make sure your employee knows when to check with you if there's any question. You will find that some subordinates have a well-honed sense of when to ask and when to just proceed. For others, a typical range for giving someone a guideline here is: (1) "Wait to be told what to do before doing anything"; (2) "ask what to do if you're not sure"; (3) "recommend, then take action if you can't reach me"; (4), "act, then report results immediately"; and (5) "take action, and report only after the fact."

AUTHORITY SHOULD EQUAL RESPONSIBILITY   A basic principle of management (remember Henri Fayol?) is that "authority should equal responsibility." The person should have enough authority to accomplish the task.

MAKE THE PERSON ACCOUNTABLE FOR RESULTS   Make it clear to the employee that he or she is accountable to you for results. This means that there must be predictable and acceptable measures of results.

BEWARE OF BACKWARD DELEGATION   A famous *Harvard Business Review* article was titled "Management Time: Who's Got the Monkey?" It explains what happens to an unsuspecting supervisor whose subordinate comes into his office to discuss a problem. The subordinate says, "I have a problem with the job you gave me to do." After a few minutes of discussion, the supervisor, pressed for time, says, "I'll handle it." Like a monkey, the job has jumped from the subordinate's to the unsuspecting supervisor's shoulder.

The point is this: Beware of backward delegation. When your employee says the task isn't working out as planned, you have several good options. You can suggest some solutions or insist that your subordinate take the initiative in solving the problem. Do not carelessly let the task you delegated bounce back to you. The following leadership feature focuses in on how to delegate to "virtual" employees.

Leadership Applications for Supervisors

Leading Virtual Teams

With more and more employees working from home, getting work done through virtual teams is increasingly popular. A virtual team *is a group of geographically dispersed employees who use information technology tools such as e-mail and video conferencing to work together to carry out some project. Their meetings and interactions are "virtual," rather than face to face.*

It's likely that at some point you'll find yourself supervising a virtual team. Leading such a team is obviously a bit tricky. For example, suppose you have to discipline someone. In the movie Up in the Air, George Clooney plays a consultant who flies around the country firing employees, until his boss decides the job can be done remotely via video conferencing. They soon discover that the drawbacks of such impersonality far outweigh the money they save on air fare.

Leading virtual teams raises some other special questions, too. For example, how do virtual team leaders go about delegating authority to subordinates whom they may never meet (or, for that matter, see)? One recent study looked at that question, and it came to two conclusions. First, the study found that virtual team leaders delegate more to competent virtual teams. So if your virtual team isn't doing too well, do not assume that the problem is "lack of authority." Get them up to speed first. The more competent teams were the ones that got more authority. Second, delegation in virtual teams correlated positively with team member satisfaction with their leader and with team member motivation.[8] So, if your team colleagues seem up to the task, then giving them more authority should yield benefits in terms of improved motivation and morale.

The Meaning of "Decentralized"

During your supervisory career, you will frequently hear the phrase "decentralized organization." A **decentralized organization** is one in which (1) authority for most decisions (sales, production, and HR, for instance) is delegated down to the department heads, while (2) control for major companywide decisions is maintained at the headquarters office. "Decentralized divisions" therefore tend to have broad authority for managing all the functions (sales, production, and so on) required to serve their end users. The company is literally decentralized, insofar as the divisions' head managers tend to have authority over all or most of the decisions (sales, and so forth) necessary to serve the divisions' customers. Companies organized around product divisions are usually also decentralized, and many business people use the terms "divisionalized" and "decentralized" interchangeably. Decentralizing is usually a top management issue.

"Decentralize" is not the same as "delegate." Delegate simply means pushing down authority from supervisor to subordinate. In contrast, *decentralizing* should always represent a shrewd balance between delegated authority and top management's centralized control of essential functions. On the one hand, department heads and supervisors get the autonomy and resources they need to service local customers. On the other hand, headquarters maintains the control it needs by centralizing major decisions regarding things like capital appropriations, incoming cash receipts, and setting profitability goals. Thus Ford may decentralize most Ford car sales and manufacturing decisions to the Ford car division head, but will insist that the payments for the cars go directly to Ford corporate headquarters.

ANDERSEN AND ENRON EXAMPLE   Enron Corporation was an energy trading company based in Houston, Texas. Possibly because Enron was a valued client, the CPA firm Arthur Andersen's Houston office wanted to let Enron account for some transactions in a way that would show higher sales for Enron. Arthur Andersen's parent in Chicago, Andersen Worldwide, was decentralized. It believed in delegating a great deal of auditing authority to its local office supervisors. However, Andersen Worldwide had a special, *centralized* Professional Standards Group (PSG) at its Chicago headquarters. Its job was to ride herd on what local Andersen supervisors were doing. In this case, Anderson's PSG apparently told local Houston Andersen supervisors *not* to use the questionable approach. It appears someone at Andersen Houston may have approved the transaction anyway, with disastrous results.

Andersen Worldwide had decentralized most decisions to its branches, with the understanding that the branches would abide by the PSG's centralized oversight and control. In this case, those controls may not have been adequate. Local Andersen supervisors overrode the PSG's decision.[9] Enron collapsed, taking Andersen Worldwide with it.

Tall and Flat Organizations and the Span of Control

Delegating authority results in a chain of command. Traditionally, that chain or hierarchy may be "flat" or "tall." We look at this next.

THE SPAN OF CONTROL   The **span of control** is the number of subordinates reporting directly to a supervisor. In the organization shown in Figure 6.5, the span of control of the country general manager is 10: There are 8 business managers, 1 innovation supervisor, and 1 manufacturing supervisor.

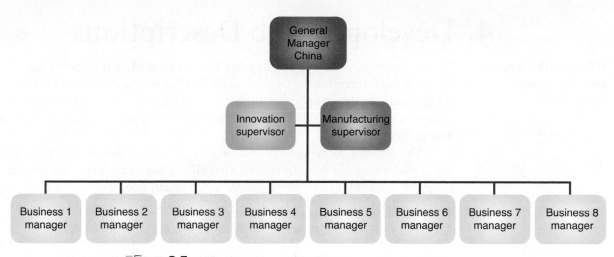

■Figure **6.5**
Spans of Control in Organization

The average span of control in a company determines how many management levels the company will have. Suppose your company has 64 workers and an average span of 8. Then there will be 8 supervisors directing 8 workers each ($8 \times 8 = 64$). And (because the 8 supervisors need their *own* supervisor) there will also be one manager directing the 8 supervisors. This would be a flat (in this case a two-management-level) organization.

However, suppose the span of control were only 4. Then supervising the same number of workers would require 16 supervisors ($16 \times 4 = 64$). And (since every 4 supervisors needs their own supervisor) the 16 supervisors would, in turn, be directed by 4 managers ($4 \times 4 = 16$). And these 4 managers would in turn of course be directed by 1 manager. So now we would have a three-management-level (a *tall*) organization. Thus, in any company, the more workers you have reporting to each supervisor, the flatter the chain of command will be. The fewer the workers, the taller the chain of command. Put a different way, when companies cut out management levels, they tend to widen spans of control.

TALL VS. FLAT ORGANIZATIONS   Now, at this point you may be asking, "So what?" That's not unreasonable. But there is a critical issue at stake here.

Whether tall or flat is best has long been a matter of debate. Classical management theorists such as Henri Fayol said that tall organizational structures (with narrow spans of control) improved performance by *guaranteeing close supervision*.[10] The thinking was that having six to eight subordinates was ideal, since beyond that it became increasingly difficult to monitor and control what your subordinates do.

The counterargument is that flat is better: Flat means wide spans, which means less meddling with (and thus *a more motivational experience* for) subordinates. Some also argue that a tall chain of command is more bureaucratic and *slows decisions* by forcing each decision to pass through more levels of supervisors.

The consensus today seems to be that flat is better. For one thing, flattening cuts out levels and supervisors, and to that extent, it may save the company money. There is also the belief that eliminating layers does push the point at which decisions are made closer to the customer (since there's less cause to check first with the boss).

4. Developing Job Descriptions

For the supervisor, as we said, the rubber hits the road when it comes to making sure that each subordinate has the right job to do. In other words, that grand-looking organization chart consists of specific jobs that have to be staffed. It is your responsibility to make sure that each job is filled with an employee who knows what his or her job is, and how to do it.

The question is, how do you know what specific duties each of those jobs for which you're responsible really entails? After all, the box on the organization chart may simply say something like "sales assistant." What exactly does that person do? The quick answer is that there should be a *job description* for each job for which one of your subordinates is responsible. A job description is a written statement of *what* the jobholder does, *how* he or she does it, and under *what conditions* the job is performed. You use the job description to identify what sort of skills the person who fills the job needs, to show the person what the job entails, and as a guide for training the employee.

Usually, the employer will give you job descriptions for the jobs for which you're responsible. Occasionally, however, that may not be the case, and you may be expected to write your own. We'll end this chapter with a brief explanation of how to do that.

Conducting a Job Analysis

Job analysis is the procedure through which you determine the duties of these jobs and the characteristics of the people who should be hired for them. The analysis produces information on the job's activities and requirements. This information is then used for developing **job descriptions** (what the job entails) and **job specifications** (what kind of people to hire for the job).[11]

First-line supervisors are rarely engaged in designing the company's organization chart. However, as Meg (in the opening scenario) quickly discovered, they still must make sure that their own subordinates are organized. And for this, they should understand how to conduct a job analysis and how to write job descriptions.

Methods for Conducting the Job Analysis

Job analysis is often a collaborative effort between the supervisor and human resource management. HR may provide the job analysis questionnaire and overall directions. Then the supervisor (who, after all, should know more about the subordinates' jobs than just about anyone) may do the actual job analysis, perhaps using a *questionnaire* like the one in Figure 6.6. Alternatively, job analysis *interviews* involve interviewing the workers themselves or supervisors who know the job. Typical interview questions include "What is the job being performed?" "What are the major duties of your position?" "What exactly do you do?" In any case, the information you're seeking typically includes information on the work activities performed (such as cleaning, selling, teaching, or painting) and information about such matters as physical working conditions and work schedule.

Job analysis information is the basis for many supervisory activities. For example, you will use information about the job's required human traits to decide what sort of people to recruit and hire. You will use information about the job's duties to decide what training the workers require, and on what basis to appraise their performance.

COMPETENCY-BASED JOB ANALYSIS   A *job* is a set of closely related activities carried out for pay, but over the past few years, the concept of job has been changing dramatically. For example, when a self-managing team is doing the work, individual team members' jobs may change daily as workers help each other out. Situations like these blur the meaning of *job* as a set of clearly delineated responsibilities. If all the members of the team need to pitch in to get some job done, you don't want some of them to say, "That's not on my job description, so that's not part of my job." There's thus a trend toward newer ways to analyze and describe jobs. One of these is Competency-Based Job Analysis.

Competencies are demonstrable characteristics of the person that enable performance. We can say that *competency-based job analysis* means describing the job in terms of measurable, observable, behavioral competencies (knowledge, skills, and/or behaviors) that an employee doing that job *must exhibit to do the job well*. This contrasts with the traditional way of describing the job in terms of job duties and responsibilities.[12]

■Figure **6.6**

Illustrative Job Analysis Questionnaire

Job Analysis Information Sheet

Job Title_____ Date _____
Job Code_____ Dept. _____
Superior's Title _____
Hours Worked _____ AM to _____ PM
Job Analyst's Name _____

1. What is the job's overall purpose?

2. If the incumbent supervises others, list them by job title; if there is more than one employee with the same title, put the number in parentheses following

3. Check those activities that are part of the incumbent's supervisory duties.
   ☐ Training
   ☐ Performance appraisal
   ☐ Inspecting work
   ☐ Budgeting
   ☐ Coaching and/or counseling
   ☐ Others (please specify) _____

4. Describe the type and extent of supervision received by the incumbent.

5. JOB DUTIES: Describe briefly WHAT the incumbent does and, if possible, HOW he/she does it. Include duties in the following categories:
   a. daily duties (those performed on a regular basis every day or almost every day)

   b. periodic duties (those performed weekly, monthly, quarterly, or at other regular intervals)

   c. duties performed at irregular intervals

6. Is the incumbent performing duties he/she considers unnecessary? If so, describe.

7. Is the incumbent performing duties not presently included in the job description? If so, describe.

8. EDUCATION: Check the box that indicates the educational requirements for the job (not the educational background of the incumbent).
   ☐ No formal education required   ☐ Eighth grade education
   ☐ High school diploma (or equivalent) ☐ 2-year college degree (or equivalent)
   ☐ 4-year college degree (or equivalent) ☐ Graduate work or advanced degree
                                              Specify: _____
   ☐ Professional license
      Specify: _____

(Continued)

9. EXPERIENCE: Check the amount of experience needed to perform the job.

☐ None   ☐ Less than one month
☐ One to six months   ☐ Six months to one year
☐ One to three years   ☐ Three to five years
☐ Five to ten years   ☐ More than ten years

10. LOCATION: Check location of job and, if necessary or appropriate, describe briefly.

☐ Outdoor   ☐ Indoor
☐ Underground   ☐ Excavation
☐ Scaffold   ☐ Other (specify)

11. ENVIRONMENTAL CONDITIONS: Check any objectionable conditions found on the job and note afterward how frequently each is encountered (rarely, occasionally, constantly, etc.).

☐ Dirt   ☐ Dust
☐ Heat   ☐ Cold
☐ Noise   ☐ Fumes
☐ Odors   ☐ Wetness/humidity
☐ Vibration   ☐ Sudden temperature changes
☐ Darkness or poor lighting   ☐ Other (specify)

12. HEALTH AND SAFETY: Check any undesirable health and safety conditions under which the incumbent must perform and note how often they are encountered.

☐ Elevated workplace   ☐ Mechanical hazards
☐ Explosives   ☐ Electrical hazards
☐ Fire hazards   ☐ Radiation
☐ Other (specify)

13. MACHINES, TOOLS, EQUIPMENT, AND WORK AIDS: Describe briefly what machines, tools, equipment, or work aids the incumbent works with on a regular basis:

14. Have concrete work standards been established (errors allowed, time taken for a particular task, etc.)? If so, what are they?

15. Are there any personal attributes (special aptitudes, physical characteristics, personality traits, etc.) required by the job?

16. Are there any exceptional problems the incumbent might be expected to encounter in performing the job under normal conditions? If so, describe.

17. Describe the successful completion and/or end results of the job.

18. What is the seriousness of error on this job? Who or what is affected by errors the incumbent makes?

19. To what job would a successful incumbent expect to be promoted?

[Note: this form is obviously slanted toward a manufacturing environment, but it can be adapted quite easily to fit a number of different types of jobs.]

Traditional job analysis therefore focuses on "what" a job is in terms of job duties and responsibilities. *Competency analysis* focuses more on what skills (or "competencies") the worker needs to do the job.[13] Traditional job analysis is more job focused. Competency-based analysis is more worker focused—specifically, what must he or she be competent to do?

AN EXAMPLE   In practice, *competency-based analysis often comes down to identifying the basic skills* an employee needs to do the job. For example, British Petroleum's (BP's) exploration division wanted to shift employees' attention from a job description "that's-not-my-job" mentality to one that would motivate them to acquire the new skills they needed to accomplish their broader, flexible responsibilities.

The solution was a skills matrix as in Figure 6.7. Human resources prepared a matrix for each job or job family (such as drilling supervisors). As in Figure 6.7, the matrix listed (1) the basic skills needed for that job (such as technical expertise) and (2) the minimum level of each skill required for that job or job family. The emphasis at BP is no longer on specific job duties. Instead, the focus is on developing the new skills needed for the employees' broader, and often relatively undefined, responsibilities.

Skills Matrix

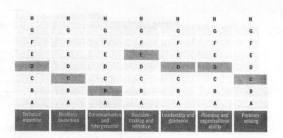

Writing Job Descriptions

The job analysis should provide the information required to write the job description. A job description is a written statement of *what* the jobholder does, *how* he or she does it, and under *what conditions* the job is performed. You can then use this information to write a *job specification* that lists the knowledge, abilities, and skills needed to perform the job satisfactorily. Figure 6.8 presents a typical job description.

As is usual, the description in Figure 6.8 contains several types of information.

■Figure **6.8**

Sample Job Description

JOB TITLE: Telesales Respresentative	JOB CODE: 100001
RECOMMENDED SALARY GRADE:	EXEMPT/NONEXEMPT STATUS: Nonexempt
JOB FAMILY: Sales	EEOC: Sales Workers
DIVISION: Higher Education	REPORTS TO: District Sales Manager
DEPARTMENT: In-House Sales	LOCATION: Boston
	DATE: April 2009

SUMMARY (Write a brief summary of joh.)

The person in this position is responsible for selling college textbooks, software, and multimedia products to professors, via incoming and outgoing telephone calls, and to carry out selling strategies to meet sales goals in assigned territories of smaller colleges and universities. In addition, the individual in this position will be responsible for generating a designated amount of editorial leads and communicating to the publishing groups product feedback and market trends observed in the assigned territory.

SCOPE AND IMPACT OF JOB
Dollar responsibilities (budget and/or revenue)

The person in this position is responsible for generating approximately $2 million in revenue, for meeting operating expense budget of approximately $4000, and a sampling budget of approximately 10,000 units.

Supervisory responsibilities (direct and indirect)

None

Other

REQUIRED KNOWLEDGE AND EXPERIENCE (Knowledge and experience necessary to do job)
Related work experience

Prior sales or publishing experience preferred. One year of company experience in a customer service or marketing function with broad knowledge of company products and services is desirable.

Formal education or equivalent

Bachelor's degree with strong academic performance or work equivalent experience.

Skills

Must have strong organizational and persuasive skills. Must have excellent verbal and written communications skills and must be PC proficient.

Other

Limited travel required (approx 5%)

(Continued)

PRIMARY RESPONSIBILITIES (List in order of importance and list amount of time spent on task.)

Driving Sales (60%)

- Achieve quantitative sales goal for assigned territory of smaller colleges and universities.
- Determine sales priorities and strategies for territory and develop a plan for implementing those strategies.
- Conduct 15–20 professor interviews per day during the academic sales year that accomplishes those priorities.
- Conduct product presentations (including texts, software, and Web site); effectively articulate author's central vision of key titles; conduct sales interviews using the PSS model; conduct walk-through of books and technology.
- Employ telephone selling techniques and strategies.
- Sample products to appropriate faculty, making strategic use of assigned sampling budgets.
- Close class test adoptions for first edition products.
- Negotiate custom publishing and special packaging agreements within company guidelines.
- Initiate and conduct in-person faculty presentations and selling trips as appropriate to maximize sales with the strategic use of travel budget. Also use internal resources to support the territory sales goals.
- Plan and execute in-territory special selling events and book-fairs.
- Develop and implement in-territory promotional campaigns and targeted email campaigns.

Publishing (editorial/marketing) 25%

- Report, track, and sign editorial projects.
- Gather and communicate significant market feedback and information to publishing groups.

Territory Management 15%

- Track and report all pending and closed business in assigned database.
- Maintain records of customer sales interviews and adoption situations in assigned database.
- Manage operating budget strategically.
- Submit territory itineraries, sales plans, and sales forecasts as assigned.
- Provide superior customer service and maintain professional bookstore relations in assigned territory.

Decision-Making Responsibilities for This Position:

Determine the strategic use of assigned sampling budget to most effectively generate sales revenue to exceed sales goals.
Determine the priority of customer and account contacts to achieve maximum sales potential.
Determine where in-person presentations and special selling events would be most effective to generate most sales.

Submitted By: Jim Smith, District Sales Manager	Date: April 2009
Approval:	Date:
Human Resources:	Date:
Corporate Compensation:	Date:

JOB IDENTIFICATION The job identification section includes the job title; this specifies the title of the job, such as marketing.

JOB SUMMARY The job summary should describe the general nature of the job, listing only its major functions or activities.

RESPONSIBILITIES AND DUTIES This is the heart of the job description and presents a complete list of the job's responsibilities and duties. Here, list and describe in several sentences each of the job's major duties. For instance, you might further define the duty "selects, trains, and develops subordinate personnel" as follows: "develops spirit of cooperation and understanding," "ensures that work group members receive specialized training as necessary," and "directs training involving teaching, demonstrating, and/or advising." Federal law requires special care in preparing the list of duties, as the accompanying new workforce feature shows.

AUTHORITY This section defines the limits of the jobholder's authority. For example, the jobholder might have authority to approve purchase requests up to $5,000, grant

Writing Job Descriptions That Comply with the ADA

Congress enacted the Americans with Disabilities Act (ADA) to reduce or eliminate serious problems of discrimination against disabled individuals. Under the ADA, the individual must have the requisite skills, educational background, and experience to perform the job's essential functions. A job function is essential when it is the reason the position exists or when the function is so specialized that the firm hired the person doing the job for his or her expertise or ability to perform that particular function. If the disabled individual can't perform the job as currently structured, the employer is required to make a "reasonable accommodation," unless doing so would present an "undue hardship."

The ADA does not require job descriptions, but it's probably advisable to have them. Virtually all ADA legal actions will revolve around the question, "What are the essential functions of the job?" Without a job description that lists such functions, it will be hard to convince a court that the functions are essential to the job. The corollary is that you should clearly identify the essential functions. Don't just list them among the job description's other duties.

time off or leaves of absence, discipline department personnel, and recommend salary increases.[14]

WORKING CONDITIONS AND PHYSICAL ENVIRONMENT This section lists the general working conditions involved in the job. These might include noise level, hazardous conditions, heat, and other conditions.

Internet-Based Job Descriptions

Most employers today write their job descriptions based wholly or in part on Internet-based services. One site (www.jobdescription.com) illustrates why. The process is simple. Search by alphabetical title, key word, category, or industry to find the desired job title. This leads you to a generic job description for that title—say, "computers & EDP systems sales representative." You can then use the wizard to customize the generic description for this position. For example, you can add specific information about your organization, such as job title, job codes, department, and preparation date.

The U.S. Department of Labor's *Occupational Information Network*, or O*NET, is another useful (free) online resource. It allow users to discover the duties and responsibilities of thousands of jobs, as well as the training, experience, education, and knowledge each job requires.

As an example, start by going to http://online.onetcenter.org (Screen A in Figure 6.9). Here, click on *Find Occupations*. Assume you want to create a job description for a retail salesperson. Type in *Retail Sales* for the occupational titles, and *Sales and Related* from the "job families" drop-down box.

Click *Find Occupations* to continue, which brings you to the *Find Occupations Search Result* (Screen B in Figure 6.9).

Clicking on *Retail Salespersons-summary* produces the job summary and specific occupational duties for retail salespersons (Screen C in Figure 6.9). For a small store, you might want to combine the duties of the "retail salesperson" with those of "first-line supervisors of retail sales workers."

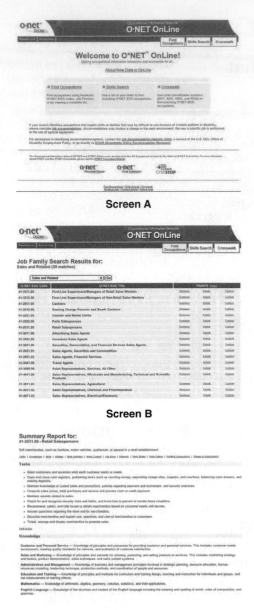

Screen A

Screen B

Screen C

Writing Job Specifications

To hire, train, and appraise employees, you don't just want to know the job's duties. You need to know what human traits and skills the job requires. Then you can try to identify these traits in your job candidates, and you'll understand what skills training they require.

The **job specification** answers the question, "What human traits and experience are required to do this job well?" A short list of illustrative experience and traits might include things such as formal education and training; job skills (such as carpentry); licenses and certifications; physical specifications such as strength and vision; and mental specifications such as math ability.[15] The job specification may be a separate section on the job description (as at the end of Figure 6.8) or a separate document entirely.

Chapter 6 Concept Review and Reinforcement

Key Terms

Review of Key Concepts

Organizing	Organizing means identifying the jobs to be done, establishing departments, delegating authority, establishing a chain of command, and coordinating the work to be done in order to accomplish the organization's goals.
Organization Chart	A chart that shows the structure of the organization including positions connected by lines to determine who is accountable to whom and who has authority for each area.
Chain of Command	The chain of command is the formal path that a directive and/or answer or request should take through each level of an organization (also called scalar chain).
Line Manager	A manager who has the authority to issue orders to subordinates down the chain of command.
Staff Manager	A manager without the authority to give orders down the chain of command (except in his or her own department); generally can only assist and advise line managers in specialized areas.
Functional Manager	A manager with narrowly limited authority to issue orders down the chain of command in a specific functional area such as personnel testing.
Authority	The right to take action, to make decisions, and to direct the work of others.
Coordination	Coordination is the process of achieving unity of action among interdepartmental activities. Techniques for achieving coordination include mutual adjustment; use of rules and procedures; standardization of targets, skills, shared values, or direct supervision; divisionalizing; the use of a staff assistant, a liaison, a committee; and/or independent integrators.

Departmentalization	Departmentalization is the process through which an organization's activities are grouped together and assigned to managers. Activities grouped together may include functions, products, customers, or geographic organization.
Informal Organization	The informal contacts, communications, and habitual way of doing things that employees develop.
Functional Departmentalization	A form of organization that groups a company's activities around functions such as manufacturing, sales, or finance.
Divisional Organization	A form of organization in which the firm's major departments are organized so that each one can manage all or most of the activities needed to develop, manufacture, and sell a particular product (or to a particular customer or geographic area).
Principles of Division of Work	
Authority/Responsibility	Supervisors need authority that correlates with their responsibilities.
Unity of Command	An employee should report and receive orders from one boss only.
Centralization	The organization must balance the extent to which decisions are centralized versus decentralized. This balance can be obtained by flattening the chain of command, by eliminating levels of middle managers, and by letting more decisions be made lower down the chain. This will allow people who are closer and more familiar with the customer to make quicker decisions.
Sources of Supervisor's Authority	
Rank or Position	Within the chain of command a hierarchy of authority evolves. Authority flows from the top of the organization, and the amount of authority delegated depends on a person's rank or position.
Personal Traits	Some people have authority because of personal traits such as intelligence or charisma. Employees follow instructions of individuals with such characteristics because of the power of their personalities.
Expertise	Some people have authority because they are experts in an area or have special knowledge that requires others to depend on them.

Rewards	A supervisor's authority over subordinates is generally proportionate to his or her ability to control their awards or punishment.
Acceptance	Authority depends on the degree of subordinate acceptance of the supervisor's orders. Employee acceptance of orders is increasingly important today, given the emphasis on empowered workers and team-based operations.
Span of Control	Span of control is the number of subordinates reporting directly to a supervisor. Employee performance is directly proportionate to the degree of supervisory control exercised effectively with a given number of subordinates at each organizational level.
Developing Job Descriptions	Job Analysis is a procedure used to determine the duties of jobs and the characteristics of the people who should be hired. This analysis generates the information for developing job descriptions (what the job entails) and job specifications (what kind of people to hire for said job).

Review and Discussion Questions

1. What is organizing?
2. Define scalar chain.
3. Why is the coordination process so important when we are organizing jobs and work?
4. Why do we refer to departmentalization as the organizational division of work?
5. How does achieving unity of action influence how a company coordinates its operations?
6. From a supervisory perspective, why is the principle of unity of command so important?
7. Explain the difference between centralization and decentralization.
8. Do you think a company can flatten its hierarchy without taking steps to prepare its employees for their new roles? Why or why not? What steps would you recommend?
9. Why do you think that functional departmentalization is a popular way to organize company activities?
10. Explain a major reason why a company would choose divisional organization.
11. List at least three of the variables that help determine the effective supervisory span of control.
12. When developing job descriptions and job specifications, what is the purpose of job analysis?

Application and Skill Building

Case Study One

Organizing Greenley Communications

Louis Greenley has to make a difficult decision. Greenley Communications was a diversified communications company that operated primarily in the western United States. The firm owned and operated newspapers and radio and television stations.

Greenley's existing structure was organized by industry. There was a newspaper division, a radio division, and a television production division. Each division had its own bookkeeping, sales, marketing, operations, and service divisions. Accounting and financial management were handled at the corporate level.

In the newspaper division, there was a clear distinction between the news and the sales/financial sides of the business. Coming from a family of journalists, Greenley was always concerned that the sale of advertising to local clients would influence the paper's coverage of the news—editors might ignore potential stories that might reflect negatively on an advertiser.

The head of broadcast operations in Greenley's television arm proposed a major structural change. The proposal called for organizing Greenley Communications geographically. This would allow regional managers to have a single sales force that could sell advertising in any form: print, radio, or TV. The approach had some appeal. There was significant overlap at Greenley—the company tended to own multiple sales forces in the same region, for instance, sometimes calling on the same customer. Certainly, there would be savings in personnel, since the company would need a far smaller sales staff. However, Greenley is not yet persuaded. He is trying to decide what to do.

Discussion Questions

1. Draw Greenley's current organization chart as best you can.
2. What factors should influence Greenley's decision to restructure?
3. What risks does the proposed restructuring create?
4. What are the pros and cons of the vice president's new proposed structure?
5. If you were Greenley, how exactly would you reorganize (if at all), and why?

Case Study Two

Carter Cleaning Company: The Job Description

Based on her review of her father's chain of cleaning stores, Jennifer Carter concluded that one of the first matters she had to attend to involved developing job descriptions for her store managers.

As Jennifer tells it, her lessons regarding job descriptions in her basic supervisory management courses were insufficient to fully convince her of the pivotal role job descriptions actually played in the smooth functioning of an enterprise. Many times during her first few weeks on the job, Jennifer found herself asking one of her store supervisors why he was violating what she knew to be recommended company policies and procedures. Repeatedly, the answers were either "Because I didn't know it was my job" or "Because I didn't know that was the way we were supposed to do it." Jennifer knew that a job description, along with a set of standards and procedures that specified what was to be done and how to do it, would go a long way toward alleviating this problem.

In general, the store supervisor is responsible for directing all store activities in such a way that quality work is produced, customer relations and sales are maximized, and profitability is maintained through effective control of labor, supply, and energy costs. In accomplishing that general aim, a specific store manager's duties and responsibilities include quality control, store appearance and cleanliness, customer relations, bookkeeping and cash management, cost control and productivity, damage control, pricing, inventory control, spotting and cleaning, machine maintenance, purchasing, employee safety, hazardous waste removal, human resource administration, and pest control.

The questions that Jennifer had to address follow.

Questions

1. What should be the format and final form of the store supervisor's job description?
2. Is it practical to specify standards and procedures in the body of the job description, or should these be kept separate?
3. How should Jennifer go about collecting the information required for the standards, procedures, and job description?
4. What, in your opinion, should the store supervisor's job description look like and contain?

Experiential Activities

Activity 1. In the opening scenario, Meg was delighted to finally be promoted to comptroller/accounting supervisor for Andean Research LLC, a 90-person company that solved pollution control problems for client companies. Andean's founder and owner had dismissed Meg's predecessor, the previous comptroller, allegedly due to an excessive number of errors emanating from that department. About one month into her new job, Meg was astonished when the president entered her office to tell her that the payroll reports for the past two months were entirely wrong. The issue had serious implications for a variety of matters, including the accuracy of the employment taxes that Andean had been withholding. "You'd better get your people organized," said the president as he stormed out.

Getting People Organized

Purpose: The purpose of this exercise is to give you practice in organizing your employees' efforts.

Required understanding: You should be thoroughly familiar with how to organize efforts, not just company-wide but for individual employees.

How to set up the exercise/Instructions: Form teams of 4–5 students and answer the following questions:

1. *Based on what you read in this chapter*, what is the first way in which Meg went wrong here?
2. What could account for the excessive number of errors?
3. Write a one-page outline summarizing the organization of the accounting department and how they can improve the accuracy of the payroll reports.
4. *Based on what you read in this chapter*, how should Meg go about getting her department organized now?

Activity 2. Colleges are interesting from an organizational viewpoint, because the employees (the faculty) tend to make so many of a college's decisions and run so many of its projects. It's not unusual, for instance, to have the faculty elect a faculty senate, which in turn appoints committees for things such as faculty promotions and curricula; the committees then often have a major say in who gets promoted, what programs the college offers, and so on. Similarly, the students often evaluate the faculty, as well as elect their own student governments, which, in turn, decide how the students' fees are spent.

Some critics say that all of this is a little like "letting the inmates run the asylum." And, indeed, the pace of criticism has picked up in the past few years. With more colleges and universities going online, students have more educational choices. As a result, tuition fees are under pressure, and universities are scrambling to cut costs and be more efficient. Since efficiency is not something most people instinctively associate with academia, the pressures to reduce costs have caused a lot of soul-searching. Boards of trustees are reviewing everything about how their colleges do things—from how many courses faculty members teach, to how professors are appraised, to how to decide which programs to offer or drop.

Form teams of four to five students and answer the following questions:

1. Draw an organization chart for your college or university. What type(s) of departmentalization does it use? How would you show, on the chart, the authority exercised by the faculty and faculty committees (teams)?
2. The chapter argues that having a decentralized structure tends to speed decisions. However, some people think that even though colleges tend to be decentralized, they are still the most bureaucratic organizations they've ever dealt with. To what extent and in what way is your college decentralized? Do you consider it bureaucratic, and, if so, what explains why a decentralized organization produces such bureaucracy?
3. How would you reorganize the college if streamlining and more efficiency were your goals?

Activity 3. In teams of 4–5 students, spend some time on the Internet or in the library obtaining the organization charts for two companies. Then together answer these questions: What forms of departmentalization can you identify in each chart? Which company would you say is more decentralized? Why do you believe each company organized the way that it did?

Role-Playing Exercise

Distinguishing Between Line and Staff Authority: The Situation

Your company has recently gone through a reorganization and you have been called into a meeting to discuss the impact of this reorganization on your job. In a memo received yesterday, top management indicated that all company positions would exercise either line or staff authority. You are not sure what it means to exercise line or staff authority, but this meeting should help explain everything.

Instructions: All students should read the situation above in addition to studying Chapter 6. The students, in class, will play the role of employees while a separate panel of four or five students will take on the roles of top management, to communicate the differences between line and staff authority.

A class discussion will follow the role-playing presentation.

Role of employees: Each student should choose a particular job as a point of discussion for this exercise. Examples of jobs to choose from can be maintenance, HR, assembly supervisor, plant manager, engineering, quality control, and so on. You are encouraged to ask for clarification regarding your authority, during the meetings with top management.

Role of Top Management Panel: Your job is to advise, assist, and enlighten your employees as to the difference between line and staff managers and regarding their authority. The points that you will want to make in your presentation should include the following:

- Degree of authority delegated.
- What is meant by staff specialist or expert?
- Why is there a need for cooperation, coordination, and communication between line and staff?
- Define and give examples of functional authority for some of the employees.

Questions for Class Discussion

1. Based on what you studied in the chapter, did the panel do a good job in communicating the differences between line and staff positions?
2. Who do you think has the more difficult and challenging jobs? Line or staff?
3. Do you feel that cooperation and coordination is important between line and staff members? Explain your answer.

7

The Supervisor's Role in Equal Employment

CHAPTER OBJECTIVES

When you finish studying this chapter, you should be able to answer the following questions:

1. What Do Supervisors Need to Know About Equal Employment Opportunity Law?
2. Why Is Sexual Harassment a Difficult Challenge for Supervisors?
3. How Does the Americans with Disabilities Act (ADA) Affect Supervisors?
4. What Are the Strict Requirements Posed by the Genetic Information Non-Discrimination Act of 2008 (GINA)?
5. How Do State and Local Equal Opportunity Laws Affect Supervisors?
6. What Defenses May Be Used Against Discrimination Allegations?
7. What Are the Steps in the EEOC Enforcement Process?
8. What Are the Recommended Steps for Establishing an Affirmative Action Program?

OPENING SNAPSHOT
The Pharmacist's Questionable Decision

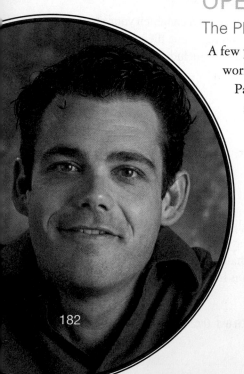

A few years ago, Walmart hired Patrick Brady, who has cerebral palsy, to work as a pharmacist's assistant in one of its stores. According to Patrick, he worked as an assistant for just one day. He says his supervisor, the store pharmacist, didn't think Patrick was fit for the pharmacy job, so the store reassigned him to collect carts and pick up trash.[1] A New York jury soon ordered Walmart to pay Patrick $7.5 million for violating the Americans with Disabilities Act.[2]

1. Discrimination and the Supervisor

The employer is responsible for instituting and managing its companywide equal employment program, but in practice it's usually individual supervisors who cause the problem.[3] It's probably quicker to list supervisory employment actions that can't lead to equal employment suits than to list those that can. However, potential problem areas include (just as a start) asking candidates how old they are or what their husbands do, "jokingly" telling a female employee to "spend her raise at Victoria's Secret," or telling a 60-year-old employee that he's "too old to be promoted." The bottom line is that carrying out just about every supervisory task such as hiring, training, evaluating, or transferring employees is fraught with peril if you don't understand the basics of equal employment law. We'll therefore focus on that in this chapter.

2. What Supervisors Need to Know About Equal Employment Opportunity Law

What Do Supervisors Need to Know about Equal Employment Opportunity Law?

American race relations were not always as tolerant as Barack Obama's inauguration might suggest. It took centuries of legislative action, court decisions, and evolving public policy to arrive at this point. For example, the Fifth Amendment to the U.S. Constitution (ratified in 1791) states that "no person shall . . . be deprived of life, liberty, or property, without due process of the law."[4] But as a practical matter, Congress and various presidents were reluctant to take dramatic action on equal employment until the early 1960s.[5] At that point, "they were finally prompted to act primarily as a result of civil unrest among the minorities and women" who eventually became protected by the then-new equal rights laws.[6]

Equal Pay Act of 1963

The **Equal Pay Act of 1963** (amended in 1972) was one of the first new laws. It made it unlawful to discriminate in pay on the basis of sex when jobs involve equal work—equivalent skills, effort, and responsibility—and are performed under similar working conditions. However, differences in pay do not violate the equal pay act if the pay difference is based on non-discriminatory criteria (such as a seniority system, a merit system, a system that measures earnings by quantity or quality of production, or a differential based on any factor other than sex).

Title VII of the 1964 Civil Rights Act

WHAT THE LAW SAYS   **Title VII of the 1964 Civil Rights Act** was another of these new laws. Title VII (amended by the 1972 Equal Employment Opportunity Act) says an employer cannot discriminate based on race, color, religion, sex, or national origin.

Specifically, it states that it shall be an unlawful employment practice for an employer:[7]

1. *To fail or refuse to hire or to discharge an individual or otherwise to discriminate against any individual* with respect to his or her compensation, terms, conditions, or privileges of employment, because of such individual's race, color, religion, sex, or national origin.

2. *To limit, segregate, or classify his or her employees or applicants for employment* in any way that would deprive or tend to deprive any individual of employment opportunities or otherwise adversely affect his or her status as an employee, because of such individual's race, color, religion, sex, or national origin.

Title VII established the **Equal Employment Opportunity Commission (EEOC)** to implement the Civil Rights Act. The EEOC consists of five members, appointed by the president with the advice and consent of the Senate. The EEOC, of course, has a staff of thousands to assist it in administering the civil rights law in employment settings.

Establishing the EEOC enhanced the federal government's ability to enforce equal employment opportunity laws. The EEOC receives and investigates job discrimination complaints. When it finds reasonable cause that the charges are justified, it attempts (through conciliation) to reach an agreement. If this conciliation fails, the EEOC has the power to go to court to enforce the law. Under the Equal Employment Opportunity Act of 1972, discrimination charges may be filed by the EEOC on behalf of an aggrieved individual, as well as by the individuals themselves. We explain this procedure in more detail later in this chapter.

Executive Orders

U.S. presidents issued executive orders 11246 and 11375 years ago. These orders don't just ban discrimination; they also require that most employers who do business with the U.S. government take affirmative action to ensure equal employment opportunity (we explain affirmative action later in this chapter). These orders also established the **Office of Federal Contract Compliance Programs (OFCCP)**. It is responsible for ensuring the compliance of federal contracts. President Obama's administration recently directed more funds and staffing to the OFCCP.[8]

Age Discrimination in Employment Act of 1967

The **Age Discrimination in Employment Act (ADEA) of 1967**, as amended, makes it unlawful to discriminate against employees or applicants for employment who are 40 years of age or older. This law effectively ended most mandatory retirement rules.[9]

Pregnancy Discrimination Act of 1978

Congress passed the **Pregnancy Discrimination Act (PDA)** in 1978 as an amendment to Title VII. The act broadened the definition of sex discrimination to encompass pregnancy, childbirth, or related medical conditions. It prohibits using these to discriminate in hiring, promotion, suspension or discharge, or any other term or condition of employment. Regarding benefits, the act basically says that if an employer offers its employees disability coverage, then pregnancy and childbirth must be treated like any other disability and included in the health plan.

Progressive human resource thinking notwithstanding, an auto dealership recently fired an employee after she revealed she was pregnant. The reason? Allegedly "in case I ended up throwing up or cramping in one of their vehicles. They said pregnant women do that sometimes, and I could cause an accident."[10]

Federal Agency Uniform Guidelines on Employee Selection Procedures

The EEOC, Civil Service Commission, Department of Labor, and Department of Justice adopted uniform equal employment guidelines.[11]

These guidelines flesh out the procedures to use in complying with equal employment laws. For example, the ADEA prohibits employers from discriminating against persons over 40 years old because of age. But what if you replace a 52-year-old employee with one who's 45? The guidelines explain that it is unlawful to discriminate by giving preference because of age to individuals *within* the 40-plus age bracket. Thus, you can't reject a 58-year-old candidate based on age and defend yourself by showing you hired a 46-year-old.[12] (Hiring someone closer in age, such as a 54-year-old, may provide a defense, though.) Separately, the American Psychological Association has published its own (non–legally binding) *Standards for Educational and Psychological Testing* that psychologists follow, for instance, when designing testing programs.

Selected Court Decisions Regarding Equal Employment Opportunity (EEO)

Several early court decisions helped employers and lawyers to better understand what they could and could not do regarding EEO laws like those we just discussed. The *Griggs* and *Albemarle Paper* cases were two early, very important ones.

GRIGGS V. *DUKE POWER COMPANY*   *Griggs* v. *Duke Power Company* (1971) was a landmark case because the Supreme Court used it to define unfair discrimination. In this case, a suit was brought against the Duke Power Company on behalf of Willie Griggs, an applicant for a job as a coal handler. The company required its coal handlers to be high school graduates. Griggs claimed that this requirement was illegally discriminatory because it wasn't related to success on the job and because it resulted in more blacks than whites being rejected for these jobs.

Griggs won the case. In his written opinion, Chief Justice Burger laid out three crucial guidelines affecting equal employment legislation. First, the court ruled that discrimination on the part of the employer need not be overt; in other words, the employer does not have to be shown to have intentionally discriminated against the employee or applicant—it need only be shown that discrimination took place. Second, the court held that an employment practice (in this case requiring the high school diploma) must be shown to be *job related* if it has an unequal impact on members of a protected class. In the words of Justice Burger:

> The act proscribes not only overt discrimination but also practices that are fair in form, but discriminatory in operation. The touchstone is business necessity. If an employment practice which operates to exclude Negroes cannot be shown to be related to job performance the practice is prohibited.[13]

Third, Burger's opinion clearly placed the burden of proof on the employer to show that the hiring practice is job related. Thus, the *employer* must show that the employment practice (in this case, requiring a high school diploma) is needed to perform the job satisfactorily if it has a disparate impact on (unintentionally discriminates against) members of a protected class.

ALBEMARLE PAPER COMPANY V. MOODY   In the *Griggs* case, the Supreme Court decided that a screening tool (such as a test) had to be job related or valid—that is, performance on the test must be related to performance on the job. The 1975 *Albemarle* case helped to clarify what the employer had to do to prove that the test or other screening tools are related to or predict performance on the job. For example, the Court ruled that before using a test to screen job candidates, the performance standards for the job in question should be clear. That way the employer can identify which employees were performing better than others (and thus whether the screening tools were effective).[14]

The Civil Rights Act of 1991

Subsequent Supreme Court rulings in the 1980s actually had the effect of limiting the protection of women and minority groups under equal employment laws; this prompted Congress to pass a new Civil Rights Act. President George H. W. Bush signed the new **Civil Rights Act of 1991 (CRA 1991)** into law in November 1991. The effect of CRA 1991 was to roll back the clock to where it stood before the 1980s decisions. For example, several Court decisions had made it more difficult for the employee or applicant to show the employer discriminated against him or her. CRA 1991 therefore addressed the issue of *burden of proof*. It did so by making it easier for an employee or applicant to make his or her case. Today, after CRA 1991, the plaintiff (say, an applicant who failed a selection test) needs to do two things. First, the person must demonstrate that the employment practice (like a test) has a significantly greater adverse impact (effect) on the members of his or her protected group than on other employees.[15] (For example, requiring a college degree for a job would have an adverse impact on some minority groups). Then, he or she must show that the apparently neutral employment practice, (such as the test, or a requirement that the jobholder "be able to lift 100 pounds"), is causing the disparity.[16] Then the burden of proving that the testing (or other) process was fair and non-discriminatory shifts to the employer.

Sexual Harassment

Sexual harassment is a type of discriminatory behavior. Because of the necessarily close and interpersonal nature of the relationship between supervisors and their subordinates, sexual harassment can be a particular problem for supervisors.

SEXUAL HARASSMENT DEFINED   The EEOC guidelines define **sexual harassment** as unwelcome sexual advances, requests for sexual favors, and other verbal or physical conduct of a sexual nature that takes place under any of the following conditions:

1. Submission is explicitly or implicitly a term or condition of an individual's employment.

2. Submission to or rejection of such conduct is the basis for employment decisions affecting such individual.

3. Such conduct has the purpose or effect of unreasonably interfering with an individual's work performance or creating an intimidating, hostile, or offensive work environment.

Sexual harassment is a violation of Title VII when such conduct has the purpose or effect of substantially interfering with a person's work performance or creating an intimidating, hostile, or offensive work environment. The EEOC's guidelines further assert that employers have a duty to maintain workplaces free of sexual harassment and intimidation. The Civil Rights Act of 1991 added teeth to this by permitting victims of intentional discrimination, including sexual harassment, to have jury trials and to collect compensatory damages for pain and suffering and punitive damages in cases in which the employer acted with "malice or reckless indifference" to the individual's rights.[17]

Sexual harassment laws do not just cover harassment of women by men. They also cover those occasions when women harass men, as well as same-sex harassment. The U.S. Supreme Court held (in *ONCALE* v. *Sundowner Offshore Services Inc.*) that "same-sex discrimination consisting of same-sex sexual harassment is actionable under Title VII." It said that same-sex subordinates, coworkers, or superiors are liable under the theory that they create a hostile work environment for the employee.[18] In one recent year, EEOC received 13,867 sexual harassment charges, 15.9% of which males filed.[19]

The **Federal Violence Against Women Act of 1994** provides another avenue that women can use to seek relief for violent sexual harassment. It provides that someone "who commits a crime of violence motivated by gender and thus deprives another of her rights shall be liable to the party injured."

PROVING SEXUAL HARASSMENT   There are three main ways an employee can prove sexual harassment.

Quid Pro Quo.   The most direct way is to show that rejecting a supervisor's advances adversely affected some "tangible employment action," like hiring, firing, promotion, demotion, undesirable assignment, benefits, or compensation. Thus in one case the employee showed that advancement was dependent on her agreeing to her supervisor's sexual demands.

Hostile Environment Created by Supervisors.   But the employee doesn't have to show that the harassment had tangible consequences such as a demotion or dismissal. For example, in one case, the court found that a male supervisor's sexual behavior had substantially affected a female employee's emotional and psychological ability so much that she felt she had to quit her job. Even though the supervisor made no direct threats or promises in exchange for sexual advances, the fact that the advances interfered with the woman's performance and created an offensive work environment were enough to prove that sexual harassment occurred.

Distinguishing between harassment and flirting can be tricky. The courts do not interpret as sexual harassment any sexual relationships that arise during the course of employment but that do not have a substantial effect on that employment. In one decision, for instance, the U.S. Supreme Court held that sexual harassment law doesn't cover ordinary "intersexual flirtation." In his ruling, Justice Scalia said courts must carefully distinguish between "simple teasing" and truly abusive behavior.[20]

Hostile Environment Created by Coworkers or Nonemployees. The advances don't have to be made by the person's supervisor to qualify as sexual harassment: An employee's coworkers or even customers can cause sexual harassment. In one case, the court held that a server's sexually provocative uniform that the employer required led to lewd comments by customers. When she complained that she would no longer wear the uniform, she was fired. Because the employer could not show there was a job-related necessity for requiring such a uniform and because the uniform was required only for female employees, the court ruled that the employer, in effect, was responsible for the sexually harassing behavior. Such abhorrent client behavior is more likely when the clients are in positions of power, and when they have less reason to think they'll be penalized.[21]

Court Decisions   The U.S. Supreme Court used a case called *Meritor Savings Bank, FSB* v. *Vinson* to broadly endorse the EEOC's guidelines on how to deal with sexual harassment. Two more recent U.S. Supreme Court decisions (*Burlington Industries* v. *Ellerth*, and *Faragher* v. *City of Boca Raton*) further clarified the law. The Court's decisions in the two latter cases have two important implications for supervisors.

First, the decisions make it clear that in a *quid pro quo* case it is *not* necessary for the employee to have suffered tangible consequences (such as being demoted) to win the case; *just making the suggestion may be enough.*

Second, the Court said that an employer could defend itself against sexual harassment liability by showing two things.

1. First, it had to show "that the employer exercised care to prevent and correct promptly any sexually harassing behavior."

2. Second, the employer had to demonstrate that the plaintiff "unreasonably failed to take advantage of any preventive or corrective opportunities provided by the employer." The Supreme Court specifically said that the employee's failing to use formal organizational reporting systems would satisfy the second component.

Sensible employers promptly took steps to show that they did take "reasonable care." For example, they publicized strong harassment policies, trained supervisors and employees regarding their responsibilities for complying with these policies, instituted reporting processes, and investigated and corrected charges promptly.[22] A form like that in the accompanying Figure 7.1 is useful here.

Figure 7.2 (page 191) summarizes what the EEOC says employers and supervisors should do. First, take steps to ensure harassment does not take place. Second, once

The University of Iowa

Office of Equal Opportunity and Diversity

CONFIDENTIAL REPORT OF INFORMAL* SEXUAL HARASSMENT COMPLAINT RESOLUTION

Please complete this form and submit it to the Office of Equal Opportunity and Diversity, 202 Jessup Hall,
As soon as reasonably possible after resolution of the complaint
Due to confidentiality considerations, please do not e-mail these forms.

Date of Incident	Date complaint received

College/Organizational Unit	Department	Today's Date
Name of Individual Completing Report	Title	Campus Telephone #

Consistent with the UI Policy on Sexual Harassment, if the person charged in the complaint has been informed of the existence of the complaint, all parties' names shall be disclosed; if the person charged has not been informed of the existence of the complaint, the parties' names shall not be disclosed.

Name of Complainant(s)

Department	Gender
	☐ Male ☐ Female ☐ Unknown

Status of Complaint(s): ☐ Academic or Administrative Officer ☐ Faculty ☐ Professional & Scientific ☐ Merit ☐ Student Employee ☐ Undergraduate Student ☐ Graduate Student ☐ Job Applicant ☐ Former Employee ☐ No current University affiliation ☐ Graduate Assistant ☐ Other _____

Ethnicity of Complainant(s): ☐ American Indian or Alaskan Native ☐ White, not of Hispanic Origin ☐ African American and Black, not of Hispanic Origin ☐ Asian or Pacific Islander ☐ Latino or Hispanic

Name of Victim(s) *(if other than Complainant)*

Department	Gender
	☐ Male ☐ Female ☐ Unknown

Status of Victim(s): ☐ Academic or Administrative Officer ☐ Faculty ☐ Professional & Scientific ☐ Merit ☐ Student Employee ☐ Undergraduate Student ☐ Graduate Student ☐ Job Applicant ☐ Former Employee ☐ No current University affiliation ☐ Graduate Assistant ☐ Other _____

Ethnicity of Victim(s): ☐ American Indian or Alaskan Native ☐ White, not of Hispanic Origin ☐ African American and Black, not of Hispanic Origin ☐ Asian or Pacific Islander ☐ Latino or Hispanic

Name of Respondent(s)

Department	Gender
	☐ Male ☐ Female ☐ Unknown

Status of Respondent(s): ☐ Academic or Administrative Officer ☐ Faculty ☐ Professional & Scientific ☐ Merit ☐ Student Employee ☐ Undergraduate Student ☐ Graduate Student ☐ Job Applicant ☐ Former Employee ☐ No current University affiliation ☐ Graduate Assistant ☐ Other _____

Ethnicity of Respondent(s): ☐ American Indian or Alaskan Native ☐ White, not of Hispanic Origin ☐ African American and Black, not of Hispanic Origin ☐ Asian or Pacific Islander ☐ Latino or Hispanic

DEFINITION: The University's Policy on Sexual Harassment defines sexual harassment as persistent, repetitive or egregious conduct directed at a specific individual or group of individuals that a reasonable person would interpret, in the full context in which the conduct occurs, as harassment of a sexual nature, when:

1. submission to such conduct is made or threatened to be made explicitly or implicitly a term or condition of an individual's employment, education, on campus living environment, or participation in a University activity;
2. submission to or rejection of such conduct is used or threatened to be used as a basis for a decision affecting an individual employment, education, on-campus living environment, or participation in a University activity; or
3. such conduct has the purpose or effect of unreasonably interfering with work or educational performance, or of creating an intimidating or offensive environment for employment, education, on-campus living, or participation in a University activity.

■ Figure **7.1**

Form for Reporting Possible Sexual Harassment

Source: http://www.uiowa.edu/~eod/policies/sexual%20harassment%20form.pdf (accessed April 28, 2009).

For the purposes of this form, "informational complaints" are those handled by department or units outside the Office of Equal Opportunity and Diversity. Pursuant to the UI Policy on Sexual Harassment, any academic or administrative officer who becomes aware of allegations of sexual harassment by any means **must** consult with the Office of Equal Opportunity and Diversity regarding appropriate steps.

Forms of Sexual Harassment: (check all forms of unwelcome behavior that apply)

☐ **Verbal Harassment**	☐ **Physical Harassment**	☐ **Visual Harassment**
☐ comments of a sexual nature ☐ unwelcome advances ☐ derogatory sex based comments ☐ verbal threats ☐ other (explain)	☐ unwelcome contact ☐ physical gestures ☐ exhibitionism ☐ stalking ☐ assault ☐ other (explain)	☐ written ☐ pictures/photos ☐ posters ☐ electronic/computer ☐ other (explain)
☐ **Conditioning employment or educational benefits on submitting to sexual requests**	☐ **retaliation for complaining about sexual harassment**	☐ **Other (explain)**

Please provide summary of the nature of the allegations below (attach additional pages if necessary):

Outcome (check only one):

☐ Founded	☐ unfounded	☐ resolved/negotiated settlement
☐ complaint pending	☐ complaint withdrawn	☐ referred to another office
☐ Other		

Discipline (check all that apply):

☐ apology	☐ educational program	☐ counseling
☐ verbal reprimand	☐ written reprimand	☐ reassignment
☐ suspension	☐ no contact order	☐ termination
☐ other (explain)		
☐ **sanctions applied under the Code of Student Life** (explain)**		

*To your knowledge, has this complaint been referred to another office? ☐ Yes ☐ No   If yes, please indicate where:
☐ Office of Equal Opportunity and Diversity ☐ Office of Student Services ☐ other (specify)

** For Office of Student Services use only: Date report Completed

Please return this form to the Office of Equal Opportunity and Diversity, 202 Jessup Hall.
Due to confidentiality considerations, please do not e-mail these forms.
Thank you for your assistance in resolving the complaint.

■Figure **7.1**
(Continued)

being apprised of such a situation, take immediate corrective action once you know (or should know) of harassing conduct.[23]

Why Is Sexual Harassment a Difficult Challenge for Supervisors?

SEXUAL HARASSMENT'S CAUSES   Sexual harassment's causes are more varied than people realize. For one thing, minority women are particularly at risk. One study found, "Women experienced more sexual harassment than men, minorities experienced more ethnic harassment than whites, and minority women experienced more harassment

The EEOC says, "Prevention is the best tool to eliminate sexual harassment in the workplace." Therefore:

1. *Issue a strong policy statement* condemning harassment. Clearly explain what's prohibited, assure protection against retaliation for employees who make complaints, and lay out a complaint process that provides confidentiality as well as prompt, thorough, and impartial investigations and corrective actions. A form like that in the accompanying Figure 7.1 is useful here.
2. *Inform all employees* about the policy prohibiting sexual harassment and of their rights under the policy.
3. *Develop and implement a complaint procedure.*
4. *Take all harassment complaints seriously.* Establish a management response system that includes an immediate reaction and investigation by senior management.
5. *Commence management training sessions* with supervisors and managers. Don't just focus on legal issues but on harassment's ethical dimension as well.[25]
6. *Discipline supervisors and employees* involved in sexual harassment.
7. *Keep thorough records* of complaints, investigations, and actions taken.
8. *Monitor the harassment climate.* For example, use periodic written attitude surveys and hotlines, as well as exit interviews that uncover complaints.

overall than majority men, minority men, and majority women."[26] Another big cause is a permissive climate, where employees conclude there's a risk to victims for complaining, or that complaints won't be taken seriously.[27]

Adding to this is the unfortunate fact that most harassment victims don't sue or complain. Instead (either due to fear of being fired or a sense that complaining is futile), they quit or try to avoid their harassers. "The few women who do formally complain do so only after encountering frequent, severe sexual harassment; at that point, considerable damage may have already occurred."[28] In one study, researchers surveyed about 6,000 U.S. military employees. Their findings made it clear that reporting incidents of harassment often triggered retaliation. Under such conditions, for many of these employees, the most "reasonable" thing to do was nothing, and to avoid reporting. The point for supervisors is that they can't just pay lip service to the company's written harassment rules and procedures. They must set a tone that discourages sexual harassment.[29]

Psychology complicates doing so. For example, what is harassment to women may be seen as innocent behavior by men. "Women perceive a broader range of socio-sexual behaviors as harassing," including behaviors like dating pressure, or physical sexual contact.[30] In one study, about 58% of employees reported experiencing at least some of the potentially harassment-type behaviors at work. Overall, about 25% found it fun and flattering and about half viewed it as benign. But on closer examination, about four times as many men as women found the behavior flattering or benign.[31] The harassers themselves sometimes don't even realize that their abominable behavior is offending others. Sexual harassment training and policies can reduce these problems.

Most people probably assume that sexual motives drive sexual harassment, but that's not always so. **Gender harassment** is "a form of hostile environment harassment that appears to be motivated by hostility toward [someone] who violates gender ideals." In one case, for instance, her bosses told a high-performing female accountant to "walk more femininely [and] dress more femininely."[32]

The supervisor's leadership has a lot to do with minimizing sexual harassment. The accompanying Leadership Applications for Supervisors feature explains why.

Leadership Applications for Supervisors

Considerate Leadership and Setting the Right Culture

If there is one guiding fact about the causes of sexual harassment at work, it's probably this: The best way to minimize such problems is to make it clear that such behavior is impermissible. Permissive cultures breed such behavior. Cultures in which everyone sees that you'll deal quickly with violators reduce it. One of your most important leadership tasks is therefore to set the right "EEO" culture.

Even insurance companies (who often pay the claims when suits are lost) put supervisors front and center in the battle against harassment. Supervision is "an area where we are lacking big time," said an insurer's risk control officer. "Supervisors hear the dirty jokes, see the dirty magazines" and, in many cases, "walk by and ignore it. . . . I'm not talking about keeping your employees under your thumb, but supervisors have to live up to their responsibilities. . . . they are paid to make the difficult, hard decisions."[33] "Establishing workplace respect must be driven by an organization's leadership. . . . They establish the culture of the organization."[34] Here are some specific supervisory leadership suggestions:

- Teach workers to show consideration for one another's differences and sensibilities.
- In turn, you can't really teach employees to be considerate by acting autocratically yourself. Tyrannical leaders breed tyrannical follower behaviors, and considerate leaders breed considerate follower behaviors. Remember that consideration and leader structure are not mutually exclusive. Exhibiting considerate leadership behaviors (being respectful, supportive, and fair) does not mean you can't also be structuring as required.
- Identify workplace problems that could lead to harassment or discrimination and communicate the need for better working relationships.
- Remember that your essential leadership role here is to make it clear you believe that it is "morally and legally right for everyone in the workplace to behave properly" and to set out the "boundaries of acceptable behavior."[35] It's always what you actually do to role model, reward, and punish, not what you say, that creates the department's culture.

WHAT THE EMPLOYEE CAN DO Suppose you or someone you know feels they've been a victim of sexual harassment. What should you do? First, know and follow the employer's sexual harassment reporting procedures. In addition, you may do the following:

1. File a verbal contemporaneous complaint or protest with the harasser and the harasser's boss stating that the unwanted overtures should cease because the conduct is unwelcome.

2. Write a polite letter that does three things: provides a detailed statement of the facts as the writer sees them, describes his or her feelings and what damage the writer thinks has been done, and states that he or she would like to request that the future relationship be on a purely professional basis.

3. If the unwelcome conduct does not cease, file verbal and written reports regarding the unwelcome conduct and unsuccessful efforts to get it to stop with the harasser's supervisor and/or the human resource director.

4. If the letters and appeals to the employer do not suffice, turn to the local office of the EEOC to file the necessary claim.

5. If the harassment is of a serious nature, the employee can also consult an attorney about suing the harasser for assault and battery, intentional infliction of emotional distress, and injunctive relief and to recover compensatory and punitive damages.

The Americans with Disabilities Act (ADA)

WHAT IS THE ADA?   The **Americans with Disabilities Act (ADA)** of 1990 prohibits employment discrimination against qualified individuals with disabilities.[36] It aims to reduce or eliminate serious problems of discrimination against individuals with disabilities. And it requires that employers make "reasonable accommodations" for physical or mental limitations, unless doing so imposes an "undue hardship" on the business.[37]

The act says that "impairment" includes any physiological disorder or condition, cosmetic disfigurement, or anatomical loss affecting one or more of several body systems, or any mental or psychological disorder.[38] However, the act does not list specific disabilities. Instead, the EEOC's implementing regulations provide that an individual is disabled if he or she has a physical or mental impairment that substantially limits one or more major life activities. On the other hand, the act does set forth certain conditions that are not to be regarded as disabilities, including homosexuality, bisexuality, voyeurism, compulsive gambling, and pyromania.[39] The ADA does protect employees with intellectual disabilities, including those with IQs below 70–75.[40] Mental disabilities account for the greatest number of claims brought under the ADA.[41]

Simply being disabled does not qualify someone for a job, of course. Instead, the act prohibits discrimination against qualified individuals—those who, with (or without) a reasonable accommodation, can carry out the essential functions of the job. This means that the individual must have the requisite skills, educational background, and experience to do the essential functions of the position. A job function is essential when, for instance, it is the reason the position exists, or because the function is so specialized that the person is hired for his or her expertise or ability to perform that particular function.[42]

REASONABLE ACCOMMODATION   If the individual can't perform the job as currently structured, the employer is required to make a reasonable accommodation, unless doing so would present an undue hardship. *Reasonable accommodation* might include modifying work schedules, or modifying or acquiring equipment or other devices to assist the person in performing the job. Court cases illustrate what "reasonable accommodation" means. For example, a Walmart door greeter was diagnosed with and treated for back problems. When she returned to work she asked if she could sit on a stool while on duty. Walmart said no, contending that standing was an essential part of the greeter's job. She sued, but the federal district court agreed with the employer. It said the door greeters must act in an "aggressively hospitable manner," which can't be done sitting on a stool.[43]

THE ADA IN PRACTICE   By most measures, workplace disabilities are on the rise, and employers need to accommodate increasing numbers of heavier and disabled employees.[44] It's thus not surprising that ADA complaints continue to flood the courts.

However, until recently, employers typically prevailed in about 96% of federal circuit court ADA decisions. A main reason is that employees were failing to show that they're disabled.[45] The employee must establish that he or she has a disability that fits under the ADA's definition. Doing so is more complicated than proving that one is a particular age, race, or gender.

A U.S. Supreme Court decision illustrates what plaintiffs faced. An assembly-line worker sued Toyota, arguing that carpal tunnel syndrome and tendonitis prevented her from doing her job (*Toyota Motor Manufacturing of Kentucky, Inc.* v. *Williams*). The U.S. Supreme Court ruled that the ADA covers carpal tunnel syndrome and tendonitis if her impairments affect not only her job performance but her daily living activities too. Here, the employee admitted that she could perform personal tasks and chores such as washing her face, brushing her teeth, tending her flower garden, and fixing breakfast and doing laundry. The court said the disability must be central to the employee's daily living (not just the job) to qualify under the ADA. The court will therefore look at each case (for instance, of carpal tunnel syndrome) individually.[46]

THE "NEW" ADA   But the era in which employers prevail in most ADA claims probably ended January 1, 2009. On that day, the ADA Amendments Act of 2008 (ADAAA) became effective. The EEOC had been interpreting the ADA's "substantially limits" phrase very narrowly, making it difficult for employees to show they were really disabled.

The new act's basic effect will be to make it easier for employees to show that their disabilities are limiting. For example, the new act makes it easier for an employee to show that his or her disability is influencing one of the employee's "major life activities." It does this by adding new examples of major life activities like reading, concentrating, thinking, sleeping, and communicating.[47] As another example, under the new act, an employee is still considered disabled even if he or she has been able to control his or her impairments through medical or "learned behavioral" modifications. The bottom line is that supervisors (and employers) must henceforth redouble their efforts to make sure they're complying with the ADA and providing reasonable accommodations.[48]

How Does the Americans with Disabilities Act (ADA) Affect Supervisors?

LEGAL OBLIGATIONS   The ADA imposes numerous legal obligations on employers. Important ones for supervisors to know about include the following:

- The timing of any inquiry about a person's disability is important. The central issue is this: In the event the hiring employer rescinds an offer, the applicant must be able to identify the specific reason for the rejection. For example, in one case, the courts found that American Airlines had violated the ADA by not making a "real" offer to three candidates before requiring them to take their medical exams, because American still hadn't yet checked their background references. In this case, the medical exams showed the candidates had HIV and American rescinded their offers, thus violating the ADA.[49]

- Employers should review job descriptions and identify the essential functions of the jobs in question.

- Employers must make a reasonable accommodation, unless doing so would result in undue hardship. As a supervisor, you may have to make suggestions such as allowing an employee to work in quieter surroundings, or with the aid of, say, voice recognition software, to accommodate an employee. The accompanying Supervising the New Workforce feature and Figure 7.3 illustrate how to do this. Figure 7.4 summarizes important ADA guidelines for supervisors and employers.

Many employers simply take a progressive approach. Research shows that common employer concerns about people with disabilities (for instance, that they have more

Providing Reasonable Accommodation

Technological innovations make it easier today for employers to accommodate disabled employees. For example, many employees with mobility impairments benefit from voice recognition software that allows them to input information into their computers and interactively communicate (for instance, via e-mail) without touching a keyboard. Special typing aids including word prediction software suggest words based on context and on just one or two letters typed.[50] The Firefox Web browser incorporates special IBM software that enables people to use the keyboard arrows rather than the mouse to access pull-down menus, aiding some disabled people.[51]

Employees with hearing and/or speech impairments have long benefited from the teletypewriter, which lets people communicate by typing and reading messages on a keyboard connected to a telephone line. Real-time translation captioning enables them to participate in lectures and meetings. Vibrating text pagers let them know when messages arrive. Employees with vision impairments benefit from add-on computer devices that, among other things, allow adjustments in font size, display color, and screen magnification for specific portions of the computer screen. Voice recognition software transcription devices transcribe and speak the written word for the employee. Special word processor software provides spoken instructions to aid the employee. Arizona had IBM Global Services create a disability-friendly Web site, "Arizona@Your Service," to help link prospective employees and others to various agencies.[52] Figure 7.3 illustrates what supervisors can do.

---

1. *Follow ADA Accessibility Guidelines*, such as regarding

   Protruding Objects.
   Ground and Floor Surfaces
   Curb Ramps
   Platform Lifts (Wheelchair Lifts)
   Doors (width, height of door handles, and so on)
   Drinking Fountains and Water Coolers
   Water Closets

2. *Modify Workplace Policies, such as regarding*

   Eating at the work site
   Hours of work
   Leave and attendance

3. *Use Technology, for example,*

   Employees with *mobility or vision impairments* may benefit from voice recognition software.
   Word prediction software suggests words based on context with just one or two letters typed.
   Real-time translation captioning enables employees to participate in meetings.
   Vibrating text pagers notify employees when messages arrive.
   Arizona created a disability-friendly Web site, "Arizona@YourService," to help link prospective employees and others to various agencies.

■Figure **7.3**

Examples of How to Provide Reasonable Accommodation

Source: Adapted from *Sexual Harassment Manual for Managers and Supervisors,* published in 1991, by CCH Incorporated, a WoltersKluwer Company, and from www.eeoc.gov/types/sexual_harrasment. html, accessed May 6, 2007.

- *Do not* deny a job to a disabled individual if the person is qualified and able to perform the essential job functions.
- *Make* a reasonable accommodation unless doing so would result in undue hardship.[54]
- *You need not* lower existing performance standards or stop using tests for a job. However, those standards or tests must be job related and uniformly applied to all employees and candidates.
- *Know* what you can ask applicants. In general, you may *not* make pre-employment inquiries about a person's disability before making an offer conditioned on passing the medical exam and reference check.[55] However, you *may* ask questions about the person's ability to perform essential job functions.[56]
- *Remove from* job application, interview procedures, and job descriptions illegal questions about health, disabilities, medical histories, or previous workers' compensation claims.[57]
- *Itemize* essential job functions on the job descriptions.
- *Do not* allow misconduct or erratic performance (including absences and tardiness), "even if that behavior is linked to the disability."[58]
- One expert advises, "*Don't treat employees as if they are disabled.*" If they can control their conditions (for instance, through medication), courts may not consider them disabled. But if you treat them as disabled, they'll normally be "regarded as" disabled and protected.[59]

accidents) are generally baseless.[60] So, for example, Walgreens has a goal of filling at least one-third of the jobs at its two large distribution centers with people with disabilities.[61]

Genetic Information Non-Discrimination Act of 2008 (GINA)

What Are the Strict Requirements Posed by the Genetic Information Non-Discrimination Act of 2008 (GINA)?

GINA prohibits discrimination by health insurers and employers based on people's genetic information. Specifically, it prohibits the use of genetic information in employment, prohibits the intentional acquisition of genetic information about applicants and employees, and imposes strict confidentiality requirements.[62]

Sexual Orientation

The federal Employment Non-Discrimination Act (ENDA) would prohibit workplace discrimination based on sexual orientation and gender identity if Congress passes it.[63] Meanwhile, a federal appeals court recently decided that a homosexual man is not necessarily barred from filing a sexual discrimination claim under Title VII of the Civil Rights Act.[64] Many states do bar discrimination at work based on sexual orientation.[65]

State and Local Equal Employment Opportunity Laws

How Do State and Local Equal Opportunity Laws Affect Supervisors?

In addition to the federal laws, all states and many local governments also prohibit employment discrimination.

In most cases, the effect of the state and local laws is to further restrict employers. For example, they often cover employers that don't fall within federal legislation (such as employers with fewer than 15 employees). Similarly, some local governments extend the protection of age discrimination laws to young people as well as those over 40. As two examples, State of Florida statutes prohibit wage rate discrimination based on sex even in those employers not subject to the federal Fair Labor Standards Act.[66] The New York City Human Rights Law prohibits (among other things) discrimination in employment based on various criteria, including arrest or conviction record and status as a victim of domestic violence.[67]

State and local equal employment opportunity agencies (often called *commissions on human relations,* or *fair employment commissions*) also play a role in the EEO process. When the EEOC receives a discrimination charge, it usually defers it for a limited time to the relevant state and local agencies. Then, if satisfactory remedies are not achieved, the charges revert back to the EEOC.

Summary

Table 7.1 summarizes these and selected other equal employment opportunity legislation, executive orders, and agency guidelines.

■ Table **7.1**

Summary of Important Equal Employment Opportunity Actions

Action	What It Does
Title VII of 1964 Civil Rights Act, as amended	Bars discrimination because of race, color, religion, sex, or national origin; instituted EEOC
Executive orders	Prohibit employment discrimination by employers with federal contracts of more than $10,000 (and their subcontractors); established office of federal compliance; require affirmative action programs
Federal agency guidelines	Indicate policy covering discrimination based on sex, national origin, and religion, as well as on employee selection procedures; for example, require validation of tests
Supreme Court decisions: *Griggs* v. *Duke Power Company, Albemarle Paper Company* v. *Moody*	Ruled that job requirements must be related to job success; that discrimination need not be overt to be proved; that the burden of proof is on the employer to prove the qualification is valid
Equal Pay Act of 1963	Requires equal pay for men and women for performing similar work
Age Discrimination in Employment Act of 1967	Prohibits discriminating against a person 40 or over in any area of employment because of age
State and local laws	Often cover organizations too small to be covered by federal laws
Pregnancy Discrimination Act of 1978	Prohibits discrimination in employment against pregnant women, or related conditions
Americans with Disabilities Act of 1990	Strengthens the need for most employers to make reasonable accommodations for disabled employees at work; prohibits discrimination
Civil Rights Act of 1991	Reverses *Wards Cove, Patterson,* and *Martin* decisions; places burden of proof back on employer and permits compensatory and punitive money damages for discrimination
Genetic Information Non-Discrimination Act of 2008 (GINA)	Prohibits discrimination by health insurers and employers based on people's genetic information.

3. Defenses Against Discrimination Allegations

What Defenses May Be Used against Discrimination Allegations?

As careful as you try to be, eventually you may find yourself accused of some discriminatory action. To understand how to help defend yourself and your employer, you should be familiar with some basic legal terminology.

What Is Adverse Impact?

ADVERSE IMPACT   Under the Civil Rights Act of 1991, it is fairly easy for an applicant or employee who thinks he or she has been *unintentionally* discriminated against to pursue a case. The person just has to show that the employer's selection (or other) procedures had an *adverse impact* on a protected minority group. **Adverse impact** "refers to the total employment process that results in a significantly higher percentage of a protected group in the candidate population being rejected for employment, placement, or promotion."[68]

What does this mean? If a minority or other protected group applicant for the job feels he or she has been discriminated against, the applicant need only show that the selection procedures resulted in an adverse impact on his or her minority group. (There are several ways to do this, for example, by showing that 80% of the white applicants passed the test, but only 20% of the black or other protected group's applicants passed; if this is the case, the minority applicant has a prima facie case proving adverse impact.)

Then, once the employee has proved his or her point, the burden of proof shifts to the employer. It becomes the employer's task to prove that its test, application blank, interview, or the like is a valid predictor of performance on the job, and that it was applied fairly and equitably to both minorities and nonminorities. (By the way, don't be lulled into thinking that such cases are ancient history. For example, a U.S. Appeals Court recently upheld a $3.4 million jury verdict against Dial Corp. Dial allegedly rejected 52 women for entry-level jobs at a meat processing plant. Supervisors had said the women failed strength tests, although strength was not a job requirement).[69]

DISPARATE IMPACT AND DISPARATE TREATMENT   Discrimination law distinguishes between disparate *treatment* and disparate *impact*. *Disparate treatment* means *intentional* discrimination. It "requires no more than a finding that women (or protected minority group members) were intentionally treated differently . . . because of their gender (or minority status)." Being caught making outrageous comments like "we never hire women for these jobs" might be an example.

Disparate impact claims do not require proof of discriminatory intent. Instead, the plaintiff must show that there is a significant disparity between the proportion of (say) women in the available labor pool and the proportion hired, and that there's an apparently neutral employment practice (such as a selection test) causing the disparity.[70]

BRINGING A CASE OF DISCRIMINATION: SUMMARY   Assume that an employer turns down a member of a protected group for a job based on a test score (or some other employment practice, such as a strength test). Further assume that the person believes that he or she was discriminated against and decides to sue the employer.

All he or she has to do is show (to the court's satisfaction) that the employer's test had an adverse impact on members of his or her minority group. Then the burden of proof shifts to the employer, which then must defend itself against the charges of discrimination.

There are two defenses that the employer can use: the **bona fide occupational qualification (BFOQ)** defense and the business necessity defense. Either can be used to justify an employment practice that has been shown to have an adverse impact on the members of a minority group. (A third defense is that the decision was made on the basis of legitimate nondiscriminatory reasons, such as poor performance, having nothing to do with the alleged prohibited discrimination.)

Bona Fide Occupational Qualification

One approach an employer can use to defend against charges of discrimination is to claim that the employment practice is a *bona fide occupational qualification* for performing the job. Title VII provides that

> it should not be an unlawful employment practice for an employer to hire an employee . . . on the basis of religion, sex, or national origin in those certain instances where religion, sex, or national origin is a bona fide occupational qualification reasonably necessary to the normal operation of that particular business or enterprise.

For example, an employer can use age as a BFOQ to defend itself against a disparate treatment (intentional discrimination) charge when federal requirements impose a compulsory age limit. For instance, the Federal Aviation Agency sets a ceiling of age 65 for pilots. Actors required for youthful or elderly roles or persons used to advertise or promote the sales of products designed for youthful or elderly consumers suggest other instances when age may be a BFOQ, although the courts set the bar high: The reason for the discrimination must go to the "essence of the business."

Unfortunately, it isn't always clear what the essence of the business is. A Texas man recently filed a complaint against Hooters of America. He alleged that one of its franchisees would not hire him as a waiter because it "merely wishes to exploit female sexuality as a marketing tool to attract customers and insure profitability" and so was limiting hiring to females.[71] Hooters argued a BFOQ defense before reaching a confidential settlement with the man.

Business Necessity

The **business necessity** defense requires showing that there is an overriding business purpose for the discriminatory practice and that the practice is therefore acceptable.

It's not easy to prove that a practice is a business necessity. Business necessity does not encompass such matters as avoiding inconvenience, or expense. The Second Circuit Court of Appeals held that *business necessity* means an "irresistible demand." It said that to be retained, the practice "must not only directly foster safety and efficiency," but also be essential to these goals.[72] For example, an employer cannot generally discharge employees whose wages have been garnished merely because garnishment (requiring the employer to divert part of the person's wages to pay his or her debts) creates an inconvenience for the employer.

On the other hand, employers use this defense successfully all the time. In one famous case, *Spurlock* v. *United Airlines*, a minority candidate sued United Airlines. He said that United's requirements that a pilot candidate have 500 flight hours and a college degree were unfairly discriminatory. The Court agreed that these requirements did have an adverse impact on members of the person's minority group. However, the Court held that in light of the cost of the training program and the tremendous human and economic risks involved in hiring unqualified candidates, the selection standards were required by business necessity and were job related.[73]

Attempts by employers to show that their selection tests or other screening practices (like interview questions) are valid are examples of the business necessity defense. Used in this context, the word *validity* means the degree to which the test or other employment practice is related to or predicts performance on the job. The bottom line is that supervisors really should only use screening tools such as interview questions and tests that they are quite sure relate to performance on the job in question.

4. Illustrative Discriminatory Supervisory Practices

A Note on What You Can and Cannot Do

In this section, we present several illustrations of what supervisors can and cannot do under equal employment laws. But before proceeding, keep in mind that most federal laws, such as Title VII, do not expressly ban preemployment questions about an applicant's race, color, religion, sex, age, or national origin.[74] For example, it is not illegal to ask a job candidate "Are you married?" (although at first glance such a question might seem discriminatory). You can ask such a question. However, you must stand ready to show either that *you do not discriminate*, or that the practice can be defended as a *BFOQ* or *business necessity*.

In other words, illustrative practices such as those we summarize on the next few pages are not illegal per se. But beware: In practice, there are two good reasons to avoid such questionable practices. First, although federal law may not bar such questions, many state and local laws do. Second, the EEOC has said that it disapproves of such practices as asking women their marital status or applicants their age. Supervisors who use practices like the following could thus increase the chances their employers will be sued.

Recruitment

WORD OF MOUTH   You cannot rely on word-of-mouth dissemination of information about job opportunities when your workforce is all (or substantially all) white or all members of some other class such as all female, all Hispanic, and so on. Doing so might reduce the likelihood that others will become aware of the jobs and thus apply for them.

MISLEADING INFORMATION   It is unlawful to give false or misleading information to members of any group or to fail to refuse to advise them of work opportunities and the procedures for obtaining them.

HELP WANTED ADS   "Help wanted—male" and "Help wanted—female" advertising classifieds are violations of laws forbidding sex discrimination in employment unless sex is a BFOQ for the job advertised.[75] Also, you cannot advertise in a way that suggests that applicants are being discriminated against because of their age. For example, you cannot advertise for a "young" man or woman.

Selection Standards

EDUCATIONAL REQUIREMENTS An educational requirement may be held illegal when (1) it can be shown that minority groups are less likely to possess the educational qualifications (such as a high school diploma), and (2) such qualifications are also not job related. Unnecessary prerequisites (such as requiring a high school diploma where one is not required to perform the job) reportedly remains a problem today.[76]

TESTS According to former Chief Justice Burger:

> Nothing in the [Title VII] act precludes the use of testing or measuring procedures; obviously they are useful. What Congress has forbidden is giving these devices and mechanisms controlling force unless they are demonstrating a *reasonable measure of job performance.*

The problem is that many employers do use tests that they buy from vendors (such as office supply stores) that may seem reasonable but that may not be distinguishing between potentially high-performing and low-performing employees. You need to make sure the test results are job-related. Do people who do better on this test really perform measurably better on the job?

PREFERENCE TO RELATIVES You cannot as a rule give preference to relatives of your current employees with respect to employment opportunities if your current employees are substantially nonminority.

HEIGHT, WEIGHT, AND PHYSICAL CHARACTERISTICS Maximum weight rules for employees don't usually trigger adverse legal rulings. However, some minority groups have a higher incidence of obesity. Therefore, employers must ensure that their weight rules aren't inadvertently adversely impacting those minorities. And in any case, supervisors should be vigilant against stigmatizing obese people. Studies leave little doubt that obese individuals are less likely to be hired, less likely to receive promotions, more likely to get less desirable sales assignments, and more likely to receive poor customer service as customers, for instance.[77]

HEALTH QUESTIONS Under the ADA, "employers are generally prohibited from asking questions about applicants' medical history or requiring preemployment physical examinations." However, such questions and exams can be used *once the job offer has been extended* to determine that the applicant can safely perform the job.[78]

ARREST RECORDS You cannot ask about or use a person's arrest record to disqualify him or her automatically for a position because there is always a presumption of innocence until proof of guilt. In addition, arrest records in general have not been shown to be valid for predicting job performance, and a higher percentage of minorities than nonminorities have been arrested.

Sample Discriminatory Promotion, Transfer, and Layoff Procedures

Fair employment laws protect not just job applicants but current employees as well.[79] Therefore, many employment practices regarding pay, promotion, termination, discipline, or benefits may be held to be illegally discriminatory. To take an obvious example, you generally can't use differences like race or gender to decide who will be trained or promoted.

UNIFORMS   When it comes to discriminatory uniforms and suggestive attire, courts frequently side with the employee. For example, requiring female employees (such as waitresses) to wear sexually suggestive attire as a condition of employment has been ruled as violating Title VII in many cases.[80]

RETALIATION   Occasionally, a misguided supervisor might be inclined to respond to a complaint of unlawful discrimination by retaliating against the complaining employee, rather than by taking appropriate action.[81] Supervisors should understand that "unlawful retaliation for engaging in protected activities, such as pursuing a claim of employment discrimination, is a separate employment offense under Title VII of the Civil Rights Act of 1964 that an employee may bring even if the primary discrimination complaint is deemed to be without merit."[82] Supervisors receiving discrimination complaints must therefore be careful to follow the proper procedures. Avoid any retaliatory behavior toward the aggrieved employee.

5. The EEOC Enforcement Process

What Are the Steps in the EEOC Enforcement Process?

It's generally the employer, not the supervisor, who will set the firm's employment policies and have to deal with the consequences of discrimination claims. However, supervisors should have a working understanding of what transpires if an EEO suit is filed (we've summarized the process in Figure 7.5.)

Processing a Charge

FILE A CLAIM   The process begins with someone filing a claim. Under the Civil Rights Act of 1991, the discrimination claim must be filed within 300 days (when there is a similar state discrimination law that may cover the employee) or 180 days (no similar state law) after the alleged incident took place. In practice the EEOC typically defers a person's charge to the relevant state or local regulatory agency. If the latter waives jurisdiction or cannot obtain a satisfactory solution to the charge, they refer it back to the EEOC.[83]

After a charge has been filed (or the state or local deferral period has ended), the EEOC has 10 days to serve notice of the charge on the employer. The EEOC then investigates the charge to determine whether there is reasonable cause to believe it is true; it is expected to make this determination within 120 days.

If no reasonable cause is found, the EEOC must dismiss the charge, in which case the person who filed the charge has 90 days to file a suit on his or her own behalf.

If reasonable cause for the charge is found, the EEOC must attempt to conciliate. If this conciliation is not satisfactory, the EEOC may bring a civil suit in a federal district court or issue a notice of right to sue to the person who filed the charge.

The Equal Employment Opportunity Commission often pursues changing initiatives (see for instance, http://eeoc.gov/eeoc/initiatives/e-race/index.cfm). For example, for fiscal years 2008–2013, it has its E-RACE Initiative. This aims to improve the EEOC's efforts to ensure workplaces are free of race and color discrimination.[84]

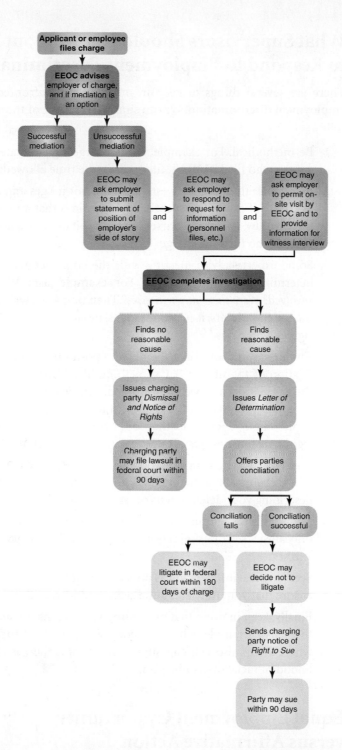

VOLUNTARY MEDIATION   The EEOC refers about 10% of its charges to a voluntary mediation mechanism. If the plaintiff agrees to mediation, the employer is asked to participate. A mediation session usually lasts up to four hours. If no agreement is reached or one of the parties rejects participation, the charge is then processed through the EEOC's usual mechanisms.[85]

What Supervisors Should Know About How to Respond to Employment Discrimination Charges

There are several things to keep in mind when confronted by a charge of illegal employment discrimination. We can summarize some of the more important items as follows:

1. Be methodical. For example, is the charge signed, dated, and notarized by the person who filed it? Was it filed within the time allowed?[86]

2. Remember that EEOC investigators are not judges and aren't empowered to act as courts. If the EEOC eventually determines that an employer may be in violation of a law, its only recourse is to file a suit or issue a notice of right to sue to the person who filed the charge.

3. Some experts advise meeting with the employee who made the complaint to determine all relevant issues. For example, ask: *What happened? Who was involved? Were there any witnesses?* Then prepare a written statement summarizing the complaints, facts, dates, and issues involved and request that the employee sign and date this.[87]

4. The employer should give the EEOC a position statement based on its own investigation of the matter. Say something like, "Our company has a policy against discrimination and we would not discriminate in the manner outlined in the complaint." Support your case with some statistical analysis of the workforce, copies of any documents that support your position, and an explanation of any legitimate business justification for the actions you took.

5. Ensure that there is information in the EEOC's file demonstrating lack of merit of the charge. Often the best way to do that is by providing a detailed statement describing your defense in its most persuasive light.

6. Limit the information supplied as narrowly as possible. For example, if the charge only alleges sex discrimination, do not provide a breakdown of employees by age and sex.

7. Seek as much information as possible about the charging party's claim in order to ensure that you understand the claim and its ramifications.

8. Finally, keep in mind that preventing such claims is usually better than litigating them. For example, when someone with racist attitudes works in a company where there's also a climate supporting racism, there is a significantly higher likelihood of racial discrimination.[88]

Equal Employment Opportunity versus Affirmative Action

Equal employment opportunity aims to ensure that anyone, regardless of race, color, disability, sex, religion, national origin, or age, has an equal chance for a job based on his or her qualifications. *Affirmative action* goes beyond equal employment opportunity by requiring the employer to make an extra effort to hire and promote those in a protected group.

Steps in an Affirmative Action Program

What Are the Recommended Steps for Establishing an Affirmative Action Program?

According to the EEOC, in an affirmative action program the employer ideally takes eight steps:

1. Issue a written equal employment policy indicating that it is an equal employment opportunity employer, as well as a statement indicating the employer's commitment to affirmative action.

2. Appoint a top official with responsibility and authority to direct and implement the program.

3. Publicize the equal employment policy and affirmative action commitment.

4. Survey present minority and female employment to determine locations where affirmative action programs are especially desirable.[89]

5. Develop goals and timetables to improve utilization of minorities, males, and females in each area where utilization has been identified.

6. Review the firm's human resource management system (including recruitment, selection, promotion, compensation, and disciplining.) Identify barriers to equal employment opportunity and to make needed changes.

7. Establish an internal audit and reporting system to monitor and evaluate progress in each aspect of the program.

8. Develop support for the affirmative action program, both inside the company (among supervisors, for instance) and outside the company in the community.[90]

AFFIRMATIVE ACTION TODAY   Affirmative action is still a significant workplace issue today. The incidence of major court-mandated programs is down. However, many employers must still engage in voluntary programs. For example, Executive Order 11246 (issued in 1965) requires federal contractors to take affirmative action to improve employment opportunities for women and racial minorities. It covers about 26 million workers—about 22% of the U.S. workforce.

In addition, in 2009, the U.S. Supreme Court decided an important "reverse discrimination" suit brought by Connecticut firefighters. In *Ricci* v. *DeStefano*, 19 white firefighters and one Hispanic firefighter said the city of New Haven should have promoted them based on their successful scores. The city argued that certifying the tests would have left them vulnerable to lawsuits by minorities for violating Title VII.[91] The Court decided in favor of the white firefighters.

Avoiding an employee backlash to affirmative action programs is important. A review of 35 years of research suggests several steps employers and supervisors can take to increase employee support. Current employees need to see that the program is fair. *Transparent selection procedures* help in this regard. *Communication* is also crucial. Make clear that the program doesn't involve preferential selection standards. Provide details on the qualifications of all new hires (both minority and nonminority). *Justifications* for the program should emphasize redressing past discrimination and the practical value of diversity, not underrepresentation.[92]

Chapter 7 Concept Review and Reinforcement

Key Terms

Adverse Impact, p. 198
Age Discrimination in
   Employment Act
   (ADEA) of 1967, p. 184
Bona Fide Occupational
   Qualification
   (BFOQ), p. 199
Business Necessity, p. 199

Civil Rights Act of 1991
   (CRA 1991), p. 186
Equal Employment
   Opportunity
   Commission
   (EEOC), p. 184
Equal Pay Act
   of 1963, p. 183

Federal Violence
   Against Women Act
   of 1994, p. 187
Gender Harassment,
   p. 191
Office of Federal Contract
   Compliance Programs
   (OFCCP), p. 184

Pregnancy
   Discrimination Act
   (PDA), p. 184
Title VII of the 1964
   Civil Rights Act,
   p. 183

Review of Key Concepts

Fifth Amendment to U.S. Constitution	(1791) States that no person shall be deprived of life, liberty, or property without due process of the law.
Equal Pay Act	(1963) Made it unlawful to discriminate in pay on the basis of sex when jobs involve equal work.
Title VII—Civil Rights Act	(1964) An employer cannot discriminate based on race, color, religion, sex, or national origin.
Equal Employment Opportunity Commission	(EEOC) To implement Civil Rights Act. Meant to enhance the federal government's ability to enforce equal employment opportunity laws.
Age Discrimination in Employment Act	(1967) Prohibits discrimination against a person 40 years of age or older due to his or her age.
Pregnancy Discrimination Act	(1978) Prohibits discrimination in employment against pregnant women.
Americans with Disabilities Act	(1990) Strengthens the need for employers to make reasonable accommodations for disabled employees.
Civil Rights Act	(1991) Places burden of proof back on employer and permits damages for discrimination.
Executive Orders	Prohibits employment discrimination by employees with federal contracts of more than $10,000.
Supreme Court Ruling: *Griggs v. Duke Power Company*	Ruled that job requirements must be related to success.

Adverse Impact	Refers to the total employment process that results in a significantly higher percentage of a protected group in the candidate population being rejected for employment, placement, or promotion.
Disparate Impact	Disparate impact claims do not require proof of discriminatory intent.
Disparate Treatment	Disparate treatment means intentional discrimination.
Bona Fide Occupational Qualification	(BFOQ) It is not unlawful to hire an employee in those certain instances where religion, sex, or national origin is a bona fide occupational qualification reasonably necessary to the normal operation of that particular business.
Affirmative Action	Affirmative action goes beyond equal employment opportunity by requiring the employer to make an extra effort to hire and promote those in a protected group.
Eight Steps in Affirmative Action Program	• Issue written policy. • Appoint a top official. • Publicize the policy. • Survey present minority and female employment. • Develop goals and timetables. • Develop and implement specific programs. • Establish an internal audit. • Develop support of in-house and community programs.

Review and Discussion Questions

1. What was the Equal Pay Act of 1963? Describe.
2. What is Title VII? What does it state?
3. Describe how the federal government enforces Title VII of the Civil Rights Act of 1964.
4. Why was the Pregnancy Discrimination Law enacted in 1978?
5. Under the Americans with Disabilities Act (ADA), name at least five reasonable accommodations that might be made for employees with disabilities.
6. What important precedents were set by the *Griggs* v. *Duke Power Company* case?
7. What is adverse impact? How can it be proven?
8. What particular group of employees is targeted by executive orders? Why?
9. What does disparate treatment mean?
10. When an employer uses a bona fide occupational qualification as a defense against charges of discrimination, what must that employer show?
11. What is the difference between affirmative action and equal employment opportunity?

Application and Skill Building

Case Study One

An Accusation of Sexual Harassment in Pro Sports

The jury in a sexual harassment suit brought by a former high-ranking New York Knicks basketball team executive recently awarded her over $11 million in punitive damages. They did so after hearing testimony during what the *New York Times* called a "sordid four-week trial." Officials of the Madison Square Garden (which owns the Knicks) said they would appeal the verdict. However, even if they were to win on appeal (which one University of Richmond Law School professor said was unlikely), the case still exposed the organization and its managers to a great deal of unfavorable publicity.

The federal suit pitted Anucha Browne Sanders, the Knicks' senior vice president of marketing and business operations (and former Northwestern University basketball star) against the team's owner, Madison Square Garden, and its president, Isiah Thomas. The suit charged them with sex discrimination and retaliation. Ms. Browne Sanders accused Mr. Thomas of verbally abusing and sexually harassing her over a two-year period, and says the Garden fired her about a month after she complained to top management about the harassment. "My pleas and complaints about Mr. Thomas' illegal and offensive actions fell on deaf ears," she said. At the trial, the Garden cited numerous explanations for the dismissal, saying she had "failed to fulfill professional responsibilities." At a news conference, Browne Sanders said that Thomas "refused to stop his demeaning and repulsive behavior and the Garden refused to intercede." For his part, Mr. Thomas vigorously insisted he was innocent, and said, "I will not allow her or anybody, man or woman, to use me as a pawn for their financial gain." According to one report of the trial her claims of harassment and verbal abuse had little corroboration from witnesses, but neither did the Garden's claims that her performance had been sub-par. After the jury decision came in, Browne Sanders's lawyers said, "This [decision] confirms what we've been saying all along, that [Browne Sanders] was sexually abused and fired for complaining about it." The Garden's statement said, in part, "We look forward to presenting our arguments to an appeals court and believe they will agree that no sexual harassment took place."

Questions

1. Do you think Ms. Browne Sanders had the basis for a sexual harassment suit? Why or why not?
2. From what you know of this case, do you think the jury arrived at the correct decision? If not, why not? If so, why?
3. Based on the few facts that you have, what steps, if any, could Garden management have taken to protect themselves from liability in this matter?
4. Aside from the appeal, what would you do now if you were the Garden's top management?

5. "The allegations against the Madison Square Garden in this case raise ethical questions with regard to the employer's actions." Explain whether you agree or disagree with this statement, and why.

Sources: "Jury Awards $11.6 Million to Former Executive of Pro Basketball Team in Harassment Case," *BNA Bulletin to Management* (October 9, 2007): 323; Richard Sandomir, "Jury Finds Knicks and Coach Harassed a Former Executive," *The New York Times,* http://www.nytimes.com/2007/10/03/sports/basketball/03garden.html?em&ex=1191556800&en=41d47437f805290d&ei=5087%0A (accessed November 31, 2007); "Thomas Defiant in Face of Harassment Claims," ESPN.com (accessed November 31, 2007).

Case Study Two

Carter Cleaning Centers

A Question of Discrimination

One of the first problems Jennifer faced when she joined her father's Carter Cleaning Centers after graduation concerned the inadequacies of the firm's current employment practices and procedures.

One problem that particularly concerned her was the lack of attention to equal employment matters. Virtually all hiring was handled independently by each store manager, and the managers themselves had received no training regarding such fundamental matters as the types of questions that should not be asked of job applicants. It was therefore not unusual—in fact, it was routine—for female applicants to be asked questions such as, "Who's going to take care of your children while you are at work?" and for minority applicants to be asked questions about arrest records and credit histories. Nonminority applicants—three store managers were white males and three were white females, by the way—were not asked these questions, as Jennifer discerned from her interviews with the managers. Based on discussions with her father, Jennifer deduced that part of the reason for the laid-back attitude toward equal employment stemmed from (1) her father's lack of sophistication regarding the legal requirements, and (2) the fact that, as Jack Carter put it, "Virtually all our workers are women or minority members anyway, so no one can really come in here and accuse us of being discriminatory, can they?"

Jennifer decided to mull that question over, but before she could, she was faced with two serious equal rights problems. Two women in one of her stores privately confided to her that their manager was making unwelcome sexual advances toward them, and one claimed he had threatened to fire her unless she "socialized" with him after hours. And during a fact-finding trip to another store, an older gentleman—he was 73 years old—complained of the fact that although he had almost 50 years of experience in the business, he was being paid less than people half his age who were doing the very same job. Jennifer's review of the stores resulted in the following questions.

Questions

1. Is it true, as Jack Carter claims, that "we can't be accused of being discriminatory because we hire mostly women and minorities anyway"?
2. How should Jennifer and her company address the sexual harassment charges and problems?
3. How should she and her company address the possible problems of age discrimination?
4. Given the fact that each store has only a handful of employees, is her company in fact covered by equal rights legislation?

Experiential Activities

Activity 1. Walmart hired Patrick Brady, who has cerebral palsy, to work as a pharmacist's assistant in one of its stores. According to Patrick, the store pharmacist didn't think Patrick was fit for the pharmacy job, so the store reassigned Patrick to pick up trash. A New York jury soon ordered Walmart to pay Patrick $7.5 million for violating the Americans with Disabilities Act. In teams of 4–5 students:

1. Do an Internet search to determine what the final decision was concerning this case. For example, did Walmart appeal the original jury decision? If so, on what basis?
2. What if anything does this case and your research into it suggest about what the pharmacist-supervisor here could have and probably should have done differently?

Activity 2. Ethics and Equal Employment If one accepts the proposition that equal employment is at least partly an ethical matter, then we should expect employers to recognize and emphasize that fact, for instance, on their Web sites. Some do. For example, you can find the ethics policy of the Duke Energy Company (which, when known as Duke Power many years ago, lost one of the first and most famous equal employment cases) posted on its Web site: http://www.duke-energy.com/about-us/ethics-and-compliance.asp (accessed November 19, 2010)

Purpose: *Ethical decision-making is an important supervisory competency.* The purpose of this exercise is to increase your understanding of how ethics and equal employment are interrelated.

Required Understanding: Be thoroughly familiar with the material presented in this chapter.

How to Set Up the Exercise/Instructions

1. Divide the class into groups of three to five students.
2. Each group should use the Internet to identify and access at least five more companies that emphasize how ethics and equal employment are interrelated.

3. Next, each group should develop answers to the following questions:
   a. Based on your Internet research, how much importance do employers seem to place on emphasizing the ethical aspects of equal employment?
   b. What seem to be the main themes these employers emphasize with respect to ethics and equal employment?
   c. Given what you've learned here, explain how you would emphasize the ethical aspects of equal employment if you were creating an equal employment training program for new supervisors.

Activity 3. Age Discrimination—Proof Larry walked into the dean's office at a large southeastern university to apply for a teaching position in the economics department. Larry had over 25 years of experience teaching in higher education together with a PhD in economics from an Indiana university. At age 58, Larry felt he had at least another 10–15 years to teach before he retired. During his interview, Larry's age was mentioned, to which the dean replied, "I'm sorry, Mr. Vaughn, but you are just too old for this position. Even though you are well qualified, we would rather hire someone younger." This ended the interview and Mr. Vaughn left the dean's office, not to pursue the issue further. This example of age discrimination is probably only one of many situations similar to Larry's that never made it to the courtroom.

In teams of 4–5 students, spend some time on the Internet or in the library researching information pertaining to the Age Discrimination Employment Act of 1967. From your research, put together a one-page summary of the steps Larry might take to prove age discrimination in the workplace. Do you agree that age discrimination can be very difficult to prove? Explain your answer.

Starting point for Internet research: http://www.ehow.com/How

Role-Playing Exercise

Sexual Harassment and the Supervisor: The Situation

The production supervisor of the Lawrence Furniture Manufacturing Company had just returned from a two-week vacation. The supervisor's primary goal was to produce first-quality lawn furniture for specialty furniture dealers and large department stores with furniture departments. It was quite a shock to the supervisor to learn, upon returning from vacation, that one of the subordinates had claimed that she had been a victim of sexual harassment. A female employee had indicated that another worker in the department had created an intimidating and hostile work environment, which had affected the employee's work performance.

The supervisor decided that immediate action was necessary because sexual harassment was a violation of Title VII of the Civil Rights Act. The supervisor was so disappointed to have had something like this happen in the department.

Instructions: All students should read the situation above.

One student will play the role of the production supervisor while a second student will play the role of the alleged sexual harasser.

Each student should reach his or her assigned role below. Then the two students should engage in a 15-minute conversation to resolve the issue.

After the role-play exercise the students should read and address the questions at the end of this exercise.

The Supervisor: The major problem you face as the supervisor is what you are going to do about this situation. Several courses of action are evident to you. You can:

- Fire the alleged offending employee (who has been with the company for over eight years).
- Transfer the alleged offending employee to another department (if there is a position open in another department and they will take the person).
- Counsel the alleged offending employee and hopefully resolve the issue.

You have chosen the third approach: counseling. An appointment has been made to meet with said employee.

A major challenge that you will face as the supervisor is that other workers in your department are going to be watching to see how you resolve the issue. You have enough worries surrounding quality and production, and now more has been added to your plate with the allegations of departmental sexual harassment. You must convince this employee that this behavior has been inappropriate and that the employee must adjust their actions accordingly or face transfer or termination.

Employee Charged with Sexual Harassment: You are a little surprised that a fellow employee has charged you with sexual harassment. Everyone tells a dirty joke or says something that may be offensive every once in a while, so what is the big deal? You've worked here for over eight years and have never been written up or sanctioned before. You wish this situation would just go away so that you can get back to work. You are hoping that you do well in this meeting with your supervisor and don't lose your job!

Questions

1. Based on what you read in this chapter, did the supervisor do a good job in taking corrective action? Explain your answer.
2. Were the reactions of the offending employee in the role-play exercise what you would expect from an employee in a similar situation?
3. If you were the supervisor, what would you have done with this employee?
4. What action would you suggest to the supervisor to keep the situation from happening again?
5. Is there any indication in this case that the offending employee is male or female? Support your answer.

8 How to Interview and Select Employees

....

CHAPTER OBJECTIVES

After studying this chapter, you should be able to answer the following questions:

1. Why Is Selecting the Right Person for the Job and Organization Important?

2. What Basic Employee Selection Concepts Should Supervisors Understand and Apply?

3. How Are an Employment Candidate's Rights Protected?

4. How Are Selection Tests Helpful in Screening Applicants?

5. Selection Interviews: What Guidelines Are Helpful for Finding the Right Person for the Job?

6. Background Checks and Other Selection Techniques: How Do They Assist the Supervisor in Choosing the Right Person for the Job?

OPENING SNAPSHOT
Cassandra Gets Deceived

Cassandra wasn't just proud to be promoted to office supervisor at the plumbing company where she worked, she was euphoric. She had spent five years working toward this position, and when she got it, she wanted to make sure that all went well.

Unfortunately, it was not to be. Two weeks into the job, her boss, the company's owner, asked her to find candidates to fill a new position, sales assistant. This person was to support the sales supervisor by calling prospective clients (mostly builders) to see if they needed supplies. Cassandra placed an ad, received about 30 applications, and called what seemed to be the five best to come in for interviews with her and with the sales supervisor. One candidate they spoke with particularly stood out: She seemed enthusiastic, motivated, outgoing, and smart. After briefly checking with her last boss, they hired her.

It was a disaster. After two weeks on the job, this person was arguing with everyone in the company. Following a

particularly tense argument with one coworker, that coworker left the office in tears. After two more weeks of this, they gave the new sales assistant one week's severance pay and dismissed her. Now Cassandra had to figure out how she could have been so wrong.

1. Why Be Careful About Whom You Hire?

It isn't easy picking good job candidates. In Chicago, a pharmaceutical firm discovered that it had hired a group of gang members to work in mail delivery and computer repair. The entrepreneurial gang members were stealing computer parts and then using the mail department to ship them to a nearby computer store they owned.[1] And at a time in which many people are creating avatars to represent idealized versions of themselves on Second Life, selecting good people is even more challenging. For example, an entire mini-industry has emerged that creates, for applicants, a "career" complete with false job references. Many retailers, seeking to reduce hiring expenses, automated their hiring processes. The retailers teamed with special online companies. These online companies posted personality and other tests for the retailers' applicants to take. The idea was to use the online tests to prescreen job candidates. Theory hasn't translated into practice, however. As the *Wall Street Journal* recently noted, "the test is also creating a culture of cheating and raising questions for applicants about its fairness."[2]

With a job to fill, you need to select the best person for it. Figure 8.1 presents a bird's-eye view of the recruitment and selection process. In large companies, the HR department typically recruits applicants and prescreens them. In small firms, the office supervisor often fulfills that function. In either case, the candidate's prospective supervisor almost always gets to interview the best candidates and to help choose one. Most people think they're better at screening employees than they really are. You therefore need to know something about interviewing and screening employees.

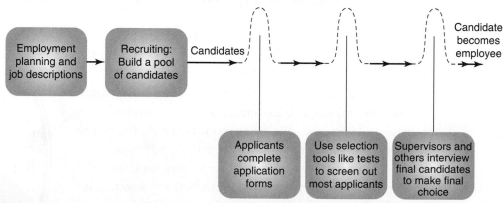

Steps in Recruitment and Selection Process. The recruitment and selection process is a series of hurdles aimed at selecting the best candidate for the job.

The selection process is a series of hurdles aimed at selecting the best candidate for the job.

■ Figure **8.1**
Overview of the Recruitment and Selection Process

Why Careful Selection Is Important

Why Is Selecting the Right Person for the Job and Organization Important?

Selecting the right employees is important for five main reasons.

- First, doing so leads to *improved employee and organizational performance.*
- Second, *your own performance* always depends on your subordinates. Subordinates with the right skills and attributes will do a better job for you and the company. Employees without these skills or who are abrasive or obstructionist won't perform effectively, and your own performance and the firm's will suffer.
- Third, screening can help reduce *dysfunctional behaviors* at work. For example, by some estimates, 33% to 75% of employees have engaged in behaviors such as theft, vandalism, and voluntary absenteeism.[3] The time to screen out undesirables is before they are in the door, not after.
- Fourth, effective screening is important because it's *costly* to recruit and hire employees. Hiring and training even a clerk can cost $10,000 or more in fees and supervisory time, after search fees, interviewing time, reference checking, and travel and moving expenses are tallied.

LEGAL IMPLICATIONS AND NEGLIGENT HIRING   Finally, careful selection is important because of the *legal implications* of incompetent selection.

There are two big legal implications. First, we saw that EEO laws and court decisions require you to avoid unfairly discriminating.

Second, courts will find employers liable when employees with criminal records or other problems use their access to customers' homes or similar opportunities to commit crimes. Hiring workers with such backgrounds without proper safeguards is called *negligent hiring.*[4]

APPLICATION EXAMPLE   A number of years ago, a crew working for a nationally known carpet cleaning company molested and then killed the child of the owner of the house in which they were working. Tragedies like that are thankfully rare. However, it illustrates an extreme example of why it's important to know whom you're hiring. Effective screening is always important. But, in situations like these, you want to be doubly sure that the person you hire has no skeletons in his or her closet. Doing so (and thus avoiding negligent hiring issues) requires carefully checking the candidate's background. This would include the following:

- Don't just rely on an application and resume. Make a systematic effort to gain relevant information about the applicant, for example, through background/reference checks.
- Verify the candidate's documentation.
- Follow up on missing records or gaps in employment.
- Keep a detailed log of all attempts to obtain information, including the names and dates of phone calls or other request (in case a problem does arise).[5]

2. Basic Employee Selection Concepts

One cannot do an effective job of screening applicants without at least a basic understanding of what industrial psychologists call reliability and validity.

What Are Reliability and Validity?

Although the supervisor usually isn't responsible for designing the company's selection procedure, you will help to select your subordinates. You do not have to be a statistician to be good at selecting employees. However, any screening tool you use—be it interview questions or employment tests—should be both *reliable* and *valid*.

RELIABILITY   Reliability refers to a test's consistency. It is "the consistency of scores obtained by the same person when retested with the identical tests or with an equivalent form of a test."[6] Test reliability is essential: If a person scored 90 on an intelligence test on Monday and 130 when retested on Tuesday, you probably wouldn't trust the test.

There are many ways that a supervisor may unintentionally poison a selection tool's reliability. For example, let one candidate take a test in a quiet, comfortable room, while the next day another must take the same test in the midst of the noisy office. Be courteous and patient asking interview questions with one candidate, and terse and impatient asking the same questions with the next candidate. Your basic guideline here is therefore to be consistent. Treat every candidate the same for testing, interviewing, and selection purposes.

VALIDITY   Validity means, "Does this test (or other screening item, such as an interview question) measure what it's supposed to measure?"[7] With respect to employee selection, the term *validity* often refers to evidence that the test is job related, in other words, that performance on the test is a *valid predictor* of performance on the job. If so, then people who do well on the test perform well on the job, and those who do poorly on the test perform poorly on the job. A selection test must be valid. After all, without proof of its validity, why use it for screening job applicants?

In employment testing, there are two main ways to show that a test is valid: **criterion validity** and **content validity**. Demonstrating criterion validity means demonstrating that those who do well on the test also do well on the job, and that those who do poorly on the test do poorly on the job. At work, a *predictor* is the measurement (in this case, the test score) that you are trying to relate to a *criterion* (such as performance on the job). In criterion validity, the two should be closely related. Validating a test this way usually requires the expertise of an industrial psychologist. The validation process is summarized in Figure 8.2. As a supervisor, you're not expected to be a psychologist. However, you should know enough so that you won't use tests or ask questions unless you believe they will actually provide useful and measurable insight into how the person will do on the job.

Content validity means that the test represents a fair sample of the content of a job. A typing test illustrates this. If the content of the typing test is a representative sample of the typist's job, then the test is probably content valid.

Validity is the weak link in many employers' selection processes. For example, they may use tests from office supply stores, which may or may not have any power to help them screen candidates for jobs in their own companies. Supervisors often interview candidates by asking questions (such as, "What's your biggest weakness?") that in fact offer little or no real insight into job performance.

The bottom line is that simply asking yourself, "What evidence do I have that scores on this test (or answers to these job interview questions) really predict job performance?" is probably the single easiest way for you to boost your employee-selection

Step 1: Analyze the Job. First, analyze the job and write job descriptions and job specifications. Specify the human traits and skills you believe are required for adequate job performance. For example, must an applicant be aggressive? Must the person be able to assemble small, detailed components?

These requirements become your predictors. They are the human traits and skills you believe to be predictive of success on the job.

In this first step, you must also define what you mean by "success on the job" because it is this success for which you want predictors. The standards of success are called *criteria*. You could focus on production-related criteria (quantity, quality, and so on), personnel data (absenteeism, length of service, and so on), or judgments (of worker performance by persons such as supervisors). For an assembler's job, predictors for which to test applicants might include manual dexterity and patience.

Criteria that you would hope to predict with your test might then include quantity produced per hour and number of rejects produced per hour.

Step 2: Choose the Tests. Next, choose tests that you think measure the attributes (predictors) important for job success. This choice is usually based on experience, previous research, and best guesses, and you usually won't start off with just one test. Instead, you choose several tests, combining them into a test battery aimed at measuring a variety of possible predictors, such as aggressiveness, extroversion, and numeric ability.

Step 3: Administer Tests. Administer the selected test(s) to employees. Predictive validation is the most dependable way to validate a test. The test is administered to applicants before they are hired.

Then these applicants are hired using only existing selection techniques, not the results of the new test you are developing. After they have been on the job for some time, you measure their performance and compare it to their performance on the earlier test. You can then determine whether their performance on the test could have been used to predict their subsequent job performance.

Step 4: Relate Test Scores and Criteria. Next, determine whether there is a significant relationship between scores (the predictor) and performance (the criterion). The usual way to do this is to determine the statistical relationship between scores on the test and performance through correlation analysis, which shows the degree of statistical relationship.

Step 5: Cross-Validate and Revalidate. Before putting the test into use, you may want to check it by cross-validating, by again performing steps 3 and 4 on a new sample of employees. At a minimum, an expert should validate the test periodically.

batting average. Be very skeptical about asking questions or administering work tests unless you're reasonably sure that they really relate to on-the-job performance.

Protecting the Candidate's Rights

You take a test at school and discover that your professor unthinkingly posted the grades for all to see.

No one who takes a test wants people who shouldn't have the results to have them. People taking employment tests also have privacy and information rights. In particular, under the American Psychological Association's standards (which guide professional psychologists but are not legally enforceable), they have the right to the *confidentiality* of the test results and the right to *informed consent* regarding the use of these results. They have the right to expect that only people *qualified* to interpret the scores will have access to them or that sufficient information will accompany the scores to ensure their appropriate interpretation. They have the right to expect that the test is *secure*; no person taking the test should have prior information concerning the questions or answers.

3. Types of Selection Tests

Employers use many tools (such as tests, interviews, and reference checks) to screen job applicants. We'll start with employment tests.

Selection tests can be very effective. For example, researchers administered an aggression questionnaire to high school hockey players prior to the season. Preseason aggressiveness as measured by the questionnaire predicted the amount of minutes they subsequently spent in the penalty box for penalties such as fighting and slashing.[8] Try the short test in Figure 8.3 to see how prone you might be to having on-the-job accidents.

How Do Employers Use Tests at Work?

Employers use tests to measure a wide range of candidate attributes, including cognitive (mental) abilities, motor and physical abilities, personality and interests, and achievement.

EXAMPLE   Outback Steakhouse has used preemployment testing since just after the company started. Outback is looking for employees who are highly social, meticulous, sympathetic, and adaptable. They use a special personality assessment test as part of a preemployment interview process. Applicants take the test, and the company then compares the candidate's results to the profile for Outback Steakhouse employees. Those who score low on certain traits (such as compassion) don't move to the next step. Those who score high move on and are interviewed by two supervisors. The supervisors ask the candidates "behavioral" questions. Behavioral interview questions ask what you'd do in a particular situation. For example, what would you do if a customer asked for a side dish we don't have on the menu?[9] The basic types of employment tests you may come across are as follows.

■Figure **8.3**

Sample Test

Source: Courtesy of NYT Permissions.

CHECK YES OR NO	YES	NO
1. You like a lot of excitement in your life.		
2. An employee who takes it easy at work is cheating on the employer.		
3. You are a cautious person.		
4. In the past three years you have found yourself in a shouting match at school or work.		
5. You like to drive fast just for fun.		

Analysis: According to John Kamp, an industrial psychologist, applicants who answered no, yes, yes, no, no to questions 1, 2, 3, 4, and 5 are statistically likely to be absent less often, to have fewer on-the-job injuries, and, if the job involves driving, to have fewer on-the-job driving accidents. Actual scores on the test are based on answers to 130 questions.

Type of Question Applicant Might Expect on a Test of Mechanical Comprehension

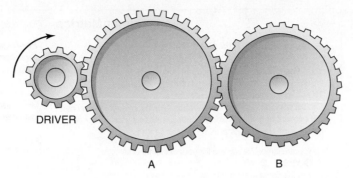

DRIVER

A   B

Which gear will turn the same way as the driver?

How Are Selection Tests Helpful in Screening Applicants?

TESTS OF COGNITIVE ABILITIES   Employers often want to assess a candidate's cognitive (mental) abilities. For example, you may want to know if a sales candidate has the intelligence to do the job's paperwork.

Intelligence tests, such as IQ tests, are tests of general intellectual abilities. They measure not a single intelligence trait, but rather a range of abilities, including memory, vocabulary, verbal fluency, and numeric ability. Today, psychologists often measure intelligence with individually administered tests such as the Stanford–Binet or the Wechsler test. Employers use other IQ tests such as the Wonderlic to provide quick measures of IQ.

Aptitude tests aim to measure the applicant's aptitudes for the job in question. For example, the Test of Mechanical Comprehension illustrated in Figure 8.4 tests the applicant's understanding of basic mechanical principles. It may therefore reflect a person's aptitude for jobs—such as engineer—that require mechanical comprehension.

TESTS OF MOTOR AND PHYSICAL ABILITIES   There are many motor or physical abilities you might want to measure, such as finger dexterity and reaction time (for instance, for machine operators or police candidates). The Stromberg Dexterity Test is an example. It measures the speed and accuracy of simple judgment as well as the speed of finger, hand, and arm movements.

MEASURING PERSONALITY   As one consultant put it, most people are hired based on qualifications, but most are fired for nonperformance. And *nonperformance* (or *performance*) "is usually the result of [personality] characteristics, such as attitude, motivation, and especially, temperament."[10]

Personality tests measure basic aspects of an applicant's personality, such as introversion, stability, and motivation. A sample personality inventory item is:

It does not make sense to work hard on something if no one will notice:

a. Definitely true.
b. Somewhat true.
c. Neither true nor false.
d. Somewhat false.
e. Definitely false.[11]

Of course, personality testing isn't limited to employment settings. Some online dating services have prospective members take online personality tests and reject those who its software judges are unmatchable. Figure 8.5 shows a sample page from one online personality inventory.

HumanMetrics

Jung Typology Test™

After completing the questionnaire, you will obtain:

- Your type formula according to Carl Jung and Isabel Myers-Briggs typology along with the strengths of the preferences
- The description of your personality type
- The list of occupations and educational institutions where you can get relevant degree or training, most suitable for your personality type - Jung Career Indicator™

For Organizations and Professionals

Organizations and specialists interested in Jung personality assessments for team building, candidate assessment, leadership, career development, psychographics - visit HRPersonality™ for practical and validated instruments and professional services.

1. You are almost never late for your appointments
   O YES   O NO
2. You like to be engaged in an active and fast-paced job
   O YES   O NO
3. You enjoy having a wide circle of acquaintances
   O YES   O NO
4. You feel involved when watching TV soaps
   O YES   O NO
5. You are usually the first to react to a sudden event: the telephone ringing or unexpected question
   O YES   O NO
6. You are more interested in a general idea than in the details of its realization
   O YES   O NO
7. You tend to be unbiased even if this might endanger your good relations with people
   O YES   O NO
8. Strict observance of the established rules is likely to prevent a good outcome
   O YES   O NO
9. It's difficult to get you excited
   O YES   O NO
10. It is in your nature to assume responsibility
    O YES   O NO
11. You often think about humankind and its destiny
    O YES   O NO
12. You believe the best decision is one that can be easily changed
    O YES   O NO
13. Objective criticism is always useful in any activity
    O YES   O NO
14. You prefer to act immediately rather than speculate about various options
    O YES   O NO
15. You trust reason rather than feelings
    O YES   O NO
16. You are inclined to rely more on improvisation than on careful planning
    O YES   O NO
17. You spend your leisure time actively socializing with a group of people, attending parties, shopping, etc.
    O YES   O NO
18. You usually plan your actions in advance
    O YES   O NO
19. Your actions are frequently influenced by emotions
    O YES   O NO
20. You are a person somewhat reserved and distant in communication
    O YES   O NO
21. You know how to put every minute of your time to good purpose
    O YES   O NO
22. You readily help people while asking nothing in return
    O YES   O NO
23. You often contemplate about the complexity of life
    O YES   O NO
24. After prolonged socializing you feel you need to get away and be alone
    O YES   O NO
25. You often do jobs in a hurry
    O YES   O NO
26. You easily see the general principle behind specific occurrences
    O YES   O NO
27. You frequently and easily express your feelings and emotions
    O YES   O NO
28. You find it difficult to speak loudly.
    O YES   O NO

A Slide from the Rorschach Test

Source: http://en.wikipedia.org/wiki/File:Rorschach1.jpg, accessed July 27, 2009.

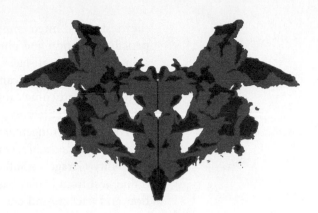

Many personality tests are *projective*. Here the person taking the test must interpret or react to an ambiguous stimulus such as an ink blot. Because the pictures are ambiguous, the person supposedly projects into the picture his or her own emotional attitudes about life. Thus, a security-oriented person might describe the ink blot image in Figure 8.6 as "That thing is coming to get me."

Personality tests—particularly the projective type—are the most difficult to evaluate and use. An expert must analyze the test taker's interpretations and reactions and infer from them his or her personality.

PERSONALITY TEST EFFECTIVENESS   The difficulties notwithstanding, personality tests can help companies hire more effective workers. Industrial psychologists often focus on the "big five" personality dimensions: extroversion, emotional stability, agreeableness, conscientiousness, and openness to experience.[12] Conscientiousness, in particular, tends to show a consistent relationship with all job performance criteria for many occupations.[13]

INTEREST INVENTORIES   *Interest inventories* compare one's interests with those of people in various occupations. Thus, if you were to take the Strong–Campbell Interest Inventory, you would receive a report comparing your interests to those of people already in occupations such as accounting, engineering, management, and medical technology. Why use a test such as this? Because people generally perform best on the jobs for which they have an interest. The Self-Directed Search is another useful online test (see http://www.self-directed-search.com).

ACHIEVEMENT TESTS   An *achievement test* measures what a person has learned. Most of the tests you take in school are achievement tests. They measure your knowledge in areas such as economics, marketing, or personnel. In addition to job knowledge, achievement tests can measure applicants' abilities; a typing test is one example.[14]

Computerized and Online Testing

Computerized and online testing is increasingly replacing conventional paper-and-pencil and manual tests. Most of the types of tests we described are available in both computerized and paper form.[15]

CITY GARAGE COMPUTERIZED TESTING EXAMPLE   One auto repair chain, City Garage, knew they'd never be able to continue growing fast without a dramatic change in how they tested and hired employees.[16] Their old hiring process consisted of a paper-and-pencil application and one interview, immediately followed by a hire/don't hire decision. This was unsatisfactory. For one thing, local shop supervisors didn't have the time to evaluate every applicant. Therefore, "if they had been shorthanded too long, we would hire pretty much anybody who had experience," said the training director. Complicating the problem was that City Garage competitively differentiates itself with an "open garage" arrangement, where customers interact directly with technicians. Therefore, finding mechanics who react positively to customer inquiries was essential.

City Garage's solution was to purchase the Personality Profile Analysis (PPA) online test from Dallas-based Thomas International USA. Now, after a quick application and background check, likely candidates take the 10-minute, 24-question PPA. City Garage staff then enter the answers into the PPA Software system and receive test results in less than two minutes.

Situational Judgment Tests

Situational judgment tests "are designed to assess an applicant's judgment regarding a situation encountered in the workplace."[17] Here is an example. "Suppose you are facing a project deadline and are concerned that you may not complete the project by the time it is due. It is very important to your supervisor that you complete the project by the deadline. It is not possible to get anyone to help you with the work. You would:"[18]

A. Ask for an extension of the deadline.

B. Let the supervisor know that you may not meet the deadline.

C. Work as many hours it as it takes to get the job done by the deadline.

D. Explore different ways to do the work so it can be completed by the deadline.

E. On the date the project is due, hand in what you have done so far.

F. Do the most critical parts of the project by the deadline and complete the remaining parts after the deadline.

G. Tell your supervisor that the deadline is unreasonable.

H. Give your supervisor an update and express your concern about your ability to complete the project by the deadline.

I. Quit your job.

Very often, the best way to test a candidate is to find out how he or she would actually respond to realistic on-the-job choices. Situational judgment tests do just that. The attractive thing about them is that supervisors can create situational judgment tests that make sense for the jobs in their departments. (For example, "What would you do if a customer said she only wants that dress in red, and we only have it in off-white or black in the store?")

Management Assessment Centers

Your employer may ask you to participate in an assessment center to select whom to promote to a supervisory or managerial job. In a **management assessment center**, supervisory candidates take tests and make decisions in simulated situations, and

How Do Employers Select Leaders?

Employers often use management assessment centers to identify leadership potential. For example, trainers in the assessment center give a group a discussion question and tell members to arrive at a group decision. They then watch and assess each member's interpersonal skills, acceptance by the group, leadership ability, and individual influence, and see who turns out to be the leader who emerges from the group.

Employers use other tools as well to identify leadership potential. For example, it often turns out that the people whom their high school classmates chose as the most likely to succeed often do better than average in life. (Perhaps this is because while people can fool recruiters and even tests, it's hard to snow one's colleagues into thinking you're something you're not, day after day.) In any case, another way to identify leadership potential is to take what you might call the "Most Likely to Succeed" approach. Some employers therefore choose who'll move up in management in part by asking the person's peers what they think of the person's leadership potential. For example, in one study of military officers, peer ratings were quite accurate in predicting which officers would be promoted.[19] Behaving like a leader with your peers and work colleagues is therefore advisable.

Employers sometimes use testing to identify which supervisory candidates have leadership potential. For example, in one study, personality traits including extraversion, conscientiousness, and openness to experience were strong predictors of leadership.[20] In another recent study, candidates for law enforcement leadership positions completed a test called the California Psychological Inventory. The test was useful for identifying leadership strengths and areas for development.[21] We

also saw, in Chapter 2, that Professor Ralph Stogdill and others have identified numerous personality traits that distinguish leaders from non-leaders. These include adaptability to situations, ambitious and achievement oriented, assertive, cooperative, decisive, dependable, dominant, energetic, persistent, self-confident, tolerant of stress, and willing to assume responsibility.[22]

The following list of Web sites allows you to take various types of online tests to help you assess different aspects of your leadership traits, styles, and abilities. (Web sites come and go, so we've presented a complete enough list so that even if some no longer work, you should have several from which to choose.)

http://www.yourleadershiplegacy.com/assessment/assessment.php

http://www.schulersolutions.com/leadership_self_test.html

http://www.mindtools.com/pages/article/newLDR_01.htm

http://www.queendom.com/tests/access_page/index.htm?idRegTest=702

http://www.quizmoz.com/quizzes/Personality-Tests/l/Leadership-Test.asp

http://www.testcafe.com/lead/

http://www.lifescript.com/Quizzes/Career/What_Is_Your_Leadership_Style.aspx?gclid=CPOYjYTX8qECFRYhnAodsE_8mg&trans=1&du=1&ef_id=1350:3:s_ebef0823e7a1e46bc9caeaf54bf0d063_2540437025:S-6WRkNIYWYAABAvZpUAAAOA:20100527155654

observers score them on their performance. For two or three days at the assessment center, 10 to 12 candidates perform realistic supervisory tasks (such as making presentations) under the observation of assessors (usually, company managers). The center may be a special room with a one-way mirror to facilitate unobtrusive observations. Examples of the simulated but realistic exercises to expect in a typical assessment center are as follows:

- **The in-basket.** In this exercise, the candidate is faced with an accumulation of reports, memos, notes of incoming phone calls, letters, and other materials. The candidate takes appropriate action on each of these materials.

- **The leaderless group discussion.** A leaderless group is given a discussion question and told to arrive at a group decision. The raters then evaluate each group member's interpersonal skills, acceptance by the group, leadership ability, and individual influence.

- **Individual presentations.** A participant's communication skills and persuasiveness are evaluated by having the person make an oral presentation on an assigned topic.

Management assessment centers are one tool employers use to decide who has the leadership potential to move up in management. The accompanying Leadership Applications for Supervisors feature on page 223 elaborates on this.

4. How to Interview Job Candidates

Supervisors may not always be involved in testing applicants, but they almost always interview the prospective employees; interviewing is thus an indispensable supervisory skill.

A selection interview is "a selection procedure designed to predict future job performance on the basis of applicants' oral responses to oral inquiries."[23]

Two Basic Interview Issues

Your employer may have a specific procedure for you to follow when interviewing job candidates. If not, then there are two issues you'll have to decide on yourself.

STRUCTURED OR NOT? First, you need to decide whether to just sort of ask questions as they come to mind (an "unstructured" interview) or to use a standardized questionnaire approach (a "structured" interview). In the former, you ask questions as they come to mind, and there is generally no set format to follow. In the more structured (or "directive" interview), such as the one summarized in Figure 8.7, you list the questions and perhaps even "ideal" responses in advance. We'll see that it's usually best to structure your interview ahead of time, rather than just to ask questions as they come to mind. Doing so makes the interview more consistent and therefore reliable.

WHAT QUESTIONS TO ASK The second issue is what sorts of questions to ask. Many supervisors think that interviews just involve obvious questions such as "What are your main strengths and weaknesses?" However, there's much more to good interviews than that. The best interviewers ask questions that force candidates to reveal insights into how they would actually perform on the job. For example:

- *Experience questions* are quite familiar. For example, you might ask, "What marketing courses did you take in school?" or, "What advertising programs have you put together yourself?"

- *Situational questions* focus on the candidate's ability to project what his or her behavior *would be* in a given situation.[24] For example, you might ask a candidate for a supervisor position how he or she would respond to a subordinate coming to work late three days in a row.

Portion of Structured Interview Guide

Source: Copyright 1992. The Dartnell Corporation, Chicago, IL. Adapted with permission.

APPLICANT INTERVIEW GUIDE

To the interviewer: This Applicant Interview Guide is intended to assist in employee selection and placement. If it is used for all applicants for a position, it will help you to compare them, and it will provide more objective information than you will obtain from unstructured interviews.

Because this is a general guide, all of the items may not apply in every instance. Skip those that are not applicable and add questions appropriate to the specific position. Space for additional questions will be found at the end of the form.

Federal law prohibits discrimination in employment on the basis of sex, race, color, national origin, religion, disability, and in most instances, age. The laws of most states also ban some or all of the above types of discrimination in employment as well as discrimination based on marital status or ancestry. Interviewers should take care to avoid any questions that suggest that an employment decision will be made on the basis of any such factors.

Job Interest

Name _____ Position applied for _____

What do you think the job (position) involves? _____

Why do you want the job (position)? _____

Why are you qualified for it? _____

What would your salary requirements be? _____

What do you know about our company? _____

Why do you want to work for us? _____

Current Work Status

Are you now employed? _____ Yes _____ No. If not, how long have you been unemployed? _____

Why are you unemployed? _____

If you are working, why are you applying for this position? _____

When would you be available to start work with us? _____

Work Experience

(Start with the applicant's current or last position and work back. All periods of time should be accounted for. Go back at least 12 years, depending upon the applicant's age. Military service should be treated as a job.)

Current or last
employer _____ Address _____

Dates of employment: from _____ to _____

Current or last job title _____

What are (were) your duties? _____

Have you held the same job throughout your employment with that company? _____ Yes _____ No. If not, describe the various jobs you have had with that employer, how long you held each of them, and the main duties of each. _____

What was your starting salary? _____ What are you earning now? _____ Comments _____
_____

Name of your last or current supervisor _____

What did you like most about that job? _____

What did you like least about it? _____

Why are you thinking of leaving? _____

Why are you leaving right now? _____

Interviewer's comments or observations _____
_____

- With *behavioral questions* you ask interviewees how they behaved *in the past* in some situation. Thus, an interviewer might ask, "Did you ever have a situation in which a subordinate came in late? If so, how did you handle the situation?" For example, when Citizen's Banking Corporation in Flint, Michigan, found that 31 of the 50 people in its call center quit in one year, Cynthia Wilson, the center's head, switched to behavioral interviews. Many of those who left did so because they didn't enjoy fielding questions from occasionally irate clients. So Wilson no longer tries to predict how candidates will act by asking them if they want to work with angry clients. Instead, she asks behavioral questions such as, "Tell me about a time you were speaking with an irate person, and how you turned the situation around." Wilson says this makes it much harder to fool the interviewer, and, indeed, only four people left her center in the following year.[25]

How Useful Are Interviews?

Research shows that the key to effective interviewing is how you do the interview itself.[26] Here's what you should know:

- With respect to predicting job performance, *situational questions* ("What would you do?") tend to be more valid than behavioral questions ("What did you do?"), but either type of question is almost always more useful than are general questions such as "What are your strengths?" Always try to ask situational or behavioral questions that really hone in on what choices the candidate would actually make (or actually made) once on the job.

- *Structured* interviews, using a standard set of questions, are more valid than unstructured interviews for predicting job performance. They are more valid partly because they are more reliable—for example, you end up asking the same questions consistently from candidate to candidate.[27]

Selection Interviews: What Guidelines Are Helpful for Finding the Right Person for the Job?

So in summary, structured situational interviews (in which you ask the candidates what they would do in a particular situation) are the most useful for predicting job performance. However, whether you are an effective interviewer also depends on avoiding common interviewing mistakes, a subject to which we now turn.

How to Avoid Common Interviewing Mistakes

Most people tend to think they're better interviewers than they really are. In one study, less than 34% of interviewers had formal interview training. However, the "interviewers were confident that they could identify the best candidates regardless of the amount of interview structure employed."[28] Several common interviewing mistakes can undermine an interview's usefulness. Here are some of these common mistakes—and suggestions for avoiding them.

SNAP JUDGMENTS   People draw conclusions about you, often before you even say a word. One London-based psychologist interviewed the chief executives of 80 top companies. She came to this conclusion about snap judgments in selection interviews:

> Really, to make a good impression, you don't even get time to open your mouth. . . . An interviewer's response to you will generally be preverbal—

how you walk through the door, what your posture is like, whether you smile, whether you have a captivating aura, whether you have a firm, confident handshake. You've got about half a minute to make an impact and after that, all you are doing is building on a good or bad first impression. . . . It's a very emotional response.[29]

If you are interviewing for a job, such findings show why it's important for you to start off right. The person interviewing you will probably make up his or her mind about you during the first few minutes of the interview. From the supervisor/interviewer's point of view, the findings show this: *You should consciously delay a decision and keep an open mind until the interview is over.*

NEGATIVE EMPHASIS   Unfortunately, interviewers often mostly use the interview to find flaws in the candidate. This means that a candidate will be hard-pressed to overcome any initial negative impression. Again, this means you should work diligently to *keep an open mind and consciously work against being preoccupied with negative impressions.*

NOT KNOWING THE JOB   Interviewers who don't know exactly what the job entails *and what sort of candidate is best suited for it* usually make decisions based on incorrect stereotypes about what makes a good applicant. They then erroneously compare candidates against these incorrect stereotypes.[30] Therefore, before the interview, use the job description to think through what type of person you really need. Supervisors should *know as much as possible about the position* for which they're interviewing and about the specific human requirements (such as interpersonal skills and job knowledge) that the job requires.

PRESSURE TO HIRE   Being under pressure to hire undermines an interview's usefulness. In one study, a group of supervisors were told to assume that they were behind in their recruiting quota. A second group was told that they were ahead of their quota. Those behind evaluated the same recruits much more highly than did those ahead.[31] So: *Don't rush.*

CANDIDATE ORDER (CONTRAST) ERROR   Candidate order (or "contrast") error means that the order in which you see applicants affects how you rate them. In one study, researchers asked supervisors to evaluate a candidate who was "just average" after first evaluating several "unfavorable" candidates. In contrast to the unfavorable candidates, the average candidate looked better than he might otherwise have.[32] This means you should *be aware of this problem*, to avoid it.

THE CANDIDATE'S "NONVERBAL BEHAVIOR"   How the applicant looks and acts will subliminally influence how you rate him or her. For example, studies show that interviewers give higher ratings to applicants who demonstrate more eye contact, head moving, smiling, and similar nonverbal behaviors. Such behaviors often account for almost all of the applicant's rating.[33] In another study, vocal cues (such as the interviewee's pitch, speech rates, and pauses) and visual cues (such as physical attractiveness and smile) correlated with the evaluator's judgments of the interviewees' likability.[34] Extroverted applicants are particularly good at self-promotion, and self-promotion makes interviewers view these candidates more positively.[35]

Bias Against Working Mothers

Would you hire someone's mother? As silly as that question seems, supervisors should be aware of a sad fact: People often tend to view working mothers negatively.[39]

Here's an example. Researchers gave 100 MBA students (34% female, and all of whom worked full time) copies of a job description summary. The job was assistant vice president of financial affairs. The MBA students also got a "promotion applicant information form" to evaluate for each fictitious "applicant." These included researcher-created information such as marital status and supervisor comments. Some "applicants" were mothers.

The student-evaluators were biased against the mothers. They viewed them as less competent and were less likely to recommend them for the job. As the researchers say, "These data are consistent with mounting evidence that women suffer disadvantages in the workplace when they are mothers, a problem that has been termed 'the maternal wall.'"[40]

The applicant's attractiveness also comes into play.[36] In general, people ascribe more favorable traits and more successful life outcomes to attractive people.[37] In one study, researchers asked subjects to evaluate candidates for promotability based on photographs. More attractive candidates, especially men, were preferred over less attractive ones.[38] The solution is to stay *consciously aware of the impact* these non-relevant attributes can have. The accompanying feature illustrates the potential problem.

INGRATIATION   It is easy to get snowed by a clever interviewee. Interviewees can boost their chances for job offers through self-promotion and ingratiation. *Ingratiation* involves, for example, agreeing with the recruiter's opinions and thus signaling that the two of you share similar beliefs. *Self-promotion* means promoting one's own skills and abilities to create the impression of competence.[41] Again, *remain aware* of this possibility.

Steps in Conducting an Effective Interview

We've talked about what makes some interviews more useful than others. Now let's pull this all together and see how to conduct a good interview.

STEP 1: BEFORE STARTING, KNOW THE JOB   First make sure you understand the job and what human skills you're looking for. Study the job description and make sure you understand what traits and skills the ideal employee in that job needs.

STEP 2: STRUCTURE THE INTERVIEW   You are best off thinking through and writing out your questions ahead of time. Avoid unstructured, off-the-cuff interviews. There are several things you can do to standardize the interview.[42] Most importantly, *write out situational or behavioral questions*. Questions that ask for opinions and attitudes, goals and aspirations, and self-descriptions and self-evaluations encourage self-promotion. They allow candidates to avoid revealing weaknesses. Examples of good questions include:

- *Situational* questions such as "Suppose you were giving a sales presentation and a difficult technical question arose that you could not answer. What would you do?"

- *Past behavior* questions such as "Can you provide an example of a specific instance where you developed a sales presentation that was highly effective?"

- *Background* questions such as "What work experiences, training, or other qualifications do you have for working in a teamwork environment?"

- *Job knowledge* questions such as "What factors should you consider when developing a TV advertising campaign?"

If possible, compile and list your questions in an interview form. Interviews based on structured guides, like the one in Figure 8.7, usually result in superior interviews.[43] At the very least, list your questions before the interview.

STEP 3: GET ORGANIZED   Conduct the interview in a private room where telephone calls are not accepted and where you can minimize interruptions. Begin by reviewing the candidate's application and résumé, and note any areas that are vague or that may indicate strengths or weaknesses. Review your questions and interview plan.

STEP 4: ESTABLISH RAPPORT   The main reason for the interview is to find out about the applicant. To do this, start by putting the person at ease. Greet the candidate and start the interview by asking a noncontroversial question, perhaps about the weather or the traffic conditions that day.

STEP 5: ASK QUESTIONS   Try to follow your structured interview guide or the questions you wrote out ahead of time. As a starter, you'll find a menu of supplemental questions (such as "Why did you choose this line of work?") in Figure 8.8. Here are some question do's and don'ts:

- **Don't** ask questions that can be answered yes or no.

- **Don't** put words in the applicant's mouth or telegraph the desired answer, for instance, by nodding or smiling when the right answer is given.

- **Don't** interrogate the applicant as if the person is a criminal, and don't be patronizing, sarcastic, or inattentive.

■ Figure **8.8**

Selected Interview Questions to Ask Candidates

1. Why did you choose this line of work?
2. What did you enjoy most about your last job?
3. What did you like least about your last job?
4. What did you study in college? How do you think those studies will help you on this job?
5. What is the first thing you would do your first day on this job?
6. What would you do if a family member was ill but you knew you had an important presentation to make here that day?
7. What would your last supervisor say your weaknesses are?
8. How can your supervisor here best help you obtain your goals?
9. How did your last supervisor rate your job performance?
10. Describe how you handled a situation in the past when you disagreed with a supervisor.
11. What did you do the last time you received instructions with which you disagreed?
12. What are some of the things about which you and your supervisor disagreed? What did you do?
13. Do you have any questions about the duties of the job for which you have applied?

- **Don't** monopolize the interview by rambling, nor let the applicant dominate the interview so you can't ask all your questions.
- **Do** ask open-ended questions.
- **Do** listen to the candidate to encourage him or her to express thoughts fully.
- **Do** draw out the applicant's opinions and feelings by repeating the person's last comment as a question (e.g., "You didn't like your last job?").
- **Do** ask for examples.[44] For instance, if the candidate lists specific strengths or weaknesses, follow up with, "What are specific examples that demonstrate each of your strengths?"
- **Do** take brief notes during the interview. Doing so may help you keep an open mind (not make a snap judgment early in the interview) and help you remember the person's answers. The research suggests that the interviewer should take notes, but not copious ones, instead noting just the key points of what the interviewee says.[45]

WHAT *NOT* TO ASK   As a rule, avoid questions that might screen out applicants based on age, race, gender, national origin, handicap, or other prohibited criteria. Can you pick out the inappropriate questions in the following list?[46]

- What kinds of things do you look for in a job?
- What types of interests or hobbies are you involved in?
- Do you have any handicaps?
- What university subjects do you like the most?
- What qualities should a successful employee possess?
- Do you have any future plans for marriage and children?
- What do you think you have to offer a company like Dandy Toys?
- What is your date of birth?
- What is the nature of your previous work experience?
- Have you ever been arrested for a crime?
- What do you consider to be your greatest strengths?

STEP 6: CLOSE THE INTERVIEW   Toward the close of the interview, leave time to answer any questions the candidate may have. If appropriate, advocate your firm to the candidate.

Try to end all interviews on a positive note. Tell the applicant whether there is any interest and, if so, what the next step will be. Similarly, make rejections diplomatically (for instance, with a statement such as "Thank you but there are other candidates whose experience is closer to our requirements"). As one recruiter says, "An interview experience should leave a lasting, positive impression of the company, whether the candidate receives and accepts an offer or not."[47]

STEP 7: REVIEW THE INTERVIEW   After the candidate leaves, review the interview while it's fresh in your mind. You might use an interview evaluation form to compile your impressions (for instance, see Figure 8.9). The accompanying Supervising the New Workforce feature presents some guidelines for a special interview situation.

Interview Evaluation Form

Source: Reprinted from http://hr.blr.com with permission of the publisher, Business and Legal Reports Inc., 141 Mill Rock Road East, Old Saybrook, CT © 2004.

Name of candidate:

Date interviewed:

Position:

Completed by:

Date:

Instructions: Circle one number for each criterion, then add them together for a total.

KNOWLEDGE OF SPECIFIC JOB AND JOB-RELATED TOPICS

0. No knowledge evident.
1. Less than we would prefer.
2. Meets requirements for hiring.
3. Exceeds our expectations of average candidates.
4. Thoroughly versed in job and very strong in associated areas.

EXPERIENCE

0. None for this job; no related experience either.
1. Would prefer more for this job. Adequate for job applied for.
2. More than sufficient for job.
3. Totally experienced in job.
4. Strong experience in all related areas.

COMMUNICATION

0. Could not communicate. Will be severely impaired in most jobs.
1. Some difficulties. Will detract from job performance.
2. Sufficient for adequate job performance.
3. More than sufficient for job.
4. Outstanding ability to communicate.

INTEREST IN POSITION AND ORGANIZATION

0. Showed no interest.
1. Some lack of interest.
2. Appeared genuinely interested.
3. Very interested. Seems to prefer type of work applied for.
4. Totally absorbed with job content. Conveys feeling only this job will do.

OVERALL MOTIVATION TO SUCCEED

0. None exhibited.
1. Showed little interest in advancement.
2. Average interest in advancement.
3. Highly motivated. Strong desire to advance.
4. Extremely motivated. Very strong desire to succeed and advance.

POISE AND CONFIDENCE

0. Extremely distracted and confused. Displayed uneven temper.
1. Sufficient display of confusion or loss of temper to interfere with job performance.
2. Sufficient poise and confidence to perform job.
3. No loss of poise during interview. Confidence in ability to handle pressure.
4. Displayed impressive poise under stress. Appears unusually confident and secure.

COMPREHENSION

0. Did not understand many points and concepts.
1. Missed some ideas or concepts.
2. Understood most new ideas and skills discussed.
3. Grasped all new points and concepts quickly.
4. Extremely sharp. Understood subtle points and underlying motives.

_____ **TOTAL POINTS**

ADDITIONAL REMARKS:

Applicant Disability and the Employment Interview

Researchers surveyed 40 disabled people from various occupations.[48] Their basic finding was that, from the disabled person's point of view, interviewers tend to avoid directly addressing the disability, and therefore they make their decisions without getting all the facts. What people with disabilities prefer is an open discussion, one that would allow the employer to fully clarify his or her concerns and reach a knowledgeable conclusion. Among the questions disabled persons said they would like interviewers to ask were these:

- Is there any kind of setting or special equipment that will facilitate the interview process for you?
- Is there any specific technology that you currently use or have used in previous jobs that assists the way you work?
- Provide an example of how you would use technology to carry out your job duties.
- Is there any technology that you don't currently have that would be helpful in performing the duties of this position?
- Other than technology, what other kind of support did you have in previous jobs? If none, is there anything that would benefit you?

5. Background Checks and Other Selection Techniques

Background Checks and Other Selection Techniques: How Do They Assist the Supervisor in Choosing the Right Person for the Job?

Even when employers don't use formal tests, they use other screening methods such as reference checks, medical exams and drug screening. About 82% of HR supervisors report checking applicants' backgrounds; 80% do criminal convictions searches; and 35% do credit history reports.[49] Let's start with background checks.

How to Conduct Effective Background Investigations and Reference Checks

There are two key reasons for checking backgrounds. One is to verify the accuracy of the information the applicant provided. The other is to uncover damaging background information such as criminal records.

WHAT TO VERIFY   The most commonly verified background areas are legal eligibility for employment (to comply with immigration laws), dates of prior employment, military service (including discharge status), education, and identification (including date of birth and address).[50] Other items should include county criminal records (current residence, last residence), motor vehicle record, credit, licensing verification, Social Security number, and reference checks.[51]

COLLECTING BACKGROUND INFORMATION   There are several ways to collect background information. Most employers try to directly verify an applicant's current position, salary, and employment dates with his or her current employer or supervisor by phone (assuming that the candidate cleared them doing so). Others try to discover more about the person's motivation, technical competence, and ability to work with others.[52]

Many employers get background reports from commercial credit rating companies and/or employment screening services. There are also thousands of online databases and sources for obtaining background information, including sex offender registries; worker's compensation histories; nurses' aid registries; and sources for criminal, employment, and educational histories.[53] Top employee background providers include Kroll Background Screenings Group (http://www.Krollworldwide.com), Choicepoint (http://www.choicepoint.com), and First Advantage (http://www.FADV.com).[54] Background checks and other selection techniques: How do they assist the supervisor in choosing the right person for the job?

CHECKING SOCIAL NETWORKING SITES   More employers are checking candidates' social networking sites' postings. One employer went to Facebook.com and found that a top candidate described his interests as smoking marijuana and shooting people. The student may have been joking, but he did not get the offer.[55] After conducting such online searches, recruiters found that 31% of applicants had lied about their qualifications and 19% had posted information about their drinking or drug use.[56] Similarly, as a *Wall Street Journal* article titled "Job References You Can't Control" noted, social networking sites can also help prospective employers identify an applicant's former colleagues, and thus contact them.[57]

However, note that while Googling is probably safe enough, checking social networking sites raises legal issues. For example, it's still probably best to get the candidate's prior approval for social networking searches.[58] And, of course, do not use a pretext or fabricate an identity.[59]

NAVIGATING THE REFERENCE CHECK MINE FIELD   Handled correctly, background checks are an inexpensive and straightforward way to verify information (such as previous job titles) about applicants.

However, they can also backfire, in two ways. Defamation is one. It is not easy for the reference to prove that the applicant warranted the bad reference. The rejected applicant thus has various legal remedies, including suing the reference for defamation of character.[60] One man was awarded $56,000 after being turned down for a job because, among other things, a former employer called him a "character."

Useless or misleading references are another issue. Fear of a lawsuit can understandably inhibit former employers and supervisors from giving candid references. However, it's not just the fear of legal reprisal that can lead to misleading references. Many supervisors don't want to diminish a former employee's chances for a job. Others would rather give incompetent employees good reviews if it will get rid of them. When checking references, therefore, be careful. Try to judge whether the reference's answers are evasive and, if so, why.

MAKING REFERENCE CHECKS MORE PRODUCTIVE   You can do several things to make your reference checking more productive.

1. First, make sure the candidate signed a release on the application form authorizing the background check.[61]

2. Second, always get at least two forms of identification and make applicants fill out job applications. Always compare the application to the résumé. People tend to be more creative on their résumés than on their application forms, where they must certify the information.[62]

3. Third, use a structured reference-checking form as in Figure 8.10.

4. Fourth, use the references offered by the applicant as merely a source for other references who may know of the applicant's performance. Thus, you might ask each

■ Figure **8.10**

Reference Checking Form

Source: Society for Human Resource Management, © 2004. Reproduced with permission of Society for Human Resource Management in the Format Textbook via Copyright Clearance Center.

(Verify that the applicant has provided permission before conducting reference checks.)

Candidate Name _____

Reference Name _____

Company Name _____

Dates of Employment
From: _____ To: _____

Position(s) Held _____

Salary History _____

Reason for Leaving _____

Explain the reason for your call and verify the above information with the supervisor (including the reason for leaving)

_____
_____
_____
_____

1. Please describe the type of work for which the candidate was responsible.

_____
_____
_____

2. How would you describe the applicant's relationships with coworkers, subordinates (if applicable), and with superiors?

_____
_____
_____

3. Did the candidate have a positive or negative work attitude? Please elaborate.

_____
_____
_____

4. How would you describe the quantity and quality of output generated by the former employee?

_____
_____
_____

5. What were his/her strengths on the job?

_____
_____
_____

6. What were his/her weaknesses on the job?

_____
_____
_____

7. What is your overall assessment of the candidate?

_____
_____
_____

8. Would you recommend him/her for this position? Why or why not?

_____
_____
_____

9. Would this individual be eligible for rehire? Why or why not?

_____
_____
_____

Other comments?

of the applicant's references, "Could you please give me the name of another person who might be familiar with the applicant's performance?" In that way, you begin getting information from references that may be more objective because they weren't referred directly by the applicant.

5. Finally, companies *giving* references should ensure that only authorized managers give them. Former employees will take legal action for defamatory references. There are dozens of reference-checking firms like Allison & Taylor Reference Checking Inc. in Jamestown, New York, doing this sort of work.[63] Many use certified court reporters to manually transcribe what the reference is saying.[64] One supervisor, describing a former city employee, reportedly "used swear words, said he was incompetent and said that he almost brought the city down on its knees."[65] Most firms therefore centralize the task of giving references within HR. *Supervisors should use caution in responding to any such reference requests.*

How to Spot Dishonesty

A famous comedian once said that he had no problem identifying dishonest people: "If someone keeps telling me how honest they are, I run for the hills." In practice, here's what one expert suggests:

- **Ask blunt questions.**[66] You can ask very direct questions in the interview. For example, there is probably nothing wrong with asking the applicant, "Have you ever stolen anything from an employer?" "Have you recently held jobs other than those listed on your application?" "Is any information on your application misrepresented or falsified?"
- **Listen, rather than talk.** Allow the applicant to do the talking so you can learn as much as possible about the person.
- **Check all references.** Rigorously pursue employment and personal references.
- **Test for drugs.** Devise a drug testing program and give each applicant a copy of the policy.
- **Conduct searches.** Prudent employers establish a search policy. The policy should state that all lockers, desks, and similar property remain the property of the company and may be inspected routinely. Give each applicant a copy of the policy and require each to return a signed copy.
- **Use caution.** Being rejected for dishonesty carries a greater stigma than does being rejected for, say, poor mechanical comprehension. Therefore, ensure that you are protecting your candidates' and employees' rights to privacy.

POLYGRAPH TESTS   The *polygraph* (or "*lie detector*") machine is a device that measures physiological changes such as increased perspiration. The assumption is that such changes reflect changes in the emotional stress that accompanies lying.

Complaints about offensiveness as well as doubts about the polygraph's accuracy culminated in the Employee Polygraph Protection Act in 1988. With few exceptions, the law prohibits most employers from conducting polygraph examinations of all applicants and most employees.[67]

PAPER-AND-PENCIL HONESTY TESTS   The virtual elimination of the polygraph as a screening device created a market for other honesty testing devices. Paper-and-pencil honesty tests are psychological tests designed to predict job applicants' proneness to dishonesty. Most of these tests measure attitudes regarding things such as tolerance of others who steal. (See, for example, http://www.queendom.com/tests/career/honesty_access.html). Psychologists have some concerns about paper-and-pencil honesty tests. For example, integrity tests may be prone to producing a high percentage of false positives (rating people dishonest when they are not), and they are susceptible to coaching.[68] However, studies tend to support these tests' validity.[69]

Realistic Job Previews

Sometimes, a dose of realism makes the best screening tool. For example, Walmart found that associates who quit within the first 90 days often did so because of conflict in their schedules or because they preferred to work in another geographic area. The firm then began explicitly explaining and asking about work schedules and work preferences.[70] One study even found that some applicants accepted jobs with the intention to quit, a fact that more realistic interviewing might have unearthed.[71]

Tapping Friends and Acquaintances

Testing and interviewing aside, don't ignore tapping the opinions of people you trust who have direct personal knowledge of the candidate. It may be an exaggeration, but as a CEO of Continental Airlines said, "The best possible interview is miniscule in value compared to somebody who's got even a couple of months of work experience with somebody."[72]

Seeing What the Candidate Can Do

Sometimes, the most straightforward way of sizing up a candidate is to see what he or she can actually do. For example, suppose you have a job opening for a cleaner-spotter for a dry cleaning store.[73] You ask yourself what specific tasks this cleaner-spotter will have to perform and the standards on which you will measure that performance. Next, think of several activities (such as removing a coffee stain from a blouse) you can ask your candidates to perform that would be similar to what you'd expect the person to do on the job. After identifying several of these activities, you might even think about the weights you'd attach to each activity based on what you think is the relative importance of each activity. Then have each candidate perform each activity, and give each candidate a score on each activity using some simple rating system (such as 1 to 5, from low to high). Then multiply each candidate's score on each activity with the weight for that activity, sum up the results, and determine which candidate scores highest.

Physical Exams

Physical examinations are often the next step in the selection process, and there are several reasons for requiring them. Such exams can confirm that the applicant qualifies for the physical requirements of the position. They can also unearth any medical limitations to take into account in placing the applicant. The examination can also detect communicable diseases that may be unknown to the applicant.

Under the ADA, a person with a disability can't be rejected for the job if he or she is otherwise qualified and if the person could perform the essential job functions with reasonable accommodation. According to the ADA, a medical exam is permitted during the period between the job offer and the commencement of work, if such exams are standard practice for all applicants for that job.[74]

Drug Screening

Employers generally conduct drug tests. The most common practice is to test new applicants just before they are formally hired. Many firms also test current employees when there is reason to believe an employee has been using drugs after a work accident, or when there are obvious behavioral symptoms such as chronic lateness. Some firms administer drug tests on a random or periodic basis, while others do so only when transferring or promoting an employee.[75] Virtually all (96%) employers that conduct such tests use urine sampling.

PROBLEMS   Unfortunately, drug testing is flawed. Drug tests in general can't measure impairment or, for that matter, addiction.[76] They're not like the breathalyzers and blood tests for alcohol (like those given at the roadside to drivers). Those do correlate closely with impairment levels. Urine and blood drug tests only show whether drug residues are present. It's also not clear that drug testing improves either safety or performance.[77] Workplace drug testing might therefore identify one's use of drugs during leisure hours, "but have little or no relevance to the job itself.[78] Furthermore, "there is a swarm of products that promise to help employees (both male and female) beat drug tests."[79]

Complying with Immigration Law

Under the Immigration Reform and Control Act of 1986, people must prove that they are eligible to be employed in the United States. A person does not have to be a U.S. citizen to be employed under this act. However, employers should ask a candidate who is about to be hired whether he or she is a U.S. citizen or an alien lawfully authorized to work in the United States.

HOW TO COMPLY   There are two basic ways prospective employees can show their eligibility for employment. One is to show a document such as a U.S. passport or alien registration card with photograph that proves both identity and employment eligibility. However, many prospective employees do not have either of these documents. Therefore, the other way to verify employment eligibility is to see a document that proves the person's identity, along with a separate document showing the person's employment eligibility, such as a work permit.

The main problem here is fraudulent documents. It's not difficult to buy what appears to be a Social Security card or ID. The solution is a careful background check. For example, you can verify Social Security cards by calling the Social Security Administration.[80]

Supervisors cannot and should not use the I-9 Employment Eligibility Verification form required to document eligibility to discriminate based on race or country of national origin.[81] The requirement to verify eligibility does not provide any basis to reject an applicant just because he or she is a foreigner, or not a U.S. citizen, or an alien residing in the United States, as long as that person can prove his or her identity and employment eligibility.

Chapter 8 Concept Review and Reinforcement

Key Terms

Criterion Validity, p. 216   Management Assessment
Content Validity, p. 216   Center, p. 222

Review of Key Concepts

Careful Selection Is Important	• Leads to improved employee and organization performance • A supervisor's performance always depends on subordinates. • Careful selection can help reduce dysfunctional behaviors. • Screening is costly—avoid repeating.
Test Reliability	Test reliability refers to a test's consistency. Scores will be consistent when the same person takes a similar test two times in a row.
Test Validity	Test validity refers to evidence that the test is job related and is a valid predictor of performance on the job.
Tests and Equal Opportunity	EEO legislation states that an employer may have to prove that his or her tests are predictive of success or failure on the job.
Intelligence Tests	Intelligence tests measure a range of abilities including memory, vocabulary, verbal fluency, and numeric ability.
Aptitude Tests	These tests measure the applicant's aptitude for the job in question.
Physical Abilities Tests	Physical abilities tests can measure finger dexterity and reaction time.
Personality Tests	Personality tests measure characteristics such as attitude, motivation, and temperament. These characteristics represent the basis for performance and nonperformance of the job after the person is hired.
Achievement Tests	Achievement tests measure what a person has learned. These tests can measure an applicant's abilities.
Management Assessment Centers	Management candidates take tests and make decisions in simulated situations and observers score them on their performance.

Situational Judgment Tests	These tests are designed to assess an applicant's judgment regarding a situation encountered in the workplace.
Selection Interview	This is a selection procedure designed to predict future job performance on the basis of applicants' oral responses to oral inquiries. This type of interview can be either structured or nonstructured.
Common Interviewing Mistakes	Common interviewing mistakes that can undermine an interview's usefulness include snap judgments, negative emphasis, not knowing the job, pressure to hire, and nonverbal behavior.
Conducting an Effective Interview	The seven steps in conducting an effective interview include: • Know the job • Structure the interview • Get organized • Establish rapport • Ask questions • Close the interview • Review the interview
Reference Checks	Reference checks verify the accuracy of the information that the applicant has provided and attempt to uncover damaging background information such as criminal records.
Physical Exams	Physical exams confirm that the applicant qualifies for the physical requirements of the position.
Drug Screenings	Employers generally conduct drug tests on a random or periodic basis.
Polygraph Tests	The polygraph (or lie detector) machine is a device that measures physiological changes such as increased perspiration. There are grave doubts about the accuracy of such tests.
Paper-and-Pencil Honesty Tests	Pencil-and-paper honesty tests are psychological tests designed to predict job applicants' proneness to dishonesty. There are some concerns as to the usefulness of such tests.

Review and Discussion Questions

1. Explain what is meant by reliability and validity. What is the difference between them?
2. Discuss why careful selection of new employees is important.
3. Give some examples of jobs that would require the use of physical abilities tests.
4. How effective do you believe the use of drug screening is in today's workplace?
5. Write a short presentation titled "How to Be Effective as an Interviewer."
6. Briefly discuss three of the most common interviewing mistakes that you feel are most important.
7. For what types of jobs do you think computerized interviews are most appropriate? Why?
8. Why is it important to conduct preemployment background investigations? How would you go about doing so?
9. What type of jobs would management assessment centers be used for? Why?
10. In what type of jobs or trades would the use of achievement tests be most effective? Why?
11. From the perspective of the company, why does the use of physical exams become so important from a legal liability standpoint?

Application and Skill Building

Case Study One

Ethics and the Out-of-Control Interview

Ethics are "the principles of conduct governing an individual or a group"—they're the principles people use to decide what their conduct should be.[82]

The apparent fairness of the selection process is important. For example, "If prospective employees perceive that the hiring process does not treat people fairly, they may assume that ethical behavior is not important in the company, and that 'official' pronouncements about the importance of ethics can be discounted."[83]

That's one reason why the situation Maria Fernandez ran into is disturbing. Maria is a bright, popular, and well-informed mechanical engineer who graduated with an engineering degree from State University in June 2009. During the spring preceding her graduation, she went out on many job interviews, most of which she thought were conducted courteously and were reasonably useful in giving both her and the prospective employer a good impression of where each of them stood on matters of importance to both of them. It was, therefore, with great anticipation that she looked forward to an interview with the one firm in which she most wanted to work: Apex Environmental. She had always had a strong interest in cleaning up the environment and firmly believed that the best use of her training and skills lay in working for a firm like Apex, where she thought she could have a successful career while making the world a better place. The interview, however, was a disaster. Maria walked into a room in which five men—the president of the company, two vice presidents, the marketing director, and another engineer—began throwing questions at her that she felt were aimed primarily at tripping her up rather than finding out what she could offer through her engineering skills. The questions ranged from unnecessarily discourteous ("Why would you take a job as a waitress in college if you're such an intelligent person?") to irrelevant and sexist ("Are you planning on settling down and starting a family anytime soon?"). Then, after the interview, she met with two of the gentlemen individually (including the president), and the discussions focused almost exclusively on her technical expertise. She thought that these later discussions went fairly well. However, given the apparent aimlessness and even mean-spiritedness of the panel interview, she was astonished when several days later she got a job offer from the firm.

The offer forced her to consider several matters. From her point of view, the job itself was perfect—she liked what she would be doing, the industry, and the firm's location. And, in fact, the president had been quite courteous in subsequent discussions, as had been the other members of the management team. She was left wondering whether the panel interview had been intentionally tense to see how she'd stand up under pressure, and, if so, why they would do such a thing.

Questions

1. How would you explain the nature of the panel interview Maria had to endure? Specifically, do you think it reflected a well-thought-out interviewing

strategy on the part of the firm or carelessness (or worse) on the part of the firm's management? If it was carelessness, what would you do to improve the interview process at Apex Environmental?

2. Do you consider the supervisors' treatment of Maria ethical? Why? If not, what specific steps would you take to make sure the interview process is ethical from now on?

3. Would you take the job offer if you were Maria? If you're not sure, is there any additional information that would help you make your decision, and if so, what is it?

4. The job of applications engineer for which Maria was applying requires: (a) excellent technical skills with respect to mechanical engineering; (b) a commitment to working in the area of pollution control; (c) the ability to deal well and confidently with customers who have engineering problems; (d) a willingness to travel worldwide; and (e) a very intelligent and well-balanced personality. List 10 questions you would ask when interviewing applicants for the job.

Case Study Two

Honesty Testing at Carter Cleaning Centers

Jennifer Carter, president of the Carter Cleaning Centers, and her father have what the latter describes as an easy but hard job when it comes to screening job applicants. It is easy because for two important jobs—the people who actually do the pressing and those who do the cleaning-spotting—the applicants are easily screened with about 20 minutes of on-the-job testing. As with typists, as Jennifer points out, "Applicants either know how to press clothes fast enough or how to use cleaning chemicals and machines, or they don't, and we find out very quickly by just trying them out on the job." On the other hand, applicant screening for the stores can also be frustratingly hard because of the nature of some of the other qualities that Jennifer would like to screen for. Two of the most critical problems facing her company are employee turnover and employee honesty. Jennifer and her father sorely need to implement practices that will reduce the rate of employee turnover. If there is a way to do this through employee testing and screening techniques, Jennifer would like to know about it because of the management time and money that are now being wasted by the never-ending need to recruit and hire new employees. Of even greater concern to Jennifer and her father is the need to institute new practices to screen out those employees who may be predisposed to steal from the company. Here is what Jennifer would like you to answer:

Questions

1. Specifically, what situational and behavioral interview questions should we ask to try to screen out candidates who are more likely to quit within the first few months here?

2. Can you think of any written tests we might use to identify high-potential candidates? Why did you suggest those tests?
3. What would be the advantages and disadvantages to Jennifer's company of routinely administering honesty tests to all its employees?
4. Specifically, what other screening techniques could the company use to screen out theft-prone and turnover-prone employees, and how exactly could these techniques be used?
5. How should her company terminate employees caught stealing, and what kind of procedure should be set up for handling reference calls about these employees when they go to other companies looking for jobs?

Experiential Activities

Activity 1. Two weeks after Cassandra was promoted to office supervisor, she was asked to fill a new position for a sales assistant. Cassandra placed an ad and after interviewing several applicants, she hired a new assistant. After just four weeks the new sales assistant was dismissed for performance-based issues. Now Cassandra can't figure out why she made the wrong decision.

Be Careful About Whom You Hire

Purpose: The purpose of this exercise is to give you practice in better preparing for the employment interviewing and screening process.

Required Understanding: You are going to develop a comprehensive interviewing and screening process for hiring the best qualified applicant for the sales assistant position and should therefore be thoroughly familiar with the discussion of interviewing and screening in this chapter.

How to Set Up the Exercise/Instructions: Divide the class into groups of four or five students.

1. You want to answer the question of how Cassandra should go about determining how she could have made such a misstep in her hiring.
2. Your group should develop an outline summarizing an interviewing and screening process. Decide which types of tests, background investigations, reference checks, and other information will be needed.
3. Next, create an interview form, including what important questions need to be covered in the interview process.
4. Have a spokesperson from each group share their outlines and summaries with each of the other groups. Follow with a class discussion involving all groups while looking at differences and similarities in the reports.

Activity 2. Assume you are the supervisor of a women's wear retail store on Madison Avenue in New York City. Customers tend to be fairly well off. Service is very important. In groups of 4–5 students, create a set of a dozen or so situational and behavioral questions you should use to evaluate applicants for sales clerk positions.

Role-Playing Exercise

The Most Important Person You'll Ever Hire

Purpose: The purpose of this exercise is to give you practice using some of the interview techniques you learned from this chapter.

Required Understanding: You should be familiar with the information presented in this chapter, and read this: For parents, children are precious. It's therefore interesting that parents who hire nannies to take care of their children usually do little more than ask several interview questions and conduct what is often, at best, a perfunctory reference check. Given the often questionable validity of interviews and the (often) relative inexperience of the father or mother doing the interviewing, it's not surprising that many of these arrangements end in disappointment. You know from this chapter that it is difficult to conduct a valid interview unless you know exactly what you're looking for and, preferably, also structure the interview. Most parents simply aren't trained to do this.

How to Set Up the Exercise/Instructions

1. Set up groups of five or six students. Two students will be the interviewees, while the other students in the group will serve as panel interviewers. The interviewees will develop an interviewer assessment form, and the panel interviewers will develop a structured situational interview for a nanny.

2. Instructions for the interviewees: The interviewees should leave the room for about 20 minutes. While out of the room, the interviewees should develop an "interviewer assessment form" based on the information presented in this chapter regarding factors that can undermine the usefulness of an interview. During the panel interview, the interviewees should assess the interviewers using the interviewer assessment form. After the panel interviewers have conducted the interview, the interviewees should leave the room to discuss their notes. Did the interviewers exhibit any of the factors that can undermine the usefulness of an interview? If so, which ones? What suggestions would you (the interviewees) make to the interviewers on how to improve the usefulness of the interview?

3. Instructions for the interviewers: While the interviewees are out of the room, the panel interviewers will have 20 minutes to develop a short structured situational interview form for a nanny. The panel interview team will interview two candidates for the position. During the panel interview, each interview should be taking notes on a copy of the structured situational interview form. After the panel interview, the panel interviewers should discuss their notes. What were your first impressions of each interviewee? Were your impressions similar? Which candidate would you all select for the position and why?

9 Training and Developing Employees

CHAPTER OBJECTIVES

After studying this chapter, you should be able to answer the following questions:

1. Orientation: Why Is It Critical to Ensure Employee Success?
2. How Do Managers Ascertain the Need for Training and Development?
3. What Training Techniques Are Available for Front-Line Employees?
4. What Training and Development Programs Are Available for Supervisors and Managers?
5. What Part Do Supervisors Play in Implementing Organizational Change Programs?
6. How Are Training and Development Efforts Evaluated?
7. How Is Employee Career Development Managed?

OPENING SNAPSHOT

That's Unbelievable, Al

After working as a chef and then head chef in several restaurants, Alex was thrilled to finally get the funding he needed to open his new French restaurant, Alex's Bistro, not far from the new Mid-Town Miami complex close to downtown Miami. For his kitchen staff he hired people with whom he'd worked closely at other restaurants, because he knew they were trained and competent and that they knew what to do. Hiring the wait staff was another thing. He had no personal experience running the "front end" of a restaurant, so he posted a *Help Wanted—Wait Staff* sign on the window and hired six people who exhibited the conscientiousness and people-orientation that he was looking for. He spent about an hour before opening day explaining details to the wait staff (such as how to use the computerized order input system) and describing how he wanted them to behave ("supportive and helpful"). Unfortunately, opening day was a disaster. Waiters and waitresses couldn't answer basic questions

such as "What's in this dish?" They got almost half the orders wrong, and when they finally did bring the orders to the tables, they didn't remember who ordered what dish, so the customers themselves ended up passing their dishes around. Later that night, after the restaurant had closed for the night, Alex went home and asked his former boss what he thought had gone wrong. "Are you actually telling me you didn't train your wait staff at all before letting them loose on your customers? That's unbelievable, Al."

1. Orienting and Training Employees

After the new employee joins the team, it's generally the supervisor's job to make sure he or she gets the necessary orienting and training.

Why Orientation Is Important

Most people feel slightly adrift when they start a new job, so it's important to put them at ease as soon as possible. A successful orientation should accomplish that, and more.[1] Of course, the **employee orientation** should give new employees the basic background information they need to do their jobs, such as information about company rules, and make them feel welcome and at home. But ideally, orientation should also start the process of socializing the new employee into the company's ways of doing thing. *Socialization* is the ongoing process of instilling in all employees the attitudes, standards, values, and patterns of behavior that the organization expects.[2]

After the orientation, your new employee should feel welcome. He or she should understand the organization in a broad sense (its past, present, culture, and vision of the future), as well as key facts such as policies and procedures. The employee should be clear about what the firm expects in terms of work and behavior. And, hopefully, the person should begin the process of becoming socialized into the firm's preferred ways of doing things.[3] For example, the Mayo Clinic's "heritage and culture" program uses videos and lectures to instill core Mayo Clinic values in new nurses and employees. These values include ones such as teamwork, responsibility, innovation, and mutual respect.[4] Training experts often refer to orientation as *onboarding* today. Promoting the company's values distinguishes onboarding from traditional orientation.[5]

Orientation: Why Is It Critical to Ensure Employee Success?

Types of Orientation Programs

Orientation programs range from brief introductions to lengthy, formal programs. The HR specialist or office manager usually performs the first part of the orientation and explains matters such as working hours and vacation. The employee then meets his or her new supervisor. The latter may then just spend an hour or two explaining the exact nature of the job, introducing the person to his or her new colleagues, and familiarizing the new employee with the workplace and the job, perhaps with a checklist like that in Figure 9.1. At the other extreme, employers such as the Mayo Clinic and Honda Motor USA may spend a week onboarding new employees. Here they include videos, lectures by company officers, and exercises covering matters like company history, vision, and values. The Apps feature shows one tool for supporting orientation.

■ Figure **9.1**

Sample Orientation Checklist

UNIVERSITY of CALIFORNIA SAN DIEGO
MEDICAL CENTER

NEW EMPLOYEE DEPARTMENTAL ORIENTATION CHECKLIST
(Return to Human Resources within 10 days of Hire)

NAME:	HIRE DATE:	SSN:	JOB TITLE:
DEPARTMENT:	NEO DATE:	DEPARTMENTAL ORIENTATION COMPLETED BY:	

TOPIC	DATE REVIEWED	N/A
1. HUMAN RESOURCES INFORMATION		
a. Departmental Attendance Procedures and UCSD Medical Center Work Time & Attendance Policy	a. _____	☐
b. Job Description Review	b. _____	☐
c. Annual Performance Evaluation and Peer Feedback Process	c. _____	☐
d. Probationary Period Information	d. _____	☐
e. Appearance/Dress Code Requirements	e. _____	☐
f. Annual TB Screening	f. _____	☐
g. License and/or Certification Renewals	g. _____	☐
2. DEPARTMENT INFORMATION		
a. Organizational Structure-Department Core Values Orientation	a. _____	☐
b. Department/Unit Area Specific Policies & Procedures	b. _____	☐
c. Customer Service Practices	c. _____	☐
d. CQI Effort and Projects	d. _____	☐
e. Tour and Floor Plan	e. _____	☐
f. Equipment/Supplies	f. _____	☐
• Keys issued	_____	☐
• Radio Pager issued	_____	☐
• Other _____	_____	☐
g. Mail and Recharge Codes	g. _____	☐
3. SAFETY INFORMATION		
a. Departmental Safety Plan	a. _____	☐
b. Employee Safety/Injury Reporting Procedures	b. _____	☐
c. Hazard Communication	c. _____	☐
d. Infection Control/Sharps Disposal	d. _____	☐
e. Attendance at annual Safety Fair (mandatory)	e. _____	☐
4. FACILITES INFORMATION		
a. Emergency Power	a. _____	☐
b. Mechanical Systems	b. _____	☐
c. Water	c. _____	☐
d. Medical Gases	d. _____	☐
e. Patient Room	e. _____	☐
• Bed	_____	☐
• Headwall	_____	☐
• Bathroom	_____	☐
• Nurse Call System	_____	☐
5. SECURITY INFORMATION		
a. Code Triage Assignment	a. _____	☐
b. Code Blue Assignment	b. _____	☐
c. Code Red–Evacuation Procedure	c. _____	☐
d. Code 10–Bomb Threat Procedure	d. _____	☐
e. Departmental Security Measures	e. _____	☐
f. UCSD Emergency Number <u>6111</u> or <u>911</u>	f. _____	☐

This generic checklist may not constitute a complete departmental orientation or assessment. Please attach any additional unit specific orientation material for placement in the employee's HR file

I have been oriented on the items listed above _____

D1999(R7-01)   **WHITE** – HR Records (8912)   **Yellow** – Department Retains

In either case, new employees usually receive printed or Web-based handbooks that cover matters such as working hours, performance reviews, getting on the payroll, and vacations, as well as a tour of the facilities. Other information might cover employee benefits, personnel policies, the employee's daily routine, company organization and operations, and safety regulations.[7] Courts may find that your employee handbook's contents represent a contract with the employee. Supervisors therefore should never say or imply that statements of company policies, benefits, and regulations constitute an employment contract. And never improvise with comments such as, "We only fire people for good cause," unless that is actually company policy.

Using Technology in Orientation

Companies increasingly use technology to improve orientation. For example, some firms provide new supervisors with preloaded personal digital assistants. These contain information such as key contact information, main tasks to undertake, and even images of employees the new supervisor should know.[8] Some firms provide all new employees with URLs or disks containing discussions of corporate culture, videos of corporate facilities, and welcoming addresses from top managers.

VIRTUAL ORIENTATION   IBM uses virtual environments like Second Life to support orientation, particularly for employees abroad. The new employees choose virtual avatars, which then interact with other company avatars, for instance, to learn how to enroll for benefits.[9]

2. The Training and Development Process

What Is Training?

Directly after orientation, training should begin. **Training** means giving new or present employees the skills they need to perform their jobs. This might mean showing a new Web designer the intricacies of your site, or a new salesperson how to sell your firm's product. Training might involve simply having the current jobholder explain the job to the new hire. Or it may involve a multiweek training program. Training experts today increasingly use the phrase "workplace learning and performance" in lieu of training, to underscore training's dual aims of employee learning and organizational performance.[10]

In any case, training is a hallmark of good supervision, and a task that supervisors ignore at their peril. Having high-potential employees doesn't guarantee they'll perform. Instead (unlike the hapless staff at Alex's Bistro), they must know what you want them to do, and how you want them to do it. If they don't, they will improvise or do nothing useful at all.

Inadequate training can also expose employers to legal liability: "It's clear from the case law that where an employer fails to train adequately and an employee subsequently does harm to third parties, the court will find the employer liable."[11] (This might occur, for instance, if you hire someone to repair plumbing who turns out to be inadequately trained and floods someone's basement.) As an agent of your employer, you should confirm the applicant/employee's claims of skill and experience, supply adequate training (particularly where employees work with dangerous equipment), and evaluate the training to ensure that it's accomplishing what it is supposed to.

We can envision the *training process* as including four steps:

1. In the first step, *needs analysis*, you identify the specific knowledge and skills the job requires and compare these with the prospective trainees' knowledge and skills.

2. In the second step, *instructional design*, you formulate specific, measurable knowledge and performance training objectives. Then review possible training program content (including workbooks, exercises, and activities), and collect and organize the methods and materials you'll use for the training program.[12]

3. The third step is to *implement* the program by actually training the person, using methods such as on-the-job or online training.

4. Finally, there may be an *evaluation* step, in which you assess the program's success (or failures).

DETERMINING TRAINING NEEDS   How do you know what sorts of training the person needs? Assessing *new employees'* training needs usually involves *task analysis*—breaking the jobs into subtasks and teaching each to the new employee.

Determining *current employees'* training needs is more complex: Is this person doing poorly because he or she needs more training, or is performance down because the person isn't motivated? Here *performance analysis* is required. We'll look at each.

NEW EMPLOYEES   Supervisors use *task analysis* to determine new employees' training needs. With inexperienced personnel, your aim is to provide the skills and knowledge required for effective performance. **Task analysis** is a detailed study of the job to determine what specific skills—such as soldering (in the case of an assembly worker) or interviewing (in the case of a supervisor)—is required. Here the job description and job specification provide useful information. The former lists the job's specific duties; the latter lists the skills someone needs to do the job. Figure 9.2 summarizes additional tools to use to uncover a job's training requirements.

CURRENT EMPLOYEES   For current employees whose performance is deficient, task analysis is usually not enough.[13] Why isn't the person doing well? You need to decide what the problem is. **Performance analysis** means verifying that there is a performance deficiency and determining whether to rectify the deficiency through training or

■Figure **9.2**

Methods for Uncovering Training Needs

Source: Adapted from P. Nick Blanchard and James Thacker, *Effective Training: Systems, Strategies and Practices* (Upper Saddle River, NJ: Prentice Hall, 1999), pp. 138–39.

Sources for Obtaining Job Data	Training Need Information
1. Job Descriptions	Outlines the job's typical duties and responsibilities but is not meant to be all-inclusive. Helps define performance discrepancies.
2. Job Specifications or Task Analysis	List specified tasks required for each job. More specific than job descriptions. Specifications may extend to judgments of knowledge and skills required of job incumbents.
3. Performance Standards	Objectives of the tasks of job, and standards by which they are judged. This may include baseline data as well.
4. Perform the Job	Most effective way of determining specific tasks, but has serious limitations in higher-level jobs because performance requirements typically have longer gaps between performance and resulting outcomes.
5. Observe Job-Work Sampling	Same as 4 above.

6. Review Literature Concerning the Job
  a. Research in other industries
  b. Professional journals
  c. Documents
  d. Government sources
  e. Ph.D. theses
	Possibly useful in comparison analyses of job structures, but far removed from either unique aspects of the job structure within any *specific* organization or specific performance requirements.

7. Ask Questions About the Job
  a. Of the job holder
  b. Of the supervisor
  c. Of higher management
	Inputs from several viewpoints can often reveal training needs or training desires.

8. Training Committees or Conferences	Same as 7 above.

9. Analysis of Operating Problems
  a. Downtime reports
  b. Waste
  c. Repairs
  d. Late deliveries
  e. Quality control
	Indications of task interference, environmental factors, etc.

through some other means (such as transferring the employee or doing something to motivate the person). Supervisors identify employees' performance deficiencies and training needs in several ways. A typical list would include:

- Reviews of past performance appraisals
- Job-related performance data (including productivity, absenteeism and tardiness, accidents, short-term sickness, grievances, waste, late deliveries, product quality, downtime, repairs, equipment utilization, and customer complaints)
- Observation by supervisors or other specialists
- Interviews with the employee or his or her supervisor
- Tests of things such as job knowledge, skills, and attendance
- Attitude surveys
- Assessment centers[14]

Your first step here is usually to appraise the employee's performance. Examples of specific performance deficiencies follow:

"I expect each salesperson to make 10 new contacts per week, but John averages only six."

"Other plants our size average no more than two serious accidents per month; we're averaging five."

Distinguishing between "can't do" and "won't do" problems is the heart of performance analysis. First, determine whether it's a "can't do" problem and, if so, its specific causes. For example, perhaps the employees don't know what to do or what your standards are, or there are obstacles such as lack of tools or supplies. Perhaps job aids are needed, such as color-coded wires that show assemblers what wire goes where; or poor screening results in hiring people who haven't the skills to do the job; or training is inadequate. On the other hand, it might be a "won't do" problem. Here employees *could* do a good job if they wanted to. If this is the case, the supervisor may have to change the reward system, perhaps by implementing an incentive plan.

COMPETENCY MODELS   More employers use competency models to summarize training needs. The aim of such a model is to compile in one place the competencies (the knowledge, skills, and behaviors) that are crucial for executing the job. At Sharp Electronics, training managers first interview senior executives to identify the firm's strategic objectives and to infer what competencies those objectives will require. Trainers also interview the job's top performers. Here they identify the competencies (such as "focuses on the customer") the latter believe comprise the job's core competencies. Subsequent training then aims to develop these competencies.[15] The **competency model** consolidates, usually in one diagram, a precise overview of the competencies someone would need to do a job well.

As an example, Figure 9.3 shows the competency model for a human resource manager. At the top of the pyramid, it shows four main roles the human resource manager needs to fill. Beneath that it shows the areas of expertise in which he or she must be expert, such as selection and training. At the base are the HR manager's essential, "foundation" competencies, such as communicating effectively.

SETTING TRAINING OBJECTIVES   After training needs have been uncovered, measurable training objectives should be set. Training, development, or (more generally) *instructional objectives* are "a description of a performance you want learners to be able to exhibit before you consider them competent."[16] For example:

> Given a tool kit and a service manual, the technician will be able to adjust the registration (black line along paper edges) on this Canon duplicator within 20 minutes according to the specifications.

Objectives specify what the trainee should be able to accomplish after successfully completing the training program. They thus provide a focus for both the trainee's and the trainer's efforts and a benchmark for evaluating the success of the training program.

TRAINING AND MOTIVATION   If you collect too many traffic tickets, you may find yourself in "driving school." Here the motor vehicles department hopes you (and the other driver "trainees") may overcome the propensity to drive through so many red lights. More often than not that school session starts with a very graphic car crash, to remind you what bad driving can do, and to grab your attention and motivate you to listen in class.

The moral is that training is futile if the trainee lacks the ability or motivation to benefit from it.[17] The supervisor can take several steps to increase the trainee's motivation to learn. Providing opportunities for *active practice* and letting the trainee *make errors* and explore alternate solutions improve motivation and learning.[18] *Feedback—*

Roles
Line Function
(Within HR)
Staff Function
(Advise, Assist)
Coordinative Function
(Monitor)
Strategic HR Function
(Formulate, Execute)

Areas of Expertise
HR Practices (Recruiting, Selection, Training, etc.)
Strategic Planning
Employment Law
Finance and Budgeting
General Management

Foundation Competencies

Personal
Competencies
• Behave Ethically
• Exercise Good Judgment
  Based on Evidence
• Set and Achieve Goals
• Manage Tasks Effectively
• Develop Personally

Interpersonal
Competencies
• Communicate Effectively
• Exercise Leadership
• Negotiate Effectively
• Motivate Others
• Work Productively
  with Others

HR/Business/
Management
• Institute Effective
  HR Systems
• Analyze Financial Statements
• Craft Strategies
• Manage Vendors

**ILLUSTRATIVE
HUMAN RESOURCE MANAGER
COMPETENCY MODEL**

including periodic performance assessments and frequent verbal critiques—is also important.[19] Also, try to *make the material meaningful*. For example, provide an overview of the material and ensure that your instructions use familiar examples and concepts to illustrate key points.[20]

Designing the Training Program

After determining the employees' training needs and setting training objectives, you can design and implement a training program. Many employers simply choose packaged on- and-offline training programs from vendors like the American Society for Training and Development. [21] Many other vendors, including HRDQ (http://www.hrdqstore.com/) also provide turnkey training packages. [22]

3. Training Techniques

We'll look at popular training techniques next.

What Training Techniques Are Available for Front-Line Employees?

On-the-Job Training

Every employee receives some on-the-job training (OJT). The most familiar type of on-the-job training is the coaching or understudy method. Here an experienced worker or the trainee's supervisor trains the employee, on the job. At lower levels, trainees may acquire skills for, say, running a machine by observing the supervisor. Job rotation, in which an employee moves from job to job at planned intervals, is another on-the-job technique.

As an example, The Men's Wearhouse, with about 500 stores nationwide, makes extensive use of on-the-job training. It has few full-time trainers. Instead, it has a formal process of "cascading" responsibility for training: Every supervisor is accountable for the development of his or her direct subordinates.[23]

In practice, OJT is probably the single most important training technique that supervisors use. The following is a useful four-step procedure supervisors can use for creating a simple on-the-job training program for various types of jobs.

Step 1. Review the Job Description. A detailed job description is the heart of the training program. It should list the daily and periodic tasks of each job, along with a summary of the steps in each task.

Step 2. Develop a Task Analysis Record Form. The supervisor may use a Task Analysis Record Form (Table 9.1) to organize the training needs. In the first column, list *tasks* (including what is to be performed in terms of each of the main tasks, and the steps involved in each task). In column B, list *performance standards* (in terms of quantity, quality, accuracy, and so on). In column C, list *trainable skills* required, things the employee must know or do to perform the task. This column provides you with specific knowledge and skills (such as "Keep both hands on the wheel") that you want to stress.

■ Table **9.1**

Sample Summary Task Analysis Record Sheet			
Task List A	**Performance Standards B**	**Trainable Skills Required C**	**Aptitudes Required D**
1. Operate paper cutter			
1.1 Start motor	Start by push-button on first try	To start machine without accidentally attempting restart while machine running	Ability to understand written and spoken instructions
1.2 Set cutting distance	Maximum +/− tolerance of 0.007 inch	Read gauge	Able to read tolerances on numerical scale
1.3 Place paper on cutting table	Must be completely even to prevent uneven edges	Lift paper correctly	At least average manual dexterity
1.4 Push paper up to paper cutter blade		Must be even with blade	At least average manual dexterity
1.5 Grasp safety release with left hand	100% of the time, for safety	Must keep both hands on releases to prevent hand contact with cutting blade	Ability to understand written and spoken warnings

Note: This shows the first five steps in one of the tasks (operate paper cutter) for which a printing factory owner would train the person doing the cutting of the paper before placing the paper on the printing presses.

Sample Job Instruction Sheet	
Steps in Task	**Key Points to Keep in Mind**
1. Start motor	None
2. Set cutting distance	Carefully read scale—to prevent wrong-sized cut
3. Place paper on cutting table	Make sure paper is even—to prevent uneven cut
4. Push paper up to cutter	Make sure paper is tight—to prevent uneven cut
5. Grasp safety release with left hand	Do not release left hand—to prevent hand from being caught in cutter
6. Grasp cutter release with right hand	Do not release right hand—to prevent hand from being caught in cutter
7. Simultaneously pull cutter and safety releases	Keep both hands on corresponding releases—avoid hands being on cutting table
8. Wait for cutter to retract	Keep both hands on releases—to avoid having hands on cutting table
9. Retract paper	Make sure cutter is retracted; keep both hands away from releases
10. Shut off motor	None

In the fourth column, list *aptitudes required*. These are the human aptitudes (such as mechanical comprehension) that the employee should have to be trainable for the task and for which the employee can be screened ahead of time.

Step 3. Develop a Job Instruction Sheet. Next develop a job instruction sheet for the job. As in Table 9.2, a job instruction training sheet shows the steps in each task as well as key points for each.

Step 4. Train the Employee. The actual on-the-job training may simply involve going through the steps in the job, as listed in the Job Instruction Sheet. Preferably, prepare a training manual for the job. This should include the job description, Task Analysis Record Form, and job instruction sheet. It might also contain an introduction to the job and a graphical and/or written explanation of how the job fits with other jobs in the plant or office.

Informal Learning

Surveys from the American Society for Training and Development estimate that as much as 80% of what employees learn on the job they learn through informal means. This often means performing their jobs in collaboration with their colleagues.[24]

Although supervisors don't arrange informal learning (that's why it's informal), there's much they can do to ensure that it occurs. For example, Siemens Power Transmission and Distribution in North Carolina places tools in cafeterias to capitalize on the work-related discussions taking place. Even simple things like installing whiteboards and keeping them stocked with markers facilitates informal learning. Sun Microsystems implemented an informal "knowledge management" learning tool it called Sun learning eXchange. This grew into an Internet site containing more than 5,000 informal learning items addressing topics ranging from eating sales to technical support.[25]

Informal learning isn't just for big companies. For example, training expert Stephen Covey says small businesses can provide job-related personal improvement without establishing expensive formal training programs. His suggestions include the following ideas:[26]

- Offer to cover the tuition for special classes.
- Identify online training opportunities.
- Provide a library of tapes and DVDs for systematic, disciplined learning during commute times.
- Encourage the sharing of best practices among associates.
- When possible, send people to special seminars and association meetings for learning and networking.

Apprenticeship Training

Apprenticeship training is a structured process by which individuals become skilled workers through a combination of classroom instruction and on-the-job training, usually under the tutelage of a master craftsperson. It is widely used to train individuals for many occupations, including electrician and plumber.[27] When steelmaker Dofasco discovered that many of their employees would be retiring during the next 5 to 10 years, the company revived its apprenticeship-training program. Applicants are prescreened. Then new recruits spend about 32 months in an internal training program. The program emphasizes apprenticeship training, learning various jobs under the tutelage of experienced crafts persons.[28]

The U.S. Department of Labor's National Apprenticeship System promotes apprenticeship programs. Over 460,000 apprentices participate in 28,000 programs, and registered programs can receive federal and state contracts and other assistance.[29] Figure 9.4 lists popular recent apprenticeships.

Behavior Modeling

Behavior modeling involves showing trainees the right (or model) way of doing something, letting each person practice the right way to do it, and providing feedback regarding each trainee's performance. The basic behavior modeling procedure is as follows:

1. Modeling. First, trainees watch videodisks that show model persons behaving effectively in a problem situation.

■ Figure **9.4**
Some Popular Apprenticeships

Source: www.doleta.gov/oa, accessed July 3, 2009.

The U.S. Department of Labor's Registered Apprenticeship program offers access to 1,000 career areas, including the following top occupations:

- Able seaman
- Carpenter
- Chef
- Child care development specialist
- Construction craft laborer
- Dental assistant
- Electrician
- Elevator constructor
- Fire medic
- Law enforcement agent
- Over-the-road truck driver
- Pipefitter

2. Role-playing. Next, the trainees are given roles to play in a simulated situation.

3. Social reinforcement. The trainer provides praise and constructive feedback based on how the trainee performs in the role-playing situation.

4. Transfer of training. Finally, trainees are encouraged to apply their new skills when they are back on their jobs.

Vestibule Training

Vestibule training is a technique in which trainees learn on the actual or simulated equipment they will use on the job but receive their training off the job. Such training is necessary when on-the-job training is too costly or dangerous. Putting new assembly-line workers right to work could slow production. And when safety is a concern, such as with pilots, vestibule training may be the only practical alternative. As an example, UPS uses a life-size learning lab to provide a 46-hour, five-day realistic training program for driver candidates.[30] Vestibule training may just take place in a separate room with the equipment the trainees will actually be using on the job (a "vestibule" is an entry room leading to the main room). However, it often involves the use of equipment simulators, as in pilot training.

Audiovisual and Traditional Distance Learning Techniques

Audiovisual techniques such as DVDs, films, closed-circuit television, and CDs can be very effective and are widely used. The Ford Motor Company uses videos in its dealer training sessions to simulate sample reactions to various customer complaints. Firms also use various distance learning methods for training. Distance learning methods include traditional correspondence courses, as well as videoconferencing and Internet-based classes.[31] For example, Macy's established the Macy's Satellite Network television-based training program, in part to provide training to the firm's employees around the country.

VIDEOCONFERENCE DISTANCE LEARNING   Videoconferencing is a popular way to train geographically dispersed employees. It is "a means of joining two or more distant groups using a combination of audio and visual equipment."[32] Vendors such as Cisco offer videoconference products such as WebEx and TelePresence (http://www.cisco.com/en/US/products/ps10352/index.html). These make it easy to create Web-based videoconference training programs.

Computer-Based Training

In a Stanford University Hospital training room, medical students wearing virtual reality headsets control computer-screen avatars in a virtual reality trauma center. The residents and medical students use their keypads to control their avatar's every move.[33]

In **computer-based training** such as this, the trainee uses a computer-based system to increase his or her knowledge or skills interactively. Today this often means (as at Stanford) presenting trainees with computerized simulations, and using multimedia including videodiscs to help the trainee learn how to do the job.[34]

But the computer-based training is often simpler. For example, in one training program, people training to be recruiters start with a computer screen that shows an "applicant's" employment application, as well as information about the job. The trainee then begins a simulated interview by typing in questions. A videotaped model acting as the applicant answers the questions using answers that the firm previously programmed into the computer. At the end of the session, the computer tells the recruiter trainee where he or she went wrong (perhaps in asking discriminatory questions, for instance) and offers further instructional material to correct these mistakes.

SIMULATED LEARNING   "Simulated learning" means different things to different people. A survey asked training professionals what experiences qualified as simulated learning experiences. The percentages of trainers choosing each experience were:

- Virtual reality-type games, 19%
- Step-by-step animated guide, 8%
- Scenarios with questions and decision trees overlaying animation, 19%
- Online role-play with photos and videos, 14%
- Software training including screenshots with interactive requests for responses, 35%
- Other, 6%[35]

Employers increasingly rely on computerized simulations to inject more realism into their training programs. For example, Orlando-based Environmental Tectonics Corporation created an Advanced Disaster Management simulation for emergency medical response trainees. One of the simulated scenarios involves a passenger plane crashing into an airport runway. So realistic that it's "unsettling", trainees including firefighters and airport officials respond to the simulated crash's sights and sounds via pointing devices and radios.[36]

Other employers capitalize on virtual environments such as Second Life to provide simulated learning. For example, British Petroleum (whose planning in some other areas of safety are in question today) uses Second Life to train new gas station employees. The aim here is to show new gas station employees how to use the safety features of gasoline storage tanks. BP built three-dimensional renderings of the tank systems in Second Life. Trainees could use these to "see" underground and observe the effects of using the safety devices.[37]

Training via the Internet and Learning Portals

Employers, of course, also use Internet-based learning to deliver training. The training itself may simply include posting videos, lectures, and PowerPoint slides, or sophisticated simulations (like BP's).

Whether to use online "e-learning" often comes down to efficiency. Web learning doesn't necessarily teach faster or better.[38] But the need to teach large numbers of trainees remotely or to enable trainees to study at their leisure often makes e-learning so much more efficient that the small differences in effectiveness don't matter.[39] Many firms simply let their employees take online courses offered by online course providers such as Click2Learn.com. Others use their proprietary internal *intranets* to facilitate computer-based training.

LEARNING PORTALS   Companies increasingly convey their employee training through their intranet portals. They often contract with *applications service providers* such as SkillSoft (www.skillsoft.com) or, for health and safety training, puresafety (www. puresafety.com) to deliver online training courses to the firms' employees.[40] Figure 9.5 lists a few of them.

In practice, many employers opt for "blended learning." Here the trainees use several delivery methods (such as manuals, in-class lectures, self-guided e-learning programs, and Web-based seminars or "webinars") to learn the material.[41]

Mobile Learning

Mobile learning (or "on-demand learning") means delivering learning content on demand via mobile devices like cell phones, laptops, and iPhones, wherever and whenever the learner wants to access it.[42] For example, using dominKnow's (http://www.dominknow.com/) iPod touch and iPhone-optimized Touch Learning Center Portal, trainees can log in and take full online courses.[43]

IBM uses mobile learning to deliver just-in-time information (for instance, about new product features) to its sales force. To increase such learning's accessibility, IBM's training department often breaks up, say, an hour-long program into 10-minute pieces.[44] The banking firm JP Morgan encourages employees to use instant messages as quick learning devices. Employers also use instant messaging to supplement classroom training, for instance, by using IM for online office hours and for group chats. One training supervisor sends a short personal development idea or quote each day for others to access via his Twitter account.[45]

THE VIRTUAL CLASSROOM   Conventional online learning tends to be limited to the sorts of learning with which many college students are already familiar—reading PowerPoint presentations and taking online exams, for instance.

The virtual classroom takes online learning to a new level. A **virtual classroom** uses special collaboration software to enable remote learners, using their PCs or laptops, to participate in live audio and visual discussions, communicate via written text, and learn via content such as PowerPoint slides. For example, Elluminate Inc. makes one popular virtual classroom system, Elluminate live! (http://www.elluminate.com/demo/live_demo.jsp) It enables learners to communicate with clear, two-way audio, build communities with user profiles and live video, collaborate with chat and shared whiteboards, and learn with shared applications such as PowerPoint slides.[46]

Training for Special Purposes

Training today does more than just prepare employees to perform their jobs. Training for special purposes—dealing with diversity, for instance—is required too. A sampling follows.

LITERACY TRAINING TECHNIQUES   Functional illiteracy—the inability to do basic reading, writing, and arithmetic—is a serious problem at work. By one estimate, about 39 million people in the United States find it challenging to read, write, or do arithmetic.[47] A recent study described the American workforce as "ill-prepared."[48] Yet today's emphasis on teamwork and quality increases employees' need to read, write, and understand numbers.

E-learning Companies

Categories

Course Authoring (58)
E-learning Portals (69)
E-learning Research (22)
Learning Management Systems (73)
Online Classrooms (16)

Related Categories:

Computers > Education > Commercial Services > Training Companies > Self-Study (39)
Reference > Education > Distance Learning > Online Courses (275)
Reference > Education > Distance Learning > Services (29)
Reference > Knowledge Management > Business and Companies (103)

Web Pages	Viewing in Google PageRank order	View in alphabetical order

Skillsoft - http://www.skillsoft.com
Providers of enterprise e-learning, a fully integrated student environment and courseware to support e-Learning initiatives in enterprises.

Plateau Systems - http://www.plateau.com
Corporate learning solutions deployed at enterprises across the world enabling global organizations to increase productivity and save millions of training dollars.

Academee - http://www.academee.com
Integrated learning programmes, blending consultancy, online e-learning and face-to-face classroom courses for management and professional development.

Enspire Learning - http://www.enspire.com
Enspire Learning develops custom e-learning courses that include interactive multimedia, simulations, and engaging scenarios.

Ninth House Network - http://www.ninthhouse.com/
A leading e-learning broadband environment for organizational development, delivering to the desktop experiential, interactive programs that leverage the world's foremost business thinkers.

Futurate Ltd - http://www.futurate.com/
Developers of eLearning content and systems that are engaging and accessible to all. They offer a 'full service' from consultancy to implementation and maintenance.

PrimeLearning - http://www.primelearning.com
E-learning company that specialises in business and professional skills courses provided off the self or can be custom made.

Intellinex - http://www.intellinex.com
Provider of e-Learning solutions for workers in Global 2000 companies, government, and educational institutions. Courseware covers PC and business skills applications.

Allen Communication - http://www.allencomm.com
Provides e-Learning solutions including learning portals, strategic planning for training, courseware development and authoring / design tools.

The Learning House, Inc. - http://www.learninghouse.com
Learning House, Inc. is an eLearning services company that creates off the shelf and custom online degree and professional development courses.

DefinITion - http://www.definition.be
DefinITion design and development e-learning courses for companies. The company is based in Belgium and their services include consultancy and support.

Intrac Design Inc - http://www.intrac.biz
The development and delivery of customizable training programs for live classroom and e-learning delivery.

Seward, Inc. - http://www.sewardinc.com
Seward, Inc. provide engaging, instructionally sound, cost-effective training solutions ranging from soft skills involved in sales to the most technically exacting fields of medicine, engineering, and finance.

Silverchair Learning Systems - http://www.silverchairlearning.com
Online employee education exclusively for the Senior Care industry.

Tata Interactive Systems - http://www.tatainteractivesystems.com
Developer of custom e-learning solutions for corporate, educational and governmental organizations.

Little Planet Learning - http://www.littleplanet.com
Provides design and development of learning experiences delivered live and through elearning, computer and web based training (CBT and WBT), and multimedia programs.

■Figure **9.5**

Some e-Learning Companies

Employers take various approaches to teaching basic skills. For example, at one Borg-Warner plant, supervisors chose employee participants and placed them in three classes of 15 students each based on test scores. There were two trainers from a local training company. Each session was to run a maximum of 200 hours. However, employees could leave when they reached a predetermined skill level. Therefore, some were in the program for only 40 hours and others stayed for the whole course.[49] Classes were 5 days per week, 2 hours per day. In this program, employees could help each other (for instance, they paired someone good with decimals with someone who was not).

Another, simple approach is for supervisors to teach basic skills. For example, if an employee needs to use a manual to find out how to change a part, use the opportunity to teach that person how to use an index to locate the relevant section.

PROVIDING EMPLOYEES WITH LIFELONG LEARNING **Lifelong learning** means providing employees with continuing learning experiences over their tenure with the firm. The aim is ensuring they have the opportunity to learn the skills they need to do their jobs and to expand their horizons. With more emphasis today on employee empowerment and decision making, programs like these might range from training in English as a second language to computer literacy. For example, one senior waiter at Rhapsody restaurant in Chicago received his undergraduate degree and began work toward a master of social work using the *lifelong learning account* (LiLA) program his employer offers. Employers and employees contribute to LiLA plans, and the employee can use these funds for self-improvement.[50]

4. Supervisory Training and Development Programs

Like their employees, supervisors need and benefit from special training programs. These typically include in-house programs such as courses, coaching, and rotational assignments; professional programs such as American Management Association (AMA) seminars; and university programs such as executive MBA programs. Many first-line supervisors—from department heads to production and sales supervisors—get supervisory training.[51]

The most popular development methods include classroom-based learning, executive coaching, action learning, 360° feedback, experiential learning, off-site retreats (where supervisors meet with colleagues for learning), mentoring, and job rotation.[52] In general, there is a trend toward supplementing traditional development methods (such as lectures and case discussions) with realistic methods like action learning projects. Here trainees solve actual company problems.[53] We'll look at some of these supervisor development methods.

What Training and Development Programs Are Available for Supervisors and Managers?

Supervisory On-the-Job Training

On-the-job training isn't just for workers. It's also popular for supervisors. Important variants include **job rotation**, the **coaching/understudy method**, and **action learning**. *Job rotation* means moving supervisors from department to department to broaden their understanding of all parts of the business. With the *coaching/understudy* method, the new supervisor receives ongoing advice, often from the person he or she is to replace.

Action Learning

Action learning means letting supervisors work full time on real projects, analyzing and solving problems, usually in departments other than their own. The trainees meet periodically within a four- or five-person project group to discuss their findings. The groups then present their recommendations to, say the plant manager and his or her staff.

The Case Study Method

The **case study method** presents a trainee with a written description of an organizational problem. The person analyzes the case, diagnoses the problem, and presents his or her findings and solutions in a discussion with other trainees.[54]

The case study method has several aims. It aims, first, to give trainees realistic experience in identifying and analyzing complex problems in an environment in which their trainer/discussion leader can subtly guide their progress. Through the class discussion of the case, trainees also learn that there are usually many ways to approach and solve organizational problems. They also learn that their own needs and values often influence the solutions they suggest.

Business Games

In computerized **business games**, trainees split into five- or six-person companies, each of which has to compete with the others in a simulated marketplace. Each company can make several decisions. For example, the group may decide what to spend on advertising, how much to hold in inventory, and how many of which product to produce. Usually, the game compresses a 2- or 3-year period into days, weeks, or months. As in the real world, each company usually can't see what decisions the other firms have made, although these decisions do affect their own sales. For example, if a competitor decides to increase its advertising expenditures, that firm may end up increasing its sales at the expense of the others.[55]

Outside Programs and Seminars

Many vendors offer supervisory development seminars and conferences. The selection of short, (one- to three-day) training programs offered by the American Management Association illustrates what's available. Recently, for instance, their offerings ranged from "developing your emotional intelligence," to "assertiveness training," "assertiveness training for women in business," dynamic listening skills for successful communication," and "fundamentals of cost accounting."[56] Programs like these are particularly appropriate in terms of length and depth for first-line supervisors.

Most of these programs offer continuing education units (CEUs) for course completion. CEUs generally can't be used to obtain degree-granting credit at most colleges or universities. However, they provide a record that the trainee completed a conference or seminar.

University-Related Programs

Colleges and universities provide several types of supervisor training and development activities. First, many schools provide continuing education programs in leadership, supervision, and the like. As with the AMA, these range from one- to four-day programs to programs lasting one to four months. Many also offer individual courses in areas such as business, supervision, and health care administration. Supervisors can take these as matriculated or nonmatriculated students to fill gaps in their backgrounds. Schools, of course, also offer degree programs such as the master of business administration (MBA).[57]

In-House Development Centers

Many firms have **in-house development centers** or "universities." These usually combine classroom learning (lectures and seminars, for instance) with other techniques such as assessment centers and online learning opportunities. For example, at General Electric's (GE) Leadership Institute, the courses range from entry-level programs in manufacturing and sales to a business course for English majors.

LEARNING PORTALS   For many firms, their online learning portals are becoming their virtual in-house development centers. Learning portals let even smaller firms have their own corporate universities on the Web. Bain & Company, a management-consulting firm, has a Web-based virtual university for its employees. It provides a means for conveniently coordinating all the company's training efforts, and also for delivering Web-based modules that cover topics from strategic management to mentoring.[58]

5. Understanding Organizational Change Programs

Companies and units within them are always having to change. Companywide, for instance, BP recently began reviewing ways to change how it organizes and oversees its safety and drilling operations. The changes will probably lead to revising the company's organization chart, appointing many new executives, and taking steps to change BP's "safety culture"—the emphasis all its employees put on safety. Another example was when GM's new CEO, in 2010, reorganized the company and sold many of its brands. Top management usually formulates and manages such big-picture changes.

What Part Do Supervisors Play in Implementing Organizational Change Programs?

However, "organizational change" isn't the sole responsibility of top or even middle managers. Hardly a week will go by when the typical supervisor doesn't have to get his or her people to execute some change, be it getting a new sales procedure implemented, or a new machine online, or ending a quality issue that's been plaguing the team.

Making changes like these are never easy, but usually the hardest part of leading the change is overcoming the resistance to it. Individual employees, groups, and even entire organizations may resist the change. They'll do so because they are accustomed to the usual way of doing things or because the changes seem to threaten their power and influence, or for some other reason.[59] Most people don't like change and may try to stymie the supervisor's efforts to implement a change.

Lewin's Process for Overcoming Resistance

Psychologist Kurt Lewin formulated a famous model to show what he believed was the best process for implementing a change with minimal resistance. To Lewin, all behavior in organizations was a product of two kinds of forces: those striving to maintain the status quo and those pushing for change. Implementing change thus meant either reducing the forces for the status quo, or building up the forces for change. Lewin's recommended change process consisted of three steps:

1. *Unfreezing* means reducing the forces that are striving to maintain the status quo. For example, present a provocative problem or event to shock your people to recognize the need for change.

2. *Moving* means developing new employee behaviors, values, attitudes, and ways of doing things. For example, the head of GM did this by reorganizing the company.

3. *Refreezing* means building in the reinforcement to make sure the organization does not slide back into its former ways of doing things. For example, change the incentive plan so that it reinforces your new sales policy.

AN 8-STEP PROCESS FOR IMPLEMENTING A CHANGE   Of course, the "devil is in the details." Actually choosing the right tactics that will help you unfreeze, change, and then refreeze your team is the difficult part. It does not really matter much if it's the CEO or the first-line supervisor. Steps to take to get the change through are as follows:[60]

1. **Establish a sense of urgency.**   For instance, create a crisis by comparing your team's performance relative to other teams doing similar work. One supervisor opened a morning team meeting by saying, "If we don't get our act together, in two months none of us will be here."

2. **Mobilize commitment to change through joint diagnosis of business problems.** Next, meet with your team to diagnose the business problems. (If you're managing a larger department, select a subgroup of employees to serve on this team.) The aim is to produce a shared understanding of what can and must be improved. Your aim is to mobilize the commitment of those who must actually implement the change.

3. **Create a guiding coalition.**   Especially in a larger department, no supervisor can accomplish any significant change alone. That's why many supervisors choose a few "employee leaders" to help you to push through and to guide the change.

4. **Develop a shared vision.**   Your employees will need a vision to which to be committed. Therefore, create a concise statement that summarizes in five or six words what the change will accomplish for the team ("We're going to be the top-rated quality team at Apex Corp. by this April").

5. **Communicate the vision.**   Use multiple meetings, repetition, and leading by example to foster support for the new vision.

6. **Remove barriers to the change.**   Accomplishing the change will require removing any barriers that stand in the way of your team being able to actually make the change. For example, make sure they have the tools and resources they need to get their jobs done.

Building Your Transformational Leadership Skills

Few of your supervisory tasks rely on leadership abilities as much as does getting your team to implement a change. Leadership means setting a direction and then getting your people to follow you, and that, in essence, is what implementing a change is about.

When it comes to shepherding through an important change, transformational leadership *skills* are especially important. Transformational leadership refers to the process of influencing major changes in the attitudes and assumptions of organization members, and building commitment for the organization's mission, objectives, and strategies.

Transformational leaders have the knack for inspiring their followers to want to make the change. They encourage and get "performance beyond expectations" by

formulating visions and then inspiring subordinates to pursue them. Here are some specific things you can do to be more transformational:

- Articulate a clear and appealing vision.
- Explain how the vision can be attained.
- Act confident and optimistic.
- Express confidence in followers.
- Provide opportunities for early successes.
- Celebrate successes.
- Use dramatic, symbolic actions to emphasize key values.
- Lead by example.
- Empower your people to achieve the vision.

7. **Generate short-term wins.** Maintain your employees' motivation to change by ensuring that they have short-term goals to achieve from which they will receive positive feedback. ("Quality up by a reasonable 2% next month.")

8. **Monitor progress and adjust as required.** For example, monitor sales or production data, or check with customers to see how things are going.

The accompanying Leadership Applications for Supervisors feature explains how supervisors can hone their transformational leadership style to be more effective in leading an organizational change.

Organizational Development

There are many ways to reduce the resistance associated with organizational change. For example, change experts suggest that supervisors *impose rewards or sanctions* to guide employee behaviors, *explain* why the change is needed, *negotiate* with employees, give *inspirational speeches*, or *ask employees to help* design the change.[61] **Organizational development** is a special approach to change in which you use the employees themselves to diagnose and formulate the change that's required and implement it. It is a method you might use yourself, or one that you may find yourself a part of because your employer has such a program.

Action research is the basis for most organizational development–type efforts. It means *gathering data* about the problem, with an eye toward solving the problem (for example, conflict between the sales and production departments); *feeding back* these data to the employees involved; and then having them *team-plan* solutions to the problems.

Sometimes companies use "survey feedback" to gather the information. **Survey feedback** uses questionnaires to survey employees' attitudes and to provide feedback.

The aim here is usually to crystallize for the employees that there is a problem to address. Then the team can use the results to turn to the job of discussing and solving it. You can also find such assessment tools at Web sites such as CPP.com.[62]

Suppose the problem is that the team is not working together productively. **Team building** refers to special organizational development activities aimed at improving teams at work. The typical team-building program begins with an outside consultant interviewing each of the group members prior to the group meeting. He or she asks them what their problems are, and what obstacles are in the way of the group performing better.[63] The consultant usually categorizes the interview or attitude survey data into themes. He or she then presents the themes to the group at the beginning of the meeting. They might include, for example, "Not enough time to get my job done," or "I can't get any cooperation around here." The group examines and discusses the issues, talks about the underlying causes of the problem, and begins work on a solution.

If there is a serious breakdown in communications, some companies may try *sensitivity training*. **Sensitivity training** seeks to accomplish its aim of increasing interpersonal sensitivity by requiring frank, candid discussions in a small, off-site, trainer-guided "T-group" meeting (the "T" is for training), specifically, discussions of participants' personal feelings, attitudes, and behavior. Because of its personal nature, this is a controversial method surrounded by heated debate.

6. Evaluating the Training and Development Effort

How Are Training and Development Efforts Evaluated?

Was the training you did successful, or not? You should find out. There are two basic issues to address when evaluating a training program. The first is how to do the evaluation study and, in particular, whether to use *controlled experimentation*. The second is what training effect to measure.

Controlled experimentation is the ideal method to use in evaluating a training program. A controlled experiment uses both a training group and a control group (the latter receives no training). Data (for instance, on quantity of production or quality of soldered junctions) are obtained both before and after the training effort in the group exposed to training, *and before and after a corresponding work period in the control (no training) group*. In this way, it is possible to determine what accounts for the change. Did the change in the "trained" group result from the training itself? Or did it result from some organizationwide change such as a raise in pay (we assume that the pay raise would have equally affected employees in both groups)? In terms of practices, however, few firms run such controlled studies (although they should). Most just try to measure the effects of the training.

Training Effects to Measure

Supervisors can measure four basic categories of training outcomes:

1. **Reaction.** First, evaluate trainees' reactions to the program. Did they like the program? Did they think it worthwhile?

2. **Learning.** Second, test the trainees to determine whether they learned the principles, skills, and facts they were supposed to learn.

3. **Behavior.** Next, ask whether the trainees' behavior on the job changed because of the training program. For example, are employees in, say, the store's complaint department more courteous toward disgruntled customers than they were previously?

4. **Results.** Finally, but probably most importantly, ask: What final results were achieved in terms of the training objectives previously set? For example, did the number of customer complaints drop? Did the reject rate improve? Did scrap decrease? Was turnover reduced?

7. Career Management Methods for Supervisors

"Developing employees" doesn't just mean training them or getting them to implement some change. For the supervisor, developing employees may also mean dealing with employee career-development issues. For example, is your employee's desire to move up to assistant supervisor realistic in terms of his or her strengths? Is there something the person can do to better prepare for such a promotion? Is the person simply on the wrong occupational track? Does he or she even have a viable career plan?

Not every supervisor will or should get into such a conversation with the subordinate. On the other hand, many employees do appreciate and benefit from a candid discussion about whether their aspirations are realistic. And there are times when the short-term discomfort that such candor may cause prompts the employee to reorient his or her career plans in a more viable direction. Letting someone waste five or 10 more years in a job that has no real future for him or her may actually be cruel. Many employers require such career-oriented discussions as part of the appraisal interview. Let's look first at some career terminology.

Career Terminology

We may define **career** as the occupational positions a person holds over the years. **Career management** is a process for enabling employees to better understand and develop their career skills and interests and to use these skills and interests most effectively. **Career development** is the series of activities (such as workshops) that contribute to a person's career exploration, establishment, success, and fulfillment. **Career planning** is the formal process through which someone becomes aware of personal skills, interests, knowledge, motivations, and other characteristics; acquires information about opportunities and choices; identifies career-related goals; and establishes action plans to attain specific goals.

The employee's supervisor and employer should both play roles in guiding and developing the employee's career. However, the employee must always accept full responsibility for his or her own career development and career success.

The Employee's Role

For the employee, career planning means matching individual strengths and weaknesses with occupational opportunities and threats. The person wants to pursue occupations, jobs, and a career that capitalizes on his or her interests, aptitudes, values, and skills.

He or she also wants to choose occupations, jobs, and a career that makes sense in terms of projected future demand for various types of occupations.

Yet it is unfortunate but true that many people just don't put much thought into their careers. Some choose majors based on class scheduling preferences, favorite professors, or unstated psychological motives. Others stumble into jobs because "that's all that was available." If there was ever anything that cried out for fact-based decisions, it is choosing one's career. The first and essential step here is for the employee to learn as much as possible about his or her interests, aptitudes, and skills.

IDENTIFY YOUR OCCUPATIONAL ORIENTATION   Career-counseling expert John Holland says that personality (including values, motives, and needs) is one career choice determinant. For example, a person with a strong people orientation might be attracted to careers that entail interpersonal rather than intellectual or physical activities and thus to occupations such as social work. Based on early research with his Vocational Preference Test (VPT), Holland found six basic personality types (or "orientations," see www.self-directed-search.com).[64]

1. **Realistic orientation.**   These people are attracted to occupations that involve physical activities requiring skill, strength, and coordination. Examples include forestry, farming, and agriculture.

2. **Investigative orientation.**   Investigative people are attracted to careers that involve cognitive activities (thinking, organizing, understanding) rather than affective activities (feeling, acting, or interpersonal and emotional tasks). Examples include biologist, chemist, and college professor.

3. **Social orientation.**   These people are attracted to careers that involve interpersonal rather than intellectual or physical activities. Examples include clinical psychology, foreign service, and social work.

4. **Conventional orientation.**   A conventional orientation favors careers that involve structured, rule-regulated activities, as well as careers in which it is expected that the employee subordinate his or her personal needs to those of the organization. Examples include accountants and bankers.

5. **Enterprising orientation.**   Verbal activities aimed at influencing others characterize enterprising personalities. Examples include supervisors, lawyers, and public relations executives.

6. **Artistic orientation.**   People here are attracted to careers that involve self-expression, artistic creation, expression of emotions, and individualistic activities. Examples include artists, advertising executives, and musicians.

In Table 9.3, we have summarized some of the occupations found to be the best match for each of these six orientations. For about $10.00, someone can take Holland's self-directed search (SDS) test online (see www.self-directed-search.com). A number of other online career assessment instruments such as the career key (www.careerkey.org/english) also reportedly provide validated and useful information.[65]

WHAT DO YOU WANT TO DO?   Another exercise can help reveal occupational inclinations. On a sheet of paper, answer the question: "If you could have any kind of job, what would it be?" Invent your own job if need be, and don't worry about what you can do—just what you want to do.[66]

Examples of Some Occupations That May Typify Each Occupational Theme					
Realistic	Investigative	Artistic	Social	Enterprising	Conventional
				A wide range of managerial occupations, including:	
Engineers	Physicians	Advertising executives	Auto Sales dealers	Military officers	Accountants
Carpenters	Psychologists	Public relations executives	School administrators	Chamber of commerce executives	Bankers
	Research and development managers			Investment managers	Credit managers
				Lawyers	

Sometimes, there's no good substitute for actually trying a variety of jobs. Another useful way to learn about, compare, and contrast occupations is through the Internet. For example, the U.S. Department of Labor's online (*www.bls.gov/oco/*) *Occupational Outlook Handbook* (updated each year) provides detailed descriptions and information on hundreds of occupations.

UsE O*NET   One can also use the U.S. government's occupational network system, O*Net, to identify occupations that are consistent with his or her skills or aptitudes. Find it at http://online.onetcenter.org/skills/.

The Employer's Role in Career Management

The employer's career development responsibilities depend partly on how long the employee has been with the firm. *Before hiring*, realistic job interviews can help prospective employees more accurately gauge whether the job is a good fit with a candidate's skills and interests.

After the person has been *on the job* for a while, new employer career-management roles arise. Career-oriented appraisals—in which the supervisor is trained not just to appraise the employee but also to match the person's strengths and weaknesses with a feasible career path and required development work—is one important step. Employers' career development initiatives may also include programs like these:[67]

1. **Provide each employee with an individual career development budget.**   He or she can use this budget for learning about career options and personal development.[68]

2. **Offer on-site or online career centers.**   These might include an on- or offline library of career development materials, for instance.

3. **Provide career-planning workshops.** A career-planning workshop is a "planned learning event in which participants are expected to be actively involved, completing career planning exercises and inventories and participating in career skills practice sessions."[69]

The Supervisor's Role

It's hard to overestimate the impact that a supervisor can have on his or her employee's career development. With little or no additional effort than realistic performance reviews and candid career advice, a competent supervisor can help the employee get on and stay on the right career track. At the other extreme, an uncaring or unsupportive supervisor may look back on years of having crippled his or her employee's career development. Career advising requires effective "servant leadership" skills, as the accompanying leadership applications feature explains.

Leadership Applications for Supervisors

Servant Leadership

As the person responsible for orienting, training, and mentoring your subordinates, your view of what your leadership role is has a big effect on how you do your job. Traditionally, you're "the person in charge." You use your authority and expertise to determine your employees' "performance gap" and to teach them what they need to know. Your employees are there to serve the company, and you are there to make sure they're doing their jobs.

But in today's changing world there's a new point of view, which management gurus call "servant leadership." As one writer says, "Serving the needs of workers so they can better serve the needs of the organization is the new direction of supervision and management today. [The] leader as Servant."[70]

If you think that the servant concept of leadership turns leadership on its head in many respects, you would be right. For example, in orienting, training, and advising subordinates, the main questions are no longer "What are they doing wrong, and what can I do to them to change them?" Instead, the servant leader might ask, "What can I do to serve these people so they'll do their jobs better?" The idea is that "as a manager or supervisor, you are only as good as the people who work for you, and they are only as good as you allow and equip them to be."[71]

Then, once your role in serving them becomes central, new solutions might quickly become obvious. In fact, it might encourage you to do everything possible to make sure that your people have, not just the training, but also the tools, incentives, working conditions, and

career advice they need to do their jobs. Here are one writer's suggestions for putting servant leadership to work as a supervisor:[72]

1. *"Get to know every employee as a unique human being." Know about each of their families and interests, and what makes them tick. That's the only way to understand fully what they need to do a better job.*

2. *Manage-While-Walking-Around (MWWA) to see what needs to be done. The point here is to see what workers need to be more productive, not to catch them doing something wrong.*

3. *Practice "open management." Keep employees fully informed, including sharing budget information.*

4. *Strive to be a teacher, mentor, coach, and cheerleader.*

5. *Buffer employees from undue pressure, distractions, or interruptions.*

6. *Provide growth opportunities for all employees. Almost everyone wants the chance to become the person they believe they have the potential to become. One way to serve them here is to give them growth opportunities.*

7. *Become a prospector for resources. Find a way to get whatever your workers need to succeed (such as more budget, time, tools, materials, and more help).*

Whether or not your employer has a career development program, the supervisor can do several things to support his or her subordinates' career development needs. For example, when the subordinate first begins his or her job, make sure (through orientation and training) that he or she *gets off to a good start*. Schedule regular performance appraisals and, at these reviews, touch on the extent to which the employee's current *skills and performance are consistent* with the person's career goals. Provide the employee with an *informal career development plan* like that in Figure 9.6. Keep subordinates *informed* about how they can utilize the firm's current career-related benefits, and encourage them to do so.[73] And, perhaps most importantly, know how to provide *mentoring* assistance. Let's look at this next.

How Is Employee Career Development Managed?

Building Your Mentoring Skills

Mentoring traditionally means having experienced senior people advising, counseling, and guiding employees' longer-term career development. An employee who agonizes over which career to pursue or how to navigate office politics might need mentoring.

Mentoring may be formal or informal. Informally, supervisors may voluntarily help less-experienced employees—for instance, by giving them career advice and helping them

■Figure **9.6**

Employee Career Development Plan

Source: Reprinted from www.HR.BLR.com with permission of the publisher *Business and Legal Reports, Inc.,* 141 Mill Rock Road East, Old Saybrook, CT © 2004.

Employee Career Development Plan

Employee: _____ **Position:** _____

Manager: _____ **Department:** _____

Date of Appraisal: _____

1. What is the next logical step up for this employee, and when do you think he or she will be ready for it?

Probable Next Job:	When Ready:			
	Now	6 Months	1 Year	2 Years
1.	☐	☐	☐	☐
2.	☐	☐	☐	☐
3.	☐	☐	☐	☐

2. What is the highest probable promotion within five years?

3. What does this employee need to prepare for promotion?

- Knowledge: _____
_____

  Action Plan: _____
_____

- Still Training: _____
_____

  Action Plan: _____
_____

- Management Training: _____
_____

  Action Plan: _____
_____

to navigate office politics. Some employers also have formal mentoring programs. Here the employer may pair protégés with potential mentors and provide training to help mentor and protégé better understand their respective responsibilities. Whether formal or informal, studies show, having a mentor act as a sounding board can significantly enhance one's career satisfaction and success.[74]

MENTORING CAVEATS   For the supervisor, mentoring is both valuable and dangerous. It can be valuable insofar as it allows you to affect, in a positive way, the careers and lives of your less experienced subordinates and colleagues. The danger lies on the other side of that same coin. *Coaching* focuses on daily work tasks that you can easily relearn, so coaching's downside is usually limited. *Mentoring* focuses on relatively hard-to-reverse longer-term issues such as what career to pursue. It often touches on the person's psychology (motives, needs, aptitudes, and how one gets along with others, for instance). Because the supervisor is usually not a psychologist or trained career advisor, he or she must be extra cautious in the mentoring advice he or she gives.

THE EFFECTIVE MENTOR   Research on what supervisors can do to be better mentors reveals few surprises. Effective mentors *set high standards*, are willing to *invest the time* and effort the mentoring relationship requires, and actively *steer protégés* into important projects, teams, and jobs.[75] Effective mentoring requires *trust*, and the level of trust reflects the mentor's *professional competence, consistency, ability to communicate,* and readiness to *share control*.[76] The accompanying new workforce feature explains another important mentoring issue.

Supervising the New Workforce

Gender Issues in Career Development

Women and men face different challenges as they advance through their careers. In one study, promoted women had to receive higher performance ratings than promoted men to get promoted, "suggesting that women were held to stricter standards for promotion."[77] Women report greater barriers (such as being excluded from informal networks) than do men, and more difficulty getting developmental assignments and geographic mobility opportunities. Women have to be more proactive than men do just to be considered for such assignments, and employers therefore need to focus on breaking down the barriers that impede women's career progress. One study concluded that three corporate career development activities—fast-track programs, individual career counseling, and career planning workshops—were less available to women than to men.[78] Many call this combination of subtle and not-so-subtle barriers to women's progress the *glass ceiling*. Because developmental experiences like these are so important, "organizations that are interested in helping female

[supervisors] advance should focus on breaking down barriers that interfere with women's access to developmental experiences."[79]

Minority Women In these matters, minority women may be particularly at risk. Women of color hold only a small percentage of professional and managerial private-sector positions. The minority women in one survey several years ago reported that the main barriers to advancement included not having an influential mentor (47%), lack of informal networking with influential colleagues (40%), lack of company role models for members of the same racial or ethnic group (29%), and lack of high-visibility assignments (28%).[80]

Adding to the problem is the fact that some corporate career development programs may actually be inconsistent with the needs of minority and nonminority women. For example, such programs may assume that career paths are sequential and continuous; yet the need to stop working for a time to attend to family needs often characterizes the career paths of many people of color and women (and perhaps men).[81] The bottom line for supervisors is to be sensitive to the potential special mentoring needs of women, and particularly minority women.

Chapter 9 Concept Review and Reinforcement

Key Terms

Action Learning, p. 260
Action Research, p. 264
Behavior Modeling, p. 255
Business Games, p. 261
Career, p. 266
Career Development, p. 266
Career Management, p. 266

Career Planning, p. 266
Case Study Method, p. 261
Coaching/Understudy Method, p. 260
Competency Model, p. 251
Computer-Based Training, p. 256
Controlled Experimentation, p. 265

Employee Orientation, p. 246
In-House Development Centers, p. 262
Job Rotation, p. 260
Lifelong Learning, p. 260
Organizational Development, p. 264
Performance Analysis, p. 249

Sensitivity Training, p. 265
Survey Feedback, p. 264
Task Analysis, p. 249
Team Building, p. 265
Training, p. 248
Vestibule Training, p. 256
Virtual Classroom, p. 258

Review of Key Concepts

Employee Orientation	Employee orientation is the socialization of the new employee into the company's ways of doing business. Orientation includes basic background information about their jobs, company rules and policies, and generally making them feel welcome.
What Is Training?	Training means giving new or present employees the skills they need to perform their jobs. Training experts today call training "workplace learning and performance."
Training Needs	New employees' training needs usually involve task analysis: breaking the jobs into subtasks and teaching each new employee. Current employees' training needs are more complex and require performance analysis to determine where there is a deficiency and how to rectify it.
Training Techniques	
On-the-Job Training	An experienced worker or trainee's supervisor trains the employee, on the job. A useful four-step procedure for creating a simple on-the-job training program includes: • Review the job's description. • Develop a task analysis record form. • Develop a job instruction sheet. • Train the employee.
Informal Learning	It has been estimated that as much as 80% of what employees learn on the job they learn through informal means.
Apprenticeship Training	Apprenticeship training is a structured process by which individuals become skilled workers through a combination of classroom instruction and on-the-job training. This process is usually under the direction of an experienced craft person.

Behavior Modeling	Behavior modeling involves showing the trainees the right (or model) way of doing something. This lets each trainee practice the model way, then provides feedback in reference to the trainee's performance.
Vestibule Training	Vestibule training is a technique in which trainees learn, off the job, on actual or simulated equipment.
Videoconference Distance Learning	Videoconferencing is a technique used to train geographically dispersed employees using audio and visual equipment.
Computer-Based Training	A computer-based system is used to increase trainees' knowledge or skills interactively. Computerized simulations and multimedia, including videodisks, are used to help the trainee learn how to do the job.
"e-Learning" Online	Internet-based learning may include posting videos, lecture, PowerPoint slides, or simulations through the Internet or internally through learning portals on the company's intranet.
Mobile Learning	Mobile learning means delivering learning content on demand via mobile devices like cell phones, laptops, and iPhones available to the learner at his or her demand.
The Virtual Classroom	The virtual classroom enables remote learners, using PCs or laptops, to participate in live audio and video discussions using two-way communications to share information with others. The learning process is enhanced through shared whiteboards, chat rooms, and collaborations.
Supervisory Training and Development	Like their employees, supervisors need and benefit from special training programs that go beyond traditional techniques like on-the-job training, coaching, and rotational assignments. These special programs include: • Action learning • Case studies • Business games • Seminars • University programs • In-house development centers
Organizational Change Programs	Organizational change programs aim at changing the company's strategy, culture, structure, technologies, or attitudes and skills of the employees. Overcoming resistance to this change is important to the supervisors' people who will ultimately have to execute these changes.

Organizational Development	Organizational development is a special approach to change in which you use the employees themselves to diagnose and formulate the change that's required and implemented.
Career Management	Career management is a process for engaging employees to better understand and develop their career skills and interests in order to identify career-related goals and establish actions plans to attain said goals.
The Supervisor as Mentor	Supervisors may voluntarily help less experienced employees by advising, counseling, and guiding said employees' long-term career development.

Review and Discussion Questions

1. Explain why the employee orientation process must precede employee training.
2. Define "employee training."
3. RSOs (Range Safety Officers) maintain order, direction, and safety on a gun range. Develop a list of training needs for new RSOs who have volunteered for the job.
4. There are many ways to approach the training needs of any organization. Why is on-the-job training the most popular and most often used technique?
5. What are some typical on-the-job training techniques?
6. Do you think that job rotation is a good method to use for management trainees? Why or why not?
7. Why do you think that apprenticeship training is not as widely used today as it was 30 years ago?
8. In what type of jobs do you think that vestibule training would be most useful?
9. What are the potential cost savings when using videoconferencing and computer-based training?
10. Describe the virtual classroom. What are its advantages?
11. How does organizational development motivate employees to overcome resistance to change?
12. How can experienced supervisors guide an employee's long-term career development by acting as his or her mentor?

Application and Skill Building

Case Study One

Reinventing the Wheel at Apex Door Company

Jim Delaney, supervisor of Apex Door Company's door design and order processing teams, has a problem. No matter how often he tells his employees how to do their jobs, they invariably "decide to do things their way," as he puts it, and arguments ensue between Delaney and the employee. The designers are expected to work with the architects to design doors that meet the specifications. Although it's not "rocket science," as Delaney puts it, the designers often make mistakes—such as designing in too much steel—a problem that can cost Apex tens of thousands of wasted dollars, especially considering the number of doors in, say, a 30-story office tower.

The order-processing team is another example. Although Jim has a specific, detailed way he wants each order written up, most of the order clerks don't understand how to use the multipage order form, and they improvise when it comes to a question such as whether to classify a customer as "industrial" or "commercial."

The current training process is as follows. None of the jobs have training manuals per se, although several have somewhat out-of-date job descriptions. The training for new employees is all on the job: Usually, the person leaving the company trains the new person during the one- or two-week overlap period, but if there's no overlap, the new person is trained as well as possible by other employees who have occasionally filled in on the job in the past. The training is basically the same throughout the company—for machinists, secretaries, assemblers, and accounting clerks, for example.

Discussion Questions

1. What do you think of Apex's training process? Could it help to explain why employees "do things their way," and if so, how?
2. What role do job descriptions play in training?
3. Explain in detail what you would do to improve the training process at Apex. Make sure to provide specific suggestions.

Case Study Two

Carter Cleaning Centers: The New Training Program

At the present time the Carter Cleaning Centers have no formal orientation or training policies or procedures, and Jennifer believes this is one reason why the standards to which she and her father would like employees to adhere are generally not followed.

The Carters would prefer that certain practices and procedures be used in dealing with the customers at the front counters. For example, all customers should be greeted with what Jack refers to as a "big hello." Garments they drop off should immediately be inspected for any damage or unusual stains so these can be brought to the customer's attention, lest the customer later return to pick up the garment and erroneously blame the store. The garments are then supposed to be immediately placed together in a nylon sack to separate them from other customers' garments. The ticket also has to be carefully written up, with the customer's name and telephone number and the date precisely and clearly noted on all copies. The counterperson is also supposed to take the opportunity to try to sell the customer additional services such as waterproofing, or simply notify the customer, for example, "Now that people are doing their spring cleaning, we're having a special on drapery cleaning all this month." Finally, as the customer leaves, the counterperson is supposed to make a courteous comment such as "Have a nice day" or "Drive safely." Each of the other jobs in the stores—pressing, cleaning and spotting, periodically maintaining the coin laundry equipment, and so forth—similarly contain certain steps, procedures, and most important, standards the Carters would prefer to see upheld.

The company has had problems, Jennifer feels, because of a lack of adequate employee training and orientation. For example, two new employees became very upset last month when they discovered that they were not paid at the end of the week, on Friday, but instead were paid (as are all Carter employees) on the following Tuesday. The Carters use the extra two days in part to give them time to obtain everyone's hours and compute their pay. The other reason they do it, according to Jack, is that "frankly, when we stay a few days behind in paying employees, it helps to ensure that they at least give us a few days' notice before quitting on us. While we are certainly obligated to pay them anything they earn, we find that psychologically they seem to be less likely to just walk out on us Friday evening and not show up Monday morning if they still haven't gotten their pay from the previous week. This way they at least give us a few days' notice so we can find a replacement."

Other matters that could be covered during orientation and training, says Jennifer, include company policy regarding paid holidays, lateness and absences, health and hospitalization benefits (there are none, other than workers' compensation), and general matters like the maintenance of a clean and safe work area, personal appearance and cleanliness, time sheets, personal telephone calls and mail, company policies regarding matters like substance abuse, and eating or smoking on the job (both forbidden).

Jennifer believes that implementing orientation and training programs would help to ensure that employees know how to do their jobs the right way. And she and her father further believe that it is only when employees understand the right way to do their jobs that there is any hope their jobs will in fact be accomplished the way the Carters want them to be accomplished.

Questions

1. What, specifically, should the Carters cover in their new employee orientation program, and how should they convey this information?
2. In the HR management course Jennifer took, the book suggested using a job instruction sheet to identify tasks performed by an employee. "Should we

use a form like this for the counterperson's job, and if so, what would the filled-in form look like?"

3. Which specific training techniques should Jennifer use to train her pressers, her cleaner–spotters, her managers, and her counterpeople, and why?

Experiential Activities

Activity 1. Unfortunately, opening day at Alex's Bistro was a disaster. Waiters and waitresses couldn't answer basic questions such as "What's in this dish?" They got almost half the orders wrong, and when they finally did bring the orders to the tables, they didn't remember who ordered what dish, so the customers themselves ended up passing their dishes around. In teams of 4–5 students, address these questions:

1. Based on an Internet survey that you do, what sorts of training programs are available for training restaurant employees?
2. List three main tasks a wait-person should typically carry out then rite a job instruction sheet for each task.

Activity 2. Flying the Friendlier Skies

Purpose: The purpose of this exercise is to give you practice in developing a training program for the job of airline reservation clerk for a major airline.

Required Understanding: You should be fully acquainted with the material in this chapter and should read the following description of an airline reservation clerk's duties:

Description: Customers contact our airlines reservation clerks to obtain flight schedules, prices, and itineraries. The reservation clerks look up the requested information on our airline's online flight schedule system, which are updated continuously. The reservation clerk must deal courteously and expeditiously with the customer and be able to find alternative flight arrangements quickly in order to provide the customer with the itinerary that fits his or her needs. Alternative flights and prices must be found quickly, so that the customer is not kept waiting, and so that our reservations operations group maintains its efficiency standards. It is often necessary to look under various routings, since there may be a dozen or more alternative routes between the customer's starting point and destination.

You may assume that we just hired 30 new clerks, and that you must create a three-day training program.

How to Set Up the Exercise/Instructions: Divide the class into teams of five or six students. Airline reservation clerks obviously need numerous skills to perform their jobs. This major airline has asked you to develop quickly the outline of a training program for its new reservation clerks. You may want to start by listing the job's main duties. In any case, please produce the requested outline, making sure to be very specific about what you want to teach the new clerks, and what methods and aids you suggest using to train them.

Activity 3. Pick out some task with which you are familiar—mowing the lawn, making a salad, or studying for a test—and develop a job instruction sheet for it.

Activity 4. Working individually or in groups, develop several specific examples to illustrate how a professor teaching supervision could use at least four of the techniques described in this chapter in teaching his or her course.

Role-Playing Exercise

Supervisory Resistance to Change: The Situation

The machine shop supervisor at the Madison Peterbilt Motors Plant had been with the company for over 35 years and had been a member of management for over half that time. With a reputation of producing high-quality machine parts and meeting production schedules, the machine shop supervisor met or exceeded all of the expectations of plant management and engineering.

Eight years ago when the plant was producing six trucks a day, the machine shop supervisor had come up with a card scheduling system for loading the different shop machines to meet schedules when parts would be required on the line. This paper system has worked well with few problems.

A new plant manager came in and, come Monday morning, what a surprise it was for the machine shop supervisor and his subordinates to see that a lot of changes had been made. Machines had been moved and a large 10' magnet had replaced the cardex system. The plant was moving from 6 to 12 trucks a day and the old system was said to not work effectively enough. The supervisor is at a loss. No one had ever told him or his subordinates about the impending change. Now he has to figure out how to make the new system work, and he is finding every reason he can to show that it won't ever work.

Instructions: All students should read the situation above. One student will play the role of the machine shop supervisor while a second student will play the role of an HR representative sent down to the machine shop to smooth out any resistance to the change and make sure that the new system is up and running.

After the Role-Play exercise all students should read and address the questions at the end of the exercise.

Role of Machine Shop Supervisor: You are embarrassed and disappointed at what has happened. You run a tight ship and your subordinates look up to you. How are you going to retain your people when you do not believe that the change was necessary? You would like to know who made this change and why. It will never work, if you have anything to say about it. You are really mad and frustrated by the whole situation. How could they have done this to you? It is going to take some fast talking to make you change your mind!

Role of HR Representative: You have only been with Peterbilt Motors for three months right out of college. You remember reading about resistance to change in a chapter of a supervisory management textbook from a course in college. You presume that you must certainly have your job cut out for you. It is up to you to get the supervisor on board with the team and make the changes work.

Questions for Class Discussion

1. Was the machine shop supervisor justified in feeling the way he did about the unannounced change?
2. How often do you feel that situations like this occur in the real world?
3. Can you make any additional recommendations on how to best persuade the machine shop supervisor to overcome his resistance to the change?

10 Using Motivation and Incentives

....

CHAPTER OBJECTIVES

After studying this chapter, you should be able to answer the following questions:

1. What Should Supervisors Know About Individual Behavior?
2. What Are Needs-Based Approaches to Motivation?
3. What Are Process Approaches to Motivation?

4. What Are Learning/Reinforcement Approaches to Motivation?
5. What Are Ten Theory-Based Methods for Motivating Employees?
6. How Are Performance-Motivation Problems Analyzed?

OPENING SNAPSHOT
Motivating Mal

Mal seemed to have everything you'd want in a travel agent. He was smart, good with numbers, sociable, and loved traveling. Lisa thought he'd make a great agent in her Chicago travel agency, so she hired him on the spot.

Three weeks later, she regretted her choice. Twice last week Mal failed to follow up when clients called, and Thursday Lisa found him sleeping at his desk. "What do I have to do to light a fire under this guy?" she asked her husband and business partner, Al. Hiring people is useless if they're not motivated. Psychologists define **motivation** as the intensity of a person's desire to engage in some activity.

Most people instinctively know a lot about motivation. They know what motivates them, such as the hobbies they'd gladly work on for hours each day. And they also know other things about motivation. That people don't like to be punished. That people do like getting rewards. That people are motivated to do jobs they love. That most people won't try to do things that they believe they can't do. That people want to

280

be treated equitably. And that supervisors have to appeal to what's important to a person to motivate him or her. This chapter should help you develop stronger supervisory motivation skills by building on what you already know about motivation.

1. What Supervisors Should Know About Individual Behavior

You know that any stimulus—an order from the boss, an offer of a raise, or the threat of being fired—has different effects on different people. John might jump whenever the boss gives orders, while Jane might laugh them off. These behavioral differences reflect what psychologists call the **law of individual differences**—that people differ in personalities, abilities, self-concept, values, and needs. As Figure 10.1 illustrates, these factors act like filters. They add to, detract from, and distort the effect of any stimulus.

We're going to focus on motivation in this chapter. However, to understand motivation better, we should first review the factors that influence individual behavior.

Personality and Behavior

Personality is probably the first thing that comes to mind when you think about what determines behavior. We tend to classify people as introverted, dominant, mature, or paranoid, for instance, and these labels invoke images of particular kinds of behavior.

PERSONALITY DEFINED   Many psychologists would define **personality** as "the characteristic and distinctive traits of an individual, and the way the traits interact to help or hinder the adjustment of the person to other people and situations." The assumption is that traits like friendliness or aggressiveness are the basis for who the person "is" and how he or she behaves.

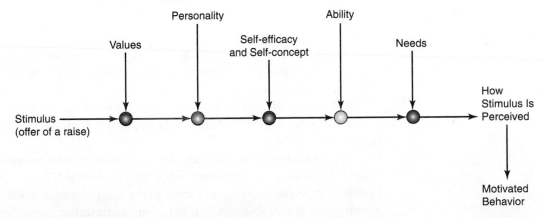

■Figure **10.1**
Some Individual Determinants of Behavior

A particular stimulus may evoke different behaviors among individuals, because each person's values, personality, self-concept, abilities, and needs influence how he or she reacts.

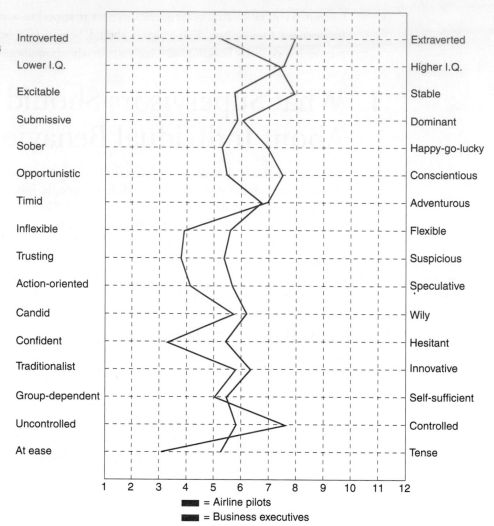

■Figure **10.2**

Comparing Traits of Pilots and Executives

Source: R. Cattel, *The Scientific Analysis of Personality* (Baltimore: Penguin Books, 1965). See also G. Northcraft and M. Neale, *Organizational Behavior* (Hinsdale, IL: Dryden Press, 1994), pp. 64–240.

Introverted	Extraverted
Lower I.Q.	Higher I.Q.
Excitable	Stable
Submissive	Dominant
Sober	Happy-go-lucky
Opportunistic	Conscientious
Timid	Adventurous
Inflexible	Flexible
Trusting	Suspicious
Action-oriented	Speculative
Candid	Wily
Confident	Hesitant
Traditionalist	Innovative
Group-dependent	Self-sufficient
Uncontrolled	Controlled
At ease	Tense

1 2 3 4 5 6 7 8 9 10 11 12

■ = Airline pilots
■ = Business executives

But what the basic traits are is a matter of debate. Psychologists today often emphasize the "big five" personality traits at work: *extraversion, emotional stability, agreeableness, conscientiousness,* and *openness to experience.*[1] For example, in one study, *conscientiousness* showed a consistent relationship with all job performance criteria for all occupations.[2] Figure 10.2 illustrates important traits—in this case, possessed by pilots and executives.

As we said, personality traits are important in part because they guide how people behave—your employee may be "extraverted," or "conscientious," for instance. At work, you will encounter many unique personalities (each supposedly growing out of a unique mix of traits). For example, the *authoritarian personality* is rigid, intolerant of ambiguity, tends to stereotype people as good or bad, and conforms to the requirements of authority, while being dictatorial to subordinates. The *Machiavellian personality* (the name refers to the writings of the sixteenth-century Italian political advisor Niccolò Machiavelli) tends to be manipulative and controlling.[3]

MEASURING PERSONALITY   The Myers-Briggs Type Indicator (MBTI) is one popular tool for measuring personality in the work setting. The MBTI classifies people as extraverted or introverted (E or I), sensing or intuitive (S or N), thinking or feeling (T or F), and perceiving or judging (P or J). The MBTI questionnaire classifies people into 16 different personality types (a 4 × 4 matrix); these 16 types are, in turn, classified into one of four cognitive (thinking or problem-solving) styles:

- Sensation–thinking (ST)
- Intuition–thinking (NT)
- Sensation–feeling (SF)
- Intuition–feeling (NF)

Classifying personality types and cognitive styles in this way has several applications. Some employers match the MBTI styles to particular occupations. Figure 10.3 illustrates this. People with the ST approach to problem solving are often well suited to occupations such as auditor and safety engineer, for instance.

Abilities and Behavior

Of course, personality traits such as conscientiousness don't determine by themselves how someone behaves. For instance, a conscientious but untalented employee may still perform poorly. Differences in talents and abilities also influence how we perform.[4] The basic rule is this: Even the most highly motivated person will not perform well unless he or she also has the ability to do the job. Conversely, the most able employee will not perform satisfactorily if not motivated. Organizational behavior experts sum that up with the pithy *Performance = Ability × Motivation.*

There are many types of abilities. Mental, cognitive, or *thinking abilities* include intelligence and verbal comprehension. *Mechanical ability* would be important for mechanical engineers or machinists. *Psychomotor abilities* include dexterity, eye–hand coordination, and motor ability. Such abilities might be important for employees who work as dealers in Las Vegas. People also differ in *visual skills*—for example, in their ability to discriminate between colors and between black and white details. In addition to these general abilities, people also have specific abilities learned through training, experience, or education, such as accounting. The point is this: Don't waste your time trying to motivate someone if he or she couldn't do the job even if he or she wanted to. The corollary is, hire people with potential and then train them.

■Figure **10.3**

Four Examples of MBTI Styles and Some Corresponding Occupations

	Thinking Style	Feeling Style
Sensation Style	People with this combined thinking/sensation style tend to be *thorough, logical,* and *practical* and to make good *CPAs* or *safety engineers.*	People with this combined sensation/feeling style tend to be *conscientious* and *responsible* and to make *good social workers* and *drug supervisors.*
Intuitive Style	People with this combined intuitive/thinking style tend to be *creative, independent,* and *critical* and to make good *systems analysts, professors,* and *lawyers.*	People with this combined intuitive/feeling style tend to be *people-oriented, sociable,* and *often charismatic* and to make good *human resource managers, public relations directors,* and *politicians.*

■Figure **10.4**

Perception Affects How We "See" the Arches' Sizes

The farthest arch looks to be about one-third the size of the closest, but we know they're actually the same size.

Perception and Behavior

We all react to stimuli that reach us via our senses. However, how we define, perceive, or "see" these stimuli reflects our experiences, needs, and personalities.[5] In other words, our behavior is motivated by our **perceptions** of stimuli, by the way our personalities and experiences cause us to interpret them.

Perception obviously affects how we see inanimate objects. In Figure 10.4, the farthest arch looks smaller than the closest one, and its perspective size is, in fact, smaller (because it is farthest away). Based on experience, however, we know that the arches are actually equal in size. Therefore, the height of the last arch *as we perceive it* is a compromise between the perspective size of the arch and its actual size. (It looks closer in size to the first arch than it actually is—try measuring them.) *Our desire to see objects as we expect them to be causes us to perceive things as we expect them to be.*

The same phenomenon applies to work relationships. For example, some people associate characteristics such as industriousness and honesty with certain socioeconomic classes, but not with others, a process called **stereotyping**. We tend to stereotype people according to age, gender, race, or national origin. We then (often unfairly) attribute the characteristics of this stereotype to everyone we meet of that age, gender, race, or national origin.[6]

Attitudes and Behavior

When people say things like "I like my job" they are expressing attitudes. An **attitude** is a tendency to respond to objects, people, or events in either a positive or a negative way.[7] Attitudes are important because they can (but don't always) influence how people behave on the job.

Job satisfaction is probably the most familiar example of attitudes at work. Satisfaction is "an evaluative judgment about one's job."[8] One popular job satisfaction survey, the Job Descriptive Index, measures the following five aspects of someone's job satisfaction:

1. *Pay.* In terms of amount of pay received, and is it equitable?
2. *Job.* Are tasks interesting?
3. *Promotional opportunities.* Are promotions available and fair?

4. *Supervisor.* Does the supervisor demonstrate interest in and concern about employees?

5. *Coworkers.* Are coworkers friendly, competent, and supportive?[9]

Good (or bad) attitudes do not necessarily translate into good (or bad) performance.[10] For example, dissatisfied engineers may continue to do their best because they adhere to their professional standards. But, of course, no one wants to have dissatisfied employees ("low morale.")

Summary

In summary, your employee's behavior—what he or she does—depends on many things. These include his or her personality, abilities, self-concept, values, and attitudes. As a result, motivation explains only part of why people do what they do. However, there is just about no chance at all that you'll get any useful work out of even talented employees if they're not motivated.[11] And the likelihood that you're going to change someone's personality is just about zero. Let's therefore turn to how to apply the three main approaches to motivation at work, starting with need-based approaches.

2. Need-Based Approaches to Motivation

The defense attorney paced back and forth in front of the jury and asked, "Ladies and gentlemen, what possible motive would my client have for committing this crime?" That question is crucial: After all, if there's no motive, then why do it?

A **motive** is something that incites the person to action or that sustains and gives direction to action.[12] When we ask why a defendant might have done what he did, or why a sales manager flies all night to meet with a client, we are asking about motives.

A motive can be aroused or unaroused. Everyone carries within him or her **motivational dispositions** or *needs*—motives that, like seeds in winter, go unaroused until the proper conditions bring them forth. You may have a motivational disposition to enjoy yourself at the movies. However, that motive is dormant until Saturday night, when you can put your work aside.[13] When the conditions are right—when the work is done, and the weekend arrives—the movie-attendance need is aroused, and it is off to the movies.

What Are Needs-Based Approaches to Motivation?

Need-based approaches to motivation focus on how needs drive people to do what they do. Which needs are most important? How and under what conditions do they become aroused and transformed into behavior? Psychologists Abraham Maslow, David McClelland, and Frederick Herzberg studied such questions.

Maslow's Needs-Hierarchy Theory

Maslow's needs-hierarchy theory is one famous need-based explanation of motivation. It is also the basis for the other two approaches in this section. Professor Abraham Maslow argued that people have a hierarchy of five increasingly higher-level needs:

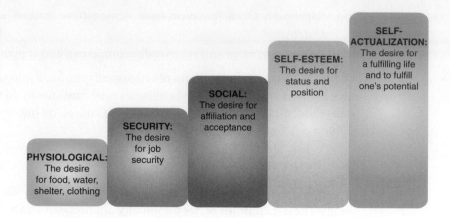

physiological, security, social, self-esteem, and self-actualization. According to his *prepotency process principle*, people are motivated first to satisfy the lower-order needs and then, in sequence, each of the higher-order needs.[14]

We usually envision Maslow's hierarchy as a stepladder or pyramid, as in Figure 10.5. Satisfying the lower-level needs triggers the higher-order needs.[15] The higher-level needs aren't too important in motivating behavior unless the lower-level needs are pretty well satisfied.

That's how psychologists usually present Maslow's theory, but there's actually not much research evidence supporting the idea that people's needs form a hierarchy.[16] On the other hand, the pyramid idea resonates with most people's day-to-day experiences. For example, employees may push much harder for promotions when they think their jobs are secure than they do when they're worried about just keeping their jobs. Maslow also wanted to emphasize that quite possibly, as they grow older and more established, people's "higher-level" needs become more important.[17] In any event, the five Maslow needs are as follows.[18]

PHYSIOLOGICAL NEEDS   People are born with physiological needs. These are the basic survival needs, including the needs for food, water, clothing, and shelter.

SECURITY NEEDS   When physiological needs are reasonably satisfied—when a person is no longer thirsty and has enough to eat, for instance—then security, or safety, needs become aroused. Thus, if you are in the middle of a desert with nothing to drink, the lower-level need for water will drive your behavior. You might risk your safety to satisfy that need. But once you have enough to drink, personal safety and security start to motivate your behavior. When Yahoo announced recently that it would lay off hundreds of employees, it activated its employees' safety needs; the announcement surely prompted many to think less about promotions and colleagues, and more about keeping their jobs.

SOCIAL NEEDS   Once you have had enough to eat and to drink and feel reasonably secure, social needs start to drive your behavior. These are the needs to give and receive affection and to have friends. At work, social needs manifest themselves in the work groups and alliances employees form, and with whom they choose to spend their time.

SELF-ESTEEM NEEDS   In Maslow's theory, *self-esteem needs* include needs for things such as independence, achievement, competence, status, recognition, position, and the respect of others.[19] Like the social, security, and physiological needs, self-esteem needs supposedly don't motivate behavior until the person has pretty much satisfied the lower-level needs.

SELF-ACTUALIZATION NEEDS   Finally, Maslow says, there's an ultimate need. This need only begins to dominate behavior once all lower-level needs have been quite satisfied. This is the need for self-actualization or fulfillment. It is the need to become the person we have the potential to become. Employees seeking to better themselves by taking evening classes toward a degree are motivated in part by the need to self-actualize.

Herzberg's Hygiene–Motivator (Two-Factor) Approach

Frederick Herzberg's famous Hygiene–Motivator motivation theory divides Maslow's hierarchy into lower-level (physiological, safety, social) and higher-level (ego, self-actualization) needs. He says higher-level needs such as for self-esteem and self-actualization are more or less insatiable—we always strive to become the person we believe we can be. Therefore, says Herzberg, the best way to motivate someone is to arrange the job so that doing the job helps satisfy the person's higher-level needs. Then the worker finds the job itself so challenging and interesting that he or she actually gets a kick out of doing it. When employers let employee work teams supervise themselves, the employers are applying (perhaps without realizing it) Herzberg's theory.

HYGIENES AND MOTIVATORS   Herzberg says the things or "hygiene factors" that satisfy lower-level needs are different from the "motivator factors" that satisfy, or partially satisfy, higher-level needs. He says that if hygiene factors (factors from outside the job itself, such as working conditions, salary, and supervision) are not adequate, employees become dissatisfied. But—and this is very important—adding more of these hygiene factors (like better working conditions or pay) to the job (what Herzberg calls *extrinsic motivation*) is a poor way to try to motivate someone. Lower-level needs are quickly satisfied, so give someone a raise, and pretty soon he or she just wants another raise.

The way to motivate employees, says Herzberg, is to appeal to their higher-order needs, by building *motivator factors* (like opportunities for achievement, recognition, responsibility, and challenge on the job) into the job itself. Then, it's the sense of achievement and accomplishment and of using all one's skills that provides the motivation, not some external factor like more pay. Motivator factors aim to appeal to the employee's self-esteem and self-actualization needs, needs that are rarely satiated. So in summary, Herzberg says that the best way to motivate employees is to build challenges and opportunities for achievement into jobs—to make sure the job provides *intrinsic motivation*, in other words. How does one do this? For example, by letting employees check their own work, deal more with customers, schedule their own time, and even supervise themselves. That way the job itself turns the employee on, much as working on a favorite hobby may motivate you. We might sum up Herzberg's conclusion as, "If you want to motivate someone, make sure [the] pay and working conditions are adequate (to prevent dissatisfaction); then build challenge and opportunities for achievement into the job to ensure intrinsic motivation."[20] Figure 10.6 summarizes Herzberg's hygienes and motivators.

Summary of Herzberg's Hygiene–Motivator Findings

Source: Adapted from Frederick Herzberg, "One More Time: How Do You Motivate Employees," *Harvard Business Review,* January–February 1968.

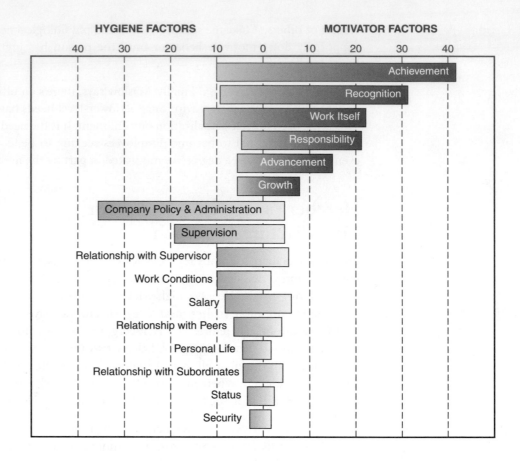

Herzberg's theory accomplished two main things. It popularized the important role of intrinsic motivation—motivation that comes from within the person—in motivating employees. And it popularized the idea that the nature of the job (how challenging it is) therefore plays a central role in employee motivation. Today's emphasis on enriching jobs (discussed later in this chapter) and on organizing work around self-managing teams largely derives from this thinking. When we say that supervisors have to be supporters and coaches more than order-givers, it's because so many more companies are using Herzberg's theory to let employees manage themselves. Herzberg's ideas have had a powerful effect on how employers design jobs and on how they motivate employees.[21]

Needs for Achievement, Power, and Affiliation

David McClelland and John Atkinson agree with Herzberg that supervisors should appeal to employees' higher-level needs. They focused on three needs they believe are especially important—the needs for *achievement, power,* and *affiliation.* To understand the nature of these needs, try the following exercise.

Take a quick look (just 10 to 15 seconds) at Figure 10.7. Now allow yourself up to five minutes to write a short essay about the picture, touching on the following questions:

1. What is happening? Who are the people?

2. What has led up to this situation? That is, what happened in the past?

What's Happening Here?

Source: David A. Kolb, Irwin M. Rubin, and James M. McIntyre, *Organizational Psychology: An Experiential Approach* (Upper Saddle River, NJ: Prentice Hall, 1971), p. 55.

3. What is being thought? What is wanted? By whom?

4. What will happen? What will be done?

The questions are only guides, so don't just answer each one. Instead, make your story continuous and let your imagination roam. Once you have finished writing, resume reading the following text.

The picture is one from the Thematic Apperception Test (TAT). McClelland and his associates use the TAT, which consists of a number of pictures, to identify a person's needs. The pictures are intentionally ambiguous, so when you wrote your essay, you were probably reading into the picture ideas that reflected your own needs and drives. McClelland says the test is useful for identifying the level of a person's achievement, power, and affiliation needs.[22]

THE NEED FOR ACHIEVEMENT   They say that achievement motivation is present in your essay when any one of the following three things occurs:

1. Someone in your story is concerned about a standard of excellence—for example, he or she wants to win or do well in a competition, or has self-imposed standards for a good performance. You can infer standards of excellence from the use of words such as *good* or *better* to evaluate performance.

2. Someone in the story is involved in a unique accomplishment, such as an invention or an artistic creation.

3. Someone in the story is involved in a long-term goal, such as having a specific career or being a success in life.

People high in the need to achieve have a predisposition to strive for success. They are highly motivated to obtain the satisfaction that comes from accomplishing a challenging task or goal. They prefer tasks for which there is a reasonable chance for success, and they avoid those that are too easy or too difficult. They prefer specific, timely feedback about their performance.

THE NEED FOR POWER   Power motivation is present in your essay when any of the following three things occurs:

1. Someone in the story is emotionally concerned about getting or maintaining control of the means of influencing a person. Wanting to win a point, to show dominance, to convince someone, or to gain a position of control—as well as wanting to avoid weakness or humiliation—are examples.[23]

2. Someone is actually doing something to get or keep control of the means of influence, such as arguing, demanding or forcing, giving a command, trying to convince, or punishing.

3. Your story involves an interpersonal relationship that is culturally defined as one in which a superior has control of the means of influencing a subordinate. For example, a boss is giving orders to a subordinate, or a parent is ordering a child to shape up.

People with a strong need for power want to influence others directly by making suggestions, giving their opinions and evaluations, and trying to talk others into things. They enjoy jobs requiring persuasion, such as teaching and public speaking, as well as positions as leaders and members of the clergy.

How the need for power manifests itself depends on the person's other needs. A person with a high need for power but a low need for warm, supportive relationships might become dictatorial, while one with high needs for friendship might become a member of the clergy or a social worker. McClelland said that "a good manager is motivated by a regimented and regulated concern for influencing others"— in other words, good supervisors do have a need for power, but one that is under control.[24]

THE NEED FOR AFFILIATION   Affiliation motivation is present in your essay when one of the following three things occurs:

1. Someone in the story is concerned about establishing, maintaining, or restoring a positive emotional relationship with another person. Friendship is the basic example. Other relationships, such as father–son, reflect affiliation motivation only if they have the warm, compassionate quality implied by the need for affiliation.

2. One person likes or wants to be liked by someone else. Affiliation motivation is also present if someone is expressing sorrow or grief about a broken relationship.

3. Affiliative activities are taking place, such as parties, reunions, visits, or relaxed small talk. Friendly actions, such as consoling or being concerned about the well-being or happiness of another person, usually reflect a need for affiliation.

People with a strong need for affiliation are highly motivated to maintain strong, warm relationships with friends and relatives. In group meetings, they try to establish friendly relationships, often by being agreeable or giving emotional support.[25]

3. Process Approaches to Motivation

What Are Process Approaches to Motivation?

Needs-based motivation theories such as Maslow's explain motivation in terms of people's needs, as in, "People are motivated to satisfy their needs." The so-called process approaches to motivation aim to explain how motivation arises in terms of the decision-making process the person goes through in deciding what to do. We'll focus on the work of psychologists J. S. Adams, Edwin Locke, and Victor Vroom.

Adams's Equity Theory

Adams's **equity theory** assumes that people are motivated to be treated fairly at work. Equity theory states that if a person perceives an inequity, a tension or drive will develop in the person's mind, and the person will be motivated to reduce or eliminate the tension and the perceived inequity. Employees can do this by reducing what they put into the job, or by boosting the magnitude of the rewards they take out (or both).

Equity theory takes reality into account. Thus, a person might not envy a colleague's higher salary if it's obvious that the colleague actually does work harder or longer. Furthermore, a person might accept a lower salary in return for, say, a more prestigious title. Again, though, what matters is perception. What matters is how the person perceives his or her relative inputs and outputs.[26]

Figure 10.8 summarizes this. For example, paying somewhat more than the going rate should lead to higher quality (if the person is on incentive pay) or to a rise in quality and quantity (for those paid a salary).

In reality, things don't always work out that way. People paid on a piece-rate basis, per item produced, typically boost quantity and reduce quality when they believe they are not earning enough. Those paid a straight hourly rate tend to reduce both quantity and quality when they think they're underpaid. However, alas, *overpayment* does not always have the positive effects on either quantity or quality that Adams's theory would predict for it.[27] But in any case, supervisors ignore employees' desire to be treated equitably at their peril.

Locke's Goal Theory of Motivation

Simply put, Edwin Locke's **goal theory of motivation** assumes that people are motivated to achieve their goals.[28] Unsatisfied goals prompt the person to seek ways to

		Employee Thinks He or She Is Underpaid	Employee Thinks He or She Is Overpaid
Piece-rate Basis	Pay	Quality down Quantity the same or up	Quantity the same or down Quality up
Salary Basis	Pay	Quantity or quality should go down	Quantity or quality should go up

■Figure **10.8**

How a Perceived Inequity Can Affect Performance

According to equity theory, how a person reacts to under- or overpayment depends on whether he or she is paid on a piece-rate or salary basis.

satisfy those goals.[29] For example, a person wants to be an artist. To become one, she must go to college for a fine arts degree. So, she sets the goal of graduating from a university's fine arts program. That goal (which is prompted by her desire to be an artist) then motivates her behavior—she signs up and goes to college.

The research here is strikingly more scientific than that on most other motivation theories (in part because goal-setting lends itself more easily to analysis).[30] The findings suggest that setting goals is a simple, effective way to motivate employees. For supervisors it means that *the most straightforward way to motivate an employee may simply be to make sure that he or she has an acceptable, challenging goal, and has the ability to achieve it.*

Vroom's Expectancy Theory

Most people won't pursue rewards they find unattractive; nor will they take on tasks where the odds of success are very low. Psychologist Victor Vroom's motivation theory echoes these commonsense observations. He says that a person's motivation to exert some level of effort is a function of three things: the person's **expectancy** (in terms of probability) that his or her effort will lead to performance;[31] **instrumentality**, or the perceived relationship between successful performance and obtaining the reward; and **valence**, which represents the perceived value the person attaches to the reward.[32] In Vroom's theory, motivation is therefore a product of these three things: Motivation = $(E \times I \times V)$, where, of course, E represents expectancy, I instrumentality, and V valence.

PRACTICAL IMPLICATIONS   Vroom's theory has three big implications for how supervisors motivate employees.

- First, without an *expectancy* that effort will lead to performance, no motivation will take place. Supervisors therefore must ensure that their employees have the skills to do the job, and that they know they *can* do the job. Put another way, some performance problems are "can't do" rather than "won't do" problems. Here employees don't know what to do or how to do it, or they think they can't do it. Here training and confidence-building are important.

- Second, employees must see the *instrumentality* of their efforts—that successful performance will lead to getting the reward. Supervisors ensure this in many ways—for instance, by creating easy-to-understand incentive plans.

- Finally, supervisors should think through how to boost the *valence* or perceived value their subordinates attach to the rewards. One person may prefer two extra days' vacation, whereas another prefers two extra days' pay.

4. Learning/Reinforcement Approaches to Motivation

Needs theories such as Maslow's and process theories like Vroom's are two ways to explain what motivates employees. Leaning/motivation theories are a third approach.

We can define **learning** as a relatively permanent change in a person that occurs as a result of experience.[33] For example, we learn as children that our parents—through their smiles or some small gift—reward being courteous. We may then be motivated to be courteous throughout our lives. Motivation like this (such as to be courteous) tends to be instinctive, rather than a product of a deliberate thought process (as is process-based motivation like Vroom's). Few people consciously think about the pros and cons of being courteous when they behave in a courteous way!

There are several theories about how people learn. We'll focus on what may be called learning/reinforcement approaches to motivating employees. These focus on how consequences of behavior mold behavior.

B. F. Skinner and Operant Behavior

Psychologist B. F. Skinner's findings provide the foundation for much of what we know about learning. Consider an example. You want to train your dog to roll over. How would you do it? You'd probably encourage the dog to roll over (perhaps by gently nudging it down), and then reward it with some treat. Your dog would soon come to associate rolling over with the treat. It would *learn* that if it wanted a treat, it would have to roll over.

In Skinner's theory, the dog's rolling over is **operant behavior**, because the act of rolling over operates on the dog's environment, specifically by causing its owner to give it a treat. The process (training the dog to roll over in return for a treat) is *operant conditioning*. The main question in operant conditioning is how to strengthen the association between the **contingent reward** (in this case the treat) and the operant behavior.[34] (For instance, what can you do to make it clear to Fido that rolling over leads to a treat?)

Behavior Modification

Supervisors and psychologists answer that question at work through behavior modification. **Behavior modification** means changing or modifying behavior through rewards or punishment that are contingent on performance. Behavior modification has two basic principles: (1) Behavior that appears to lead to a positive consequence (reward) tends to be repeated, whereas behavior that appears to lead to a negative consequence (punishment) tends not to be repeated. (2) Therefore, you can get a person to learn to change his or her behavior by providing the properly scheduled rewards.[35] We'll look at how to actually apply behavior modification (and the other motivation theories we discussed) next.

5. Motivation in Action: 10 Methods for Motivating Employees

Supervisors apply motivation theories such Skinner's, Maslow's, Herzberg's, Locke's, and Vroom's through various methods. We'll explain 10 of these methods, such as "goal setting" and "pay for performance" next. As Table 10.1 shows, each of these 10 methods is based on one or more motivation theories. For example, the *job redesign* method reflects Herzberg's attempts to find a practical way to apply his ideas about how to build intrinsic motivation into employees' jobs. We start with method 1, Setting Goals to motivate employees.

1. Set Goals

The supervisor's first choice for motivating employees is usually simply to ensure that the employee has a doable goal and that he or she agrees with it. It makes little sense to

The Motivational Underpinnings of 10 Motivation Methods		
Foundation Theories of Behavior and Motivation	Goal Setting	Pay for Performance
Self-Actualization: People seek to fulfill their potential.		
Self-Efficacy: People differ in their estimates of how they'll perform on a task: self-efficacy influences effort.		
Maslow's Needs Hierarchy: Higher-level needs are never totally satisfied and aren't aroused until lower-level needs are satisfied.		
Maslow and others: All needs may be active, to some degree, at the same time.		
McClelland's (Achievement, Power, Affiliation): Needs for achievement, power, and affiliation are especially important in the work setting.		
Herzberg's Dual Factor: Extrinsic factors prevent dissatisfaction; intrinsic factors motivate workers.		
Vroom's Expectancy Approach: Motivation is a function of expectancy that effort leads to performance, performance leads to reward, and reward is valued.		x
Locke's Goal Setting: People are motivated to achieve goals they consciously set.	x	
Adams's Equity Theory: People are motivated to maintain balance between their perceived inputs and outputs.	x	
Reinforcement: People will continue behavior that is rewarded and cease behavior that is punished.		X

Source: Copyright © 1997 by Gary Dessler, Ph.D.

try to motivate employees in other ways (such as with financial incentives) if they don't know their goals or don't agree with them. Psychologist Edwin Locke and his colleagues have consistently found that specific, challenging goals lead to higher task performance than specific, unchallenging goals, vague goals, or no goals. Recall that suggestions for setting effective goals include the following:

- Set *SMART* goals—make them *specific, measurable, attainable, relevant,* and *timely.*
- Choose *performance measures* (sales revenue, costs, and so forth) that are *relevant* and *complete.*
- Assign *specific* goals.
- Assign *measurable* goals.
- Assign doable but *challenging* goals.
- Encourage *participation.*

2. Use Pay for Performance and Incentives

Incentive pay is obviously another important motivation method. **Pay for performance** or incentive pay refers to any pay plan that ties pay to the quantity or quality of work the person produces. In terms of motivation theory, pay for performance motivates employees by *reinforcing* desirable behaviors, and (in line with expectancy theory), by making it clear that performance is *instrumental* in (leads to) producing a coveted reward.

Piecework is the oldest incentive plan and still the most commonly used. Pay is tied directly to what the worker produces: The person is paid a "piece rate" for each unit

Merit Raises	Spot Rewards	Skill-Based Pay	Recognition Awards	Job Redesign	Empower Employees	Positive Reinforcement	Lifelong Learning
		X			X		X
X	X		X	X	X		X
X	X		X	X	X		X
		X	X	X	X		X
				X	X		X
X	X		X				
					X		
X	X		X				
X	X		X			X	

he or she produces. Thus, if Tom Smith gets $0.40 apiece for finding addresses on the Web, then he would make $40 for finding 100 a day and $80 for 200.

SALES INCENTIVES   Most companies pay their salespeople a combination of salary and commissions. Typical is a 70% base salary/30% incentive mix. Sales supervisors should know that a recent survey reveals that salespeople at high-performing companies:

- Receive 38% of their compensation in the form of *sales-related pay*, compared with 27% of compensation for salespeople at low-performing companies;
- Spend 264 more hours per year on *high-value sales activities* (e.g., prospecting, making sales presentations, and closing) than salespeople at low-performing companies;
- Spend 40% more time each year with their *best potential customers*— qualified leads and prospects they know—than salespeople at low-performing companies; and,
- Compared with salespeople at low-performing companies, spend nearly 25% *less time on administration*, allowing them to allocate more time to core sales activities, such as prospecting leads and closing sales.[36]

MANAGING SALES INCENTIVES   To maximize performance, the sales supervisor needs information such as, "Do the sales team members know how we measure and reward performance? Is there a positive correlation between performance and commission earnings?"[37]

Gathering this data requires special software programs.[38] Several vendors supply these systems. One is VUE Software, which supplies VUE Compensation Management.[39] With

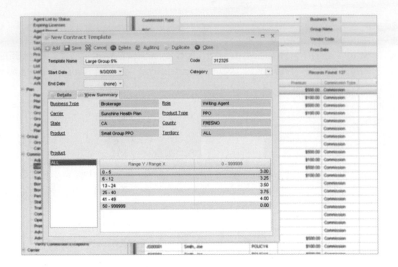

the aid of charts such as that in the accompanying Figure 10.9, VUE Compensation enables the sales supervisor to conduct the necessary analyses. For example, he or she can trend and analyze compensation and performance data, and conduct "What-if" analyses and reports.

■ Application Example

How to Design Effective Incentive Plans

Incentives can be effective. Two researchers compared performance over time in convenience stores that did and did not use financial and nonfinancial incentives.[40] Each store had about 25 workers and two supervisors. The researchers trained the supervisors to identify observable, measurable employee behaviors that were currently deficient but that could influence store performance. Example behaviors included "keeping both hands moving at the drive-through window," "working during idle time," and "repeating the customer's order back to him or her."[41]

Some employees in some of the stores received financial incentives for exhibiting the desired behaviors. For example, if the supervisor observed a work team exhibiting up to 50 of the good behaviors during the observation period, he or she added $25 to the paychecks of all store employees that period.

The researchers also trained the supervisors in some stores to deliver nonfinancial incentives in the form of feedback and recognition. For example, they placed charts by the time clocks, so all the store employees could keep track of their store's performance on things like drive-through times. They also gave *recognition* to employees, such as, "I noticed that today the drive-through times were really good. That is great since that is what we're really focusing on these days."[42]

Both the financial and nonfinancial incentives improved employee and store performance.[43] For example, store profits rose 30% for those units where supervisors used financial rewards. Store profits rose 36% for those units where supervisors used nonfinancial rewards.

GUIDELINES   Supervisors should create their incentive plans based on motivation theory.[44] For example, Vroom's expectancy approach says that motivation depends on employees' seeing the link between performance and rewards, and on the value of the reward to the recipient. The following lists important motivation-based steps for implementing an effective incentive plan.

- **Make sure effort and rewards are directly related.** The incentive plan should reward employees in direct proportion to increased productivity or quality.

- **Make the plan easy to understand.** Employees should be able to calculate their rewards for various levels of effort.

- **Set specific, effective standards.** Make standards high but reasonable—there should be about a 60% to 70% chance of success.

- **View the standard as a contract with your employees.** Once the plan is working, use caution before decreasing the size of the incentive.

- **Provide quick reinforcement.** Employees should find out quickly how they've done.

- **Get employee support for the plan.** Restrictions by peers can undermine the plan.

- **Use good measurement systems.** Make sure the standard and the employees' performance are both easy to measure.

- **Take the system into account.** For example, trying to motivate employees with a new incentive plan when they either don't have the skills to do the job or are demoralized by unfair supervisors might well fail.[45]

- **Be scientific.** Don't waste money on incentives that seem logical but that may not be contributing to performance. *Gather evidence* and analyze the effects of the incentive plan over time. Ascertain whether it is indeed influencing the measures (such as employee turnover, and so on) that you intended to improve through your plan.[46]

3. Improve Merit Pay

A **merit raise** is a salary increase—usually permanent—based on individual performance. The motivational basis for such raises is sound. Pursuing the raise should focus the employee on the link between his or her effort, performance, and rewards, consistent with Vroom's expectancy model. Getting the raise should provide reinforcement, consistent with learning theory. The merit raise should also reflect the fact that rewards are distributed equitably, consistent with equity theory.

Unfortunately, merit raises often fail on all three counts.

1. Many supervisors try to avoid bad feelings by awarding raises across the board, regardless of merit. They thus sever the performance–reward link.

2. Merit plans depend on annual appraisals, but some firms' appraisal procedures don't effectively distinguish between those who do well or poorly. (In one study, the researchers found a "very modest relationship between merit pay increase and performance rating.")[47]

3. A year is a long time to wait for a reward, so the reinforcement benefits of merit pay are suspect.[48]

The solution is for supervisors to use merit raises more intelligently. Do three things. First, *clarify performance standards* before the measurement period begins.

Incentives for Top Performers

In challenging economic times employers tend to reduce the pool of dollars available for raises, but that's not necessarily true for all employers. As one expert from the consulting firm Mercer puts it, "in this less than robust economic environment . . . top-performing employees are an organization's best competitive weapon and they are rewarding them accordingly."[49]

So as the United States slipped into recession, employers were broadening the performance differentials they awarded to top performers. For example, in 2009, expected base pay increases for the highest-ranked employees were 5.6%, compared with only 0.6% for the lowest-rated employees. Middle-rated employees could expect about 3.3%. The same is true for incentive payouts. For example, the highest-paid office clerical employees could expect short-term incentive payouts of 13%, while lowest-rated employees could expect 3%, and mid-rated employees 8%.[50] So the bottom line seems to be that in challenging times it's even more important to focus on keeping and incentivizing your top employees.[51]

Second, make sure your performance appraisals are *fair and unbiased*. Third, make sure to award merit pay *based on merit*, not across the board (top people get merit pay, bottom people don't). The Supervising in Challenging Times feature expands on this.

4. Use Recognition

Recognizing an employee's contribution is a simple and effective way for supervisors to motivate employees. It provides an inexpensive and timely form of feedback, and it contributes to a person's needs for achievement and self-esteem.

We saw that recognition has a positive impact on performance, either alone or in combination with financial rewards. For example, in one study, combining financial rewards with nonfinancial ones (like recognition) produced a 30% performance improvement in service firms—almost twice the effect of using each reward alone.[52]

RECOGNITION AWARDS SUPERVISORS CAN USE   Supervisors need not (and should not) rely just on the employer's incentive plans for motivating subordinates. Think back for a moment to the last time you worked hard to submit a great assignment or to cook a great meal, and consider how let down you felt when no one even said "Thanks." It's just too easy (and effective, given the research) to recognize a job well done. There are numerous informal ways that supervisors can recognize a job well done. A short list would include the following:[53]

- Challenging work assignments
- Freedom to choose own work activity
- Having fun built into work
- More of preferred task
- Role as boss's stand-in when he or she is away
- Role in presentations to top management
- Job rotation
- Encouragement of learning and continuous improvement
- Being provided with ample encouragement
- Being allowed to set own goals
- Compliments

- Expression of appreciation in front of others
- Note of thanks
- Employee-of-the-month award
- Special commendation
- Bigger desk
- Bigger office or cubicle

In terms of informal "motivators," the supervisor's leadership style also has important effects on employee motivation, as the accompanying feature illustrates.

Leadership Applications for Supervisors

Role of Charismatic and Transactional Leadership in Motivation

When many people think of how leaders motivate their followers, charismatic leadership usually pops to mind. We think of the general leading his or her troops to victory, or the movie star leading the cavalry charge, or someone like Steve Jobs coming back to take over a sputtering Apple Computer and ener-

gizing his employees to turn it into a company selling millions of iPods and iPads.

Charismatic leadership also has a long and distinguished history in leadership theory.[54] Charismatic leadership generally refers to leaders whom people follow, not because they're the appointed heads of some organization but because of the leader's personal magnetism and exceptional personal qualities and vision. To most leadership theorists who study charismatic leadership, charismatic leaders usually arise in response to crises. Their followers follow them because they believe that the leader has the vision and wherewithal to get followers through the crisis. At the risk of oversimplifying things, motivating people, for charismatic leaders, is relatively straightforward: Followers are motivated to pursue the charismatic leader's vision because the followers believe that the charismatic leader has what it takes to get them out of the crisis.

While that's all well and good for charismatic leaders, most people come up a little short when it comes to charisma. Even former president George H. W. Bush, a war hero and former CIA head and vice president, once said he thought he'd lost his bid to be reelected president in part "because perhaps I needed another quart of charisma."

Perhaps this shortage of charisma is just as well, because one study concludes that supervisors shouldn't let things like charisma blind them to the fact that old-fashioned, reward-based transactional leadership

may actually be more potent. As they say, "One unfortunate consequence of the focus on "charismatic," "transformational," and "visionary" leader behaviors during the past few decades has been the tendency to diminish the importance that transactional leadership behaviors have on leadership effectiveness."[55] Their analysis led them to conclude that one of the most powerful things that supervisors do to motivate employees is to recognize and reward performance day to day. So, do not be too distracted by the need to be "charismatic" or "transformational." Instead, stick to the basic blocking and tackling of leadership. Here's what they suggest leaders do to motivate employees:[56]

- **Make rewards, recognition, and positive feedback linked to—or made contingent upon—performance.**

- **Specify the reasons for rewards and punishments.** Recognition, praise, and rewards should focus on the specific behaviors or outcomes that are desirable.

- **Personalize rewards and punishments.** Show that you truly appreciate specific behaviors. This requires a leader to get to know employees and find out what they value.

- **Provide timely recognition and discipline.** The recognition should closely follow an employee's performance of the desired behavior. Similarly, discipline should also follow—as closely as possible—the employee's performance of the undesired behavior.

- **Match the magnitude of the reward or punishment to the behavior.** Leaders should match the magnitude of the feedback—positive or negative—given to employees to the level of performance exhibited by the employee.

5. Use Positive Reinforcement

"Positive reinforcement" is one of the most loosely used terms in business. Every time a supervisor thanks an employee, recognizes an employee, awards a raise, or gives out a promotion, he or she probably thinks, "I'm using positive reinforcement." More technically, however, positive reinforcement means something more. We may define **positive reinforcement** as any *formal organizational program* aimed at improving employee performance by using rewards to reinforce good behavior. Recognition programs like those we discussed previously tend to be more informal and between the supervisor and his or her employees.

Positive reinforcement's popularity stems from its solid basis in motivation theory. Numerous studies of learning and reinforcement (such as Skinner's) confirm the motivational benefits of providing employees with positive rewards.

Many companies therefore formalize the employee recognition process. According to one survey, 78% of CEOs and 58% of HR vice presidents said their firms were using performance recognition programs.[57] One survey of 235 supervisors found that the most-used rewards to motivate employees were (from most used to least):[58]

- Employee recognition
- Gift certificates
- Special events
- Cash rewards
- Merchandise incentives
- E-mail/print communications
- Training programs
- Work/life benefits
- Variable pay
- Group travel
- Individual travel
- Sweepstakes

Figure 10.10 lists other positive reinforcement rewards.

ONLINE AWARD PROGRAMS   If there's a downside to programs like prizes and rewards, it's that they're expensive to administer. Many firms—including Levi Strauss & Co., Barnes and Noble, Citibank, and Walmart—now collaborate with online incentive firms to expedite the whole process. Management consultant Hewitt Associates uses http://www.bravanta.com to help its supervisors more easily reward exceptional employee service with special awards. Other Internet incentive/recognition sites include http://www.giveanything.com, http://incentivecity.com, and http://www.kudoz.com.

SPOT AWARDS   In learning theory, the most powerful reinforcement usually comes at once. A **spot award** is one you give "on the spot," as soon as you observe the praiseworthy performance.[59] For example, Scitor, a systems engineering consulting firm based in Sunnyvale, California, has a program called Be Our Guest.[60] Be Our Guest bonuses (which usually range from $100 to $300) are given by employees to their coworkers for

MONETARY
Salary increases or bonuses
Company-paid vacation trip
Discount coupons
Company stock
Extra paid vacation days
Profit sharing
Paid personal holiday (such as birthday)
Movie or athletic event passes
Free or discount airline tickets
Discounts on company products or services
Gift selection from catalog

JOB AND CAREER RELATED
Empowerment of employee
Challenging work assignments
Job security (relatively permanent job)
Favorable performance appraisal
Freedom to choose own work activity
Promotion
Having fun built into work
More of preferred task
Role as boss's stand-in when he or she is away
Role in presentations to top management
Job rotation
Encouragement of learning and continuous improvement
Being provided with ample encouragement
Being allowed to set own goals

FOOD AND DINING
Business luncheon paid by company
Company picnics
Department parties
Holiday turkeys and fruit baskets

SOCIAL AND PRIDE RELATED
Compliments
Encouragement
Comradeship with boss
Access to confidential information
Pat on back
Expression of appreciation in front of others
Note of thanks
Employee-of-the-month award
Wall plaque indicating accomplishment
Special commendation
Company recognition plan

STATUS SYMBOLS
Bigger desk
Bigger office or cubicle
Exclusive use of fax machine
Freedom to personalize work area
Private office
Cellular phone privileges
Online service privileges

■Figure **10.10**

Some Positive Reinforcement Rewards

Source: Several items under the job- and career-related category are from Dean R. Spitzer, "Power Rewards: Rewards That Really Motivate," *Management Review,* May 1996, p. 48.

doing something beyond the call of duty. If (in the giver's eyes) the recipient does something exceptional—stays late to work on a project, for instance—the giver fills out a card indicating the amount of the bonus. Then it's the recipient's to spend as he or she likes.

6. Use Behavior Management

Some experts would challenge using the label *positive reinforcement* to cover such a wide array of reward programs. Some prefer to limit the term to formal *behavior management* programs. These apply Skinner's concepts and principles of learning/reinforcement (discussed earlier) to motivating employees.

Suppose you have what you think is a "motivation" problem. For example, your employee, Pierre, comes in a few minutes late almost every day. How could you use behavior management to solve this familiar problem? Supervisors applying behavior modification at work must address two basic issues: the *type of reinforcement* (reward or punishment) and the *schedule of reinforcement.*

TYPES OF REINFORCEMENT   There are four types of reinforcement. **Positive reinforcement** is a positive consequence, or reward, such as praise or a bonus, that results when the desired behavior occurs. In **extinction**, supervisors *withhold* reinforcement so that the undesired behavior disappears over time. For example, Pierre learns that arriving late invariably leads to a scolding by you, which, in turn, leads to laughter from the worker's peers. Here, use extinction: Discipline Pierre in the privacy of your office, thereby removing the laughter—the reward. **Negative reinforcement** means reinforcing the desirable behavior *by removing something undesirable* that results from performing the behavior. Making safety helmets more comfortable is an example.

Punishment is in a class by itself. It means adding something undesirable to change Pierre's behavior. Reprimands and discipline are familiar examples. Punishment is the most controversial method of modifying behavior. Skinner recommends extinction rather than punishment for decreasing the frequency of the undesired behavior.

As in Figure 10.11, using behavior modification successfully is like balancing a scale. Suppose wearing a safety helmet is the desired behavior, and not wearing it is the undesired behavior. One way to increase the desired behavior (positive reinforcement) is to add a positive consequence—for instance, by praising the worker each time he or she wears the helmet. Another option (negative reinforcement) is to remove the negative consequences of wearing the helmet, perhaps by making the helmet less cumbersome. Most psychologists say it's best to focus on improving desirable behaviors rather than on decreasing undesirable ones.

THE SCHEDULE OF REINFORCEMENT   In behavior modification, it's not just the type of reinforcement, but the *schedule* you use to apply it that's important. The research findings suggest the following:

1. The fastest way to get someone to learn is not to put him or her on a schedule at all. Instead, reinforce the desired behavior every time it occurs. This is *continuous reinforcement.* The drawback is that the desired behavior also diminishes very quickly once you stop reinforcing it.

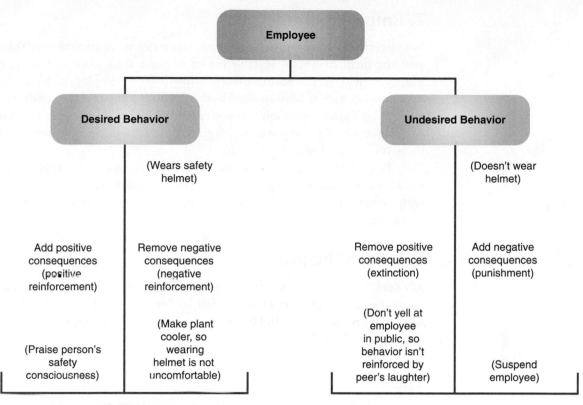

■Figure **10.11**
Options for Modifying Behavior with Reinforcement

2. *Variable* (also called partial) *reinforcement* is the most powerful at sustaining behavior. Here, you don't reinforce the desired behavior each time it occurs, but every few times, around some average number of times. As they do when playing Las Vegas–type slot machines, people always hope to "hit the jackpot" on the next try. They therefore continue producing the desired behavior for a long time even without reinforcement. The following example illustrates this.

■ **Application Example**

Emery Air Freight

The Emery Air Freight Company program grew out of management's discovery that the containers used to consolidate air freight shipments were not being fully utilized.[61] In this case, the workers used containers only about 45% of the time. Management wanted them to boost the actual usage rate to 90% to 95%.

Consultants installed a behavior management program. It included an instruction book for supervisors that showed how to use recognition, rewards, feedback, and various other types of social, intrinsic, and tangible consequences. Each dockworker also received a checklist to mark each time he or she used a container (so the worker, in effect, gave him- or herself positive feedback). In 80% of the offices where Emery installed it, container usage rose from 45% to 95% in a single day.

7. Empower Employees

Empowerment means giving employees some degree of control over their jobs and enabling them to employ suitable power to make their work lives more effective.[62] Empowerment, in motivation theory, helps to satisfy employees' higher-level needs. Psychologists such as Maslow and Herzberg would argue that the satisfaction one gets from doing a challenging job that you're empowered to do is highly motivating. As in working on a hobby that you love, you get positive reinforcement by doing well at something you're proud of and love to do.

Empowering employees requires taking specific steps, such as providing employees with a clear vision and goals, fostering their personal mastery, and providing them with needed support. Table 10.2 lists actions supervisors can take to empower employees.[63]

8. Enrich the Job

Job enrichment means making a job more interesting and challenging, and therefore motivational. Supervisors often do this by "vertically loading" the job—giving the worker more autonomy, and allowing the person to do much of the planning and

■ Table **10.2**

Practical Suggestions for Empowering Others
ARTICULATE A CLEAR VISION AND GOALS
[ ] Create a picture of a desired future.
[ ] Use word pictures and emotional language to describe the vision.
[ ] Identify specific actions and strategies that will lead to the vision.
[ ] Establish SMART goals.
[ ] Associate the vision and goals with personal values.
FOSTER PERSONAL MASTERY EXPERIENCES
[ ] Break apart large tasks and assign one part at a time.
[ ] Assign simple tasks before difficult tasks.
[ ] Highlight and celebrate small wins.
[ ] Incrementally expand job responsibilities.
[ ] Give increasingly more responsibility to solve problems.
MODEL SUCCESSFUL BEHAVIORS
[ ] Demonstrate successful task accomplishment.
[ ] Point out other people who have succeeded.
[ ] Facilitate interaction with other role models.
[ ] Find a coach.
[ ] Establish a mentor relationship.
PROVIDE SUPPORT
[ ] Praise, encourage, express approval for, and reassure.
[ ] Send letters or notes of praise to family members of coworkers.

Practical Suggestions for Empowering Others

[ ] Regularly provide feedback.
[ ] Foster informal social activities to build cohesion.
[ ] Supervise less closely and provide time slack.
[ ] Hold recognition ceremonies.

AROUSE POSITIVE EMOTIONS

[ ] Foster activities to encourage friendship formation.
[ ] Periodically send lighthearted messages.
[ ] Use superlatives in giving feedback.
[ ] Highlight compatibility between important personal values and organizational goals.
[ ] Clarify impact on the ultimate customer.
[ ] Foster attributes of recreation in work: clear goals, effective scorekeeping and feedback systems, and out-of-bounds behavior.

PROVIDE INFORMATION

[ ] Provide all task-relevant information.
[ ] Continuously provide technical information and objective data.
[ ] Pass along relevant cross-unit and cross-functional information.
[ ] Provide access to information or people with senior responsibility.
[ ] Provide access to information from its source.
[ ] Clarify effects of actions on customers.

PROVIDE RESOURCES

[ ] Provide training and development experiences.
[ ] Provide technical and administrative support.
[ ] Provide needed time, space, or equipment.
[ ] Ensure access to relevant information networks.
[ ] Provide more discretion to commit resources.

CONNECT TO OUTCOMES

[ ] Provide a chance to interact directly with those receiving the service or output.
[ ] Provide authority to resolve problems on the spot.
[ ] Provide immediate, unfiltered, direct feedback on results.
[ ] Create task identity or the opportunity to accomplish a complete task.
[ ] Clarify and measure effects as well as direct outcomes.

CREATE CONFIDENCE

[ ] Exhibit reliability and consistency.
[ ] Exhibit fairness and equity.
[ ] Exhibit caring and personal concern.
[ ] Exhibit openness and honesty.
[ ] Exhibit competence and expertise.

Source: David A. Whetton and Kim S. Cameron, *Developing Management Skills* (Upper Saddle River, NJ: Prentice Hall, 2002), pp. 426–27.

inspection normally done by the supervisor. Job enrichment is the method Frederick Herzberg recommends for applying his motivator-hygiene approach.

USING JOB ENRICHMENT   Successfully applying this approach requires answering two questions. The first question is, "*How does one know if a job (or set of jobs) is ripe for this approach?*"[64] Figure 10.12 provides a guide. It is a form for evaluating the appropriateness of job enrichment. According to the form's creators, "a lower rating (1.0–1.9) indicates that a job is a prime candidate for enrichment; and if properly implemented, it has a high expected return on investment. A job enrichment rating of 2.0–3.9 identifies jobs that can be enriched that may have a marginal return on investment in terms of productivity pleasures. A high rating (4.0–5.0) identifies jobs that for all practical purposes cannot be enriched at the present time."[65]

The second question is, "*What specific actions can I take that will 'enrich' an employee's job?*" Supervisors can enrich jobs in several ways:[66]

1. **Form natural work groups.**   For example, put a team in charge of an identifiable body of work, such as building the entire engine.
2. **Combine tasks.**   Let one person assemble a product from start to finish instead of having it go through separate operations performed by different people.
3. **Establish client relationships.**   Let the worker have contact as often as possible with the client of that person's work.
4. **Vertically load the job.**   Have the worker, rather the supervisor, plan, schedule, troubleshoot, and control his or her job.
5. **Open feedback channels.**   Find more and better ways for the worker to get quick feedback on performance.

JOB DESIGN   Job enrichment is one example of a motivation method called job design (or job redesign). **Job design** refers to manipulating the number and nature of activities in a job. The basic issue is whether jobs should be more specialized or, at the other extreme, more enriched. **Job enlargement** assigns workers additional similar tasks. For example, the worker who previously only bolted the seat to the chair legs might also attach the back. **Job rotation** systematically moves workers from job to job. *Job enrichment* is more extensive. Here the supervisor also takes steps to vertically load the job (perhaps letting employees, for instance, check their own work and communicate with their clients.).

9. Use Skill-Based Pay

Most firms pay employees based on specific job titles. Presidents make more than vice presidents do, and sales supervisors make more than assistant sales supervisors do. How do you pay workers when you want to encourage workers who work in teams to move from one team job to another, when the jobs may entail different skill levels?

Skill-based pay is one solution. Here, employers pay employees for their skills and knowledge, rather than for the jobs they currently hold.[67] As an example, a General Mills plant boosted the skill level of its workforce by implementing a pay plan that

The Job Itself (For each item, circle the number that best applies)

1.	Quality is important and attributable to the worker	1/2/3/4/5	Quality is not too important and/or is not controllable by the worker.
2.	Flexibility is a major contributor to job efficiency.	1/2/3/4/5	Flexibility is not a major consideration.
3.	The job requires the coordination of tasks or activities among several workers.	1/2/3/4/5	The job is performed by one worker acting independently of others.
4.	The benefits of job enrichment will compensate for the efficiencies of task specialization.	1/2/3/4/5	Job enrichment will eliminate substantial efficiencies realized from specialization.
5.	The conversion and one-time set-up costs involved in job enrichment can be recovered in a reasonable period of time.	1/2/3/4/5	Training and other costs associated with job enrichment are estimated to be much greater than expected results.
6.	The wage payment plan is not based solely on output.	1/2/3/4/5	Workers are under a straight piece-work wage plan.
7.	Due to the worker's ability to affect output, an increase in job satisfaction can be expected to increase productivity.	1/2/3/4/5	Due to the dominance of technology, an increase in job satisfaction is unlikely to significantly affect productivity.

Technology

8.	Changes in job content would not necessitate a large investment in equipment and technology	1/2/3/4/5	The huge investment in equipment and technology overrides all other considerations.
9.	Employees are accustomed to change and respond favorably to it.	1/2/3/4/5	Employees are set in their ways and prefer the status quo.
10.	Employees feel secure in their jobs; employment has been stable.	1/2/3/4/5	Layoffs are frequent, many employees are concerned about the permanency of employment.
11.	Employees are dissatisfied with their jobs and would welcome changes in job content and work relationships.	1/2/3/4/5	Employees are satisfied with their present jobs and general work situation.
12.	Employees are highly skilled blue- and white-collar workers, professionals, and supervisors.	1/2/3/4/5	Employees are semi- and unskilled blue- and white-collar workers.
13.	Employees are well educated, with most having college degrees.	1/2/3/4/5	The average employee has less than a high school education.
14.	Employees are from a small town and rural environment.	1/2/3/4/5	The company is located in a large, highly industrialized metropolitan area.
15.	The history of union–management (if no union, worker–management) relations has been one of cooperation and mutual support.	1/2/3/4/5	Union–management (worker–management) relations are strained, and the two parties are antagonistic to one another.

Management

16.	Supervisors are committed to job enrichment and are anxious to participate in its implementation.	1/2/3/4/5	Supervisors show little interest in job enrichment and even less interest in having it implemented in their departments.
17.	Supervisors have attended seminars, workshops, and so forth; are quite knowledgeable of the concept; and have had experience in implementing it.	1/2/3/4/5	Supervisors lack the training and experience necessary to develop and implement job enrichment projects.
18.	Management realizes that substantial payoffs from job enrichment usually take one to three years to materialize.	1/2/3/4/5	Management expects immediate results (within six months) from job enrichment projects.

Total Score _____ ÷ 18 = _____

Job Enrichment Rating

■Figure **10.12**

A Job Enrichment Evaluation Form

Source: Theodore T. Herbert, *Organizational Behavior: Readings and Cases* (New York: Macmillan Publishing Co., Inc., 1976), pp. 344–45.

encouraged employees to develop greater skills.[68] The plan paid workers based on attained skill levels, rather than based on their job titles. For each of the several types of jobs in the plant, workers could attain three levels of skill: *limited ability*, *partial proficiency*, and *full competence.*

After starting a job, workers got tests periodically to see if they had earned certification at the next higher skill level. If they had, they received higher pay even though they kept the same job. The plant's overall skill level increased, as did its ability to switch employees from job to job. Your employer will determine whether to implement such a special pay plan. But the supervisor can still take steps to encourage employees to learn more about their and others' jobs, for instance, by recognizing those who do so.

10. Provide Lifelong Learning

Just about everyone is motivated by the desire to learn new things and to keep getting better. **Lifelong learning** is a formal, usually companywide effort aimed at making sure employees have the skills they need—from remedial skills to decision-making techniques to college degrees—to work effectively throughout their careers.

Lifelong learning is inherently motivational. It boosts employees' sense of competence. It also enhances an employee's opportunity to self-actualize, fulfill his or her potential, and gain the sense of achievement that psychologists argue is important in motivation.

Lifelong learning isn't the sort of tool (like incentives or merit pay) that typically springs to mind when one thinks about motivating employees. However, the motivational effect of giving employees an opportunity to develop their skills and to self-actualize is considerable. Supervisors have numerous opportunities to provide employees with lifelong learning opportunities. These include, for instance, sending them to courses to hone their skills, recommending them for educational programs, and enabling them to serve on workplace problem-solving teams.

Putting It All Together: How to Solve Performance-Motivation Problems

Your employee is not performing up to par. You want to understand what is happening— and why—and correct the problem.

To help you reduce the vast number of potential causes and to simplify your analysis, you may find Figure 10.13 useful. The model, based on what we discussed in this chapter, assumes that inadequate performance may have three main sources:

1. The person does not know what to do in terms of his or her goals.
2. Or could not do the job if he or she wanted to.
3. Or is not motivated to do the job.

How Are Performance-Motivation Problems Analyzed?

Use the flowchart and the guidelines in the model to analyze and solve the performance-motivation problem. How could Lisa (in the chapter opener) use this flowchart to analyze and hopefully improve Mal's performance?

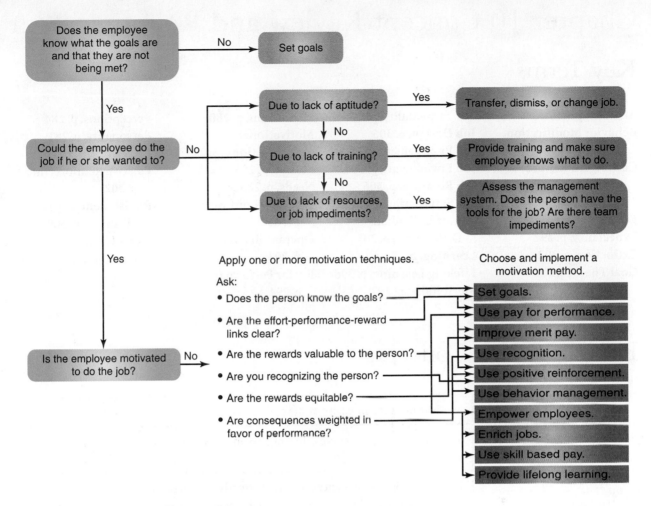

■Figure **10.13**

How to Solve Motivation Problems

Source: Copyright Gary Dessler, Ph.D. Suggested in part by "Performance Diagnosis Model," David Whetton and Kim Cameron, *Developing Management Skills* (Upper Saddle River, NJ: Prentice Hall, 2001), p. 339.

Chapter 10 Concept Review and Reinforcement

Key Terms

Attitude, p. 284
Behavior Modification,
  p. 293
Contingent Reward,
  p. 293
Empowerment, p. 304
Equity Theory, p. 291
Expectancy, p. 292
Extinction, p. 302
Goal Theory of
  Motivation, p. 291

Instrumentality, p. 292
Job Design, p. 306
Job Enlargement, p. 306
Job Enrichment, p. 304
Job Rotation, p. 306
Job Satisfaction, p. 284
Law of Individual
  Differences, p. 281
Learning, p. 292
Lifelong Learning, p. 308
Merit Raise, p. 297

Motivation, p. 280
Motivational
  Dispositions, p. 285
Motive, p. 285
Needs, p. 285
Negative Reinforcement,
  p. 302
Operant Behavior,
  p. 293
Pay for Performance,
  p. 294

Perceptions, p. 284
Personality, p. 281
Piecework, p. 294
Positive Reinforcement,
  p. 302
Punishment, p. 302
Spot Award, p. 300
Stereotyping, p. 284
Valence, p. 292

Review of Key Concepts

Motivation	Motivation is the intensity of the person's desire to engage in some activity.
Law of Individual Differences	This law states that people differ in personalities, abilities, self-concept, values, and needs.
Personality	Personality is the characteristic and distinctive traits of an individual measured by extraversion, emotional stability, agreeableness, conscientiousness, and openness to experience.
Perception	We all react to stimuli that reach us via our senses. How we perceive, define, or "see" these stimuli reflects our experiences, needs, and personality.
Attitude	Attitude is a tendency to respond to objects, people, or events in either a positive or a negative way.
Motive	A motive is something that incites a person to action or that sustains and gives direction to action.
Maslow's Needs Hierarchy	Maslow's theory states that people have a hierarchy of five increasingly higher-level needs: • Physiological • Security • Social • Self-esteem • Self-actualization Maslow argued that people are motivated first to satisfy the lower-order needs before they move to higher-order needs.

Herzberg's Two-Factor Approach	Herzberg's Hygiene–Motivator theory divides Maslow's hierarchy into lower-level (psychological, safety, and social) and higher-level (ego, self-actualization) needs. The theory states that the way to motivate someone is to satisfy higher-level needs. Herzberg goes on to say that employees can become dissatisfied when hygiene factors are not adequate but that adding more of these factors will do a poor job of motivating employees.
Needs for Achievement, Power, and Affiliation	McClelland and Atkinson agree with Herzberg that supervisors should appeal to employees' higher-level needs. They focused on three needs they felt are especially important, needs for: • Achievement • Power • Affiliation
Equity Theory	Equity theory states that if a person perceives an inequity, a tension or drive will develop in the person's mind, and the person will be motivated to reduce or eliminate the tension.
Goal Theory	Goal theory assumes that people are motivated to seek ways to satisfy unsatisfied needs.
Expectancy Theory	Vroom says that a person's motivation to exert some level of effort is in part a function of the person's expectancy that his or her effort will lead to performance.
Behavior Modification	Behavior modification means changing or modifying behavior through rewards or punishment that are dependent on performance.
Use Recognition	Recognizing an employee's contribution is a simple and effective way for supervisors to motivate employees.
Positive Reinforcement	Positive reinforcement is any formal organizational program aimed at improving employee performance by using rewards to reinforce good behavior.
Types of Reinforcement	There are four types of reinforcement: • Positive • Extinction • Negative • Punishment
Empowerment	Empowerment means giving employees some degree of control over their jobs, enabling them to employ suitable power to make their work lives more effective.

Job Enrichment	Job enrichment means making a job more interesting and challenging, and therefore motivational.
Lifelong Learning	Lifelong learning is a formal effort aimed at making sure employees have the skills they need to work effectively throughout their careers.

Review and Discussion Questions

1. What is "personality"?

2. Describe the law of individual differences and how it affects motivation.

3. Describe what a motive is. Give an example.

4. Briefly explain Maslow's motivation theory.

5. Why, according to Herzberg, is giving someone better working conditions an ineffective way to motivate the person?

6. Describe Vroom's expectancy theory.

7. Compare Herzberg's motivator factors with McClelland's needs for achievement, power, and affiliation. How are these needs similar?

8. Explain how you would empower an employee.

9. Give three examples of positive reinforcement.

10. Define job enrichment. Give an example of how you would enrich someone's job.

11. Why is it to the advantage of an organization to offer their employees lifelong learning?

Application and Skill Building

Case Study One

Dayton-Hudson Corporation: Learning to Motivate Employees

Dayton-Hudson Corporation (DHC) wants to run "the best stores in town." The owner of Dayton's, Hudson's, Mervyn's, Marshall Fields, and Target, DHC understands that to have the best stores, it needs to attract, retain, and motivate the best employees. Since women consumers account for most of the retail-shopping dollars spent, DHC also wants to attract and motivate women managers; it has therefore developed various policies to make the company attractive to prospective women employees.

DHC has been successful in its efforts to promote women managers. The company's most recent Equal Employment Opportunity (EEO) report noted that in senior management, 26% of DHC managers at the level of vice president or higher are women. Of middle management at the company, 37% are women. Women recently comprised more than 66% of DHC's employee population.

Each of DHC's major divisions has its own program of compensation-related HR policies and benefits, but they all have several common features:

- Pretax salary employees can set aside tax free to pay for dependent care
- Child-care resource and referral information
- Employee participation in alternative work arrangements, such as telecommuting, job-sharing, working at home, flex-time, and part-time employment
- Time off to care for a sick child or seriously ill family member
- Generous leaves for pregnancy
- Additional programs in individual divisions, such as expense reimbursement for adoption and prenatal and well-baby care programs

Working Mother magazine has six times named DHC one of the top workplaces for women with children. It has noted a number of key features in the DHC programs, including the publication of its overall benefits program.

The stakes are very high in the retail industry. Consider the Target division of DHC. Since opening the first Target store in suburban St. Paul, Minnesota, the company has grown to nearly 900 stores in 44 states. Target provides employment for approximately 189,000 people. The parent company, DHC, is America's fourth largest general merchandise retailer, with more than a quarter of a million team members. However, profit margins have been eroding for years as customers seek ever-better sales, and it's obvious that only the most efficient retailers are going to survive.

Discussion Questions

1. DHC has hired you as a consultant to evaluate the motivational potential of its various compensation programs. Write a brief report titled "The Motivational Potential of DHC's Current Family-Friendly Compensation Program." Please make sure to explain (in terms of the motivation theories

in this chapter) the extent to which each program (such as preset salary set-asides) is or is not motivational.

2. Why (if at all) do you think DHC's compensation programs would help to motivate working parents in particular to work in its stores and/or offices?

3. In your opinion, does DHC have all the programs it needs to motivate managers? Why or why not? Based on what you know about the retail store business, propose three specific motivational programs you would recommend that Target use for the salespeople in its stores.

Case Study Two

JetBlue: Keeping the Troops Happy

One reason JetBlue Airline's costs are low is that it doesn't have labor unions. It therefore can "require higher productivity from its 2,100 employees while paying them lower wages than unionized airlines."[69]

However, employees are not foolish; they know when they're working harder than their colleagues at other airlines for about the same pay. The question is, "How does JetBlue keep morale and motivation up so that its workers are willing to work harder for the same or less pay?"

JetBlue accomplishes this in several ways. One is by providing flexible work. For example, its staff of 350 or so reservation agents work from special minicall centers in their homes, and so they needn't travel to work.[70] JetBlue also lets its flight attendants decide how many hours they want to work. For example, they have some flight attendants on traditional schedules and some on a more flexible college student flight attendant program. The JetBlue Friend's Crew Program is another example. In this program, JetBlue hires people to share a schedule. Thus, two friends might share one flight attendant's schedule, and decide between themselves who flies when.

JetBlue also has several pay and benefits programs aimed at keeping morale and motivation high. Its new, high-tech planes and new systems mean JetBlue can fly with fewer employees per plane. That means pay at JetBlue is quite competitive. Furthermore, JetBlue employees like the company's profit-sharing plan. Asked how the company's profit-sharing plan increases employees productivity, former CEO David Neeleman gave the following answer: "One day in December, there were a lot of cancellations in the New York City area, and we operated our flights deep into the night, but we got them all done. I got e-mail from employees who picked up passengers off canceled flights from all these other carriers from LaGuardia, and they wrote 'profit sharing' in big bold letters."[71]

JetBlue also keeps some employee benefits higher than those at other airlines. For example, rather than wait until a new employee has completed his or her 90-day probationary period, he or she starts getting benefits almost at once. Similarly, whereas most airlines don't pay for new employees benefits (such as hotel expenses) while they're being trained, JetBlue pays them during training.

However, a recent news item might raise some concern for JetBlue's management. Southwest Airlines has been running into some unexpected turbulence with regard to its employee relations. Its mechanics want a federal mediator to help settle a two-year contract battle. Ground workers sued the airline because of how Southwest is disciplining its employees. And its pilots were reluctantly voting on a Southwest contract offer that their own pilot union leaders said was insufficient.[72] Since Southwest is, in many respects, the model that David Neeleman used when he created JetBlue about 20 years ago, Southwest's employee turbulence may be a warning sign. As one writer noted at the time, "Neeleman obsesses over keeping employees happy, and with good reason. Airline watchers say JetBlue's ability to stay union free is critical to its survival as a low-cost carrier."[73] The question is, "Can they do what's necessary to avoid the sorts of problems that Southwest seems to be running into?"

You and your team are consultants to JetBlue's top management, which is depending on your management expertise to help in navigating the launch and management of JetBlue. Here's what JetBluewants to know from you now.

Assignment

1. What are the pros and cons of the JetBlue profit-sharing incentive plan? Are there any changes you would recommend?
2. Assume that a consultant has recommended to JetBlue that, if it wants to keep its labor costs down, it should use job enrichment for its pilots, mechanics, or flight attendants. Do you agree that JetBlue can substitute "job enrichment" for "pay"—in other words, make the job itself so motivating that people will willingly work hard even if the pay is not as good as it might be at another airline? Next, choose the pilots', mechanics', or flight attendants' jobs. Ascertain (from what you know about such jobs) if the job is amenable to job enrichment, and explain in detail how you would enrich it.
3. Former CEO David Neeleman and his managerial colleagues worked very hard to make sure they hired sociable, friendly people to be JetBlue employees, because they wanted to make sure JetBlue's customer service remains among the best in the industry. Assume that you want to develop a behavior management program for flight attendants. You want to focus on improving "customer service." Define the specific activity you will use to measure customer service, and then develop a behavior management program for this activity for the flight attendants.

Experiential Activities

Activity 1. Mal seemed to be a good hiring choice as a travel agent. Three weeks after hiring Mal, Lisa (a partner in the travel agent company) regretted her choice. Mal was not getting his job done, and Lisa wondered what she had to do to light a fire under this guy.

Employee Motivation—The Challenge

Purpose: The purpose of this exercise is to give you practice in determining how to motivate employees to succeed in their jobs.

Required Understanding: You are going to develop a comprehensive plan for motivating this newly hired travel agent and therefore you need to be thoroughly familiar with the discussion of motivation covered in this chapter.

How to Set Up the Exercise/Instructions: Divide the class into groups of 4–5 students.

1. You want to determine the process needed to light a fire under Mal.
2. Next, your group should develop an outline summarizing the steps you propose to use in this motivation process.
3. Have a spokesperson from each group share their proposed motivation plan for Mal with the other groups. Follow up with a class discussion involving all of the student groups and look at the similarities in the groups' reports.

Activity 2. In teams of 4–5 students, use Figure 10.12 to analyze a supermarket cashier's job for its enrichment potential. What specifically would you do to enrich it more?

Activity 3. You like everything your company's training director does, with one glaring exception: He insists on spending much of each lecture with his back toward the group. His excuse is that he's busy writing on the board. However, in an average 50-minute training session, he probably turns his back to the group and talks 30 to 35 times, and it is driving everyone to distraction. One trainee said, half in jest, that it would be less distracting if he'd at least give his lectures with a baseball cap on backwards. In teams of 4–5 students, develop a behavior management program to cure your training director of his annoying behavior.

Role-Playing Exercise

Empowering Employees: The Situation

The personnel manager of Nashville Insurance Company has just completed a one-week class on how to motivate their employees. The manager's goal is to persuade the office supervisor to use some of the ideas learned on their office staff. The manager is really excited at using a motivational tool called empowerment. The manger learned in class that famous psychologists like Maslow and Herzberg would argue that the satisfaction one gets from doing a challenging job that you're empowered to do is highly motivating. The personnel manager realizes that when you empower employees to make decisions, you delegate a portion of the power you have as a supervisor. The manager must convey to the supervisor that empowerment means giving employees some degree of control over their jobs.

Instructions: All students should read the situation above. One student will play the role of personnel manager and a second student will play the role of the office supervisor.

Important: Each student should only read his or her assigned role below. Then the two students should engage in a 15-minute conversation. After the 15-minute role play has ended, the class (including the two role-play students) should read and address the questions at the end of the exercise.

Role of Personnel Manager: You must impress on the supervisor how important to the organization this motivation tool is:

- Better employee attitudes
- Increased quality of work
- Better time management
- Fewer mistakes
- Increased productivity
- Higher self-esteem

The supervisor is not going to be sure about giving up some authority. You must persuade the supervisor that it will benefit both of them as well as their employees.

Role of Office Supervisor: You're not sure how this meeting with the personnel manager is going to work out. You have great concerns about giving up part of your authority (that you have always had). Some of the questions you should include in your conversation should be:

- How will this change my job as a supervisor? Will it make it easier or more difficult?
- Are these office employees ready to be held responsible for their decisions?
- Will I need to train them?
- What is in it for me?

Questions for Class Discussion

1. Based on what you read in this chapter, did the personnel manager do a good job in persuading the supervisor to use employee empowerment?
2. If you were the supervisor, how would you react to the personnel manager's request?
3. Do you agree with the advantages in using empowerment discussed in the meeting?
4. What additional reasons for using empowerment would you suggest be used?

11 Leading the Team Effort

....

CHAPTER OBJECTIVES

After studying this chapter, you should be able to answer the following questions:

1. Teams: Why Are They Important?
2. How Do Group Dynamics Impact the Development of Effective Teams?
3. What Types of Teams Might Be Found in an Organization?
4. What Should a Supervisor Expect During the Formation of Self-Directing Work Teams?
5. How Does a Supervisor Evaluate Team Performance?

6. What Are the Keys to Building a High-Performing Team?
7. What Behaviors Do Leaders of Effective Teams Practice?
8. What Might Be Expected When Transitioning from Supervisor to Team Leader?
9. What Tools Does a Supervisor Use to Develop Sound Decision-Making Skills in Team Members?

OPENING SNAPSHOT
The Out-of-Control Team

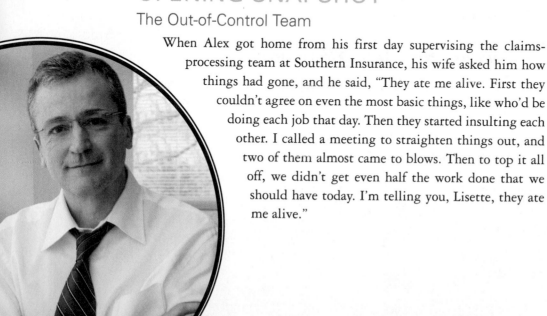

When Alex got home from his first day supervising the claims-processing team at Southern Insurance, his wife asked him how things had gone, and he said, "They ate me alive. First they couldn't agree on even the most basic things, like who'd be doing each job that day. Then they started insulting each other. I called a meeting to straighten things out, and two of them almost came to blows. Then to top it all off, we didn't get even half the work done that we should have today. I'm telling you, Lisette, they ate me alive."

1. Why Teams Are Important

Chances are, you're not going to supervise employees who go about their jobs independently; instead, you'll supervise some sort of team. It may be a work team (such as the unfortunate Alex's claims-processing team.) Or it may a team that's working on a special project (a "project team"), or one analyzing a special problem (a "problem-solving team"), or even one whose members only meet online (a "virtual team"). In the United States, about 82% of companies with more than 100 employees use teams to get their work done.[1] Reasons why companies organize around teams include "improving product quality" (chosen by 69% of these respondents), "improving productivity" (64%), "improving employee morale" (17%), and "improving staffing flexibility" (13%).[2] A **team** is a small number of people with complementary skills who are "committed to a common purpose, set of performance goals, and approach for which they hold themselves mutually accountable."[3] More simply put, a team is a group of people who work together and share a common objective.

Is Teamwork New?

In some ways, there's nothing new about doing the work with teams. Companies have always had "top management teams" and even work teams (like the cleaning crews that sweep into offices each night). And of course, there are all those baseball, soccer, and hockey teams.

But today's interest in teams stems from something more. Years of experience have shown companies just how powerful organizing work around teams can be. A close-knit and cohesive team of employees with high performance goals can produce spectacularly higher output and quality than can a mere group of workers. And left to its own devices, a well-trained team of even minimum-wage employees can often study and solve workplace problems that even high-priced consultants wouldn't see. In a competitive world, companies need all the quality and productivity they can muster. More often than not today, they get that by having teams do the work.

What Using Teams Means for Supervisors

Supervising teams is different from supervising individuals, and so requires new skills. Traditional supervisory skills like planning, budgeting, training, and even motivating aren't enough. You also need to know how to take a diverse group of individuals and forge them into a cohesive team, and then how to lead the team's efforts. We'll address these team leadership skills in this chapter. First, though, much of what we know about effective teams comes from research into how small groups of people behave. We'll therefore start by looking at what behavioral scientists call *group dynamics*.

2. How Group Dynamics Affect Teamwork

For many years, behavioral scientists studied what happens when small groups of people interact. They asked questions such as, "What factors determine whether people work together harmoniously when they're in groups?" and, "What determines how committed each member is to the group's welfare?" The behavioral scientists called their field of study **group dynamics**, which literally means studying group activity. *Group norms* is one subject they focus on. *Group cohesiveness* is another.

Group Norms

One of the first thing these scientists discovered was that when you create a group, the new group takes on a life of its own. The people in the group behave (and, indeed, even think) differently than they did before they joined the group. Supervisors forget that simple fact at their peril.

For one thing, it takes a very strong-willed employee to defy one's group. For example, one study (aptly named *Monkey See, Monkey Do: The Influence of Workgroups on the Antisocial Behavior of Employees*) looked at how the antisocial behavior of coworkers influenced each team members' antisocial behavior.[4] The researchers found that the more antisocial the group, the more it was able to pressure its individual members into taking antisocial actions.[5] So, do not ever forget, when you're supervising, just how powerful an influence the group can have on its members. Your threats and incentives may be meaningless to the employee, compared to the pressure he or she can expect from group-mates.

Groups exert this extraordinary influence largely through group norms. **Group norms** are "the informal rules that groups adopt to regulate and regularize group members' behavior."[6] They are "rules of behavior, proper ways of acting, which have been accepted as legitimate by members of a group [and which] specify the kind of behaviors that are expected of group members."[7]

Very often, it doesn't matter how skilled your employee is, or even if he or she wants to do a great job. His or her frame of reference will be, "What will my group say?" Studies show that "group norms may have a greater influence on the individual's performance than the knowledge, skills and abilities the individual brings to the work setting."[8] Indeed, this was one of the key findings from the first formal exploration into human relations at work. Researchers during a project known as the Hawthorne Studies described, for instance, how production levels that exceeded the group's norms triggered what the workers called "binging." Here, the worker's teammates slapped her hand for exceeding group production norms.[9]

Group norms may have a positive or negative (or neutral) effect from the company's point of view. At the Toyota assembly plant in Kentucky, positive group norms include "always do your best". Creating an environment that leads to the right norms requires effective team leadership skills, which we'll address later in this chapter.

◢ Group Cohesiveness

In turn, the extent to which a group can enforce its norms and influence its members' behavior depends to a large extent on the group's attraction for its members—on its **group cohesiveness.**[10] This makes sense. If a group's members don't feel a strong bond, the group is less likely to influence its members. The last thing you want to face as a supervisor is a very cohesive team with bad norms. Indeed, if your group is hopelessly anticompany, your best bet might sometimes be to undercut its cohesiveness.

Group cohesiveness depends on several things, some of which are under the supervisor's control:

- One is *proximity*. One way to undercut a group is to split its members up, placing them each in different locations.
- Individuals tend to be attracted to a group when they find its activities or goals attractive. Therefore *agreement on goals* boosts cohesiveness, while differences reduce it.[11]
- The saying "opposites attract" is sometimes true, but people usually choose friends (and group colleagues), at least initially, based on *similarities*, such as age, gender, and (to some extent) academic achievement and intelligence.[12] At least in the short run, bringing diverse members in undercuts cohesiveness; reducing diversity increases it.
- Intergroup competition can boost cohesiveness (particularly for the winning group), whereas *intra*group competition (among the group's members) tends to undermine it.[13] Want to build cohesiveness? Help your group to win. Want to undercut its cohesiveness? Set them up to lose.
- *Abrasive*, antagonistic, or inflexible team members can undermine group cohesiveness.
- Group cohesiveness tends to decline as group size increases beyond five to six members.[14] "Members are generally less satisfied with the group if the size is increased [beyond five to seven members]."[15] Larger groups tend to split into two or more, often opposing, subgroups.[16]

How Do Group Dynamics Impact the Development of Effective Teams?

So in summary, a Machiavellian (scheming) supervisor who wanted to undercut a hostile work group's influence might try dispersing its members to various locations or work schedules, setting up competitions with other groups where the errant group is likely to lose, adding one or two obnoxious group members, and adding, say, eight or nine new people to the group.

RESEARCH INSIGHT   Sometimes cohesiveness is a matter of survival. Researchers analyzed mortality rates for Pennsylvania heart surgeons who each practiced at more than one hospital.[17] It turned out that patients usually did best in the hospital where the surgeon performed more operations. This is probably because in the hospital where the surgeon did most operations, his or her interactions with the surgical team (consisting of nurses, technicians, and anesthesiologist) were smoother and more predictable. Similarly (although the results here are hardly as grave) National Basketball Association teams whose players are together longer tend to win more games. This may be because these are more cohesive, and its members can more easily anticipate what colleagues are going to do as they move down the court.

BUILDING GROUP COHESIVENESS   Unlike our Machiavellian supervisor (who weakens group cohesiveness by adding obnoxious members) you will almost surely do all you can to promote your group's cohesiveness. A list of research-based cohesiveness suggestions would include the following:[18]

- **Make it easy for the group to be close together.** Physical proximity enhances cohesiveness. Use video cams, frequent virtual meetings, and other information technology devices such as group decision-making software where distance makes physical proximity impractical.
- **Focus on and foster similarities among group members.** Do what you can to highlight and emphasize the group members' similarities, rather than their differences.
- **Put a positive spin on the group's performance.** In general, winning builds cohesiveness and losing diminishes it. Set some early tasks that you're pretty sure your group will "nail." And if they fail at something, find some positive aspect to emphasize.
- **Help the group build identity.** Whether it's T-shirts with a team logo or some other team-builder, help your group crystallize what their mission is and what makes them special.
- **Keep the group size manageable.** To the extent you can, don't let your immediate group exceed more than, say, 10 or so people.
- **Challenge the group.** Give them an attainable goal or challenge to achieve, and reward them when they succeed.

In this chapter, we'll show you how supervisors use knowledge like this to improve the effectiveness of their teams. First, though, let's briefly discuss the types of teams you might encounter at work.

3. The Basic Types of Teams at Work

Work Teams

Employers use teams at work in several ways.[19] *Work teams*, "continuing work units responsible for producing goods or providing services," are the most familiar.[20] An engine-installation team at Ford, the claims-processing team at Southern Insurance, and the team of miners who go underground each day at the Colorado Peabody Energy coal mine are work teams. The *management team* is a special work team responsible for the performance of a business unit (which might be the whole company, or a division.) At Ford, the engine installation team is a special type of work team in that it *self-manages* what it does (a "self-managing work team"). Sometimes the work team is *virtual,* insofar as its geographically separated members mostly meet online. We'll look closer at self-managing and virtual teams in a moment.

Work teams are parts of the regular organization, for instance, they do the work of assembling cars in a Ford factory. Sometimes, though, companies must pull together employees from various departments to serve on special temporary cross-functional teams, for instance, problem-solving teams. Some management experts call such teams *parallel teams*, because they exist in parallel with the regular organization to solve special problems.[21] We'll address special types of teams and their unique needs next.

Suggestion Teams, Problem-Solving Teams, and Quality Circles

It is often said that no one knows as much about workplace problems and how to solve them as do the employees themselves. Three types of teams exist to enable employers to tap employees' knowledge, with the aim of improving workplace functioning.

Suggestion teams are temporary teams whose members work on specific analytical assignments, such as how to cut costs or raise productivity. Some employers formalize this process by appointing semipermanent **problem-solving teams**. These teams identify and research work processes and develop solutions to work-related problems.[22] They usually consist of the supervisor and five to eight employees from a common work area.[23]

A **quality circle** is a special type of formal problem-solving team, usually composed of 6 to 12 specially trained employees who meet once a week to solve problems affecting their work area.[24] The team first gets training in problem-analysis techniques (including basic statistics). Then it applies the problem-analysis process (problem identification, problem selection, problem analysis, solution recommendations, and solution review by top management) to solve problems in its work area.[25]

Project Teams

Project or **development teams** operate, often "semi-autonomously," outside the usual chain of command to manage creating, delivering, or building a new product or service.[26] They often consist of professionals like marketing experts, editors, or engineers. They work on specific projects like designing new processes (process-design teams), new products (product-development teams), or new businesses (venture teams).[27]

Virtual Teams

Problem-solving and project teams sometimes don't physically meet at all. For example, the project team overseeing the construction of a large chemical plant in China may consist of members from vendors and suppliers in many different countries. **Virtual teams** are groups of geographically and/or organizationally dispersed workers who are assembled and who interact using a combination of telecommunications and information technologies to accomplish an organizational task. Being virtual, they require some special supervisory skills.

TECHNOLOGY AND VIRTUAL TEAMS   Virtual teams depend on information technology for communications. Desktop videoconferencing systems are often the heart around which firms build virtual technologies. Communication here can thus include the body language and nuances of face-to-face communications.[28] These teams also use collaborative software systems. For example, Microsoft offers a NetMeeting conference system. WebOffice (http://www.weboffice.com/) enables geographically separated employees to meet together online. When WebOffice is combined with products like Framework Technologies Corp.'s ActiveProject 5.0, virtual team members can hold live project reviews and discussions and then store the sessions on the project's Web site.[29]

BUILDING TRUST IN VIRTUAL TEAMS   One big challenge in supervising a virtual team is this: "Given the lack of in-person interaction, how do you build trust among team members?" Supervisors should know that according to one study, virtual teams with the highest levels of trust had several characteristics.

1. First, team members began their projects by *introducing themselves* and providing some personal background. They didn't just start off by focusing on the team's task.[30]

2. Second, each member had a *specific task and role.*

3. Third, high-trust virtual teams had the *right attitude.* Team members "consistently displayed eagerness, enthusiasm, and an intense action orientation in all their messages."

4. Fourth, effective teams also respected *cultural differences.* For example, team members avoided using cultural idioms (like "apples to oranges").[31]

GUIDELINES FOR IMPROVING VIRTUAL TEAM EFFECTIVENESS   One study found that the main challenges a virtual team faces are building trust, cohesion, and team identity, and overcoming isolation among virtual team members. The supervisor can help meet these virtual team challenges as follows:[32]

- Make sure everyone responds rapidly to virtual teammates (to foster trust).
- Establish norms encouraging open and honest communications.
- Use decision-making software to facilitate problem solving and decision making.
- Give virtual team members a realistic preview of the potential for feeling detached.
- Give virtual team members opportunities for occasional face-to-face contact.
- Use current virtual team members to help recruit and select new team members.
- Use "richer" communication media, including videoconferencing for performance evaluation feedback.[33]

Supervising Self-Directed Work Teams

In many facilities today, specially trained teams of self-managing employees do their jobs with little or no oversight from supervisory personnel. A **self-managing/self-directed work team** is "a highly trained group of around eight employees, fully responsible for turning out a well-defined segment of finished work."[34] The "well-defined segment" might be an entire jet engine, an Acura dashboard, or a fully processed insurance claim. In any case, the distinguishing features of self-directed teams are that (1) they are empowered to supervise and do virtually all of their own work, and (2) their work results in a singular, well-defined item or service. Supervising a team like this is therefore in a class by itself.

Some companies organize the work of entire facilities around self-managing teams. For example, the GE aircraft engine plant in Durham, North Carolina, is a self-managing team-based facility. The plant's 170 workers work in teams, all of which report to one boss, the factory manager.[35] In teams like these, employees "train one another, formulate and track their own budgets, make capital investment proposals as needed, handle quality control and inspection, develop their own quantitative standards, improve every process and product, and create prototypes of possible new products."[36] Getting this much autonomy can be very motivational. As the vice president of one company said about organizing his firm around teams, "People on the floor were talking about world markets, customer needs, competitors' products, making process improvements—all the things managers are supposed to think about."[37]

STAGES IN THE DEVELOPMENT OF A SELF-DIRECTED TEAM Employers typically go through several stages in organizing the company's work around self-directed teams. First, an executive steering committee ascertains the feasibility of a team-based organization. It then writes a mission statement for the program and selects the initial sites that will have the teams. Next the company designs a multilevel network of teams, such as the plant management team and the design, purchasing, and assembly teams. It then specifies what tasks each team will do, and how the teams will overlap, and assigns employees to the teams. Then each new team goes through several predictable stages, which the supervisor should be aware of.

What Should a Supervisor Expect During the Formation of Self-Directing Work Teams?

Forming Stage.   At start-up, the teams and their leaders begin working out their specific responsibilities in what experts call the forming stage. Here they also start building friendships and working through questions they may have with the team's purpose, structure, and leadership.[38] At this stage, the employees have to learn how to communicate and how to listen, how to use budgets, and how to work together as a team.[39]

The main supervisory task here is training for all involved.[40] Team members must learn how to communicate and how to listen, how to use budgets, and how to develop other similar skills. Supervisors must learn how to become facilitators and coaches rather than bosses.

Storming Stage.   Once the initial enthusiasm wears off, doubts may surface. In this "storming" stage, questions typically arise regarding who is leading the team and what its structure and purpose should be. With the initial enthusiasm diminished, team members may become concerned about whether their new (self-imposed) higher work standards may backfire at raise time. Supervisors start becoming concerned about their apparently shrinking roles.

The chief danger here is that a vacuum develops. Rather than remaining self-directed, the team lets a team member become its de facto boss. The supervisor needs to make sure everyone has an equal opportunity to lead, and that consensus decision-making prevails.[41]

Norming Stage.   Here team members agree on matters like purpose, structure, and leadership, and on important norms such as for cooperation and quality. Now they are a true self-managing team.

Misplaced loyalty is the potential problem now. The team's newfound cohesiveness, loyalty, and norms can prompt it to cover up for underperforming members. The supervisor's job is to emphasize the need for the team to temper loyalty with the responsibility to supervise its own members.[42]

Performing Stage.   The *performing* stage is hopefully a period of productivity, achievement, and pride as the team members work together to get the job done.

Adjourning Stage.   Finally, there may be an *adjourning* stage as the team splits up. Here, the team members face the mixed emotions of separation and of satisfaction over a job well done.

4. How to Evaluate Team Performance

Throwing several people together doesn't make the group a team, and certainly not a productive one. Before the supervisor can address a team's problems, he or she needs to be able to recognize what the problems may be. You need to be able to size up how the team is doing.

Does Teamwork Work?

The evidence regarding work-team productivity is quite mixed. After one Kodak division organized its work activities around teams, its unit costs declined by 6% per year and its productivity rose by over 200% in six years.[43] On the other hand, one highly publicized failure occurred in the U.S. factories of Levi Strauss.[44] As competitors with cheaper sources overseas cut into Levi's sales, the firm sought higher productivity in its U.S. factories. It decided to reorganize around teams.

LEVI'S EXAMPLE   At the time, most of the firm's U.S. plants operated on a piece-work incentive system. The firm paid each worker a sum for each specialized task (like attaching belt loops) that he or she finished.[45] The new Work Team Program changed that. Now a team of 10 to 35 workers constructed each pair of pants together, sharing all the tasks. The team was paid according to the total number of pants it finished each day. Levi's assumption was that this new arrangement would encourage employees to do several jobs instead of one, hopefully reducing boredom and boosting productivity.

It didn't work out that way. Faster workers found their wages pulled down by slower ones. Morale fell and arguments ensued. At some plants, such as in Morrilton, Arkansas, Dockers that previously cost $5 to stitch together now cost $7.50.

The results weren't entirely grim. Teams that were more homogeneous (in terms of work skills) did see productivity rise. Levi Strauss decided to continue the Work Team Program at its remaining U.S. plants. But for 6,000 of its U.S. employees, that is now irrelevant. Levi's soon announced it would close 11 U.S. plants and dismiss one-third of its U.S. employees.

RESEARCH INSIGHT   Unfortunately, studies suggest that team incentives are often counterproductive. A researcher studied business students enrolled in a graduate online MBA program who worked in teams.[46]

The fundamental problem was inequity. In many cases, each team member's financial compensation was the same, although one or two people "did the lion's share of the work." In other cases, the employer chose one or two team members for promotion, leaving others to feel they'd worked hard to support someone else's career. The bottom line is that unless you minimize inequities, it's probably best to pay employees based on their individual contributions to the team, rather than on collective team performance.

Results such as these underscore the fact that the supervisor needs to remain vigilant for signs of team ineffectiveness. There are several signs to look for.

Symptoms of Unproductive Teams

POOR PERFORMANCE   Various symptoms should signal to you that you have a problem team.[47] Of these low performance is often the first sign. As at Levi Strauss, the team's performance falls off, often dramatically. But first, more subtle early-warning signs may signal that trouble is brewing.

Conflict within the team. Problem teams are often characterized by a breakdown in team cohesiveness. Particularly be attentive to a suspicious, combative situation and arguments among team members

Lack of agreement or disagreement. Lack of either agreement or disagreement among team members may reflect team members' mistrust, and therefore their unwillingness to share their feelings and ideas.

Cautious or guarded communication. Conflict and mistrust may reveal itself in team members being guarded in what they do or say.

Lots of personal criticism. Personal criticism, such as "That's just the sort of ridiculous idea we can always expect of you," is a sign of unhealthy team relations.

Malfunctioning meetings. Unproductive teams often have malfunctioning meetings characterized by arguments, boredom, lack of enthusiasm, failure to reach decisions, and dominance by one or two people.

Unclear goals. Productive teams have a clear sense of mission. Members of unproductive teams often can't recite their teams' objectives.[48]

Signs of Productive Teams

Of course, you don't want unproductive teams, you want productive ones.

What are the signs of a healthy team situation? For one thing, the team exhibits few of the issues above (like conflict, or cautious communications). Beyond this, the following characteristics typically signal that the team will be effective.[49]

A CLEAR AND COMMITTED DIRECTION   Effective teams are never aimless, but instead have a clear direction. This requires three things. Effective teams have a *clear mission or purpose*, such as "Build a world-class quality car." Next, they then translate their common purpose (such as "build world-class quality cars") into tangible team *goals* (such as "reduce new-car defects to no more than four per vehicle"). Finally, effective teams are *committed to their mission*. Whether it's a work team at Boeing or Tom Hanks's team in the 1990s movie *Saving Private Ryan*, team members are committed to achieving their missions. When you speak to them on the factory floor, team members view themselves as mutually accountable and as "all in this together."

CIVILITY   Behavior in effective teams is civil, meaning courteous, respectful, and polite. Team members are willing to listen to others in order to achieve interpersonal understanding. There are open communications, and members openly share their opinions and provide timely feedback. Team members are tolerant of other members' style and behavioral differences. When disagreements do arise, the team handles them productively and courteously.

CLEAR ROLES AND ASSIGNMENTS   Team members know what their jobs are. They agree about who does particular jobs, how schedules are set and followed, what skills need to be developed, what members have to do to earn continuing membership in the team, and how to make decisions.

HEALTHY INFORMAL RELATIONS   Interpersonal relations within the team are comfortable and relaxed. There is a willingness to share, in that members seek out and willingly accept the knowledge, experience, and support of other team members.

CONSENSUS DECISION MAKING   If it's a self-managing team, look for evidence of consensus decision making. In expressing ideas and suggestions, all members "have their day in court." Some members may believe that there is a better alternative. But they still accept the wisdom of letting, say, a "consensus" vote of 80% prevail. Participation by everyone in discussing the pros and cons of decisions facilitates member buy-in.

How Does a Supervisor Evaluate Team Performance?

5. How to Build a High-Performing Team

To this point, we've looked at sizing up teams, and at the symptoms of unproductive teams and of productive ones. The question now is, "What exactly can I do to improve my team's effectiveness?

Hire Team Players

Unfortunately, the first (and probably most important) step is one over which you may have little control. When forming a new team, you may have the luxury of choosing people with the technical and interpersonal skills the team and its mission require.[50] However, that's usually not the case when you're supervising intact groups, where the team already exists. Everyone has served on teams with someone who did more harm than good. Perhaps the person wouldn't do his or her share of the work, or was disruptive. As one writer put it, "Some people . . . find it difficult to subordinate their inner drive to that of their team members. Like it or not, they end up being labeled as 'not team players' and may have hurt their career potential because of their behavior."[51] In such situations, the supervisor may just have to make do with the people he or she is assigned.

But in most instances you probably will have some discretion. If so, you should use your interviewing skills to pick the people you think will best fit.

The actual mix of traits you seek in new members depends on several things, including "the type of team being formed (such as problem analysis team vs. permanent work team), tasks performed, the team's level in the organization, the length of time it has been in existence, and the ease of substitutability of existing members."[52] Thus for a temporary problem-solving team you may look for problem analysis skills and be more willing to tolerate some abrasiveness. For a permanent work team, the latter trait might be unacceptable. Agreeableness is more important in a self-managing team than it might be in, say, a commando group in Iraq. In general, though, there are some traits that most teams can benefit from; we'll look at these next.

GENERAL "TEAMWORK" TRAITS   You are, first, usually looking for someone who'll fit in. In most (but not all) instances, teams with *agreeable* and *conscientious* team members usually do best. *Abrasive, obstructionist* individuals will tend to have a centrifugal impact on the team.

In general, the likelihood of someone being a team player reflects his or her tendency to be "individualistic" or "collectivist" in how they approach things. Individualists tend to prefer doing things their own way and working alone. *Collectivists* prefer working with others. Figure 11.1 provides a rough measure. Circle your answers, and then add up your score. In one study of 492 undergraduate students, the average score was about 89. Scores below 65 to 70 may suggest a strong preference for working alone. Scores above 110 or so may indicate a "preference for collaborating with others."[53]

THE RIGHT STUFF   But again, what is "best" for one team situation or task will be different in another. For example, choosing shuttle astronauts traditionally requires finding candidates who have what one popular book (and film) called "The Right Stuff"—that perfect combination of judgment, stress tolerance, courage, collegiality, and flying skills.

As another example, Nucor Steel's former CEO, H. David Aycock, looks for "positive thinkers" and "unselfish people."[54] Each Big Apple Traveling Circus comprises a diverse group. It includes "Chinese acrobats, Russian and Polish aerialists, elephant trainers from the United States, a French clown, the Danish equestrian, and a bird trainer from England."[55] Big Apple's founder and director, Paul Binder, says "The most important part of putting together and managing a great diverse team is picking the right people at the start. . . . They're people with talent, of course. But they're also people who get along—who can engage with others."[56] Here's how he selects his performers:

> When I find out about potential acts for the Circus, I visit with them and I watch them. I'm looking for skill. They have to be a great act. . . . But along with that, I try to spend quite a bit of time talking with them. What I'm listening for is a certain kind of flexibility—a willingness to work outside their own conceptions of what "has to be." For instance, I might say to them, "You know, I think we might want to change your costumes or music. How do you feel about that?" I want to hear openness. I want to get a sense right off that they're willing to create something bigger than their individual act.[57]

Sometimes it comes down to choosing people who have the right decision-making style for the job. For example, Kolbe WAREwithal® online (http://www.warewithal.com) lets

Do You Have a Team Mentality?

Source: Adapted from J. A. Wagner III, "Studies of Individualism—Collectivism: Effects on Cooperation in Groups," *Academy of Management Journal*, February 1995, p. 162.

Circle the answer that most closely resembles your attitude.

		Strongly Disagree				Strongly Agree		
1. Only those who depend on themselves get ahead in life.		7	6	5	4	3	2	1
2. To be superior, a person must stand alone.		7	6	5	4	3	2	1
3. If you want something done right, you must do it yourself.		7	6	5	4	3	2	1
4. What happens to me is my own doing.		7	6	5	4	3	2	1
5. In the long run, the only person you can count on is yourself.		7	6	5	4	3	2	1
6. Winning is everything.		7	6	5	4	3	2	1
7. I feel that winning is important in both work and games.		7	6	5	4	3	2	1
8. Success is the most important thing in life.		7	6	5	4	3	2	1
9. It annoys me when other people perform better than I do.		7	6	5	4	3	2	1
10. Doing your best is not enough; it is important to win.		7	6	5	4	3	2	1
11. I prefer to work with others in a group rather than work alone.		7	6	5	4	3	2	1
12. Given a choice, I would rather do a job where I can work alone rather than doing a job where I have to work with others in a group.		7	6	5	4	3	2	1
13. Working with a group is better than working alone.		7	6	5	4	3	2	1
14. People should be made aware that if they are going to be part of a group, then they are sometimes going to have to do things they do not want to do.		7	6	5	4	3	2	1
15. People who belong to a group should realize that they are not always going to get what they personally want.		7	6	5	4	3	2	1
16. People in a group should realize that they sometimes are going to have to make sacrifices for the sake of the group as a whole.		7	6	5	4	3	2	1
17. People in a group should be willing to make sacrifices for the sake of the group's well-being.		7	6	5	4	3	2	1
18. A group is most productive when its members do what *they* want to do rather than what the group wants to do.		7	6	5	4	3	2	1
19. A group is most efficient when its members do what *they* think is best rather than do what the group wants them to do.		7	6	5	4	3	2	1
20. A group is most productive when its members follow their own interests and concerns.		7	6	5	4	3	2	1

Add your answers to calculate your score. The higher your score, the higher your collectivist orientation, so high scores are more compatible with being a team player.

potential team members take an online test. This classifies employees based on four basic styles—fact finder, follow-through, quick start, and implementer.[58] Others use the Myers-Briggs test (see Chapter 10) to build teams around employees' sensing-intuitive-thinking-feeling styles.

Guidelines for Building Higher Performing Teams

What Are the Keys to Building a High-Performing Team?

Faced with an underperforming team, the actions you take will depend on what you think is the problem. We've seen that what your team *should* exhibit is:

- A clear and committed direction
- Civility
- Clear roles and assignments
- Healthy informal relations
- Consensus decision making (as appropriate)

Therefore, as far as solutions for poor team performance go, the low-hanging fruit is to make sure that your team understands its mission and that each member knows how you measure the team's success. Then, foster civility. Set a good "civility" example by being supportive and by encouraging and reinforcing positive interactions and cohesiveness within the team. Effective teams have rules of conduct to help them achieve their performance goals. The most critical rules (norms) pertain to attendance (for example, "no interruptions to take phone calls"), discussions ("nothing is off the table"), confidentiality, using an analytic approach, and constructive confrontation (no finger-pointing). If necessary, try to rehabilitate obstructionist team members; if that's impossible, a change may be required. Table 11.1 provides a checklist for turning an underperforming team around.

■ Table **11.1**

A Checklist for Turning the Team Around

- **Goal Setting** (Clarify Expectations as to Desired Team Behaviors)
- **Leadership**—Model Desired Team Behaviors
- **Structural Changes**—Such as Reporting Relationships, Required Relationships, Required Interactions, Pairing, Task Enrichment
- **Empowering Group** as a Whole—e.g., Allow for Group Decision Making and Problem Solving
- **Changing Performance Management** System—Especially Reward/Behavior Links
- **Formal Training** in Deficient Areas
- **Team Member Coaching** by Team Leader or Peers
- **Behavior Modification**
- **Constructive Feedback**
- **Changing Membership** (Such as Transfers, and Infusion of New Members)
- **Holding a Retreat** to Kick-Start Change

Source: Laird Mealiea and Ramon Baltazar, "A Strategic Guide for Building Effective Teams." *Public Personnel Management*, Volume 34, No. 2, Summer 2005.

6. Leading Productive Teams

What Do We Know About How to Lead Effective Teams?

What Behaviors Do Leaders of Effective Teams Practice?

It's probably no wonder that when a professional sports team is doing badly, the first to go is usually—you guessed it—the coach. Leadership is certainly a main factor determining a team's effectiveness. We'll therefore look next at what we know about how the leaders of effective teams behave.

THE LIKERT STUDIES   Some years ago, psychologist Rensis Likert conducted what was then, and perhaps still is, one of the most extensive series of studies of work groups and how to lead such groups. His observations are probably as relevant now as they were when he first made them. He first laid out the rationale for organizing the work around teams. He said,

> Most persons are highly motivated to behave in ways consistent with the goals and values of their work group in order to obtain recognition, support, security, and favorable reactions from this group. It can be concluded, therefore, that *management will make full use of the potential capacities of its human resources only when each person in an organization is a member of one or more effectively functioning work groups that have a high degree of group loyalty, effective skills of interaction, and high performance goals.*[59]

Based on his studies, Likert also drew several conclusions about how the leaders of the most effective groups behave. His observations provide a roadmap for just about anyone leading a team today. Here's what he said:

> The high-producing supervisors and managers *make clear to their subordinates what the objectives are* and what needs to be accomplished and then *give them freedom to do the job.* These subordinates can pace themselves and can use their own ideas and experiences to do the job in the way they find works best. Supervisors in charge of low-producing units tend to spend more time with their subordinates than do the high-producing supervisors, but the time is broken into many short periods in which they give specific instructions, "do this, do that, do it this way, etc."[60]

And he went on to explain that,

> The leadership and other processes of the organization must be such as to ensure a maximum probability that in all interactions and all relationships with the organization each member will, in light of his background, values, and expectations, *view the experience as supportive* and one which builds and maintains his sense of personal worth and importance.[61]

WHAT EFFECTIVE TEAM LEADERS DO   In 2010, two behavioral scientists published a paper that summarized much of what is known about what effective team leaders do.[62] One of their main conclusions is that how the team's leader behaves depends on whether the leader is (1) getting the team organized and started, or (2) leading an ongoing team. Here's what they found.

First, they found that during the team's organizational, "start-up" phase, the leader's main focus should be on "structuring the team, planning the team's work, and evaluating the team's performance such that the team will ultimately be able to achieve its goal or objective."[63]

So here, as the supervisor charged with leading the team through this start-up phase, your important team leadership functions will include

> *ensuring the right mix of people* in the team; *defining the team's overall mission, goals, and standards* of performance; *structuring roles and responsibilities* in the team; ensuring all team members *are capable of performing* effectively; *making sense* of the team environment; and *facilitating feedback* processes in the team.[64]

Second, they found that the team's leader then must shift gears once the team is up and operating. During this second, "action phase," important team leadership functions include

> *monitoring the team* and its performance environment, *managing the boundaries* between the team and the broader organizational environment, *challenging the team* to continually improve, becoming involved in *performing the team's work, solving problems* that the team encounters, *acquiring resources* for the team, *encouraging the team to act autonomously*, and *cultivating a positive social climate* within the team.[65]

A Snapshot of How Effective Team Leaders Behave

From studies we get quite a clear image of how the leaders of effective teams behave and what they do. Here's a snapshot. Effective team leaders:

- Clarify their subordinates' objectives, what needs to be accomplished, and the standards of performance.
- Give team members the freedom to do the job.
- Ensure that each team member views the team experience as supportive.
- Ensure there is the right mix of people in the team.
- Ensure all team members are capable of performing effectively.
- Facilitate feedback to the team.
- Monitor the team and its performance.
- Manage the boundaries between the team and the rest of the company.
- Challenge the team to continually improve.
- Become involved in performing the team's work.
- Solve problems that the team encounters.
- Acquire resources for the team.
- Encourage the team to act autonomously.
- Cultivate a positive social climate within the team.

What Values Should Team Leaders Exhibit?

If you look back through that list, it's probably apparent that leading teams today means supervisors can't get away with being "the boss." In most situations, the best team leaders really are more like coaches. They don't get things done by saying, "You do this now, and you do that." Certainly, especially during the important start-up phase, they make sure everyone's on-board regarding the team's mission and performance standards. But mostly, the best team leaders view themselves as facilitators.[66] They ask themselves, "What can I do to help my team to succeed?" They focus on giving team members the self-confidence, authority, information, and tools they need to get their jobs done. They share decision-making responsibility and delegate decisions to the team.

Not everyone is cut out for this type of supportive leadership role. For one thing, it takes someone with the right personality. If you're not inherently a sociable, supportive-type person, leading teams may not be for you.

Similarly, not every leader is philosophically prepared to surrender the trappings of "being the boss" that leading teams requires. Supervising a team—and particularly empowered, self-managing teams—requires a special set of guiding personal values. Those supervising teams need to buy into four especially important values:

TEAM MEMBERS WILL DO THEIR BEST   Some supervisors bring to the job what professor Douglas McGregor called "Theory X" values. Deep down, they believe that people are lazy, need to be controlled, need to be motivated, and are not very smart. Assumptions like these will torpedo leaders of most types of teams. Instead, these leaders need to adhere to what McGregor called "Theory Y" values: that people like to work, have self-control, can motivate themselves, and are smart.

TEAM MEMBERS COME FIRST   Supervising effective teams requires people who genuinely respect other people. At the former Saturn auto plant in Spring Hill, Tennessee, for instance, team members used to carry a card that listed the firm's values, one of which is,

> We have nothing of greater value than our people. We believe that demonstrating respect for the uniqueness of every individual builds a team of confident, creative members possessing a high degree of initiative, self-respect, and self-discipline.[67]

I'M HERE TO COACH, NOT TO BOSS   Supervisors who can't break out of the "I give the orders around here" mold won't do well supervising teams. The best supervisors here believe that their main job is to facilitate and coach, not to boss.

TEAMWORK WORKS   It may seem obvious, but you have to believe in the wisdom and potential of getting things done via teams, or you're not likely to act in a way that supports teamwork.

Making the Transition from Supervisor to Team Leader

For many supervisors, moving from a traditional in-charge supervisor to a team's facilitator-coach is a shock. As one former executive put it:

> Working . . . under the autocratic system was a lot easier, particularly when you want something done quickly and you are convinced you know the

What Might Be Expected When Transitioning from Supervisor to Team Leader?

right way to do it. It is a lot easier to say, "OK, we're going to Chicago tomorrow," rather than sit down and say, "All right, first of all, do we want to go out of town? And where do we want to go—east or west?"[68]

In making the transition, the supervisor can expect four big things to change. Knowing what to expect can make the transition easier.

PERCEIVED LOSS OF POWER OR STATUS   Moving from supervisor to team leader often involves a loss of power and/or status.[69] One day you're the boss, with the authority to give orders and have others obey. The next day, you're a facilitator/coach, focused on making sure that your team has what it needs to do its job—to a large extent, without you. The accompanying leadership feature expands on how to deal with this leadership issue.

UNCLEAR TEAM LEADER ROLES   Team leadership—particularly when the team is a self-managing one—leaves the leader in an ambiguous situation: What exactly does the leader of a self-managing team do, anyway? This can leave the supervisor unsure of what he or she is there to do. Some companies worsen the situation by overemphasizing what the former supervisor (now team leader) is not: They'll tell you you're not the boss; you are not to control or direct anymore; and you are not to make all the hiring decisions any more.

In fact, team leaders do have vital duties (again see the leadership feature), for instance, as coaches and facilitators making sure that the team gets the resources that it needs. Top management's job is to ensure that the new team leaders understand what their new duties are.

JOB SECURITY CONCERNS   Telling former supervisors/new team leaders that "you're not in charge any more" understandably undermines their sense of security. After all, it's not

---

Leadership Applications for Supervisors

Distributed or Shared Leadership

As you can see, one of the more uncomfortable aspects of team leadership (at least to some supervisors) is that they're not conventional leaders any more. Instead, leadership is literally "distributed" or shared among team members. As one leadership paper says, "while 'Great Man or Woman' theories persist, the majority of leadership scholars now recognize that successful organizations are marked by a distributive, collective, complementary form of leadership."[70]

Leadership researchers say that shared leadership "refers to a team property whereby leadership is distributed among team members rather than focused on a single designated leader."[71] Thus on a team, everyone (collectively and individually) is expected to exhibit leadership, for instance, in terms of assuming responsibility for the direction of certain team projects, clarifying

what's to be done, and taking steps to motivate and influence team colleagues as they go about their tasks.

Of course, shared leadership doesn't just emerge by itself, so (ironically) the supervisor/leader must take steps to nurture it. One study found there were several things the supervisor could do here. These include (1) fostering an environment that encourages a shared purpose, social support, and "voice" (team members' ability to express their suggestions and concerns), and then (2) providing coaching as required.[72] The bottom line: Don't view the switch to leading a team as a loss of power; instead, take steps to make your team more effective by encouraging everyone on the team to act more like a leader.

unreasonable for someone to ask, "Just how secure is the job of managing a self-managing team?" For example, General Mills claimed much of the productivity improvement from its self-directed work teams came from eliminating middle managers.

Companies handle this security problem in several ways. Suppose a company decides to organize, say, a production facility around self-managing teams. Here many of the former line supervisors will find new jobs as facilitator/coaches in the new teams. As another example, when chemical firm Rohm and Haas's Louisville, Kentucky, plant changed over to self-directing work teams, it turned the redundant supervisors into training coordinators. The firm made them responsible for managing the continuing educational requirements of the plant's new teams.[73]

THE DOUBLE STANDARD PROBLEM   With their authority apparently usurped by the new self-managing teams, some supervisors feel like second-class citizens. Career-minded

Supervising the New Workforce

Leading Diverse Work Teams

With the workforce increasingly diverse, eventually you'll find yourself supervising a team composed of people of diverse ages, nationalities, and backgrounds. What sorts of problems can you expect? How should you address those problems? A recent study answers these questions.[74]

The researchers looked at 55 diverse teams in companies ranging from Nokia to Reuters Group PLC to the BBC. Most of the teams were diverse in terms of gender (32% women), age, nationality (26% British, 23% American, 23% European, 15% Asian, and 13% rest of world), and education (7% high school diploma, 50% undergraduate degree, 37% master's degree, and 6% doctorate).

In many cases, the teams crashed and burned. As the researchers say, "some could not deliver on time; others fell short of the hoped-for productivity. . . . Some teams broke up in acrimony and bad feeling; some foundered in incompetence." When they did fail, it was usually because team members just stopped communicating. They lacked trust and goodwill; team members withheld their individual knowledge from other team members.

The problem was not just the diversity, but the nature of the diversity and how the leader of each team dealt with it. In some teams, strong "faultlines" emerged between subgroups (for example, women versus men, French versus Asian, or young versus old) within the teams. Strong faultlines were particularly likely to emerge when demographic attributes multiplied. For example, if all women in a team were over 50 years old and all the men were under 30, gender and age formed a single, strong faultline.

Most of the teams suffered from such faultlines, but some still managed to be very successful teams. Why?

The most important factor in determining whether destructive faultlines emerged was the style of leader, and in particular the extent to which the group's leader was task-oriented or relationship-oriented. Some leaders in the study were able to adjust their leadership styles as the project progressed, say, beginning with a task orientation and then switching to a relationship orientation (or vice versa).[75]

Here's what the researchers suggest for supervisors of diverse teams:

1. **Diagnose the Probability of Faultlines Emerging** At the outset, think carefully about the diversity in the team and the likelihood of faultlines emerging among subgroups.

2. **Focus on Task Orientation When a Team Is Newly Formed** When many of the team leaders saw faultlines forming, their first reaction seemed sensible but was wrong: They focused on the relationships between members of the subgroups. They tried to help team members get to know one another better, hoping that socializing would reduce the faultlines. It turns out it made more sense for the leaders to instead focus the team's attention on the task at hand and on clarifying the team's mission, assigning tasks, clarifying the performance standards, and making sure the team had the resources that it required.

3. **Learn When to Make the Switch** Focusing on the task is crucial in the early stage to get the team so focused on the task that they get beyond the faultlines. But at some point, as in almost all effective teams, the leader needs to switch to a facilitator/coach/supportive role. "If the leader fails to make this switch, the team will slowly become less effective."[76]

supervisors should make sure that their employer has in place a transition plan for supervisors. This plan should clarify the (former) supervisors' new duties and pinpoint the training they'll receive as they (hopefully) transition from supervisor to team leader or some other role.

The accompanying New Workforce feature addresses the special team leadership issues involved with supervising diverse teams.

7. How to Use Groups to Make Better Decisions

Whether they're analyzing problems, working through a project management issue, or deciding how to assign the week's tasks, the team is making decisions. Unfortunately, as anyone who has been on a committee knows, in making decisions, groups can be a force for good or ill. Luckily, there's a solid body of knowledge we can tap regarding how leaders can improve a team's decision-making. We'll look at this next.

Pros and Cons of Group Decision Making

It's useful to first understand the potential pros and cons of having a group make a decision.

PROS   The advantages or pros are considerable. Pooling the experiences and points of view of several people means you may bring *more points of view* to bear. This may lead to more ways to define the problem, more possible solutions, and more creative decisions in general. Groups that come up with their own decisions also tend to *buy into* those decisions. This acceptance boosts the likelihood that the group will work harder to implement the decision once it's put into effect.[77]

CONS   However, while advocates say "two heads are better than one," detractors say "a camel is a horse put together by a committee." The desire to be accepted tends to *silence disagreement* and to favor consensus. That can actually reduce creative decisions instead of enhancing them.[78] In many groups, a *dominant individual* emerges who effectively cuts off debate and channels the rest of the group to his or her point of view. When groups are confronted by a problem, there is also a tendency for individual members to become committed to their own solutions; the goal then becomes *winning the argument* rather than solving the problem. Groups also take longer to make decisions.

Other strange things happen when groups make decisions. In one study, researchers had group members read an example of poor performance. Then they asked the group how it would discipline the poor-performing employee. Individually, each group member's decision was rather lenient. But when the group got together to discuss the punishment, its consensus decision was *more severe* than the average of the individual decisions.[79]

Groupthink is a special problem. It is "a mode of thinking that people engage in when they are deeply involved in a cohesive group, when the members' desire for unanimity overrides their personal motivation to realistically appraise alternative courses of action."[80] Many national disasters, including at least one space shuttle explosion, reportedly stemmed from group members' reluctance to go against the apparent will of

■Figure **11.2**

**Signs That
Groupthink May
Be a Problem**

Source: Adapted from information provided in Irving James, *Group Think: Psychological Studies of Policy Decisions and Fiascos*, 2nd ed. (Boston: Houghton Mifflin, 1982).

"Don't ask, don't question."	Group members censor themselves, refuse to ask probing questions, and withhold disagreement.
"You must conform."	Someone, probably a group member, pressures others to withhold dissent and to go along with the group decisions.
"We all agree."	Group members press on with making their decisions under the erroneous impression that all group members agree—possibly due to dissenters' silence.
"We're on a mission."	Group members frame their arguments in terms of what's right for the group's mission—electing the U.S. president, attacking a country, or beating a competitor, for instance—and assume, therefore, that what they're doing is right and ethical.
"Masters of the world."	Group members come to believe that the group is totally in command of the mission and can, therefore, do anything, regardless of the risks—they come to feel invulnerable.

the majority. Figure 11.2 presents groupthink's warning signs. (The first hint is usually an influential person pressing others, "Don't ask, don't question what we're doing here.")

Some Basic Tools for Improving Group Decision Making

As the supervisor, your job is to lead the team discussion in such a way that the advantages of group decision making outweigh its disadvantages. This really is a leadership issue. You need to exercise your influence to help the team make its decision. There are three popular tools you can use.[81]

DEVIL'S-ADVOCATE APPROACH   One way to avoid groupthink is to formalize the process of injecting criticism. With the "devil's-advocate approach" the group chooses an advocate to defend the proposed solution, and one to be the devil's advocate. The latter prepares a detailed counterargument. That person lists what is wrong with the solution and why the group should not adopt it.

BRAINSTORMING   With "brainstorming," the group members introduce all possible solutions without criticizing any of them, and then turn to evaluating them.[82] The technique is aimed at fostering creative solutions by encouraging everyone to make suggestions *without fear of criticism*. Brainstorming has four main rules:

1. Avoid criticizing others' ideas until all suggestions are out on the table.
2. Share even wild suggestions.
3. Offer as many suggestions and supportive comments as possible.[83]
4. Build on others' suggestions to create your own.[84]

PC-BASED DECISION SUPPORT SYSTEMS   Some teams use "electronic brainstorming." Group members interact anonymously via PCs instead of face-to-face, using special group decision-making software. This method generally results in a large increase in the number of high-quality ideas generated by the group, compared with face-to-face groups, perhaps because it reduces inhibitions.[85] Computerized group decision support systems can also improve a group's decision-making effectiveness by reducing problems like groupthink.[86]

**What Tools Does a
Supervisor Use to
Develop Sound
Decision-Making Skills
in Team Members?**

How to Lead a Group Decision-Making Discussion

Based on group decision-making studies, here's what you should do to lead an effective group decision-making effort:

1. *Make sure that all group members participate* and contribute. As discussion leader, this is your responsibility. Don't monopolize (or let someone monopolize) the discussion. Ensure that different points of view emerge.

2. *Distinguish between idea getting and idea evaluation.* These studies found that evaluating and criticizing proposed solutions and ideas actually inhibits the process of getting or generating new ideas. Yet in most group discussions, that's exactly what happens. One person presents an alternative, and others begin immediately discussing its pros and cons. Discussion leaders should distinguish between the idea-getting and idea-evaluation stages—forbid criticism until all ideas are on the table.

3. *Do not respond to each participant or dominate* the discussion. Remember that the discussion leader's main responsibility is to elicit ideas from the group, not to supply them.

4. *Focus on solving the problem* rather than on discussing historical events that you cannot change. As discussion leader, your job is to focus the group on obstacles that the team can overcome and on solutions it can implement.[87]

Chapter 11 Concept Review and Reinforcement

Key Terms

Development Teams, p. 323

Group Cohesiveness, p. 321

Group Dynamics, p. 320

Group Norms, p. 320

Groupthink, p. 337

Problem-Solving Teams, p. 323

Project Teams, p. 323

Quality Circle, p. 323

Self-Managing/Self-Directed Work Team, p. 324

Suggestion Teams, p. 323

Team, p. 319

Virtual Teams, p. 323

Review of Key Concepts

Work Teams	Work teams are examples of employee involvement programs, which allow employees to participate in formulating important work decisions or in supervising all or most of their work activities.
Group Dynamics	Group dynamics defines the building blocks of teams including group norms and group cohesiveness.
Group Norms	Group norms are the informal rules that groups adopt to regulate and standardize group members' behavior.
Group Cohesiveness	Group cohesiveness is the extent to which a group can enforce its norms and influence its members' behavior. Group members must feel a strong bond if the group is likely to influence its members.
Types of Teams	
Suggestion Teams	Temporary teams whose members work on specific analytical assignments.
Problem-Solving Teams	These teams identify, research, and develop solutions to work-related problems.
Quality Circles	A type of formal problem-solving team that meets regularly to solve problems affecting their work area.
Project Teams	Small groups of employees who manage and coordinate creating, developing, or building a new product or service.
Virtual Teams	Virtual teams are group of geographically dispersed workers who are assembled and who interact using a combination of telecommunication and information technologies to accomplish an organizational task.

Self-Directed Work Teams	A self-directed work team is a highly trained group of employees, fully responsible for turning out a well-defined segment of finished work. This team is empowered to supervise and do virtually all of their own work.
Unproductive Teams	Symptoms of unproductive teams include: • Poor performance • Team conflict • Disagreements • Guarded communication • Personal criticism • Unclear goals
Improving Team Effectiveness	Building a high-performing team depends first on hiring team players. Unfortunately, supervisors may have little control over who is chosen for the team.
Building Higher Performance Teams	Higher performing teams should exhibit: • A clear and committed direction • Civility • Clear roles • Healthy informal regulations • Concise decision making
Transition from Supervisor to Team Leader	Moving from supervisor to team leader often involves a loss of power and/or status. One day you're the boss and the next day you're a facilitator/coach. The supervisor moves from giving orders that others must follow to focus on making sure your team has what it needs to get the job accomplished with or without you.
Effective Leaders of Self-Managing Teams	Not everyone has the values to be an effective leader of a self-managing team. A successful team leader must adhere to the right values including: • Respecting people • Putting team members first • Trusting Team Members to do their best
Pros of Group Decision Making	Advantages of group decision making include: • Pooling experiences • Having more ways to define the problem • More possible solutions • More creative decisions • The likelihood that group members will work harder to implement their own decisions

Cons of Group Decision Making	Disadvantages of group decision making include: • The desire to be accepted leads to silence and disagreement • A dominant individual emerges and cuts off debate. Winning the argument becomes more important than solving the problem.
Group Discussion Leader Skills	These leader skills include: • Making sure all members participate • Distinguishing between idea gathering and idea evaluation • Not responding to each participant or dominating the discussion • Directing the group's effort toward overcoming surmountable obstacles.

Review and Discussion Questions

1. What is the difference between a group and a team?

2. Define group dynamics.

3. What influences group cohesion?

4. Give some examples of group norms.

5. Why have virtual teams become so popular in recent years? Explain.

6. In what type of organizational setting would we be most likely to see quality circles?

7. What are the symptoms of unproductive teams?

8. Why do supervisors not always have a choice in hiring their team members?

9. Why do many supervisors have difficulty in moving from supervisor to team leader?

10. What are some of the advantages of group decision making?

11. What are some of the disadvantages of group decision making?

12. What would you do to make a team you're in charge of more productive?

Application and Skill Building

Case Study One

Team Building at the Colorado Symphony Orchestra

Anyone checking the Web site of the Colorado Symphony Orchestra (CSO) a few years ago would have found a friendly message that the weekend concert series was sold out. A first-time visitor to the site would not realize that this orchestra, both artistically and financially successful, was largely the same group of musicians who watched the Denver Symphony Orchestra (DSO) declare bankruptcy a few years earlier. The musicians then decided to create a new team approach to orchestra management, and a new orchestra, the CSO, was born.

DSO's traditional orchestra management approach was complicated. Ticket sales were never enough to fund the full cost of production, so orchestras relied heavily on contributions from patrons to cover costs. These patrons often had advisory roles, and they could exert financial pressure by withholding gifts. An executive director usually manages the business side of an orchestra, while a music director manages the artistic side. Musicians were usually unionized. At DSO, there was a long history of labor–management problems. There were four work stoppages, the longest of which lasted more than 11 weeks.

The newly reorganized musicians opted for a cooperative team approach to running the orchestra. The basic concept was that all the stakeholders—musicians, staff members, and board—were to share in making decisions that affected the outcomes for the CSO. They planned to share the risks and potential rewards of running the orchestra as a team.

One of the key elements that made the agreement unique was the high level of musician involvement in managing the business. The musicians made a substantial financial commitment to the orchestra. They agreed to accept a low salary for the potential to share in surpluses generated at year-end. The goal was to keep musicians' salaries at no more than 50% of the operating budget. Since the musicians were making such a strong financial commitment, they also got a stronger voice in the operation of the orchestra. They held one-third of the seats on all governing committees and the majority of seats on the artistic committee (an area usually under the sole control of the artistic director).

The results were extraordinary. Ticket sales, a direct measure of customer satisfaction, soon increased more than 2.5 times. There were also substantial increases in contributions. However, the CSO isn't standing still. It has hired an experienced professional as executive director. The organization has also invested in developing future audiences with an aggressive youth education program, including two series of free concerts for school groups.

Although the orchestra has still not achieved the level of contributions it had hoped for, it is financially stable. The team-based structure at the CSO has proved to be a solid base from which to lead the orchestra.

1. Based on what you read in this chapter, what team-building values, concepts, and techniques did the CSO musicians (perhaps inadvertently) apply to build their new team approach to managing the orchestra? List at least eight reasons why you believe the CSO team does or does not have the necessary building blocks to function effectively as a team.
2. Specifically, what supervisory team leadership roles do you see the new executive director playing in CSO's team-based organization? What skills do you think he'll need? Why? How do you believe the addition of a new strong executive director will change the dynamics of the CSO's team-based structure?
3. To what extent could CSO's team-based structure work in other orchestras? Why?
4. Do you think the orchestra could apply the same team approach to conducting its presentations without a conductor? Why or why not?

Case Study Two

Building Teamwork at JetBlue

Although JetBlue is organized departmentally rather than around teams, teamwork plays a central role in the company's success. For one thing, at any point in time, JetBlue does have 30 or 40 "Tiger teams" working on specific, short-term projects. Furthermore, JetBlue knows that maintaining its lead as a low-cost, high-quality airline means making sure that in everything it does, JetBlue emphasizes teamwork—and it does this in a variety of ways.

First, it makes sure that the employees it hires are team players. The company uses a screening device known as "targeted selection." Targeted selection is a structured interview aimed at uncovering the extent to which the candidate follows (and has followed in the past) the company's five basic values of safety, caring, integrity, fun, and passion. The targeted-selection interview questions go far beyond the usual "tell me your strengths and weaknesses" types of questions that other companies tend to emphasize during interviews. For example, the JetBlue interviewer might ask a pilot candidate, "Describe a situation that challenged your skills as a pilot, and how you dealt with it." Similarly, JetBlue does extensive background screening to screen out those who might not fit well into the JetBlue team. For example, rather than just check with the 6–7 personal references the candidate provides, JetBlue interviewers ask these references, "Who do you know who might be able to give me some insights into this candidate?"—and then the interviewers check with those people.

JetBlue takes other steps to foster a sense of teamwork. For example, everyone makes a conscious effort to avoid unproductive meetings and in general to be very respectful of one another's time. In fact, every meeting the company holds typically has one or two self-appointed "time cops," who make sure the meeting doesn't last any longer than is necessary.

In general, therefore, there is a pervasive effort, both formally and informally, to hire team players, as well as to encourage a sense that "we're all in this together" and that teamwork is crucial for JetBlue's success. However, from a practical point of view, it seems likely that as JetBlue grows, it will become harder to maintain this team atmosphere (particularly as more employees get more specialized assignments). JetBlue is working hard to maintain its start-up, entrepreneurial atmosphere, and it knows that doing so was always going to be easier when the company was small than when it's much larger.

Assignment

You and your team are consultants to JetBlue's CEO, who is depending on your supervisory expertise to help him navigate the tough competition JetBlue is running into now. Here's what he wants to know from you:

1. What do you think of the steps JetBlue is now taking to ensure that it hires only team players? Create and list five specific structured interview questions you would use to help screen out nonteam players in order to supplement the current targeted selection interview.
2. Many of JetBlue's meetings now have "time cops" to make sure that everyone's time is respected and that the meetings last no longer than necessary. Based on the information in this chapter, list five other specific steps you would suggest JetBlue take in order to ensure that meetings are as short and productive as possible.
3. Show, in organization-chart form, what JetBlue's organization might look like if it made the decision to organize the company around teams.

Experiential Activities

Activity 1. Alex had a rough first day supervising a claims-processing team at an insurance company. His team members couldn't agree on who would be doing what job. They insulted each other and almost came to blows. Not much work was accomplished that first day. Alex felt as if he'd been eaten alive.

Supervising Team Effort

Purpose: The purpose of this exercise is to give you a better understanding of the importance of developing and leading team effort as a supervisor.

Required Understanding: You are going to develop a one-page summary plan, using the discussion of leading the team effort included in this chapter.

How to Set Up the Exercise/Instructions: Divide the class into groups of 4–5 students.

1. You want to answer the question of how Alex, starting his first day as a new supervisor, could have avoided the resulting problems indicating a lack of team cohesiveness.
2. Your group should develop an outline that Alex could have used to direct the efforts of his team members toward a cohesive team effort, making sure to avoid the potential reasons why some teams do not perform effectively.
3. Next, have a spokesperson from each group share their outlines with the other groups.
4. Follow with a class discussion involving all of the student groups and answer the question: Are there any other variables that could affect the formation and development of successfully functioning groups?

Activity 2. In many of the exercises throughout this book, you have been working in teams. Now, in teams of 4 or 5 students, compare team cohesiveness as the semester or quarter has progressed. Has it increased or decreased? What accounts for this? What group norms have evolved? How have these influenced group functioning? List the ways your team does or does not have the necessary building blocks to be a highly effective team.

Activity 3. You have undoubtedly worked on teams at school, at work, or socially with someone who obviously did not have what it takes to be a team player. In teams of 4 or 5 students, discuss your nominees for "the worst team player I ever worked with" (no names, please), including what he or she did to win your nomination. List five reasons why you believe the person is not suited to be a team player.

Role-Playing Exercise

The Dysfunctional Problem-Solving Team: The Situation

Northern Telecom of North America, with offices in Nashville, Tennessee, has been using customer service teams to answer and solve problems that businesses have with their telephone systems for over five years. They have, up to now, had great success in randomly placing 5–6 employees into these service teams, which after 3–4 months have developed a high level of group cohesiveness. Team 5A does not fit this success mold. The six members of this service team have never been productive; they argue with customers; and basically they do not get along with each other very well. The team has worked together for over one year and the company is thinking about disbanding the team altogether. This problem-solving team is dysfunctional, and they need to get their act together. A team spokesperson has asked to meet with their supervisors, as a team, to request that they reform as a self-managing team.

Instructions: All students should read the situation above. One student will play the role of the supervisor for Team 5A and the second student will play the role of team spokesperson. Each student should only read his or her assigned role below. Then both students should engage in a 15-minute conversation.

A class discussion will follow the role-playing presentation.

Team Spokesperson: Your role is to represent your work group. You admit that your team is not always on the same page and that you really do not like some of your teammates, but you want to make the case that your team could function better if it had more authority to direct itself. You want to convince your supervisor that you all want to and can self-manage.

Supervisor: You have seen how dysfunctional this team has been. They seem to represent a group of six different people going six different ways. Your argument is that if they can't make it as a problem-solving team, how do they expect to make it as a self-directed team? As far as you are concerned, you need to break up this group and start over. This team better have some good arguments for moving to self-management with little or no oversight from management personnel.

Questions for Class Discussion

1. Based on what you studied in this chapter, did the supervisor do a good job in discouraging this team from transitioning to a self-directed team?
2. If you were a team member, would you have said anything different in your approach to the supervisor?
3. As a problem-solving team, dealing with the customers, do you feel that these six members can be more functional and productive in the future?
4. If you were the supervisor in this situation, how would you go about saving this team?

12 Coaching and Communicating Skills for Leaders

CHAPTER OBJECTIVES

After studying this chapter, you should be able to answer the following questions:

1. Clear Communication: Why Is It Important for a Supervisor?
2. Can Understanding the Communication Process Improve the Message?
3. What Barriers Might Prevent Effective Communication?
4. What Specific Steps Can a Supervisor Take to Improve Interpersonal Communication?
5. What Are the Basic Principles That Govern Powerful Persuasion?
6. What Guidelines Do Experienced Negotiators Use to Improve Their Bargaining Positions?
7. How Can a Supervisor Improve Upward and Downward Communication from/to Team Members?
8. How Do Supervisors Use Coaching and Mentoring to Bring Out the Best in Team Members?
9. Besides Face to Face, What Other Forms of Communication Do Supervisors Use?
10. How Do Work Group Support and Decision Systems Facilitate Accomplishment of Goals?

OPENING SNAPSHOT
Sara Gets No Respect

Sara was fit to be tied. The office supervisor for a small law firm, she was telling her friend over coffee that "my employees disobey my instructions constantly." In the latest episode, "I told Hal to get someone in who could upgrade the office PCs' virus protection, and he hired some guy for a week who charged us $2,000, instead of a vendor like Best Buy's Geek Squad. How could he do such a thing? They never listen to me."

Supervising is an interpersonal vocation. Supervisors spend almost all their time with people, meeting with them, coaching them, and communicating, persuading, and negotiating with them. For example, one study found supervisors spent 53% of their time meeting with people, 15% writing and reading, and 9% on the phone.[1] Another found that, including meetings and interacting with customers and colleagues, supervisors spent 60% to 80% of their time communicating.[2] So to succeed in supervising, you have to be good at communicating.

Clear Communication: Why Is It Important for a Supervisor?

Furthermore, being good at communicating isn't just crucial for you; it's also crucial for your employees. Poor communicators have less satisfied subordinates. One study concluded, "Communication with one's superior was a significant predictor of job satisfaction, irrespective of job level."[3]

Some people think communicating just means talking or sending e-mails, but it really involves much more. The word *communication* derives from the Latin verb *communicare*, "to make common."[4] So how you communicate—whether by talking, Skyping, e-mailing, or some other way—is beside the point. Those are all just means to an end. **Communication** means exchanging information in such a way that you create a common basis of understanding and feeling. If (like Sara) you're not creating that common understanding, you're not communicating. This chapter explains how to communicate effectively.

1. Why There's More to Communicating Than Just Talking

A man drove up to a gasoline pump to fill his tank. The gas station attendant noticed three penguins in the back seat of the car and, curious, asked about them.

"I don't know how they got there," the driver said. "The penguins were there when I took the car out of the garage this morning."

The attendant thought for a moment. "Why don't you take them to the zoo?"

"Good idea," the driver said.

The next day, the same man returned to the station. In the back seat were the same three penguins, but now they wore sunglasses.

The attendant looked at them in surprise. "I thought you took them to the zoo!" said the attendant. "I did," the driver said, "and they had such a good time that now I'm taking them to the beach."

As you know from your own experiences, many things—misunderstandings or even fear—can distort the meaning of what people think you're trying to say.[5] Problems like these can cripple even the simplest supervisory leadership tasks, such as setting goals. In this first section we'll look more closely at what these communications barriers are.

The Communication Process

Because you've been communicating since you were young, you may think it's excessive to describe communicating in terms of a "process." But to better understand how

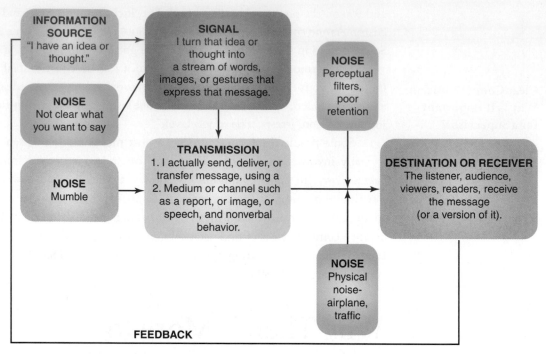

■Figure **12.1**

The Communication Process

Source: © Gary Dessler, Ph.D.

Can Understanding the Communication Process Improve the Message?

communication problems arise, it does help to visualize communication in terms of a process—one with a beginning, an end, and with various factors influencing how well (and even whether) the "message" gets from one end to the other.

Figure 12.1 shows that process. The process includes five main components (information source, signal, transmission, receiver, and noise). Problems (what communications experts call "noise") can arise at any step.[6]

For example, suppose you've appraised your subordinate, Joe, and now want to give him some constructive feedback. Let's work through the communications process to see where communication problems might arise.

- **The information source.** The information source is the message, idea, thought, or fact that you want to communicate. In this case, your subordinate has not performed well. The basic thought and understanding you want to communicate is this: "Your performance is below par. If it doesn't improve by the end of the year, we're going to have to let you go. However, we think you can do better and want to help you do so."

- **The signal.** The signal is the stream of words, images, or gestures you *actually* use to express the message. The signal *is what you actually "say"* to the employee when you meet with him, including the gestures and facial expressions you use to help communicate your point.

- **The transmission, and the channel or medium.** The day of the appraisal interview arrives, and you sit down with Joe. The *transmission* is the act of actually sending, delivering, or transferring the message, which you do using a *medium* or *channel*. The channel might be a report, image, speech, or some other; in this case it's a one-on-one interview.

- **The destination or receiver.** The destination or receiver is the listener, audience, viewer, or reader that you're actually aiming your message at—in this case, Joe the interviewee.
- **The noise.** Noise is any barrier that blocks, distorts, or in any way changes the *information source* (the idea, thought, or fact that you originally started out to communicate) as it makes its way to the destination/receiver. Noise can arise at any step in the communication process.

The interview does not go well. Hoping to lighten things up, you start the meeting with an irrelevant comment about the local football team, thus sending a muddled signal. Joe, having worried about this meeting for weeks, gets agitated. The more agitated he gets, the more you start mumbling. Annoyed, you finally blurt out, "Your performance this past six months has been unsatisfactory, and if you don't improve by the end of the year, we're going to have to let you go."

At this point, Joe, who is turning purple, is not getting the message. He hears "have to let you go," and insists that you can't fire him without warning, especially "considering my family situation" (his mother has been ill). You have not delivered your message. There is no "common basis of understanding and feeling." You both ignored the potential noise/problems/barriers at each step of the communication process. There is little chance that this meeting will prompt Joe's performance to improve.

What Barriers Might Prevent Effective Communication?

Noise: Barriers to Effective Communication

The situation with Joe didn't have to arise. You could have had a productive meeting by (1) keeping the goal of "creating a common basis for understanding and feeling" in mind, and (2) by anticipating the communication barriers/problems that could arise.[7] Again, *noise* is any barrier that blocks, distorts, or in any way changes the idea, thought, or fact that you originally started out to communicate. The main potential "noise" barriers include the following.[8]

AMBIGUOUS, MUDDLED MESSAGES   Few things cause communication breakdowns more often than ambiguous, muddled messages. "Say what you mean, and mean what you say" should be the rule. *Ambiguity of meaning* means the person receiving the message isn't sure what the person who sent it meant. (Does "We're going to have to let you go" mean immediately or next year?) *Ambiguity of intent* means the words may be clear, but the sender's intentions aren't. ("This is an appraisal interview. Why is he talking to me about the weather?") *Ambiguity of effect* means the receiver is uncertain about what the message's consequences might be. ("Is he actually going to fire me?") In any case, the solution is to send an unambiguous message.

The point is, be meticulous in translating what you *want to say* into what you *actually say*. Know what you want to say. Then, "Say what you mean, and mean what you say."

SEMANTICS   Words mean different things to different people. The attendant said, "Take the penguins to the zoo," but he didn't mean as tourists. Luckily for the penguins, the driver misinterpreted his words. Telling a hospital administrator that she has "scabs" in her hospital may signal a sign of recuperation to her, but something different to the head of the local union.

PHYSICAL BARRIERS   Physical barriers range from obvious to subtle. Street noise, frequent interruptions, and the clattering of machines are obvious distractions. Indecipherable writing and tiny fonts are less obvious sources of noise. Even discomfort is a source of noise. A recent ad for a desk chair says, "Think of what your brain could be accomplishing now, if it didn't have to worry about your back."

LOST IN TRANSMISSION   Everyone with cable TV is familiar with this problem, but loss of transmission is not limited to cables. People rarely relay messages without snipping from (or adding to) them in some way. You, therefore, cannot assume that the message you send will be exactly the one that reaches the destination.

FAILING TO COMMUNICATE   All these problems assume that you've actually sent a message. However, sometimes a message isn't even sent. For example, the supervisor may just assume that "everyone knows," and not follow up by sending a message.

COMPETITION BARRIERS   When you're communicating, the person you're speaking to is not "yours" alone. The students in a lecture hall will have matters they want to discuss among themselves or on Facebook; the employee you're appraising may have his mind on his sick mother; and that e-mail you sent may simply get lost among the two dozen messages your boss has to deal with that day. Many other things are competing for your audience's time and attention. Don't assume that you've got the person's full attention.

NOT LISTENING   Many communication efforts fail because one of the parties simply does not listen. This is why we'll see that "active listening" skills are crucial for supervisors.

Nonverbal Communication

The comment, "It's not what you say, but how you say it" is true. "It has been estimated that in a conversation involving two people, verbal aspects of a message account for less than 5% of the meaning, whereas nonverbal aspects of a message account for 95% of the meaning."[9] In other words (to use our terms), the *channel or medium* you use is not always what you think it is. You may think that you're just communicating with words. However, people also draw conclusions about who you are and what you mean from your manner of speaking, facial expressions, posture, and so on—from your **nonverbal communication**. And this can present a problem.

For example, here's how one expert interprets some common nonverbal behaviors:

1. Scratching your head indicates confusion or disbelief.
2. Biting your lips signals anxiety.
3. Rubbing the back of your head or neck suggests frustration or impatience.
4. A lowered chin conveys defensiveness or insecurity.
5. Avoiding eye contact conveys insincerity, fear, evasiveness, or (at the very least) lack of interest in what's being discussed.
6. A steady stare suggests a need to control, intimidate, and dominate.
7. Crossing your arms in front of your chest communicates defiance, defensiveness, resistance, aggressiveness, or a closed mind.

8. Handwringing is a strong sign of anxiety verging on terror.

9. In North America, getting a limp, dead-fish handshake is almost always a disappointment.[10]

CULTURE, DIVERSITY, AND NONVERBAL COMMUNICATIONS   The nonverbal aspect of communication especially complicates the task of communicating with people from different cultures. For example, gestures have different meanings in different cultures. The A-OK sign means "everything's fine" in New York, but may be a crude insult in South America. Supervisors often relax with their feet on their desks in America, but you'd insult someone in Saudi Arabia by showing them the soles of your shoes.

The nonverbal part of communicating is more important in some societies than in others.[11] For example, a sales supervisor in Michigan might e-mail an unsolicited sales pitch to a customer in Taiwan and be surprised when the person ignores the message. Yet, to the Taiwanese, ignoring such a message is quite understandable. In the United States, Canada, and northern Europe, the verbal content of a message tends to be more important. The setting (the sender's tone of voice and facial expression, for instance) in which you deliver the message is not so important. In such "low-context" cultures, people usually accept an e-mail as an efficient substitute for an in-person meeting.[12]

However, in many "high-context" countries (mostly in Asia and the Middle East), context or setting, including nonverbal signals, is hugely important. People from these areas rely on the context of the message to convey and understand the message's meaning. In that part of the world, business transactions tend to follow a ritual (such as not getting to the point of the visit until you've spent time on small talk). There's more emphasis on face-to-face interaction and on after-hours socializing. An unsolicited curt message to a person in Asia might well be ignored. Similarly, communicating with people from these cultures even here in the United States may well require, for instance, avoiding unsolicited and cryptic messages, and providing a more personal background for the message.

The accompanying Supervising the New Workforce feature expands on some potential cultural barriers in communicating.

Psychological Barriers

In addition to barriers like semantics, ambiguity, and nonverbal cues, *psychology* affects how we hear things. Psychological communications barriers include perception, experience, emotions, and defenses.

PERCEPTUAL BARRIERS   Misperceptions ruin communications. This is because people's needs and situations shape how they actually see (perceive) things, so that what they hear isn't what you said. If you're concerned about losing your job, you may be jumpy if your boss schedules a meeting with you.

Perception problems manifest themselves in several ways. For example, there's *selectivity*: Here, people block out unpleasant things that they don't want to hear, or "hear" things that may not be there. (After buying a new car, people tend to notice good news about the car and to screen out negative news about it). There's *retention*: People remember things that feel good and tend to forget those that are painful.

Cultural, Linguistic, and Diversity Barriers

There is always the potential for a Tower of Babel effect in today's diverse and globalized organizations. Words and gestures often mean different things in different ethnic and cultural groups. The classic (and much repeated example) occurred some years ago when General Motors marketers decided to sell the then-popular Chevy Nova in South America with the same name. The fact that *"no va"* means no-go in Spanish was lost on them.

Table 12.1 summarizes the results of a relevant study comparing communication tendencies of U.S. and Japanese managers. For example, the Japanese tend to be indirect and relationship-oriented, while U.S. managers are more direct and "get to the point"–oriented.

An informal survey of supervisors from 15 countries helps highlight this point. The supervisors listed "lack of cultural understanding" as the biggest challenge in communicating with people around the world. Other challenges (in order) were "being thorough and very careful with interpretations," "careful audience research," "keeping communication simple," "respecting everyone," "using technology as an asset," "knowing similarities as well as differences," and "teaching the value of a globally accepted language."[13]

■ Table **12.1**

Some Differences Between Japanese and American Communication Styles	
Japanese *Ningensei* Style of Communication	**U.S. Adversarial Style of Communication**
Indirect verbal and nonverbal communication	More direct verbal and nonverbal communication
Strategically ambiguous communication	Prefers more to-the-point communication
Delayed feedback	More immediate feedback
Cautious, tentative	More assertive, self-assured
Makes decisions in private venues, away from public eye	Frequent decisions in public at negotiating tables
Decisions via *ringi* and *nemawashi* (complete consensus process)	Decisions by majority rule and public compromise are more commonplace
Uses go-betweens for decision making	More extensive use of direct person-to-person, player-to-player interaction for decisions
Understatement and hesitation in verbal and nonverbal communication	May publicly speak in superlatives, exaggerations, nonverbal projection
Uses qualifiers; tentative; humility as communicator	Favors fewer qualifiers; more ego-centered
Shy, reserved communicators	More publicly self-assertive
Distaste for purely business transactions	Prefers to "get down to business" or the "nitty-gritty"
Utilizes *matomari*, or "hints," for achieving group adjustment and saving face in negotiating	More directly verbalizes management's preference at negotiating tables

Source: Adapted from *International Journal of Intercultural Relations* 18, no. 1, A. Goldman, "The Centrality of 'Ningensei' to Japanese Negotiating and Interpersonal Relationships: Implications for U.S.-Japanese Communications," copyright 1994.

EXPERIENCE BARRIERS   People's experiences also affect how they perceive things. Most people find it more difficult to understand things that they haven't experienced for themselves. So, convincing employees who've never been injured at work that it's important to work safely may fall on deaf ears.

On the other hand, people find it easier to understand things they can identify with. The director of one large research lab wanted to make the point to his firm's board of directors that managing research scientists wasn't easy. He made it by saying that managing the lab "is like trying to herd a pack of alley cats." Most of the board members had never experienced managing research scientists (or cats). However, they could identify with the difficulty of getting two dozen screaming alley cats all going in the same direction. He made his point by linking to something his audience could understand. So the moral here is to present plenty of recognizable examples.

EMOTIONAL BARRIERS   An angry or frustrated person may ignore even the most persuasive argument. Someone in a good mood may be more agreeable.

DEFENSIVENESS BARRIERS   Defenses are adjustments people make to avoid acknowledging personal inadequacies that might reduce their self-esteem. Accuse someone of poor performance, and his or her first reaction may well be *denial.* By denying reality, the person avoids having to confront his or her own competence. People who react this way aren't consciously distorting what was said. They're simply "hearing" and reacting to it in a way that protects their self-esteem.[14]

2. How to Improve Interpersonal Communication

We've just seen that a host of barriers can intervene between what you meant to say to someone, and what that person actually hears. There is *noise,* in the form of ambiguous muddled messages, semantics, physical barriers, loss in transmission, cultural misunderstandings, competition barriers, and not listening. There's the influence of *nonverbal* aspects of the interchange (such as when your apparent anger belies the gentleness of your words). And there are the *psychological factors* to consider, as when the subordinate's nervousness renders him or her incapable of understanding what you're trying to say.

And yet, you need to be able to get around these potential barriers. Tasks that require **interpersonal communication**—communication between two people—will fill your day. The supervisor disciplines an employee for breaking a rule, shows a new employee how to improve her performance, or tries to convince production employees to work harder. Barriers like ambiguity and defensiveness can cripple your efforts to make yourself understood, and thus your ability to lead. Your task is to make sure this does not happen. We therefore look next at how to become a better person-to-person communicator. Let's start with general interpersonal communications guidelines, and then turn to improving your persuasiveness and negotiating skills.

Guidelines for Improving Interpersonal Communications

What Specific Steps Can a Supervisor Take to Improve Interpersonal Communication?

First, what we know about the various communications barriers suggests following these interpersonal communications guidelines.

MAKE YOURSELF CLEAR   If you garble the initial message, then you're starting off at less than zero, as far as making yourself understood is concerned.

The fact is, most people are lazy when it comes to communicating their ideas. They do not take the time to conscientiously translate what they're thinking into words. Ambiguous, unclear communiqués therefore usually reflect sloppy thinking. Or, to restate this, fuzzy words reflect fuzzy thinking. Make sure you say what you mean. For example, if you mean immediately, say "immediately"; don't leave the timing open-ended or say something like "as soon as you can." Someone once said that good communicating is essentially a moral matter; not taking the time to translate what you're thinking into words is just lazy.

BE CONSISTENT   We know that much of what the other person hears reflects not just your words but your nonverbal tone and eye contact. Therefore, endeavor to be consistent. Make sure your tone, expression, and words send a consistent meaning. In terms of body language, come across as open and receptive. Maintain eye contact, smile, keep hands away from your face and mouth, use open-handed gestures. If you must achieve some subtle domination, direct your glance at the subordinate's forehead rather than meet his or her eyes directly.[15]

CONSIDER THE DISTRACTIONS   You'll rarely have the luxury of communicating with someone under perfect (distraction-less) physical conditions. There will almost certainly be interruptions, background noise, trucks driving by, and numerous other distractions. In delivering a particularly important message (a performance assessment or dismissal notice, for instance), try to do so under relatively tranquil conditions. And in delivering any message, factor in the potential distractions (for instance, by speaking louder, or by not shouting across the room).

CONFIRM "MESSAGE RECEIVED"   Airport flight controllers know that many sources of noise—static, cockpit noise, a pilot's preoccupation, language barriers—can undermine a message. Both pilot and controller are therefore trained to confirm and reconfirm the message ("Landing runway 13/31, over"). You should do the same.

DON'T ATTACK THE PERSON'S DEFENSES   There will be many times when communicating requires that you point out a subordinate's deficiencies. This just comes with the supervisor's territory. Yet doing so raises the risk that you'll run full speed into the other person's defenses. No one likes being criticized. The normal reaction is to mount a defense (as in, "No, I never said I'd do that").

The important thing here is, don't attack the other person's defenses. For example, don't try to "explain a person to him- or herself" by saying things like, "You know the reason you're saying that is that you can't bear to be blamed for anything." Comments like that will lead down a slippery slope of increasingly more bitter comments and counter-comments. Don't criticize the person. Instead, focus on the act itself ("Production levels are too low"). To minimize defensive reactions, words to avoid include *blame, catastrophe, demand, destroyed, idiotic*, and *misguided*. Phrases to avoid include *better shape up, don't come to me about it, don't want to hear it, figure it out for yourself, you don't understand*, and *you'd better*.[16]

BE AN ACTIVE LISTENER   As we said earlier, there's more to communicating than just talking. Your aim is not just to communicate the words, but to create a common understanding.

Psychological barriers make doing so particularly challenging. Our perceptions, emotions and defenses often mean that what one person says is different from what the other person hears. Behavioral scientist Carl Rogers said the way to get around this is with **active listening**. Active listening means taking steps to listen not just to what the speaker says, but to understand and respond to the feelings behind the words.[17] Active listeners try to understand the person from his or her point of view and to convey the message that they do understand. They use the following listening tools:[18]

- **Listen for total meaning.** For example, if the salesperson says, "We can't sell that much this year," the supervisor's typical knee-jerk response might be, "Sure you can." An active listener would instead strive to understand the underlying feelings (such as the pressure the salesperson is under): "I know how you feel, so let's see what we can work out."

- **Reflect feelings.** Show the person that his or her message is getting through. For example, say something like, "They're pushing you pretty hard, aren't they?"

- **Note all cues.** Remember that not all communication is verbal. Facial expressions and gestures reveal feelings, too.

- **Give the person your full attention.** Turn off the cell phone, ignore the computer screen, don't look at your watch.

- **Show that you are listening with an open mind.** Do not rush to interrupt the person or to finish his or her sentences. Avoid conversation-stopping phrases such as, "You've got to be kidding" and "Yes, but . . . " and judgmental body language such as rolling one's eyes.

- **Encourage the speaker to give complete information.** Ask open-ended questions. Confirm your understanding by paraphrasing, summarizing, and asking if your paraphrase or summary was the message the speaker intended.

How to Be More Persuasive

We often underestimate the importance of persuasion. As someone who studied business leaders said, "Persuasion is widely perceived as a skill reserved for selling products and closing deals."[19]

In fact, persuasiveness is a skill supervisors need in many situations. For example, if you are asking for a raise or trying to get your team to work harder, you need persuasiveness. We'll look at this special type of communicating next.

HOW TO BE UNPERSUASIVE If you think of the worst salesperson you've ever met, you'll probably agree that he or she made some glaring mistakes. Studies suggest that the typical mistakes people make when trying to persuade others include these:[20]

- **Ignore.** They ignore your point of view. They're so focused on selling their idea (why you should buy the car, why you should settle the lawsuit, or whatever) that they *ignore your wants and needs.*

- **Don't listen.** The corollary is that bad salespeople *don't listen.* They don't listen to your objections and ignore the feelings that underlie your inquiries.

- **Overwhelm.** They assume that the way to persuade you is to *overwhelm you* with a barrage of ideas, facts, and figures. Actually, this is more often a turnoff.

- **Resist.** *They resist compromise.* By failing to compromise, the person signals that he or she has a closed mind and isn't interested in reaching a common basis of understanding.

- **Argue.** *They assume the secret of persuasion lies in presenting great arguments.* In fact (unless you're on the debate team), logic is usually less influential than are the "seller's" credibility and ability to make the proposal in a way that appeals to you, the "buyer."

HOW TO BE MORE PERSUASIVE   The flip side is that there's a lot you can do to be more persuasive. Research shows that persuasion involves appealing to "deeply rooted human drives and needs." Therefore powerful persuasion "is governed by basic principles that can be taught, learned, and applied."[21] We can summarize these rules for you as follows:

- **Establish your credibility.** It's difficult to persuade anyone to do anything if they think you don't know what you're talking about, or if they don't trust you. To establish your creditability: *Marshal the facts* underlying your position; underscore your *expertise* (perhaps by listing your related accomplishments); and cultivate and mention *relationships* that help prove your credibility.

- **Persuade based on common ground.** Present your argument in terms that appeal to the other person. For example, relate your proposal to examples the person can relate to. ("Your friend Harry was in last week and bought the same type of car from me.")

- **Connect emotionally.** Car ads typically don't just sell transportation, but emphasize emotions such as family safety (Volvo) and prestige (Rolls-Royce). They do this because car buying is often as emotional as it is analytical. The same is true at work. It helps to understand the emotions underlying the other person's point of view. For example, a job transfer means uncertainty and possible loss of influence, not just a new title. Therefore, endeavor to link the "sale" to some deep-seated emotional need (such as for job security) that you believe you can address.

- **Provide evidence.** Once you've established your credibility, found common ground, and connected emotionally, persuasion becomes a matter of presenting supporting evidence. "The most effective persuaders . . . supplement numerical data with examples, stories, metaphors, and analogies to make their positions come alive."[22]

- **Use peer power whenever it's available.** It's easier to persuade someone to do something once you've established that others they identify with have done something similar.[23] A few years ago, the collapse of a big investment advisor wiped out about $50 billion of investors' savings in a pyramid scheme. Almost all those investors had apparently been drawn into doing business with him, not by ads, but by the word-of-mouth recommendations and referrals of friends.

- **Have the person make the commitment active, public, and voluntary.** People tend to align their actions with the goals they've set and with the commitments they've made. Therefore, if possible, get the person to declare his or her acceptance publicly.

What Are the Basic Principles that Govern Powerful Persuasion?

How to Improve Your Negotiating Skills

People are always negotiating at work. For example, obtaining more resources for your team, getting a raise, trying to get employees to cut their hours, and dealing with the union steward all require good negotiating skills.

FOUR WAYS TO HURT THE NEGOTIATIONS   One expert says that negotiators typically make four big mistakes, such as those in the following list, and suggests these ways to prevent them:[24]

- **Neglecting the other side's problems.** Like all communication, negotiations go best when they achieve a common basis of understanding. Ignoring or neglecting the other side's point of view makes it unlikely you'll reach an agreement.

- **Letting price overwhelm other interests.** There's a tendency for negotiators to focus on price, and for price to cause negotiations to fail. Ironically, discussing the deal's other terms might have saved the day. For example, a high price may look less foreboding if a store will finance the purchase.

- **Being preoccupied with searching for common ground.** Sometimes, it's best to accept that the parties have different agendas. For example, the potential buyer for a small company wants to do the deal but is much less optimistic about the firm's future prospects than is the firm's current owner. Here, structure a deal that takes into account these differences. For example, agree on a deal whereby an initial payment is followed by a series of payments contingent on the business's performance.

- **Neglecting BANTAs.** In their book *Getting to Yes*, Robert Fisher, Bill Ury, and Bruce Patton stress the importance of knowing your "best alternative to a negotiated agreement" (BANTA). For example, the best alternative may not be "doing" the deal, but walking away, or approaching another buyer. Don't become so wrapped up in finalizing a deal that you "give away the farm."

NEGOTIATING GUIDELINES   Experienced negotiators use *leverage, desire, time, competition, information, credibility, and judgment* to improve their bargaining positions.

- *Leverage* means using factors that help or hinder the negotiator.[25] Factors you can leverage include necessity, desire, competition, and time. For example, the seller who must sell (of *necessity*) is at a disadvantage. It's being able to walk away from a deal (or to look as if you can!) that wins the best terms.

- Similarly, the new car may not be a necessity, but if your *desire* is too obvious, it will undercut your bargaining power. Don't seem desirous. *Time* (and particularly your having to meet a deadline) can also tilt the table for or against you.

- There is no more convincing ploy than telling the other party that they've got *competition*—that someone else wants to make the deal.

- In negotiations, "knowledge is power." Having *information* about the other side and about the situation puts you at a relative advantage. It's imperative to go in armed with the facts.

- *Credibility* is important: The people on the other side will be trying to decide if you're bluffing, so convincing them otherwise is an important negotiating skill.

What Guidelines Do Experienced Negotiators Use to Improve Their Bargaining Positions?

- Finally, good negotiators need *judgment*: the ability to "strike the right balance between gaining advantages and reaching compromises, in the substance as well as in the style of [their] negotiating technique."[26]

3. Communicating Upward and Communicating Downward

A famous management article once described the first-line supervisor as "the man or woman in the middle." You've got a boss above you. And you have your subordinates below you. You're often the go-between, relaying your boss's instructions downward, and your employee's concerns upwards.

Much of the communicating you'll do, therefore, isn't just interpersonal, but also downward and upward. Downward, you'll want to keep your team apprised of where the firm is heading, what the company's new vacation policy means for them, and what the firm's required procedures and practices are. Upward, you'll want to keep your finger on the pulse of what's happening in your team or department (for instance, in terms of problems with new work procedures and suggestions for work improvements). Let's therefore look next at ways to improve upward and downward communications.

How to Encourage Upward Communication

There are good reasons to encourage upward communication. From a practical point of view, the one thing you do *not* want is to be blindsided by problems in your group, a likely occurrence if you never bother to check on how things are going. Beyond this, finding out what your people are thinking encourages subordinates to volunteer ideas. It also provides you with valuable input on which to base decisions,[27] encourages gripes and grievances to surface (so you can deal with them),[28] and cultivates acceptance and commitment by giving employees an opportunity to express ideas.[29] Upward communication helps you verify that subordinates understand orders and instructions, and helps them "cope with their work problems and strengthen their involvement in their jobs and with the organization."[30] And in general, it enables you to see how your subordinates feel about their jobs, superiors, and the organization.

INFORMAL STEPS TO TAKE   Given that it's so beneficial, the question is, "How do I improve the upward communications between me and my team?"

One expert says, "By far the most effective way of tapping the ideas of subordinates is sympathetic listening in the many day-to-day, informal contacts within the department and outside the workplace."[31] Never at a loss to complicate things, management gurus sometimes call this kind of listening "Management by Walking Around." As one executive put it, "Go visit the department heads—chat with them, ask questions, learn what they do for a living. Ask them what is frustrating for them in their business process, and they will talk all day if you let them. You'll learn a great deal about how the cogs mesh."[32]

A classic example of how *not* to do this occurred at Harvard University several years ago. Lawrence Summers, then Harvard University's new president (and then for two years chief economic advisor for President Obama) had an interesting way of eliciting upward communication. He started debates (some say arguments) with the groups with whom he was talking.[33] For example, shortly after arriving at Harvard, Summers reportedly astonished law school professors who had invited him to meet Harvard's legal scholars. In this instance, he triggered a heated debate by arguing that it was fair to use age as a factor in awarding tenure to professors. He went on to get into a public feud with Professor Cornell West about the latter's performance. (West subsequently accepted a professorship at Princeton.) Summers then alienated many others by suggesting that women were unsuited to excelling in science. Summers's actions hardly reflected "sympathetic listening in the many day-to-day, informal contacts within the department and outside the workplace." Members of the university's governing board, after trying to get him to tone down his approach, soon accepted his resignation.

Beyond "sympathetic listening," other simple, effective methods for promoting upward communication include the following:

- *Hold social gatherings* (including departmental parties, picnics, and recreational events) to provide opportunities for informal, casual communication.

- *Regular meetings* with subordinates, in addition to the informal contacts that take place every day, can be a good source of information.

- *Use performance appraisal meetings* to seek employees' opinions about their jobs and job attitudes.

- Remember that *grievances* provide insights into operational problems.

- *Attitude surveys* provide answers to (and help management address) questions like, "Are working hours and shift rotations perceived as reasonable?"

- A *suggestion system*, even a suggestion box, encourages upward communication. (Figure 12.2 illustrates one firm's suggestion program).

- *An open door* policy lets employees express concerns through a channel outside the normal chain of command—and thus acts as a safety valve.

- *Use indirect measures*, including absences, turnover rates, and safety records, because they are useful indicators of festering personnel problems.

FORMAL STEPS TO TAKE   Many employers install formal programs to encourage upward communication. Some use "hotlines" that let employees voice mail or e-mail concerns to the human resource department, anonymously. Others have formal grievance processes.

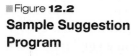

■ Figure **12.2**
Sample Suggestion Program

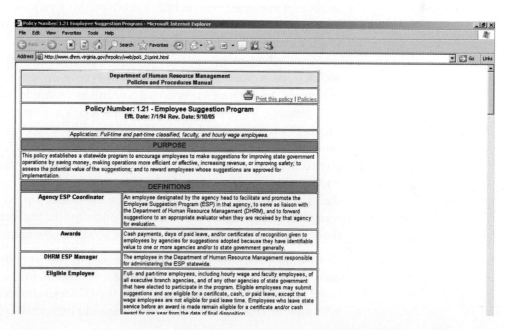

These enable employees to appeal a supervisor's decision by filing formal grievances up the line to the supervisor's boss, and up through a committee that may include the CEO.

UPWARD APPRAISALS   Some firms encourage upward communication by letting employees formally appraise their supervisors. In one study, researchers collected subordinates' ratings for 238 supervisors in a large firm at two points six months apart.[34] Subordinates were asked to rate a variety of supervisory behaviors, such as "Treated me fairly and with respect."[35]

The prospect of upward appraisals didn't seem to affect the performance of supervisors whose original appraisals were high; their ratings were about the same six months later. It was a different story with those whose initial appraisals were moderate or low. Six months later, their ratings shot up.[36]

Interestingly, it didn't seem to matter whether these supervisors actually got feedback in six months regarding how they were doing. They even improved with no feedback. It seemed that just knowing they'd be appraised was enough to get the supervisors to improve their behavior at work. Shrewd supervisors act every day as if their employees will be evaluating them tomorrow.

UPWARD COMMUNICATIONS AND THE SUPERVISOR   If you sense that programs such as hotlines, grievance processes, and upward appraisals aim in part to catch and head off unfair supervisory behavior, you're right. In an ideal world, every supervisor would be unbiased and fair, and none would treat employees with disrespect. Unfortunately, that's not always so. As a result, programs like these function in part to remind supervisors that the employer is monitoring their actions. Your employer may have no such formal program. But again, as a rule, you would still do well to treat your employees as if your actions will routinely come to light, and as if you will have to defend your actions to your employer.

Improving Downward Communication

Downward communication (from you to your team) embraces information on many important matters. These include job instructions, rationales for jobs (including how jobs are related to other jobs in the company), organizational policies and practices, and the company's mission.[37] In fact, the whole apparatus for getting things done at work, including giving orders, training employees, and informing employees about policies and procedures, fits under the heading of "downward communication."[38] Informal daily meetings as you walk around are a simple way to do this.

Employers facilitate downward communications in many ways. Some install closed-circuit TV screens in break areas. They use these to keep employees apprised of how the company is doing. Sea Island Shrimp House in San Antonio, Texas, keeps employees in its seven restaurants communicating with what it calls "cascading huddles."[39] As in football, the huddles are very quick meetings. At 9 a.m. top management meets in the day's first "huddle." The next huddle is a conference call with store supervisors. Then, store supervisors meet with hourly employees at each location before the restaurants open to communicate the day's news. "It's all about alignment and good, timely communications," says Sea Island.

OPEN-BOOK MANAGEMENT   As another example, your employer may institute an open-book management program. **Open-book management** means literally opening the company's books to its employees.[40] The firm shares its financial data, explains its numbers, and rewards workers for improvements in performance.[41]

The basic idea is to foster trust and commitment by treating employees more like partners. Manco, a Cleveland-based manufacturer of industrial products, illustrates this.[42] Every month, each department gets four books, designated by color, with financial information broken down by company, department, product line, and customer. Monthly meetings are held so that employees can see whether they're on track to earn their bonuses and what can be done to stay on track. Between meetings, management posts daily companywide sales totals. Employees can take accounting classes to help them understand the numbers.

DEALING WITH RUMORS   Dealing with rumors is one of the trickier aspects of delivering information to your team. Professor Keith Davis said that there are three main reasons rumors get started: Lack of information, insecurity, and conflicts.[43] When employees *lack information*, they are likely to speculate—and a rumor is born. (Thus, employees who observe an unscheduled disassembly of a machine may erroneously assume that the firm will soon lay off the machine's operators.) *Insecure* employees are especially prone to react that way. Finally, *conflicts*, such as between union and management, may trigger rumors, each side uses propaganda to show itself in a favorable light. Davis advises releasing the truth as quickly as possible, since the more the rumor spreads, the more people will believe it.

Unfortunately, many employers don't get the word out fast enough. In one classic study of 100 employees, the researcher found that when management made an important change, most employees heard the news first through the grapevine. Hearing news from a supervisor and official memorandums ran a poor second and third.[44] A few years ago the Web site www.greedyassociates.com (a big hit with associates at major law firms, but now gone) announced, "I heard Shearman [& Sterling, a Wall Street law firm] partners are sacrificing, in a bloody, gruesome manner, 1 of each 10 associates at midnight during the next full moon." The firm did soon lay off about that many.[45]

SHARING INFORMATION   One way to head off rumors while helping to boost morale is to take your employees into your confidence. Of course, "doing so demands good judgment."[46] Some information that comes down to you from your boss needs to be restricted. But as one writer says, "When there is a choice about sharing news of the department or of the company, playing it safe may be unwise."[47] Doing so may simply encourage rumors and low morale. "Withholding knowledge that would scotch the rumors simply contributes to confusion. It is in the best interests of both the manager and the company to give employees the straight scoop whenever possible."[48] The bottom line: Get the truth out to your people as soon as practical.

How Can a Supervisor Improve Upward and Downward Communication from/to Team Members?

4. Coaching, Counseling, and Mentoring Employees

Great supervisors tend to be great coaches, because they bring out the best in their teams. Coaching (and the closely related *mentoring*) are thus key supervisory skills. **Coaching** means educating, instructing, and training subordinates. **Mentoring** means advising, counseling, and guiding. Coaching focuses on learning shorter-term job-related skills, mentoring on traversing longer-term career-type hazards. Supervisors have coached and mentored employees from the dawn of management (in Greek mythology, *Mentor* advised Odysseus's son Telemachus). But with more supervisors leading highly trained employees and self-managing teams, supporting, coaching, and mentoring are fast replacing formal authority for getting things done.

Supervisors rely on coaching and mentoring for some of their most important tasks. For example, you'll need coaching and mentoring skills when appraising employees, and coaching is the most common form of on-the-job training.[49] Many firms use "executive coaches"—special, independent management development experts—to improve their supervisors' performance. You may have to mentor a new employee to learn the ropes. Firms like AT&T assign mentors to those employees they send abroad to ensure that the expats' careers stay on track while they're gone.

Employers understand coaching and mentoring's importance. One consulting firm surveyed about 2,500 senior human resource and training and development managers.[50] The survey found that the top skills these firms' leadership development programs addressed were *coaching a performance problem* (72%), *communicating performance standards* (69%), *coaching a development opportunity* (69%), and *conducting a performance appraisal* (67%). We'll look more closely at coaching and mentoring skills in this section.

Building Your Coaching Skills

Being an effective coach requires both analytical and interpersonal skills. It requires *analysis*, because it's futile to coach someone if you don't know what the problem is. It takes *interpersonal* skills, because it's equally futile to know the problem if you can't get the person to change. Here are the steps.

WHAT'S THE PROBLEM?   Some situations don't require coaching. For example, if your new employee learns the first time how to do the job, if your current employees use the new machine flawlessly, and if your employee's performance review is faultless, you won't need to do much coaching. But things rarely go so smoothly. And when they don't, you're probably going to have to coach the employee. You can best think of coaching in terms of a four-step process: *preparation, discussion, active coaching, and follow-up*.[52]

PREPARATION   *Preparation* means understanding the problem, and the employee, and the employee's skills. Your aim here is to formulate a hypotheses about what the problem is. Preparation is partly an observational process. You'll need to watch the employee to see what he or she is doing, and observe the job's larger context, including the workflow and how coworkers interact with the employee. In addition to observation, you may want to review objective data. Review things like productivity, tardiness, accidents, short-term sickness, grievances, waste, quality, repairs, equipment utilization, customer complaints, and the employee's previous performance reviews and training.

In formulating your hypothesis, you may also want to use the *ABC (antecedent, behavior, consequences) approach*. The basic idea of ABC is that poor motivation doesn't always explain poor performance.

- Faced with a performance problem, first review the *antecedents*—those things that come before the person does the job. Most important, does the employee know what the performance standards are, and that they're not being met?

- Next review the employee's *behavior*. Here, particularly ask whether the person could do the job if he or she wanted to. For example, was training adequate? Does the person have the necessary aptitudes? Does he or she have the tools and raw materials to do the job?

- Finally, think through, from the employee's vantage point, the *consequences* of doing the job right. Do you reward the person for doing well? Might there be negative consequences (such as complaints from peers) for performing up to standard?

DISCUSSION   Next, engage your employee in a discussion to (1) reach an agreement on the nature of the problem, and to (2) formulate a plan for getting performance back up to par. This plan typically includes *steps to take, measures of success,* and *date to complete.* Having this discussion requires you to apply the interpersonal communications skills we covered earlier in this chapter. These include avoiding nonverbal and psychological barriers, as well as following our guidelines, such as "make yourself clear," "be consistent," and "consider the distractions."

■Figure **12.3**

**Self-Evaluation
Coaching Checklist**

Source: Richard Luecke, *Coaching and Mentoring: How to Develop Top Talent and Achieve Stronger Performance* (Boston: Harvard Business School Press, 2004), p. 140.

The questions below relate to the skills and qualities needed to be an effective coach. Use this tool to evaluate your own effectiveness as a coach.

Question	Yes	No
1. Do you show interest in career development, not just short-term performance?		
2. Do you provide both support and autonomy?		
3. Do you set high yet attainable goals?		
4. Do you serve as a role model?		
5. Do you communicate business strategies and expected behaviors as a basis for establishing objectives?		
6. Do you work with the individual you are coaching to generate alternative approaches or solutions which you can consider together?		
7. Before giving feedback, do you observe carefully, and without bias, the individual you are coaching?		
8. Do you separate observations from judgments or assumptions?		
9. Do you test your theories about a person's behavior before acting on them?		
10. Are you careful to avoid using your own performance as a yardstick to measure others?		
11. Do you focus your attention and avoid distractions when someone is talking to you?		
12. Do you paraphrase or use some other method to clarify what is being said in a discussion?		
13. Do you use relaxed body language and verbal cues to encourage a speaker during conversations?		
14. Do you use open-ended questions to promote sharing of ideas and information?		
15. Do you give specific feedback?		
16. Do you give timely feedback?		
17. Do you give feedback that focuses on behavior and its consequences (rather than on vague judgments)?		
18. Do you give positive as well as negative feedback?		
19. Do you try to reach agreement on desired goals and outcomes rather than simply dictate them?		
20. Do you try to prepare for coaching discussions in advance?		
21. Do you always follow up on a coaching discussion to make sure progress is proceeding as planned?		
TOTALS		

When you have these characteristics and use these strategies, people trust you and turn to you for both professional and personal support.
If you answered "yes" to most of these questions, you are probably an effective coach.
If you answered "no" to some or many of these questions, you may want to consider how you can further develop your coaching skills.

ACTIVE COACHING   With agreement on a plan, you can start the actual coaching sessions. Here you may want to apply what you learned about on-the-job training in Chapter 9 ("review the job description," "produce a job instruction sheet," and so on). Most important, remember that coaching means helping the person to understand, *not* trying to force him or her to change. As one writer says, "[a]n effective coach offers ideas and advice in such a way that the subordinate can hear them, respond to them, and appreciate their value."[53]

FOLLOW-UP   Follow-up means checking periodically to ensure your employee is still on the right track. Bad habits sometimes repeat themselves. It's therefore essential to observe the person's progress periodically.

Figure 12.3 presents a self-evaluation checklist for assessing your on-the-job coaching skills.

Finally, remember that effective coaching is a two-way street: It takes not just leader-coaches but also good follower-"coach-ees." The accompanying leadership feature explains how to capitalize on that fact.

Leadership Applications for Supervisors

Dyads and Followership

The old saying that it "takes two to tango" also applies to coaching and communicating, because processes like these are so interactive. As we said, you're not really "communicating" if you simply come up to someone, give some instructions, and then walk away. Both coaching and communicating assume that you and the person you're dealing with both understand where you're coming from, and that takes two-way interaction.

Interestingly, some earlier theories of leadership pretty much assumed that leadership is a one-way street and ignored the fact that how the leader behaves also reflects the follower's reactions. Therefore, some of the newer leadership theories (such as leader-member exchange theory, or LMX) are "dyadic" (as in "two"). In other words, they explicitly take into account the fact that the leader's behavior reflects the follower's reactions, and vice versa.

But if good leading (and coaching) is a two-way street, does that mean that there is something about some followers that cause their leaders to look better? (To take an extreme example, some baseball teams might make even a mediocre manager look good.) That possibility has prompted a growing interest in "followership" (namely, what it is about followers that makes leaders look good). After all, if we knew what it was about a follower that made his or her leader look good, then all "followers" (subordinates) might benefit from that knowledge.

So, what are the characteristics of good followers? Leadership expert Gary Yukl summarized the knowledge in this area and lists the following guidelines for anyone at work who wants to be a good follower—for instance, when in a coaching situation.[54]

- *Find out what you are expected to do.*
- *Take the initiative to deal with problems.*
- *Keep the boss informed about your decisions.*
- *Verify the accuracy of information you give the boss.*
- *Encourage the boss to provide honest feedback to you.*
- *Support leader efforts to make necessary changes.*
- *Show appreciation and provide recognition when appropriate.*
- *Challenge floor plans and proposals made by leaders.*
- *Resist inappropriate influence attempts by the boss.*
- *Provide upward coaching and counseling (to your boss) when appropriate.*

5. Using Other Important Communications Media

Supervisors don't just communicate face to face. They also present their ideas in writing, give presentations, and use e-mail and instant messaging, for instance. To this point we've focused mostly on communicating verbally one-on-one or with your team. In this final section we'll turn to using some other important communications media.

Guidelines for Written Work

Supervisors have to put their ideas in writing all the time. They write reports for their colleagues and bosses, memos for their teams, and e-mails to suppliers and customers, for instance. If you're reading this book, then you already know quite a bit about writing. However, there are several *good writing guidelines* that can help anyone, including the following.[55]

Get to the point. It's annoying to have to read through five or six paragraphs before finding out what the memo is about. Particularly for business documents, start with your main point first, and then elaborate.

Make sense. Remember that good communications is "essentially a moral matter." Taking the time to faithfully translate what you mean to say into the written (or spoken) word takes effort and intellectual honesty. It's always easier to take the easy way out. As we said earlier, for instance, if you mean "immediately," say that. Don't leave the timing open-ended, or say "as soon as you can." Use your word processor's thesaurus to find the pithiest word.

Back up your assertions. Use examples, anecdotes, citation of authorities, statistics, and other forms of support.

Write for your audience. Use language, length, arguments, and evidence that suit your audience.

Edit and revise. Eliminate dead words (like all those unnecessary *ands*, *thats*, and *thes*), provide transitions between ideas, and repair grammar and spelling.

Format for readability. Create easy-to-read, attractive documents. For example, how would you like reading this page in this book, if it was just one long paragraph with no headings or subheadings? Your letter (or e-mail or memo, etc.) should be interesting to look at.

Favor common language over difficult verbiage. That's why Mark Twain vowed "never to write 'metropolis' when I get paid the same for writing 'city.'"

Use graphic aids to capture and highlight ideas. For many written documents (and especially reports) the saying "a picture is worth a thousand words" is true. Graphics not only make your document look more interesting, they can also make a point with more impact than the dozens of words they replace.

Write with conviction. There's a certain amount of "nonverbal communications" in written work, too. It's not just what you say, but how you say it. Make your point early, back it up with data, use short, punchy sentences, and underscore and highlight for emphasis.

Guidelines for Making Presentations

Some people are naturally more adept at giving presentations than are others. When you see them "on stage," they seem confident, they command attention, and they don't exhibit the nervousness that most people do.

Not everyone is blessed with the ability to make great presentations. Most of us will always be a bit nervous getting up in front of a crowd. However, experts suggest the following guidelines for making your presentation as tension-free and effective as possible.[56]

Know your audience. Find out ahead of time whom the audience will consist of. You want to gear the presentation's level, length, and technical aspects to your audience.

Don't plan on making more than three points. It's hard for most people to remember what someone says during a 10-minute conversation, let alone a 30- or 60-minute lecture or presentation. Experienced presenters therefore generally try to limit themselves to making no more than three main points during their presentations. They then use examples and illustrations to fill out the time.

Achieve rapport quickly. There's a reason why many experienced presenters start with a joke, or by getting the audience to interact right away, for instance, by asking questions like "Who's from New York?" Doing so helps to make everyone more comfortable and to establish the sort of rapport that will make your audience want to tune in to what you're saying.

Use notes (if necessary) as unobtrusively as possible. Notes and PowerPoint slides function best as "thought triggers." The last thing you want is to stand there reading from your notes (it would be easier to just distribute your notes and let the listeners read them at their leisure!), or to make them plod through heavily annotated PowerPoint slides. Use brief, outlined notes or slides just as thought triggers.

Speak up. Have you noticed how famous newscasters always seem to speak forcefully and several decibels louder than most other people? They understand that it's more interesting to listen to someone who doesn't sound bored, and who speaks so that everyone can hear them.

Look at your listeners. It's best to make eye contact and to let your gaze wander from listener to listener. If you find doing that uncomfortable, still let your gaze wander, but focus instead at points just above or between listeners. Try to watch your audience for signs of comprehension or misunderstanding (or, alas, boredom).

Look interesting. Maintain your audience's interest level by looking interesting yourself. Three things here. *Move freely*, without pacing, using the available space to move naturally. Use *gestures* to express your ideas. And be conscious of what you do with your *hands*; it's best to let them hang by your side (when you're not gesturing). Do not put them in your pockets, and keep them away from your face.

End with a roar, not a whimper. Make your concluding words memorable.

Electronic Mail

As e-mail (and IM, and tweeting, and blog) use has proliferated, it's become more important to ensure you're using your employer's e-mail system properly. There are several things to keep in mind.[57]

KNOW YOUR EMPLOYER'S RULES   Most employers have (or should have) strict rules regarding employees' use of the company e-mail system (check the system's opening page, or your employee manual). In general, here's what you should know.

- E-mail messages you send, receive, save, or delete on your employer's system generally are *not* private. Your employer owns the system, so it's not like the e-mail you send via public systems such as Gmail and Hotmail. Your employer generally *does* have the right to review the messages you route *via its system* (even those you send via Hotmail or Gmail.). Many employers specifically advise against using their systems for your personal messages.

- E-mail messages do *not* disappear after you click delete (even if you delete them from "deleted"). They remain on your employer's servers, and the firm can access them.

- If you send or forward salacious material (inappropriate jokes, comments, or photos, for instance), you not only put yourself in legal jeopardy, but you may endanger your employer as well.

Besides Face to Face, What Other Forms of Communication Do Supervisors Use?

THINK BEFORE YOU PRESS THE "SEND" KEY   Don't send anything that you wouldn't want posted in a public place.[58] A few years ago, a U.S. Senate committee demanded an appearance by Goldman Sachs executives to explain e-mails from them that some thought implied Goldman was treating customers less than fairly.

While just about everyone who uses e-mail knows you've got to be careful, even CEOs still make mistakes. For example, the following e-mail from one corporate CEO quickly ended up on several Internet bulletin boards:

> Hell will freeze over before this CEO implements any other employee benefit in this culture. We are getting less than 40 hours of work from a large number of our KC-based employees. . . . As managers—you either do not know what your employees are doing; or you do not care. . . . You have a problem and you will fix it or I will replace you. . . . What you're doing, as managers, with this company makes me sick.[59]

BE PROFESSIONAL   The preceding example illustrates what not to do. You *should* be concise, clear, respectful, and also sensible about who you add to your distribution list.

RESPOND QUICKLY   In one survey, about half of the workers polled said they considered it rude not to get an e-mail reply within a day, and many felt it was rude not to get a reply within five minutes.

USE THE RIGHT MEDIUM FOR THE MESSAGE   One company supposedly once used a mass text message to let warehouse employees know they were fired. Dealing with sensitive topics or trying to be persuasive is probably best left to more personal, rich media (such as face-to-face discussions).

Work Group Support Systems

Your employer will likely make available *work group support systems.* These are technology-based systems that make it easier for work-group members to work together. Group members might meet at a single site, or they may be dispersed around the world.

Table 12.2 summarizes popular information technology (IT)–based work group support systems, along with a brief list of the issues to keep in mind when using each system.

■ Table **12.2**

IT-Based Work Group Support and Collaboration Systems		
Work Group Support System	**What It Does**	**Some Issues to Keep in Mind**
E-mail systems	Messaging infrastructures such as e-mail or instant messenger systems	• rules governing use • security
Electronic meeting systems	Real-time conferencing systems that may be managed by either local or remote sources	• scheduling meetings • post-meeting follow-up • cost • number of people who can work on system simultaneously and efficiently
Document handling systems	Group document management, storage, and editing tools	• security • work flow • data integrity • page mark-up standards • standard systems • ensuring user compatibility
Online communities	Web sites organized by subject matter where members access interactive discussion areas and share content, reference tools, and Web links	• value of shared content • updating of content and resources
Workflow management systems	Project management, process diagramming, and routing tools	• establishing workflow standards • making decisions • establishing processes and systems
Group decision-support systems	Tools used to integrate collaboration and team management systems across computer platforms, operating systems, and network architectures	• security • updating of systems

Source: Adapted from Jennifer Salopek, "Digital Collaboration," *Training and Development* 54 (June 2000): 6, 38. See also http://www.ifm.eng.cam.ac.uk/dstools/ (accessed April 26, 2010).

Chapter 12 Concept Review and Reinforcement

Key Terms

Active Listening, p. 357
Coaching, p. 363
Communication, p. 349

Interpersonal
  Communication, p. 355
Mentoring, p. 363

Nonverbal
  Communication, p. 352

Open-Book
  Management, p. 362

Review of Key Concepts

Communication	Communication means exchanging information in such a way that you create a common basis of understanding and feeling.
Communication Process	The five elements of the communication process are: • Information source • Signal • Transmission • Channel • Destination or receiver • Noise Errors can occur in any one of these elements.
Interpersonal Communication Barriers	
Ambiguity	Ambiguity means that the words may be clear, but the sender's intentions aren't, or the person receiving the message isn't sure what the person who sent it meant.
Semantics	Words mean different things to different people.
Physical Barriers	Obvious physical barriers include street noise, interruptions, and machine clatter. Less obvious sources include tiny fonts and indecipherable writing.
Nonverbal Communication	People draw conclusions about who you are and what you mean from your manner of speaking, facial expressions, and posture.
Perceptual Barriers	People's needs and situations shape how they actually see (perceive) things, so what they hear may not be what you said.
Experiential Barriers	People's experiences affect how they perceive things. People find it easier to understand things they can identify with through personal experience.

Improving Interpersonal Communications	Good-practice guidelines include: • Making yourself clear • Being consistent • Considering distractions • Confirming "Message received" • Being an active listener
Active Listening	Active listening means taking steps to listen, not just to what the speaker says, but to understand and respond to the feelings behind the words.
How to Be More Persuasive	Persuasion involves appealing to "deeply rooted human drives and needs." The basic principles of powerful persuasion include: • Establish your credibility • Persuade based on common ground • Connect emotionally • Provide evidence • Use peer power • Have person make a commitment
Communicating Upward	Upward communication should be encouraged. Upward communication helps you verify that subordinates understand orders and instructions, and give you valuable input on which to base decisions.
Communicating Downward	Downward communication embraces information on many important matters including job instructions, rationales for jobs, and organizational policies and procedures.
Open-Book Management	Open-book management attempts to foster trust and commitment by treating employees more like partners. The firm shares its financial data, explains its numbers, and rewards workers for improvements in performance.
Coaching and Mentoring Employees	Coaching means educating, instructing, and training subordinates. Mentoring means advising, counseling, and guiding. With more supervisors leading self-managing teams, coaching and mentoring are fast replacing formal authority for getting things done.
Telecommunications and the Internet	Telecommunications and the Internet play an important role in managing communications. Work group support systems allow geographically dispersed employees to interact in real-time, substantially reducing communication costs.

Review and Discussion Questions

1. What are the main steps in the communication process? Include examples.
2. Ambiguity is a major barrier to interpersonal communications. What steps do you suggest taking to remove this barrier?
3. Define communication.
4. What can a manager do to improve downward communications? Upward communications?
5. What value does open-book management have in motivating employees?
6. What are the rules for active listening?
7. What are the roles of telecommunications and the Internet in managing communications?
8. What can a person do to be more persuasive?
9. What are five examples of noise that affect communications?
10. What are the good-practice guidelines for improving interpersonal communications?

Application and Skill Building

Case Study One

Approaching Diversity: Barriers or Breakthroughs?

You have just been retained by a restaurant chain that has been successfully sued by former employees and by customers four times in the last five years for racial and gender discrimination. The company is losing business because of its poor image in the community. Employees are also leaving, and others are threatening to sue if conditions do not improve. The workforce is 65% women, of which 55% are women of color. Twenty-one percent of the male workforce consists of men of color. Ninety percent of middle management and above are white males.

The board of directors has fired the CEO and replaced him with a young Latina to try to change the company. You are the new consultant. The new CEO has asked you to help her implement a communications program so she can find out what employees are thinking, and let them know that she plans to take steps to improve the situation. She needs your report by the end of the week.

Discussion Questions

1. What communications barriers and problems might you expect to unearth in this situation?
2. What means of communication might you use to help the new CEO reach the employees? What exactly would you suggest?
3. Given that you are new on the job, how would you collect information to do your analysis in less than a week?

Source: Gillian Flynn, "Do You Have the Right Approach to Diversity?" *Personnel Journal,* October 1995, 68–76.

Case Study Two

Keeping Communication Open at JetBlue

Management has built JetBlue based on five values—safety, caring, integrity, fun, and passion—and keeping communications open and transparent is vital for adhering to all of them. Indeed, the company feels so strongly about these values that they appear on all employees' identification cards.

Most employees' first exposure to JetBlue's brand of open communication comes during their initial one-hour orientation, when the company's president and CEO explain how JetBlue makes money. The officers go so far as to do the math with the new employees, and then show how each of the employees' jobs affects every aspect of the company's expenses and revenues. The basic idea is to get the new employee to think, "If I do this—that's what happens." The basic theme is that JetBlue can succeed as a low-cost, high-quality airline only if every employee gives his or her best, and so employees have to think of themselves more as partners than employees. Indeed, there are no employees at JetBlue—just "crewmembers."

JetBlue's monthly "pocket sessions" provide another example of open communications. The pocket sessions meetings include the company CEO, president, and head of HR with about 200 JetBlue employees at the company's main crew lounge at JFK airport. These meetings usually involve short presentations by each officer and then a period of frank and open questions and answers between officers and employees. Again, given JetBlue's emphasis on open, transparent communication, the officers work hard to answer even the thorniest questions forthrightly. For example, at one recent meeting, a flight attendant asked why the officers get stock options, while the flight attendants do not. (The answer was that they play different roles and that early on management and the board of directors made the decision that only managers, pilots, and others in the company requiring professional licensing and degrees would be eligible for stock options. However, other employees are eligible for profit sharing and other benefits.)

Another employee pointed out that because of bad weather, many employees had to work mandatory overtime for three days. This particular employee "didn't like the fact that it was mandatory" and complained that the supervisor shouldn't have put the order in "mandatory" terms. Management responded that if the order was less than courteous, they would look into it, but the bottom line was that everyone joining JetBlue had to understand that it is everyone's responsibility to pitch in and help during periods like these and that those who could not do so might not be happy at JetBlue. Finally, the company also issues periodic "Blue notes"—companywide e-mails covering important news and press releases—as another communication aid.

However, JetBlue does not have some of the trappings of formal communication you might expect from a company this size. For example, there is no employee manual. (The company is considering publishing one, tentatively titled "the JetBlue route map," sometime in the future.) New employees do get a "Blue book"—a 13-page pamphlet summarizing major policy issues, for instance, concerning equal employment opportunity and sexual harassment. There are also several benefits documents describing matters such as sick leave and vacation pay. The company has disciplinary procedures but does not publicize them or distribute them to employees. JetBlue simply emphasizes that it will treat employees with respect. Then, if there is a problem, employees receive a warning and a description of the progressive disciplinary policy.

Employee appraisal at JetBlue similarly tends to be an open, give-and-take discussion, one in which the employee's commitment to JetBlue looms large. JetBlue managers call the annual appraisal the "Flight plan." JetBlue also has a yearly crew member experience survey. This is an attitude survey that monitors employee impressions of various matters, ranging from supervision to pay. Generally, according to the company's head of HR, this survey contains few surprises, but rather tends to validate things that management already knows. This is because managers, and particularly top managers, spend so much time out in the field—in the terminal, in the aircraft, and so on—talking to and interacting with employees and passengers.

1. Are there any interpersonal or organizational communication barriers that JetBlue seems to be ignoring, and if so, how would you suggest the company remedy the situation?
2. List and explain the things you would do to improve organizational communication at JetBlue.
3. Make a list of the specific vehicles JetBlue is currently using to encourage upward communication, downward communication, and interdepartmental communication. Do you think these are adequate for a company in JetBlue's situation? What would you suggest JetBlue do to improve organizational communication?

Experiential Activities

Activity 1. Sara could not figure out why her employees were constantly disobeying her instructions. As an example, she had told a subordinate to hire someone outside the company to upgrade their computers, but Sara felt the wrong person had been hired. Sara could not figure out why she had been disobeyed.

Communication Skills and the Supervisor

Purpose: The purpose of this exercise is to give you practice in developing your communication skills in order to be a more effective manager and leader.

Required Understanding: You are going to develop a comprehensive communication plan that could have aided Sara in avoiding the communication problem she encountered; therefore, you should be thoroughly familiar with the discussion of coaching and communication as discussed in this chapter.

How to Set Up the Exercise/Instructions: Divide the class into groups of 5 or 6 students.

1. Your group should develop a communication plan that supports clear and concise messages while avoiding the barriers to effective communication.
2. Next, using group consensus, arrange your group communication plan into a one-page outline.
3. Have a spokesperson from each group share their outline with the other groups.
4. Next, answer the question of how Sara could have approached her subordinate differently using a communication plan you have developed.
5. Follow with a class discussion involving all of the student groups. Answer the question: What will the impact of the supervisor have on the success or failure of effective communication?

Activity 2. As the example about Larry Summers at Harvard shows, different executives have different ways of communicating with their employees. Form teams of 4–5 students and answer the following questions: What methods has the president of your college or university used to elicit upward communication from members of the college or university community? What methods does he or she use to foster downward communication from the president to the students? What do the president's communication methods tell you about the organizational culture that person is trying to create (or is inadvertently creating) at your university or college?

Activity 3. You have probably faced a situation in which you had to speak with a supervisor about a problem—you thought your appraisal should be higher, for instance. In teams of 4–5 students, discuss the experiences you've had along these lines. Then make a list of what that supervisor did right and wrong with respect to the interpersonal communication skills (how to be an active listener, and so on) in this chapter. What communication barriers did this person seem to be ignoring?

Activity 4. You need to take a training class, but it's not offered this year. HR has made you this proposition: If you can persuade 15 other supervisors to sign up for the course, the company will offer it. In teams of 4–5 students, use what you learned in this chapter to write a script you will use to persuade other supervisors to join you in this class.

Role-Playing Exercise

Communication Skills and the Supervisor: The Situation

Libby Proster has been a timekeeper for Muessler Brass Company for over four years. As a timekeeper, she has access to all the plant employees who are doing electronic assembly for the computer industry. Libby has been tagged as "the Mouth of the South" for her ability to quickly spread rumors throughout the plant. Before becoming a timekeeper, Libby had worked most all of the assembly jobs in the plant and was considered a hard worker. The plant management does not feel that they have done a good job communicating with the plant workers, thus Libby has been busy spreading rumors almost daily. Libby would like a better paying job with more responsibility, like a supervisor position. A trade union is currently trying to organize the hourly workers in this plant, and Libby is contemplating being the first union president if their unionization effort is successful. The plant manager would like to remove Libby from this environment by promoting her to a department supervisor position.

A meeting is planned where Libby and the HR manager will discuss this proposed promotion.

Instructions: All students should read the situation above. One student will play the role of Libby Proster and the second student should play the role of the HR manager. Each student should only read his or her assigned role below. Then, both students should engage in a 15-minute conversation. A class discussion will follow the role-playing presentation.

Timekeeper—Libby Proster: You have heard a rumor that when you meet with the HR director today, they are going to offer you a job as a supervisor. If they offer you this position, you must decide whether you want to stay where you are as timekeeper or become a department supervisor. The management job will pay more and open you up to future promotion opportunities, but if the union comes in, you have the opportunity to be its first president with status, prestige, and power. The decision is not going to be easy.

HR Manager: Your role is to represent what is best for the company. Libby has the potential to be a good manager. You would like to remove her from her timekeeper position. Moving her to supervisor will not only cut down on the rumor mill, but it will keep her from joining the new union if it wins certification.

Questions for Class Discussion

1. After talking with the HR manager, do you concur with the employment decision Libby made? Why?
2. What steps do you suggest to management to improve communications with employees while dealing with rumors?
3. What factor will influence Libby's decision to take the supervisory position? The union position?
4. If placed in a similar situation, which decision would you have made? Why?

13 Appraising and Managing Performance

OPENING SNAPSHOT

"I'm Rating You a 6.5 out of 10!"

Gladys had only worked for Ocean Engineering for about six months, but she loved her job as a junior engineer and the people she worked with. It was therefore with enthusiasm that she sat down with her supervisor, Phyllis, to get and discuss Gladys's first performance appraisal. Unfortunately, the meeting was a disaster. Phyllis came in armed with a long list of errors that Gladys had supposedly made in the past few months. She followed that up by telling Gladys that she wasn't even doing half the things that the job called for. "Overall," said Phyllis, "I'm rating you a 6.5 out of 10," and then she walked out. Gladys sat there stunned.

1. The Performance Appraisal Cycle

Few things supervisors do are fraught with more peril than appraising subordinates' performance. Employees tend to be overly optimistic about what their ratings will be. And they know that their raises, careers, and peace of mind may hinge on how you rate them. As if that's not enough, few appraisal processes are as fair and above-board as employers think they are. Hundreds of obvious and not-so-obvious problems (such as bias, and the tendency for supervisors to rate everyone "fair") undermine the process. However, the perils notwithstanding, performance appraisal is part of what supervisors do. The point of this chapter is therefore to make sure that you understand the potential pitfalls and can excel at appraising your employees.

What Is Performance Appraisal and Management?

What Is Performance Appraisal?

Performance appraisal means evaluating an employee's performance relative to his or her performance standards. Stripped to its essentials, performance appraisal always involves (1) setting work standards, (2) assessing the employee's actual performance relative to those standards, and (3) providing feedback to the employee with the aim of motivating him or her to eliminate performance deficiencies or to continue to perform above par. As Figure 13.1 summarizes, supervisors call these three steps the **performance appraisal cycle**.

PERFORMANCE MANAGEMENT   As Gladys discovered, traditional performance appraisals suffer from some potential problems, one of which is blindsiding unsuspecting employees with surprise appraisals. When that happens, no one gains. The employee feels bad, the supervisor feels useless, and the company still ends up with poor performance. Many employers have therefore switched to a better way.

For example, if you were to spend time in Toyota's Lexington, Kentucky, Camry plant, the absence of "appraisal" would soon be apparent. Supervisors don't sit with

■Figure **13.1**

The Three-Step Performance Appraisal Cycle

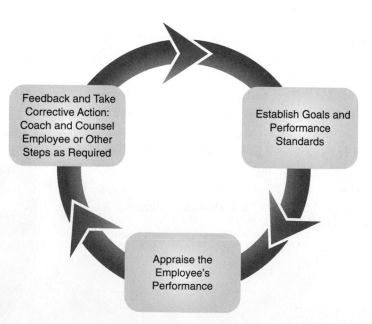

- Feedback and Take Corrective Action: Coach and Counsel Employee or Other Steps as Required
- Establish Goals and Performance Standards
- Appraise the Employee's Performance

individual employees to fill out forms and appraise them. Instead, teams of employees monitor their own results. They continuously align those results with the work team's standards and with the plant's overall quality and productivity needs. They do this by continuously adjusting how they and their team members do things. Team members who need coaching and training receive it, and procedures that need changing are changed. This is *performance management* in action. **Performance management** is the *continuous* process of identifying, measuring, and developing the performance of individuals and teams and *aligning* their performance with the organization's *goals*.[1] We'll look at it more closely later in the chapter. Let's first focus on appraisal.

Why Appraise Performance?

Why Appraise Performance?

There are five reasons to appraise subordinates' performance.

- First, from a practical point of view, most employers still base pay, promotion, and retention decisions on the employee's appraisal.[2]
- Second, the appraisal lets you and the subordinate develop a plan for correcting any deficiencies and reinforce what the subordinate does right.
- Third, appraisals should provide an opportunity to review the employee's career plans in light of his or her exhibited strengths and weaknesses.
- Fourth, appraisal serves a performance management function by helping to ensure that the employee's performance results are in synch with the company's goals.
- Finally, supervisors use appraisals to identify employees' training and development needs. Specifically, the appraisal should enable the supervisor to identify if there is a "performance gap" between the employee's performance and his or her standards. And it should help identify the cause of any such gap and the remedial steps required.

Figure 13.2 summarizes why you appraise employees' performance.

The Importance of Immediate Feedback

For accomplishing several of these aims, the traditional annual (or semiannual) appraisal review meeting makes sense. For example, promotions and raises tend to be periodic decisions. Similarly, you probably wouldn't want to hold career discussions more than once or twice per year.

However, when you see a performance problem, the time to take action is immediately—there is no substitute for nudging your employee's performance back into line continuously and incrementally. Similarly, when someone does something well, the best reinforcement comes immediately, not six months later.

Specifying Employees' Goals and Work Standards

As Gladys's supervisor Phyllis should know, your employees ought to know ahead of time the basis on which you will appraise them.

In practice, you do this in one of two ways. Many employers simply use appraisal forms with preprinted generic criteria like "quality of work" or "gets along with others." These generic criteria are the standards by which you appraise your employees.

The second approach is to appraise employees based on specific standards you set in advance, such as "add 10 new customers next year."[3] We've already explained how to set effective goals in Chapter 3. In brief, the guidelines for doing so include the following:

- **Set SMART goals.** These are *specific, measurable, attainable, relevant,* and *timely*.
- **Assign Specific Goals.** Employees who have *specific goals* usually perform better than those who do not.
- **Assign Measurable Goals.** Always try to express the goal in terms of numbers, and include target dates or deadlines.
- **Assign Challenging but Doable Goals.** Make them challenging, but not so difficult that they appear impossible or unrealistic.
- **Encourage Participation.** Participatively set goals usually produce higher performance.

How Are Employees' Goals and Work Standards Specified?

THE JOB DESCRIPTION   The job description should provide an up-to-date list of the job's specific duties. It is therefore the logical starting point for understanding the job's duties, goals, and performance standards. It should be a focal point of your discussions when you first assign and train the employee to a new job, and a main reference point for comparing, for each duty, actual to planned performance.

The Supervisor's Role in Appraising Performance

Appraising performance is both a difficult and an essential supervisory skill. The supervisor—not HR—usually does the actual appraising. Supervisors must therefore be familiar with appraisal tools, understand and avoid problems that can cripple appraisals, and know how to conduct appraisals fairly.

The human resources department serves an advisory role. Generally, human resource managers provide advice and assistance regarding what appraisal tool to use. They generally leave final decisions on procedures to operating supervisors.

Why It's Important to Be Candid with the Subordinate

To paraphrase GE's former CEO, Jack Welch, "There is nothing crueler than telling someone who's doing a mediocre job that he or she is doing well."[4] A candid review might have given the subordinate the chance to correct bad behavior or to find a more appropriate vocation. Instead, a soft review may leave him or her in a dead-end job for years, only to have to leave when a more demanding boss comes along.

What Is the Supervisor's Role in Appraising Performance?

There are many practical motivations for giving soft appraisals: the fear of having to hire and train someone new; the appraisee's unpleasant reactions; or a company appraisal process that's not conducive to candor, for instance. Ultimately, you must decide if the potential negatives of less-than-candid appraisals outweigh the assumed benefits. They rarely do.

2. Tools for Appraising Performance

Supervisors usually don't have much choice about the tool they use for appraising subordinates. The employer and/or the human resource management department usually make that choice from among six or so standard methods. However, each tool has pros, cons, and its own idiosyncrasies. You should be familiar with them before using them.

What Methods Are Used for Appraising Performance?

Graphic Rating Scale Method

The graphic rating scale is the most common tool for appraising performance. Figure 13.3 shows one graphic rating scale. A **graphic rating scale** lists traits (such as "quality" or "teamwork") and a range of performance (such as from "unsatisfactory" to "outstanding") for each trait. The supervisor rates each employee by circling or checking the score that best describes the employee's performance for each trait. The scores for the traits are then totaled.

Usually, as in Figure 13.3, you'll rate subordinates along *generic job dimensions* such as communications, teamwork, and quantity. Some forms will require that you appraise the *job's actual duties*. For example, Figure 13.4 (page 386) shows part of an appraisal form for a pizza chef. You'd use such a form to assess the main job-specific duties. One of these is "Maintain adequate inventory of Pizza dough." Here you would assess how well the employee did in exercising each of these duties.

Some graphic rating forms measure several things. For example, Figure 13.5 (Sections I, II, page 386–387) assesses the employee's performance in terms of competencies and objectives. With respect to *competencies*, the employee is expected to develop and exhibit competencies (Section II) such as "identifies and analyzes problems" (Problem Solving).

Sample Performance Rating Form

Employee's Name _____   Level Entry-level employee

Manager's Name _____

Key Work Responsibilities   Results/Goals to Be Achieved

1. _____   1. _____

2. _____   2. _____

3. _____   3. _____

4. _____   4. _____

Communication

1	2	3	4	5
Below Expectations		Meets Expectations		Role Model
Even with guidance, fails to prepare straightforward communication, including forms, paperwork, and records, in a timely and accurate manner; products require minimal correction. Even with guidance, fails to adapt style and materials to communicate straightforward information.		With guidance, prepares straightforward communications, including forms, paperwork, and records, in a timely and accurate manner; products require minimal corrections. With guidance, adapts style and materials to communicate straightforward information.		Independently prepares communications, such as forms, paperwork, and records, in a timely, clear, and accurate manner; products require few, if any, corrections. Independently adapts style and materials to communicate information.

Organizational Know-How

1	2	3	4	5
Below Expectations		Meets Expectations		Role Model
<performance standards appear here>		<performance standards appear here>		<performance standards appear here>

Personal Effectiveness

1	2	3	4	5
Below Expectations		Meets Expectations		Role Model
<performance standards appear here>		<performance standards appear here>		<performance standards appear here>

Teamwork

1	2	3	4	5
Below Expectations		Meets Expectations		Role Model
<performance standards appear here>		<performance standards appear here>		<performance standards appear here>

Achieving Business Results

1	2	3	4	5
Below Expectations		Meets Expectations		Role Model
<performance standards appear here>		<performance standards appear here>		<performance standards appear here>

Results Assessment

Accomplishment 1: _____

1	2	3	4	5
Low Impact		Moderate Impact		High Impact
The efficiency or effectiveness of operations remained the same or improved only minimally.		The efficiency or effectiveness of operations improved quite a lot.		The efficiency or effectiveness of operations improved tremendously.
The quality of products remained the same or improved only minimally.		The quality of products improved quite a lot.		The quality of products improved tremendously.

Accomplishment 2: _____

1	2	3	4	5
Low Impact		Moderate Impact		High Impact
The efficiency or effectiveness of operations remained the same or improved only minimally.		The efficiency or effectiveness of operations improved quite a lot.		The efficiency or effectiveness of operations improved tremendously.
The quality of products remained the same or improved only minimally.		The quality of products improved quite a lot.		The quality of products improved tremendously.

Narrative

_____

_____

_____

_____

_____

Areas to Be Developed	Actions	Completion Date

Manager's Signature _____ Date _____

Employee's Signature _____ Date _____

The above employee signature indicates receipt of, but not necessarily concurrence with, the evaluation herein.

■Figure **13.4**
**One Item from
a Graphic Rating
Form Assessing
Employee's
Performance on
Specific Job-Related
Duties**

Position: Pizza Chef				
Duty 1: Maintain adequate inventory of Pizza dough		Rating		
Each round pizza dough must be between 12 and 14 ounces each, kneaded at least 2 minutes before being placed in the temperature- and humidity-controlled cooler, and kept there for at least 5 hours prior to use. There should be enough, but no more for each day's demand.		Needs improvement	Satisfactory	Excellent

You and the employee would fill in the *objectives* section (Section I) at the start of the year, and then assess results and set new ones as part of the next appraisal.

Alternation Ranking Method

Ranking employees from best to worst is another option. Since it is usually easier to distinguish between the worst and best employees, an **alternation ranking method** is most

SECTION I	Responsibilities of Objectives and Performance Standards in Support of Departmental Goals "Maximizing one's professional qualifications to make a difference"	
Primary Performance Expectations: Responsibilities of Objectives and Standards	Mid-Year Progress Notes	End of Period Rating of Success and Effectiveness Comment and Place X on Scale to Rate Not Strong Very Strong
Objective 1:		├──┼──┼──┼──┤
Objective 2:		├──┼──┼──┼──┤
Objective 3:		├──┼──┼──┼──┤
Objective 4:		├──┼──┼──┼──┤
Objective 5:		├──┼──┼──┼──┤
Objectives for new rating period reviewed and agreed to:		Mid-Year Review:
Evaluator Date Employee Date		Evaluator Date Employee Date

■Figure **13.5**
Rating Employee Based on Objectives (top) and Competencies (bottom)

Performance Competencies
"Making a Difference by Working and Learning Together."

	Mid-Year Progress Notes	End of Period Rating of Success and Effectiveness Comment and Place X on Scale to Rate Not Strong Very Strong
Job Knowledge/Competency: Demonstrates the knowledge and skills necessary to perform the job effectively. Understands the expectations of the job and remains current regarding new developments in areas of responsibility. Performs responsibilities in accordance with job procedures and policies. Acts as a resource person upon whom others rely for assistance.		
Quality/Quantity of Work: Completes assignments in a thorough, accurate, and timely manner that achieves expected outcomes. Exhibits concern for the goals and needs of the department and others that depend on service or work products. Handles multiple responsibilities in an effective manner. Uses work time productively.		
Planning/Organization: Establishes dear objectives and organizes duties for self based on the goals of the department, division, or management center. Identifies resources required to meet goals and objectives. Seeks guidance when goals or priorities we unclear.		
Initiative/Commitment: Demonstrates personal responsibility when performing duties. Offers assistance to support the goals and objectives of the department and division. Performs with minimal supervision. Meets work schedule/attendance expectations for the position.		
Problem Solving/Creativity: Identifies and analyzes problems. Formulates alternative sections. Takes or recommends appropriate actions. Follows up to ensure problems are reserved.		
Teamwork and Cooperation: Maintains harmonious and effective work relationships with co-workers and constituents. Adapts to changing priorities and demands. Shares information and resources with others to promote positive and collaborative work relationships.		
Interpersonal Skills: Deals positively and effectively with coworkers and constituents. Demonstrates respect for all individuals.		
Communication (Oral and Written): Effectively conveys information and ideas both orally and in writing. Listens carefully and seeks clarification to ensure understanding.		

Competencies Reviewed and Discussed:	Mid-Year Review	
Evaluator	Date	Employee Date

■Figure **13.5**
(Continued)

popular. First, list all subordinates to be rated, and then cross out the names of any not known well enough to rank. Then, on a form like that in Figure 13.6, indicate the employee who is the highest on the trait being measured and the one who is the lowest. Then choose the next highest and the next lowest, alternating between the highest and lowest employee until all employees have been ranked.

ALTERNATION RANKING SCALE

Trait: _____

For the trait you are measuring, list all the employees you want to rank. Put the highest ranking employee's name on line 1. Put the lowest ranking employee's name on line 20. Then list the next highest ranking on line 2, the next lowest ranking on line 19, and so on. Continue until all names are on the scale.

Highest ranking employee

1. _____   11. _____
2. _____   12. _____
3. _____   13. _____
4. _____   14. _____
5. _____   15. _____
6. _____   16. _____
7. _____   17. _____
8. _____   18. _____
9. _____   19. _____
10. _____   20. _____

Lowest ranking employee

Forced Distribution Method

The **forced distribution method** is similar to grading on a curve. With this method, you place predetermined percentages of ratees into several performance categories. The proportions in each category need not be symmetrical; GE used top 20%, middle 70%, and bottom 10% for supervisors.

Many employers use forced ranking. Sun Microsystems (now part of Oracle) force-ranks its 43,000 employees. Supervisors appraise employees in groups of about 30; those in the bottom 10% of each group get 90 days to improve. If they're still in the bottom 10% in 90 days, they can resign and take severance pay. Some decide to stay, but "if it doesn't work out," the firm fires them without severance.[5] This dismissal policy seems somewhat standard. It reflects the fact that top employees often outperform average or poor ones by as much as 100%.[6] About a fourth of *Fortune* 500 companies including Microsoft, Conoco, and Intel use versions of forced distribution.[7]

As most students know, forced grading systems are unforgiving. With forced distribution, you're either in the top 5% or 10% (and thus get that A), or you're not. And if you're in the bottom 5% or 10%, you get an F, no questions asked. The professor hasn't the wiggle room to give everyone As, Bs, and Cs. Some students must fail. One survey found that 77% of responding employers using this approach were at least "somewhat satisfied" with forced ranking, while the remaining 23% were dissatisfied. The biggest complaints: 44% said it damages morale.[8] Some writers refer unkindly to forced rankings as "Rank and Yank."[9]

Given this, you need to be doubly careful here.[10] There should be a committee to review any employee's low ranking. Some employers wisely use multiple raters in conjunction with forced distribution.

Examples of Critical Incidents for Assistant Plant Supervisor		
Continuing Duties	**Targets**	**Critical Incidents**
Schedule production for plant	90% utilization of personnel and machinery in plant; orders delivered on time	Instituted new production scheduling system; decreased late orders by 10% last month; increased machine utilization in plant by 20% last month
Supervise procurement of raw materials and inventory control	Minimize inventory costs while keeping adequate supplies on hand	Let inventory storage costs rise 15% last month; overordered parts "A" and "B" by 20%; underordered part "C" by 30%
Supervise machinery maintenance	No shutdowns due to faulty machinery	Instituted new preventive maintenance system for plant; prevented a machine breakdown by discovering faulty part

Using Critical Incidents

Rather than quantifying ratings, some employers take a more subjective approach. With the **critical incident method**, you keep a log of positive and negative examples (critical incidents) of a subordinate's work-related behavior. Every six months or so, supervisor and subordinate meet to discuss the latter's performance, using the incidents as examples.

Even if you have to use graphic ratings or ranking, compiling incidents is still useful. Doing so provides you with examples of performance you can use to explain the person's rating. It makes you think about the subordinate's appraisal all during the year (so the rating does not just reflect the employee's most recent performance). In Table 13.1, one of the assistant plant supervisor's jobs was to supervise procurement and minimize inventory costs. The critical incident log shows that she let inventory storage costs rise 15%; this provides an example of what performance she must improve in the future.

Narrative Forms

All or part of the written appraisal may be in narrative form. Figure 13.7 presents one example. Here, the supervisor is responsible for assessing the employee's past performance and areas of required improvement. The supervisor's narrative helps the employee to understand where his or her performance was good or bad, and how to improve that performance.

Behaviorally Anchored Rating Scales

Some employers (a relative few) use a behaviorally anchored rating scale (BARS). A **behaviorally anchored rating scale** is an appraisal tool that anchors a numerical rating scale (say, from 1 Low to 9 High) with specific examples (critical incidents) of good or poor performance.[11]

The BARS is a relatively precise and scientific way to appraise performance. Developing a BARS typically requires these steps:

1. **Write critical incidents.** Ask supervisors to describe specific illustrations (critical incidents) of effective and ineffective performance on this job, such as , "Checked sales flyer . . .".

■ Figure **13.7**

Appraisal-Coaching Worksheet

Source: Reprinted from www.HR.BLR.com with permission of the publisher Business and Legal Reports, Inc., 141 Mill Rock Road East, Old Saybrook CT © 2004.

Appraisal-Coaching Worksheet

Instructions: This form is to be filled out by supervisor and employee prior to each performance review period.

Employee: _____ Position: _____

Supervisor: _____ Department: _____

Date: _____ Period of Work under Consideration: from _____ to _____

1. What areas of the employee's work performance are meeting job performance standards?

2. In what areas is improvement needed during the next six to twelve months?

3. What factors or events that are beyond the employee's control may affect (positively or negatively) his or her ability to accomplish planned results during the next six to twelve months?

4. What specific strengths has the employee demonstrated on this job that should be more fully used during the next six to twelve months?

5. List two or three areas (if applicable) in which the employee needs to improve his or her performance during the next six to twelve months (gaps in knowledge or experience, skill development needs, behavior modifications that affect job performance, etc.).

6. Based on your consideration of items 1-5 above, summarize your mutual objectives:
A. What supervisor will do:

B. What employee will do:

C. Date for next progress check or to re-evaluate objective:

D. Data/evidence that will be used to observe and/or measure progress.

_____
Employee Signature   Supervisor Signature

_____
Date

2. **Develop performance dimensions.**   Have these people classify the incidents into 5 or 10 dimensions, such as "conscientiousness."

3. **Scale the incidents.**   This group then rates the incident as to how effectively or ineffectively it represents performance on the dimension (7- to 9-point scales are typical). In Figure 13.8, "Checked sales flyer . . ." deserves a rating between 6 and 7, for instance.

4. **Develop a final instrument.**   Choose about six or seven of the incidents to use as the dimension's behavioral anchors.[12]

Here's an example. Three researchers developed a BARS for grocery checkout clerks.[13] They collected many critical incidents and then grouped these into the following performance dimensions:

1. Knowledge and judgment

2. Conscientiousness

3. Skill in human relations

4. Skill in operation of register
5. Skill in bagging
6. Skill in monetary transactions
7. Observational ability

They then developed behaviorally anchored rating scales or BARS (similar to the one in Figure 13.8) for each of these seven dimensions. Each BARS contained a scale (ranging from 1 to 9) for rating performance from "extremely poor" to "extremely good." Then a specific critical incident (such as "Carefully but expeditiously checked the date of each coupon to ensure it was still valid") helped anchor or specify what was meant by "extremely good" (9) performance. Similarly, they used several other critical incident anchors along the performance scale from (8) down to (1).

BARS are probably the most accurate way to appraise employees' performance. Most important, the critical incidents along the scale make clear what to look for in terms of superior performance, average performance, and so forth.[14]

Management by Objectives

Most supervisors use the term "MBO" (Management by Objectives) quite loosely. Strictly speaking, MBO means a formal, companywide goal-setting program. Many

■Figure **13.8**

Example of a Behaviorally Anchored Rating Scale for the Checkout Clerk Performance Dimension: Conscientiousness

Grocery Store Checkout Clerk: *Conscientiousness* Being careful and precise in checking out the customer's groceries. Meticulous in ensuring prices are accurately charged and that coupons are rung up correctly.		
Extremely Good	9-	
		Carefully but expeditiously checked the date of each coupon to ensure it was still valid.
	8-	
		Looked for unmarked items and had a bagger go back to check the price when received an item with an un-marked price.
	7-	
		Checked sales flyer when customer pointed out an item was on sale.
	6-	
		Weighed produce but failed to check price listed Price per pound, instead depending on memory.
	5-	
		Asked clerk at next register for price of unmarked item.
	4-	
		Noticed unmarked item and asked customer what the price should be.
	3-	
		Instead of checking item, rang up produce item as "plain" rather than as "deluxe", undercharging by 40%.
	2-	
		Seen talking on cell phone and texting while checking customer's groceries, failing to charge for six items as a result.
Extremely Poor	1-	

employers use formal MBO programs (like those we outlined in Chapter 4) as the main appraisal method. Here you appraise your subordinate based on how well he or she achieved the goals you set for him or her. Other supervisors use MBO informally to supplement a graphic rating or other appraisal method. They engage in informal "MBO programs" with subordinates by setting goals and periodically providing feedback.

Computerized and Web-Based Performance Appraisal

Employers increasingly use computerized or Web-based performance appraisal systems. These enable supervisors to keep computerized notes on subordinates during the year, and then to merge these with ratings of employees on several performance traits. The software then generates written text to support each part of the appraisal. Most appraisal software combines several of the basic methods we discussed, such as graphic ratings plus critical incidents or BARS.

EXAMPLES   There are several good ones from which to choose. *PerformancePro* from HRN Management Group (illustrated in Figure 13.9) presents the supervisor with a behaviorally anchored scale with which to appraise subordinates. *Employee Appraiser* (developed by the Austin-Hayne Corporation, San Mateo, California) presents a menu of more than a dozen evaluation dimensions, including dependability, initiative, communication, decision making, leadership, judgment, and planning and productivity.[15] Within each dimension are various performance factors, again in menu form. For example, under "Communication" are separate factors for things like writing, verbal communication, and receptivity to feedback and criticism. When the user clicks on a performance factor, he or she is presented with a version of a graphic rating scale. However, instead of numbers (such as Good 5 or Poor 1), Employee Appraiser uses behaviorally anchored examples. For example, for *verbal communication* there are six choices, ranging from "presents ideas clearly" to "lacks structure." The supervisor picks the phrase that most accurately describes the worker. Then Employee Appraiser generates an appraisal with sample text.

Appraisal in Practice

The best appraisal forms merge several approaches. Figure 13.3 (page 384–385) was an example. It supports a graphic rating scale with behavioral anchors such as "Even with guidance, fails to. . . ."

This form also illustrates an important point about appraisals. Even if the company uses a graphic rating scale with traditional dimensions such as "Below Expectations," it can benefit from anchoring the scale, as here, with behavioral descriptions. Doing so improves the reliability and validity of the appraisal. Figure 13.3 is a graphic rating scale supported with specific behavioral competency expectations (across the top). These expectations pinpoint what raters should look for.

Who Should Do the Appraising?

Traditionally, the employee's direct supervisor appraises his or her performance. However, other options are available and used. We'll look at the main ones.

■Figure **13.9**

Online Performance Appraisal Tool

Source: http://www.hrnonline.com/per_about.asp (accessed April 29, 2009).

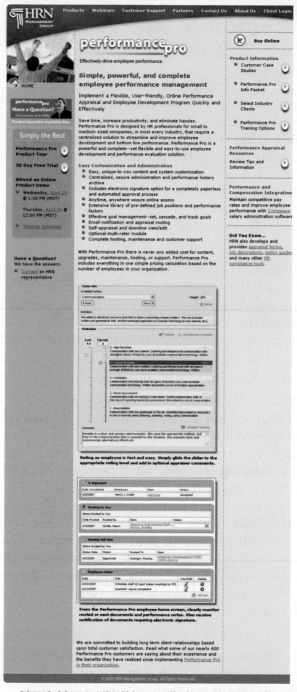

THE IMMEDIATE SUPERVISOR   Supervisors' ratings are the heart of most appraisals. This makes sense: The supervisor usually is in the best position to evaluate the subordinate's performance and is responsible for that person's performance.

PEER APPRAISALS   With more firms using self-managing teams, peer or "team" appraisals—the appraisal of an employee by his or her peers—are popular. Typically, an employee chooses an appraisal chairperson. That person then selects one supervisor and three or four other peers to evaluate the employee's work.

Peer ratings have benefits. In one study, the researchers found that requiring peer appraisals had "an immediate positive impact on [improving] perception of open communication, task motivation, social loafing, group viability, cohesion, and satisfaction."[16]

Peer appraisals are also good for predicting who will or will not succeed in management. In one study of military officers, peer ratings were quite accurate in predicting which officers would be promoted.[17]

RATING COMMITTEES   Many employers use rating committees. These committees usually contain the employee's immediate supervisor and two or three other supervisors.

Using multiple raters makes sense. The composite ratings tend to be more reliable, fair, and valid.[18] Using several raters can also help cancel out problems like bias and halo effects. Furthermore, when there are differences in ratings, they usually stem from the fact that raters at different levels observe different facets of an employee's performance. Even when a committee is not used, it is customary to have the supervisor immediately above the one who makes the appraisal review it.

SELF-RATINGS   Should employees appraise themselves? The problem, of course, is that employees usually rate themselves higher than they are rated by supervisors or peers. One study found that when asked to rate their own job performances, 40% of employees in jobs of all types placed themselves in the top 10% ("one of the best"), while virtually all remaining employees rated themselves either in the top 25% ("well above average"), or at least in the top 50% ("above average").[19] Similarly, group members tend to give their groups unrealistically high ratings.[20]

Supervisors requesting self-appraisals from employees should know they're potentially opening a hornet's nest. Doing so may accentuate differences and rigidify positions, rather than aid the process. Furthermore, even if you don't ask for a self-appraisal, your employees will almost certainly come to the performance review with their (relatively high) self-appraisals in mind. Therefore, come prepared for a dialogue, with specific critical incidents to make your point.

APPRAISAL BY SUBORDINATES   Many employers let subordinates anonymously rate their supervisor's performance, a process some call *upward feedback*. The process helps top managers diagnose leadership styles, identify potential "people" problems, and take corrective action as required.

Subordinate ratings are especially valuable when used for developmental rather than evaluative purposes. Supervisors who receive feedback from subordinates who identify themselves view the upward appraisal process more positively than do supervisors who receive anonymous feedback. However, subordinates (not surprisingly) are more comfortable giving anonymous responses. Sample upward feedback items include, "I can tell my supervisor what I think," and "My supervisor tells me what is expected."

The evidence suggests that subordinate appraisals, used properly, can have impressive results. One study involved 92 supervisors.[21] The subordinates rated themselves and their supervisors on 33 behavioral statements.

The results were striking. According to the researchers, "managers whose initial level of performance was 'low' (as defined as the average rating from subordinates) improved between administrations one and two [of the employee surveys], and sustained this improvement two years later."[22] In fact, the low-performing managers seemed to improve over time even if they didn't receive any feedback. Just learning what the critical supervisory behaviors were and knowing their subordinates would be appraising them may have been enough to prompt the improved behavior.[23]

360-DEGREE FEEDBACK   Many firms expand the idea of upward and peer feedback into "360-degree feedback." Here ratings are collected from supervisors, subordinates, peers, and internal or external customers.[24] The surveys include items such as "returns phone calls promptly," "listens well," or "[my supervisor] keeps me informed." Computerized and Web-based systems then compile this feedback into individual reports, just for the ratees. They then meet with their own supervisors and sometimes with their subordinates and share the information they feel is pertinent for self-improvement. Employers generally use the feedback for development rather than for pay increases.

Some doubt the practicality of 360-degree feedback. Employees usually do these reviews anonymously, so those with an ax to grind can misuse them. A "Dilbert" cartoon, announcing that evaluations by coworkers will help decide raises, has one character asking, "If my coworkers got small raises, won't there be more available in the budget for me?"[25] Using 360-degree feedback generally requires collecting and compiling the individual survey results via computerized surveys; Figure 13.10 illustrates one such survey.

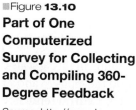

■Figure **13.10**

Part of One Computerized Survey for Collecting and Compiling 360-Degree Feedback

Source: http://www.hr-survey.com/sd3609q.htm (accessed April 28, 2009).

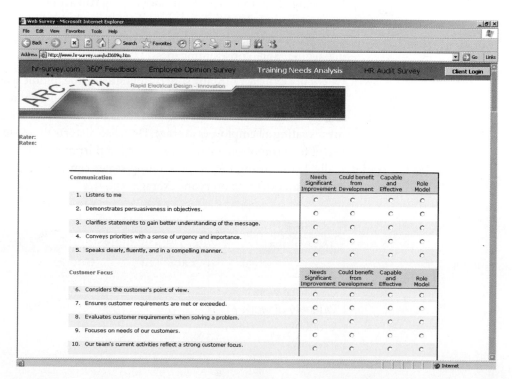

3. Appraisal Problems and How to Handle Them

Employers' 360-degree appraisals aren't the only ones susceptible to problems. Graphic ratings and the other appraisal tools have idiosyncrasies of their own. Left unattended, these problems will undermine the fairness and usefulness of your appraisals. Let's therefore look next at these problems and how to avoid them.

Potential Appraisal Issues

Appraisals that rely on graphic rating scales are susceptible to several problems. These include unclear standards, halo effect, central tendency, leniency or strictness, and bias.

UNCLEAR STANDARDS   Table 13.2 illustrates the **unclear standards** problem. This graphic rating scale seems objective. However, it would probably result in unfair appraisals, because the traits and degrees of merit are ambiguous. For example, different supervisors might define "good" performance, "fair" performance, and so on differently. The same is true of traits such as "quality of work" or "creativity."[26]

The way to fix this problem is to include descriptive phrases that define or illustrate each trait and standard, as in Figure 13.3. That form spells out what measures like "Role Model" or "Below Expectations" mean.

HALO EFFECT   Experts define **halo effect** as "the influence of a rater's general impression on ratings of specific ratee qualities."[27] For example, supervisors often rate unfriendly employees lower on all traits, rather than just on "gets along well with others." Just being aware of this problem should help you avoid it. Halo effect helps explain why employers use behaviorally anchored rating scales (BARS). Because of the behavioral anchors, the ratings the supervisor gives to each performance dimension (such as "skill in bagging" and "conscientiousness") tend to be more independent of each other.

CENTRAL TENDENCY   Many supervisors stick to the middle when filling in rating scales. For example, if the rating scale ranges from 1 to 7, they tend to avoid the highs (6 and 7) and lows (1 and 2) and rate most of their people between 3 and 5. **Central tendency** means rating all employees average. Doing so distorts the evaluations, making them less useful for promotion, salary, or counseling purposes. Ranking employees (even informally, before using the graphic rating scale) can reduce this problem, since ranking means you can't rate everyone average.

■ Table **13.2**

A Graphic Rating Scale with Unclear Standards				
	Excellent	Good	Fair	Poor
Quality of work Quantity of work Creativity Integrity				

Note: For example, what exactly is meant by "good," "quantity of work," and so forth?

LENIENCY OR STRICTNESS   Other supervisors tend to rate all their subordinates consistently high or low, just as some instructors are notoriously high or low graders. This **strictness/leniency** problem is especially severe with graphic rating scales. On the other hand, ranking forces supervisors to distinguish between high and low performers.

There are several solutions. Some employers insist that supervisors avoid giving all their employees high (or low) ratings. A stronger position is to require a distribution—that, say, about 10% of the people should be rated "excellent," 20% "good," and so forth.[28]

RECENCY EFFECTS   The recency effect means letting what the employee has done recently blind you to what his or her performance has been over the year. The main solution is to accumulate critical incidents all year long.

BIAS   The number of things that can lead to biased appraisals is limitless. One study focused on the rater's personality. Raters who scored higher on "conscientiousness" tended to give lower ratings—they were stricter, in other words; those scoring higher on "agreeableness" gave higher ratings—they were more lenient.[29] Even the appraisal's purpose biases the results. In one study, performance appraisal ratings obtained for pay raises or promotions were nearly one-third higher than were those obtained for employee development purposes.[30] Then there is interpersonal dynamics between supervisor and subordinate. "Good relationships tend to create good [appraisal] experiences, bad relationships bad ones."[31]

Unfortunately, the subordinates' personal characteristics (such as age, race, and sex) also affect their ratings. A 36-year-old supervisor ranked a 62-year-old subordinate at the bottom of the department's rankings, and then fired him. The court held that the younger boss's discriminatory motives might have prejudiced the dismissal decision.[32] In one study, women had to receive higher performance ratings than men to be promoted, "suggesting that women were held to stricter standards for promotion."[33] Another study found that raters might actually penalize successful women for their success.[34] The Supervising the New Workforce feature expands on this.

The bottom line is that the appraisal often says more about the supervisor than about the subordinate.[37] This is a powerful reason for having the supervisor's boss review

---

Supervising the New Workforce

The Gender Gap in Appraisals

A study illustrates how bias can influence the way one person appraises another. In this study, researchers sought to determine the extent to which pregnancy biases performance appraisals.[35] The subjects were 220 undergraduate students between the ages of 17 and 43 attending a Midwestern university.

The researchers showed two videos of a female "employee." Each video showed three five-minute scenarios in which this "employee" interacted with another woman. For example, she acted as a customer representative to deal with an irate customer, tried to sell a computer system to a potential customer, and dealt with a problem subordinate. In each case, the employee's performance level was designed to be average or slightly above average. The employee was the same in both videotapes, and the videotapes were identical—except for one difference. Researchers shot the first video in the employee's ninth month of pregnancy, the second about five months later.

Several groups of student raters watched either the "pregnant" or "not pregnant" tape. They rated the "employee" on a 5-point rating scale for individual characteristics such as "ability to do the job," "dependability," and "physical mannerisms." Despite seeing otherwise identical behavior by the same woman, the student raters "with a remarkably high degree of consistency" assigned lower performance ratings to a pregnant woman as opposed to a nonpregnant one.[36]

the rating. Some employers even have "calibration" meetings. Here supervisors discuss among themselves their reasons for the appraisals they gave each of their subordinates.[38]

Let's look next at some general rules or guidelines for improving appraisals.

Five Guidelines for Effective Appraisals

Problems like bias can make an appraisal worse than no appraisal at all. Would an employee not be better off with no appraisal than with a seemingly objective but actually biased one? However, problems like these aren't inevitable, and you can minimize them. Do five things to have effective appraisals.

KNOW THE PROBLEMS *First*, learn and understand the potential appraisal problems. Understanding and anticipating the problem (halo effect, recency, and so on) can help you avoid it.

USE THE RIGHT APPRAISAL TOOL *Second*, to the extent you have a choice, use the right appraisal tool—or combination of tools. Table 13.3 summarizes each tool's pros and cons.

In practice, employers choose appraisal tools based on several criteria. Accessibility and *ease-of-use* is probably first. That is why graphic rating scales are still so popular, even within computerized appraisal packages. Ranking produces clearer results, but many employers (and supervisors) prefer to avoid the *push-back* from employees that rankings provoke. For those for whom *accuracy* is a great concern, BARS are superior, but require much more time to develop and use. Critical incidents by themselves are seldom sufficient for making salary raise decisions.

KEEP A DIARY *Third*, keep a diary of employees' performance over the year.[39] One study involved 112 first-line supervisors. Some attended a special diary-keeping

■ Table **13.3**

Important Advantages and Disadvantages of Appraisal Tools		
Tool	**Advantages**	**Disadvantages**
Graphic rating scale	Simple to use; provides a quantitative rating for each employee.	Standards may be unclear; halo effect, central tendency, leniency, bias can also be problems.
BARS	Provides behavioral "anchors." BARS is very accurate.	Difficult to develop.
Alternation ranking	Simple to use (but not as simple as graphic rating scales). Avoids central tendency and other problems of rating scales.	Can cause disagreements among employees and may be unfair if all employees are, in fact, excellent.
Forced distribution method	End up with a predetermined number or % of people in each group.	Employees' appraisal results depend on your choice of cutoff points.
Critical incident method	Helps specify what is "right" and "wrong" about the employee's performance; forces supervisor to evaluate subordinates on an ongoing basis.	Difficult to rate or rank employees relative to one another.
MBO	Tied to jointly agreed-upon performance objectives.	Time-consuming.

- Base the performance review on duties and standards from a job analysis.
- Try to base the performance review on observable job behaviors or objective performance data.
- Make it clear ahead of time what your performance expectations are.
- Use a standardized performance review procedure for all employees.
- Make sure whoever conducts the reviews have frequent opportunities to observe the employee's job performance.
- Either use multiple raters or have the rater's supervisor evaluate the appraisal results.
- Include an appeals mechanism.
- Document the appraisal review process and results.
- Discuss the appraisal results with the employee.
- Let the employees know ahead of time how you're going to conduct the reviews and use the results.
- Let the employee provide input regarding your assessment of him or her.
- Indicate what the employee needs to do to improve.
- Thoroughly train supervisors. For example, make sure you understand the procedure to use; how problems (like leniency) arise; and how to deal with them.

training program. Compiling a history of critical incidents as they occurred did reduce appraisal problems.[40]

GET AGREEMENT ON A PLAN   *Fourth*, the aim of the appraisal is to improve unsatisfactory performance (or to reinforce exemplary performance). The appraisal's outcome should therefore always be a plan for what the employee must do to improve.

What Are the Guidelines for Compiling Effective Appraisals?

BE FAIR   *Fifth*, make sure that every appraisal you give is fair. One study found that several best practices, such as "have an appeal mechanism" distinguish fair appraisals from unfair ones. Figure 13.11 summarizes these guidelines.

Appraisals and the Law

Inept appraisals are one surefire way to cause legal problems for your employer.[42] For example, one court held that an employer violated Title VII when it laid off several Hispanic-surnamed employees based on poor performance ratings. The court concluded that doing so was illegal because:

1. The firm based the ratings only on subjective supervisory observations.
2. It didn't administer and score the appraisals in a standardized fashion.
3. Two of the three supervisors did not have daily contact with the employees they rated.

How Does the Law Impact Appraisals?

If your case gets to court, what will judges look for? Actions reflecting fairness and due process are most important.[43] Figure 13.12 lists guidelines for developing a legally defensible appraisal process.[44]

4. The Appraisal Interview and Taking Corrective Action

The appraisal typically culminates in an **appraisal interview**. Here, you and the subordinate review the appraisal and make plans to correct deficiencies and reinforce strengths. Interviews like these are often uncomfortable. Few people like to receive—or give—

1. Preferably, conduct a job analysis to establish performance criteria and standards.
2. Make sure you and your employee know what the latter's performance standards are, in writing.
3. When using graphic rating scales, avoid undefined abstract trait names (such as "loyalty" or "honesty").
4. Use subjective narrative comments as only one component of the appraisal.
5. Make sure you know how to use the rating instrument properly.
6. Make sure you've had substantial daily contact with the employees you're evaluating.
7. Using a single overall rating of performance is usually not acceptable to the courts.[45] Use specific performance dimensions, such as quality and conscientiousness.
8. When possible, have more than one appraiser, and conduct all such appraisals independently.
9. One appraiser should never have absolute authority to determine a personnel action.
10. Give employees the opportunity to review and make comments, and have a formal appeals process.
11. Document everything: "Without exception, courts condemn informal performance evaluation practices that eschew documentation."[46]
12. Where appropriate, provide corrective guidance to assist poor performers in improving.

negative feedback. Interviews that culminate in warnings are never likely to be pleasant. However, no appraisal interview should ever raise the specter of unfairness. And no employee should ever walk away feeling that your actions abused his or her sense of respect or identity. Adequate preparation and effective implementation are therefore essential.

Types of Appraisal Interviews

As a supervisor, you will face four types of appraisal interviews, each with its unique objectives:

> *Satisfactory—Promotable* is the easiest interview: The person's performance is satisfactory and there is a promotion ahead. Your objective is to discuss the person's career plans and to develop a specific plan for educational and professional development.

> *Satisfactory—Not promotable* is for employees whose performance is satisfactory but for whom promotion is not possible. The objective here is to maintain satisfactory performance. The best option is usually to find incentives that are sufficient to maintain performance. These might include extra time off, a small bonus, and reinforcement, perhaps in the form of an occasional "well done!"

When the person's performance is *unsatisfactory but correctable*, the interview objective is to lay out an action plan for correcting the unsatisfactory performance.

Finally, if the employee is *unsatisfactory* and the situation is *uncorrectable*, you can usually skip the interview. You either tolerate the person's poor performance for now, or (more likely) dismiss the person.

How to Conduct the Appraisal Interview

If you put yourself in your subordinate's place, it's not hard to imagine what you would want from the appraisal interview. At a minimum, you would probably prefer:

1. Not feeling threatened during the interview
2. Having an opportunity to present your ideas and feelings and to influence the course of the interview

3. Having a helpful and constructive supervisor conduct the interview

4. Having a clear understanding of what you're doing well and not so well, and a plan to rectify the latter

There are thus five main things to keep in mind when conducting the interview:

1. **Preparation is essential.** Beforehand, review the employee's job description, compare performance to the standards, and review the previous appraisals. Give the employee at least a week's notice to review his or her work. Set a mutually agreeable time for the interview and allow enough time.

2. **Talk in terms of objective work data.** Use examples such as absences, tardiness, quality records, orders processed, productivity records, order processing time, accident reports, and so on.

3. **Don't get personal.** Don't say, "You're too slow in producing those reports." Instead, try to compare the person's performance to a standard. ("These reports should normally be done within 10 days.") Similarly, don't compare the person's performance to that of other people. ("He's quicker than you are.")

4. **Encourage the person to talk.** Stop and listen to what the person is saying; ask open-ended questions such as, "What do you think we can do to improve the situation?" Use a command such as "Go on." Restate the person's last point as a question, such as, "You don't think you can get the job done?"

5. **Get agreement.** Make sure the person leaves knowing specifically what he or she is doing right and doing wrong and with agreement on how things will improve, and by when. Write up an action plan with targets and dates. The accompanying Leadership Applications for Supervisors feature expands on the leadership aspects of these five points.

What Are the Guidelines for Conducting an Appraisal Interview?

Taking Corrective Action

For employees whose performance is meritorious, the action plan may range from recognition to promotion and a pay raise.

Other appraisal interviews will necessitate some corrective action. Corrective actions may range from a critical review of the person's performance, to counseling, training, or, if appropriate, a warning.

HOW TO CRITICIZE A SUBORDINATE   When you must criticize, do so in a manner that lets the person maintain his or her dignity—in private and constructively. Provide examples of critical incidents and specific suggestions of what to do and why. Avoid once-a-year "critical broadsides" by giving feedback periodically, so that the formal review contains no surprises. Never say the person is "always" wrong (since no one is ever "always" wrong or right). Criticism should be objective and free of personal bias.

HOW TO HANDLE A DEFENSIVE SUBORDINATE   Defenses are a familiar aspect of our lives. When a supervisor tells someone his or her performance is poor, the first reaction is often denial (as in, "That's not true; I have been working hard"). Denial is a defense mechanism. By denying the fault, the person avoids having to question his or her own competence. Others react with anger and aggression. This helps them let off steam and postpones confronting the immediate problem.

The Appraisal Interview and the Quality of the Leader-Member Exchange (LMX)

As we saw in Chapter 2 (Leading a Diverse Workforce), leader-member exchange theory (LMX) draws a simple and clear conclusion: that leaders treat people they like (those in their in-groups) better than they treat those they don't like as much (those in their out-groups). A recent research study shows that higher quality supervisor-subordinate relationships manifest themselves in more open and congenial communications, and thus in more useful appraisal interviews.[47]

We know from other research that how employees react to appraisal interviews, and whether the interviews get them to change, depend largely on whether the employees think they have a chance to express their opinions. In the present study, the researchers therefore asked the participants to respond to items such as, "To what extent did you discuss what you felt your strengths and weaknesses are?" and, "To what extent did you influence how your supervisor evaluates your work?" The researchers found that employees in lower quality exchange relationships with their supervisors seemed to get fewer opportunities to express their opinions in the interview. They therefore reacted less favorably to their supervisors' performance suggestions and information.

So as usual, the leaders' unfortunate out-group employees lost out.

The solution isn't necessarily for the leader/supervisor to expand his or her in-group (though that would be nice). A simpler option is to make sure that you give all your subordinates an adequate opportunity to talk and to express themselves during the interview. You can do this by "asking team members for their thoughts . . . asking clarifying questions, taking notes, and rephrasing members' statements, and acknowledging their inputs when communicating your final decision."[48] Doing so "could help minimize employee resistance and decrease the likelihood of legal challenges."[49]

On the other hand, just letting appraisees talk is not enough. Giving appraisees an opportunity to express themselves and then not considering their opinions can backfire. The optimal solution, the researchers say, is that when supervisors "work to create common ground throughout the year, this can be a social foundation on which to build aligned efforts, understanding, and more positive reactions to [performance appraisal] systems."[50]

In any event, as we saw earlier in this book, understanding and dealing with defensiveness is an important supervisory leadership skill. In his book *Effective Psychology for Managers*, psychologist Mortimer Feinberg suggests the following:

1. Recognize that defensive behavior is normal.

2. Never attack a person's defenses. Don't try to "explain someone to themselves" by saying things like, "You know the real reason you're using that excuse is that you can't bear to be blamed." Instead, concentrate on the facts ("sales are down").

3. Postpone action. Sometimes it is best to do nothing. Employees may react to sudden threats by instinctively hiding behind their defenses. But given sufficient time, a more rational reaction takes over.

4. Recognize your own limitations. The supervisor should not try to be a psychologist. Offering understanding is one thing; trying to deal with psychological problems is another.

HOW TO HANDLE A FORMAL WRITTEN WARNING   An employee's performance may be so weak that it requires a formal written warning. Such warnings serve two purposes: (1) They may serve to shake your employee out of his or her bad habits, and (2) they can help you defend your rating, both to your own boss and (if needed) to the courts.

Sample Employee Development Plan

Employee Name: __J. Citizen__   Position Title: __HR Analyst__   Date Developed: _____   Date Last Revised: _____

A. Key objectives and core competencies

List top 3-5 business objectives for this year:	List core competencies for position:
1. Implement revised employee development system	1. Employee Development 4. Communication
2. Provide organization development support	2. Recruitment 5. Conflict Management
3. Reduce employee turnover by 5%	3. Organization Development 6. Grievance Management

B. Competency gaps and action plan

List top 2-3 core competencies that need development	List key gaps for each core competency	Briefly state how you will close each gap	Target completion date	Status R/Y/G
1. Employee Dev.	1. Succession Plng.	1. Participate in succession planning reviews in sister company to learn about process		G
2. Grievance Mgmt.	2. Elevation Process	2. Attend refresher training. Develop draft process. Pilot draft process and review.		Y
3.	3.	3.		

Written warnings should do four things: *identify* the employee's standards, make it clear that the employee was *aware* of the standard, specify any *deficiencies* relative to the standard, and show the employee had an *opportunity* to correct his or her performance.

The Development Plan

As appropriate, the corrective action should manifest itself in a development plan. As in Figure 13.13, the development plan should identify the performance deficiency, the steps involved in correcting the deficiencies, and a timeline for accomplishing these steps.

Figure 13.14 provides a checklist to make sure you cover all the appraisal interview bases.

CHECKLIST DURING THE APPRAISAL INTERVIEW

	Yes	No
• Did you discuss each goal or objective established for this employee?	☐	☐
• Are you and the employee clear on the areas of agreement? Disagreement?	☐	☐
• Did you and the employee cover all positive skills, traits, accomplishments, areas of growth, etc.? Did you reinforce the employee's accomplishments?	☐	☐
• Did you give the employee a sense of what you thought of his or her potential or ability?	☐	☐
• Are you both clear on areas where improvement is required? Expected? Demanded? Desired?	☐	☐
• What training or development recommendations did you agree on?	☐	☐
• Did you indicate consequences for noncompliance, if appropriate?	☐	☐
• Did you set good objectives for the next appraisal period?	☐	☐
• Objective?	☐	☐
• Specific?	☐	☐
• Measurable?	☐	☐
• Did you set a standard to be used for evaluation?	☐	☐
• Timeframe?	☐	☐
• Did you set a time for the next evaluation?	☐	☐
• Did you confirm what your part would be? Did the employee confirm his or her part?	☐	☐
• Did you thank the employee for his or her efforts?	☐	☐

5. Using Performance Management

What Is Performance Management?

As we said earlier in the chapter, the sorts of problems that traditional appraisals trigger prompted many employers to try an alternative approach, *performance management*. Thus we saw that at Toyota's Kentucky Camry plant, supervisors don't sit with individual employees to appraise them. Instead, teams of employees monitor their own results, continuously aligning those results with the work team's standards and with the plant's overall quality and productivity needs. **Performance management** is the *continuous* process of identifying, measuring, and developing the performance of individuals and teams and *aligning* their performance with the organization's *goals*.[51]

Comparing Performance Appraisal and Performance Management

In comparing performance management and performance appraisal, "the distinction is the contrast between a year-end event—the completion of the appraisal form—and a process that starts the year with performance planning and is integral to the way people are managed throughout the year."[52]

Three main things distinguish performance management from performance appraisal.

1. First, performance management never means just meeting with a subordinate once or twice a year to "review your performance." It means *continuous daily or weekly* interactions and feedback to ensure continuous improvement.[53]

2. Second, performance management is always *goal-directed*. The continuing performance reviews always involve comparing the employee's or team's performance against goals that specifically stem from and link to the company's strategic goals.

3. Third, performance management means continuously reevaluating and (if need be) *modifying how the employee and team get their work done*. Depending on the issue, this may mean additional training, changing work procedures, or instituting new incentive plans, for instance.

Using Performance Management

Any supervisor can apply these steps and thus "performance management-ize" how he or she appraises employees. Specifically, *continuously* compare the employee's performance to goals that make sense in terms of the department's goals, provide *continuous constructive feedback*, and take steps to continuously nudge the employee's performance back into alignment, for instance, with coaching or additional training.

Using Information Technology to Support Performance Management

Performance management needn't be high-tech. For example, each day those Toyota work teams meet to review their performance and to get their efforts and those of their members aligned with their performance standards and goals.

What Is Performance Management?

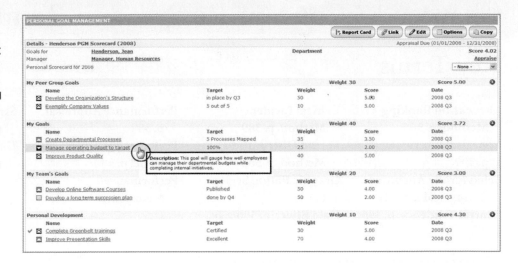

But information technology does enable management to automate performance management. We can sum up this IT-supported performance management process as follows:

- Assign financial and nonfinancial goals to each team's activities. (For example, Southwest Airlines might measure ground crew aircraft turnaround time in terms of "Improve turnaround time from an average of 30 minutes per plane to 26 minutes per plane this year.")
- Inform all employees of their goals.
- Use IT-supported tools like "digital dashboard" reports (see Figure 13.15) to continuously monitor and assess each team's and employee's performance.
- Take corrective action at once.

IT-supported performance management gives supervisors a real-time overview of each team's performance, and a way to take corrective action before things swing out of control. Apps like the following one are available, too.

APPs

Mobile Performance Management

A new iPhone app enables supervisors and employees to monitor their performance management goals and progress while on the go. ActiveStrategy (http://www.activestrategy. com) recently demonstrated what they call "the first enterprise performance management application for the iPhone," ActiveStrategy Mobile™.

Linked in to this vendor's ActiveStrategy Enterprise software, the new application "allows business users to keep in close touch with the strategic performance of their business, making it an ideal enterprise application for the iPhone."[54]

Chapter 13 Concept Review and Reinforcement

Key Terms

Review of Key Concepts

Performance Appraisal	Performance appraisal means evaluating an employee's performance relative to his or her performance standards.
Performance Management	Performance management is the continuous process of identifying, measuring, and developing the performance of individuals and teams and aligning their performance with the organization's goals.
Why Appraise Performance?	Reasons to appraise subordinates' performance include: • Basis for pay, promotion, and retention decisions. • Appraisals play integral role in the performance management process. • Basis for subordinate to develop a plan for correcting any deficiencies. • Appraisals serve as a useful career planning purpose. • Helps supervisors identify training and development needs.
	**Tools for Appraising Performance**
Graphic Rating Scale Method	A scale that lists a number of traits and a range of performance for each. The employee is then rated by identifying the score that best describes his or her level of performance for each trait.
Alternation Ranking Method	With the alternation ranking method, you can rank employees from best to worst on a particular trait.
Forced Distribution Method	The forced distribution method is similar to grading on a curve. Here you place predetermined percentages of appraisees in various performance categories.

Behaviorally Anchored Rating Scale	A behaviorally anchored rating scale anchors a quantified scale with specific narrative examples of good and poor performance.
Critical Incidents Method	With the critical incident method, you keep a log of positive and negative examples (critical incidents) of a subordinate's work-related behavior. During a performance review, these incidents are used as examples.
Management by Objectives	With MBO programs, supervisors together with subordinates set goals and then periodically review and provide feedback. Here you appraise your subordinate based on how well he or she achieved the goals you set for him or her.
Dealing with Performance Appraisal Problems	Potential appraisal problems include: • Unclear standards • The halo effect • Central tendency • Leniency/strictness • Recent effects • Appraisals need to be legally defensible
Appraisal Interview	In an appraisal interview, the supervisor and the subordinate review the performance appraisal and make plans to correct deficiencies and reinforce strengths.
Types of Appraisal Interviews	There are four types of appraisal interviews, each with its own unique objectives: • Satisfactory—promotable • Satisfactory—not promotable • Unsatisfactory but correctable • Unsatisfactory and uncorrectable
Conducting the Appraisal Interview	Points the supervisor needs to keep in mind during the appraisal interview: • Preparation is essential. • Talk in terms of objective work data. • Don't get personal. • Encourage the person to talk. • Get agreement.

Review and Discussion Questions

1. Describe five reasons why we appraise subordinates' performance. Why is this appraisal important to an employee meeting or exceeding the performance expectations of the organization?
2. What is the difference between using the graphic rating scale method and the alternation ranking method?
3. Which method is most used to appraise performance? Why?
4. What are the advantages to using the critical incidents method to appraise performance?
5. How effective, do you think, is using management by objectives (MBO) to appraise subordinate performance?
6. Be specific in your answer. If you ranked the potential appraisal problems, which problems would you rank number 1 and number 2? Why?
7. Identify and briefly discuss the objectives of using appraisal interviews.
8. When conducting an appraisal interview, why do you not want to get personal with the subordinate?
9. Discuss why it is important to align the employee's efforts with the job standards.
10. Discuss why having current job descriptions is so critical to effective job performance appraisals.

Application and Skill Building

Case Study One

Appraising the Professor

Your friend Dr. Adams, the dean of the school of business, has come to you with a problem. Knowing that you are an experienced human resource management professional, she wants you to tell her the advantages and disadvantages of using the online faculty appraisal form in Figure 13.16.

■ Figure **13.16**

Online Faculty Evaluation Form

Source: Used with permission of Central Oregon Community College.

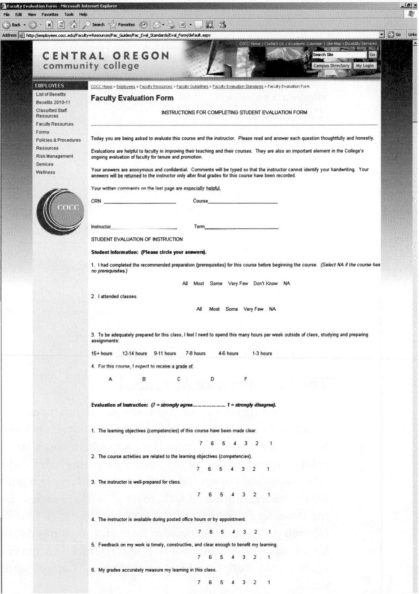

(*Continued*)

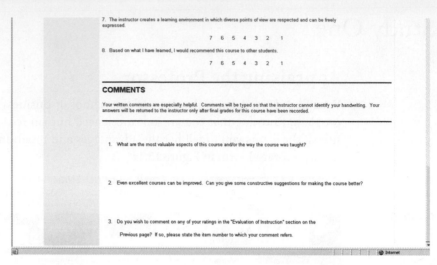

7. The instructor creates a learning environment in which diverse points of view are respected and can be freely expressed.

7 6 5 4 3 2 1

8. Based on what I have learned, I would recommend this course to other students.

7 6 5 4 3 2 1

COMMENTS

Your written comments are especially helpful. Comments will be typed so that the instructor cannot identify your handwriting. Your answers will be returned to the instructor only after final grades for this course have been recorded.

1. What are the most valuable aspects of this course and/or the way the course was taught?

2. Even excellent courses can be improved. Can you give some constructive suggestions for making the course better?

3. Do you wish to comment on any of your ratings in the "Evaluation of Instruction" section on the previous page? If so, please state the item number to which your comment refers.

■ Figure **13.16**
(*Continued*)

Questions

Specifically, evaluate the pros and cons of using this form for the faculty at her school, list any pitfalls one might expect from using the form, and suggest any changes that you believe might improve the form and how it is used.

Case Study Two

Carter Cleaning Centers

The Performance Appraisal

After spending several weeks on the job, Jennifer was surprised to discover that her father had not formally evaluated any employee's performance for all the years that he had owned the business. Jack's position was that he had "a hundred higher-priority things to attend to," such as boosting sales and lowering costs, and, in any case, many employees didn't stick around long enough to be appraisable, anyway. Furthermore, contended Jack, manual workers such as those doing the pressing and the cleaning did periodically get positive feedback in terms of praise from Jack for a job well done, or criticism, also from Jack, if things did not look right during one of his swings through the stores. Similarly, Jack was never shy about telling his managers about store problems so that they, too, got some feedback on where they stood.

This informal feedback notwithstanding, Jennifer believes that a more formal appraisal approach is required. She believes that there are criteria such as quality, quantity, attendance, and punctuality that should be evaluated periodically even if a worker is paid on piece rate. Furthermore, she feels quite strongly that the supervisors need to have a list of quality standards for matters such as store cleanliness, efficiency, safety, and adherence to budget on which they know they are to be formally evaluated.

Questions

1. Is Jennifer right about the need to evaluate the workers formally? The supervisors? Why or why not?
2. Develop a performance appraisal method for the workers and supervisors in each store.

Experiential Activities

Activity 1. Gladys had only worked for Ocean Engineering for six months, but she really loved her job as a junior engineer. She looked forward to getting and discussing her first performance appraisal. The meeting with her supervisor was a disaster. Gladys was told that she was making a lot of errors and wasn't doing even half of her job requirements. Overall, Gladys received a very low rating.

The Management of Performance Appraisals

Purpose: The purpose of this exercise is to give you practice in preparing for appraising and managing performance.

Required Understanding: You are going to develop a comprehensive guideline for performance reviews. You should be familiar with the discussion of appraising and managing performance from this chapter.

How to Set Up the Exercise/Instructions: Divide the class into groups of 4 or 5 students.

1. Your group should develop a one-page outline summarizing the guidelines for effective performance reviews.
2. Next, you want to answer the question of how Gladys's supervisor could have managed her performance appraisal differently to have avoided a poor performance evaluation, using your guidelines.
3. Have a spokesperson from each group share their outline with each of the other groups.
4. Follow with a class discussion involving all groups. Look at the similarities of these outlines. What are the potential problems in using these outlines?

Activity 2. Many organizations, such as Habitat for Humanity, depend heavily on volunteers in order to fulfill their mission. These volunteers come from all walks of life, each with special talents or skills. They are required to help build homes or support the Habitat for Humanity stores located mostly in communities where donated-surplus materials are resold to the public or used to furnish new homes. These volunteers are not paid a wage and can come and go as they please. They represent a challenge to Habitat supervisors when it comes to appraising their performance. This appraisal is important, though, as it is a basis for job placement and gives direction to the volunteers who need to correct deficiencies in how they are performing their work.

Purpose: The purpose of this exercise is to give you practice in appraising the performance of volunteer workers.

Required Understanding: You are going to develop a comprehensive outline for appraising volunteer workers. You should be familiar with the discussion of appraising and managing performance covered in this chapter.

How to Set Up the Exercise/Instructions: Divide the class into groups of 4 or 5 students.

1. Develop an outline of a performance appraisal for volunteer workers at Habitat for Humanity.
2. Next, have a spokesperson from each group share their outlines with each of the other groups. Follow with a class discussion involving all of the student groups. Look at the difficulties and questions raised in completing this assignment.

Role-Playing Exercise

Managing Office Performance: The Situation

Joyce, the office supervisor at Ajax Manufacturing Company has been a manager for over 10 years, but lately the low morale of her 10-person staff is making Joyce's job very difficult. She has been going through an annual practice of performance reviews and must now conduct an appraisal interview with each of her subordinates. Joyce uses the graphic rating scale method for appraising performance. She has been requested to rank her workers from best to worst, despite the fact that the lowest ranked employee is still doing the job satisfactorily. It is Joyce's understanding that the first or second highest ranked employees will receive a merit raise in addition to a cost-of-living adjustment for all employees. The problem is that no merit raises, no cost-of-living allowances, and no promotions have been awarded during the past three years. Most of the office employees realize what's happening. Joyce has her first appraisal interview scheduled for tomorrow.

Instructions: All students should read the situation above. One student will play the role of an office worker while the other will play the role of the office supervisor. Each student should only read his or her assigned role below. The two students should engage in a 15-minute conversation (appraisal interview).

After the role-play exercise all students in the class should read and address the questions at the end of the exercise.

Office Worker: Here we go again! Another performance review that is most likely going to be a waste of time. It is not fair; workers in our office have not even gotten a cost-of-living raise over the past three years. The company seems to be doing well financially, so why don't we get a raise? I do a good job at what I do and deserve better. When I go into my appraisal interview, I'm going to ask some questions. Maybe I can get some answers.

Office Supervisor: Morale is really low in the office and I know why. During the past three years, I have suggested merit raises and cost-of-living adjustments for all of my staff, but have been told by my superior that no money is available for raises or adjustments. My first appraisal interview is coming up tomorrow, and I know there will be questions. I just hope I can give them the right answers.

Questions for Discussion

1. Did the office supervisor do a good job in answering the office workers' questions?
2. Can you suggest additional comments or questions that the office worker could have asked?
3. In studying the material in this chapter, can you explain why there is low morale among the office workers?
4. If you were the supervisor, how would you have handled this situation?

14 Supervising Ethics, Fair Treatment, and Discipline at Work

....

CHAPTER OBJECTIVES

After studying this chapter, you should be able to answer the following questions:

1. What Constitutes Fair Treatment of Employees and Why Is It Important?
2. What Causes Unfair Treatment of Employees?
3. What Are Important Fair Treatment Principles?
4. What Is the Role of Ethics at Work?
5. What Are the Guidelines for Managing Employee Discipline and Privacy?

OPENING SNAPSHOT
Last Train out of Coney Island

Enrique had worked as a waiter at a well-known all-night restaurant in the Coney Island section of Brooklyn, New York, for several years. He enjoyed the job, but not the commute. Unless he left the restaurant promptly at 1 a.m., he'd miss his Q train connection to his home in Queens. Then, what should be a 45-minute train and bus ride would take him 2½ hours. One night, two noisy out-of-town men sat down at one of his tables at about 12:45 a.m. When he explained he'd have to leave in 15 minutes, they objected loudly. Enrique's supervisor came over and told him he'd just have to stay until they finished their meal. That could keep him working until 3 a.m. Enrique followed his supervisor back to the kitchen and told him, "Let someone else take over; you know I have to get home." His supervisor smiled and said, "Enrique, if you don't like your job here, I know many people who would."

414

1. Treating Subordinates Fairly

Someone once famously said, "Life is unfair," and to some extent that's true. We can all recount examples of good people suffering misfortune through no fault of their own.

However, this chapter isn't about unavoidable injustices. It's about preventing the sorts of injustices, dismissals, and emotional bullying that many employees suffer due to the intentional or unintentional actions of supervisors.

The Effects of Workplace Unfairness

Unfortunately, such behavior seems to be widespread. For example, executive recruiters Korn/Ferry commissioned a study of workplace unfairness. The study estimated that each year more than two million professionals and managers leave their corporate employers due solely to workplace unfairness. That costs U.S. employers about $64 billion per year in needless turnover. The study also concluded that people of color were three times more likely and gays and lesbians twice as likely as heterosexual Caucasian males to have left their jobs solely due to workplace unfairness. "The study highlights that unfairness in the form of everyday inappropriate behaviors is a very real, prevalent and damaging part of today's work environment," the study said.[1]

Workplace unfairness is often subtle, but it can be blatant. Some supervisors are workplace bullies, yelling at or even threatening subordinates. Not surprisingly, employees of abusive supervisors are more likely to report lower job and life satisfaction and higher stress.[2] (Even MayoClinic.com says, "You can reduce workplace stress by creating and maintaining a good relationship with your supervisor.")[3] Mistreatment also makes it more likely the employee will not do his or her best.[4] Mistreated employees also exhibit more workplace deviance, for instance, in terms of stealing and sabotage.[5] So, at all levels it makes sense to treat employees fairly. How can you tell unfairness when you see it? In practice, fair treatment reflects concrete actions like those in Figure 14.1.[6] These include "employees are treated with respect."[7]

Why Treat Employees Fairly?

For most people the answer to "Why treat employees fairly?" is obvious, since most learn, early on, some version of the Golden Rule.

But there are also tangible reasons supervisors should treat employees fairly. As we just said, unfairness is *counterproductive*—people you treat unfairly perform less well and quit more often. Unjust behavior will also *backfire* on you, by poisoning your reputation as a person and as a supervisor. *Arbitrators and the courts* will consider the fairness of the employer's disciplinary procedures when reviewing disciplinary decisions. Treating people fairly (not *un*fairly) also relates to a wide range of *positive employee outcomes*. These include enhanced employee commitment; satisfaction with the employer, job, and leader; and "organizational citizenship behaviors" (the steps employees take to support their employers' interests).[8] *Job applicants* who feel treated unfairly express more desire to appeal the outcome.[9]

RESEARCH INSIGHT   A study illustrates the practical effects of being fair. College instructors completed attitude surveys. These surveys asked whether they felt their

■Figure **14.1**

Perceptions of Fair Interpersonal Treatment Scale

Note: R = the item is reverse scored.

Source: Michelle A. Donovan et al., "The Perceptions of Their Interpersonal Treatment Scale: Development and Validation of a Measure of Interpersonal Treatment in the Workplace," *Journal of Applied Psychology* 83, no. 5 (1998), p. 692.

What is your organization like most of the time? Circle Yes if the item describes your organization, No if it does not describe your organization, and ? if you cannot decide.

IN THIS ORGANIZATION:

1. Employees are praised for good work.	Yes	?	No
2. Supervisors yell at employees. (R)	Yes	?	No
3. Supervisors play favorites. (R)	Yes	?	No
4. Employees are trusted.	Yes	?	No
5. Employees' complaints are dealt with effectively.	Yes	?	No
6. Employees are treated like children. (R)	Yes	?	No
7. Employees are treated with respect.	Yes	?	No
8. Employees' questions and problems are responded to quickly.	Yes	?	No
9. Employees are lied to. (R)	Yes	?	No
10. Employees' suggestions are ignored. (R)	Yes	?	No
11. Supervisors swear at employees. (R)	Yes	?	No
12. Employees' hard work is appreciated.	Yes	?	No
13. Supervisors threaten to fire or lay off employees. (R)	Yes	?	No
14. Employees are treated fairly.	Yes	?	No
15. Coworkers help each other out.	Yes	?	No
16. Coworkers argue with each other. (R)	Yes	?	No
17. Coworkers put each other down. (R)	Yes	?	No
18. Coworkers treat each other with respect.	Yes	?	No

colleges treated them with procedural and distributive justice. *Procedural justice* questions included, "In general, the department/college's procedures allow for requests for clarification for additional information about a decision." *Distributive justice* questions included, "I am fairly rewarded considering the responsibilities I have." The attitude surveys also included questions such as, "I am proud to tell others that I am part of this department/college." Their students also completed surveys. These contained items such as, "The instructor put a lot of effort into planning the content of this course," "The instructor was sympathetic to my needs," and "The instructor treated me fairly."

The results were impressive. Instructors who felt their colleges treated them fairly were more committed to the college and to their jobs. Their students reported higher levels of instructor effort, prosocial behaviors, and fairness.[10]

EMPLOYEE RIGHTS   Of course, few societies rely solely on supervisors' sense of fairness to ensure that they do what's right by their employees. They also establish various laws. Laws like Title VII give employees numerous *rights*. For example, the Occupational Safety and Health Act gave employees the right to refuse to work under unsafe conditions.[11] Figure 14.2 lists some other legislated areas under which workers have rights.[12]

Aside from legislation, employees also have certain rights under common law (the law that evolves from judges' decisions).[13] For example, under common law, an employee may have the right to sue the employer whose supervisor publicizes embarrassing personal information about the employee.[14]

What Constitutes Fair Treatment of Employees and Why Is It Important?

What Causes Unfair Behavior?

Some of the things that prompt supervisors to be fair or unfair aren't surprising. For one thing, some supervisors just may not have the fairness gene: For whatever reason, they derive an unhealthy pleasure from being hypercritical. Others may just be oblivious to

- Leave of absence and vacation rights
- Injuries and illnesses rights
- Noncompete agreement rights
- Employee rights on employer policies
- Discipline rights
- Rights on personnel files
- Employee pension rights
- Employee benefits rights
- References rights
- Rights on criminal records
- Employee distress rights
- Defamation rights
- Employee rights on fraud
- Rights on assault and battery
- Employee negligence rights
- Rights on political activity
- Union/group activity rights
- Whistleblower rights
- Worker's compensation rights

the adverse affects they're having on others. For example, on interest inventories (such as John Holland's Self-Directed Search, http://www.self-directed-search.com), the best supervisor candidates generally score high on the Social dimension. They tend to be empathetic, people-oriented people who enjoy working with, helping, advising, and supporting other people.

The *subordinate* also influences how fairly he or she is treated. For one thing, the saying, "The squeaky wheel gets the grease" is true. One study found that it paid to be assertive.[15] Supervisors treated pushier employees more fairly: "Individuals who communicated assertively were more likely to be treated fairly by the decision maker." Furthermore, supervisors who see themselves as treated unjustly tend to be abusive, particularly toward subordinates who they see as vulnerable.[16] So be particularly cautious when dealing with vulnerable subordinates. There's a tendency to be tougher on those who can't fight back.

Finally, the *employer* has a lot to do with how fairly their supervisors behave.[17] Many firms call attention to fairness with antiharassment policies. (For example, at one state agency, "It is the policy of the department that all employees, customers, contractors, and visitors to the work site are entitled to a positive, respectful, and productive work environment.")[18] Many employers establish channels through which employees can air their concerns. For example, the FedEx Survey Feedback Action (SFA) program includes an anonymous survey. This lets employees express their feelings about the company and their supervisors. Sample questions include the following:

- I can tell my supervisor what I think.
- My supervisor tells me what is expected.
- My supervisor listens to my concerns.
- My supervisor keeps me informed.

**What Causes Unfair
Treatment of
Employees?**

Each supervisor then has an opportunity to discuss the department results with subordinates and create an action plan for improving work group commitment.

Supervisors' Fairness Guidelines

But the bottom line is that it's usually the front-line supervisor who must ensure employees are treated fairly.

Doing so isn't always easy. For one thing, what seems "fair" to one person may seem unfair to another. For example, your employees will tend to rate their own performance more highly than will you. So, even when you try to be fair, employees may say, "You treated me unfairly." One study concluded that supervisors could do three things to influence how fairly their subordinates perceive their actions:[19]

1. *Involve employees* in the decisions that affect them by asking for their input and allowing them to refute the others' ideas and assumptions.

2. Ensure that everyone involved and affected *understands why* final decisions are made and the thinking that underlies the decisions.

3. Make sure everyone knows up front by what *standards* you will judge him or her.

PRACTICAL COMMUNICATIONS   You can see that providing opportunities for two-way communication is important in fostering perceptions of fairness. Guidelines here include the following:

- Ask questions and listen carefully. For example, say, "Can you tell me exactly what you see as unfair about my decision?"[20]

- Set aside your defensive reactions. Instead, perhaps say something like, "I can see why you might feel that way."

- Tactfully deflect distracting statements. For instance, don't get into debates comparing the person's salary raise to someone else's. Instead say, "In fairness to that other person, let's just discuss your situation."

- Ask, "What would you like me to do?" It could turn out the employee just wants to be heard.

- Deal with specifics. If the employee does want you to change the decision, ask him or her to outline specific reasons.

What Are Important Fair Treatment Principles?

2. Understanding the Role of Ethics at Work

Every society needs principles their citizens use to decide what is right and what is wrong. Thus in most societies, people take it for granted that bosses should treat employees fairly, that doing so is the ethical thing to do. Ethics refers to the principles we all use to make those sorts of "what's the right thing to do?" decisions.

What Are Ethics?

To be precise, by **ethics**, we mean "the principles of conduct governing an individual or a group; specifically, the standards you use to decide what your conduct should be."[21]

(handwritten margin note: Enron's normative judgment was misdirected toward financial success or the appearance of financial success, which overrode all other ethics.)

Making ethical decisions always involves two things. First, it always involves *normative judgments.*[22] A normative judgment means that something is good or bad, right or wrong, better or worse. "You are wearing a skirt and blouse" is a non-normative statement. "That's a great outfit!" is a normative one.

Second, ethical decisions always involve questions of morality. *Morality* is society's highest accepted standards of behavior. Moral standards guide behaviors of the most serious consequence to society's well-being, such as murder, lying, and slander. Violating moral standards often makes someone feel ashamed or remorseful.[23]

It would simplify things if it were always clear when one's decisions were ethical. Unfortunately, it is not. If the decision makes you feel ashamed or remorseful, or involves doing something with serious consequence such as murder, then, chances are, it's unethical.

People face ethical choices every day. Is it wrong to use a company credit card for personal messages? Is a $50 gift to a client unacceptable? Compare your answers by answering the quiz in Figure 14.3.

What Is the Role of Ethics at Work?

Why Study Ethics?

Almost everyone reading this book rightfully views him- or herself as an ethical person, so we should ask, "Why include ethics in a book about supervision?" For two reasons. First, ethics greases the wheels that make businesses work. Supervisors who promise raises but don't deliver, salespeople who say, "The order's coming" when it's not,

■Figure **14.3**
Ethics Quiz

Source: Wall Street Journal (October 21, 1999): B1–B4. Ethics Offer Association Belmont, MA: Ethics Leadership Group.

The Wall Street Journal Workplace–Ethics Quiz

The spread of technology into the workshop has raised a variety of new ethical questions and many old ones still linger. Compare your answers with those of other Americans surveyed, on page 438.

Office Technology

1. Is it wrong to use company e-mail for personal reasons?
   ☐ Yes   ☐ No

2. Is it wrong to use office equipment to help your children or spouse do schoolwork?
   ☐ Yes   ☐ No

3. Is it wrong to play computer games on office equipment during the workday?
   ☐ Yes   ☐ No

4. Is it wrong to use office equipment to do Internet shopping?
   ☐ Yes   ☐ No

5. Is it unethical to blame an error you made on a technological glitch?
   ☐ Yes   ☐ No

6. Is it unethical to visit pornographic Web sites using office equipment?
   ☐ Yes   ☐ No

Gifts and Entertainment

7. What's the value at which a gift from a supplier or client becomes troubling?
   ☐ $25   ☐ $50   ☐ $100

8. Is a $50 gift to a boss unacceptable?
   ☐ Yes   ☐ No

9. Is a $50 gift *from* the boss unacceptable?
   ☐ Yes   ☐ No

10. Of gifts from suppliers: Is it OK to take a $200 pair of football tickets?
    ☐ Yes   ☐ No

11. Is it OK to take a $120 pair of theater tickets?
    ☐ Yes   ☐ No

12. Is it OK to take a $100 holiday food basket?
    ☐ Yes   ☐ No

13. Is it OK to take a $25 gift certificate?
    ☐ Yes   ☐ No

14. Can you accept a $75 prize won at a raffle at a supplier's conference?
    ☐ Yes   ☐ No

Truth and Lies

15. Due to on-the-job pressure, have you ever abused or lied about sick days?
    ☐ Yes   ☐ No

16. Due to on-the-job pressure, have you ever taken credit for someone else's work or idea?
    ☐ Yes   ☐ No

---

production supervisors who take kickbacks from suppliers—they all corrode the trust that day-to-day business transactions depend on. According to one recent lawsuit, marketers for Pfizer Inc. influenced the company to suppress unfavorable studies about one of its drugs.[24] Plaintiffs are suing for billions.

Second, just about everything supervisors do has ethical consequences.[25] Workplace safety, employee records security, employee theft, affirmative action, performance appraisal, employee privacy rights are just some examples.[26] For example:

- You know that your team shouldn't start work on the new machine until all the safety measures have been checked, but your boss is pressing you to get started. What should you do?

- You dismissed an employee in an angry moment, and now she has applied for unemployment insurance, saying you never warned her. Should you create and place in her file a note of warning to protect your employer from paying higher unemployment taxes?

- You have an incompetent employee who you would like to get rid of, and someone just called you to get a job reference for that person. How honest should you be?

- You've just taken over as the plant supervisor of a company in a depressed economic area, only to find that it has been hiring illegal aliens. If you complain, the company will probably close, putting 600 area residents out of work. What should you do?

3. What Determines Ethical Behavior at Work?

Whether someone acts ethically at work is usually not a consequence of just one thing. For example, could it be that every manager running some of the banks that triggered the subprime mortgage mess was simply unethical? That's not likely. There must have been more to it. *But what?*

There's No One Smoking Gun

The short answer is that you can't assume it's just "unethical people" who do the damage. The problems more often emerge from a sort of perfect storm of factors.

A recent review of ethics research illustrates this well.[27] The authors titled their paper "Bad Apples, Bad Cases, and Bad Barrels." This title highlighted their conclusion that no single "smoking gun" determines ethical behavior. Instead, "bad apples" (people who are inclined to make unethical choices), "bad cases" (ethical dilemmas ripe for unethical choices), and "bad barrels" (environments that foster unethical choices) combine to determine what the employee's ethical choices will be. Here's what they found.

INDIVIDUAL CHARACTERISTICS: WHO ARE THE BAD APPLES?   Some people are just more inclined to make unethical choices. Most importantly, people differ in their level of moral development. The most principled people with the highest level of moral development *think through the implications of their decisions and apply ethical principles.*

But most adults don't operate at this high level. Instead, most base their judgment about what is right *on their colleagues' expectations, or on company policies and what the law says.*

Finally, people at the lowest level make their ethical choices solely based on *obeying what they're told and on avoiding punishment.*

WHICH ETHICAL SITUATIONS MAKE FOR BAD (ETHICALLY DANGEROUS) SITUATIONS? Similarly, some ethical dilemmas are more likely to prompt unethical choices. Interestingly, it's often the "smaller" ethical situations that prompt the worst choices. In deciding whether to do something they suspect is wrong, people calibrate the total harm that can befall victims, the likelihood that the action will result in harm, and the number of people potentially affected by the act. In seemingly less serious situations, it's more likely that someone might say, in effect, "It's okay to do this, even though I know it's wrong, because it's not a big deal."

WHAT ARE THE "BAD BARRELS"? WHAT OUTSIDE FACTORS MOLD ETHICAL CHOICES? The employer sets the stage for unethical decisions. These researchers found that companies that promote an "everyone for him- (or her-) self" atmosphere are more likely to suffer unethical choices. Those emphasizing that their employees should focus on the well-being of everyone tend to elicit more good ethical choices.[28]

Let's look next at specifically what the supervisor, employee, and employer can do to boost the chances that everyone's decisions will be ethical.

What the Employee Can Do

Because people bring to their jobs their own ideas of what is morally right and wrong, the individual must shoulder much of the credit (or blame) for ethical choices (you don't want to be, as the researchers said, a "bad apple"). Do you think through the implications of the pending action, relative to what's right or wrong? Or do you say, "It's not likely I'll get caught, so I'll do it anyway"? How would you rate your own ethics? Figure 14.4 presents a short self-assessment survey to help you answer that question.[29]

The Supervisor as Leader: What the Supervisor Can Do

Supervisors have a huge influence on their employees' ethics. You are your subordinates' leader. It's hard to resist even subtle pressure, let alone coercion, from the person who is leading you, someone who is also your boss.

The evidence supports that commonsense conclusion. For instance, according to one report, "the level of misconduct at work dropped dramatically when employees said their supervisors exhibited ethical behavior." Only 25% of employees who agreed that their supervisors "set a good example of ethical business behavior" said they had observed misconduct in the last year. Seventy-two percent of those who said their supervisors *did not* set good examples observed misconduct.[30] Here are examples of how supervisors knowingly (or unknowingly) lead subordinates astray:

- Tell staffers to do whatever is necessary to achieve results.
- Overload top performers to ensure that the work gets done.
- Look the other way when wrongdoing occurs.
- Take credit for others' work or shift blame.[31]

■Figure **14.4**

How Do My Ethics Rate?

Source: Adapted from A. Reichel and Y. Neumann, *Journal of Instructional Psychology,* March 1988, pp. 25–53.

Instrument

Indicate your level of agreement with these 15 statements using the following scale:

1 = Strongly disagree
2 = Disagree
3 = Neither agree nor disagree
4 = Agree
5 = Strongly agree

1. The only moral of business is making money.	1	2	3	4	5
2. A person who is doing well in business does not have to worry about moral problems.	1	2	3	4	5
3. Act according to the law, and you can't go wrong morally.	1	2	3	4	5
4. Ethics in business is basically an adjustment between expectations and the ways people behave.	1	2	3	4	5
5. Business decisions involve a realistic economic attitude and not a moral philosophy.	1	2	3	4	5
6. "Business ethics" is a concept for public relations only.	1	2	3	4	5
7. Competitiveness and profitability are important values.	1	2	3	4	5
8. Conditions of a free economy will best serve the needs of society. Limiting competition can only hurt society and actually violates basic natural laws.	1	2	3	4	5
9. As a consumer, when making an auto insurance claim, I try to get as much as possible regardless of the extent of the damage.	1	2	3	4	5
10. While shopping at the supermarket, it is appropriate to switch price tags on packages.	1	2	3	4	5
11. As an employee, I can take home office supplies; it doesn't hurt anyone.	1	2	3	4	5
12. I view sick days as vacation days that I deserve.	1	2	3	4	5
13. Employees' wages should be determined according to the laws of supply and demand.	1	2	3	4	5
14. The business world has its own rules.	1	2	3	4	5
15. A good businessperson is a successful businessperson.	1	2	3	4	5

ANALYSIS AND INTERPRETATION

Rather than specify "right" answers, this instrument works best when you compare your answer to those of others. With that in mind, here are mean responses from a group of 243 management students. How did your responses compare?

1. 3.09	6. 2.88	11. 1.58
2. 1.88	7. 3.62	12. 2.31
3. 2.54	8. 3.79	13. 3.36
4. 3.41	9. 3.44	14. 3.79
5. 3.88	10. 1.33	15. 3.38

Three way supervisors foster ethical behavior are creating the right organizational culture, appraising fairly, and using reward and disciplinary systems.

CREATE THE RIGHT ORGANIZATIONAL CULTURE   The examples illustrate that the supervisor's ethical influence is often unintentional. The supervisor sends signals about the right way to behave. Those signals then create the culture to which employees react. We can define **organizational culture** as the "characteristic values, traditions, and behaviors a company's employees share." A *value* is a basic belief about what is right or wrong, or about what you should or shouldn't do. ("Honesty is the best policy" would be a value.)

Values are important because they guide and channel behavior. Supervising people, therefore, depends on influencing the values they use as behavioral guides. For example, if you really believe that "honesty is the best policy," your actions should support your words. Supervisors should "walk the talk." They can't say, "Don't fudge the financials," and then do so themselves.

APPRAISE FAIRLY   Studies (and practical experience) confirm that some supervisors ignore accuracy in performance appraisals. Instead, they use them for political purposes (such as encouraging employees with whom they don't get along to leave).[32] Few things can send a worse signal about how fair and ethical the company is. For fair appraisals, standards should be clear, your employees should understand the basis upon which you're going to appraise them, and the appraisal should be objective.

USE REWARD AND DISCIPLINARY SYSTEMS   Employees' behavior tends to reflect the consequences of that behavior. If employees see that cheating pays, it's more likely they'll start cheating. The solution is, reward ethical behavior and penalize unethical behavior. Research suggests, "Employees expect the organization to dole out relatively harsh punishment for unethical conduct."[33]

What the Company Can Do

Do you work in an ethically toxic company? Some think so. An *ethically toxic company* is one in which all the usual procedures that normally militate against bad behavior are missing. For example, supervisors pressure or even reward employees for bad behavior; no one publicizes ethical standards such as "don't bribe officials"; and no one takes the time to follow up on or audit bad behavior. Having ethical blowups at companies like these is perhaps understandable. What's strange is that things can go wrong in companies that at least seem to be ethically normal.

The thing the supervisor must beware of is that it may not be so strange. Some years ago, the U.S. government accused the CFO of a large company of instructing subordinates to file false statements with the SEC. Why would the CFO do this? "I took these actions, knowing they were wrong, in a misguided attempt to preserve the company to allow it to withstand what I believed were temporary financial difficulties."[34]

So the scary thing about unethical behavior at work is that it's usually not just personal interests driving it. Table 14.1 summarizes the results of one survey. It shows the principal causes of ethical lapses, as reported by six levels of employees and managers. As you can see, *being under the gun to meet scheduling pressures* was the number-one reported factor. For most of these employees, "meeting overly aggressive financial or business objectives," and "helping the company survive" were the two other top causes. "Advancing my own career or financial interests" ranked toward the bottom. Thus (at least in this case), most ethical lapses seemed to occur because employees shifted their ethical compasses to "I must help my company." Avoiding such pressure tactics is one way supervisors head off ethical lapses.

In summary, people tend to reorient their ethical compasses when they get to work. Suddenly, the question isn't "Is this right?" but "Will this help the company?" Employers try to head this off with ethics codes, whistleblowers, and improved employee selection and training.

ETHICS CODES   An **ethics code** lays out the ethical standards to which the employer expects its employees to adhere (for instance, with respect to accepting expensive gifts from vendors). All publicly traded companies in the United States need one. The Sarbanes-Oxley Act (passed after a series of top corporate management ethical lapses) requires companies to declare if they have a code of conduct. Federal sentencing guidelines reduce penalties for companies convicted of ethics violations if they have codes of conduct.

Principal Causes of Ethical Compromises	Senior Mgmt.	Middle Mgmt.	Front-Line Supv.	Professional Non-Mgmt.	Admin. Salaried	Hourly
Meeting schedule pressure	1	1	1	1	1	1
Meeting overly aggressive financial or business objectives	3	2	2	2	2	2
Helping the company survive	2	3	4	4	3	4
Advancing the career interests of my boss	5	4	3	3	4	5
Feeling peer pressure	7	7	5	6	5	3
Resisting competitive threats	4	5	6	5	6	7
Saving jobs	9	6	7	7	7	6
Advancing my own career or financial interests	8	9	9	8	9	8
Other	6	8	8	9	8	9

Note: 1 is high, 9 is low.
Sources: O. C. Ferrell and John Fraedrich, *Business Ethics*, 3rd ed. (New York: Houghton Mifflin, 1997), p. 28; adapted from Rebecca Goodell, *Ethics in American Business: Policies, Programs, and Perceptions* (1994), p. 54. Permission provided courtesy of the Ethics Resource Center, 1120 6th Street NW, Washington, DC: 2005.

To ensure compliance with ethics codes, some companies actually encourage *whistleblowers*. Whistleblowers are individuals, frequently employees, who use procedural or legal channels to report incidents of unethical behavior to company ethics officers or to legal authorities. While many employers fear whistleblowers, others encourage them, for instance, by instituting ethics hotlines.[35]

Some companies urge employees to apply a quick *ethics test* to evaluate whether what they're about to do fits the company's code of conduct. For example, the Raytheon Company asks employees who face ethical dilemmas to ask:

- Is the action legal?
- Is it right?
- Whom will the decision affect?
- Does it fit Raytheon's values?
- How will it "feel" afterwards?
- How will it look in the newspaper?
- Will it reflect poorly on the company?[36]

SELECTION   One writer says, "The simplest way [a company can] tune up an organization, ethically speaking, is to hire more ethical people."[37] Employers can start by creating recruitment materials that emphasize ethics. (The Microsoft site in Figure 14.5 is an example.) Employers also use honesty tests and background checks to screen out undesirables.[38] You can also ask behavioral questions such as, "Have you ever observed someone stretching the rules at work? What did you do about it?[39]

ETHICS TRAINING   For all practical purposes, ethics training by employers is mandatory. Federal sentencing guidelines reduce penalties for employers accused of misconduct who implemented codes of conduct and ethics training.[40] Ethics training usually

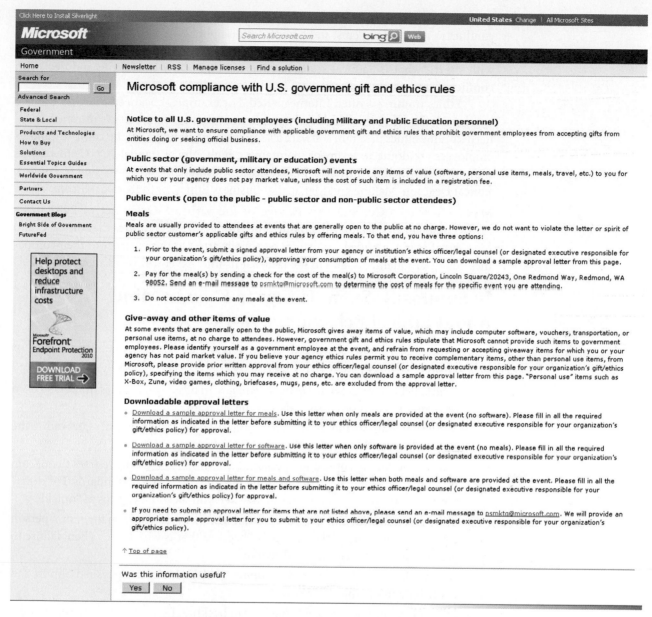

United States Change | All Microsoft Sites

Microsoft

Government

Home

Newsletter | RSS | Manage licenses | Find a solution |

Search for
[   ] Go

Advanced Search

Federal
State & Local

Products and Technologies
How to Buy
Solutions
Essential Topics Guides

Worldwide Government

Partners

Contact Us

Government Blogs
Bright Side of Government
FutureFed

Help protect
desktops and
reduce
infrastructure
costs

Forefront
Endpoint Protection
2010

DOWNLOAD
FREE TRIAL →

Microsoft compliance with U.S. government gift and ethics rules

Notice to all U.S. government employees (including Military and Public Education personnel)
At Microsoft, we want to ensure compliance with applicable government gift and ethics rules that prohibit government employees from accepting gifts from entities doing or seeking official business.

Public sector (government, military or education) events
At events that only include public sector attendees, Microsoft will not provide any items of value (software, personal use items, meals, travel, etc.) to you for which you or your agency does not pay market value, unless the cost of such item is included in a registration fee.

Public events (open to the public - public sector and non-public sector attendees)
Meals
Meals are usually provided to attendees at events that are generally open to the public at no charge. However, we do not want to violate the letter or spirit of public sector customer's applicable gifts and ethics rules by offering meals. To that end, you have three options:

1. Prior to the event, submit a signed approval letter from your agency or institution's ethics officer/legal counsel (or designated executive responsible for your organization's gift/ethics policy), approving your consumption of meals at the event. You can download a sample approval letter from this page.

2. Pay for the meal(s) by sending a check for the cost of the meal(s) to Microsoft Corporation, Lincoln Square/20243, One Redmond Way, Redmond, WA 98052. Send an e-mail message to psmktg@microsoft.com to determine the cost of meals for the specific event you are attending.

3. Do not accept or consume any meals at the event.

Give-away and other items of value
At some events that are generally open to the public, Microsoft gives away items of value, which may include computer software, vouchers, transportation, or personal use items, at no charge to attendees. However, government gift and ethics rules stipulate that Microsoft cannot provide such items to government employees. Please identify yourself as a government employee at the event, and refrain from requesting or accepting giveaway items for which you or your agency has not paid market value. If you believe your agency ethics rules permit you to receive complementary items, other than personal use items, from Microsoft, please provide prior written approval from your ethics officer/legal counsel (or designated executive responsible for your organization's gift/ethics policy), specifying the items which you may receive at no charge. You can download a sample approval letter from this page. "Personal use" items such as X-Box, Zune, video games, clothing, briefcases, mugs, pens, etc. are excluded from the approval letter.

Downloadable approval letters

- Download a sample approval letter for meals. Use this letter when only meals are provided at the event (no software). Please fill in all the required information as indicated in the letter before submitting it to your ethics officer/legal counsel (or designated executive responsible for your organization's gift/ethics policy) for approval.

- Download a sample approval letter for software. Use this letter when only software is provided at the event (no meals). Please fill in all the required information as indicated in the letter before submitting it to your ethics officer/legal counsel (or designated executive responsible for your organization's gift/ethics policy) for approval.

- Download a sample approval letter for meals and software. Use this letter when both meals and software are provided at the event. Please fill in all the required information as indicated in the letter before submitting it to your ethics officer/legal counsel (or designated executive responsible for your organization's gift/ethics policy) for approval.

- If you need to submit an approval letter for items that are not listed above, please send an e-mail message to psmktg@microsoft.com. We will provide an appropriate sample approval letter for you to submit to your ethics officer/legal counsel (or designated executive responsible for your organization's gift/ethics policy).

↑ Top of page

Was this information useful?
[Yes] [No]

■Figure **14.5**

Source: http://www.microsoft.com/industry/government/GovGiftingCompliance.mspx (accessed April 28, 2009).

includes showing employees how to recognize ethical dilemmas, how to use codes of conduct to resolve problems, and how to use disciplinary practices in ethical ways.

Such training needn't be complicated. Lockheed Martin provides its employees with short, "what-if" ethical scenarios that highlight how to identify and deal with conflict of interest situations.[41]

Ethics training is often Internet-based. For example, Lockheed Martin's 160,000 employees also take ethics and legal compliance training via the firm's intranet. Lockheed's online ethics program software also keeps track of how well the company and its employees are doing in terms of maintaining high ethical standards.[42] Online ethics training tools include Business Ethics from skillsoft.com, and two online courses, Ethical Decision-Making and Managerial Business Ethics, both from netG.com.[43]

MANAGING ETHICS COMPLIANCE   Passage of the Sarbanes-Oxley Act of 2002 made ethics compliance obligatory.[44] Among other things, the act requires that the CEO and the CFO of publicly traded companies personally attest to the accuracy of their companies' financial statements, and to the fact that its internal controls are adequate.[45]

In Summary: Some Things to Keep in Mind About Ethical Behavior at Work

Several experts reviewed the research concerning things that influence ethical behavior in organizations. Here's what their findings suggest for supervisors:[46]

- Ethical behavior starts with *moral awareness.* In other words, does the person even recognize that a moral issue exists in the situation?
- *Supervisors* can do a lot to influence employee ethics by carefully cultivating the right values, leadership, reward systems, and culture.
- Ethics slide when people undergo *moral disengagement.* Doing so frees them from the guilt that would normally go with violating one's ethical standards. For example, you're more likely to harm others when you view the victims as "outsiders."
- The most powerful morality comes from *within.* In effect, when the moral person asks, "Why be moral?" the answer is, "because that is who I am." Then, failure to act morally creates emotional discomfort.[47]
- Beware the seductive power of an *unmet goal.* Unmet goals pursued blindly can contribute to unethical behavior.[48]
- Offering *rewards* for ethical behavior can backfire. Doing so may actually undermine the intrinsic value of ethical behavior.
- Don't inadvertently reward someone for *bad behavior.* For example, don't promote someone who got a big sale through devious means.[49]
- Supervisors should *punish unethical behavior.* Employees who observe unethical behavior expect you to discipline the perpetrators.
- The degree to which employees *openly talk about ethics* is a good predictor of ethical conduct. Conversely, organizations characterized by "moral muteness" suffer more ethically problematic behavior.
- Remember that people tend to alter their *moral compasses* when they join organizations. They uncritically equate "what's best for this organization (or team, or department)" with "what's the right thing to do?"

4. Managing Employee Discipline and Privacy

The purpose of *discipline* is to encourage employees to adhere to rules and regulations. Discipline is necessary when an employee violates a rule.[50] Protecting your employer's rights, but doing so fairly and ethically, is the heart of effective discipline.

Proper disciplinary procedures are important for several reasons. They help to ensure that the discipline is fair. And they help protect you and your employer against having your rulings overturned. (One study surveyed 45 arbitration awards in which employee tardiness had triggered discipline. When arbitrators overturned supervisors' decisions, it was usually because the employer had failed to clarify what it meant by "tardy," or used overly severe penalties.) Furthermore, unfair discipline can actually encourage misbehavior.[51]

Establishing a fair disciplinary process isn't easy. The accompanying Managing the New Workforce feature illustrates one reason for this.

What Are the Guidelines for Managing Employee Discipline and Privacy?

Basics of a Fair and Just Disciplinary Process

The employer wants its discipline process to be both effective (in terms of discouraging unwanted behavior) and fair. Employers base such a process on clear rules and regulations, progressive penalties, and an appeals process.

Supervising the New Workforce

Comparing Males and Females in a Discipline Situation

Watching a movie like *King Arthur* may lead you to conclude that chivalry in general and a protective attitude toward women in particular is a well-established value in many societies, but that may not be the case. Not only is chivalry not necessarily a prevailing value, there is even a competing theory.[52] What several researchers unfortunately call the "Evil Woman Thesis" certainly doesn't argue that women are evil. Instead, it argues that women who commit offenses that violate stereotypic assumptions about the "proper" behavior of women "will [then] be penalized for their inappropriate sex role behavior in addition to their other offenses." In other words, it argues that when a woman doesn't act the way other men and women think she should act, the men and women tend to overreact and treat her more harshly than they might if a man committed the same act.

While such a thesis might seem ridiculous on its face, the results of at least one careful study seem to support it. In this study, 360 graduate and undergraduate business school students reviewed a labor arbitration case. The case involved two employees, one male and one female, with similar work records and tenure with their employers. Both were discharged for violation of company rules related to alcohol and drugs. The case portrays one worker's behavior as a more serious breach of company rules: That worker (a male in half the study and a female in the other half) had brought an intoxicant to work. The students had to choose between two alternative approaches to settling the dispute that arose after the discharge.

In their study, the researchers found bias against the supposedly culpable females by both the male and female students. The female workers in the case received recommendations for harsher treatment from both the men and women students. As the researchers conclude, women "appear to be as willing as men to impose harsher discipline on women than upon men . . . [especially when it involves what they view as inappropriate sex role behavior]."

RULES AND REGULATIONS   First, rules and regulations address issues such as theft, destruction of company property, drinking on the job, and insubordination. Examples include the following:

- **Poor performance is not acceptable.** Each employee is expected to perform his or her work properly and efficiently.
- **Alcohol and drugs are prohibited at work.** The use of either during working hours and reporting for work under the influence are both prohibited.

Rules inform employees ahead of time what is and is not acceptable behavior. Upon hiring, tell employees, preferably in writing, what is not permitted. The employee handbook usually contains the rules and regulations.

PROGRESSIVE PENALTIES   A system of progressive penalties is a second requirement of effective discipline. Penalties typically range from oral warnings to written warnings to suspension from the job to discharge.

The severity of the penalty is usually a function of the offense and the number of times it has occurred. For example, most companies issue warnings for the first unexcused lateness (see form in Figure 14.6). For a fourth offense, discharge is the usual disciplinary action.

FORMAL DISCIPLINARY APPEALS PROCESSES   In addition to rules and progressive penalties, the disciplinary process requires an appeals procedure.

■ Figure **14.6**

Disciplinary Action Form

Source: Reprinted from www.HR.BLR.com with permission of the publisher *Business and Legal Reports, Inc.*, 141 Mill Rock Road East, Old Saybrook CT © 2004.

Disciplinary Action Form

Date: _____

Name: _____

Dept.: _____

Disciplinary Action:

❑ Verbal*   ❑ Written   ❑ Written & Suspension   ❑ Discharge

To the employee:

Your performance has been found unsatisfactory for the reasons set forth below. Your failure to improve or avoid a recurrence will be cause for further disciplinary action.

Details: _____

_____

_____

_____

_____

_____

A copy of this warning was personally delivered to the above employee by:

Supervisor: _____

Date: _____

I have received and read this warning notice. I have been informed that a copy of this notice will be placed in my personnel file.

Employee: _____

Date: _____

*If action is *verbal,* completion of this form shall serve as documentation only and should not be filed in the employee's personnel file.

Virtually all union agreements contain disciplinary appeal procedures, but such procedures are not limited to unionized firms. For example, FedEx calls its appeals procedure *guaranteed fair treatment:*

- In *step 1, management review,* the complainant submits his or her written complaint to a member of management (such as a supervisor or senior manager).

- If not satisfied with that decision, then in *step 2, officer complaint,* the complainant submits a written appeal to the vice president or senior vice president of the division.

- Finally, in *step 3, executive appeals review,* the complainant may submit a written complaint to the employee relations department. This department then investigates and prepares a case file for the executive review appeals board. The appeals board—the CEO, the COO, the chief personnel officer, and three senior vice presidents—then reviews all relevant information and makes a decision to uphold, overturn, or to take other appropriate action.

Some companies establish independent ombudsmen, neutral counselors outside the normal chain of command to whom employees can turn for confidential advice.[53]

DISCIPLINE WITHOUT PUNISHMENT   Traditional discipline has two potential downsides. First, no one likes to be punished. Second, punishment tends to gain short-term compliance, but not the long-term cooperation employers often prefer.

Discipline without punishment (or **nonpunitive discipline**) aims to avoid these drawbacks. It does this by gaining employees' acceptance of the rules while reducing the punitive nature of the discipline itself. Here is how it works:[54]

1. **First, issue an oral reminder.**   The goal is to get the employee to agree to avoid future infractions.

2. **Should another incident arise within six weeks, issue a formal written reminder, a copy of which is placed in the employee's personnel file.**   In addition, hold a second private discussion with the employee, again without any threats.

3. **Give a paid, one-day "decision-making leave."**   If another incident occurs in the next six weeks or so, tell the employee to take a one-day leave with pay, and to stay home and consider whether the job is right for him or her and whether he or she wants to abide by the company's rules. When the employee returns to work, he or she meets with you and gives you a decision regarding whether or not he or she will follow the rules.

4. **If no further incidents occur in the next year or so, purge the one-day paid suspension from the person's file.**   If the behavior reoccurs, typically the next step is dismissal.

The process would not apply to exceptional circumstances. Criminal behavior or in-plant fighting might be grounds for immediate dismissal, for instance. And if several incidents occurred at very close intervals, you might skip step 2—the written warning.

IN SUMMARY: THE HOT STOVE RULE   Supervisors traditionally apply what they call the "hot stove rule" when applying discipline. When touching a hot stove that is labeled "Don't touch," the person has *prior warning* (in this case, of the rule) and the pain is *consistent, impersonal,* and *immediate.* Figure 14.7 summarizes useful fair discipline guidelines.

- Make sure the evidence supports the charge.
- Protect the employee's due process rights.
- Warn the employee of the disciplinary consequences.
- The rule that was allegedly violated should be "reasonably related" to the efficient and safe operation of the work environment.
- Fairly and adequately investigate the matter before administering discipline.
- The investigation should produce substantial evidence of misconduct.
- Apply all rules, orders, or penalties evenhandedly.
- The penalty should be reasonably related to the misconduct and to the employee's past work.
- Maintain the employee's right to counsel.
- Don't rob a subordinate of his or her dignity.
- Remember that the burden of proof is on you.
- Get the facts. Don't base a decision on hearsay or on your general impression.
- Don't act while angry.
- In general, do not attempt to deal with an employee's "bad attitude." Focus on improving the specific behaviors creating the workplace problem.[56]

Discipline sometimes brings out the worst in some supervisors. The employee, having broken a rule, is vulnerable. On occasion, a supervisor may take advantage of his or her power to throw his or her weight around. Effective discipline therefore draws heavily on the supervisor's leadership skills, as the following leadership feature illustrates.

Leadership Applications for Supervisors

Using Power and Coercion in Disciplining Employees

Many supervisors have what you might call a love-hate relationship with leadership power and coercion. On the one hand, like most people, supervisors instinctively understand that fear can be a great motivator. You may recall that we summed up this point of view in Chapter 2 (leadership) by quoting Machiavelli as follows:

> One ought to be both feared and loved, but as it is difficult for the two to go together, it is much safer to be feared than loved, for love is held by a chain of obligation which, men being selfish, is broken whenever it serves their purpose; but fear is maintained by a dread of punishment which never fails.[57]

And yet, most supervisors would probably agree that one should use brute force and coercion sparingly, if at all. If you check the thesaurus, it's easy to see why. Synonyms for coercion include intimidation, bullying, compulsion, force, and fear, and most would agree that such behavior usually has no place in work organizations. Even the famous Harvard Professor B. F. Skinner, who studied the effects of rewards and punishment on rats (and people), discouraged using punishment except in the most extraordinary situations.

However, there is one situation in which even leadership experts agree that coercion might be appropriate, and that is to "deter behavior detrimental to the organization, such as illegal activities, theft, violation of safety rules, reckless acts that endanger others, and direct disobedience of legitimate requests."[58] In such cases, the supervisor in his or her leadership role might legitimately use coercive power to threaten a subordinate with punishment (such as dismissal or suspension). Of course, using coercion successfully requires meeting several standards. The threats need to be seen as credible (make sure you really have the power to pull the threat off). The threat itself needs to be persuasive (as opposed to, "You want to suspend me for one day, go ahead; I don't care"). And the leader needs to maintain respect by not personalizing the situation or making rash or uncommonly discourteous threats, and by ensuring that he or she followed the system of warnings and penalties the company set up.

■ Figure **14.8**

Source: http://www.
imonitorsoft.com/ (accessed
April 28, 2009).

Employee Privacy

For most people, invasions of privacy are neither ethical nor fair.[59] The four main types of employee privacy violations supervisors should avoid are intrusion (locker room and bathroom surveillance), publication of private matters, disclosure of medical records, and appropriation of an employee's name or likeness for commercial purposes.[60] Background checks, monitoring off-duty conduct and lifestyle, drug testing, workplace searches, and monitoring of workplace activities trigger most privacy violations.[61]

Employee Monitoring

Supervisors should be aware of their employer's monitoring policies. Over half of employers say they monitor their employees' incoming and outgoing *e-mail*; 27% monitor internal e-mail as well.[62] One survey found that 41% of employers with more than 20,000 employees have someone reading employee e-mails.[63] Ninety-six percent monitor and block access to adult Web sites, 61% to game sites.[64] (See Figure 14.8.) Biometrics—using physical traits such as fingerprints or iris scans for identification—is another example.[65] Bronx Lebanon Hospital in New York uses biometric scanners, for instance, to ensure that the employee that clocks in the morning is really who he or she says he is. The Federal Aviation Authority uses iris scanning to control employees' access to its network information systems.[66]

Location monitoring is becoming pervasive.[67] Employers ranging from United Parcel Service to the City of Oakland, California, use GPS units to monitor their truckers' and street sweepers' whereabouts.[68]

RESTRICTIONS   Supervisors should know something about what employers can and can't do with respect to monitoring.

There are two main restrictions on workplace monitoring. These are the **Electronic Communications Privacy Act (ECPA),** and *common-law protections* against invasion of privacy. The ECPA is a federal law intended to help restrict interception and monitoring of oral and wire communications. It contains two exceptions. The "business purpose exception" permits employers to monitor communications if they can show a legitimate business reason for doing so. The second, "consent exception," lets employers monitor communications if they have their employees' consent to do so.[69]

Electronic eavesdropping is thus legal—up to a point. Federal law and most state laws allow employers to monitor employees' phone calls in the ordinary course of business. However, they must stop listening once it becomes clear that a conversation is personal rather than business related. Employers can also generally monitor their e-mail systems, which are, after all, their property. However, supervisors should warn employees to use those systems for business purposes only.[70] Employers should have employees sign monitoring acknowledgment statements like that in Figure 14.9. The APPS feature shows another problem.

■Figure **14.9**
Sample E-Mail Monitoring Acknowledgment Statement

> I understand that XYZ Company periodically monitors any e-mail communications created, sent, or retrieved using this company's e-mail system. Therefore I understand that my e-mail communications may be read by individuals other than the intended recipient. I also understand that XYZ Company periodically monitors telephone communications, for example, to improve customer service quality.
>
> Signature   Date
>
> Print Name   Department

5. Managing Dismissals

Dismissal is the most drastic disciplinary step the employer can take. Because of this, it requires special care. There should be sufficient cause for the dismissal. And (as a rule) you should only dismiss someone after taking reasonable steps to rehabilitate the employee. However, there will be times when dismissal is required, perhaps at once.

The best way to "handle" a dismissal is to avoid it in the first place. Many dis-missals start with bad hiring decisions. Using effective selection practices including assessment tests, reference and background checks, drug testing, and clearly defined job descriptions can reduce the need for many dismissals.

Termination at Will and Wrongful Discharge

For more than 100 years, *termination at will* was the prevailing dismissal-related rule in the United States. **Termination at will** means that without a contract, either the employer or the employee could *terminate at will* the employment relationship. The employee can resign for any reason, at will, and the employer can dismiss an employee for any reason, at will.[73]

Today, however, dismissed employees increasingly take their cases to court. Many employers are discovering they no longer have a blanket right to fire. Instead, EEO and other laws limit supervisors' right to dismiss. For example, firing a whistleblower might trigger "public policy" exceptions to firing at will. Or, a statement in an employee hand-book may imply a contractual agreement to keep an employee. In practice, plaintiffs only win a tiny fraction of such suits. However, the cost of defending the suits is still huge.[74]

PROTECTIONS AGAINST WRONGFUL DISCHARGE   **Wrongful discharge** refers to a dis-missal that violates the law or that fails to comply with contractual arrangements stated or implied by the employer, for instance, in employee manuals.

There are three main protections against wrongful discharge—*statutory excep-tions, common-law exceptions*, and *public policy exceptions*.

First, in terms of *statutory exceptions*, federal and state equal employment and workplace laws prohibit specific types of dismissals. As just one example, occupational safety laws prohibit firing employees for reporting dangerous workplace conditions.[75]

Second, numerous *common-law exceptions* exist. For example, some state courts recognize the concept of *implied contracts* in employment. Thus, a court may decide that an employee handbook promising termination only "for just cause" may create an exception to the at-will rule.

Finally, under the *public policy exception*, courts have held a discharge to be wrongful when it was against an explicit, well-established public policy. (For instance, the employer fired the employee for refusing to break the law.)

Grounds for Dismissal

There are four bases for dismissal: unsatisfactory performance, misconduct, lack of qualifications for the job, and changed requirements of (or elimination of) the job.

Unsatisfactory performance means persistent failure to perform assigned duties or to meet prescribed job standards.[76] Specific grounds include excessive absenteeism, tardiness, a persistent failure to meet normal job requirements, or an adverse attitude toward the company, supervisor, or fellow employees.

Misconduct is deliberate and willful violation of the employer's rules and may include stealing, rowdy behavior, and insubordination. Sometimes the misconduct is more serious, as when it potentially causes someone harm. For example, a few years ago, someone video recorded (and posted on YouTube) a cook at a national pizza chain apparently putting vile foreign matter into the pizzas. Putting things like that in food is pretty clearly misconduct. Figure 14.10 shows how to identify such *gross misconduct* (in this case "gross" means "extreme," not "yuck").

Lack of qualifications for the job is an employee's inability to do the assigned work although he or she is diligent. If the employee may be trying to do the job, it is reasonable to do what's possible to salvage him or her—perhaps by assigning the person to another job.

"Changed requirements of the job" refers to an employee's inability to do the job after the employer changed the nature of the job. Again, the employee may be industrious, so it is reasonable to retrain or transfer this person, if possible.

INSUBORDINATION   **Insubordination** is a form of misconduct and means disobedience and/or rebelliousness. While things like stealing, chronic tardiness, and poor-quality work are easily understood grounds for dismissal, insubordination is sometimes harder

■Figure **14.10**
Was It Gross Misconduct?[77]

- Was anyone physically harmed? How badly?
- Did the employee realize the seriousness of his or her actions?
- Were other employees significantly affected?
- Was the employer's reputation severely damaged?
- Will the employer lose significant business or otherwise suffer economic harm because of the misconduct?
- Could the *employer* lose its business license because of the employee's misconduct?
- Will the *employee* lose any license needed to work for the employer (e.g., driver's license)?
- Was criminal activity involved?
- Was fraud involved?
- Was any safety statute violated?
- Was any civil statute violated?
- Was the conduct purposeful?
- Was the conduct on duty?
- Is the policy violated well known to employees?
- Does the conduct justify immediate termination?
- Has the employer immediately fired other employees who did something similar?

to translate into words. However, some acts are usually clearly insubordination. These include, for instance:

1. Direct disregard of the boss's authority
2. Direct disobedience of, or refusal to obey, the boss's orders, particularly in front of others
3. Deliberate defiance of clearly stated company policies, rules, regulations, and procedures
4. Public criticism of the boss
5. Blatant disregard of reasonable instructions
6. Contemptuous display of disrespect
7. Disregard for the chain of command, shown by frequently going around the immediate supervisor with complaints, suggestions, or political maneuvers
8. Participation in (or leadership of) an effort to undermine and remove the boss[78]

FAIRNESS IN DISMISSALS   Dismissals are never pleasant. However, you can do three things to make sure the dismissal is fair.[79] First, "individuals who said that they were given *full explanations* of why and how termination decisions were made were more likely to perceive their layoff as fair . . . and indicate that they did not wish to take the past employer to court."

Second, follow your employer's formal *multistep procedure* (including warning and appeal) process.

Third, *who actually does the dismissing* is important. Employees in one study whose supervisors informed them of an impending layoff viewed the dismissal procedure as fairer than did those told by, say, human resources. (Some employers take a less diplomatic approach. About 10% of respondents in one survey said they've used e-mail to fire employees.)[80]

SECURITY MEASURES   Security measures are important whenever dismissals occur. Prudence requires using a checklist to ensure that dismissed employees return all keys and company property, and (often) accompanying them out of their offices and out of the building. The supervisor should also ensure that the former employee's passwords and accounts are disabled, and ensure return of company laptops and handhelds.[81]

Avoiding Wrongful Discharge Suits

The last thing you need or want is to have the employee you dismiss accuse you or your employer of "wrongful discharge." As noted earlier, wrongful discharge occurs when an employee's dismissal does not comply with the law or with the contractual arrangement stated or implied by the employer.[82]

Avoiding wrongful discharge suits is not entirely under the supervisor's control. The employer's policies play a big role.[83]

First, the employer should have employment policies including grievance procedures and severance pay that help make employees feel you treated them fairly.[84] You can't make termination pleasant, but the first line of defense is to handle it justly.[85]

Second, your employer should review periodically all its employment-related policies, procedures, and documents to limit challenges. Make sure applicants sign the employment application. Make sure it contains a statement that the employer can terminate at any time. Pay particular attention to the employee handbook. Employers should probably delete statements such as "Employees can be terminated only for just cause." Supervisors should keep careful confidential records of all employee actions such as appraisals, warnings or notices, and memos outlining how improvement should be accomplished.

Third, make sure you clearly communicated job expectations to the employee.[86] Make sure he or she knows what the job entails, what the performance standards are, and that those standards are not being met. The courts will look to see if the employee knew what you expected in terms of behavior, and that he or she received fair warning.

Personal Supervisory Liability

Courts sometimes hold supervisors *personally* liable for certain supervisory actions.[87] For example, the Fair Labor Standards Act defines *employer* to include "any person acting directly or indirectly in the interest of an employer in relation to any employee." This can mean the individual supervisor.

There are several ways to avoid personal liability, for instance, for a particularly acrimonious dismissal. Make sure you have a working knowledge of the main *employment-related laws* such as Title VII (for instance, in terms of not discriminating against minorities). *Follow company policies and procedures* (for instance, regarding dismissals). The essence of many charges is that the plaintiff was treated differently than others, so *consistent application* of the rules is essential. Administer the discipline in a manner that does not add to the *emotional hardship* on the employee (as dismissing them publicly would). Most employees will try to present *their side* of the story, and allowing them to do so can provide the employee some measure of satisfaction. *Do not act in anger,* since doing so undermines any appearance of objectivity. Finally, *utilize the human resources department* for advice on how to handle difficult disciplinary matters.

The Termination Interview

Dismissing an employee is one of the most difficult tasks you will face at work. During one five-year period, physicians interviewed 791 working people who had just undergone heart attacks to find out what might have triggered them. The researchers concluded that the stress associated with firing someone doubled the usual risk of a heart attack for the person doing the firing, during the week following the dismissal.[88] Furthermore, the dismissed employee, even if warned many times, may still react with disbelief or even violence.[89] Guidelines for the **termination interview** itself are as follows:

1. **Plan the interview carefully.** According to experts at Hay Associates, this includes:
   - Make sure the employee keeps the appointment time.
   - Allow 10 minutes as sufficient time for the interview.
   - Use a neutral site, not your own office.
   - Have employee agreements and release announcements prepared in advance.
   - Have phone numbers ready for medical or security emergencies.
2. **Get to the point.** Avoid small talk. *As soon as the employee enters,* give the person a moment to get comfortable and then inform him or her of your decision.

3. **Describe the situation.**   Briefly explain why the person is being let go. For instance, "Production in your area is down 6%. We have talked about these problems several times in the past three months. We have to make a change." Stress the situation, rather than the employee's shortcomings. Emphasize that the decision is final and irrevocable.

4. **Listen.**   To the extent practical, continue the interview for several minutes until the person seems to be talking freely and reasonably calmly.

5. **Review all elements of the severance package.**   Briefly describe severance payments, benefits, access to office support people, and how references will be handled. However, make no promises beyond those already in the support package.

6. **Identify the next step.**   The terminated employee may be disoriented and unsure what to do next. Explain where the employee should go upon leaving the interview. It's often best to have someone escort him or her until the person is out the door.

Layoffs, Downsizing, and the Plant Closing Law

Nondisciplinary separations are a fact of corporate life. For the employer, reduced sales or profits may require *layoffs* or *downsizing*. *Layoff* generally refers to having selected employees take time off, with the expectation that they'll come back to work. *Downsizing* refers to permanently dismissing a relatively large proportion of employees in an attempt to improve competitiveness. Other employees may *resign* to *retire* or to look for better jobs. Supervisors need to be familiar with how to handle such nondisciplinary separations.

THE PLANT CLOSING LAW   In 1989, Congress passed the Worker Adjustment and Retraining Notification Act (the so-called *plant closing law*). It requires employers of 100 or more employees to give 60 days' notice before closing a facility or starting a layoff of 50 people or more. The law does not prevent the employer from closing down. It simply gives employees time to seek other work or retraining by giving them advance notice.

THE LAYOFF PROCESS   Supervisors usually play an important role in layoffs. For example, in one company, senior management first met to make strategic decisions about the size and timing of the layoffs. These managers also debated the relative importance of the skills they thought the firm needed going forward. First-line supervisors then assessed their subordinates, rating their nonunion employees either A, B, or C. The first-line supervisors than informed each of their subordinates about his or her A, B or C rating, and told each that those employees with C grades were designated "surplus" and most likely to be laid off.[90]

SUPERVISING IN CHALLENGING TIMES   As the United States slipped into recession, the number of large layoffs climbed ominously. How do employers prepare for the layoffs that result from such challenging times?

Interestingly, the initial focus isn't on the layoffs but on the employer's appraisal systems, so the supervisor plays a pivotal role. One expert says that in preparing for large-scale layoffs, management needs to do the following:[91]

- Make sure appraisals are up-to-date.
- Identify top performers and get them working on the company's future.
- Have leaders committed to the company's turnaround.

Another consultant says that companies that "don't closely manage their performance appraisal systems suddenly learn during a reduction in force that everyone has been ranked a 'four' out of 'five.' That information is meaningless."[92]

So the essential point about layoffs is to prepare in advance by making sure you have effective performance appraisals for your employees. If you don't, then when the time comes to lay off significant numbers of employers, you may find yourself with no rational basis on which to decide who stays or leaves.

BUMPING/LAYOFF PROCEDURES   As noted above, *layoff* generally refers to having some employees take time off, with the expectation that they'll come back to work. With layoffs, three conditions are usually present: (1) There is no work available for these employees; (2) management expects the no-work situation to be temporary and probably short term; and (3) management intends to recall the employees. Some employers, however, use the term *layoff* as a euphemism for discharge or termination. (Others have taken to calling them "productivity transformation programs.")[93]

Employers who encounter frequent business slowdowns may have bumping/layoff procedures. These let employees use their seniority to remain on the job. Most such **bumping/layoff procedures** have these features in common:

1. Seniority is usually the ultimate determinant of who will work.

2. Seniority can give way to merit or ability, but usually only when no senior employee is qualified for a particular job.

3. Seniority is usually based on the date the employee joined the organization, not the date he or she took a particular job.

4. Because seniority is usually companywide, an employee in one job can usually bump or displace an employee in another job, provided the more senior person can do the job.

Ethics Quiz Answers
Quiz is on Page 419—Figure 14-3

1. 34% said personal e-mail on company computers is wrong.
2. 37% said using office equipment for schoolwork is wrong.
3. 49% said playing computer games at work is wrong.
4. 54% said Internet shopping at work is wrong.
5. 61% said it's unethical to blame your error on technology.
6. 87% said it's unethical to visit pornographic sites at work.
7. 33% said $25 is the amount at which a gift from a supplier or client becomes troubling, while 33% said $50, and 33% said $100.
8. 35% said a $50 gift to the boss is unacceptable.
9. 12% said a $50 gift *from* the boss is unacceptable.
10. 70% said it's unacceptable to take the $200 football tickets.
11. 70% said it's unacceptable to take the $120 theater tickets.
12. 35% said it's unacceptable to take the $100 food basket.
13. 45% said it's unacceptable to take the $25 gift certificate.
14. 40% said it's unacceptable to take the $75 raffle prize.
15. 11% reported they lie about sick days.
16. 4% reported they take credit for the work or ideas of others.

Chapter 14 Concept Review and Reinforcement

Key Terms

Bumping/Layoff
Procedures, p. 438
Dismissal, p. 433
Electronic
Communications
Privacy Act
(ECPA), p. 432

Ethics, p. 418
Ethics Code, p. 423
Insubordination,
p. 434
Nonpunitive Discipline,
p. 429

Organizational Culture,
p. 422
Termination at Will,
p. 433

Termination Interview,
p. 436
Wrongful Discharge,
p. 433

Review of Key Concepts

Treating Employees Fairly	• Mistreated employees report lower job and life satisfaction, higher stress, workplace deviance, and the employee will not do his or her best. • Treating people fairly can enhance employee commitment and enhance satisfaction with the employer, job, leader, and organization.
Supervisors' Fairness Guidelines	• Involve employees in decisions that affect them. • Ensure that everyone involved and affected understands why final decisions are made. • Make sure everyone knows up front by what standards you will judge him or her.
What Are Ethics?	Ethics are the principles of conduct governing an individual or a group.
Normative Judgments	A normative judgment means that something is good or bad, right or wrong, better or worse.
What Is Morality?	Morality is a society's highest accepted standards of behavior. Moral standards guide behaviors of the most serious consequence to a society's well-being, such as murder, lying, and slander.
Why Study Ethics?	• Ethics greases the wheels that make businesses work. • Just about everything supervisors do has ethical consequences.
Determinates of Ethical Behavior at Work	Moral awareness, the supervisors themselves, moral engagement, morality, unmet goals, and rewards all influence ethical behavior.
The Supervisor as Leader	Supervisors can influence their employees' ethics by: • Creating the right organizational culture • Appraising fairly • Using reward and disciplinary systems fairly

Ethically—What the Company Can Do	
Ethic Codes	An ethics code memorializes the standards to which the employer expects its employees to adhere.
Whistleblower Policies	Whistleblowers are individuals, frequently employees, who use procedural or legal channels to report incidents of unethical behavior.
Personnel Selection Procedure	The simplest way to maintain an ethical organization is to hire ethical people.
Ethics Training	Ethics training usually includes showing employees how to recognize ethical dilemmas, how to use codes of conduct to resolve problems, and how to use disciplinary practices in ethical ways.
Why Discipline Employees?	The purpose of discipline is to encourage employees to adhere to rules and regulations, which, when violated, require discipline.
Disciplinary Process— Fair and Just	The employer wants its disciplinary process to be both effective and fair, based on clear rules and regulations, a system of progressive penalties, and an appeals process.
Nonpunitive Discipline	Discipline without punishment attempts to gain employee' acceptance of the rules while reducing the punitive nature of the discipline itself.
Hot Stove Rule	The hot stove rule means administering discipline in such a way that the person has warning, and the pain is consistent, impersonal, and immediate.
Employee Monitoring	With more employers using Internet monitoring and technologies such as biometrics, monitoring is widespread.
ECPA	The Electronic Communications Privacy Act (ECPA) protects against invasion of privacy by helping restrict interception and monitoring of oral and wire communications.
Managing Dismissals	Dismissal is the most drastic disciplinary step the employer can take. There should be sufficient cause for the dismissal and you should only dismiss someone after taking reasonable steps to rehabilitate.

Grounds for Dismissal	The four bases for dismissal are: • Unsatisfactory performance • Misconduct • Lack of qualifications for the job • Changed requirements of the job
Insubordination	Insubordination is a form of misconduct and basically refers to disobedience and/or rebelliousness including direct disregard of the boss's authority.
Fairness in Dismissals	The supervisor should make sure the dismissal is fair by giving full explanations of why and how termination decisions were made, following a multistep procedure, and making the actual dismissal.
Termination Interview	The termination interview should be planned carefully, and the supervisor should the get to the point, describe the situation, listen, review all elements of the severance package, and then identify the next step.
The Plant Closing Law	The Worker Adjustment and Retraining Notification Act requires employers of 100 or more employees to give 60 days' notice before closing a facility or starting a layoff of 50 people or more.
Layoff Procedures	A layoff generally refers to having some employees take time off, with the expectation that they will come back to work.

Review and Discussion Questions

1. Describe how treating employees fairly will enhance the position of the organization in the eyes of the employees and the community.
2. Why is it important in our highly litigious society to manage dismissals properly?
3. List 10 things your college or university does to encourage ethical behavior by students and/or faculty.
4. If you had a subordinate who stood up to you and refused a direct order, what would you do about it?
5. If you were a supervisor who had just dismissed a subordinate for a reason, what process would you have gone through to justify that this dismissal was fair?
6. If your company plans to close a plant and has given 60 days' advance notice as per the plant closing law, should you have any concerns as to the behavior of those employees during that 60-day period? If so, why?
7. Why should the termination interview be planned carefully?
8. As an organization leader, what can a supervisor do to influence his or her employees to be ethically responsible?
9. If your company has a whistleblower policy in place, what impact might this policy have on you as supervisor?
10. Describe why it is important for a company to use ethics training as an educational tool for their supervisors.
11. Describe the disciplinary process that would be both effective and fair.

Application and Skill Building

Case Study One

Enron, Ethics, and Organizational Culture

For many people, a company called Enron Corporation still ranks as one of history's classic examples of ethics run amok. During the 1990s and early 2000s, Enron was in the business of wholesaling natural gas and electricity. Rather than actually owning the gas or electricity, Enron made its money as the intermediary (wholesaler) between suppliers and customers. Without getting into all the details, the nature of Enron's business and the fact that Enron didn't actually own the assets meant that its accounting procedures were unusual. For example, the profit statements and balance sheets listing the firm's assets and liabilities were unusually difficult to understand.

It turned out that the lack of accounting transparency enabled the company's managers to make Enron's financial performance look much better than it actually was. Outside experts began questioning Enron's financial statements in 2001. In fairly short order, Enron's house of cards collapsed, and courts convicted several of its top executives of things such as manipulating Enron's reported assets and profitability. Many investors (including former Enron employees) lost all or most of their investments in Enron.

It's probably always easier to understand ethical breakdowns like this in retrospect, rather than to predict they are going to happen. However, in Enron's case the breakdown is perhaps more perplexing than usual. As one writer recently said,

> Enron had all the elements usually found in comprehensive ethics and compliance programs: a code of ethics, a reporting system, as well as a training video on vision and values led by [the company's top executives].[94]

Experts subsequently put forth many explanations for how a company that was apparently so ethical on its face could actually have been making so many bad ethical decisions without other managers (and the board of directors) noticing. The explanations ranged from a "deliberate concealment of information by officers" to more psychological explanations (such as employees not wanting to contradict their bosses), and the "surprising role of irrationality in decision-making."[95]

But perhaps the most persuasive explanation of how an apparently ethical company could go so wrong concerns organizational culture. The reasoning here is that it's not the rules but what employees feel they should do that determines ethical behavior. For example (speaking in general, not specifically about Enron), the executive director of the Ethics Officer Association put it this way:

> [W]e're a legalistic society, and we've created a lot of laws. We assume that if you just knew what those laws meant that you would behave properly. Well, guess what? You can't write enough laws to tell us what to do at all times every day of the week in every part of the world. We've got to develop the critical thinking and critical reasoning skills of our people because most of the ethical issues that we deal with are in the ethical gray areas. Virtually

every regulatory body in the last year has come out with language that has said in addition to law compliance, businesses are also going to be accountable to ethics standards and a corporate culture that embraces them.[96]

How can one tell or measure when a company has an "ethical culture"? Key attributes of a healthy ethical culture include the following:

- Employees feel a sense of responsibility and accountability for their actions and for the actions of others.[97]
- Employees freely raise issues and concerns without fear of retaliation.
- Managers model the behaviors they demand of others.
- Managers communicate the importance of integrity when making difficult decisions.

Discussion Questions

1. Based on what you read in this chapter, summarize in one page or less how you would explain Enron's ethical meltdown.
2. It is said that when one securities analyst tried to confront Enron's CEO about the firm's unusual accounting statements, the CEO publicly used vulgar language to describe the analyst, and that Enron employees subsequently thought doing so was humorous. If true, what does that say about Enron's ethical culture?
3. This case and chapter both had something to say about how organizational culture influences ethical behavior. What role do you think culture played at Enron? Give five specific examples of things Enron's CEO could have done to create a healthy ethical culture.

Case Study Two

Carter Cleaning Centers

Guaranteeing Fair Treatment

Being in the laundry and cleaning business, the Carters have always felt strongly about not allowing employees to smoke, eat, or drink in their stores. Jennifer was therefore surprised to walk into a store and find two employees eating lunch at the front counter. There was a large pizza in its box, and the two of them were sipping colas and eating slices of pizza and submarine sandwiches off paper plates. Not only did it look messy, but also there were grease and soda spills on the counter and the store smelled of onions and pepperoni, even with the four-foot-wide exhaust fan pulling air out through the roof. In addition to being a turnoff to customers, the mess on the counter increased the possibility that a customer's order might actually become soiled in the store.

While this was a serious matter, neither Jennifer nor her father felt that what the counter people were doing was grounds for immediate dismissal, partly because the store manager had apparently condoned their actions. The problem was, they didn't know what to do. It seemed to them that the matter called for more than just a warning but less than dismissal.

Discussion Questions

1. What would you do if you were Jennifer, and why?
2. Should a disciplinary system be established at Carter's Cleaning Centers?
3. If so, what should it cover? How would you suggest it deal with a situation such as the one with the errant counter people?
4. How would you deal with the store manager?

Experiential Activities

Activity 1. Enrique worked as a waiter at an all-night restaurant in Brooklyn, New York. At 1 a.m., if he missed his 45-minute train ride home, his bus ride would take 2½ hours. One night two men sat down at 12:45 a.m., 15 minutes before Enrique normally left. When he asked his supervisor to let someone else take over, he was told that if he didn't stay until to 3 a.m., he would most likely no longer have a job.

Treating Subordinates Fairly

Purpose: The purpose of this exercise is to give you practice identifying unfair treatment of subordinates as well as developing guidelines that represent fair treatment.

Required Understanding: You are going to develop a comprehensive process for treating your employees fairly.

How to Set Up the Exercise/Instructions: Divide the class into groups of 4–5 students.

1. You want to answer the question of how Enrique could have been treated differently (more fairly) in this situation.
2. Your group should develop an outline summarizing the use of the supervisors' fairness guidelines to determine how this situation could have been averted.
3. Next, outline a checklist, deciding what steps can be taken in the future to assure fairness in treatment.
4. Have a spokesperson from each group share their outlines and checklists with the other groups. Follow with a discussion looking at differences and similarities in these plans.

Activity 2. Working individually or in groups, obtain copies of the student handbook for your college and determine to what extent there is a formal process through which students can air grievances. Based on your contacts with other students, has it been an effective grievance process? Why or why not?

Activity 3. In a research study at Ohio State University, a professor found that even honest people, left to their own devices, would steal from their employers.[98] In this study, the researchers gave financial services workers the opportunity to steal a small amount of money after participating in an after-work project for which the pay was inadequate. Would the employees steal to make up for the underpayment? In most cases, yes. Employees who scored low on an honesty test stole whether or not their office had an ethics program that said stealing from the company was illegal. Employees who scored high on the honesty test also stole, but only if their office did not have such an employee ethics program—the "honest" people didn't steal if there was an ethics policy.

In groups of four or five students, answer these questions: Do you think findings like these are generalizable? In other words, would they apply across the board to employees in other types of companies and situations? If your answer is yes, what do you think this implies about the need for and wisdom of having an ethics program?

Role-Playing Exercise One

Safety Is First! Or Is It? The Situation

The new finishing department supervisor at a GM foundry has just returned from a two-week orientation in Detroit, Michigan. Dave is excited about putting to use what he learned about management at Indiana University as a business student. General Motors is a big corporation with many opportunities for advancement, and Dave feels up to the challenge after his orientation at the corporate offices. One of the most impressive directives he remembers is that GM places "safety first," "quality next," and "production" after that. Every sign, advertisement, and public message supports that sentiment. Dave fully agrees that safety must always come first in order to protect his subordinates from work-related injuries. After only one month on the job, Dave realizes that in reality, things are different. His supervisor, the plant director, has impressed upon Dave that meeting production quotas (at any price) is the number-one goal. Safetywise, the real sentiment was don't get anyone hurt, but make production, and if quality is not up to standard, then don't worry, because someone in the next plant will catch the flaw before a part gets put into a new car. This represents an ethical dilemma for Dave, who believes that these standards will have ethical consequences down the road. Dave believes that he may have made the wrong employment decision, but he has asked for a meeting with his general foreman to discuss the issue.

Instructions: All students should read the situation above. One student will play the role of Dave while the other will play the role of his general foreman. Each student should only read his or her assigned role below. The two students should engage in a 15-minute conversation.

A class discussion will follow the role-playing exercise.

Dave (Supervisor): Your role is to attempt to solve your ethical dilemma involving safety, quality, and productivity. At corporate orientation, why did they tell you something different from the way things are done in the plant? Your goal is to persuade the general foreman that ethically, safety and quality should come before production. You do not want to purchase a new GM car with a defective crankshaft, which could turn into a safety situation.

Plant Director: Your role is to clarify your position regarding safety, quality, and production issues at this plant. You, as general foreman, are under great pressure from your supervisor to meet production standards (at any cost). You *must* meet these production standards while not getting anyone hurt. Qualitywise, you say put the broken castings in the bottom of the box and maybe inspection will overlook them. Anyway, the bad parts, if they get through, will be caught by the machining operation later at the next plant (maybe).

Questions for Discussion

1. What are the ethical issues in this situation?
2. Has the plant director done a respectable job in supporting his job directives involving safety, quality, and production?
3. How prevalent do you feel situations like this are in real manufacturing plants?
4. What course of action do you think Dave should take after his meeting with the plant director?

Role-Playing Exercise Two
Discipline or Not?

Purpose: The purpose of this exercise is to provide you with some experience in analyzing and handling an actual disciplinary action.

Required Understanding: Students should be thoroughly familiar with the following case, titled "Botched Batch." **Do not read the "award" or "discussion" sections until after the groups have completed their deliberations.**

How to Set Up the Exercise/Instructions: Divide the class into groups of four or five students. Each group should step into the arbitrator's role and assume that they are to analyze the case and make the arbitrator's decision. Review the case again at this point, but please do not read the award and discussion sections.

Each group should answer the following questions:

1. Based on what you read in this chapter, including all relevant guidelines, what would your decision be if you were the arbitrator? Why?
2. Do you think that after their experience in this arbitration the parties will be more or less inclined to settle grievances by themselves without resorting to arbitration?

Botched Batch

Facts: A computer department employee made an entry error that botched an entire run of computer reports. Efforts to rectify the situation produced a second set of improperly run reports. Because of the series of errors, the employer incurred extra costs of $2,400, plus a weekend of overtime work by other computer department staffers. Management suspended the employee for three days for negligence, and revoked a promotion for which the employee had previously been approved.

Protesting the discipline, the employee stressed that she had attempted to correct her error in the early stages of the run by notifying the manager of computer operations of her mistake. Maintaining that the resulting string of errors could have been avoided if the manager had followed up on her report and stopped the initial run, the employee argued that she had been treated unfairly, because the manager had not been disciplined even though he compounded the problem, whereas she was severely punished. Moreover, citing her "impeccable" work record and management's acknowledgment that she had always been a "model employee," the employee insisted that the denial of her previously approved promotion was "unconscionable."

(*Please do **not** read beyond this point until after you have answered the two questions.*)

Award: The arbitrator upholds the three-day suspension, but decides that the promotion should be restored.

Discussion: "There is no question," the arbitrator notes, that the employee's negligent act "set in motion the train of events that resulted in running two complete sets of reports reflecting improper information." Stressing that the employer incurred substantial costs because of the error, the arbitrator cites "unchallenged" testimony that management had commonly issued three-day suspensions for similar infractions in the past. Thus, the arbitrator decides, the employer acted with just cause in meting out an "evenhanded" punishment for the negligence.

Turning to the denial of the already approved promotion, the arbitrator says that this action should be viewed "in the same light as a demotion for disciplinary reasons." In such cases, the arbitrator notes, management's decision normally is based on a pattern of unsatisfactory behavior, an employee's inability to perform, or similar grounds. Observing that management had never before reversed a promotion as part of a disciplinary action, the arbitrator says that by tacking on the denial of the promotion in this case, the employer substantially varied its disciplinary policy from its past practice. Because this action on management's part was not "evenhanded," the arbitrator rules, the promotion should be restored.[99]

15 Supervising Grievances and Labor Relations

....

CHAPTER OBJECTIVES

After studying this chapter, you should be able to answer the following questions:

1. How Do Unions Impact Organizations?
2. What Are the Laws That Govern Labor Relations?
3. What Should the Supervisor Know About the Union Drive and Election?
4. What Is to Be Expected During the Collective Bargaining Process?
5. How Are Grievances Handled?
6. What's Next for Unions?

OPENING SNAPSHOT
The Baristas Organize

The U.S. Department of Labor's National Labor Relations Board (NLRB) accused Starbucks of breaking the law. Among other things, it accused supervisors in some New York stores of retaliating against workers who wanted to unionize by interrogating them about their union inclinations. A Starbucks spokesperson said the company believes the allegations are baseless, and that the firm will vigorously defend itself.[1]

1. Do Unions Matter?

These Starbucks supervisors discovered that you can't underestimate unions.[2] Just over 17.7 million U.S. workers belong to unions—around 12.4% of the men and women working in this country.[3] Many are still blue-collar workers. But workers including doctors, psychologists, government office workers, and even fashion models are forming or joining unions.[4] Over 40% of America's 20 million federal, state, and municipal public employees belong to unions.[5] (In 2009, for the first time, just over half of all union members were in the public sector.)[6] And in some industries—including transportation and public utilities—it's hard to get a job without joining a union.[7] Union membership in other countries is declining, but still high (over 35% of employed workers in Canada, Mexico, Brazil, and Italy, for instance).

Union membership also ranges widely by state, from over 20% in Michigan and New York, down to about 4% in North Carolina. Several big unions recently formed their own federation with the aim of aggressively organizing workers (more on this below). U.S. union membership peaked at about 34% in 1955. It has fallen since then due to things such as the shift from manufacturing to service jobs. But for the first time in many years, union membership in America actually rose a bit in 2008–2009.[8] So if you're supervising in the public sector, or in many states, or (increasingly) in a great many other industries and situations, you've got to know how to deal with unions.

Furthermore, don't assume that unions are bad for employers. For example, perhaps by systematizing company practices, unionization may actually improve performance. In one study, researchers found that heart attack mortality among patients in hospitals with unionized registered nurses were 5%–9% lower than in nonunion hospitals.[9] Another study found a negative relationship between union membership and employees' intent to quit.[10]

How Do Unions Impact Organizations?

Why Do Workers Organize?

People have spent much time analyzing why workers unionize, and they've proposed many theories. Yet there is no simple answer, although supervisor behavior plays a role.

It's clear that workers don't unionize just to get more pay, although union members do earn more than nonunion members do. For example, recent median weekly wages for union workers was $781, while nonunion workers' was $612.[11]

But pay usually isn't the main issue. Instead—and this is important for supervisors to know—the urge to unionize seems to boil down to the workers' belief that it's only through unity that they can protect themselves from arbitrary supervisory whims. One labor relations lawyer put it this way, "The one major thing unions offer is making you a 'for cause' instead of an 'at will' employee, which guarantees a hearing and arbitration if you're fired."[12] For example, a butcher hired by Walmart said his new supervisor told him he'd be able to start management training and possibly move up to supervisor. The butcher started work, and bought a car for the commute. However, after the butcher hurt his back at work, his supervisor never mentioned the promotion again. Faced with high car payments and feeling cheated, the butcher went to the Grocery Workers Union. It sent an organizer. The store's meat cutters voted to unionize. A week later Walmart announced it would switch to prepackaged meats, and that its store no longer required butchers.[13]

The Bottom Line for Supervisors

The bottom line is that employees often turn to unions because they seek protection against what they view as supervisors' whims.[14] Several years ago, Kaiser Permanente's San Francisco Medical Center cut back on vacation and sick leave. The pharmacists' union won back the lost vacation days. As one staff pharmacist said, "Kaiser is a pretty benevolent employer, but there's always the pressure to squeeze a little."[15] Supervisors, therefore, play a central role in the union process. Perhaps most importantly, as a supervisor, you'll be one of or the most important determiner of whether your employees feel they're fairly treated.

What Do Unions Want? What Are Their Aims?

We can generalize by saying that unions have two sets of aims, one for union security and one for improved wages, hours, working conditions, and benefits for their members.

UNION SECURITY   First and probably foremost, unions seek to establish "security" for themselves. They fight hard for the right to represent a firm's workers and to be the *exclusive* bargaining agent for all employees in the unit. (As such, they negotiate contracts for all employees, including those who are not members of the union.) Five types of union security are possible:

1. **Closed shop.**[16]   The company can hire only current union members. Congress outlawed closed shops in interstate commerce in 1947, but they still exist in some states for particular industries (such as printing). They account for less than 5% of union contracts.

2. **Union shop.**   The company can hire nonunion people, but they must join the union after a prescribed period and pay dues. (If not, they can be fired.) This category accounts for about 73% of union contracts.

3. **Agency shop.**   Employees who do not belong to the union still must pay the union an amount equal to union dues (on the assumption that the union's efforts benefit *all* the workers).

4. **Preferential shop.**   Union members get preference in hiring, but the employer can still hire nonunion members.

5. **Maintenance of membership arrangement.**   Employees do not have to belong to the union. However, union members employed by the firm must maintain membership in the union for the contract period. These account for about 4% of union agreements.

Not all states give unions the right to require union membership as a condition of employment.

Right to work "is a term used to describe state statutory or constitutional provisions banning the requirement of union membership as a condition of employment."[17] Labor law permits states to forbid the negotiation of compulsory union membership provisions. Right-to-work laws don't outlaw unions. They do outlaw (within those states) any form of union security. This understandably inhibits union formation in those states. There are 23 right-to-work states.[18]

IMPROVED WAGES, HOURS, WORKING CONDITIONS, AND BENEFITS FOR MEMBERS   Once their security is assured, unions fight to better the lot of their members—to improve their wages, hours, and working conditions, for example. The typical labor agreement also gives the union a role in other employment activities, including recruiting, selecting, compensating, promoting, training, and discharging employees.

The AFL-CIO

The American Federation of Labor and Congress of Industrial Organizations (AFL-CIO) is a voluntary federation of about 56 national and international labor unions in the United States. It resulted from the merger of the AFL and CIO in 1955.

For many people, the AFL-CIO is synonymous with the word *union*, but union federation membership is in flux. Several years ago, six big unions—the Service Employees' International Union (SEIU), the International Brotherhood of Teamsters, the United Food and Commercial Workers, the United Farm Workers, the Laborers International Union, and UNITE HERE (which represents garment and service workers) left the AFL-CIO and established their own federation, called the Change to Win Coalition. Together, the departing unions represented over one-fourth of the AFL-CIO's membership and budget. Change to Win plans to be more aggressive about organizing workers than they say the AFL-CIO was. Then in 2009, UNITE HERE rejoined the AFL-CIO, possibly slowing Change to Win's momentum.[19] About 7 million workers belong to unions not affiliated with the AFL-CIO.

2. Unions and the Law

Until about 1930, there were no special labor laws. Employers were virtually unrestrained in their behavior toward unions; the use of spies and firing of union agitators were widespread.

What Are the Laws that Govern Labor Relations?

This one-sided situation lasted until the Great Depression (around 1930). Since then, Congress and various administrations have passed a series of labor relations laws.[20] Supervisors need a working knowledge of these laws, because the laws lay out guidelines for what you can and cannot do.

The Norris-LaGuardia (1932) and National Labor Relations or Wagner Acts (1935)

The **Norris-LaGuardia Act of 1932** set the stage for a new era in which union activity was encouraged. It guaranteed to each employee the right to bargain collectively "free from interference, restraint, or coercion." Three years later, Congress passed the **National Labor Relations (or Wagner) Act** to expand Norris-LaGuardia. It expanded Norris-LaGuardia by (1) banning certain "unfair labor practices"; (2) providing for secret-ballot elections and majority rule for determining whether a firm's employees would unionize; and (3) creating the **National Labor Relations Board (NLRB)** to enforce these two provisions.

UNFAIR EMPLOYER LABOR PRACTICES   The Wagner Act deemed "statutory wrongs" (but not crimes) five unfair labor practices used by employers (and their supervisors):

1. It is unfair for employers to "interface with, restrain, or coerce employees" in exercising their legally sanctioned right of self-organization.

2. It is unfair for company representatives to dominate or interfere with either the formation or the administration of labor unions (for example, by attempting to bribe employees).

3. Employers are prohibited from discriminating in any way against employees for their legal union activities.

4. Employers are forbidden to discharge or discriminate against employees simply because the latter file unfair practice charges against the company.

5. Finally, it is an unfair labor practice for employers to refuse to bargain collectively with their employees' duly chosen representatives.

Unions file an unfair labor practice charge (see Figure 15.1) with the National Labor Relations Board. The board then investigates the charge and decides if it should take action.

The Taft-Hartley Act (1947)

Union membership increased quickly after the Wagner Act in 1935. But, largely because of a series of massive strikes, public policy began to shift against what many viewed as union excesses.

The **Taft-Hartley (or Labor Management Relations) Act of 1947** reflected the public's less enthusiastic attitude toward unions. It amended the National Labor Relations (Wagner) Act by limiting unions in four ways: (1) prohibiting unfair *union* labor practices, (2) enumerating the rights of employees as union members, (3) enumerating the rights of employers, and (4) allowing the president of the United States to bar temporarily national emergency strikes.

UNFAIR UNION LABOR PRACTICES   The Taft-Hartley Act prohibited unions from engaging in several labor practices:

1. First, it banned unions from *restraining or coercing employees* from exercising their guaranteed bargaining rights.

2. It is also an unfair labor practice for a union to *cause an employer to discriminate* in any way against an employee in order to encourage or discourage his or her membership in a union. For example, the union generally cannot try to force an employer to fire a worker because he or she doesn't attend union meetings or refuses to join a union.

3. It is an unfair labor practice for a union to *refuse to bargain in good faith* with the employer about wages, hours, and other employment conditions.

4. It is an unfair labor practice for a union to engage in *featherbedding* (requiring an employer to pay an employee for services not performed).

RIGHTS OF EMPLOYEES   The Taft-Hartley Act protected the rights of employees against their unions in other ways. For example, many people felt that compulsory unionism violated the right of freedom of association. Under Taft-Hartley, new *right-to-work* laws

INTERNET
FORM NLRB-501
(2-08)

UNITED STATES OF AMERICA
NATIONAL LABOR RELATIONS BOARD
CHARGE AGAINST EMPLOYER

DO NOT WRITE IN THIS SPACE

Case	Date Filed

INSTRUCTIONS:
File an original with NLRB Regional Director for the region in which the alleged unfair labor practice occurred or is occurring.

1. EMPLOYER AGAINST WHOM CHARGE IS BROUGHT

a. Name of Employer	b. Tel. No.
	c. Cell No.
	f. Fax No.

d. Address *(Street, city, state, and ZIP code)*	e. Employer Representative	g. e-Mail
		h. Number of workers employed

i. Type of Establishment *(factory, mine, wholesaler, etc.)*	j. Identify principal product or service

k. The above-named employer has engaged in and is engaging in unfair labor practices within the meaning of section 8(a), subsections (1) and *(list subsections)* _____ of the National Labor Relations Act, and these unfair labor practices are practices affecting commerce within the meaning of the Act, or these unfair labor practices are unfair practices affecting commerce within the meaning of the Act and the Postal Reorganization Act.

2. Basis of the Charge *(set forth a clear and concise statement of the facts constituting the alleged unfair labor practices)*

3. Full name of party filing charge *(if labor organization, give full name, including local name and number)*

4a. Address *(Street and number, city, state, and ZIP code)*	4b. Tel. No.
	4c. Cell No.
	4d. Fax No.
	4e. e-Mail

5. Full name of national or international labor organization of which it is an affiliate or constituent unit *(to be filled in when charge is filed by a labor organization)*

6. DECLARATION
I declare that I have read the above charge and that the statements are true to the best of my knowledge and belief.

	Tel. No.
By _____ _____	Office, if any, Cell No.
(signature of representative or person making charge) *(Print/type name and title or office, if any)*	Fax No.
	e-Mail
Address_____ *(date)*	

WILLFUL FALSE STATEMENTS ON THIS CHARGE CAN BE PUNISHED BY FINE AND IMPRISONMENT (U.S. CODE, TITLE 18, SECTION 1001)

PRIVACY ACT STATEMENT

Solicitation of the information on this form is authorized by the National Labor Relations Act (NLRA), 29 U.S.C. § 151 *et seq.* The principal use of the information is to assist the National Labor Relations Board (NLRB) in processing unfair labor practice and related proceedings or litigation.The routine uses for the information are fully set forth in the Federal Register, 71 Fed. Reg. 74942-43 (Dec.13, 2006). The NLRB will further explain these uses upon request. Disclosure of this information to the NLRB is voluntary; however, failure to supply the information will cause the NLRB to decline to invoke its processes.

■Figure **15.1**

Form for Unfair Labor Practice

Source: http://www.nlrb.gov/nlrb/shared_files/forms/nlrbform501.pdf (accessed April 28, 2009).

quickly sprang up in some states (mainly in the South and Southwest). That's one reason why today union membership varies widely by state.[21]

RIGHTS OF EMPLOYERS   The Taft-Hartley Act also explicitly gave *employers* certain rights. For example, you as a supervisor can tell your employees that in your opinion unions are worthless, dangerous to the economy, and immoral. You can even (generally) hint that unionization and subsequent high-wage demands might result in the permanent closing of the plant (but *not* its relocation). Supervisors can set forth the union's record concerning violence and corruption, if appropriate.

In fact, the only major restraint is that supervisors and employers *must avoid threats, promises, coercion, and direct interference* with workers who are trying to reach a decision.[22] Management also (1) cannot meet with employees on company time within 24 hours of an election or (2) suggest to employees that they vote against the union while they are at home or in the employer's office. (However, they can do so while in their work area or where they normally gather.)

The Landrum-Griffin Act (1959)

In the 1950s, Senate investigations revealed unsavory practices on the part of some unions. The result was the **Landrum-Griffin Act** (officially, the **Labor Management Reporting and Disclosure Act) of 1959**. Its overriding aim was to protect union members from possible wrongdoing by their unions. The law contains a bill of rights for union members. It provides for certain rights in the nomination of candidates for union office. It also affirms a member's right to sue his or her union and ensures that the union cannot fine or suspend a member without due process.

3. What the Supervisor Should Know About the Union Drive and Election

What Should the Supervisor Know about the Union Drive and Election?

It is through the union drive and election that a union tries to be recognized to represent employees. The union drive and election are dangerous times for supervisors. A wrong step can trigger accusations of unfair labor practices and even overturn an election that the employer won (remember those Starbucks supervisors in the opening snapshot). Supervisors therefore need to be familiar with this union drive process, which has five basic steps.

Step 1. Initial Contact

During the initial contact stage, the union sizes up the employees' interest in organizing and establishes an organizing committee.

The initiative for the first contact between the employees and the union may come from the employees, from a union already representing other employees of the firm, or from a union representing workers elsewhere. In any case, there is an initial contact.

Union iPod organizing

Unions are using mobile devices to support their organizing efforts. The accompanying screen grab (Figure 15.2) shows one slide from a presentation from the National Education Association union.[23] For example, they'll use smartphones to send text messages and iPods to discuss issues.

■Figure **15.2**

Web Resources and Techniques Unions Use

Web Resources and Techniques for Organizing and Membership Development

Tools	Techniques	Function/Activity
Smartphone/PDA	o Spreadsheets and databases o SMS	o tracking contacts made with potential members o text messaging a quick thank you.
IPOD	o Pod casts	o talk about the issues o benefits of membership
Face-to-Face	Smile, handshake, real conversation, print brochure, flyer, etc...	Personal touch is always most effective

Once an employer becomes a target, a union official usually assigns a representative to assess employee interest. The representative visits the firm to determine whether enough employees are interested to make a campaign worthwhile. He or she also identifies employees who would make good leaders in the organizing campaign and calls them together to create an organizing committee.

Supervisors (like those at Starbucks) should know that unions must follow certain rules when contacting employees. The law allows organizers to solicit employees for membership as long as the effort doesn't endanger employee performance or safety. Therefore, much of the contact takes place off the job, perhaps at eating places near work. Organizers can also safely contact employees on company grounds during off hours (such as lunch or break time). Yet, in practice, there will be much informal organizing going on at the workplace as employees debate organizing. Much soliciting today will be via e-mail (see the APPs feature above).

UNION SALTING   The National Labor Relations Board defines union **salting** as "placing of union members on nonunion job sites for the purpose of organizing."[24] For supervisors, the solution is to make sure you know whom you're hiring. However, not hiring someone simply because, as a member of the local union, he or she might be pro-union or a union salt would be discriminatory.[25]

Step 2. Obtaining Authorization Cards

For the union to petition the NLRB for the right to hold an election, it must show that enough employees may be interested in organizing. The next step is thus for union organizers to get employees to sign **authorization cards**. These usually authorize the union to seek a representation election and state that the employee has applied to join the union. Thirty percent of the eligible employees in an appropriate bargaining unit must sign before the union can petition the NLRB for an election.

During this stage, both union and management use propaganda. The union claims it can improve working conditions, raise wages, increase benefits, and generally get the workers better deals. Management can attack the union on ethical and moral grounds and cite the cost of union membership. Management can also explain its accomplishments, express facts and opinions, and explain the law applicable to organizing campaigns. However, remember that neither side can threaten, bribe, or coerce employees. And an employer (or supervisor) may not make "promises of benefits to employees or make unilateral changes in terms and conditions of employment that were not planned to be implemented prior to the onset of union organizing activity."

WHAT CAN SUPERVISORS DO?   It is an unfair labor practice to tell employees they cannot sign a card. What you *can* do is explain what the card actually authorizes the union to do—including seeking a representation election, designating the union as bargaining representative, and subjecting the employee to union rules and dues.

One thing you should *not* do is look through signed authorization cards if confronted with them by union representatives. The NLRB could construe that as an unfair labor practice, as spying on those who signed.

Step 3. Hold a Hearing

Once the union collects the authorization cards, it usually contacts the NLRB, which requests a hearing. The regional director of the NLRB then sends a hearing officer to investigate. The examiner sends both management and union a notice of representation hearing (NLRB Form 852), which states the time and place of the hearing.

The hearing addresses several issues. First, is there enough evidence to hold an election? (For example, did 30% or more of the employees in an appropriate bargaining unit sign the authorization cards?) Second, the examiner must decide what the bargaining unit will be. The **bargaining unit** is the group of employees that the union will be authorized to represent and bargain for collectively.

If the results of the hearing are favorable for the union, the NLRB will order holding an election. It will issue a Notice of Election (NLRB Form 707) to that effect for the employer to post.

Step 4. The Campaign

During the campaign that precedes the election, union and employer appeal to employees for their votes. The union will emphasize that it will prevent unfairness, set up grievance and seniority systems, and improve wages. Union strength, they'll say, will give employees a voice in determining wages and working conditions. Supervisors will say that improvements like those don't require unions and that wages are equal to or better than they would be with a union. Supervisors will also emphasize the financial cost of union dues; the fact that the union is an "outsider"; and that if the union wins, a strike may follow. You can even attack the union on ethical and moral grounds, while insisting that employees will not be as well off and may lose freedom. But neither side can threaten, bribe, or coerce employees.

| UNITED STATES OF AMERICA |
| National Labor Relations Board |
| **OFFICIAL SECRET BALLOT** |
| FOR CERTAIN EMPLOYEES OF |

Do you wish to be represented for purposes of collective bargaining by —

MARK AN "S" IN THE SQUARE OF YOUR CHOICE

YES ☐   NO ☐

DO NOT SIGN THIS BALLOT. Fold and drop in ballot box.
If you spoil this ballot return it to the Board Agent for a new one.

Step 5. The Election

The election is by secret ballot; the NLRB provides the ballots (see Figure 15.3), voting booth, and ballot box; counts the votes; and certifies the results.

The union becomes the employees' representative if it wins the election, and winning means getting a majority of the votes *cast*, not a majority of the total workers in the bargaining unit. (Also keep in mind that if a supervisor commits an unfair labor practice, the NLRB may reverse a "no union" election. As representatives of their employer, supervisors must therefore be careful not to commit unfair practices.)

What Can Supervisors Expect the Union to Do to Win the Election?

A researcher analyzed 261 NLRB elections. She found that the best way for unions to win is to pursue what she calls a "rank and file strategy." The supervisor can expect such a campaign to include these union tactics.[26]

1. "Reliance on a slow, underground, person-to-person campaign." The union will use "house calls, small group meetings, and pre-union associations to develop leadership and union commitment, and prepare workers for employer anti-union strategies before the employer becomes aware of the campaign."

2. The union will try to build rank-and-file participation, including a large rank-and-file organizing committee reflecting the different interest groups in the bargaining unit.

3. The union will pressure for a contract early in the organizing process.

4. The union will use "inside and outside pressure tactics to build worker commitment and compel the employer to run a fair campaign."

5. The union will emphasize issues such as respect, dignity, and fairness, not just traditional bread-and-butter issues like wages, benefits, and job security.

6. The union will go all out to win. This includes the use of rank-and-file volunteers from already organized bargaining units.

The Supervisor's Role

Supervisors are an employer's first line of defense when it comes to the unionizing effort. They are often in the best position to sense evolving employee attitude problems, for instance, and to discover the first signs of union activity. Unfortunately, there's another side to that coin: They can also inadvertently do things that hurt their employer's union-related efforts.

Supervisors therefore must be knowledgeable about what they can and can't do legally to hamper organizing activities. Unfair labor practices could (1) cause the NLRB to hold a new election after your company has won a previous election, or (2) cause your company to forfeit the second election and go directly to contract negotiation.

In one case, a plant superintendent reacted to a union's initial organizing attempt by prohibiting distribution of union literature in the plant's lunchroom. Since solicitation of off-duty workers in nonwork areas is generally legal, the company subsequently allowed the union to distribute literature. However, the NLRB still ruled that the initial act of prohibiting distribution of the literature was an unfair labor practice. The NLRB used the superintendent's action as one reason for invalidating an election that the company had won.[27]

SOME TIPS   Supervisors can use the acronym **TIPS** to remember what *not* to do during the organizing or preelection campaigns:[28] *Do not* Threaten, Interrogate, make Promises to, or Spy on employees.

Use **FORE** for what you may do. *You may* give employees Facts (such as what signing the authorization card means), express your Opinion about unions, explain factually correct Rules (such as that the law permits replacing striking employees), and share your Experiences about unions. Figure 15.4 summarizes some detailed things supervisors should keep in mind.

Useful Rules for Supervisors Regarding Union Literature and Solicitation

What sorts of steps might supervisors take to restrict union organizing activity?[29]

1. Supervisors can always bar *non*employees from soliciting employees when the employee is on duty and not on a break.

2. Supervisors can usually stop employees from soliciting other employees for any purpose if one or both employees are on paid-duty time and not on a break.

3. Most employers (generally not including retail stores, shopping centers, and certain other employers) can bar nonemployees from the building's interiors and work areas as a right of private property owners.[30]

4. Supervisors can deny on- or off-duty employees access to interior or exterior areas only if they can show the rule is required for reasons of production, safety, or discipline.

■ Figure **15.4**

Union Avoidance: What Not to Do

Source: From the BLR Newsletter "Best Practices in HR." Business & Legal Reports, Inc., 141 Mill Rock Road East, Old Saybrook, CT © 2004. Reprinted with permission of the publisher.

Supervisors must be very careful to do the following during union activities at their companies:

- Watch what you say. Angry feelings of the moment may get you in trouble.
- Never threaten workers with what you will do or what will happen if a union comes in. Do not say, for example, that the business will move, that wages will go down or overtime will be eliminated, that there will be layoffs, and so on.
- Don't tell union sympathizers that they will suffer in any way for their support. Don't terminate or discipline workers for engaging in union activities.
- Don't interrogate workers about union sympathizers or organizers.
- Don't ask workers to remove union screensavers or campaign buttons if you allow these things for other organizations.
- Don't treat pro-union or anti-union workers differently.
- Don't transfer workers on the basis of union affiliation or sympathies.
- Don't ask workers how they are going to vote or how others may vote.
- Don't ask employees about union meetings or any matters related to unions. You can listen, but don't ask for any details.
- Don't promise workers benefits, promotions, or anything else if they vote against the union.
- Avoid becoming involved—in any way—in the details of the union's election or campaign, and don't participate in any petition movement against the union.
- Don't give financial aid or any support to any unions.

Any one of these practices may result in a finding of "unfair labor practices," which may in turn result in recognition of a union without an election, as well as fines for your company.

Such restrictions are valid only if the supervisor and employer do not discriminate against the union. For example, if your employer lets employees collect money for baby gifts, or to sell things like Avon products or Tupperware, it may not be able lawfully to prohibit them from union soliciting during work time.

4. What to Expect During the Collective Bargaining Process

What Is Collective Bargaining?

When and if the union becomes your employees' representative, a day is set for management and labor to meet and negotiate a labor agreement. This agreement will contain specific provisions covering wages, hours, and working conditions. First-line supervisors don't usually have a big role in negotiating the agreement. But they do play roles in some aspects, such as letting management know what sorts of concerns employees have.

What exactly is **collective bargaining**? In plain language, to bargain collectively means that both management and labor are required by law to negotiate wage, hours, and terms and conditions of employment "in good faith."

What Is Good Faith?

Good faith bargaining is the cornerstone of labor–management relations. It means that both parties communicate and negotiate, that they match proposals with counterproposals, and that both make every reasonable effort to arrive at an agreement. It does not mean that one party compels another to agree to a proposal. Nor does it require that either party make any specific concessions (although as a practical matter, some may be necessary).[31]

How can one tell if bargaining is *not* in good faith? Here are some examples.

1. **Inadequate concessions.** Unwillingness to compromise, even though no one is required to make a concession.

2. **Inadequate proposals and demands.** The NLRB considers the advancement of proposals to be a positive factor in determining overall good faith.

3. **Dilatory tactics.** The law requires that the parties meet and "confer at reasonable times and intervals." Obviously, refusal to meet with the union does not satisfy the positive duty imposed on the employer.

4. **Imposing conditions.** Attempts to impose conditions that are so onerous or unreasonable as to indicate bad faith.[32]

The Negotiating Team

Both union and management will send a negotiating team to the bargaining table, and both will have "done their homework." Union representatives will have sounded out union members on their desires and conferred with representatives of related unions.

Management uses several techniques to prepare for bargaining.[33] First, it compiles data on pay and benefits that include comparisons with local pay rates. Internal data regarding cost of benefits, overall earnings levels, and the amount and cost of overtime are important as well. Management will also "cost" the current labor contract and determine the increased cost—total, per employee, and per hour—of the union's demands.

It will use information from grievances and feedback from supervisors to determine what the union's demands might be. It will use this information to prepare counteroffers and arguments.[34]

Bargaining Items

In practice, saying one must bargain over "wages, hours, and working conditions" is too broad. Labor law sets out categories of specific items that are subject to bargaining: These are mandatory, voluntary, and illegal items.

Table 15.1 presents some of the 70 or so **mandatory bargaining items** over which bargaining is mandatory under the law. They include wages, hours, rest periods, layoffs, transfers, benefits, and severance pay. Others, such as drug testing, are added as the law evolves.

Voluntary (or permissible) bargaining items are neither mandatory nor illegal; they become a part of negotiations only through joint management and union agreement. Benefits for retirees might be an example.

What Is to Be Expected During the Collective Bargaining Process?

Illegal bargaining items are forbidden by law. A clause agreeing to hire union members exclusively would be illegal in a right-to-work state, for example.

Bargaining Stages

The actual union-management bargaining will involve several stages.[35] First, each side presents its demands. Here, both parties are usually quite far apart. Second, there is a

■ Table **15.1**

Bargaining Items		
Mandatory	**Permissible**	**Illegal**
Rates of pay	Indemnity bonds	Closed shop
Wages	Management rights as to union affairs	Separation of employees based
Hours of employment	Pension benefits of retired employees	on race
Overtime pay	Scope of the bargaining unit	Discriminatory treatment
Shift differentials	Including supervisors in the contract	
Holidays	Additional parties to the contract such	
Vacations	as the international union	
Severance pay	Use of union label	
Pensions	Settlement of unfair labor changes	
Insurance benefits	Prices in cafeteria	
Profit-sharing plans	Continuance of past contract	
Christmas bonuses	Membership of bargaining team	
Company housing, meals,	Employment of strike breaker	
and discounts		
Employee security		
Job performance		
Union security		
Management–union		
relationship		
Drug testing of employees		

Source: Adapted from Michael R. Carrell and Christina Heavrin, *Labor Relations and Collective Bargaining: Cases, Practices, and Law* (Upper Saddle River, NJ: Prentice Hall, 2001), p. 177.

reduction of demands. Here, each side trades off some demands to gain others. Third are subcommittee studies; the parties form joint subcommittees to try to work out reasonable alternatives. Fourth, the parties reach an informal settlement, and each group goes back to its sponsor. Union representatives check with their superiors and the union members; management representatives check with top management. Finally, the parties fine-tune and sign a formal agreement.

Impasses, Mediation, and Strikes

In collective bargaining, an **impasse** occurs when the parties are not able to move further toward settlement. This usually occurs because one party is demanding more than the other will offer. Sometimes an impasse can be resolved through a third party such as an arbitrator. If the impasse is not resolved in this way, the union may call a work stoppage, or strike, to put pressure on management.[36]

THIRD-PARTY INVOLVEMENT   Negotiators use three types of "third-parties" to overcome an impasse: mediation, fact finding, and arbitration. With **mediation**, a neutral third party tries to assist the principals in reaching agreement. The mediator usually holds meetings with each party to determine where each stands regarding its position. He or she then uses this information to try to find common ground for further bargaining.

A **fact finder** is a neutral party who studies the issues in a dispute and makes a public recommendation for a reasonable settlement.[37] Presidential emergency fact-finding boards have successfully resolved impasses in certain critical transportation disputes.

Arbitration is the most definitive type of third-party intervention, because the arbitrator often has the power to dictate the settlement terms. With *binding arbitration,* both parties are committed to accepting the arbitrator's award. With *nonbinding arbitration,* they are not. Arbitration may also be voluntary or compulsory (in other words, imposed by a government agency). In the United States, voluntary binding arbitration is the most prevalent.

STRIKES   A **strike** is a withdrawal of labor, and there are four main types of strikes. An **economic strike** results from a failure to agree on the terms of a contract. Unions call **unfair labor practice strikes** to protest illegal conduct by the employer. A **wildcat strike** is an unauthorized strike occurring during the term of a contract. A **sympathy strike** occurs when one union strikes in support of the strike of another union.[38] For example, in sympathy with employees of the *Detroit News,* the United Auto Workers enforced a nearly six-year boycott. This prevented the papers from being sold at Detroit-area auto plants, cutting sales by about 25,000 copies a day.[39]

Picketing, or having employees carry signs announcing their concerns near the employer's place of business, is one of the first activities to occur during a strike. Its purpose is to inform the public about the existence of the labor dispute and often to encourage others to refrain from doing business with the struck employer.

Your employer can respond in several ways to a strike. One is to shut down the affected area and halt operations until the strike is over. A second is to contract out work in order to blunt the effects of the strike. A third response is to continue operations, perhaps using supervisors and other nonstriking workers to fill in for the striking workers. A fourth alternative is hiring replacements for the strikers.

When a strike is imminent, the employer should make plans to deal with it. For example, as negotiations between the Hibbing Taconite Steel Plant in Minnesota and the United Steelworkers of America headed toward a deadline, the firm brought in security workers and trailers to house them.

OTHER ALTERNATIVES   Management and labor each have other weapons to break an impasse and achieve their aims. The union, for example, may resort to a corporate campaign. A **corporate campaign** is an organized effort by the union to exert pressure on the employer by pressuring the company's other unions, shareholders, corporate directors, customers, and creditors. For example, the union might surprise individual members of the board of directors by picketing their homes, and organize a **boycott** of the company's banks.[40]

The Web is a potent union tool here. For example, when the Hotel Employees and Restaurant Employees Union, Local 2, wanted to turn up the heat on the San Francisco Marriott, it launched a new Web site. The site explained the union's eight-month boycott and provided a helpful list of union-backed hotels where prospective guests could stay.[41]

Inside games are another union tactic, one that may hit first-line supervisors hard. **Inside games** are union efforts to convince employees to disrupt production— for example, by slowing the work pace, refusing to work overtime, refusing to do work without receiving detailed instructions from supervisors, and engaging in other disruptive activities such as sick-outs.[42] In one inside game at Caterpillar's Aurora, Illinois, plant, United Auto Workers' grievances rose from 22 to 336. The effect was to tie up workers and supervisors in unproductive endeavors on company time.[43]

For their part, employers can try to break an impasse with lockouts. A **lockout** is a refusal by the employer to provide opportunities to work. It (sometimes literally) locks out employees and prohibits them from doing their jobs (and being paid).

Both employers and unions can seek an injunction from the courts if they believe the other side is taking actions that could cause irreparable harm to the other party. An **injunction** is a court order compelling a party or parties either to resume or to desist from a certain action.[44]

The Contract Agreement

The actual contract agreement may be a 20- or 30-page document; or even longer. It may contain just general declarations of policy, or detailed rules and procedures. The tendency today is toward the longer, more detailed contract. This is largely a result of the increased number of items the agreements have been covering.

The main sections of a typical contract cover subjects such as these:

1. management rights,
2. union security and automatic payroll dues deduction,
3. grievance procedures,
4. arbitration of grievances,
5. disciplinary procedures,
6. compensation rates,
7. hours of work and overtime,
8. benefits: vacations, holidays, insurance, pensions,
9. health and safety provisions,
10. employee security seniority provisions, and
11. contract expiration date.

5. How to Handle Grievances

Hammering out a labor agreement is not the last step in collective bargaining. No labor contract can cover all contingencies. For example, suppose the contract says you can only discharge an employee for "just cause." You subsequently discharge someone for speaking back to you in harsh terms. Was speaking back to you harshly "just cause"?

The labor contract's grievance procedure usually handles problems like these. The **grievance procedure** provides an orderly system whereby both employer and union determine whether some action violated the contract.[45] It is the vehicle for administering the contract on a day-to-day basis. The grievance process allows both parties to interpret and give meaning to various clauses. Remember, though, that this involves interpretation only. It usually does not involve negotiating new terms or altering existing ones.

Knowing how to handle grievances is an important supervisory skill. Avoiding (and, if necessary, dealing with) grievances is probably the supervisor's most important role in labor relations.

Sources of Grievances

From a practical point of view, it is probably easier to list those items that *don't* cause grievances than to list the ones that do. Employees may use just about any factor involving wages, hours, or conditions of employment as the basis of a grievance.

However, certain grievances are more serious, since they're usually more difficult to settle. Discipline cases and seniority problems including promotions, transfers, and layoffs would top this list. Others would include grievances growing out of job evaluations and work assignments, overtime, vacations, incentive plans, and holidays.[46] Here are three examples of grievances:

- **Absenteeism.** An employer fired an employee for excessive absences. The employee filed a grievance stating that there had been no previous warnings related to excessive absences.

- **Insubordination.** An employee on two occasions refused to obey a supervisor's order to meet with him, unless a union representative was present at the meeting. As a result, the employee was discharged and subsequently filed a grievance protesting the discharge.

- **Plant rules.** The plant had a posted rule barring employees from eating or drinking during unscheduled breaks. The employees filed a grievance claiming the rule was arbitrary.[47]

A grievance is often a symptom of an underlying problem. Sometimes, bad relationships between supervisors and subordinates are to blame: This is often the cause of grievances over "fair treatment," for instance. Organizational factors such as ambiguous job descriptions that frustrate employees also cause grievances. Union activism is another cause; the union may solicit grievances from workers to underscore ineffective supervision. Problem employees are yet another cause. These are individuals, who, by their nature, are negative and prone to complaints. Discipline and dismissals, explained in Chapter 14, are other big sources of grievances.

The Grievance Procedure

Most collective bargaining contracts contain a specific grievance procedure. It lists the steps in the procedure, time limits associated with each step, and specific rules such as "all charges of contract violation must be reduced to writing." (Nonunionized employers need such procedures, too, as explained in Chapter 14, "Ethics.")

Union grievance procedures differ from firm to firm. Some contain simple, two-step procedures. Here the grievant, union representative, and company representative meet to discuss the grievance. If they don't find a satisfactory solution, the grievance goes before an independent, third-party arbitrator, who hears the case, writes it up, and makes a decision. Figure 15.5 shows a Grievance Record Form.

UNITED STATES POSTAL SERVICE ®

Date Received at Step B *(MM/DD/YYYY)*

USPS-NALC Joint Step A Grievance Form

INFORMAL STEP A — NALC Shop Steward Completes This Section

1. Grievant's Name *(Last, first, middle initial)*	2. Home Telephone No.

3. Seniority Date *(MM/DD/YYYY)*	4. Status *(Check one)* ☐ FT ☐ FTF ☐ PTR ☐ PTF ☐ TE	5. Grievant's SSN

6. Installation/Work Unit	7. Finance Number

8. NALC Branch No.	9. NALC Grievance No.	10. Incident Date *(MM/DD/YYYY)*	11. Date Discussed with Supervisor *(Filing Date)*

12a. Companion MSPB Appeal? ☐ Yes ☐ No	12b. Companion EEO Appeal? ☐ Yes ☐ No

13a. Supervisor's Printed Name and Initials *(Completed by Supervisor)*	13b. Steward's Printed Name and Initials *(Completed by Steward)*

FORMAL STEP A — Formal Step A Parties Complete This Section

14. USPS Grievance No.

15. Issue Statement/Provide Contract Provision(s) and Frame the Issue(s)

16. Undisputed Facts *(List and Attach **All** Supporting Documents)*   Attachments? ☐ No ☐ Yes   Number_____

17. **UNION'S** full, detailed statement of disputed facts and contentions *(List and Attach **All** Supporting Documents)*   Attachments? ☐ No ☐ Yes   Number_____

18. **MANAGEMENT'S** full, detailed statement of disputed facts and contentions *(List and Attach **All** Supporting Documents)*   Attachments? ☐ No ☐ Yes   Number_____

19. Remedy Requested/Offered

20. Disposition and Date *(Check one)* ☐ Resolved ☐ Withdrawn ☐ Not Resolved	Date of Formal Step A Meeting *(MM/DD/YYYY)*

21a. USPS Representative Name	21b. Telephone No. *(Include Area Code)*
21c. USPS Representative Signature	21d. Date *(MM/DD/YYYY)*
22a. NALC Representative Name	22b. Telephone No. *(Include Area Code)*
22c. NALC Representative Signature	22d. Date *(MM/DD/YYYY)*

PS Form **8190**, August 2002 *(Page 1 of 2)*

■Figure **15.5**

Grievance Record Form

Source: http://www.nalc.org/depart/cau/pdf/drp/8190f0802.pdf (accessed April 28, 2009).

Instructions

If the initial Filing discussion between steward (and/or employee) and supervisor at Informal Step A does not resolve the grievance, the union steward may appeal the grievance by:

- Completing the "Informal Step A" section at the top of the form,
- Obtaining the supervisor's initials in Item 13, and
- Forwarding the form to union and management Formal Step A representatives within 7 days of the discussion.

INFORMAL STEP A—NALC Shop Steward Completes This Section

Item	Explanation
1-9	Self-explanatory. All items are essential.
10	Enter the date when the event causing the grievance occurred or when the employee or union first became aware of the event.
11	Enter the date the employee and/or the union first discussed the grievance with the immediate supervisor at Informal Step A. This is the Step A filing date.
12a-b	Determine and indicate whether the grievant has filed an MSPB and/or EEO complaint on the same issue.
13a	The supervisor's printed name and initials confirm the date of the Informal Step A discussion.
13b	The steward's printed name and initials confirm the date of the Informal Step A discussion.

FORMAL STEP A—Formal Step A Parties Complete This Section

14	The USPS grievance number is assigned by computer.
15	Frame the issue statement in the form of a question. Examples: "Was there just cause for the letter of warning dated 2/15/2002 issued to the grievant for unsatisfactory work performance, and if not, what is the appropriate remedy?" "Did management violate Article 8.5.G when the grievant was required to work overtime on 3/15/2002, and if so, what is the appropriate remedy?" If discipline is involved, always indicate the type of discipline (letter of warning, 7-day suspension, indefinite suspension, etc.) in the issue statement. Also, list specific contractual or handbook provisions involved in the grievance.
	Note: The union steward may write a suggested issue in Item 15 when appealing to Formal Step A. The parties at Formal Step A are responsible for defining the issue as they see fit.
Note:	**If the grievance is resolved at Formal Step A, skip to Item 20 and note there the principles of the agreement. If the grievance is not resolved, complete Items 16 through 20.**
16	Management and/or Union Representative: List all relevant facts not in dispute.
17	Union Representative: List any facts in dispute based on your understanding of the facts. Provide concise, descriptive statements outlining the union's position on the grievance.
18	Management Representative: List any facts in dispute based on your understanding of the facts. Provide concise, descriptive statements outlining management's position on the grievance.
19	Management Representative: Indicate remedy management is willing to offer.
	Union Representative: Provide a specific statement of the remedy the union is requesting. Example: "The LOW should be expunged from the record and the grievant made whole for all loss of wages, benefits, and rights."
20	Management and/or Union Representative: Note whether the case is resolved, withdrawn or not resolved. If resolved, note the principles of the agreement.
21-22	Enter names, telephone numbers, signatures, and date form is completed.

PS Form **8190**, August 2002 (Page 2 of 2)

■Figure **15.5**

(Continued)

At the other extreme, the grievance procedure may contain six or more steps. The first step might be for the grievant and union shop steward to meet informally with the supervisor of the grievant to try to find a solution. If they don't find one, the employee files a formal grievance, and there's a meeting with the employee, shop steward, and the supervisor's boss. The next steps involve the grievant and union representatives meeting with higher-level managers. Finally, if top management and the union can't reach agreement, the grievance may go to arbitration.

Sometimes the grievance process gets out of hand. For example, in one short period members of American Postal Workers Union, Local 482, filed 1,800 grievances at the Postal Service's Roanoke mail processing facility (the usual rate is about 800 grievances per year). The employees apparently were responding to job changes, including efforts to automate its processes.[48]

Supervisor's Guidelines for Handling Grievances

The best way for a supervisor to handle a grievance is to develop a work environment in which grievances don't arise in the first place. Hone your ability to avoid, recognize, diagnose, and correct the causes of potential employee dissatisfaction (such as unfair appraisals or poor communications) before they become grievances.

Given that many factors (including union pressure) prompt grievances, it would be naïve to think that grievances only arise due to supervisor unfairness. However, there's little doubt that the quality of the interpersonal relations among you and your subordinates will influence your team's grievance rate. You should be thoroughly familiar with our discussions of supervisory fairness in Chapter 14.

The supervisor is on the firing line and must steer a course between treating employees fairly and maintaining management's rights and prerogatives. One expert has developed a list of supervisor do's and don'ts as useful guides in handling grievances.[49] Some critical do's and don'ts include the following:

Do:

1. Investigate and handle each case as though it may eventually result in arbitration.
2. Talk with the employee about his or her grievance; give the person a full hearing.
3. Require the union to identify specific contractual provisions allegedly violated.
4. Comply with the contractual time limits for handling the grievance.
5. Visit the work area of the grievance.
6. Determine whether there were any witnesses.
7. Examine the grievant's personnel record.
8. Fully examine prior grievance records.
9. Treat the union representative as your equal.
10. Hold your grievance discussions privately.
11. Fully inform your own supervisor of grievance matters.

Don't:

12. Discuss the case with the union steward alone—the grievant should be there.
13. Make arrangements with individual employees that are inconsistent with the labor agreement.

14. Hold back the remedy if the company is wrong.

15. Admit to the binding effect of a past practice.

16. Relinquish to the union your rights as a supervisor.

17. Settle grievances based on what is "fair." Instead, stick to the labor agreement.

18. Bargain over items not covered by the contract.

19. Treat as subject to arbitration claims demanding the discipline or discharge of supervisors.

20. Give long written grievance answers.

21. Trade a grievance settlement for a grievance withdrawal.

22. Deny grievances because "your hands have been tied by management."

23. Agree to informal amendments in the contract.

Grievance handling requires effective leadership skills, as the accompanying feature explains.

Leadership Applications for Supervisors

Role of Leader Consideration and Support in Grievances

As we said in this chapter, it's probably easier to list the things that don't cause grievances than to list the ones that do. However, in many instances, the filing of grievances reflects poor or tense relationships between the supervisor and his or her employees. It just makes sense that people who believe they're not being treated courteously or fairly are more likely to seek ways to let their feelings be known. For example:

> I filed a grievance . . . to the issue [of an incorrect leave balance] directly to my supervisor. He was very detached about it. I just wanted an apology [for my leave balance being calculated incorrectly]. He said there would be no apology by the clerk who made the mistake. I then took the written grievance to the second step level manager. He yelled at me and was mad that I even sent it to the second step.[50]

In situations like that and in many others, leader consideration, "leader behavior indicative of mutual trust, friendship, support, respect, and warmth" can often cut the grievance off at its knees, and often prevent it in the first place.

Again, have no doubt that nonleadership issues contribute to many (or even most) grievances. Union militancy, poor labor–management relations, unfair employment practices, and genuine disagreements over matters such as time off won't disappear just because a department has a supervisor whose leadership style is considerate and supportive. But the fact is that even some of the earliest leadership studies (such as those at Ohio State University) concluded that leaders who are more considerate had fewer grievances.

Considerateness manifests itself in healthier supervisor-employee relations. With considerate supervisors:[51]

- Friendliness, helpfulness, and less obstructiveness are expressed in discussions.

- A feeling of agreement with the ideas of others and a sense of basic similarity in beliefs and values are expressed.

- A willingness to enhance the employee's power to accomplish the employee's goals is shown.

- Defining conflicting interests as a mutual problem to be solved by collaborative effort facilitates recognizing the legitimacy of each other's interests and the necessity to search for a solution responsive to the needs of all.

---

6. What's Next for Unions?

For years, construction trade unions in western New York State placed a huge inflatable rat balloon in front of construction sites that they were protesting. However, they recently gave up the rat and are now taking a more "business friendly approach." As the business manager for the local plumbers and steamfitters union put it, "our philosophy for the past 15 years hasn't created any more market share for us. We have been viewed as troublemakers . . . Now we are going to use [public relations] to dispel those perceptions."[52]

Why the Union Decline?

We saw early in this chapter that several factors contributed to the decline in union membership over the past 60 or so years. Unions traditionally appealed mostly to blue-collar workers, and the proportion of blue-collar jobs has been decreasing as service-sector jobs have increased. Furthermore, globalization increases competition, and competition increases pressures on employers to cut costs and boost productivity. Other factors pressuring employers and unions include the deregulation of trucking, airlines, and communications, and laws (such as Title VII) that somewhat reduced the need for unions.

The effect of all this has been the permanent layoff of hundreds of thousands of union members, the permanent closing of company plants, the relocation of companies to nonunion settings (either in the United States or abroad), and mergers and acquisitions that eliminated union jobs.

Card Check and Other New Union Tactics

Of course, unions are not sitting idly by and just watching their numbers dwindle.[53] And, in fact, union membership actually inched up a bit recently.[54] The priorities of the Change to Win Coalition (whose members broke off from the AFL-CIO) illustrate the new union strategies:

> Make it our first priority to help millions more workers form unions so we can build a strong movement for rewarding work in America [and] unite the strength of everyone who works in the same industry so we can negotiate with today's huge global corporations for everyone's benefit.[55]

MORE AGGRESSIVE   Unions are in fact becoming much more aggressive.[56] Unions are pushing Congress to pass the *Employee Free Choice Act*. This would make it more difficult for employers to inhibit workers from organizing. Instead of secret ballot elections, the act would institute a "card check" system. Here the union would win recognition when a majority of workers signed authorization cards saying they want the union. (Several large companies, including Cingular Wireless, already have agreed to the card check process.)[57] The act would also require binding arbitration to set a first contract's terms if the company and union can't negotiate an agreement within 120 days.[58] Unions are also using *class action lawsuits* to support employees in nonunionized companies, to pressure employers. For example, unions recently used class action lawsuits to support workers' claims under the fair labor standards act and the equal pay act.[59]

Coordination Unions are becoming more proactive in terms of coordinating their efforts.[60] For example, consider what UNITE (the Union of Needletrades, Industrial and Textile Employees, now part of UNITE HERE) did. They used their "Voice at Work" campaign to coordinate 800 workers at one employer's distribution center with others at the employer's New York City headquarters and with local activists and international unions throughout Europe. This forced the employer's parent company, a French conglomerate, to cease resisting the union's organizing efforts.

Cooperative Arrangements Another, somewhat more risky (for the unions) approach is to agree to enter into cooperative pacts with employers. For instance, they work with them in developing employee participation programs. About half of all collective bargaining agreements encourage cooperative labor–management relationships.[61] *Cooperative clauses* cover things like joint committees to review drug problem, health care, and safety issues.[62]

Chapter 15 Concept Review and Reinforcement

Key Terms

Arbitration, p. 462
Authorization Cards, p. 455
Bargaining Unit, p. 456
Boycott, p. 462
Collective Bargaining, p. 459
Corporate Campaign, p. 462
Economic Strike, p. 162
Fact Finder, p. 462
FORE, p. 458
Good Faith Bargaining, p. 459

Grievance Procedure, p. 463
Illegal Bargaining Items, p. 460
Impasse, p. 461
Injunction, p. 463
Inside Games, p. 462
Labor Management Reporting and Disclosure Act of 1959, p. 454
Landrum-Griffin Act, p. 454
Lockout, p. 463

Mandatory Bargaining Items, p. 460
Mediation, p. 461
National Labor Relations Board (NLRB), p. 451
National Labor Relations (or Wagner) Act, p. 451
Norris-LaGuardia Act of 1932, p. 451
Picketing, p. 462
Right to Work, p. 450
Salting, p. 455
Strike, p. 462
Sympathy Strike, p. 462

Taft-Hartley (or Labor Management Relations) Act of 1947, p. 452
TIPS, p. 458
Unfair Labor Practice Strikes, p. 462
Voluntary (or Permissible) Bargaining Items, p. 460
Wildcat Strike, p. 462

Review of Key Concepts

Labor Movement	The labor movement is important. Almost 18 million U.S. workers belong to unions, about 12.4% of the total. Unions aim for union security and then for improved wages, hours, and working conditions and benefits for their members.
Union Security	
Closed Shop	The company can hire only current union members.
Union Shop	The company can hire nonunion workers, but they must join the union later and pay dues.
Agency Shop	Employees who do not belong to the union still must pay an amount equal to union dues.
Preferential Shop	Union member get preference in hiring but companies can still hire nonunion members.
Maintenance of Membership Arrangement	Employees do not have to belong to the union. Union members employed by the firm must maintain membership in the union for the contract period.
How Do Workers Unionize?	It's clear that workers don't unionize just to get more pay, benefits, hours, and better working conditions. Although these issues are important, the motivation to unionize seems to boil down to the workers' belief that it's only through unity that they can protect themselves from arbitrary supervisory whims.

Unions and the Law	
Norris-La Guardia Act	(1932) The Norris-La Guardia Act set the stage for a new era in which union activity was encouraged.
Wagner Act	(1935) The National Labor Relations Act expanded Norris-La Guardia to include: • Banning certain "unfair" labor practices • Providing secret ballot elections • Creating the National Labor Relations Board (NLRB) to enforce these provisions
Taft-Hartley Act	(1947) The Labor–Management Relations Act reflected the public's less enthusiastic attitude towards unions. It amended the Wagner Act by limiting unions in four ways: • Prohibiting unfair union labor practices • Enumerating the rights of employees as union members • Enumerating the rights of employers • Allowing the president of the United States to bar temporary national emergency strikes
Landrum-Griffin Act	(1959) The Labor Management Reporting and Disclosure Act had an overriding aim to protect union members from possible wrongdoing by their own unions.
Unfair Labor Practices—Employer	Five unfair labor practices used by employers: • Unfair to retain or coerce employees • Unfair to interfere with union formation • Unfair to discriminate • Unfair to discharge employees because they file unfair labor charges • Unfair to refuse bargain collectively
Unfair Labor Practices—Union	Four unfair labor practices used by unions: • Unfair to restrain or coerce employees from exercising their rights • Unfair to discriminate against an employee to encourage or discourage union membership • Unfair for a union to refuse to bargain in good faith • Unfair to engage in "featherbedding"
Union Drive and Election	It is very important that supervisors know and understand the union drive and election process, which has five basic steps: • Initial contact • Obtaining authorization cards • Holding a hearing—NLRB • The campaign • The election

Supervisor's Role During an Unionizing Effort	Supervisors are an employers' first line of defense and are often in the best position to sense employee attitude problems. Supervisors must be knowledgeable about what they can and cannot do legally to hamper organizing activities.
Collective Bargaining	To bargain collectively means that both management and labor are required by law to negotiate wage, hours, and terms and conditions of employment "in good faith."
Good Faith Bargaining	Good faith bargaining means that both parties communicate and negotiate, that they match proposals with counterproposals, and that both sides made every reasonable effort to arrive at an agreement.

Review and Discussion Questions

1. Why do employees join unions? What are the advantages and disadvantages of being a union member?

2. What are the differences between a closed shop, a union shop, and an agency shop?

3. Describe the most important feature of the Wagner Act, passed in 1935.

4. Why was the Landrum-Griffin Act passed in 1959?

5. If an employer commits an unfair labor practice, what is the potential impact to the collective bargaining process?

6. Discuss some things a supervisor might do to make it likely the employer will lose an NLRB election.

7. Explain in detail each step in a union drive election.

8. Briefly outline the supervisor's role during a unionizing effort.

9. What is meant by good faith bargaining? Using examples, explain when bargaining is not in good faith.

10. When management and labor sit down to negotiate "in good faith," why is it called collective bargaining?

Application and Skill Building

Case Study One

Negotiating with the Writers Guild of America

The talks between the Writers Guild of America (WGA) and the Alliance of Motion Picture & Television Producers (producers) began tense in 2007, and then got tenser. In their first meeting, the two sides got nothing done. As *Law & Order* producer Dick Wolf said, "Everyone in the room is concerned about this."[63]

The two sides were far apart on just about all the issues. However, the biggest issue was how to split revenue from new media, such as when television shows move on to CDs or the Internet. The producers said they wanted a profit-splitting system rather than the current residual system. Under the residual system, writers continue to receive "residuals" or income from shows they write every time they're shown (such as when the Jerry Seinfeld show appears in reruns, years after they shoot the last original show). Writers Guild executives did their homework. They argued, for instance, that the projections showed producers' revenues from advertising and subscription fees jumped by about 40% between 2002 and 2006.[64]

The situation grew tenser. After the first few meetings, one producers' representative said, "We can see after the dogfight whose position will win out. The open question there, of course, is whether each of us takes several lumps at the table, reaches an agreement, then licks their wounds later—none the worse for wear—or whether we inflict more lasting damage through work stoppages that benefit no one before we come to an agreement."[65] Even after meeting six times, it seemed that "the parties' only apparent area of agreement is that no real bargaining has yet to occur."[66]

In October 2007, the Writers Guild asked its members for strike authorization, and the producers claimed that the Guild was just trying to delay negotiations until the current contract expired (at the end of October). As the president of the television producers association said, "We have had six across the table sessions and there was only silence and stonewalling from the WGA leadership. . . . We have attempted to engage on major issues, but no dialogue has been forthcoming from the WGA leadership. . . . The WGA leadership apparently has no intention to bargain in good faith."[67] As evidence, the producers claimed that the WGA negotiating committee left one meeting after less than an hour at the bargaining table.

Both sides knew timing in these negotiations was very important. During the fall and spring, television series production is in full swing. So, a strike now by the writers would have a bigger impact than waiting until, say, the summer to strike. Perhaps not surprisingly, by January 2008 some movement was discernible. In a separate set of negotiations, the Directors Guild of America reached an agreement with the producers that addressed many of the issues that the writers were focusing on, such as how to divide the new media income.[68] In February 2008, the WGA and producers finally reached agreement. The new contract was "the direct result of renewed negotiations between the two sides, which culminated Friday with a marathon session including top WGA officials and the heads of the Walt Disney Co. and News Corp."[69]

Discussion Questions

1. The producers said the WGA was not bargaining in good faith. What did they mean by that, and do you think the evidence is sufficient to support the claim?
2. The WGA did eventually strike. What tactics could the producers have used to fight back once the strike began? What tactics do you think the WGA used?
3. This was a conflict between professional and creative people (the WGA) and TV and movie producers. Do you think the conflict was therefore different in any way from the conflicts between, say, the auto workers or teamsters unions against auto and trucking companies? Why?
4. What role (with examples, please) did negotiating skills seem to play in the WGA–producers negotiations?

Case Study Two

Carter Cleaning Centers

The Grievance

On visiting one of Carter Cleaning Centers' stores, Jennifer was surprised to be taken aside by a long-term Carter employee, who met her as she was parking her car. "Murray (the store manager) told me I was suspended for two days without pay because I came in late last Thursday," said George. "I'm really upset, but around here the store manager's word seems to be law, and it sometimes seems like the only way anyone can file a grievance is by meeting you or your father like this in the parking lot." Jennifer was very disturbed by this revelation and promised the employee she would look into it and discuss the situation with her father. In the car heading back to headquarters, she began mulling over what Carter Cleaning Centers' alternatives might be.

Discussion Questions

1. Do you think it is important for Carter Cleaning Centers to have a formal grievance process? Why or why not?
2. Based on what you know about Carter Cleaning Centers, outline the steps in what you think would be the ideal grievance process for this company.
3. In addition to the grievance process, can you think of anything else that Carter Cleaning Centers might do to make sure grievances and gripes like this one are expressed and are heard by top management?

Experiential Activities

Activity 1. The National Labor Relations Board (NLRB) has accused Starbucks of breaking the law by retaliating against workers who were attempting to unionize. The company believes the allegations are baseless and plans to defend itself.

Unions and the Law

Purpose: The purpose of this exercise is to give you practice in understanding the impact that labor laws have on businesses like Starbucks.

Required Understanding: You are going to develop a checklist of do's and don'ts based on your understanding of labor laws. Therefore, be thoroughly familiar with the discussion of labor relations and labor laws from this chapter.

How to Set Up the Exercise/Instructions: Divide the class into groups of 4–5 students.

1. Your group should develop a checklist of do's and don'ts based on existing labor laws.
2. Next, apply your checklist to the chapter scenario. According to labor law, is Starbucks breaking the law if the allegations are true?
3. Discuss what impact, if the allegations are true, this could have on the employees if they attempt to unionize Starbucks.
4. Have a spokesperson from each group share their checklists and have a class discussion. Look at steps that companies can follow to avoid being unionized or to bargain in good faith if the union is accepted.

Activity 2. The Union-Organizing Campaign at Pierce U.

Purpose: The purpose of this exercise is to give you practice in dealing with some of the elements of a union organizing campaign.[70]

Required Understanding: You should be familiar with the material covered in this chapter, as well as the following incident, "An Organizing Question on Campus."

Incident: An Organizing Question on Campus: Art Tipton is the human resource director of Pierce University, a private university located in a large urban city. Ruth Zimmer, a supervisor in the maintenance and housekeeping services division of the university, has just come into Art's office to discuss her situation. Zimmer's division is responsible for maintaining and cleaning the physical facilities of the university. Zimmer is one of the department supervisors who supervise employees who maintain and clean on-campus dormitories.

Zimmer proceeds to express her concerns about a union organizing campaign that has begun among her employees. According to Zimmer, a representative of the Service Workers Union has met with several of her employees, urging them to sign union authorization cards. She has observed several of her employees "cornering" other employees to talk to them about joining the union and to urge them to sign union authorization (or representation) cards. Zimmer even observed this during working hours as employees were going about their normal duties in the dormitories. Zimmer reports that a number of her employees have come to her asking for her opinions about the union. They told her that several other supervisors in the department had told their employees not to sign any union authorization cards and not to talk about the union at any time while they were on campus. Zimmer also reports that one of her fellow supervisors told his employees that anyone who was caught talking about the union or signing a union authorization card would be disciplined and perhaps dismissed.

Zimmer says that her employees are very dissatisfied with their wages and with the conditions that they have endured from students, supervisors, and other staff people. She says that several employees told her that they had signed union cards because they believed that the only way university administration would pay attention to their concerns was if the employees had a union to represent them. Zimmer says that she made a list of employees whom she felt had joined or were interested in the union, and she could share these with Tipton if he wanted to deal with them personally. Zimmer closed her presentation with the comment that she and other department supervisors needed to know what they should do in order to stomp out the threat of unionization in their department.

How to Set Up the Exercise/Instructions: Divide the class into groups of four or five students. Assume that you are labor relations consultants the university retained to identify the problems and issues involved and to advise Art Tipton on the university's rights and what to do next. Each group will spend about 45 minutes discussing the issues. Then, outline those issues, as well as an action plan for Tipton. What should he do next?

If time permits, a spokesperson from each group should list on the board the issues involved and the group's recommendations. What should Art do?

Activity 3. Working individually or in groups, use Internet resources to find situations where company management and the union reached an impasse at some point during their negotiation process, but eventually resolved the impasse. Describe the issues on both sides that led to the impasse. How did they move past the impasse? What were the final outcomes?

Role-Playing Exercise

Why Do Workers Organize? The Situation

Fred Heifner has worked as a supervisor at Apex Plastics since they opened their doors five years ago. Apex manufactures plastic parts for the automotive industry and has functioned as a nonunion plant from day one. Within the last six months, the United Auto Workers (UAW) has collected enough cards from the employees to petition the NLRB for a union certification election to be held next month. Fred, as a member of management, does not want to see a union come into his plant for a number of reasons. He feels that the workers will be better off without a union, but he has not had the opportunity to share his views and feelings with his workers. That was until yesterday when Bob, one of the workers in his department, came into his office wanting to talk about unions and how they could affect his job.

This is going to be a rare opportunity to "tell the rest of the story" and persuade Bob to say "No" to unionization. Fred has set aside 30 minutes tomorrow to sit down with Bob and discuss the pros and cons of unions.

Instructions: All students should read the situation above in addition to studying the chapter. One student will play the role of supervisor while the other will play the role of one of his workers. Each student should only read his or her assigned role below. The two students should engage in a 15-minute conversation.

A class discussion will follow the role-playing exercise.

Supervisor: Your role is to convince Bob that it is to his advantage not to bring in a union to represent him. Some points (from the chapter) that you should cover include the following:

- With a union, you must pay dues.
- Without a union, you can communicate directly with your supervisor.
- You will receive the same or better pay, working conditions, and benefits as you would with the union.
- The company will set up a procedure to handle grievances.

Worker: Your role is to attempt to find out where you (as an employee) stand with the company. The union has already promised higher pay, shorter hours, better working conditions, and health benefits. They have been told that with a union representing them, workers can protect themselves from arbitrary whims. Is this true? Some points to include in your discussion:

- Higher pay
- Shorter hours
- Communications with management
- New benefit plans
- How grievances will be handled

Questions for Discussion

1. Did the supervisor take advantage of the opportunity to tell it like it is?
2. How knowledgeable do you feel the worker was about unions? Why?
3. What additional points would you suggest should have been brought up by the supervisor? The worker?
4. When labor unions are seeking certification, do you believe that many times communications and knowledge on both sides is lacking? Why?

16 Protecting Your Employees' Safety and Health

CHAPTER OBJECTIVES

After studying this chapter, you should be able to answer the following questions:

1. Why Is Safety Important?
2. What Is the Employer's Role in Safety?
3. What Should Supervisors Know About Occupational Safety Law?
4. What Causes Accidents?
5. How Can Employers and Supervisors Prevent Accidents?

6. What Is the Supervisor's Role in Controlling Workers' Compensation Costs?
7. Workplace Health Hazards: What Are the Problems and Remedies?
8. What Should Supervisors Know About Violence at Work?
9. What Is Enterprise Risk Management?

OPENING SNAPSHOT
A Warning Unheeded

It must have been a frightening way to die. The worker, 30 years old, "suffocated when the tumbling dirt and debris rose to his chest, creating pressure so great that he could not breathe, even though his head remained uncovered."[1] Other workers had warned the owner of the Brooklyn construction site that the trench was an accident waiting to happen. He allegedly did nothing about it. The prosecutor subsequently charged the owner with manslaughter.

1. Why Is Safety Important?

Safety and accident prevention should concern supervisors for several reasons, one of which is the staggering numbers involved. In one recent year, 5,559 U.S. workers died in workplace incidents.[2] Workplace accidents in the United States cause over 3.8 million occupational injuries and illnesses per year—roughly 4.4 cases per 100 full-time workers.[3] And such figures may actually underestimate the real number of injuries and illnesses by two or three times.[4]

Injuries aren't just a problem in dangerous industries like construction. For example, every year over 15,000 reportable injuries or illnesses occur at manufacturers of computers and computer peripherals. Commercial kitchens have hazards like knives and slippery floors.[5] New computers contribute to "sick building syndrome" symptoms like headaches and sniffles, which some experts blame on poor ventilation.[6] (New computers emit chemical fumes, which diminish after about a week.)[7] And office work is susceptible to other health problems, including repetitive trauma injuries related to computer use.[8] Effective supervision can short-circuit many such problems.

Why Is Safety
Important?

The Employer's Role in Safety

Safety experts would agree that safety always starts at the top. Historically, for instance, DuPont's accident rate has been much lower than that of the chemical industry as a whole. This good safety record is partly due to an organizational commitment to safety, which is evident in the following description:

> One of the best examples I know of in setting the highest possible priority for safety takes place at a DuPont plant in Germany. Each morning at the DuPont Polyester and Nylon Plant, the director and his assistants meet at 8:45 to review the past 24 hours. The first matter they discuss is not production, but safety. Only after they have examined reports of accidents and near misses and satisfied themselves that corrective action has been taken do they move on to look at output, quality, and cost matters.[9]

In September 2010, BP's new CEO wanted to send the signal that his company would henceforth be more aggressive about ensuring safety. He announced the formation of a new company-wide safety department. Representatives of this department would be assigned to each BP operating division. Their jobs are to ensure that every manager, supervisor, and employee in every division is committed to carrying out BP's new safety processes. On the next few pages, we'll see that reducing accidents largely boils down to taking steps to reduce accident-causing conditions and accident-causing acts. However, telling employees to "work safely" is futile unless the supervisor sends a clear and unambiguous signal that he or she really puts safety above all other considerations.

What Is the Employer's
Role in Safety?

What Top Management Can Do

Policies like these start at the top. Ideally, "safety is an integral part of the system, woven into each management competency and a part of everyone's day-to-day responsibilities."[10] Your employer should institutionalize top management's commitment with a safety policy, and publicize it, and should give safety matters high priority in meetings.

For example, Louisiana-Pacific Corp., which makes building products, starts all meetings, including board of directors meetings, with a brief safety message.[11]

What the Supervisor Can Do

After inspecting a work site where workers were installing pipes in a four-foot trench, OSHA inspectors cited an employer for violating the rule requiring employers to have a "stairway, ladder, ramp, or other safe means of egress" in deep trench excavations.[12] In the event the trench caved in, workers needed a quick way out. As usual, the employer had the primary responsibility for safety, and the local supervisor was responsible for the day-to-day inspections. Here, the supervisor did not properly do his daily inspection. The trench collapsed, and several employees were severely injured.

The moral is that safety inspections should always be part of the supervisor's daily routine. For example, "a daily walk-through of your workplace—whether you are working in outdoor construction, indoor manufacturing, or any place that poses safety challenges—is an essential part of your work."[13]

Leadership Applications for Supervisors

Leader Consideration, Culture, and Safety

Leadership means influencing others to move in the desired direction, and few "desired directions" are as important as acting safely at work.

Some of the things that the supervisor as leader can do to improve safety are more obvious than are others. For example, creating a safety-conscious culture—taking steps to role model, reward, and attend to an emphasize safe procedures— is one option. Here, one safety expert says there are four basic ways that supervisors "may inadvertently encourage at-risk behavior: fail to reinforce a safe behavior; fail to coach an at-risk behavior; reinforce production more than (or instead of) safety; and model (use) at-risk behaviors."[14] Conversely, reinforcing safety behaviors in everything that you do, coaching any employees who engage in at-risk behaviors about the correct way to do the job, reinforcing safety overproduction, and avoiding being a role model for at-risk behaviors will send a signal that safe behavior is crucial and telegraph how you expect your employees to behave.

Not so obvious is the fact that safety research also suggests that considerate and supportive leaders have healthier and safer employees.[15] One research report appeared in the Journal of Occupational and Environmental Medicine. *The researchers analyzed 27 previous studies to try to ascertain the relationship (if any) between effective leadership, and employee safety, health, and* well-being. *Here, safety-effective leadership included behaviors such as "treating employees considerately and truthfully, providing social support, and providing inspirational motivation and intellectual stimulation."[16] The research team found a "moderately strong" relationship between effective leadership and increased employee well-being. For example, employees with the more effective leaders (in terms of considerateness) "were 40% more likely to be in the highest category of job well-being, meaning they had low rates of anxiety, depression, and job stress symptoms. In addition, moderate evidence linked good leadership with reduced sick days and disability. Good leadership was associated with a 27% reduction in sick leave and a 46% reduction in disability pensions.[17] So, not surprisingly, caring about one's subordinates seems to translate into safer behaviors. Some specific supportive leadership steps the supervisor can take include:*

- *Show acceptance and positive regard for safety.*
- *Be polite and diplomatic.*
- *Bolster others' self-esteem.*
- *Actively listen for safety (maintain attention, suspend biases, use restatements, show empathy, ask questions to draw the person out).[18]*

I. GENERAL HOUSEKEEPING

Adequate and wide aisles—no materials protruding into aisles

Parts and tools stored safely after use—not left in hazardous positions that could cause them to fall

Even and solid flooring—no defective floors or ramps that could cause falling or tripping accidents

Waste cans and sand pails—safely located and properly used

Material piled in safe manner—not too high or too close to sprinkler heads

Floors—clean and dry

Firefighting equipment—unobstructed

Work benches orderly

Stockcarts and skids safely located, not left in aisles or passageways

Aisles kept clear and properly marked; no air lines or electric cords across aisles

II. MATERIAL HANDLING EQUIPMENT AND CONVEYANCES

On all conveyances, electric or hand, check to see that the following items are all in sound working conditions:

Brakes—properly adjusted

Not too much play in steering wheel

Warning device—in place and working

Wheels—securely in place; properly inflated

Fuel and oil—enough and right kind

No loose parts

Cables, hooks, or chains—not worn or otherwise defective

Suspended chains or hooks conspicuous

Safely loaded

Properly stored

III. LADDERS, SCAFFOLD, BENCHES, STAIRWAYS, ETC.

The following items of major interest to be checked:

Safety feet on straight ladders

Guardrails or handrails

Treads, not slippery

No cracked, or rickety

Properly stored

Extension ladder ropes in good condition

Toeboards

IV. POWER TOOLS (STATIONARY)

Point of operation guarded

Guards in proper adjustment

Gears, belts, shafting, counterweights guarded

Foot pedals guarded

Brushes provided for cleaning machines

Adequate lighting

Properly grounded

Tool or material rests properly adjusted

Adequate work space around machines

Control switch easily accessible

Safety glasses worn

Gloves worn by persons handling rough or sharp materials

No gloves or loose clothing worn by persons operating machines

V. HAND TOOLS AND MISCELLANEOUS

In good condition—not cracked, worn, or otherwise defective

Properly stored

Correct for job

Goggles, respirators, and other personal protective equipment worn where necessary

VI. WELDING

Arc shielded

Fire hazards controlled

Operator using suitable protective equipment

Adequate ventilation

Cylinder secured

Valves closed when not in use

VII. SPRAY PAINTING

Explosion-proof electrical equipment

Proper storage of paints and thinners in approved metal cabinets

Fire extinguishers adequate and suitable; readily accessible

Minimum storage in work area

VIII. FIRE EXTINGUISHERS

Properly serviced and tagged

Readily accessible

Adequate and suitable for operations involved

■ Figure **16.1**

Checklist of Mechanical or Physical Accident-Causing Conditions

Source: Courtesy of the American Insurance Association. From "A Safety Committee Man's Guide," pp. 1–64.

What to look for depends on the situation. For example, construction sites and dry cleaners have unique hazards. However, in general you can use a checklist of unsafe conditions such as the one in Figure 16.1 to spot problems.

However, the supervisor's safety responsibilities go beyond simply checking for slippery floors and dangerous machines. He or she must cultivate the right safety attitudes. The leadership feature on page 481 explains why.

2. What Supervisors Should Know About Occupational Safety Law

Congress passed the **Occupational Safety and Health Act of 1970** "to assure so far as possible every working man and woman in the nation safe and healthful working conditions and to preserve our human resources."[19] It covers just about all employers (except, for instance, farms in which only immediate members of the employer's family work). Supervisors need a working knowledge of this law to understand what to look for at work and what their responsibilities are under the act.

The act created the **Occupational Safety and Health Administration (OSHA)** within the Department of Labor. OSHA's main purpose is to set and enforce safety and health standards. The Department of Labor enforces the standards, and OSHA has inspectors working out of branch offices to ensure compliance.

What Should Supervisors Know about Occupational Safety Law?

OSHA Standards and Record Keeping

OSHA operates under the "general" standard clause that each employer:

> . . . shall furnish to each of his [or her] employees employment and a place of employment which are free from recognized hazards that are causing or are likely to cause death or serious physical harm to his [or her] employees.

To perform this basic mission, OSHA put in place legally enforceable standards. The standards are very complete and seem to cover in detail just about every conceivable hazard. (Figure 16.2 presents a small part of the standard governing handrails for scaffolds.) And the regulations don't just list standards to which employers should adhere. They also lay out "how." For example, OSHA's respiratory protection standard also covers program administration and employee training.[20]

Guardrails not less than 2– *4– or the equivalent and not less than 36– or more than 42– high, with a midrail, when required, of a 1– * 4– lumber or equivalent, and toeboards, shall be installed at all open sides on all scaffolds more than 10 feet above the ground or floor. Toeboards shall be a minimum of 4– in height. Wire mesh shall be installed in accordance with paragraph [a](17) of this section.

■Figure **16.2**

OSHA Standards Example

Source: http://www.osha.gov/pls/oshaweb/owadisp.show_document?p_id=9720&p_table=STANDARDS (accessed May 25, 2007).

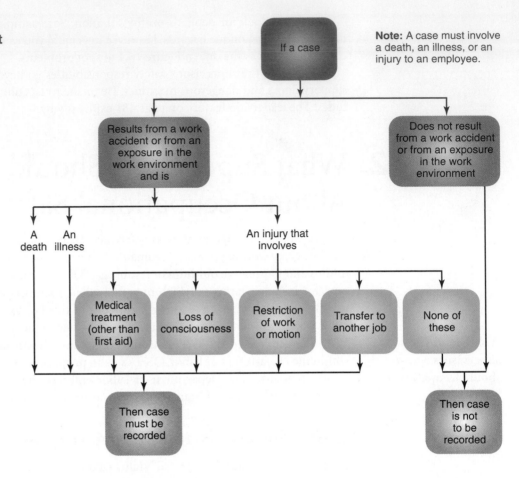

■ Figure **16.3**

What Accidents Must Be Reported Under the Occupational Safety and Health Act?

Employers with 11 or more employees must maintain records of and report certain occupational injuries and occupational illnesses. An **occupational illness** is any abnormal condition or disorder caused by exposure to environmental factors associated with employment. This includes, for instance, acute and chronic illnesses caused by inhalation, or direct contact with toxic substances.

WHAT YOUR EMPLOYER MUST REPORT   As summarized in Figure 16.3, employers must report *all* occupational illnesses.[21] They must also report most occupational injuries, specifically those that result in *medical treatment* including needlestick injuries and cuts (other than first aid), *loss of consciousness*, restriction of work (one or more *lost workdays*), *restriction of motion*, or *transfer* to another job.[22] If an on-the-job accident results in the death of an employee or in the hospitalization of five or more employees, all employers, regardless of size, must report the accident to the nearest OSHA office. OSHA will look for record-keeping violations during its inspections. Figure 16.4 shows the OSHA form for reporting occupational injuries or illness.

Inspections and Citations

OSHA enforces its standards through inspections and (if necessary) citations. OSHA may not conduct warrantless inspections without an employer's consent. However, it may inspect after acquiring an authorized search warrant or its equivalent.[23] With a

OSHA's Form 301
Injury and Illness Incident Report

U.S. Department of Labor
Occupational Safety and Health Administration

Form approved OMB no. 1218-0176

This *Injury and Illness Incident Report* is one of the first forms you must fill out when a recordable work-related injury or illness has occurred. Together with the *Log of Work-Related Injuries and Illnesses* and the accompanying *Summary*, these forms help the employer and OSHA develop a picture of the extent and severity of work-related incidents.

Within 7 calendar days after you receive information that a recordable work-related injury or illness has occurred, you must fill out this form or an equivalent. Some state workers' compensation, insurance, or other reports may be acceptable substitutes. To be considered an equivalent form, any substitute must contain all the information asked for on this form.

According to Public Law 91-596 and 29 CFR 1904, OSHA's recordkeeping rule, you must keep this form on file for 5 years following the year to which it pertains.

If you need additional copies of this form, you may photocopy and use as many as you need.

Completed by _____

Title _____

Phone (_____) ____ – _____   Date ___/___/___

Information about the employee

1) Full name _____

2) Street _____

City _____ State _____ ZIP _____

3) Date of birth ____/____/____

4) Date hired ____/____/____

5) ☐ Male
☐ Female

Information about the physician or other health care professional

6) Name of physician or other health care professional _____

7) If treatment was given away from the worksite, where was it given?

Facility _____

Street _____

City _____ State _____ ZIP _____

8) Was employee treated in an emergency room?
☐ Yes
☐ No

9) Was employee hospitalized overnight as an in-patient?
☐ Yes
☐ No

Information about the case

10) Case number from the Log _____ *(Transfer the case number from the Log after you record the case.)*

11) Date of injury or illness ____/____/____

12) Time employee began work _____ AM / PM

13) Time of event _____ AM / PM ☐ Check if time cannot be determined

14) **What was the employee doing just before the incident occurred?** Describe the activity, as well as the tools, equipment, or material the employee was using. Be specific. *Examples:* "climbing a ladder while carrying roofing materials"; "spraying chlorine from hand sprayer"; "daily computer key-entry."

15) **What happened?** Tell us how the injury occurred. *Examples:* "When ladder slipped on wet floor, worker fell 20 feet"; "Worker was sprayed with chlorine when gasket broke during replacement"; "Worker developed soreness in wrist over time."

16) **What was the injury or illness?** Tell us the part of the body that was affected and how it was affected; be more specific than "hurt," "pain," or sore." *Examples:* "strained back"; "chemical burn, hand"; "carpal tunnel syndrome."

17) What object or substance directly harmed the employee? *Examples:* concrete floor ; chlorine ; "radial arm saw." If this question does not apply to the incident, leave it blank.

18) **If the employee died, when did death occur?** Date of death ____/____/____

■Figure **16.4**

Form Used to Record Occupational Injuries and Illnesses

Source: U.S. Department of Labor.

limited number of inspectors, OSHA recently has focused on OSHA–employer cooperative programs (such as its "Voluntary Protection Programs").[24]

INSPECTION PRIORITIES   However, OSHA still makes extensive use of inspections. OSHA takes a "worst-first" approach in setting inspection priorities. Priorities include, from highest to lowest, imminent dangers, catastrophes and fatal accidents, employee complaints, high-hazard industries inspections, and follow-up inspections.[25]

OSHA inspectors look for all types of violations, but some potential problem areas—such as scaffolding and fall protection—grab more of their attention. The five most frequent OSHA inspection violation areas are scaffolding, fall protection, hazard communication, lockout/tagout (electrical disengagement), and respiratory problems. Figure 16.5 lists the hazards that accounted for the greatest number of citations in one recent year.

SUPERVISOR'S INSPECTION GUIDELINES   What should you do when OSHA inspectors unexpectedly show up? Guidelines include:

Initial Contact

- First, restrict admittance until the manager in charge/OSHA coordinator are on site.[26]
- Check the inspector's credentials.

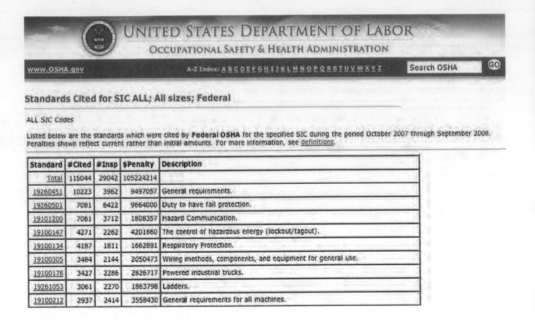

UNITED STATES DEPARTMENT OF LABOR
OCCUPATIONAL SAFETY & HEALTH ADMINISTRATION

www.OSHA.gov   A-Z Index: A B C D E F G H I J K L M N O P Q R S T U V W X Y Z   Search OSHA   GO

Standards Cited for SIC ALL; All sizes; Federal

ALL *SIC Codes*

Listed below are the standards which were cited by **Federal OSHA** for the specified SIC during the period October 2007 through September 2008. Penalties shown reflect current rather than initial amounts. For more information, see definitions.

Standard	#Cited	#Insp	$Penalty	Description
Total	115044	29042	105224214	
19260451	10223	3962	9497057	General requirements.
19260501	7081	6422	9664000	Duty to have fall protection.
19101200	7061	3712	1808357	Hazard Communication.
19100147	4271	2262	4201860	The control of hazardous energy (lockout/tagout).
19100134	4187	1811	1662891	Respiratory Protection.
19100305	3484	2144	2050473	Wiring methods, components, and equipment for general use.
19100178	3427	2286	2826717	Powered industrial trucks.
19261053	3061	2270	1863798	Ladders.
19100212	2937	2414	3558430	General requirements for all machines.

- Ask the inspector why he or she is inspecting your workplace. Is it complaints? A scheduled visit?
- If the inspection stems from a complaint, you are entitled to know whether the person is a current employee, though not the person's name.
- Notify your counsel, who should review all documents and information.

Opening Conference

- Establish the focus and scope of the planned inspection.
- Discuss the procedures for protecting trade secret areas.
- Show the inspector you have safety programs in place. He or she may not even go to the work floor if paperwork is complete and up-to-date.

Walk-Around Inspection

- Accompany the inspector and take detailed notes.
- If the inspector takes a photo or video, you should, too.
- Ask for duplicates of all physical samples and copies of all test results.
- Be helpful and cooperative, but don't volunteer information.
- To the extent possible, immediately correct any violation the inspector identifies.[27]

WHAT NOT TO DO   The magazine *EHS* (*Environment, Health, and Safety*) conducted a survey of 12 safety experts, and asked them to identify the "10 best ways" to get into trouble with OSHA.[28] Several "best ways" were inspection-related. They include the following:

1. Antagonize or lie to OSHA during an inspection.
2. Keep inaccurate OSHA logs and have disorganized safety files.
3. Fail to control the flow of information during and after an inspection. (Do not give the OSHA inspector any information he or she does not ask for, and keep tabs on everything that you give to the inspector.)

Responsibilities and Rights of Employers and Employees

Both employers and employees have responsibilities under the Occupational Safety Health Act. *Employers* are responsible for providing "a workplace free from recognized hazards" and for examining workplace conditions to make sure they conform to OSHA standards.

Employees also have responsibilities, but OSHA cannot cite them for violations of their responsibilities. Employees are responsible, for example, for complying with all applicable OSHA standards and for following all employer safety and health rules and regulations.

DEALING WITH EMPLOYEE RESISTANCE   While employees have a responsibility to comply with OSHA standards, they often resist. The refusal of some workers to wear hard hats typifies this. Supervisors often try to defend themselves against penalties for such non-compliance by citing worker intransigence. In most cases, courts still hold employers liable for workplace safety violations.

Yet employers can reduce their liability.[29] In the event of a problem, the courts may take into consideration facts such as whether the employer's safety procedures were adequate, and whether the supervisor really required employees to follow the procedures. The independent three-member Occupational Safety and Health Review Commission that reviews OSHA decisions says employers must make "a diligent effort to discourage, by discipline if necessary, violations of safety rules by employees."[30] (See Figure 16.6.) First-line supervisors play a crucial role in this process, for instance, by requiring good safety practices. However, the only surefire way to eliminate liability is to ensure that no accidents occur. For that, you need to know what causes accidents and how to prevent them.

3. What Causes Accidents?

What Causes Accidents?

There are three basic causes of workplace accidents: chance occurrences, unsafe conditions, and employees' unsafe acts. Chance occurrences (such as walking past a window just as someone hits a ball through it) are more or less beyond the supervisor's control. We will therefore focus on unsafe conditions and unsafe acts.

Unsafe Conditions and Other Work-Related Factors

Unsafe conditions are a main cause of accidents. They include things such as:

- Improperly guarded equipment
- Defective equipment
- Hazardous procedures in, on, or around machines or equipment
- Unsafe storage—congestion, overloading
- Improper illumination—glare, insufficient light
- Improper ventilation—insufficient air change, impure air source[31]

The solution here is for the supervisor to identify and eliminate the unsafe conditions. The main aim of the OSHA standards is to address these mechanical and physical

accident-causing conditions. The employer's safety department (if any) and its human resource managers and top managers have overall responsibility for identifying unsafe conditions. But the supervisor must take responsibility here on a day-to-day basis.

DANGER ZONES   While accidents can happen anywhere, there are some high-danger zones. About one-third of industrial accidents occur around forklift trucks, wheelbarrows, and other handling and lifting areas. The most serious accidents usually occur by metal and woodworking machines and saws, or around transmission machinery such as gears, pulleys, and flywheels. Falls on stairs, ladders, walkways, and scaffolds are the third most common cause of industrial accidents. Hand tools (like chisels and screwdrivers) and electrical equipment (extension cords, electric droplights, and so on) are other major causes of accidents.[32]

Work schedules and fatigue also affect accident rates. Accident rates usually don't increase too noticeably during the first five or six hours of the workday. But after that, the accident rate increases faster. This is due partly to fatigue and partly to the fact that accidents occur more often during night shifts.

Unfortunately, some of the most important working-condition-related causes of accidents are not as obvious, because they involve workplace "climate" or psychology.[33] Thus, a strong pressure to complete the work as quickly as possible, employees who are under stress, and supervisors who never mention safety all contribute to accidents. Similarly, accidents occur more frequently in plants with high seasonal layoff rates.

What Causes Workers to Act Unsafely?

The problem is that employee misconduct will short-circuit all your attempts to reduce unsafe conditions, and, of course, there's no one silver bullet for eliminating unsafe acts.

There is no one explanation for why an employee may behave in an unsafe manner. Sometimes, as noted, the working conditions may set the stage for unsafe acts. For instance, stressed-out employees may behave unsafely even if they know better. Sometimes, employees aren't trained in safe work methods. Some supervisors don't supply employees with the right safety procedures, and employees may simply develop their own (often bad) work habits. For example, in one accident, a maintenance worker followed the plant's lockout/tagout procedure by calling the control room to have them shut off the roof exhaust fan he was about to work on. When he arrived on the roof, he noticed the fan was still turning, and he assumed that the wind was turning the blades. After waiting several minutes, he wrapped a rag around his hand and tried to stop the blade with his hand, causing serious injury. He had followed the procedure by calling the control room. But the supervisor should have emphasized in the training that the point of the procedure was not just to call to disconnect the power, but "to make sure that the fan is not turning before you touch it."[34]

ACCIDENT-PRONE EMPLOYEES   Some workers may just be accident prone. For example, people who are impulsive, sensation seeking, extremely extroverted, and less dependable are more likely to have accidents.[35] That's particularly true on certain jobs, like driving. For example, personality traits that correlate with vehicular insurance claims include *entitlement* ("think there's no reason they should not speed"), *impatience* ("were 'always in a hurry'"), and *aggressiveness* ("the first to move when the light turns green").[36] (So, be careful if you have an impatient, aggressive employee with a sense of entitlement driving routes for you.) Or your employee may just lack the knowledge, training, or motivation required to do the job safely. In any case, there are things you can do to prevent accidents.

4. How Employers and Supervisors Can Prevent Accidents

In practice, accident prevention boils down to two basic activities:

1. Reducing unsafe conditions
2. Reducing unsafe acts

How Can Employers and Supervisors Prevent Accidents?

In large facilities, the safety officer (often called the "Environmental Health and Safety Officer") is responsible for designing safety programs.[37] In smaller firms, managers including those from human resources, plant management, and first-line supervisors share these responsibilities.

Reducing Unsafe Conditions

Reducing unsafe conditions is always an employer's first line of defense in accident prevention. Safety engineers (if your firm has one) should design jobs to remove or reduce physical hazards. For machinery, for example, employees can use emergency stop devices to cut power to hazardous machines.[38] In addition, we saw that supervisors play a major role. Checklists like those in Figures 16.1 (p. 482) and 16.7 (pp. 491–494) can help identify and remove potential hazards.

Sometimes the solution for eliminating an unsafe condition is obvious, and sometimes it's more subtle. For example, slips and falls are often the result of debris or slippery floors.[39] Obvious remedies include floor mats and better lighting. Perhaps less obviously, personal safety gear, like slip-resistant footwear with grooved soles, can also reduce slips and falls. Cut-resistant gloves reduce the hazards of working with sharp objects.[40] (Hand injuries account for about one million emergency department visits annually by U.S.workers).[41] Figure 16.8 (page 494) illustrates some of what's available.

Personal Protective Equipment

Getting employees to wear personal protective equipment (PPE) is famously difficult. Wearability is important.[42] In addition to providing reliable protection, protective gear should fit properly; be easy to care for, maintain, and repair; be flexible and lightweight; provide comfort and reduce heat stress; and be relatively easy to put on and take off.[43] Of course, it makes sense to require wearing the personal protective equipment before the accident, rather than after it. For example, a combustible dust explosion at a sugar refinery recently killed 14 employees and burned many others. The employer subsequently required that all employees wear fire-resistant clothing, unfortunately too late for the victims.[44]

Note, though, that reducing unsafe conditions (such as enclosing noisy equipment) is always the first line of defense. Then use administrative controls (such as job rotation to reduce long-term exposure to the hazard). Only then, turn to PPE.[45]

The accompanying Supervising the New Workforce feature expands on this.

Supervising the New Workforce

Protecting Vulnerable Workers

Employers need to pay special attention to vulnerable workers, those who are "unprepared to deal with hazards in the workplace," due to lack of education, ill-fitting personal protective equipment, physical limitations, or cultural reasons. Among others, these may include young workers, immigrant workers, aging workers, and women workers.[46]

For example, although about half of all workers today are women, most machinery and PPE (like gloves) are designed for men.[47] (Hand injuries account for about one million emergency department visits annually by U.S. workers).[48] Women may thus have to use makeshift platforms or stools to reach machinery controls, or safety goggles that don't really fit. The solution is to make sure the equipment and machines women use are appropriate for their size.[49]

Similarly, with more workers postponing retirement, older workers are doing more manufacturing jobs.[50] For example, at one Allegany Ludlam Stainless Steel Corp. facility, about two-thirds of the workers are within 10 years of retirement.[51] They can do these jobs very effectively. However, there are potential physical changes associated with aging, including loss of strength, loss of muscular flexibility, and reduced reaction time.[52] This means that employers should make special provisions, such as designing jobs to reduce heavy lifting.[53] The fatality rate for older workers is about three times that of younger workers.[54]

FORM **CD-574**
(9/02)

U.S. Department of Commerce
Office Safety Inspection Checklist for
Supervisors and Program Managers

Name:	Division:
Location:	Date:
Signature:	

This checklist is intended as a guide to assist supervisors and program managers in conducting safety and health inspections of their work areas. It includes questions relating to general office safety, ergonomics, fire prevention, and electrical safety. Questions which receive a "**NO**" answer require corrective action. If you have questions or need assistance with resolving any problems, please contact your safety office. More information on office safety is available through the Department of Commerce Safety Office website at http://ohrm.doc.gov/safetyprogram/safety.htm.

Work Environment

Yes	No	N/A	
○	○	⊙	Are all work areas clean, sanitary, and orderly?
○	○	⊙	Is there adequate lighting?
○	○	⊙	Do noise levels appear high?
○	○	⊙	Is ventilation adequate?

Walking / Working Surfaces

Yes	No	N/A	
○	○	⊙	Are aisles and passages free of stored material that may present trip hazards?
○	○	⊙	Are tile floors in places like kitchens and bathrooms free of water and slippery substances?
○	○	⊙	Are carpet and throw rugs free of tears or trip hazards?
○	○	⊙	Are hand rails provided on all fixed stairways?
○	○	⊙	Are treads provided with anti-slip surfaces?
○	○	⊙	Are step ladders provided for reaching overhead storage areas and are materials stored safely?
○	○	⊙	Are file drawers kept closed when not in use?
○	○	⊙	Are passenger and freight elevators inspected annually and are the inspection certificates available for review on-site?
○	○	⊙	Are pits and floor openings covered or otherwise guarded?
○	○	⊙	Are standard guardrails provided wherever aisle or walkway surfaces are elevated more than 48 inches above any adjacent floor or the ground?
○	○	⊙	Is any furniture unsafe or defective?
○	○	⊙	Are objects covering heating and air conditioning vents?

■ Figure **16.7**

Safety Inspection Checklist

Source: http://ocio.os.doc.gov/s/groups/public/@doc/@os/@ocio/@oitpp/documents/content/dev01_002574.pdf (accessed April 28, 2009).

FORM CD-574
(9/02)

Ergonomics

Yes	No	N/A	
○	○	◉	Are employees advised of proper lifting techniques?
○	○	◉	Are workstations configured to prevent common ergonomic problems? (Chair height allows employees' feet to rest flat on the ground with thighs parallel to the floor, top of computer screen is at or slightly below eye level, keyboard is at elbow height. Additional information on proper configuration of workstations is available through the Commerce Safety website at http://ohrm.doc.gov/safetyprogram/safety.htm)
○	○	◉	Are mechanical aids and equipment, such as; lifting devices, carts, dollies provided where needed?
○	○	◉	Are employees surveyed annually on their ergonomic concerns?

Emergency Information (Postings)

Yes	No	N/A	
○	○	◉	Are established emergency phone numbers posted where they can be readily found in case of an emergency?
○	○	◉	Are employees trained on emergency procedures?
○	○	◉	Are fire evacuation procedures/diagrams posted?
○	○	◉	Is emergency information posted in every area where you store hazardous waste?
○	○	◉	Is established facility emergency information posted near a telephone?
○	○	◉	Are the OSHA poster, and other required posters displayed conspicuously?
○	○	◉	Are adequate first aid supplies available and properly maintained?
○	○	◉	Are an adequate number of first aid trained personnel available to respond to injuries and illnesses until medical assistance arrives?
○	○	◉	Is a copy of the facility fire prevention and emergency action plan available on site?
○	○	◉	Are safety hazard warning signs/caution signs provided to warn employees of pertinent hazards?

Fire Prevention

Yes	No	N/A	
○	○	◉	Are flammable liquids, such as gasoline, kept in approved safety cans and stored in flammable cabinets?
○	○	◉	Are portable fire extinguishers distributed properly (less than 75 feet travel distance for combustibles and 50 feet for flammables)?
○	○	◉	Are employees trained on the use of portable fire extinguishers?
○	○	◉	Are portable fire extinguishers visually inspected monthly and serviced annually?
○	○	◉	Is the area around portable fire extinguishers free of obstructions and properly labeled ?
○	○	◉	Is heat-producing equipment used in a well ventilated area?
○	○	◉	Are fire alarm pull stations clearly marked and unobstructed?
○	○	◉	Is proper clearance maintained below sprinkler heads (i.e., 18" clear)?

■Figure **16.7**

(Continued)

FORM **CD-574**
(9/02)

Emergency Exits

Yes	No	N/A	
O	O	⊙	Are doors, passageways or stairways that are neither exits nor access to exits and which could be mistaken for exits, appropriately marked "NOT AN EXIT," "TO BASEMENT," "STOREROOM," etc.?
O	O	⊙	Are a sufficient number of exits provided?
O	O	⊙	Are exits kept free of obstructions or locking devices which could impede immediate escape?
O	O	⊙	Are exits properly marked and illuminated?
O	O	⊙	Are the directions to exits, when not immediately apparent, marked with visible signs?
O	O	⊙	Can emergency exit doors be opened from the direction of exit travel without the use of a key or any special knowledge or effort when the building is occupied?
O	O	⊙	Are exits arranged such that it is not possible to travel toward a fire hazard when exiting the facility?

Electrical Systems

(Please have your facility maintenance person or electrician accompany you during this part of the inspection)

Yes	No	N/A	
O	O	⊙	Are all cord and cable connections intact and secure?
O	O	⊙	Are electrical outlets free of overloads?
O	O	⊙	Is fixed wiring used instead of flexible/extension cords?
O	O	⊙	Is the area around electrical panels and breakers free of obstructions?
O	O	⊙	Are high-voltage electrical service rooms kept locked?
O	O	⊙	Are electrical cords routed such that they are free of sharp objects and clearly visible?
O	O	⊙	Are all electrical cords grounded?
O	O	⊙	Are electrical cords in good condition (free of splices, frays, etc.)?
O	O	⊙	Are electrical appliances approved (Underwriters Laboratory, Inc. (UL), etc)?
O	O	⊙	Are electric fans provided with guards of not over one-half inch, preventing finger exposures?
O	O	⊙	Are space heaters UL listed and equipped with shutoffs that activate if the heater tips over?
O	O	⊙	Are space heaters located away from combustibles and properly ventilated?
O	O	⊙	In your electrical rooms are all electrical raceways and enclosures securely fastened in place?
O	O	⊙	Are clamps or other securing means provided on flexible cords or cables at plugs, receptacles, tools, equipment, etc., and is the cord jacket securely held in place?
O	O	⊙	Is sufficient access and working space provided and maintained about all electrical equipment to permit ready and safe operations and maintenance? (This space is 3 feet for less than 600 volts, 4 feet for more than 600 volts)

■Figure **16.7**

(Continued)

FORM **CD-574**

(9/02)

Material Storage

Yes	No	N/A	
○	○	⊙	Are storage racks and shelves capable of supporting the intended load and materials stored safely?
○	○	⊙	Are storage racks secured from falling?
○	○	⊙	Are office equipment stored in a stable manner, not capable of falling?

■Figure **16.7**

(Continued)

Reducing unsafe acts—by emphasizing safety and through screening, training, or incentive programs, for example—is the second basic way to reduce accidents. Let's look at how supervisors and employers do this.[55]

Reducing Unsafe Acts through Careful Screening

Proper employee screening reduces unsafe acts. Some employers administer safety tests. For example, the Employee Reliability Inventory (ERI) (see http://www.ramsaycorp.

■Figure **16.8**

Illustrative Safety Equipment

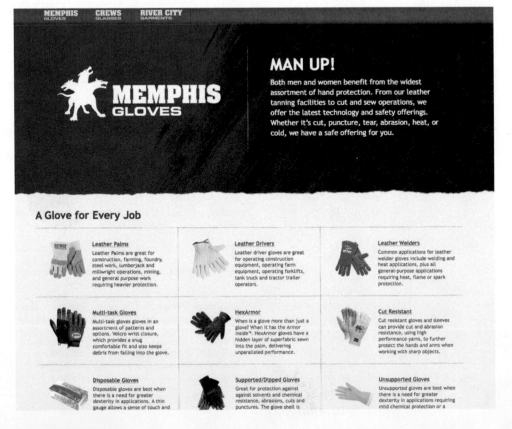

com/products/eriphone.asp) measures reliability in terms of things such as emotional maturity, conscientiousness, and safe job performance.[56] Making sure the applicant has the necessary *physical capabilities* for the job (testing for things such as muscle strength and motion) is another way to identify people who might have difficulties.[57]

Supervisors can also easily use behavioral interview questions. For example, ask, "What would you do if you saw another employee working in an unsafe way?" and "What would you do if I gave you a task, but didn't explain how to perform it safely?"[58]

Reducing Unsafe Acts through Training

Safety training reduces unsafe acts, especially for new employees. You should instruct them in safe practices and procedures, warn them of potential hazards, and work on developing a safety-conscious attitude. OSHA, NIOSH (National Institute for Occupational Safety and Health), and private vendors provide online safety training programs.[59] Use a job instruction training sheet like the one we described in Chapter 9 (Training) to itemize what the new employee should watch for.

The accompanying Supervising the New Workforce feature provides an additional perspective.

Your employer may also turn to the Web to support its safety training program.[62] For example, PureSafety (http://www.puresafety.com) enables firms to create their own training Web sites, complete with a "message from the safety director." Once an employer installs the PureSafety Web site, it can populate the site with courses from companies that supply health and safety courses.[63]

Supervising the New Workforce

Safety Training for Hispanic Workers

With increasing numbers of Spanish-speaking workers in the United States, experts express concern about their safety. For example, the number of Hispanic fatalities in construction rose by almost 50% in the early 2000s, because so many more Hispanics are now working in construction jobs.[60]

Faced with statistics like these, many construction companies are offering specialized training programs for Hispanic workers. One example is a 40-hour training course provided for construction workers at the Dallas–Fort Worth Airport expansion project. The construction firms here credit part of the airport site's safety record improvements to the new training program.

Based on this program's apparent success, there are several useful conclusions one can draw about what a program like this should look like.

- First, the program should *speak the workers' language*.
- Second, teaching the program in Spanish (or another appropriate language) is only part of "speaking the workers' language." The employer should also recruit instructors who are from the ethnic groups they are training.
- Third, provide for some *multilingual cross-training* for specific phrases. For example, the course teaches non-Hispanic trainees to say *"peligro"* [danger] or *"cuidado"* (be careful).[61]
- Fourth, *don't skimp on training*. Because of the added cultural and multilingual aspects, experts contend that a 24-hour course is the absolute minimum. The 40-hour course at Dallas–Fort Worth Airport cost about $500 tuition per student (not counting the worker's wages).

Reducing Unsafe Acts through Motivation: Posters, Incentives, and Positive Reinforcement

The simplest way to motivate employees to work safely is to show them the safe way to do it, and then to reinforce their safe behavior with recognition (such as, "Well done!")

Employers also use safety posters (Figure 16.9). These can motivate safe behavior, but not by themselves. As a supervisor, you should reinforce the desired behavior (such as correct lifting) and explain why it's important. And posters are no substitute for a comprehensive safety program (although some employers try to use them as such). Combine them with other techniques (like screening and training) to reduce unsafe conditions and acts, and change the posters often.

Incentive programs are also useful.[64] Management at the Golden Eagle refinery in California instituted one such safety incentive plan. Employees earn "WINGS" points for engaging in one or more of 28 safety activities, such as conducting safety meetings and taking emergency response training. Employees can earn up to $20 per month per person by accumulating points.[65]

Some contend that safety incentive programs are misguided. OSHA has argued, for instance, that they don't cut down on actual injuries or illnesses, but only on injury and illness *reporting*. However, no one argues against using nonmaterial incentives like recognition (such as, "Great job!").[66]

■Figure **16.9**

Safety Poster

Source: http://www.osha-safety-training.net/POS/pictures/page801.html (accessed April 28, 2009).

■ Figure **16.10**

Employee Safety Responsibilities Checklist

Source: Reprinted from www.HR.BLR.com with permission of the publisher Business and Legal Reports, Inc., 141 Mill Rock Road East, Old Saybrook, CT © 2004.

Employee Safety Responsibilities Checklist

- ☐ Know what constitutes a safety hazard.
- ☐ Be constantly on the lookout for safety hazards.
- ☐ Correct or report safety hazards immediately.
- ☐ Know and use safe work procedures.
- ☐ Avoid unsafe acts.
- ☐ Keep the work area clean and uncluttered.
- ☐ Report accidents, injuries, illnesses, exposures to hazardous substances, and near misses immediately.
- ☐ Report acts and conditions that don't seem right even if you aren't sure if they're hazards.
- ☐ Cooperate with internal inspections and job hazard analyses.
- ☐ Follow company safety rules.
- ☐ Look for ways to make the job safer.
- ☐ Participate actively in safety training.
- ☐ Treat safety as one of your most important job responsibilities.

Use Employee Participation

There are two good reasons to involve your employees in improving safety at your workplace. First, employees are often your best source of ideas about what the problems are and how to solve them. Second, employee involvement tends to encourage employees to accept the safety program.

Once they are committed to the idea of safety, a checklist as in Figure 16.10 can provide employees with a useful reminder.

Conduct Safety and Health Audits and Inspections

Again, however, reducing unsafe acts is no substitute for eliminating hazards. Supervisors should therefore routinely inspect for possible problems, using safety checklists as aids (see the APPs feature). Investigate all accidents and "near misses." Make it easy for employees to notify you about hazards.[67]

Table 16.1 summarizes actions for reducing unsafe conditions and acts.[70]

The Supervisor's Role in Controlling Workers' Compensation Costs

In the event an accident does occur, the employee may turn to the employer's workers' compensation insurance to cover his or her losses. In turn, the employer's workers'

PDA Safety Audits

Supervisors expedite safety audits by using personal digital assistants.[68] For example, Process and Performance Measurement (PPM) is a Windows application for designing and completing safety audit questionnaires. To use this application, the supervisor gives the safety audit a name, enters the audit questions, and lists possible answers. Typical questions for a fire extinguisher audit might include, "Are fire extinguishers clearly identified and accessible?" and "Are only approved fire extinguishers used in the workplace?"[69] The supervisor or employee then uses his or her PDA to record the audit and transmit it to the firm's safety office.

Reducing Unsafe Conditions and Acts: A Summary

Reduce Unsafe Conditions
Identify and eliminate unsafe conditions.
Use administrative means, such as job rotation.
Use personal protective equipment.

Reduce Unsafe Acts
Emphasize top management commitment.
Emphasize safety.
Establish a safety policy.
Reduce unsafe acts through selection.
Provide safety training.
Use posters and other propaganda.
Use positive reinforcement.
Use behavior-based safety programs.
Encourage worker participation.
Conduct safety and health inspections regularly.

compensation premiums reflect the number and size of its claims. Workers' compensation claims tend to spike on Mondays, possibly because some workers represent weekend injuries as work-related ones.[71] The supervisor plays a big role in controlling workers' compensation costs.

BEFORE THE ACCIDENT   The time to start "controlling" workers' compensation claims is before the accident happens. This involves taking all the safety steps described previously.[72] The approach doesn't have to be complicated. For example, LKL Associates, Inc., of Orem, Utah, cut its workers' compensation premiums in half. They did this by communicating written safety and substance abuse policies to workers and then strictly enforcing those policies.[73]

AFTER THE ACCIDENT   The injury can be traumatic for the employee. How you handle it is important. The employee will have questions, such as where to go for medical help and whether he or she is paid for time off. It's also usually at this point that the employee decides whether to retain a workers' compensation attorney.

Here it is important that the supervisor be supportive and proactive. Provide first aid and make sure the worker gets quick medical attention; make it clear that you are interested in the injured worker; document the accident; file required accident reports; and encourage a speedy return to work.[74]

It doesn't help that half the employees who return after workers' comp leaves face indifference, criticism, or dismissal.[75] Perhaps the most important thing an employer can do is to develop an aggressive return-to-work program, including making light-duty work available. The best solution, for both employer and employee, is for the worker to become a productive member of the company again instead of a victim living on benefits.[76]

What Is the Supervisor's Role in Controlling Workers' Compensation Costs?

Controlling safety and health costs of all types becomes a more pressing issue in challenging times, as the accompanying feature explains.

Cutting Safety Costs Without Cutting Costs

When economic times turn challenging, it's hard to think of a more dubious way to cut costs than by cutting what the employer spends on employee safety and health. Reducing expenditures on activities like safety training or safety incentives may reduce expenses short term. But they may well drive up accident-related costs, including workers' compensation, almost as quickly. The solution isn't to cut safety costs across the board, but to cut costs selectively and intelligently. For example, employers are migrating from more expensive classroom training to less expensive online training. And within online safety training, many in these challenging times are migrating from paid programs to free online programs, like those offered by NIOSH, or at Web sites such as http://www.freetraining.com.

Supervisors are also applying practices we explained in this chapter, such as more diligently reviewing workers' compensation claims and reducing accidents before they occur, for instance, with more safety checks and better employee background checks. For keeping track of things such as accident statistics, there are online safety management Web sites (which charge a monthly fee) as well as PC-based packages for this that reside on your company's server. ZeraWare (http://www.zeraware.com) is one example.[77]

5. Workplace Health Hazards: Problems and Remedies

Workplace Health Hazards: What Are the Problems and Remedies?

Most workplace hazards aren't obvious ones, such as unguarded equipment or slippery floors. Many are unseen hazards (like chemicals) that the company produces as part of its production processes. Other problems, such as drug abuse, the employees may create for themselves. In either case, these hazards are often more dangerous to workers' health and safety than are obvious hazards like slippery floors. Typical workplace exposure hazards include chemicals and other hazardous materials such as asbestos, as well as alcohol abuse, stressful jobs, ergonomic hazards (such as uncomfortable equipment), infectious diseases, smoking, and biohazards (such as mold and anthrax).[78] We'll look at several of these.

Chemicals and Industrial Hygiene

OSHA standards list exposure limits for about 600 chemicals. Hazardous substances like these require air sampling and other precautionary measures. They are also more widespread than most people realize. For example, manufacturers use ethyl alcohol as a solvent in industrial processes.[79]

Managing such exposure hazards comes under the area of *industrial hygiene* and involves recognition, evaluation, and control. First, the supervisor or the facility's health and safety officers must *recognize* possible exposure hazards. This involves activities like conducting plant/facility walk-around surveys.

Having identified a possible hazard, the *evaluation* phase involves determining how severe the hazard is. This means measuring the exposure, comparing the measured exposure to some benchmark, and determining whether the risk is within tolerances.[80]

Finally, the hazard *control* phase involves eliminating or reducing the hazard. Personal protective gear (such as face masks) is generally the *last* option. Before relying on these, the employer must install engineering controls (such as ventilation) and administrative controls (including training); doing so is mandatory under OSHA.[81]

Asbestos Exposure at Work

There are four major sources of occupational respiratory diseases: asbestos, silica, lead, and carbon dioxide. Of these, asbestos is a major concern, in part because of publicity surrounding asbestos in buildings constructed before the mid-1970s. Major efforts are still underway to rid these buildings of the substance.

OSHA standards require several actions with respect to asbestos. Employers must monitor the air whenever they expect the level of asbestos to rise to one-half the allowable limit (which is 0.1 fibers per cubic centimeter). Engineering controls—walls, special filters, and so forth—are required to maintain an asbestos level that complies with OSHA standards. Only then can employers use respirators if additional efforts are required to achieve compliance.

Infectious Diseases

With many employees traveling to and from international destinations, and with infections like flu closing schools and businesses, monitoring and controlling infectious diseases is an important health issue.[82]

Employers and supervisors can take steps to prevent the spread of infectious diseases into their workplaces. These steps include:

1. Monitor Centers for Disease Control (CDC) travel alerts. These inform travelers about health concerns and provide precautions. Access this information at http://www.cdc.gov.
2. Provide daily medical screenings for employees returning from infected areas.
3. Deny access to your facility for 10 days to employees or visitors returning from affected areas.
4. Tell employees to stay home if they have a fever or respiratory system symptoms.
5. Clean work areas and surfaces regularly.
6. Stagger breaks. Offer several lunch periods to reduce overcrowding.
7. Emphasize the importance of frequent hand washing, and make sanitizers containing alcohol easily available.

Special situations prompt special requirements. For example, in 2009 the Centers for Disease Control and Prevention advised employers that health care workers working with H1N1 patients should use special respirators to reduce virus inhalation risks.[83]

Alcoholism and Substance Abuse

Alcoholism and substance abuse are widespread problems at work. About two-thirds of people with an alcohol disorder work full-time.[84] About 15% of the U.S. workforce (just over 19 million workers) "has either been hung over at work, been drinking shortly before showing up for work, or been drinking or impaired while on the job at least once during the previous year."[85] Some experts say that as many as 50% of all "problem employees" are actually alcoholics.[86] Drug-using employees are over three and a half times more likely to be involved in workplace accidents.[87]

EFFECTS OF ALCOHOL ABUSE   The effects of alcoholism on the worker and work are severe.[88] Both the quality and quantity of the work decline, in the face of a sort of on-the-job absenteeism. The alcoholic's on-the-job accidents usually don't increase significantly (apparently, he or she becomes much more cautious). The morale of other workers drops, as they have to shoulder the alcoholic's burdens.

Recognizing the alcoholic on the job isn't easy. Early symptoms such as tardiness are similar to those of other problems and thus hard to classify. The supervisor is not a psychiatrist, and without specialized training, identifying—and dealing with—the alcoholic is difficult.

The supervisor can use a chart as in Table 6.2 to identify behaviors that indicate alcohol-related problems. As you can see, possible signs range from tardiness in the earliest stages of alcohol abuse to prolonged, unpredictable absences in its later stages.

DEALING WITH SUBSTANCE ABUSE   Screening out abusers is the first line of defense. Most employers therefore at least test job candidates for substance abuse. Many states are instituting mandatory random drug testing for high-hazard workers. For example, New Jersey requires random drug testing of electrical workers.[89]

There's some debate about whether drug tests reduce workplace accidents. The answer seems to be that *preemployment* tests pick up only about half the workplace drug users, so *ongoing* random testing is advisable.[90] Preemployment drug testing also discourages those on drugs from applying for work or going to work for employers who test.[91]

■ Table **16.2**

Observable Behavior Patterns Indicating Possible Alcohol-Related Problems		
Alcoholism Stage	**Some Possible Signs of Alcoholism Problems**	**Some Possible Alcoholism Performance Issues**
Early	Arrives at work late	Reduced job efficiency
	Untrue statements	Misses deadlines
	Leaves work early	
Middle	Frequent absences, especially Mondays	Accidents
		Warnings from boss
	Colleagues mentioning erratic behavior	Noticeably reduced performance
	Mood swings	
	Anxiety	
	Late returning from lunch	
	Frequent multi-day absences	
Advanced	Personal neglect	Frequent falls, accidents
	Unsteady gait	Strong disciplinary actions
	Violent outbursts	Basically incompetent performance
	Blackouts and frequent forgetfulness	
	Possible drinking on job	

Source: Gopal Patel and John Adkins Jr., "The Employer's Role in Alcoholism Assistance," *Personnel Journal* 62, no. 7 (July 1983), p. 570; Mary-Anne Enoch and David Goldman, "Problem Drinking and Alcoholism: Diagnosis and Treatment," *American Family Physician*, February 1, 2002, www.aafp.org/afp/20020202/441.html, accessed July 20, 2008; and Ken Pidd et al., "Alcohol and Work: Patterns of Use, Workplace Culture, and Safety," www.nisu.flinders.edu.au/pubs/reports/2006/injcat82.pdf, accessed July 20, 2008.

Some applicants or employees may try to evade the test, for instance, by purchasing "clean" specimens to use. Several states have laws making drug-test fraud a crime.[92] A newer oral fluid drug test eliminates the "clean specimen" problem and is less expensive to administer.[93]

For *current* employees who test positive, disciplining, discharge, in-house counseling, and referral to an outside agency are the usual prescriptions. Most professionals emphasize that whether it's the supervisor or just a friend that notices the employee's problem, the worst thing to do is ignore it.

SUBSTANCE ABUSE POLICIES   Employers usually establish and communicate a substance abuse policy. This policy should state management's position on alcohol and drug abuse and on the use and possession of illegal drugs on company premises. It should also list the methods (such as urinalysis) used to determine the causes of poor performance; state the company's views on rehabilitation, including workplace counseling; and specify penalties for policy violations.

SUPERVISOR GUIDELINES   The employee's supervisor is in a tricky position. You're the company's first line of defense in noticing and combating workplace drug abuse, but you should avoid becoming a detective or medical diagnostician. Guidelines supervisors should follow include these:

- Follow your employer's substance abuse policies.
- If an employee appears to be under the influence of drugs or alcohol, ask how the employee feels and look for signs of impairment such as slurred speech. (See Table 16.2.) Send an employee judged unfit home.
- Make a written record of your observations and follow up each incident. In addition, inform workers of the number of warnings the company will tolerate before requiring termination.
- Refer troubled employees to the company's employee assistance program.

LEGAL ASPECTS OF WORKPLACE SUBSTANCE ABUSE   Several types of employers have specific legal obligations with respect to substance abuse. The federal Drug-Free Workplace Act requires *employers with federal government contracts* or grants to ensure a drug-free workplace by taking a number of steps. For example, these employers must agree to:

- Publish a policy prohibiting the unlawful manufacture, distribution, dispensing, possession, or use of controlled substances in the workplace.
- Inform employees that they are required, as a condition of employment, not only to abide by the employer's policy but also to report any criminal convictions for drug-related activities in the workplace.[94]

The U.S. Department of Transportation has rules that require random breath alcohol tests (as well as preemployment, postaccident, reasonable suspicion, and return-to-duty testing) for workers in safety-sensitive jobs in transportation industries.[95]

Supervisors also face special legal risks. If you mishandle the situation (for instance, by publicizing the worker's supposed drug habit, or by baselessly discharging someone without sufficient evidence), employees may sue for invasion of privacy, wrongful discharge, defamation, and illegal searches. Therefore, be careful. Make sure that your employer has taken precautions like clarifying its abuse policy in its employee handbooks and bulletin board postings, and the like. Then, make sure that you personally follow your employer's substance abuse notification and disciplinary procedures, and that you respect your subordinate's privacy rights.

Dealing with Stress, Burnout, and Depression

Problems such as alcoholism and drug abuse sometimes reflect underlying psychological stress and depression. In turn, a variety of workplace factors can lead to stress. These include work schedule, pace of work, job security, workplace noise, poor supervision, and the number and nature of customers or clients.[96]

Personal factors also influence stress. For example, Type A personalities—people who are workaholics and who feel driven to always be on time and meet deadlines—normally place themselves under greater stress than do others. Then there is the stress caused by nonjob issues like divorce and money problems.

Job stress has serious consequences for both employer and employee. For the employee, the consequences include anxiety, depression, anger, cardiovascular disease, headaches, accidents, and even early onset Alzheimer's disease.[97] For the employer, consequences include diminished performance and increased absenteeism and turnover. A study of 46,000 employees concluded that high-stress workers' health care costs were 46% higher than those of their less-stressed coworkers.[98] Yet only 5% of surveyed U.S. employers say they're addressing workplace stress.[99]

REDUCING JOB STRESS   There are a number of ways to alleviate unwanted stress. These range from commonsense remedies (such as getting more sleep and eating better) to remedies like biofeedback and meditation. Finding a more suitable job, getting counseling, and planning and organizing each day's activities are other sensible responses.[100] In his book *Stress and the Manager*, Dr. Karl Albrecht suggests the following ways for a person to reduce job stress:[101]

- Build rewarding, pleasant, cooperative relationships with colleagues and employees.
- Don't bite off more than you can chew.
- Build an especially effective and supportive relationship with your boss.
- Negotiate with your boss for realistic deadlines on important projects.
- Learn as much as you can about upcoming events and get as much lead time as you can to prepare for them.
- Find time every day for detachment and relaxation.
- Take a walk around the office to keep your body refreshed and alert.
- Find ways to reduce unnecessary noise.
- Reduce the amount of trivia in your job; delegate routine work whenever possible.
- Limit interruptions.
- Don't put off dealing with distasteful problems.
- Make a constructive "worry list" that includes solutions for each problem.
- Get more and better-quality sleep.[102]

Meditation is another option. Choose a quiet place with soft light and sit comfortably. Then meditate by focusing your thoughts, for instance, by counting breaths, or by visualizing a calming location such as a beach. When your mind wanders, bring it back to focusing your thoughts back on your breathing, or the beach.[103]

Supervisors play a big role in reducing stress. You may have noticed that conflict with a supervisor is one big source of stress. Supportive supervision and fair treatment are thus two obvious steps. Other steps include reducing personal conflicts on the job, and encouraging open communication between management and employees.

BURNOUT   **Burnout** is a phenomenon closely associated with job stress. Experts define burnout as the total depletion of physical and mental resources caused by excessive striving to reach an unrealistic work-related goal. Burnout builds gradually, manifesting itself in symptoms such as irritability, discouragement, exhaustion, cynicism, entrapment, and resentment.[104]

What can a burnout candidate do? In his book, *How to Beat the High Cost of Success*, Dr. Herbert Freudenberger suggests:

- **Break your patterns.** First, are you doing a variety of things or the same one repeatedly? The more well rounded your life is, the better protected you are against burnout.

- **Get away from it all periodically.** Schedule occasional periods of introspection during which you can get away from your usual routine.

- **Reassess your goals in terms of their intrinsic worth.** Are the goals you've set for yourself attainable? Are they really worth the sacrifices?

- **Think about your work.** Could you do as good a job without being so intense?

EMPLOYEE DEPRESSION   *Employee depression* is a serious problem at work. Experts estimate that depression results in more than 200 million lost workdays in the United States annually, and may cost U.S. businesses $24 billion or more per year just in absenteeism and lost productivity.[105] Depressed people also tend to have worse safety records.[106]

Employers and supervisors need to do more to ensure that depressed employees utilize available support services. One survey found that while about two-thirds of large firms offered employee assistance programs covering depression, only about 14% of employees with depression said they ever used one.[107]

Supervisors should therefore know how to identify depression's warning signs, and how to counsel those who need help.[108] Depression is a disease. It does no more good to tell a depressed person to "snap out of it" than it would to tell someone with a heart condition to stop acting tired. Typical warning signs of depression (if they last for more than two weeks) include persistent sad, anxious, or "empty" moods; sleeping too little; reduced appetite; loss of interest in activities once enjoyed; restlessness or irritability; and difficulty concentrating.[109]

Solving Computer-Related Health Problems

Even with advances in computer screens, there's still a risk of monitor-related health problems at work. Problems include short-term eye burning, itching, and tearing, as well as eyestrain and eye soreness. Backaches and neck aches are also widespread. These often occur because employees try to compensate for monitor problems (such as glare) by maneuvering into awkward body positions. There may also be a tendency for computer users to suffer from repetitive motion disorders, such as carpal tunnel syndrome.[110]

NIOSH (the National Institute of Occupational Safety and Health) provided general recommendations regarding computer screens. Most relate to *ergonomics* or design of the worker-equipment interface. These include the following:

1. Employees should take a 3–5 minute break from working at the computer every 20–40 minutes and use the time for other tasks, like making copies.
2. Design maximum flexibility into the workstation so it can be adapted to the individual operator. For example, use adjustable chairs.
3. Reduce glare with devices such as indirect lighting.
4. Give workers a complete preplacement vision exam to ensure properly corrected vision.[111]
5. Allow the user to position his or her wrists at the same level as the elbow.
6. Put the screen at or just below eye level, at a distance of 18 to 30 inches from the eyes.
7. Let the wrists rest lightly on a pad for support.
8. Put the feet flat on the floor, or on a footrest.[112]

What Supervisors Should Know About Violence at Work

A disgruntled professor, apparently disappointed to be denied tenure, walked into a faculty meeting in Alabama recently and allegedly shot and killed three colleagues.

Violence against employees is a huge problem at work. Homicide is the second biggest cause of fatal workplace injuries. Surveys by NIOSH found that nonfatal workplace assaults resulted in more than one million lost workdays in one recent year. While robbery was the main motive for homicide at work, a coworker or personal associate committed roughly one of seven workplace homicides.[113]

WHO IS AT RISK?   Violence is more likely on some jobs. Jobs with a high likelihood for violence include those that involve physical care of others or decisions that influence other people's lives; involve handling guns; exercise security functions; exercise physical control over others; require interacting with frustrated individuals; and involve handling weapons other than guns.[114]

While men have more fatal occupational injuries than do women, the *proportion* of women who are victims of assault is much higher. The Gender-Motivated Violence Act (part of the Violence against Women Act) imposes significant liabilities on employers whose women employees become victims.[115] Most women (many working in retail establishments) murdered at work were victims of random criminal violence by an assailant unknown to the victim, as during a robbery. Coworkers, family members, or previous friends or acquaintances carried out the remaining homicides.

Supervisors can predict and avoid many workplace incidents. *Risk Management Magazine* estimates that about 86% of past workplace violence incidents were apparent earlier to coworkers, who had brought them to supervisors' attention prior to the incidents. Yet, in most cases, supervisors did little or nothing.[116] Employers and supervisors can take several steps to reduce workplace violence. Let's look at them.

HEIGHTENED SECURITY MEASURES   Heightened security measures are the first line of defense. For example (because about half of workplace homicides occur in the retail industry), OSHA has voluntary recommendations aimed at reducing homicides and injuries in such establishments. Particularly for late-night or early-morning retail workers, the suggestions include the following: Install mirrors and improved lighting; provide silent and personal alarms; reduce store hours during high-risk periods; install drop safes and signs that indicate little cash is kept on hand; erect bullet-resistance enclosures; and increase staffing during high-risk hours.[117] Employers in general should have a workplace violence policy that outlines unacceptable employee behavior and a zero-tolerance policy toward workplace violence.[118]

IMPROVED EMPLOYEE SCREENING   That testing can screen out those prone to workplace aggression is clear. In one study the researchers concluded that measurable individual differences like trait anger (for instance, how someone reacts when he or she does not receive recognition for doing good work) "account for more than 60% of the variance in our measure of the incidence of workplace aggression."[119]

At a minimum, carefully check references. Obtain a detailed employment application. Solicit and verify the applicant's employment history, educational background, and references. Sample interview questions to ask might include, "What frustrates you?" and "Who was your worst supervisor and why?"[120]

Certain background facts suggest the need for a more in-depth background investigation. Red flags include the following:[121]

- An unexplained gap in employment
- Incomplete or false information on the résumé or application
- A negative, unfavorable, or false reference
- Prior insubordinate or violent behavior on the job
- A criminal history involving harassing or violent behavior
- A prior termination for cause with a suspicious (or no) explanation
- A history of significant psychiatric problems
- A history of drug or alcohol abuse
- Strong indications of instability in the individual's work or personal life, for example, frequent job changes or geographic moves
- Lapsed or lost licenses or accreditations[122]

PAY ATTENTION TO RED FLAGS AT WORK   Red flags supervisors should watch for include the following:

- Typical traits. The typical perpetrator is male, between 25 and 40 years old, and exhibits an inability to handle stress, manipulative behavior, and steady complaining. Many nonviolent people exhibit such traits, too. However, perpetrators also tend to exhibit other behaviors, such as the following.[123]
- Verbal threats. They harbor grudges and often talk about what they may do, such as, "That propane tank in the back could blow up easily."
- Frustration. Most cases involve an employee who has a frustrated sense of entitlement, to a promotion, for example.
- Obsession. An employee may hold a grudge against a coworker or supervisor, and some cases stem from romantic interest.[124]
- An act of violence on or off the job.
- Erratic behavior evidencing a loss of awareness of actions.

- Overly defensive, obsessive, or paranoid tendencies.
- Overly confrontational or antisocial behavior.
- Sexually aggressive behavior.
- Isolationist or loner tendencies.
- Insubordinate behavior with a suggestion of violence.
- Tendency to overreact to criticism.
- Exaggerated interest in war, guns, violence, catastrophes.
- The commission of a serious breach of security.
- Possession of weapons, guns, knives at the workplace.[125]
- Violation of privacy rights of others such as searching desks or stalking.
- Chronic complaining and frequent, unreasonable grievances.
- A retribution-oriented or get-even attitude.[126]

DEALING WITH ANGRY EMPLOYEES   What to do when confronted by an angry, potentially explosive employee? Here are some suggestions:[127]

- Make eye contact.
- Stop what you are doing and give your full attention.
- Speak in a calm voice and create a relaxed environment.
- Be open and honest.
- Let the person have his or her say.
- Ask for specific examples of what the person is upset about.
- Be careful to define the problem.
- Ask open-ended questions and explore all sides of the issue.
- Listen. As one expert says, "Often, angry people simply want to be listened to. They need a supportive, empathic ear from someone they can trust."[128]

DISMISSING VIOLENT EMPLOYEES   The supervisor should use caution when firing or disciplining potentially violent employees.

In dismissing potentially violent employees,

- Plan all aspects of the meeting, including its time, location, the people present, and the agenda.
- If possible, involve security enforcement personnel.
- Analyze and anticipate, based on the person's history, the aggressive behavior to expect.
- Conduct the meeting in a room with a door leading to the outside of the building.
- Keep the termination brief and to the point.
- Make sure the person returns all company-owned property at the meeting.
- Clear away furniture and things the person might throw.
- Don't wear loose clothing that the person might grab.
- Don't make it sound as if you're accusing the employee; instead, say that according to company policy, you're required to take action.
- Maintain the person's dignity and try to emphasize something good about the employee.[129]

- Consider obtaining restraining orders against those who exhibited a tendency to act violently in the workplace. Your employer's human resource manager should understand restraining orders and the process for obtaining them.[130]
- Don't let the person return to his or her workstation.
- Protect the employee's dignity by not advertising the event.[131]

YOUR BEHAVIOR COUNTS   When employees behave violently at work, it is the employee and not "the situation" that's to blame. But realistically, you can't ignore the fact that, as three researchers said, "[Violence] typically occurs in response to a perceived injustice."[132]

These researchers asked respondents to reply to this: "Think back over your time as an employee in your current organization when you've been offended by another person." The researchers also asked the respondents how they reacted to the offense. An employee who blamed another for some personal affront was more likely to try to seek revenge and less likely to seek reconciliation.[133]

There's no telling how a thoughtless slight is liable to mushroom into a disaster. Consider, though, the executive suspected of sabotaging his former employer's computer system, causing up to $20 million in damage. He'd been earning $186,000 a year. What made him do it? A note he wrote anonymously to the president provides some chilling insight:

> I have been loyal to the Company in good and bad times for over thirty years. . . . What is most upsetting is the manner in which you chose to end our employment. I was expecting a member of top management to come down from his ivory tower to face us directly with a layoff announcement, rather than sending the kitchen supervisor with guards to escort us off the premises like criminals. . . . We will not wait for God to punish you—we will take measures into our own hands.[134]

What Should Supervisors Know about Violence at Work?

The moral is, the supervisor's behavior counts; to reduce violence, strive for fairness.

Enterprise Risk Management

A majority of employers have security arrangements.[135] For example, about 85% of employers in one survey have a formal disaster plan.[136] Many firms have also instituted special handling procedures for suspicious mail packages and hold regular emergency evacuation drills. Employers don't just need emergency plans for terrorist attacks. It's also important to have employer emergency plans in place for dealing with health issues such as swine flu epidemics—for instance, in terms of how the employer will communicate with employees and deal with extraordinary sick leave issues.[137]

What Is Enterprise Risk Management?

Identifying security and other corporate risks falls within the domain of *enterprise risk management*, which means identifying risks, and planning to and actually mitigating these risks. Thus, as part of its risk management, Walmart asks questions such as, "What are the risks? And what are we going to do about these risks?"[138]

Setting Up a Basic Security Program

The employer (rather than the supervisor) is responsible for the security plan. However, the supervisor in each work area should understand his or her place and role in the overall security plan.

In simplest terms, actually instituting a basic facility security program requires four steps: analyzing the current *level of risk*, and then installing *mechanical, natural,* and *organizational* security systems.[139]

Security programs ideally start with an analysis of the facility's *current level of risk.* The employer, preferably using security experts, should assess the company's exposure. For example, what is the neighborhood like? Does your facility (such as the office building you're in) house other businesses or individuals (such as law enforcement agencies) that might bring unsafe activities to your doorstep? As part of this initial threat assessment, also review at least these six matters:

1. *Access to the reception area*, including number of access points, and need for a "panic button" for contacting emergency personnel

2. *Interior security*, including possible need for key cards, secure restrooms, and better identification of exits

3. *Authorities' involvement*, in particular emergency procedures developed with local law enforcement authorities

4. *Mail handling*, including how employees screen and open mail and where it enters the building

5. *Evacuation*, including a full review of evacuation procedures and training

6. *Backup systems*, for instance, that let the company store data off-site if disaster strikes

Having assessed the potential current level of risk, the employer and supervisor then turn their attention to assessing and improving natural, mechanical, and organizational security.[140]

NATURAL SECURITY   *Natural security* means taking advantage of the facility's natural or architectural features in order to minimize security problems. For example, "Are there unlit spots in your parking lot?"

MECHANICAL SECURITY   *Mechanical security* is the utilization of security systems such as locks, intrusion alarms, access control systems, and surveillance systems to reduce the need for continuous human surveillance.[141] Technological advances are making this easier. Many mail rooms now use scanners to check the safety of incoming mail. And for access security, biometric scanners that read thumb or palm prints or retina or vocal patterns make it easier to enforce plant security.[142]

ORGANIZATIONAL SECURITY   Finally, *organizational security* means using effective supervision to improve security. For example, it means properly training and motivating security staff and lobby attendants. And it means ensuring that the security staff have written orders that define their duties, especially in situations such as fire, elevator entrapment, hazardous materials spills, medical emergencies, suspicious packages, and workplace violence.[143] Finally, as we said earlier, it's the supervisor's job to help screen employees properly. For example, are you properly investigating the backgrounds of new hires? Are you requiring the same types of background checks for the contractors who supply security and other personnel to your facility? And do you provide new employees with security orientations?

Chapter 16 Concept Review and Reinforcement

Key Terms

Burnout, p. 504
Occupational Illness,
  p. 484

Occupational Safety and
  Health Act of 1970,
  p. 483

Occupational Safety and
  Health Administration
  (OSHA), p. 483

Unsafe Conditions,
  p. 487

Review of Key Concepts

Safety and Top Management	Policies concerning safety start at the top. Every employer should institutionalize top management's commitment with a safety policy and publicize it.
Occupational Safety and Health Act	(1970) OSHA's main purpose is to set and enforce the safety and health standards that apply to almost all workers in the United States.
Occupational Illness	An occupational Illness is any abnormal condition or disorder caused by exposure to environmental factors associated with employment.
Inspection Priorities	OSHA takes a "worst-first" approach in setting inspection priorities (imminent dangers, catastrophes, and fatal accidents, employee complaints, high-hazard industries inspections, and follow-up inspections).
OSHA Standards—Employee Resistance	Employers are held liable for workplace safety violations even if workers resist complying with OSHA standards. Employers must make a diligent effort to discourage, by discipline if necessary, violations of safety rules by employees.
**What Causes Accidents?**	
Unsafe Conditions	Unsafe conditions are the main cause of accidents, including: • Defective equipment • Improperly guarded equipment • Hazardous procedures • Unsafe storage • Improper illumination • Improper ventilation
Unsafe Acts	Eliminating unsafe conditions won't eliminate unsafe employee acts, which can cause accidents. Poor working conditions, inadequate training, or accident proneness can lead to unsafe acts.
**Preventing Accidents**	
Reducing Unsafe Conditions	Reducing unsafe conditions is an employer's first line of defense in accident prevention. Also, jobs should be designed to remove or reduce physical hazards.

Reducing Unsafe Acts	Careful screening and safety training of new employees reduces unsafe acts. Instruction in safe practices and procedures, warning of potential hazards, and development of a safety-conscious attitude can reduce unsafe acts.
Use Employee Participation	It's good sense to involve your employees in improving safety at your workplace. Participation tends to encourage employees to accept the safety program.
Workplace Health Hazards	OSHA standards list exposure limits for about 600 chemicals. Other health hazards include asbestos, exposure, infectious diseases, alcohol abuse, stressful jobs, smoking, and ergonomic hazards.
Dealing with Stress	Job stress has serious consequences for both employer and employee. For the employee: anxiety, depression, anger, cardiovascular disease, headaches, and accidents. For the employer: diminished performance, increased absenteeism, turnover, and burnout.
Burnout	Burnout is the total depletion of physical and mental resources caused by excessive striving to reach an unrealistic work-related goal.

Review and Discussion Questions

1. Why should policies concerning safety emanate from top management?

2. Discuss the basic facts about OSHA—its purpose, standards, inspections, and rights and responsibilities.

3. Define occupational illness and give three examples of abnormal conditions or disorders caused by exposure to environmental factors.

4. When OSHA takes a "worst-first" approach in setting inspection priorities, why are imminent dangers ranked first?

5. Describe why employees resist complying with posted OSHA standards. What can employers do to discourage these violations?

6. Explain what causes unsafe acts.

7. What can the employer do to reduce unsafe conditions? Be specific.

8. Explain the supervisor's role in safety.

9. What are the major reasons that employers use employee participation when trying to improve safety in the workplace?

10. Analyze the legal issues concerning AIDS.

11. Explain three ways that you would use to reduce stress at work.

12. Describe the steps employers can take to deal with angry employees.

Application and Skill Building

Case Study One

The New Safety and Health Program

At first glance, a dot-com company is one of the last places you'd expect to find potential safety and health hazards—or so the owners of LearnInMotion.com thought. There's no danger of moving machinery, no high-pressure lines, no cutting or heavy lifting, and certainly no forklift trucks. However, there are safety and health problems.

In terms of accident-causing conditions, for instance, the one thing dot-com companies have lots of is cables and wires. There are cables connecting the computers to each other and to the servers, and in many cases separate cables running from some computers to separate printers. There are 10 telephones in this particular office, all on 15-foot phone lines that always seem to be snaking around chairs and tables. There is, in fact, an astonishing amount of cable considering this is an office with less than 10 employees. When the installation specialists wired the office (for electricity, high-speed cable, phone lines, burglar alarms, and computers), they estimated they used well over five miles of cables of one sort or another. Most of these are hidden in the walls or ceilings, but many of them snake their way from desk to desk, and under and over doorways. Several employees have tried to reduce the nuisance of having to trip over wires whenever they get up by putting their plastic chair pads over the wires closest to them. However, that still leaves many wires unprotected. In other cases, they brought in their own packing tape and tried to tape down the wires in those spaces where they're particularly troublesome, such as across doorways.

The cables and wires are only one of the more obvious potential accident-causing conditions. The firm's programmer, before he left the firm, had tried to repair the main server while the unit was still electrically alive. To this day, they're not sure exactly where he stuck the screwdriver, but the result was that he was "blown across the room," as one manager put it. He was all right, but it was still a scare. And while they haven't received any claims yet, every employee spends hours at his or her computer, so carpal tunnel syndrome is a risk, as are a variety of other problems such as eyestrain and strained backs.

One recent accident particularly scared the owners. The firm uses independent contractors to deliver the firm's book- and DVD-based courses in New York and two other cities. A delivery person was riding his bike east at the intersection of Second Avenue and East 64th Street in New York when he was struck by a car going south on Second Avenue. Luckily, he was not hurt, but the bike's front wheel was wrecked, and the narrow escape got the firm's two owners, Mel and Jennifer, thinking about their lack of a safety program.

It's not just the physical conditions that concern the two owners. They also have some concerns about potential health problems such as job stress and burnout. While the business may be (relatively) safe with respect to physical conditions, it is also relatively stressful in terms of the demands it makes in hours and deadlines. It is not at all unusual for employees to get to work by 7:30 or 8 o'clock in the morning and to work through until 11 or 12 o'clock at night, at least five and sometimes six or seven days per week.

The bottom line is that both Jennifer and Mel feel quite strongly that they need to do something about implementing a health and safety plan. Now, they want you, their management consultants, to help them do it. Here's what they want you to do for them.

Discussion Questions

1. Based upon your knowledge of health and safety matters and your actual observations of operations that are similar to theirs, make a list of the potential hazardous conditions employees and others face at LearnInMotion.com. What should they do to reduce the potential severity of the top five hazards?
2. Would it be advisable for the company to set up a procedure for screening out stress-prone or accident-prone individuals? Why or why not? If so, how should they screen them?
3. Write a short position paper on the subject, "What should we do to get all our employees to behave more safely at work?"
4. Based on what you know and on what other dot-coms are doing, write a short position paper on the subject, "What can we do to reduce the potential problems of stress and burnout in our company?"

Case Study Two

Carter Cleaning Centers

Carter's New Safety Program

Employees' safety and health are very important matters in the laundry and cleaning business. Each facility is a small production plant in which machines, powered by high-pressure steam and compressed air, work at high temperatures washing, cleaning, and pressing garments, often under very hot, slippery conditions. Chemical vapors are produced continually, and caustic chemicals are used in the cleaning process. High-temperature stills are almost continually "cooking down" cleaning solvents in order to remove impurities so that the solvents can be reused. If a mistake is made in this process—like injecting too much steam into the still—a boil-over occurs, in which boiling chemical solvent erupts out of the still and over the floor, and on anyone who happens to be standing in its way.

As a result of these hazards and the fact that chemically hazardous waste is continually produced in these stores, several government agencies (including OSHA and the EPA) have instituted strict guidelines regarding the management of these plants. For example, posters have to be placed in each store notifying employees of their right to be told what hazardous chemicals they are dealing with and the proper method for handling each chemical. Special waste-management firms must be used to pick up and properly dispose of the hazardous waste.

A chronic problem the Carters (and most other laundry owners) have is the unwillingness on the part of the cleaning–spotting workers to wear safety goggles. Not all the chemicals they use require safety goggles, but some—like the hydrofluoric acid used to remove rust stains from garments—are very dangerous. The latter is kept in special plastic containers, since it dissolves glass. The problem is that wearing safety goggles can be troublesome. They are somewhat uncomfortable, and they become smudged easily and thus cut down on visibility. As a result, Jack has always found it almost impossible to get these employees to wear their goggles.

Discussion Questions

1. How should the firm go about identifying hazardous conditions that should be rectified? Use checklists such as those in Figures 16.1, and 16.7 to list at least 10 possible dry cleaning store hazardous conditions.
2. Would it be advisable for the firm to set up a procedure for screening out accident-prone individuals? How should they do so?
3. How would you suggest the Carters get all employees to behave more safely at work? Also, how would you advise them to get those who should be wearing goggles to do so?

Experiential Activities

Activity 1. A construction worker suffocated when tumbling dirt and debris rose to his chest, creating pressure so great that he could not breathe. Other workers had warned the owner of the construction site that the trench was dangerous. Nothing, allegedly, was done and the owner was charged with manslaughter.

Protecting Employee Safety

Purpose: The purpose of this exercise is to help you develop an understanding of employee safety and the law.

Required Understanding: You are going to develop a comprehensive checklist that can be used by a supervisor to assure a safe working environment for employees.

How to Set Up the Exercise/Instructions: Divide the class into groups of 4–5 students.

1. You want to develop a safety checklist that the owner of the construction site could have used to prevent the regretful incident involving the construction worker. Make sure you are thoroughly familiar with the discussion of employee safety and the supervisor's role in safety discussed in this chapter.
2. Next, your group should reach a consensus on which questions and what steps should be included on your checklist. (Recommended: Go online and research OSHA's accident prevention steps.)
3. Hand out a typed checklist that your group has developed to each of the other groups in class.
4. Compare the checklists of all the groups. How different or similar are these lists?

Activity 2. Working individually or in groups, answer the question, "Is there such a thing as an accident-prone person?" Develop your answer using examples of actual people you know who seemed to be accident prone at some endeavor.

Activity 3. Working individually or in groups, compile a list of the factors at work or in school that create dysfunctional stress for you. What methods do you use for dealing with the stress?

Activity 4. How Safe Is My University?

Purpose: The purpose of this exercise is to give you practice in identifying unsafe conditions.

Required Understanding: You should be familiar with material covered in this chapter and the safety checklists in Figures 16.1 and 16.7.

How to Set Up the Exercise/Instructions: Divide the class into groups of four.

Assume that each group is a safety committee retained by your college or university's safety engineer to identify and report on any possible unsafe conditions in and around the school building. Each group will spend about 45 minutes in and around the building you are now in for the purpose of identifying and listing possible unsafe conditions. (Make use of the checklists in this chapter.)

Return to the class in about 45 minutes. A spokesperson for each group should list on the board the unsafe conditions you think you have identified. How many were there? Do you think these also violate OSHA standards? How would you go about checking?

Role-Playing Exercise

OSHA and the Supervisor: The Situation

The United Carpet Workers (UCW) has represented the workers in your manufacturing plant for over 15 years. As a production supervisor, your relationship with the UCW represents where "the rubber meets the road." You and the union don't always agree, but you have a contract that you both must abide by. Lately, as you approach a new contract negotiation, the union has been making your life a real misery. They are using the OSHA inspection priorities as a way to harass you and affect your supervisory job performance. The union is accomplishing this by filing imminent danger claims instead of employee complaints. This practice is keeping you in the office answering complaints instead of leading on the production floor. Also, imminent danger complaints require OSHA inspectors to come to your plant to investigate. You have a meeting with the union representative in order to discuss this situation and redirect your efforts to maintain a safe working environment for your workers.

Instructions: All students should read the situation above in addition to studying the chapter. One student will play the role of supervisor while the other will play the role of union representative. Each student should only read his or her assigned role below. The two students should engage in a 15-minute conversation.

A class discussion will follow the role-playing exercise.

Supervisor: From reading the situation, you can see what you are up against. Somehow, you must persuade the union representative not to use the OSHA law to their advantage and thus potentially endanger their own union members when facing a real safety danger. You also need to educate the union representative in what you, as the supervisor, are doing to inspect and deal with employee resistance to comply with OSHA standards.

Union Representative: Your role is to represent all of the workers in the bargaining unit, and if it takes a little arm bending, using OSHA, to control management, then so be it. You know the contract well, most likely better than management. You have been employed by this company for over 15 years and you know that wearing hard hats and eye protection is not always necessary, even if OSHA says so. Management has to respect the fact that the union is also concerned about employee safety and that you are keeping your eyes open, too.

Questions for Discussion

1. Can you see any potential legal issues as to how the union is using OSHA law to their advantage?
2. How well has the supervisor argued to the union to stop using OSHA law illegally?
3. Do you believe that there are unions in business that would use OSHA law in this way? Why?
4. What would you suggest in terms of changes in the next union–management contract that would avoid this situation in the future?

Endnotes

Chapter 1

1. This section adapted from Gary Dessler, *Management: Principles and Practices for Tomorrow's Leaders,* rev. 3rd ed. (Boston: Houghton-Mifflin, 2007), chap. 1.

2. M. A. Huselid, "The Impact of Human Resource Management Practices on Turnover, Productivity, and Corporate Financial Performance," *Academy of Management Journal* (1995): 647; SHRM® *Human Capital Benchmarking Study* (2007).

3. Peter Drucker, *An Introductory View of Management* (New York: Harper's College Press, 1977), 15.

4. Christina Cheddar, "Boardroom Vets Move to Power Technology—Sector Has Shed Founders Who Thrived in Labs as Skill Needs Change," *Wall Street Journal* (September 11, 2001): B8.

5. These are based on Henry Mintzberg, "The Manager's Job: Folklore and Fact," *Harvard Business Review* (July–August 1975): 489–561.

6. Ibid.

7. See, for example, ibid.; and Jenny McCune, "The Changemakers," *Management Review* (May 1999): 16–22.

8. Ibid.

9. John Holland, *Making Vocational Choices: A Theory of Careers* (Upper Saddle River, NJ: Prentice Hall, 1973), and http://self-directed-search.com/ (accessed September 20, 2010).

10. Edgar Schein, *Career Dynamics: Matching Individual and Organizational Needs* (Reading, MA: Addison-Wesley, 1978), 128–29. See also, J. Hempel, "How LinkedIn Will Fire Up Your Career", *Fortune* v. 161 no. 5 (April 12, 2010) p. 74–8, 80, 82; J. Wagner, "Personalize Your Career Development Plan", *Strategic Finance* v. 91 no. 9 (March 2010) p. 17–18.

11. Unless otherwise noted, the following discussion is based on Gary Yukl, *Leadership in Organizations* (Upper Saddle River, NJ: Prentice Hall, 1998), 251–55.

12. Joan Lloyd, "Derailing Your Career," *Baltimore Business Journal* 19 (October 19, 2000): 21, 33.

13. Yukl, op. cit., 252.

14. Shelley Kirkpatrick and Edwin Locke, "Leadership: Do Traits Matter?" *Academy of Management Executive* (May 1991): 49.

15. Yukl, op. cit., 253.

16. Quoted in William Holstein, "Why Big Ideas Often Fall Flat," *New York Times* (May 26, 2002): B5. See also Judith Chapman, "The Work of Managers in New Organizational Context," *Journal of Management Development* 20, no. 1 (January 2001): 55.

17. "Occupational Employment Projections 2006–2016," *Occupational Outlook Quarterly* (Spring 2008): 8–12.

18. http://online.onetcenter.org/link/summary/ 41-1011.00 (accessed May 2010).

19. Timothy Appel, "Better Off a Blue-Collar," *Wall Street Journal* (July 1, 2003): B-1.

20. "Charting the Projections: 2004–2014," *Occupational Outlook Quarterly* (Winter 2005–2006): 48–50; and http://www.bls.gov/ emp/emplabor01.pdf (accessed October 20, 2008).

21. Tony Carnevale, "The Coming Labor and Skills Shortage," *Training & Development* (January 2005): 39.

22. "Talent Management Leads in Top HR Concerns," *Compensation & Benefits Review* (May/June 2007): 12.

23. Bruce Tulgan, quoted in Stephanie Armour, "Generation Y: They've Arrived at Work with a New Attitude," *USA Today,* http://www.usatoday.com/ money/workplace/2005-11-06-gen-y_x.htm (accessed May 10, 2010).

24. Stephanie Armour, "Generation Y: They've Arrived at Work with a New Attitude," *USA Today,* http://www.usatoday.com/money/ workplace/2005-11-06-gen-y_x.htm (accessed May 10, 2010).

25. Nadira Hira, "You Raised Them, Now Manage Them," *Fortune* (May 2007): 38–46; Katheryn Tyler, "The Tethered Generation," *HR Magazine* (May 2007): 41–46; Jeffrey Zaslow, "The Most Praised

Generation Goes to Work," *Wall Street Journal* (April 20, 2007): W1, W7; T. Fallon, "Retain and Motivate the Next Generation: 7 Ways to Get the Most out of Your Millenial Workers", *Supervision* v. 70 no. 5 (May 2009) p. 5–7

26. Armour, "Generation Y: They've Arrived at Work with a New Attitude."

27. "Talent Management Leads in Top HR Concerns," *Compensation & Benefits Review* (May/June 2007): 12.

28. Jennifer Schramm, "Exploring the Future of Work: Workplace Visions," *Society for Human Resource Management*, no. 2 (2005): 6; Rainer Strack, Jens Baier, and Anders Fahlander, "Managing Demographic Risk," *Harvard Business Review* (February 2008): 119–28.

29. Michael Schroeder, "States Fight Exodus of Jobs," *Wall Street Journal,* (June 3, 2003): 84. See also, Monica Belcourt, "Outsourcing—The Benefits and the Risks," *Human Resource Management Review* 16 (2006): 69–279; D. Blanchard, "Offshoring May Have Extended the Recession", *Industry Week* v. 259 no. 8 (August 2010) p. 51–69.

30. See, for example, Michael Carrell and Everett Mann, "Defining Work-Force Diversity in Public Sector Organizations," *Public Personnel Management* 24, no. 1 (Spring 1995): 99–111; Richard Koonce, "Redefining Diversity," *Training and Development Journal* (December 2001): 22–33; Kathryn Cañas and Harris Sondak, *Opportunities and Challenges of Workplace Diversity* (Upper Saddle River, NJ: Pearson, 2008), 3–27.

31. Kerry Capell, "Zara Thrives by Breaking All the Rules," *Business Week* (October 20, 2008): 66.

32. See "Charting the Projections: 2004–2014," *Occupational Outlook Quarterly* (Winter 2005–2006), and http://www.bls.gov/news.release/ecopro.t01.htm (accessed May 10, 2010).

33. Peter F. Drucker, "The Coming of the New Organization," *Harvard Business Review on Knowledge Management* (1998): 45.

34. Taylor Cox, Jr., *Cultural Diversity in Organizations* (San Francisco, CA: Berrett-Koehler Publishers, 1993), 88.

35. Ibid., 64.

36. Ibid., 179–80.

37. J. H. Greenhaus and S. Parasuraman, "Job Performance Attributions and Career Advancement Prospects: An Examination of Gender and Race Affects," *Organizational Behavior and Human Decision Processes* 55 (July 1993): 273–98.

38. Madeline Heilman and Lois Saruwatari, "When Beauty Is Beastly: The Effects of Appearance and Sex on Evaluation of Job Applicants for Managerial and Nonmanagerial Jobs," *Organizational Behavior and Human Performance* (June 1979): 360–72. See also Tracy McDonald and Milton Hakel, "Effects of Applicant Race, Sex, Suitability, and Answers on Interviewer's Questioning Strategy and Ratings," *Personnel Psychology* (Summer 1985): 321–34; and D. Kopecki, "Women on Wall Street Fall Further Behind", *Business Week* no. 4199 (October 11–17, 2010) p. 46, 48.

39. Carol Heimowitz, "The New Diversity," *Wall Street Journal* (November 14, 2005): R1.

40. Ibid., R3.

41. David Thomas, "Diversity as Strategy," *Harvard Business Review* (September 2004): 98–104. See also J. T. Childs Jr., "Managing Global Diverity at IBM: A Global HR Topic That Has Arrived," *Human Resource Management* 44, no. 1 (Spring 2005): 73–77; and E. McKeown, "Quantifiable Inclusion Strategies", *T+D* v. 64 no. 10 (October 2010) p. 16.

42. Thomas, op. cit., 99.

43. Heimowitz, op. cit., R3.

44. Patricia Digh, "Creating a New Balance Sheet: The Need for Better Diversity Metrics," *Mosaics*, from the Society for Human Resource Management (September/October 1999): 1. For diversity management steps see Cox, *Cultural Diversity in Organizations*, 236. See also Richard Bucher, *Diversity Consciousness* (Upper Saddle River, NJ: Pearson, 2004), 109–37; and V. Myers, et. al., "The Transformational Power of a Mission-Driven Strategy: Extraordinary Diversity Management Practices and Quality of Care", *Organizational Dynamics* v. 38 no. 4 (October/December 2009) p. 297–304.

Chapter 2

1. See David Waldman, Gabriel Ramirez, Robert J. House, and Phanish Puranam, "Does Leadership Matter? CEO Leadership Attributes and Profitability Under Conditions of Perceived Incremental Uncertainty," *Academy of Management Journal* 44, no. 1 (2001): 134–43; and S.J. Peterson, et. al., "CEO Positive Psychological Traits, Transformational Leadership, and Firm

Performance in High-Technology Start-up and Established Firms", *Journal of Management* v. 35 no. 2 (April 2009) p. 348–68

2. See, for example, Gary Yukl, *Leadership in Organizations*, 3rd ed. (Upper Saddle River, NJ: Prentice Hall, 1998), 235.

3. In thinking about what it is inside leaders that make them great, experts usually talk of both traits and skills. Traits (such as self-confidence) are characteristics of the person that predispose someone to act in a particular way. Skill "refers to the ability to do something in an effective manner." Intelligence and self-confidence are examples of traits. Skills include technical skills (such as knowing how to program a computer), interpersonal skills (such as being able to empathize with other people), and conceptual skills (such as creativity and being able to solve complex problems). Yukl, op. cit., 235.

4. Ralph Stogdill, *Handbook of Leadership: A Survey of the Literature* (New York: Free Press, 1974), 81, quoted in Yukl, op. cit., 236.

5. Shelley Kirkpatrick and Edwin A. Locke, "Leadership: Do Traits Matter?" *Academy of Management Executive* (May 1991) 49.

6. Ibid., 50.

7. Except as noted, this section is based on ibid., 48–60.

8. Kim-Yin Chan and Fritz Drasgow, "Toward a Theory of Individual Differences and Leadership: Understanding the Motivation to Lead," *Journal of Applied Psychology* 86, no. 3 (2001): 481–98.

9. Kirkpatrick and Locke, op. cit., 53.

10. Jerry Useem, "What It Takes," *Fortune* (November 12, 2001): 126.

11. Ibid., 55. Note that recent research suggests, "The relationship between intelligence and leadership is considerably lower than previously thought." Timothy Judge, et al., "Intelligence and Leadership: A Quantitative Review and Test of the Theoretical Propositions," *Journal of Applied Psychology* 89, no. 3 (2004): 542–52.

12. Ibid., 5–6.

13. Niccoló Machiavelli, *The Prince*, trans. W. K. Marriott (London: J. M. Dent & Sons, 1958).

14. Chester Barnard, *The Functions of the Executive* (Cambridge, MA: Harvard University Press, 1938). See also Roger Dawson, *Secrets of Power Persuasion* (Upper Saddle River, NJ: Prentice Hall, 1992);

Sydney Finkelstein, "Power in Top Management Teams: Dimensions, Measurement, and Validation," *Academy of Management Journal* (August 1992); and Jeffrey Pfeffer, *Managing with Power: Politics and Influence in Organizations* (Boston: Harvard Business School Press, 1992).

15. See, for example, Kirkpatrick and Locke, op. cit., 49.

16. Ibid., 56.

17. See John Kotter, "What Leaders Really Do," *Harvard Business Review* (December 2001): 86–95.

18. Ralph Stogdill, *Managers, Employees, Organizations* (Columbus: Bureau of Business Research, Ohio State University, 1965).

19. Ralph Stogdill and A. E. Coons, "Leader Behavior: Its Description and Measurement" (Columbus: Bureau of Business Research, Ohio State University, 1957). See also Bernard M. Bass, *Bass & Stogdill's Handbook of Leadership: Theory, Research, & Managerial Applications*, 3rd ed. (New York: The Free Press, 1990).

20. Gary Yukl, "Towards a Behavioral Theory of Leadership," *Organizational Behavior and Human Performance* (July 1971): 414–40. See also Gary Yukl, *Leadership in Organizations*, 3rd ed. (Upper Saddle River, NJ: Prentice Hall, 1998).

21. Chester Schriesheim, Robert J. House, and Steven Kerr, "Leader Initiating Structure: A Reconciliation of Discrepant Research Results and Some Empirical Tests," *Organizational Behavior and Human Performance* (April 1976).

22. Robert Blake and Jane Mouton, *The Managerial Grid* (Houston: Gulf Publishing, 1964).

23. Hal Lancaster, "Herb Kelleher Has One Main Strategy: Treat Employees Well," *Wall Street Journal* (August 31, 1999): B1.

24. Rensis Likert, *New Patterns of Management* (New York: McGraw-Hill, 1961), 102–6.

25. Robert Day and Robert Hamblin, "Some Effects of Close and Punitive Styles of Leadership," *American Journal of Psychology* 69 (1964): 499–510. See also, H.P. Sims, et. al., "When should a leader be directive or empowering? How to develop your own situational theory of leadership", *Business Horizons* v. 52 no. 2 (March/April 2009) p. 149–58.

26. Jim Collins, "Level 5 Leadership," *Harvard Business Review* (January 2001): 67–76.

27. Daniel Goleman, "Leadership That Gets Results," *Harvard Business Review* (March–April 2000) 78; and Daniel Goleman, "What Makes a Leader?"

Harvard Business Review (November–December 1998): 90.

28. Goleman, "Leadership," 80. See also, "Hard and soft styles for leadership". *People Management* (July 1, 2010) p. 24.

29. J. M. Burns, *Leadership* (New York: Harper, 1978).

30. For a discussion, see Ronald Deluga, "Relationship of Transformational and Transactional Leadership with Employee Influencing Strategies," *Group and Organizational Studies* (December 1988): 457–58. See also D. Lindebaum, et. al., "A Critical Examination of the Relationship between Emotional Intelligence and Transformational Leadership". *Journal of Management Studies* v. 47 no. 7 (November 2010) p. 1317–42.

31. Joseph Seltzer and Bernard Bass. "Transformational Leadership: Beyond Initiation and Consideration," *Journal of Management* 4 (1990): 694. See also Bernard M. Bass, "Theory of Transformational Leadership Redux," *Leadership Quarterly* (Winter 1995): 463–78. Note that recent studies show that transformational and transactional leadership are not mutually exclusive. Many leaders seem to exhibit transformational and transactional behaviors at the same time. For example, they simultaneously provide a vision, while also offering their subordinates the prospect of rewards. Timothy Judge and Ronald Piccolo, "Transformational and Transactional Leadership: A Meta-Analytic Test of Their Relative Validity," *Journal of Applied Psychology* 89, no. 5 (2004): 755–68.

32. N. M. Tichy and M. A. Devanna, *The Transformational Leader* (New York: Wiley, 1986). See also, P. P. Fu, et. al., "Pursuit of Whose Happiness? Executive Leaders' Transformational Behaviors and Personal Values", *Administrative Science Quarterly* v. 55 no. 2 (June 2010) p. 222–54.

33. Seltzer and Bass, op. cit., 694.

34. Gary Yukl, *Leadership in Organizations*, 298–99.

35. Deluga, op. cit., 457.

36. F. J. Yammarino and B. M. Bass, "Transformational Leadership and Multiple Levels of Analysis," *Human Relations* 43 (1980): 975–995.

37. J. M. Howell and C. A. Higgins, "Champions of Technological Innovation," *Administrative Science Quarterly* 35 (1990) 317–41.

38. From Yukl, *Leadership in Organizations*, op. cit., 342.

39. C. M. Solomon, "Careers Under Glass," *Personnel Journal* 69, no. 4 (1990): 96–105. See also Alice Eagly and Linda Carli, "The Female Leadership Advantage: An Evaluation of the Evidence," *Leadership Quarterly* 14, no. 6 (December 2003) 807–34.

40. See, for example, James Bowditch and Anthony Buono, *A Primer on Organizational Behavior* (New York: John Wiley, 1994), 238.

41. Russell Kent and Sherry Moss, "Effects of Sex and Gender Role on Leader Emergence," *Academy of Management Journal* 37, no. 5 (1994) 1335–46; Jane Baack, Norma Carr-Ruffino, and Monica Pelletier, "Making It to the Top: Specific Leadership Skills," *Women in Management Review* 8, no. 2 (1993): 17–23.

42. S. M. Donnell and J. Hall, "Men and Women as Managers: A Significant Case of No Significant Difference," *Organizational Dynamics* 8 (1980): 60–77. For an interesting application, see for example, D. Kalette, "Does Leadership Need a Gender?", *National Real Estate Investor* v. 52 no. 7 (October 2010) p. 33–5.

43. M. A. Hatcher, "The Corporate Woman of the 1990s: Maverick or Innovator?" *Psychology of Women Quarterly* 5 (1991): 251–59.

44. D. G. Winter, *The Power Motive* (New York: The Free Press, 1975).

45. L. McFarland Shore and G. C. Thornton III, "Effects of Gender on Self and Supervisory Ratings," *Academy of Management Journal* 29, no. 1 (1986): 115–29; quoted in Bowditch and Buono, op. cit., 238.

46. G. H. Dobbins and S. J. Paltz, "Sex Differences in Leadership: How Real Are They?" *Academy of Management Review* 11 (1986): 118–27; R. Drazin and E. R. Auster, "Wage Differences Between Men and Women: Performance Appraisal Ratings versus Salary Allocation as the Locus of Bias," *Human Resource Management* 26 (1987): 157–68. On the other hand, see for example, H. Ibarra, et. al., "Women and the Vision Thing", *Harvard Business Review* v. 87 no. 1 (January 2009) p. 62–70. Here women scored lower in "envisioning".

47. M. Jelinek and N. J. Alder, "Women: World-Class Managers for Global Competition," *Academy of Management Executive* 2, no. 1 (1988): 11–19; J. Grant, "Women as Managers: What Can They Offer to Organizations?" *Organizational Dynamics* 16, no. 3 (1988): 56–63. On the other hand, one author suggests that women should be

more Machiavellian: "War favors the dangerous woman. Women may love peace and seek stability, but these conditions seldom serve them." From Harriet Rubin, *The Princessa: Machiavelli for Women* (New York: Doubleday/Currenly, 1997), quoted in Anne Fisher, "What Women Can Learn from Machiavelli," *Fortune* (April 1997): 162. See also Laura Bilski, "What Makes a Good Leader?" *American Bankers Association: ABA Banking Journal* 97, no. 12 (December 2005): 21–25.

48. Frederick E. Fiedler, *A Theory of Leadership Effectiveness* (New York: McGraw-Hill, 1967), 147. See also David Stauffer, "Once a Leader, Always a Leader?" *Across the Board* (April 1999): 14–19.

49. Ibid., 143.

50. See, for example, Fred Fiedler and J. E. Garcia, *New Approaches to Effective Leadership: Cognitive Resources and Organizational Performance* (New York: John Wiley and Sons, 1987); and Robert Vecchio, "Cognitive Resource Theory: Issues for Specifying a Test of the Theory," *Journal of Applied Psychology* (June 1992).

51. Robert J. House and Terence Mitchell, "Path–Goal Theory of Leadership," *Journal of Contemporary Business* 3 (Autumn 1974): 81–97; reprinted in Donald White, *Contemporary Perspectives in Organizational Behavior* (Boston: Allyn & Bacon, 1982), 228–35.

52. Robert J. House, "A Path–Goal Theory of Leader Effectiveness," *Administrative Science Quarterly* 16, no. 3 (September 1971); reprinted in Henry Tosi and W. Clay Hamner, *Organizational Behavior and Management* (Chicago: St. Clair Press, 1974), 459–68.

53. Steve Kerr and J. M. Jermier, "Substitutes for Leadership: Their Meaning and Measurement," *Organizational Behavior and Human Performance* 22 (1978): 374–403.

54. Ibid. See also Philip M. Podsakoff and Scott B. MacKenzie, "An Examination of Substitutes for Leadership Within a Levels-of-Analysis Framework," *Leadership Quarterly* (Fall 1995): 289–328. David Alcorn, "Dynamic Followership: Empowerment at Work," *Management Quarterly* (Spring 1992): 11–13.

55. Alcorn, op. cit., 11–13.

56. Jon Howell, David Bowen, Peter Dorfman, Steven Kerr, and Philip Podsakoff, "Substitutes for Leadership: Effective Alternatives to Ineffective Leadership," *Organizational Dynamics* (Summer 1990): 23.

57. Ibid.

58. Victor Vroom and Arthur Jago, "On the Validity of the Vroom-Yetton Model," *Journal of Applied Psychology* 63, no. 2 (1978): 151–62; Madeleine Heilman et al., "Reactions to Prescribed Leader Behavior as a Function of Role Perspective: The Case of the Vroom-Yetton Model," *Journal of Applied Psychology* (February 1984): 50–60. See also Donna Brown, "Why Participative Management Won't Work Here," *Management Review* (June 1992).

59. See Robert Vecchio, "Situational Leadership Theory: An Examination of a Prescriptive Theory," *Journal of Applied Psychology* (August 1987): 444–51; and Jerald Greenberg, *Managing Behavior in Organizations* (Upper Saddle River, NJ: Prentice Hall, 1996), 226.

60. Andrew DuBrin, *Leadership: Research Findings, Priorities, and Skills* (Boston: Houghton Mifflin, 1995).

61. Fiedler, op. cit., 250.

62. Richard Bucher, *Diversity Consciousness: Opening Our Minds to People, Cultures, and Opportunities* (Upper Saddle River, NJ: Pearson Prentice Hall, 2004), 132–33.

63. Ibid., 133.

64. G. B. Graen and T. A. Scandura, "Toward a Psychology of Dyadic Organizing," in *Research in Organizational Behavior*, Vol. 9, ed. L. L. Cummings and B. M. Staw (Greenwich, CT: J.A.I. Press, 1987), 208. See also David Schneider and Charles Goldwasser, "Be a Model Leader of Change," *Management Review* (March 1998): 41–48; K.S. Wilson, et. al., "What about the Leader in Leader-Member Exchange? The Impact of Resource Exchanges and Substitutability on the Leader", *The Academy of Management Review* v. 35 no. 3 (July 2010) p. 358–72, and J.D. Nahrgang, et. al., "The development of leader-member exchanges: Exploring how personality and performance influence leader and member relationships over time", *Organizational Behavior and Human Decision Processes* v. 108 no. 2 (March 2009) p. 256–66.

65. Greenberg, op. cit., 215.

66. Phillips and Bedeian, op. cit.

67. Except as noted, this section is based on Robert D. Ramsey, "Supervising Immigrant Workers," *Supervision* 62, no. 11 (2001): 13–15.

68. Luke J. Larsen, *The Foreign-Born Population in the United States: 2003*. Current Population Reports, P20-551. U.S. Census Bureau, Washington, DC, 2004.

69. Ramsey, op. cit.

Chapter 3

1. Max Bazerman, *Judgment in Managerial Decision Making* (New York: John Wiley, 1994), 3.

2. Matthew Karnitschnig and Marcus Walker, "Merkel Faces Loss of Political Clout," *Wall Street Journal* (May 24, 2010): A11.

3. "The Decider," *The Economist* (November 28, 2009): 11, 31–31.

4. As reported in Gary Yukl, *Leadership in Organizations* (Upper Saddle River, NJ: Prentice Hall, 1998), 236, 410.

5. Kathleen Melymuka, "Why Good Leaders Make Bad Decisions . . . and What You Can Do About It," *Computerworld* 43, no. 7 (February 16, 2009): 26.

6. See, for example, Herbert Simon, *The New Science of Management Decision* (Upper Saddle River, NJ: Prentice Hall, 1971), 45–47.

7. George Lowenstein, "The Creative Destruction of Decision Research," *Journal of Consumer Research* 38, no. 4 (December 2001): 499–505. See also Leigh Buchanan and Andrew O'Connell, "A Brief History of Decision Making," *Harvard Business Review* 84, no. 1 (January 2006): 32(10).

8. For a discussion, see, for example, Bazerman, op. cit., 4–5.

9. Ibid., 4.

10. John Hammond, Ralph Keeney, and Howard Raiffa, *Smart Choices* (Boston: Harvard Business School Press, 1999), 19–30.

11. Of course, this also assumes that Harold wants to stay in marketing.

12. Except as noted, the titles of the steps and the ideas for this section are based on Hammond et al., op. cit., 35–47.

13. Ibid., 47.

14. Bazerman, op. cit., 4. See also Max H. Bazerman and Dolly Chugh, "Decisions without Blinders," *Harvard Business Review* 84, no. 1 (January 2006): 88(10).

15. Based on Hammond et al., op. cit, 67–72.

16. See Bazerman, op. cit., 108.

17. Quoted from ibid., 105–106.

18. Prasad Padmanabhan, "Decision Specific Experience in Foreign Ownership and Establishment Strategies: Evidence from Japanese Firms," *Journal of International Studies* (Spring 1999): 25–27.

19. Quoted in Robert L. Heilbroner, "How to Make an Intelligent Decision," *Think* (December 1990): 2–4.

20. Ibid. See also Theodore Rubin, *Overcoming Indecisiveness: The Eight Stages of Effective Decision Making* (New York: Avon Books, 1985); Hammond et al., op. cit.; and J. Frank Yates, "Decision Management: How to Assure Better Decisions in Your Company," *Global Cosmetic Industry* 174, no. 2 (February 2006): 33(1).

21. This anecdote is quoted and paraphrased from Bill Breen, "What's Your Intuition?" *Fast Company* (September 2000): 294–95.

22. Ibid., 296.

23. Alden Hayashi, "When to Trust Your Gut," *Harvard Business Review* (February 2001): 64. See also David A. Garvin, "All the Wrong Moves," *Harvard Business Review* 84, no. 1 (January 2006): 18(9).

24. J. Wesley Hutchinson and Joseph Alba, "When Business Is a Confidence Game," *Harvard Business Review* (June 2001): 20–21. For an additional perspective see, for example, John Middlebrook and Peter Tobia, "Decision-Making in the Digital Age," *USA Today* 130, no. 2676 (September 2001): 50; and Linda Freeman, "Disney Exec Suggests Matrix for Decision-Making," *Credit Union Journal* 5, no. 35 (September 3, 2001): 7.

25. Robert Cross and Susan Brodt, "How Assumptions of Consensus Undermined Decision-Making," *MIT Sloan Management Review* 42, no. 2 (Winter 2001): 86.

26. See, for example, Lisa Burke and Monica Miller, "Taking the Mystery out of Intuitive Decision-Making," *Academy of Management Executive* 13, no. 4 (1999), and I. Kutschera, et. al., "Implications of Intuition for Strategic Thinking: Practical Recommendations for Gut Thinkers", *Advanced Management Journal* v. 74 no. 3 (Summer 2009) p. 12–20.

27. Kenneth Laudon and Jane Price Laudon, *Management Information Systems* (Upper Saddle River, NJ: Prentice Hall, 1996), 125. See also Bob F. Holder, "Intuitive Decision Making," *CMA* (October 1995): 6.

28. See, for example, Christopher W. Allinson and John Hayes, "The Cognitive Style Index: A Measure of Intuition—Analysis for Organizational Research," *Journal of Management Studies* (January 1996): 119–35, and E. Salas, et. al., "Expertise-Based Intuition and Decision Making in Organizations", *Journal of Management* v. 36 no. 4 (July 2010) p. 941–7.

29. This and the following guideline are from Heilbroner, op. cit.

30. Helga Drummond, "Analysis and Intuition in Technological Choice: Lessons of Taurus," *International Journal of Technology Management* (April 1999): 459–67.

31. For an additional perspective see, for example, Ruth Weiss, "How to Foster Creativity at Work," *Training & Development* (February 2001): 61–67; A. Muoio, "Where Do Great Ideas Come From?" *Fast Company* (January–February 2000): 149–64: Michael Michalko, "Jumpstart Your Company's Creativity," *Supervision* 62, no. 1 (January 2001): 14; and F. Gino, et. al., "First, get your feet wet: The effects of learning from direct and indirect experience on team creativity", *Organizational Behavior and Human Decision Processes* v. 111 no. 2 (March 2010) p. 102–15.

32. Gary Dessler and Jean Phillips, *Managing Now* (Boston: Cengage, 2008), Chapter 1.

33. Yukl, *Leadership in Organizations*, 133.

34. Lowenstein, op. cit.

35. Lester Lefton and Laura Valvatne, *Mastering Psychology* (Boston: Allyn & Bacon, 1992), 248–49. See also Daphne Main and Joyce Lambert, "Improving Your Decision Making," *Business and Economic Review* (April 1998): 9–12; and John Hammond, Ralph L. Keeney, and Howard Raiffa, "The Hidden Traps in Decision Making," *Harvard Business Review* 84, no. 1 (January 2006): 1, 18(8).

36. In fact, this apparently is common. Alleged harassers often say "Yes, I did it, but . . .," and then explain they meant no harm. However, intent is usually not the issue to the court. The issues are whether the conduct was unwelcome and objectively offensive to a reasonable person. Jonathan Segal, "I Did It, But . . . : Employees May Be as Innocent as They Say, but Still Guilty of Harassment," *HR Magazine* (March 2008): 91.

37. Maria Rotundo et al., "A Meta-Analysic Review of Gender Differences in Perceptions of Sexual Harassment," *Journal of Applied Psychology* 86, no. 5 (2001): 914–22. See also Nathan Bowling and Terry Beehr, "Workplace Harassment from the Victim's Perspective: A Theoretical Model and Meta-Analysis," *Journal of Applied Psychology* 91, no. 5 (2006): 998–1012.

38. From Armando X. Estrada and Colin R. Harbke, "Gender and Ethnic Differences in Perceptions of Equal Opportunity Climate and Job Outcomes of US Army Reserve Component Personnel," *International Journal of Intercultural Relations* 32, no. 5 (September 2008): 466–78.

39. "Examining Unwelcome Conduct in a Sexual Harassment Claim," *BNA Fair Employment Practices* (October 19, 1995): 124. See also Michael Zugelder et al., "An Affirmative Defense to Sexual Harassment by Managers and Supervisors: Analyzing Employer Liability and Protecting Employee Rights in the US," *Employee Responsibilities and Rights* 18, no. 2 (2006): 111–22.

Chapter 4

1. Dominique Morisano et al., "Setting, Elaborating, and Reflecting on Personal Goals Improves Academic Performance," *Journal of Applied Psychology* 95, no. 2 (2010): 255–64.

2. http://www.bp.com/genericarticle.do?categoryId=2012968&contentId=7061663 (accessed June 2010).

3. Ibid.

4. See, for example, Gary Latham and Gary Yukl, "A Review of Research on the Application of Goal Setting in Organizations," *Academy of Management Journal* 18, no. 4 (1964): 824. See also Gary Latham and Terrance A. Mitchell, "Importance of Participative Goal Setting and Anticipated Rewards on Goal Difficulty and Job Performance," *Journal of Applied Psychology* 63 (1978): 163–71; and Sandra Hart, William Moncrief, and A. Parasuraman, "An Empirical Investigation of Sales People's Performance, Effort, and Selling Method During a Sales Contest," *Journal of the Academy of Marketing Science* (Winter 1989): 29–39. Governments are even starting to use more citizen participation to win approval for budget cuts; see for example, J. Borget, "Provo Brings Employees and Citizens Together to Identify Budget Cuts", *Government Finance Review* v. 26 no. 4 (August 2010) p. 59–61.

5. See, for example, Latham and Yukl, op. cit. See also Latham and Mitchell, op. cit.; and Hart, Moncrief, and Parasuraman, op. cit.; and Libby, op. cit.

6. These are based on Gary Latham, Terence Mitchell, and Denise Dorsett, "Importance of Participative Goal Setting and Anticipated Rewards on Goal Difficulty and Job Performance," *Journal of Applied Psychology* 63 (1978): 170; John Wagner III, "Cognitive and Motivational Frameworks in U.S. Research on Participation: A Meta-Analysis of Primary Effects," *Journal of Organizational Behavior* (January 1997): 49–66; Robert Renn, "Further Examination of the Measurement Properties of Leiter & McGannon's 1986 Goal Acceptance and Goal Commitment Scales," *Journal of Occupational and Organizational Psychology* (March 1999): 107–14.

7. www.mygoals.com/content/action-plan.HTML (accessed June 2010).

8. Ray Faidley, "Keys to Success," *Supervision* (2010).

9. Ibid.

10. John Chambers, Santinder Mullick, and Donald Smith, "How to Choose the Right Forecasting Technique," *Harvard Business Review* (July–August 1971): 45–74. See also Moore, *Handbook of Business Forecasting* (New York: Harper Information, 1990), 265–90; and John Mentzer et al., "Benchmarking Sales Forecasting Management," *Business Horizons* (May–June 1999): 48–57. This study of 20 leading U.S. firms found widespread dissatisfaction regarding their current sales forecasting techniques.

11. E. Jerome McCarthy and William Perreault Jr., *Basic Marketing* (Homewood, IL: Irwin, 1990), 131–2; for an application, see for example, P. Vicente, et. al., "Marketing Research With Telephone Surveys: Is It Time to Change?", *Journal of Global Marketing* v. 23 no. 4 (September/October 2010) p. 321–32.

12. Kenneth Laudon and Jane Laudon, *Management Information Systems* (Upper Saddle River, NJ: Prentice Hall, 1998), 57.

13. Janet Perna, "Reinventing How We Do Business," *Vital Speeches of the Day* 67, no. 19 (July 15, 2001): 587–91.

14. Based on "Case Study JetBlue," *Flight International* (April 9, 2002): 39; Sally Donnelly, "Blue Skies," *Time* 158, no. 4 (July 30, 2001): 24–27; Katherine Yung, "Collapse of Two Startup Carriers Puts Focus on Frontier, JetBlue Airlines," *Knight-Ridder/Tribune Business News* (December 24, 2000): item 0036000a; Jeremy Kahn, "Air Startups Hit Unexpected Turbulence," *Fortune* 143, no. 2 (January 22, 2001): 42; Joan Feldman, "JetBlue Loves New York," *Air Transport World* (June 2001): 78; and "JetBlue Airways Corp. Signs Contract with Port Authority of New York and New Jersey," *Airline Industry Information* (November 29, 2005).

Chapter 5

1. Kenneth Merchant, "The Control Function of Management," *Sloan Management Review* (Summer 1982): 44.

2. This section is based on William Newman, *Constructive Control* (Upper Saddle River, NJ: Prentice Hall, 1995), 6–9.

3. Melanie Warner, "Confessions of a Control Freak," *Fortune* (September 4, 2000): 130–40.

4. Thomas Connellan, *How to Improve Human Performance: Behaviorism in Business and Industry* (New York: Harper & Row, 1978), 68–73.

5. This classification is based on Robert Simons, *Levers of Control: How Managers Use Innovative Control Systems to Drive Strategic Renewal* (Boston: Harvard Business School Press, 1995), 80.

6. Daniel Wren, *The Evolution of Management Thought* (John Wiley & Sons, 1994), 115.

7. Based on Kenneth Merchant, *Modern Management Control Systems* (Upper Saddle River, NJ: Prentice Hall, 1998), 642.

8. Ibid., 542–45.

9. Sydney Baxendale, "Activity Based Costing for the Small Business: A Primer," *Business Horizons* 44, no. 1 (January 2001): 61. For another example, see F. Öker, et. al., "Time-Driven Activity-Based Costing: An Implementation in a Manufacturing Company", *Journal of Corporate Accounting & Finance* v. 22 no. 1 (November/December 2010) p. 75–92.

10. Peter Brewer, "Putting Strategy into the Balanced Scorecard," *Strategic Finance* 83, no. 7 (January 2002): 44–52. See also Michael Mankin and Richard Steele, "Turning Great Strategy into Great Performance," *Harvard Business Review* (July/August 2005): 65–72; and T.L. Albright, et. al., "How to Transition from Assessing Performance to Enhancing Performance With Balanced Scorecard Goal Action Plans", *Journal of Corporate Accounting & Finance* v. 21 no. 6 (September/October 2010) p. 69–74.

11. See, for example, Matt Hicks, "Tuning In to the Big Picture for a Better Business," *PC Week* (July 15,

1999): 69. See also Mary Sumner, *Enterprise Resource Planning* (Upper Saddle River, NJ: Pearson Education, 2005).

12. "The Software War," *Fortune* (December 7, 1998): 102.

13. Robin Cooper and Tobert Kaplan, "The Promise and Peril of Integrated Costs Systems," *Harvard Business Review* (July–August 1998): 109. See also "Midsize Company Turns to Process-Driven ERP System; Biotech Firm Rolls Out ERP System from Exact Software in 18 Months to 48 Offices Worldwide," *Information Week*, no. 9750-6874 (December 23, 2004).

14. Hicks, op. cit.

15. Simons, op. cit., 81.

16. Jonathon Rockoff, "J&J Is Accused of Kickbacks to Omnicare on Drug Sales," *Wall Street Journal* (January 16–17, 2010): B1, B6.

17. Jeffrey Stanton and Janet Barnes-Farrell, "Effects of Electronic Performance Monitoring on Personal Control, Task Satisfaction, and Task Performance," *Journal of Applied Psychology* (December 1996): 738. See also Paul Greenlaw, "The Impact of Federal Legislation to Limit Electronic Monitoring," *Public Personnel Management* (Summer 1997): 227–45.

18. Norihiko Shirouzu and Jon Bigness, "7-Eleven Operators Resist System to Monitor Managers," *Wall Street Journal* (June 16, 1997): B1–B6.

19. The following, except as noted, is based on Kenneth Merchant, *Control in Business Organizations* (Boston: Pitman, 1985), 71–120. See also Robert Kaplan, "New Systems for Measurement and Control," *The Engineering Economist* (Spring 1991): 201–18.

20. The studies cited in this feature are all discussed in Rupa Banerjee, "An Examination of Factors Affecting Perception of Workplace Discrimination," *Journal of Labor Research* 29, no. 4 (Fall 2008): 380–401.

21. "Ethics Policies Are Big with Employers, But Workers See Small Impact on the Workplace," *BNA Bulletin to Management* (June 29, 2000): 201.

22. From Guy Brumback, "Managing Above the Bottom Line of Ethics," *Supervisory Management* (December 1993): 12.

23. "Mass Layoffs at Lowest Level Since July 2008, BLS Says," *BNA Bulletin to Management* (January 12, 2010): 13.

24. Gary Dessler, "How to Earn Your Employees' Commitment," *Academy of Management Executive* 13, no. 2 (1999): 58–67. For other reviews see James McElroy, "Managing Workplace Commitment by Putting People First," *Human Resource Management Review* 11 (2001): 329–34; and K. Kwon, et. al., "High Commitment HR Practices and Top Performers: Impacts on Organizational Commitment", *Management International Review* v. 50 no. 1 (2010) p. 57–80.

25. Rosabeth Moss Kanter, *Commitment and Community* (Cambridge, MA: Harvard University Press, 1972), 24–25.

26. Abraham Maslow, *Motivation and Personality* (New York: Harper & Row, 1954), 336.

27. Dessler, "How to Earn Your Employees' Commitment," personal interview (March 1992).

Chapter 6

1. Rob Walker, "Down on the Farm," *Fast Company* (February–March 1997): 112–22.

2. Jay Galbraith, "Organizational Design: An Information Processing View," *Interfaces* 4, no. 3 (1974): 28 36; and Jay Galbraith, *Organizational Design* (Reading, MA: Addison-Wesley, 1977). See also Henry Mintzberg, *Structures in Fives: Designing Effective Organizations* (Upper Saddle River, NJ: Prentice Hall, 1983), 4–9; and J. R. Galbraith, "The Multi-Dimensional and Reconfigurable Organization", *Organizational Dynamics* v. 39 no. 2 (April/June 2010) p. 115–25.

3. Except as noted, this section is based on Carl Rodrigues, "Fayol's 14 Principles of Management Then and Now: A Framework for Managing Today's Organizations Effectively," *Management Decision* 39, no. 10 (2001): 80–89.

4. Gary Yukl, *Leadership and Organizations* (Upper Saddle River, NJ: Prentice Hall, 1998), 47.

5. Ibid., 274.

6. These principles are based on Stephen Robbins and Philip Hunsaker, *Training in Interpersonal Skills* (Upper Saddle River, NJ: Prentice Hall, 1996), 91–95; and David Whetter and Kim Cameron, *Developing Management Skills* (Upper Saddle River, NJ: Prentice Hall, 2002), 435.

7. Larry Bossidy, "The Job No CEO Should Delegate," *Harvard Business Review*, March 2001, 47–49.

8. Suling Zhang, Marilyn Tremaine, Rich Egan, Allen Milewski, Patrick O'Sullivan, and Jerry Fjermestad,

"Occurrence and Effects of Leader Delegation in Virtual Software Teams," *International Journal of e-Collaboration* 5, no. 1 (2009): 47–68.

9. Tom Hamburger et al., "Auditor Who Questioned Accounting for Enron Speaks to Investigators," *Wall Street Journal* (April 1, 2001): C1.

10. See, for example, Henri Fayol, *General and Industrial Management,* trans. Constance Storrs (London: Sir Isaac Putnam, 1949).

11. Frederick Morgeson and Michael Campion, "Accuracy in Job Analysis: Toward an Inference Based Model," *Journal of Organizational Behavior* 21, no. 7 (November 2000): 819–27. See also Frederick Morgeson and Stephen Humphrey, "The Work Design Questionnaire (WDQ): Developing and Validating a Comprehensive Measure for Assessing Job Design and the Nature of Work," *Journal of Applied Psychology* 91, no. 6 (2006): 1321–39.

12. Jeffrey Shippmann et al., "The Practice of Competency Modeling," *Personnel Psychology* 53, no. 3 (2000): 703.

13. Ibid.

14. Ibid., 18.

15. For a complete list, see, for example, http://www.humanresources.hrvinet.com/contents-of-a-job-specification/ (accessed January 19, 2010).

Chapter 7

1. Lauren Weber, "Jury Awards Worker $7.5 Million in Wal-Mart Disability Discrimination," *Knight-Ridder/Tribune Business News* (February 25, 2005).

2. http://www.mmmglawblog.com/tp-080318191354/post-080702212644.shtml (accessed March 27, 2010). This chapter is adapted from Gary Dessler, *Human Resource Management* (Upper Saddle River, NJ: Pearson Prentice Hall, 2011) 30–69.

3. In another case, a supervisor with an alleged history of bias at a Coca-Cola bottling plant apparently enmeshed his employer in a discrimination suit when he fired a black subordinate. Mark A. Hofmann, "High Court to Rule on Supervisor Bias Case," *Business Insurance* 41, no. 3 (January 15, 2007): 1, 21.

4. Note that private employers are not bound by the U.S. Constitution.

5. Based on or quoted from *Principles of Employment Discrimination Law* (Washington, DC: International Association of Official Human Rights Agencies). See also Bruce Feldacker, *Labor Guide to Labor Law* (Upper Saddle River, NJ: Prentice Hall, 2000); "EEOC Attorneys Highlight How Employers Can Better Their Nondiscrimination Practices," *BNA Bulletin to Management* (July 20, 2008): 233; and http://www.eeoc.gov (accessed December 23, 2010). Employment discrimination law is a changing field, and the appropriateness of the rules, guidelines, and conclusions in this chapter and book may also be affected by factors unique to the employer's operation. They should be reviewed by the employer's attorney before implementation.

6. James Higgins, "A Manager's Guide to the Equal Employment Opportunity Laws," *Personnel Journal* 55, no. 8 (August 1976): 406. For guidelines also see, www.eeoc.gov, accessed December 23, 2010.

7. The Equal Employment Opportunity Act of 1972, Subcommittee on Labor of the Committee of Labor and Public Welfare, United States Senate, March 1972, p. 3. In general, it is not discrimination, but unfair discrimination against a person merely because of that person's race, age, sex, national origin, or religion that is forbidden by federal statutes. In the federal government's *Uniform Employee Selection Guidelines,* unfair discrimination is defined as follows: "Unfairness is demonstrated through a showing that members of a particular interest group perform better or poorer on the job than their scores on the selection procedure (test, etc.) would indicate through comparison with how members of the other groups performed." For a discussion of the meaning of fairness, see James Ledvinka, "The Statistical Definition of Fairness in the Federal Selection Guidelines and Its Implications for Minority Employment," *Personnel Psychology* 32 (August 1979): 551–62. In summary, a selection device (such as a test) may discriminate—for example, between low performers and high performers. However, unfair discrimination—discrimination that is based solely on the person's race, age, sex, national origin, or religion—is illegal.

8. "Restructured, Beefed Up OFCCP May Shift Policy Emphasis, Attorney Says," *BNA Bulletin to Management* (August 18, 2009): 257.

9. Note that the U.S. Supreme Court (in *General Dynamics Land Systems Inc.* v. *Cline,* 2004) held that the ADEA does *not* protect younger workers

from being treated worse than older ones. "High Court: ADEA Does Not Protect Younger Workers Treated Worse Than Their Elders," *BNA Bulletin to Management* 55, no. 10 (March 4, 2004): 73–80. The U.S. Supreme Court recently held that the plaintiff must show that age was the determining factor in the employer's personnel action. See "Justices, 5–4, Reject Burden Shifting," *BNA Bulletin to Management* (June 20, 2009): 199.

10. Nancy Woodward, "Pregnancy Discrimination Grows," *HR Magazine* (July 2005): 79.

11. http://www.uniformguidelines.com/ uniformguidelines.html (accessed November 23, 2007).

12. See, for example, Gillian Flynn, "The Maturing of the ADEA," *Workforce Management* (October 2002): 86–87.

13. *Griggs* v. *Duke Power Company,* 3FEP cases 175.

14. IOFEP cases 1181.

15. Feldacker, *Labor Guide to Labor Law,* 513.

16. "The Eleventh Circuit Explains Disparate Impact, Disparate Treatment," *BNA Fair Employment Practices* (August 17, 2000): 102. See also Kenneth York, "Disparate Results in Adverse Impact Tests: The 4/5ths Rule and the Chi Square Test," *Public Personnel Management* 31, no. 2 (Summer 2002): 253–62, and M. Ouyang, "A Look at Disparate Treatment Law After Gross v. FBL Financial Services, Inc.", *Employee Relations Law Journal* v. 35 no. 4 (Spring 2010) p. 61–71.

17. Larry Drake and Rachel Moskowitz, "Your Rights in the Workplace," *Occupational Outlook Quarterly* (Summer 1997): 19–20.

18. Richard Wiener et al., "The Fit and Implementation of Sexual Harassment Law to Workplace Evaluations," *Journal of Applied Psychology* 87, no. 4 (2002): 747–64.

19. http://www.eeoc.gov/types/sexual_harassment.html (accessed April 24, 2009).

20. Edward Felsenthal, "Justice's Ruling Further Defines Sexual Harassment," *Wall Street Journal* (March 5, 1998): B1, B5. Similarly, a series of compliments and "requests for a hug" were not sufficient to rise to the level of sexual harassment in one case involving a female supervisor and her female subordinate. "Compliments, Request for Hug Were Not Harassment by Female Supervisor, Court Says," *Human Resources Report, BNA* (November 20, 2003): 1193.

21. Hilary Gettman and Michele Gelfand, "When the Customer Shouldn't Be King: Antecedents and Consequences of Sexual Harassment by Clients and Customers," *Journal of Applied Psychology* 92, no. 3 (2007): 757–70.

22. See Mindy D. Bergman et al., "The (Un)reasonableness of Reporting: Antecedents and Consequences of Reporting Sexual Harassment," *Journal of Applied Psychology* 87, no. 2 (2002): 230–42; see also W. Kirk Turner and Christopher Thrutchley, "Employment Law and Practices Training: No Longer the Exception—It's the Rule," *Society for Human Resource Management Legal Report* (July–August 2002): 1–2.

23. See the discussion in "Examining Unwelcome Conduct in Sexual Harassment Claim," *BNA Fair Employment Practices* (October 19, 1995): 124. See also Molly Bowers et al., "Just Cause in the Arbitration of Sexual Harassment Cases," *Dispute Resolution Journal* 55, no. 4 (November 2000): 40–55.

24. http://www.eeoc.gov/ (accessed November 11, 2007).

25. Shereen Bingham and Lisa Scherer, "The Unexpected Effects of a Sexual Education Program," *Journal of Applied Behavioral Science* 37, 2 (June 2001): 125–53.

26. Jennifer Berdahl and Celia Moore, "Workplace Harassment: Double Jeopardy for Minority Women," *Journal of Applied Psychology* 91, no. 2 (2006): 426–36.

27. Chelsea Willness, et al., "A Meta-Analysis of the Antecedents and Consequences of Workplace Sexual Harassment," *Personnel Psychology* 60, no. 60 (2007): 127–62.

28. Lilia Cortina and S. Arzu Wasti, "Profile to Coping: Response to Sexual Harassment Across Persons, Organizations, and Cultures," *Journal of Applied Psychology* 90, no. 1 (2005): 182–92.

29. Bergman et al., op. cit., 237.

30. Maria Rotundo et al., "A Meta-Analytic Review of Gender Differences in Perceptions of Sexual Harassment," *Journal of Applied Psychology* 86, no. 5 (2001): 914–22. See also Nathan Bowling and Terry Beehr, "Workplace Harassment from the Victim's Perspective: A Theoretical Model and Meta-Analysis," *Journal of Applied Psychology* 91, no. 5 (2006): 998–1012.

31. Jennifer Berdahl and Karl Aquino, "Sexual Behavior at Work: Fun or Folly?" *Journal of Applied Psychology* 94, no. 1 (2009): 34–47.

32. Jennifer Berdahl, "The Sexual Harassment of Uppity Women," *Journal of Applied Psychology* 92, no. 2 (2007): 425–37.

33. Michael Bradford, "Culture of Consideration Can Lessen Harassment, Discrimination Claims," *Business Insurance* 40, no. 26 (June 26, 2006): 4, 6.

34. Ibid.

35. Ibid.

36. Elliot H. Shaller and Dean Rosen, "A Guide to the EEOC's Final Regulations on the Americans with Disabilities Act," *Employee Relations* 17, no. 3 (Winter 1991–1992); and http://www.eeoc.gov/ada/ (accessed November 20, 2007).

37. On February 1, 2001, President George W. Bush announced his New Freedom Initiative to promote the full participation of people with disabilities in all areas of society.

38. Shaller and Rosen, "A Guide to the EEOC's Final Regulations on the Americans with Disabilities Act," 408. The ADEA does not just protect against intentional discrimination (disparate treatment). Under the Supreme Court's *Smith v. Jackson, Miss.* decision, it also covers employer practices that seem neutral but that actually bear more heavily on older workers (disparate impact). "Employees Need Not Show Intentional Bias to Bring Claims under ADEA, High Court Says," *BNA Bulletin to Management* 56, no. 14 (April 5, 2005): 105.

39. Shaller and Rosen, op. cit., 409.

40. "EEOC Guidance on Dealing with Intellectual Disabilities," *Workforce Management* (March 2005): 16.

41. James McDonald, Jr., "The Americans with Difficult Personalities Act," *Employee Relations Law Journal* 25, no. 4 (Spring 2000): 93–107.

42. See, for example, Paul Starkman, "The ADA's 'Essential Job Function' Requirements: Just How Essential Does an Essential Job Function Have to Be?" *Employee Relations Law Journal* 26, no. 4 (Spring 2001): 43–102, and "Plaintiff's Statements on Social Security and State Disability Forms That He Was Disabled Did Not Bar His Claim That He Was Able to Perform Essential Elements of His Job", *Employee Benefit Plan Review* v. 64 no. 12 (June 2010) p. 18–19.

43. "No Sitting for Store Greeter," *BNA Fair Employment Practices* (December 14, 1995): 150.

44. M. P. McQueen, "Workplace Disabilities Are on the Rise," *Wall Street Journal* (May 1, 2007): A1.

45. "Odds Against Getting Even Longer in ADA Cases," *BNA Bulletin to Management* (August 20, 2000): 229. See also Barbara Lee, "The Implications of ADA Litigation for Employers: A Review of Federal Appellate Court Decisions," *Human Resource Management* 40, no. 1 (Spring 2001): 35–50.

46. "Supreme Court Says Manual Task Limitation Needs Both Daily Living, Workplace Impact," *BNA Fair Employment Practices* (January 17, 2002): 8.

47. The EEOC's recent implementing rules add sitting, reaching, and interacting with others to the number of major life activities. "EEOC OKs Proposed Rule to Implement ADA Amendments Act," *BNA Bulletin to Management* (September 20, 2009): 303.

48. Lawrence Postol, "ADAAA Will Result in Renewed Emphasis on Reasonable Accommodations," *Society for Human Resource Management Legal Report* (January 2009): 1–3.

49. "Airline Erred in Giving Test Before Making Formal Offer," *BNA Bulletin to Management* (March 15, 2005): 86.

50. Joe Mullich, "Hiring Without Limits," *Workforce Management* (June 2004): 52–58.

51. Chris Reiter, "New Technology Aims to Improve Internet Access for the Impaired," *Wall Street Journal* (September 22, 2005): 4–6.

52. IOFEP cases 1181. See also Mullich, op. cit.

53. Unless otherwise noted, these are adapted from Wayne Barlow and Edward Hane, "A Practical Guide to the Americans with Disabilities Act," *Personnel Journal* 72 (June 1992): 59.

54. "Tips for Employers with Asymptomatic HIV-Positive Employees," *BNA Fair Employment Practices* (November 27, 1997): 141.

55. The timing of any medical test is important: In the event the hiring employer rescinds an offer after the medical exam, the applicant must be able to unambiguously identify the reason for the rejection as being medical. In one case, the courts found that American Airlines had not made a "real" offer to three candidates before requiring them to take their medical exams, because (even if they passed the medical exam) the offer was still contingent on American checking their references. The medical exams showed the candidates had HIV, and American rescinded their offers. This left open the question of whether it was the exams or the reference checks that torpedoed the offers, and

American lost the case. "Airline Erred in Giving Test Before Making Formal Offer," *BNA Bulletin to Management* (March 15, 2005): 86.

56. Similar limitations apply to medical exams for *current* employees. In one case, superiors ordered a Chicago police officer to take a blood test to determine if the level of Prozac his physician prescribed would seriously impair his ability to do his job. At the time, the officer had not engaged in any behavior that suggested any performance problems. The court said the blood test was therefore not job related and violated the ADA's prohibition against inquiries into the nature or severity of an individual's disability. *Krocka v. Bransfield*, DC N111, #95C627 (June 24, 1997); reviewed in "Test for Prozac Violates ADA," *BNA Fair Employment Practices* (August 7, 1997): 91. See also Sue Willman, "Tips for Minimizing Abuses of the Americans with Disabilities Act," *Society for Human Resource Management Legal Report* (January–February 2003): 8.

57. Elliot Shaller, "Reasonable Accommodation Under the Americans with Disabilities Act: What Does It Mean," *Employee Relations Law Journal* 16, no. 4 (Spring 1991): 445–446. See also, "Circuit Court Decides That ADA Can Obligate Employer to Accommodate Employee's Disability-Related Difficulties in Getting to Work, If Reasonable", *Employee Benefit Plan Review* v. 65 no. 1 (July 2010) p. 17–18.

58. Lee, op. cit.

59. Timothy Bland, "The Supreme Court Focuses on the ADA," *HR Magazine* (September 1999): 42–46. See also James Hall and Diane Hatch, "Supreme Court Decisions Require ADA Revision," *Workforce* (August 1999): 60–66. Note also that courts traditionally defined "disabilities" quite narrowly. Employers may therefore require that the employee provide documentation of the disorder, and assess what effect that disorder has on the employee's job performance. Supervisors should therefore ask questions such as: Does the employee have a disability that substantially limits a major life activity? Is the employee qualified to do the job? Can the employee perform the essential functions of the job? Can any reasonable accommodation be provided without creating an undue hardship on the employer?

60. Mark Lengnick-Hall et al., "Overlooked and Underutilized: People with Disabilities Are an Untapped Human Resource," *Human Resource Management* 47, no. 2 (Summer 2008): 255–73.

61. Susan Wells, "Counting on Workers with Disabilities," *HR Magazine* (April 2008): 45. Similarly, Verizon Wireless has a formal program aimed at assisting current employees to better manage a transition from healthy to disabled. For example, they train supervisors to identify potentially disability-related deterioration in their employees' performance and to speak with these employees to try to identify what the issues are. If it becomes necessary for an employee to take a disability leave, the program encourages the employee to remain in contact with Verizon's HR professionals and to work with them to set realistic return dates. J. Adam Shoemaker, "A Welcome Back for Workers with Disabilities," *HR Magazine* (October 2009): 30–32.

62. http://www.eeoc.gov/press/2-25-09.html (accessed April 3, 2009).

63. Bill Leonard, "Bill to Ban Sexual Orientation Bias Introduced," *HRMagazine* 54, no. 8 (August 2009): 18.

64. Judy Greenwald, "Ruling Opens Door to Gender Stereotyping Suits," *Business Insurance* 43, no. 31 (September 7, 2009): 3.

65. http://employment.findlaw.com/employment/ employment-employee-discrimination-harassment/employment-employee-gay-lesbian-discrimination.html.

66. http://www.leg.state.fl.us/Statutes/index.cfm?App_mode= Display_Statute&Search_String=&URL=Ch0448/ SEC07.HTM&Title=-%3E2009-%3ECh0448-%3ESection%2007#0448.07, accessed January 22, 2011.

67. http://www.nyc.gov/html/cchr/.

68. John Klinefelter and James Thompkins, "Adverse Impact in Employment Selection," *Public Personnel Management* (May/June 1976): 199–204. For a recent discussion, see, for example, http://www.hr-guide.com/data/G702.htm (accessed November 21, 2007).

69. "Eighth Circuit OKs $3.4 Million EEOC Verdict Relating to Pre-Hire Strength Testing Rules," *BNA Bulletin to Management* (November 28, 2006): 377.

70. "Eleventh Circuit Explains Disparate Impact, Disparate Treatment," op. cit., 102.

71. http://www.foxnews.com/story/0,2933,517334,00.html (accessed January 7, 2010).

72. *U.S.* v. *Bethlehem Steel Company,* 3FEP cases 589.

73. *Spurlock* v. *United Airlines,* 5FEP cases 17.

74. Ledvinka and Gatewood, "EEO Issues with Preemployment Inquiries," 22–26.

75. Howard Anderson and Michael Levin-Epstein, *Primer of Equal Employment Opportunity* (Washington, DC: The Bureau of National Affairs, 1982), p. 28.

76. "Many Well-Intentioned HR Policies Hold Legal Headaches, Consultant Says," *BNA Bulletin to Management* (February 17, 2000): 47.

77. Jenessa Shapiro, et al., "Expectations of Obese Trainees: How Stigmatized Trainee Characteristics Influence Training Effectiveness," *Journal of Applied Psychology* 92, no. 1 (2007): 239–49. See also Lisa Finkelstein et al., "Bias Against Overweight Job Applicants: Further Explanations of When and Why," *Human Resource Management* 46, no. 2 (Summer 2007): 203–22.

78. "American Airlines, Worldwide Flight Sued by EEOC over Questioning of Applicants," *BNA Fair Employment Practices* (October 12, 2000): 125.

79. This is based on Anderson and Levin-Epstein, *Primer of Equal Opportunity*, 93–97.

80. Matthew Miklaue, "Sorting Out a Claim of Bias," *Workforce* 80, no. 6 (June 2001): 102–103. Dress codes are a different matter. For example, the U.S. Court of Appeals for the Third Circuit recently upheld the city of Philadelphia's decision to refuse to relax its dress code to permit a female Muslim police officer to wear a headscarf while in uniform. "City Can Bar Muslim Police Woman from Wearing Scarf," *BNA Bulletin to Management* (April 20, 2009): 126.

81. Mary-Kathryn Zachary, "Threats and Retaliation," *Supervision* 70, no. 5 (May 2009): 22–26.

82. Ibid.

83. In 2007, the U.S. Supreme Court in *Ledbetter v. Goodyear Tire & Rubber Company* held that employees claiming Title VII pay discrimination must file their claims within 180 days of when they first receive the allegedly discriminatory pay. In 2009, Congress formulated and the president signed new legislation enabling employees to file claims at any time, as long as the person is still receiving a paycheck.

84. http://eeoc.gov/eeoc/initiatives/e-race/index.cfm.

85. "EEOC Has 18 Nationwide, 300 Local Accords with Employers to Mediate Job Bias Claims Charges," *BNA Human Resources Report* (October 13, 2003): H-081.

86. Timothy Bland, "Sealed Without a Kiss," *HR Magazine* (October 2000): 85–92.

87. "Conducting Effective Investigations of Employee Bias Complaints," *BNA Fair Employment Practices* (July 13, 1995): 81.

88. Jonathan Ziegert and Paul Hanges, "Employment Discrimination: The Role of Implicit Attitudes, Motivation, and a Climate for Racial Bias," *Journal of Applied Psychology* 90, no. 3 (2005): 553–62.

89. Frank Jossi, "Reporting Race," *HR Magazine* (September 2000): 87–94.

90. U.S. Equal Employment Opportunity Commission, *Affirmative Action and Equal Employment* (Washington, DC: January 1974). See also David Kravitz and Steven Klineberg, "Reactions to Two Versions of Affirmative-Action Among Whites, Blacks, and Hispanics," *Journal of Applied Psychology* 85, no. 4 (2000): 597–611.

91. http://newsfeedresearcher.com/data/articles_n17/tests-city-court.html (accessed April 24, 2009).

92. David Harrison et al., "Understanding Attitudes Toward Affirmative Action Programs in Employment: Summary and Meta-Analysis of 35 Years of Research," *Journal of Applied Psychology* 91, no. 5 (2006): 1031–36.

Chapter 8

1. Based on Samuel Greengard, "Have Gangs Invaded Your Workplace?" *Personnel Journal* (February 1996): 47–57; See also, Carroll Lachnit, "Protecting People and Profits with Background Checks," *Workforce* (February 2002): 52, and M. Patel, "Ten Red Flags of Insider Threat", *Risk Management* v. 56 no. 5 (June 2009) p. 9.

2. Vanessa O'Connell, "Test for Dwindling Retail Jobs Spawns a Culture of Cheating," *The Wall Street Journal,* January 7, 2009 p. A1, A10.

3. See Rebecca Bennett and Sandra Robinson, "Development of a Measure of Workplace Deviance," *Journal of Applied Psychology* 85, no. 3 (2000): 349.

4. "Wal-Mart to Scrutinize Job Applicants," *CNN Money,* August 12, 2004, http://money.cnn.com/2004/08/12/News/fortune500/walmart_jobs/index.htm, downloaded August 8, 2005.

5. Fay Hansen, "Taking 'reasonable' action to avoid negligent hiring claims," *Workforce Management* (September 11, 2006): 31.

6. Anne Anastasi, *Psychological Patterns* (New York: Macmillan, 1968). See also Kevin Murphy and

Charles David Shafer, *Psychological Testing* (Upper Saddle River, NJ, Prentice Hall, 2001); pp. 108–24.

7. Robert M. Guion, "Changing Views for Personnel Selection Research," *Personnel Psychology* 40, no. 2 (summer 1987): 199–213.

8. Brad Bushman and Gary Wells, "Trait Aggressiveness and Hockey Penalties: Predicting Hot Tempers on the Ice," *Journal of Applied Psychology* 83, no. 6 (1998): 969–74.

9. Sarah Gale, "Three Companies Cut Turnover with Tests," *Workforce* (April 2002): 66–69.

10. William Wagner, "All Skill, No Finesse," *Workforce* (June 2000): 108–16. See also, for example, James Diefendorff and Kajal Mehta, "The Relations of Motivational Traits with Workplace Deviance," *Journal of Applied Psychology* 92, no. (2007): 967–977.

11. Elaine Pulakos, *Selection Assessment Methods* (SHRM Foundation, 2005): 9.

12. See, for example, Douglas Cellar et al., "Comparison of Factor Structures and Criterion-Related Validity Coefficients for Two Measures of Personality Based on the Five Factor Model," *Journal of Applied Psychology* 81, no. 6 (1996): 694–704; Jesus Salgado, "The Five Factor Model of Personality and Job Performance in the European Community," *Journal of Applied Psychology* 82, no. 1 (1997): 30–43; Joyce Hogan et al., "Personality Measurement, Faking, and Employee Selection," *Journal of Applied Psychology* 92, no. (2007): 1270–85.

13. Murray Barrick and Michael Mount, "The Big Five Personality Dimensions and Job Performance: A Meta Analysis," *Personnel Psychology* 44, no. 1 (Spring 1991): 1–26. See also Paula Caligiuri, "The Big Five Personality Characteristics as Predictors of Expatriate's Desire to Terminate the Assignment and Supervisor Rated Performance," *Personnel Psychology* 53 (2000): 67–68, and H. Zhao, et. al., "The Relationship of Personality to Entrepreneurial Intentions and Performance: A Meta-Analytic Review", *Journal of Management* v. 36 no. 2 (March 2010) p. 381–404.

14. Kathryn Tyler, "Put Applicants' Skills to the Test," HR *Magazine* (January 2000): 75–79.

15. Hal Whiting and Theresa Kline, "Assessment of the Equivalence of Conventional versus Computer Administration of the Test of Workplace Essential Skills," *International Journal of Training and Development* 10, no. 4 (December 2006): 285–290.

16. Gilbert Nicholson, "Automated Assessments," *Workforce* (December 1, 2000): 102–7.

17. Ibid.

18. Quoted from Deborah Whetzel and Michael McDaniel, "Situational Judgment Tests: An Overview of Current Research," *Human Resource Management Review* 19 (2009): 188–202.

19. R. G. Downey, F. F. Medland, and L. G. Yates, "Evaluation of a Peer Rating System for Predicting Subsequent Promotion of Senior Military Officers," *Journal of Applied Psychology* 61 (April 1976); see also Julie Barclay and Lynn Harland, "Peer Performance Appraisals: The Impact of Rater Competence, Rater Location, and M.E. Purcell, et. al., "Piloting External Peer Review as a Model for Performance Improvement in Third-Sector Organizations", *Nonprofit Management & Leadership* v. 20 no. 3 (Spring 2010) p. 357–74.

20. Timothy Judge et al., "Personality and Leadership: A Qualitative and Quantitative Review," *Journal of Applied Psychology* 87, no. 4 (2002), p. 765.

21. Miller, Holly A., Rita J. Watkins, and David Webb, "The Use of Psychological Testing to Evaluate Law Enforcement Leadership Competencies and Development," *Police Practice & Research: An International Journal* 10, no. 1 (February 2009): 49–60.

22. Gary Yukl, Leadership and Organizations, Upper Saddle River, NJ: Prentice Hall, 1998): 237.

23. Michael McDaniel et al., "The Validity of Employment Interviews: A Comprehensive Review and Meta-Analysis," *Journal of Applied Psychology* 79, no. 4 (1994): 599. See also Richard Posthuma et al., "Beyond Employment Interview Validity: A Comprehensive Narrative Review of Recent Research and Trends over Time," *Personnel Psychology* 55 (2002): 1–81.

24. McDaniel, op. cit., 601. See also Allen Huffcutt et al., "Comparison of Situational and Behavior Description Interview Questions for Higher Level Positions," *Personnel Psychology* 54 (Autumn 2001): 619–44; Stephen Maurer, "A Practitioner Based Analysis of Interviewer Job Expertise and Scale Format as Contextual Factors in Situational Interviews," *Personnel Psychology* 55 (2002): 307–27, and L.S. Kleiman, et. al., "A four-step model for teaching selection interviewing skills", *Business Communication Quarterly* v. 73 no. 3 (September 2010) p. 291–305.

25. Bill Stoneman, "Matching Personalities with Jobs Made Easier with Behavioral Interviews," *American Banker* 165, no. 229 (November 30, 2000): 8a.

26. Timothy Judge et al., "The Employment Interview: A Review of Recent Research and Recommendations for Future Research," *Human Resource Management* 10, no. 4 (2000): 392. There is disagreement regarding the relative superiority of individual versus panel interviews. See, for example, Marlene Dixon et al., "The Panel Interview: A Review of Empirical Research and Guidelines for Practice," *Public Personnel Management* (Fall 2002): 397–28.

27. Frank Schmidt and Ryan Zimmerman, "A Counterintuitive Hypothesis about Employment Interview Validity and Some Supporting Evidence," *Journal of Applied Psychology* 89, no. 3 (2004): 553–61.

28. Derek Chapman and David Zweig, "Developing a Nomological Network for Interview Structure: Antecedents and Consequences of the Structured Selection Interview," *Personnel Psychology* 58 (2005): 673–702.

29. Anita Chaudhuri, "Beat the Clock: Applying for a Job? A New Study Shows That Interviewers Will Make Up Their Minds about You Within a Minute," *The Guardian* (June 14, 2000): 2–6.

30. Don Langdale and Joseph Weitz, "Estimating the Influence of Job Information on Interviewer Agreement," *Journal of Applied Psychology* 57 (1973): 23–27.

31. R. E. Carlson, "Selection Interview Decisions: The Effects of Interviewer Experience, Relative Quota Situation, and Applicant Sample on Interview Decisions," *Personnel Psychology* 20 (1967): 259–80.

32. R. E. Carlson, "Effects of Applicant Sample on Ratings of Valid Information in an Employment Setting," *Journal of Applied Psychology* 54 (1970): 217–22.

33. See, for example, Scott Fleischmann, "The Messages of Body Language in Job Interviews," *Employee Relations* 18, no. 2 (Summer 1991): 161–76. See also James Westpall and Ithai Stern, "Flattery Will Get You Everywhere (Especially If You're a Male Caucasian): How Ingratiation, Board Room Behavior, and a Demographic Minority Status Affect Additional Board Appointments at US Companies," *The Academy of Management Journal* 50, no. 2 (2007): 267–88.

34. Tim DeGroot and Stephen Motowidlo, "Why Visual and Vocal Interview Cues Can Affect Interviewer's Judgments and Predicted Job Performance," *Journal of Applied Psychology* (December 1999): 968–84.

35. Amy Kristof-Brown et al., "Applicant Impression Management: Dispositional Influences and Consequences for Recruiter Perceptions of Fit and Similarity," *Journal of Management* 28, no. 1 (2002): 27–46. See also Linda McFarland et al., "Impression Management Use and Effectiveness Across Assessment Methods," *Journal of Management* 29, no. 5 (2003): 641–61.

36. See, for example, Cynthia Marlowe, Sondra Schneider, and Carnot Nelson, "Gender and Attractiveness Biases in Hiring Decisions: Are More Experienced Managers Less Biased?" *Journal of Applied Psychology* 81, no. 1 (1996): 11–21; see also Shari Caudron, "Why Job Applicants Hate HR," *Workforce* (June 2002): 36, and T. DeGroot, et. al., "Can Nonverbal Cues be Used to Make Meaningful Personality Attributions in Employment Interviews?", *Journal of Business & Psychology* v. 24 no. 2 (June 2009) p. 179–92.

37. Marlowe et al., op. cit., 11.

38. Ibid., 18.

39. Madeline Heilman and Tyler Okimoto, "Motherhood: A Potential Source of Bias in Employment Decisions," *Journal of Applied Psychology* 93, no. 1 (2008): 189–98.

40. Ibid., p. 196.

41. Chad Higgins and Timothy Judge, "The Effect of Applicant Influence Tactics on Recruiter Perceptions of Fit and Hiring Recommendations: A Field Study," *Journal of Applied Psychology* 89, no. 4 (2004): 622–32.

42. Laura Gollub-Williamson, James E. Campion, and Stanley B. Malos, "Employment Interview on Trial: Linking Interview Structure with Litigation Outcomes," *Journal of Applied Psychology* 82, no. 6 (1997): 901; Michael Campion, David Palmer, and James Campion, "A Review of Structure in the Selection Interview," *Personnel Psychology* 50 (1997): 655–702. See also, J.M. McCarthy, et. al., "Are Highly Structured Job Interviews Resistant to Demographic Similarity Effects?", *Personnel Psychology* v. 63 no. 2 (Summer 2010) p. 325–59

43. Robert E. Carlson, "Selection Interview Decisions: The Effect of Interviewer Experience, Relative Quota Situation, and Applicant Sample on Interviewer Decisions," *Personnel Psychology* 20, no. 3 (September 1967): 259–80.

44. Pam Kaul, "Interviewing Is Your Business," *Association Management* (November 1992): 29. See also Nancy Woodward, "Asking for Salary Histories," *HR Magazine* (February 2000): 109–12. Gathering information about specific interview dimensions such as social ability, responsibility, and independence (as is often done with structured interviews) can improve interview accuracy, at least for more complicated jobs. See for example, Andrea Poe, "Graduate Work: Behavioral Interviewing Can Tell You If an Applicant Just Out of College Has Traits Needed for the Job," *HR Magazine* 48, no. 10 (October 2003): 95–96.

45. Catherine Middendorf and Therese Macan, "Note Taking in the Employment Interview: Effects on Recall and Judgment," *Journal of Applied Psychology* 87, no. 2 (2002): 293–303.

46. These are from Alan M. Saks and Julie M. McCarthy, "Effects of Discriminatory Interview Questions and Gender on Applicant Reactions," *Journal of Business and Psychology* 21, no. 2 (Winter 2006): 175–191.

47. Kristen Weirick, "The Perfect Interview," *HR Magazine* (April 2008): 85.

48. Andrea Rodriguez and Fran Prezant, "Better Interviews for People with Disabilities," *Workforce*, downloaded from http:www.workforce.com on November 14, 2003.

49. "Are Your Background Checks Balanced? Experts Identify Concerns Over Verifications," *BNA Bulleting to Management* (May 13, 2004): 153.

50. Adler, "Verifying a Job Candidate's Background," 6.

51. Lachnit, op. cit., 52. See also Robert Howie and Lawrence Shapero, "Preemployment Criminal Background Checks: Why Employers Should Look Before They Leap," *Employee Relations Law Journal* (Summer 2002): 63–77. See also J. Greenwald, "Ex-convicts in workforce pose liability problems", *Business Insurance* v. 43 no. 32 (September 14, 2009) p. 1, 21.

52. See, for example, A. M. Forsberg et al., "Perceived Fairness of a Background Information Form and a Job Knowledge Test," *Public Personnel Management* 38, no. 1 (Spring 2009): 33–46.

53. Ibid., 50ff.

54. "Top employee background checking and screening providers," *Workforce Management* (November 7, 2005): 14.

55. *Alan Finder, "When a Risque'* Online Persona Undermines a Chance for a Job," *The New York Times,* June 11, 2006: 1.

56. "Vetting via Internet Is Free, Generally Legal, But Not Necessarily Smart Hiring Strategy," *BNA Bulletin to Management* (February 20, 2007): 57–58.

57. Anjali Athavaley, "Job References You Can't Control," *The Wall Street Journal* (September 27, 2007): B1.

58. Rita Zeidner, "How Deep Can You Probe?" *HR Magazine* (October 27, 2007): 57–62.

59. "Web Searches on Applicants Are Potentially Perilous for Employers," *BNA Bulletin to Management* (October 14, 2008): 335.

60. For example, see Lawrence Dube Jr., "Employment References and the Law," *Personnel Journal* 65, no. 2 (February 1986): 87–91. See also Mary Mayer, "Background Checks in Focus," *HR Magazine* (January 2002): 59–62.

61. Diane Cadrain, "Job Detectives Dig Deep for Defamation," *HR Magazine* 49, no. 10 (October 2004): 34ff.

62. Lachnit, op. cit., 54; Shari Caudron, "Who Are You Really Hiring?" *Workforce* (November 2002): 31.

63. Kris Maher, "Reference Checking Firms Flourish, but Complaints about Some Arise," *Wall Street Journal* (March 5, 2002): B8. See also, A. Fox, "Automated Reference Checking Puts Onus On Candidates", *HR Magazine* (2009 HR Trendbook supp) p. 66–9.

64. Cadrain, op. cit.

65. "Undercover Callers Tipoff Job Seekers to Former Employers' Negative References," *BNA Bulletin to Management* (May 27, 1999): 161.

66. Based on "Divining Integrity Through Interviews," *BNA Bulletin to Management*, June 4, 1987, and Commerce Clearing House, *Ideas and Trends* (December 29, 1998): 222–23.

67. Polygraphs are still widely used in law enforcement, and reportedly quite useful. See, for example Laurie Cohen, "The Polygraph Paradox," *The Wall Street Journal* (March 22–23, 2008): A1.

68. Ronald Karren and Larry Zacharias, "Integrity Tests: Critical Issues," *Human Resource Management Review*, 17 (2007): 221–34.

69. John Bernardin and Donna Cooke, "Validity of an Honesty Test in Predicting Theft Among Convenience Store Employees," *Academy of Management Journal* 36, no. 5 (1993): 1097–1108. HR in Practice suggestions adapted from "Diving Integrity Through Interviews," *BNA Bulletin to Management*, June 4, 1987, p. 184; and Commerce

Clearing House, *Ideas and Trends* (December 29, 1998): 222–223. Note that some suggest that by possibly signaling mental illness, integrity tests may conflict with the Americans with Disabilities Act, but one review concludes there such tests pose little legal risk to employers. Christopher Berry et al., "A Review of Recent Developments in Integrity Test Research," *Personnel Psychology* 60 (2007): 271–301.

70. Coleman Peterson, "Employee Retention: The Secrets Behind Wal-Mart's Successful Hiring Policies," *Human Resource Management* 44, no. 1 (Spring 2005): 85–88.

71. Murray Barrick and Ryan Zimmerman, "Reducing Voluntary, Avoidable Turnover Through Selection," *Journal of Applied Psychology* 90, no. 1 (2005): 159–66. See also James Breaugh, "Employee Recruitment: Current Knowledge and Important Areas for Future Research," *Human Resource Management Review* 18 (2008): 106–7.

72. Lawrence Kellner, quoted in "Corner Office," by Adam Bryant, *The New York Times* (September 27, 2009): BU2.

73. This is based on ibid.

74. Mick Haus, "Pre-Employment Physicals and the ADA," *Safety and Health* (February 1992): 64–65.

75. Scott MacDonald, Samantha Wells, and Richard Fry, "The Limitations of Drug Screening in the Workplace," *International Labour Review* 132, no. 1 (1993): 98.

76. Ibid., 103.

77. Lewis Maltby, "Drug Testing: A Bad Investment," *Business Ethics* 15, no. 2 (March 2001): 7.

78. MacDonald et al., op. cit., 105–6.

79. Diane Cadrain, "Are Your Employees' Drug Tests Accurate?" *HR Magazine* (January 2003): 40–45.

80. Russell Gerbman, "License to Work," *HR Magazine* (June 2000): 151–60.

81. Note that the acceptable documents on page 3 of the current (as of 2009) I-9 form do not reflect the current list of acceptable documents. For this, refer to the website of the U.S. Department of Homeland Security. Margaret Fiester et al., "Affirmative Action, Stock Options, I-9 Documents," *HR Magazine* (November 2007): 32. "Conflicting State E-Verify Laws Troubling for Employers," *BNA Bulletin to Management* (November 4, 2008): 359.

82. Manuel Velasquez, *Business Ethics: Concepts and Cases* (Upper Saddle River, NJ: Prentice Hall, 1992),

p. 9. See also O. C. Ferrell, John Fraedrich, and Linog Ferrell, *Business Ethics* (Boston: Houghton Mifflin, 2008)

83. Weaver and Trevino, "The Role of Human Resources," p. 123. See also Linda Andrews, "The Nexus of Ethics," *HR Magazine* (August 2005): 53–58.

Chapter 9

1. Marjorie Derven, "Management Onboarding," *Training & Development* (April 2008): 49–52. This chapter is largely adapted from Gary Dessler, *Human Resource Management* (Upper Saddle River, NJ: Pearson Prentice Hall, 2011), 262–302.

2. For a good discussion of socialization see, for example, Talya Bauer et al., "Newcomer Adjustment During Organizational Socialization: A Meta-Analytic Review of Antecedents, Outcomes, and Methods," *Journal of Applied Psychology* 92, no. 3 (2007): 707–21.

3. Sabrina Hicks, "Successful Orientation Programs," *Training & Development* (April 2000): 59. See also Howard Klein and Natasha Weaver, "The Effectiveness of an Organizational Level Orientation Program in the Socialization of New Hires," *Personnel Psychology* 53 (2000): 47–66; and Laurie Friedman, "Are You Losing Potential New Hires at Hello?" *Training & Development* (November 2006): 25–27.

4. Sheila Hicks et al., "Orientation Redesign," *Training and Development* (July 2006): 43–46.

5. Charlotte Garvey, "The Whirlwind of a New Job," *HR Magazine* (June 2001): 111. See also Bauer et al., op. cit.

6. http://www.workday.com/company/news/workday_mobility.php (accessed March 24, 2009).

7. John Kammeyer-Mueller and Connie Wanberg, "Unwrapping the Organizational Entry Process: Disentangling Multiple Antecedents and Their Pathways to Adjustments," *Journal of Applied Psychology* 88, no. 5 (2003): 779–94.

8. This section is based on Darin Hartley, "Technology Kicks Up Leadership Development," *Training and Development* (March 2004): 22–24.

9. Ed Frauenheim, "IBM Learning Programs Get a 'Second Life,'" *Workforce Management* (December 11, 2006): 6. See also J. T. Arnold, "Gaming Technology Used to Orient New Hires," *HR Magazine* (2009 HR Trendbook supp.): 36, 38.

10. Brenda Sugrue et al., "What in the World Is WLP?" *Training and Development* (January 2005): 51–54.

11. Mindy Chapman, "The Return on Investment for Training," *Compensation & Benefits Review* (January/February 2003): 32–33.

12. Employers increasingly utilize learning content management systems (LCMS) to compile and author training content. See, for example, Bill Perry, "Customized Content at Your Fingertips," *Training & Development* (June 2009): 29–30.

13. Jay Bahlis, "Blueprint for Planning Learning," *Training & Development* (March 2008): 64–67.

14. P. Nick Blanchard and James Thacker, *Effective Training: Systems, Strategies, and Practices* (Upper Saddle River, NJ: Prentice Hall, 1999), 154–56.

15. Richard Montier et al., "Competency Models Develop Top Performance," *Training and Development* (July 2006): 47–50. See also Jennifer Salopek, "The Power of the Pyramid," *Training & Development* (May 2009): 70–73.

16. Richard Camp et al., *Toward a More Organizationally Effective Training Strategy and Practice* (Upper Saddle River, NJ: Prentice Hall, 1986), 100.

17. Kenneth Wexley and Gary Latham, *Development and Training Human Resources in Organizations* (Upper Saddle River, NJ: Prentice Hall, 2002), 107.

18. Ibid., 82.

19. Ibid., 87.

20. Ibid., 90.

21. The American Society for Training & Development (ASTD) offers thousands of packaged training programs, such as "Be a Better Manager," "Strategic Planning 101," "12 Habits of Successful Trainers," "Mentoring," and "Using Job Aids." *American Society for Training & Development, Spring and Fall Line catalog.* American Society for Training & Development, 1640 King St., Box 1443, Alexandria, VA 22313; http://expo365.astd.org/bg/public/enter.aspx accessed January 2011.

22. See, for example, http://www.hrdqstore.com/ accessed January 2011.

23. Donna Goldwaser, "Me a Trainer?" *Training* (April 2001): 60–66.

24. Robert Weintraub and Jennifer Martineau, "The Just in Time Imperative," *Training and Development* (June 2002): 52; and Andrew Paradise, "Informal Learning: Overlooked or Overhyped?" *Training & Development* (July 2008): 52–53.

25. Aparna Nancherla, "Knowledge Delivered in Any Other Form Is . . . Perhaps Sweeter," *Training & Development* (May 2009): 54–60.

26. Stephen Covey, "Small Business, Big Opportunity," *Training* 43, no. 11 (November 2006): 40.

27. Harley Frazis, Maury Gittleman, Michael Horrigan, and Mary Joyce, "Results from the 1995 Survey of Employer-Provided Training," *Monthly Labor Review* 121, no. 6 (1998): 4.

28. Cindy Waxer, "Steelmaker Revives Apprentice Program to Address Graying Workforce, Forge Next Leaders," *Workforce Management* (January 30, 2006): 40.

29. Kermit Kaleba, "New Changes to Apprenticeship Program Could Be Forthcoming," *Training & Development* (February 2008): 14.

30. Paula Ketter, "What Can Training Do for Brown?" *Training & Development* ( ): 30–36.

31. Michael Blotzer, "Distance Learning," *Occupational Hazards* (March 2000): 53–54. See also, "How One Association Makes Distance Learning Work", *Associations Now* v. 6 no. 9 (August 2010) p. 69

32. Michael Emery and Margaret Schubert, "A Trainer's Guide to Videoconferencing," *Training* (June 1993): 60. See also E. Shein, "Face to (Virtual) Face", *Computerworld* v. 44 no. 8 (April 19, 2010) p. 18–20, 22–3.

33. For a slide show of a similar training process, see http://www.slideshare.net/magistra12/a-second-life-virtual-clinic-for-medical-student-training-presentation (accessed October 4, 2009).

34. See, for example, Kim Kleps, "Virtual Sales Training Scores a Hit," *Training & Development* (December 2006): 63–64.

35. Michael Laff, "Simulations: Slowly Proving Their Worth," *Training & Development* (June 2007): 30–34.

36. Jenni Jarventaus, "Virtual Threat, Real Sweat," *Training & Development* (May 2007): 72–78.

37. Pat Galagan, "Second That," *Training & Development* (February 2008): 34–37. See also David Wilkins, "Learning 2.0 and Workplace Communities," *Training & Development* (April 2009): 28–31.

38. Traci Sitzmann et al., "The Comparative Effectiveness of Web-Based and Classroom Instruction: A Meta-Analysis," *Personnel Psychology* 59 (2006): 623–64.

39. For a list of guidelines for using e-learning, see, for example, Mark Simon, "E-Learning Know-How," *Training & Development* (January 2009): 34–39.

40. Tom Barron, "A Portrait of Learning Portals," http://www.learningcircuits.com/may2000/barron.html (accessed May). See also Paul Giguere and Jennifer Minotti, "Rethinking Web-Based E-Learning," *Training and Development* (January 2005): 15–16.

41. "The Next Generation of Corporate Learning," *Training and Development* (June 2004): 47; and Jennifer Hofmann and Nanatte Miner, "Real Blended Learning Stands Up," *Training & Development* (September 2008): 28–31.

42. Jennifer Taylor Arnold, "Learning on-the-Fly," *HR Magazine* (September 2007): 137.

43. http://www.dominknow.com/ (accessed March 23, 2009).

44. For a similar program at Accenture, see Don Vanthournout and Dana Koch, "Training at Your Fingertips," *Training & Development* (September 2008): 52–57.

45. Marcia Conner, "Twitter 101: Are You Reading?" *Training & Development* (August 2009): 24–26.

46. Traci Sitzmann et al.,"The Comparative Effectiveness of Web-Based and Classroom Instruction: A Meta-Analysis," *Personnel Psychology* 59 (2006): 623–64.

47. Paula Ketter, "The Hidden Disability," *Training and Development* (June 2006): 34–40.

48. Jeremy Smerd, "New Workers Sorely Lacking Literacy Skills," *Workforce Management* (December 10, 2008): 6.

49. Valerie Frazee, "Workers Learn to Walk So They Can Run," *Personnel Journal* (May 1996): 115–120. See also Kathryn Tyler, "I Say Potato, You Say Patata: As Workforce and Customer Diversity Grow, Employers Offer Foreign Language Training to Staff," *HR Magazine* 49, no. 1 (January 2004): 85–87.

50. Susan Ladika, "When Learning Lasts a Lifetime," *HR Magazine* (May 2008): 57.

51. See, for example, Jeff Kristick, "Filling the Leadership Pipeline," *Training & Development* (June 2009): 4951.

52. Mike Czarnowsky, "Executive Development," *Training & Development* (September 2008): 44–45.

53. Jack Zenger, Dave Ulrich, and Norm Smallwood, "The New Leadership Development," *Training & Development* (March 2000): 22–27. See also Ann Locke and Arlene Tarantino, "Strategic Leadership Development," *Training & Development* (December 2006): 53–55.

54. Kenneth N. Wexley and Gary P. Latham, *Developing and Training Human Resources in Organizations* (Upper Saddle River, NJ: Prentice Hall Series in Human Resources, 2002), 193.

55. See, for example, Michael Laff, "Serious Gaming: The Trainer's New Best Friend," *Training & Development* (January 2007): 52–56. See also Jean Thilmany, "Acting Out," *HR Magazine* (January 2007): 95–100.

56. "AMA Seminars," The American Management Association, http://www.AMA seminars.org (October 2009–2010).

57. Chris Musselwhite, "University Executive Education Gets Real," *Training & Development* (May 2006): 57.

58. Russell Gerbman, "Corporate Universities 101," *HR Magazine* (February 2000): 101–106. Before creating an in-house university, the employer needs to ensure that the corporate university's vision, mission, and programs support the company's strategic goals. See also Michael Laff, "Centralized Training Leads to Nontraditional Universities," *Training & Development* (January 2007): 27–29.

59. For an example of a successful organizational change see, for example, Jordan Mora et al., "Recipe for Change," *Training & Development* (March 2008): 42–46.

60. The 10 steps are based on Michael Beer et al., "Why Change Programs Don't Produce Change," *Harvard Business Review* (November/December 1990): 158–66; John Kotter, *Leading Change* (Boston: Harvard Business School Press, 1996). See also David Herold et al., "Beyond Change Management: A Multilevel Investigation of Contextual and Personal Influences on Employees' Commitment to Change," *Journal of Applied Psychology* 92, no. 4 (2007): 949. See also Remco Schimmel and Dennis Muntslag, "Learning Barriers: A Framework for the Examination of Structural Impediments to Organizational Change," *Human Resource Management* 48, NO. 3 (May–June 2009): 399–416; and John Austin, "Mapping Out a Game Plan for Change," *HR Magazine* (April 2009): 39–42.

61. Stacie Furst and Daniel Cable, "Employee Resistance to Organizational Change: Managerial Influence Tactics and Leader Member Exchange," *Journal of Applied Psychology* 3, no. 2 (2008): 453.

62. Darin Hartley, "OD Wired," *Training and Development* (August 2004): 20–24.

63. Wendell French and Cecil Bell Jr., *Organization Development* (Upper Saddle River, NJ:

Prentice Hall, 1999). See also P. Nick Blanchard and James Thacker, *Effective Training* (Upper Saddle River, NJ: Pearson, 2007), 38–46.

64. John Holland, *Making Vocational Choices: A Theory of Careers* (Upper Saddle River, NJ: Prentice Hall, 1973).

65. Edward Levinson et al., "A Critical Evaluation of the Web-Based Version of the Career Key," *Career Development Quarterly* 50, no. 1 (September 1, 2002): 26–36.

66. This example is based on Richard Bolles, *The Three Boxes of Life* (Berkeley, CA: Ten Speed Press, 1976). See also Richard Bolles, *What Color Is Your Parachute?*

67. See also Yehuda Baruch, "Career Development in Organizations and Beyond: Balancing Traditional and Contemporary Viewpoints," *Human Resource Management Review* 16 (2006): 131.

68. Barbara Greene and Liana Knudsen, "Competitive Employers Make Career Development Programs a Priority," *San Antonio Business Journal* 15, no. 6 (July 20, 2001): 27.

69. Fred Otte and Peggy Hutcheson, *Helping Employees Manage Careers* (Upper Saddle River, NJ: Prentice Hall, 1992): 143.

70. Robert Ramsey, "The New Buzz Word," *Supervision* 66, no. 10 (October 2005).

71. Ibid.

72. Summarized or paraphrased from ibid. For a further view, see M. Jenkins, et. al., "The importance of a servant leader orientation", *Health Care Management Review* v. 35 no. 1 (January/March 2010) p. 46–54.

73. Bill Hayes, "Helping Workers with Career Goals Boosts Retention Efforts," *Boston Business Journal* 21, no. 11 (April 20, 2001): 38. See also, K. Goff, "Help Your Manager & Help Yourself: How Your Supervisor Can Help You Climb the Corporate Ladder", *Supervision* v. 71 no. 1 (January 2010) p. 25–6.

74. Michael Doody, "A Mentor Is a Key to Career Success," *Health-Care Financial Management* 57, no. 2 (February 2003): 92–94. See also, J. C. Meister, et. al., "Mentoring Millennials", *Harvard Business Review* v. 88 no. 5 (May 2010) p. 68–7.

75. Richard Luecke, *Managing Change and Transition* (Boston, MA: Harvard Business School Press, 2002), 100–101.

76. Ferda Erdem and Janset Özen Aytemur, "Mentoring—A Relationship Based on Trust: Qualitative Research," *Public Personnel Management* 37, no. 1 (Spring 2008): 55–65.

77. Karen Lyness and Madeline Heilman, "When Fit Is Fundamental: Performance Evaluations and Promotions of Upper-Level Female and Male Managers," *Journal of Applied Psychology* 91, no. 4 (2006): 777(9).

78. Jan Selmer and Alicia Leung, "Are Corporate Career Development Activities Less Available to Female than to Male Expatriates?" *Journal of Business Ethics* (March 2003): 125–37.

79. Karen Lyness and Donna Thompson, "Climbing the Corporate Ladder: Do Female and Male Executives Follow the Same Route?" *Journal of Applied Psychology* 85, no. 1 (2000): 86–101. For another, interesting perspective, see A. Maitland, "The Other Gender", *Conference Board Review* v. 47 no. 1 (Winter 2010) p. 68–9.

80. "Minority Women Surveyed on Career Growth Factors," *Community Banker* 9, no. 3 (March 2000): 44.

81. In Ellen Cook et al., "Career Development of Women of Color and White Women: Assumptions, Conceptualization, and Interventions from an Ecological Perspective," *Career Development Quarterly* 50, no. 4 (June 2002): 291–306.

Chapter 10

1. See, for example, Jesus Delgado, "The Five Factor Model of Personality and Job Performance in the European Community," *Journal of Applied Psychology* 82, no. 1, 1997, pp. 30–43; and Robert Beck, *Motivation* (Upper Saddle River, NJ: Prentice Hall, 2000), 323–25.

2. Murray Barrick and Michael Mount, "The Big Five Personality Dimensions and Job Performance: A Meta-Analysis," *Personal Psychology* (Spring 1991): 1–26. See also, W.A. Scroggins, et. al., "Psychological Testing in Personnel Selection, Part III: The Resurgence of Personality Testing", *Public Personnel Management* v. 38 no. 1 (Spring 2009) p. 67–77.

3. James Bowditch and Anthony Buono, *A Primer on Organizational Behavior* (New York: John Wiley, 1994), 115.

4. Based on Ernest J. McCormick and Joseph Tiffin, *Industrial Psychology* (Upper Saddle River, NJ: Prentice Hall, 1974), 136–74. See also M.g. Seo, et. al.,

"The role of self-efficacy, goal, and affect in dynamic motivational self-regulation", *Organizational Behavior and Human Decision Processes* v. 109 no. 2 (July 2009).

5. Ernest R. Hilgard, *Introduction to Psychology* (New York: Harcourt Brace and World, 1962), 86.

6. Benson Rosen and Thomas Jerdee, "The Influence of Age Stereotypes on Managerial Decisions," *Journal of Applied Psychology* (August 1976): 428–32.

7. Martin Fishbein and Icek Ajzen, *Attitude, Intention and Behavior: An Introduction to Theory and Research* (Reading, MA: Addison-Wesley, 1975).

8. Craig Pinder, *Work Motivation in Organizational Behavior* (Upper Saddle River, NJ: Prentice Hall, 1998), 245.

9. The Job Descriptive Index is copyrighted by Bowling Green State University. It can be obtained from Dr. Patricia C. Smith, Department of Psychology, Bowling Green State University, Bowling Green, Ohio, 43403.

10. See, for example, M. T. Iaffaldano and M. P. Muchinsky, "Job Satisfaction and Job Performance: A Meta-Analysis," *Psychological Bulletin* (March 1985): 251–73, and S.A. Way, et. al., "What Matters More?: Contrasting the Effects of Job Satisfaction and Service Climate on Hotel Food and Beverage Managers' Job Performance", *Cornell Hospitality Quarterly* v. 51 no. 3 (August 2010) p. 379–97.

11. As one of many examples, see Francie Dalton, "Motivating the Unmotivated," *Supervision* 68, no. 7 (July 2007): 18–19.

12. Ibid.

13. Ernest R. Hilgard, *Introduction to Psychology* (New York: Harcourt Brace and World, 1962), 124–25.

14. Ibid., p. 124. See also Hugo Kehr, "Integrating Implicit Motives, Explicit Motives, and Perceived Abilities: The Compensatory Model of Work Motivation and Volition," *Academy of Management Review* 29, no. 3 (2004): 479–99.

15. See, for instance, R. Kanfer, "Motivation Theory," in M. D. Dunnette and L. M. Hough (eds.), *Handbook of Industrial and Organizational Psychology* (Palo Alto, CA: Consulting Psychologists Press, 1990). See also Robert Hersey, "A Practitioner's View of Motivation," *Journal of Managerial Psychology* (May 1993): 110–15; and T. Fallon, "Retain and Motivate the Next Generation: 7 Ways to Get the Most out of Your Millenial Workers", *Supervision* v. 70 no. 5 (May 2009) p. 5–7.

16. See Douglas M. McGregor, "The Human Side of Enterprise," ed. Michael Matteson and John M. Ivancevich, *Management Classics* (Santa Monica, CA: Goodyear, 1977), 43–49. See also Ewart Woolridge, "Time to Stand Maslow's Hierarchy on Its Head?" *People Management* (December 21, 1995): 17.

17. One expert says that illustrating Maslow's theory in the form of a pyramid (with the physiological needs on the bottom and the self-actualization needs on top) "is one of the worst things that has happened to the theory." John Rowan, "Maslow Amended," *Journal of Humanistic Psychology* (Winter 1998): 81–83.

18. See, for example, Clay Alderfer, "Theories Reflecting My Personal Experience and Life Development," *Journal of Applied Behavioral Science* (November 1989): 351–66.

19. Abraham Maslow, *Toward a Psychology of Being*, 2nd ed. (New York: Van Nostrand Reinhold, 1968).

20. McGregor, op. cit., 45.

21. Frederick Herzberg et al., *Job Attitudes: Review of Research and Opinion* (Pittsburgh, PA: Pittsburgh Psychological Services, 1957).

22. See, for example, Howard Hyden, "Seven Ways to Fuel the Fire in Employee Performance," *Supervision* 70, no. 1 (January 2009): 7–9.

23. This is based on David Kolb, Irwin Rubin, and James McIntyre, *Organizational Psychology: An Experiential Approach* (Upper Saddle River, NJ: Prentice Hall, 1971), 65–69. For an example of achievement motivation in practice, see Douglas Amyx and Bruce Alford, "The Effects of Salesperson Need for Achievement and Sales Manager Leader Reward Behavior," *Journal of Personal Selling and Sales Management* 25, no. 4 (Fall 2005): 345–60.

24. These are all from Kolb et al., op. cit.

25. David McClelland and David Burnham, "Power Is the Great Motivator," *Harvard Business Review* (January–February 1995): 126–36.

26. George Litwin and Robert Stringer Jr., *Motivation and Organizational Climate* (Boston: Harvard University Press, 1968), 20–24.

27. Pinder, op. cit., 288–99.

28. See, for example, J. Greenberg, "A Taxonomy of Organizational Justice Theories," *Academy of Management Review* 12 (1987): 9–22. See also Armin Falk, "Intrinsic Motivation and Extrinsic Incentives in a Repeated Game with Incomplete Contracts," *Journal of Economic Psychology* (June 1999): 251–54.

29. Edwin A. Locke and D. Henne, "Work Motivation Theories," eds. C. L. Cooper and I. Robertson, *International Review of Industrial and Organizational Psychology* (Chichester, England: Wiley, 1986), 1–35. See also Maureen Ambrose, "Old Friends, New Faces: Motivation Research in the 1990s," *Journal of Management* (May–June 1999): 231–37.

30. Kanfer, op. cit., p. 125. See also Yitzhak Fried and Linda Haynes Slowik, "Enriching Goal Setting with Time: An Integrated Approach," *Academy of Management Review* 29, no. 3 (2004): 404–22; and Frederick Reichheld and Paul Rogers, "Motivating Through Metrics," *Harvard Business Review* 83, no. 9 (September 2005): 20–22.

31. Pinder, op. cit., 377.

32. Kanfer, p. 113.

33. For a discussion, see John P. Campbell and Robert Pritchard, "Motivation Theory in Industrial and Organizational Psychology," ed. Marvin Dunnette, *Industrial and Organizational Psychology* (Chicago: Rand McNally, 1976), 74–75; and Kanfer, op. cit., 115–16.

34. For a definition of learning, see Lefton and Valvatne, op. cit., 161.

35. For a review of operant conditioning, see Fred Luthans and R. Kreitner, *Organizational Behavior Modification and Beyond: An Operant and Social Learning Approach* (Glenview, IL: Scott, Foresman, 1985). See also Nancy Chase, "You Get What You Reward," *Quality* (June 1999): 104.

36. W. Clay Hamner, "Reinforcement Theory in Management and Organizational Settings," eds. Henry Tosi and W. Clay Hamner, *Organizational Behavior and Management: A Contingency Approach* (Chicago: Saint Claire, 1974), 86–112. See also Donald J. Campbell, "The Effects of Goal-Contingent Payment on the Performance of a Complex Task," *Personnel Psychology* (Spring 1984): 23–40; and E.C. Dierdorff, et. al., "If You Pay for Skills, Will They Learn? Skill Change and Maintenance Under a Skill-Based Pay System", *Journal of Management* v. 34 no. 4 (August 2008) p. 721–43.

37. "Driving Profitable Sales Growth: 2006/2007 Report on Sales Effectiveness," http://www.watsonwyatt.com/research/resrender.asp?id=2006-US-0060&page=1 (accessed May 20, 2007).

38. Bob Conlin, "Best Practices for Designing New Sales Compensation Plans," *Compensation & Benefits Review* (March/April 2008): 51.

39. Ibid., p. 53.

40. http://www.vuesoftware.com/Product/Compensation_Management.aspx (accessed March 4, 2009).

41. Suzanne Peterson and Fred Luthans, "The Impact of Financial and Non-Financial Incentives on Business Unit Outcomes over Time," *Journal of Applied Psychology* 91, no. 1 (2006): 156–65.

42. Ibid., 159.

43. Ibid., 159.

44. Ibid., 162.

45. Reed Taussig, "Managing Cash Based Incentives," *Compensation and Benefits Review* (March/April 2002): 65–68. See also Nigel Nicholson, "How to Motivate Your Problem People," *Harvard Business Review* (January 2003): 57–65, and "Incentives, Motivation and Workplace Performance," Incentive Research Foundation, http://www.incentivescentral.org/ employees/whitepapers (accessed May 19, 2007).

46. Adapted from Gary Dessler, *Human Resource Management* (Upper Saddle River, NJ: Prentice Hall, 2011), 453–455.

47. Theodore Weinberger, "Evaluating the Effectiveness of an Incentive Plan Design within Company Constraints," *Compensation and Benefits Review* (November/December 2005): 27–33; Howard Risher, "Adding Merit to Pay for Performance," *Compensation & Benefits Review* (November/December 2008): 22–29.

48. Michael Harris et al., "A Longitudinal Examination of a Merit Pay System," *Journal of Applied Psychology* 83 (1998): 825–31.

49. James Brinks, "Is There Merit in Merit Increases?" *Personnel Administrator* (May 1980): 60. See also Atul Migra et al., "The Case of the Invisible Merit Raise: How People See Their Pay Raises," *Compensation & Benefits Review* (May 1995): 71–76.

50. "Base Pay Will Rise More Slowly in 2009," *Compensation & Benefits Review* (November/December 2008): 5.

51. Employers need to beware of piling so many new stock incentives on top performers during challenging times that when buoyant economic times return the employees receive a windfall. See, for an example, Jack Dolmat-Connell et al., "Potential Implications of the Economic Downturn for Executive Compensation," *Compensation & Benefits Review* 41, no. 1 (January/February 2009): 33–38.

52. Cheryl Comeau-Kirschner, "Improving Productivity Doesn't Cost a Dime," *Management Review* (January 1999): 7. See also Bob Nelson, *1001 Ways to Reward Employees* (New York: Workman Publishing, 1994), 19 and Kevin McManus, "A Simple Thank You," *Industrial Engineer* 37, no. 2 (February 2005): 19.

53. Nelson, op. cit., 19. See also Sunny C. L. Fong and Margaret A. Shaffer, "The Dimensionality and Determinants of Pay Satisfaction: A Cross-Cultural Investigation of a Group Incentive Plan," *International Journal of Human Resource Management* 14, no. 4 (June 2003): 559(22).

54. This is based on Gary Yukl, *Leadership in Organizations* (Upper Saddle River, NJ: Prentice Hall, 1998), 298–323.

55. Nathan P. Podsakoff, Philip M. Podsakoff, and Valentina V. Kuskovab, "Dispelling Misconceptions and Providing Guidelines for Leader Reward and Punishment Behavior," *Business Horizons* 53 (2010): 291–303.

56. Ibid.

57. Scot Hays, "Pros and Cons of Pay for Performance," *Workforce* (February 1999): 69–74.

58. Charlotte Huff, "Recognition That Resonates," *Workforce Management* (September 11, 2006): 25–29. See also Scott Jeffrey and Victoria Schaffer, "The Motivational Properties of Tangible Incentives," *Compensation & Benefits Review* (May/June 2007): 44–50.

59. Nelson, op. cit., 47.

60. Cora Daniels, "Thank You Is Nice, But This Is Better," *Fortune* (November 22, 1999): 370.

61. This is based on W. Clay Hamner and Ellen Hamner, "Behavior Modification on the Bottom Line," *Organizational Dynamics* (Spring 1976). For recent applications, see L. Esola, "Building a Better safety incentive program", *Business Insurance* v. 44 no. 30 (July 26, 2010) p. 10–11.

62. Adapted from Pinder, op. cit., 203.

63. Whetten and Cameron, op. cit., 420–21.

64. Sharon Parker, Toby Wall, and John Cordery, "Future Work Design Research and Practice: Towards an Elaborated Model of Work Design," *Journal of Occupational and Organizational Psychology* 74, no. 4 (November 2001): 413–40. See also Robert Simons, "Designing High-Performance Jobs," *Harvard Business Review* 83, no. 7 (July–August 2005): 54–63.

65. Quoted in Theodore T. Herbert, *Organizational Behavior: Readings and Cases* (New York: Macmillan, 1976), 344–45.

66. See, for example, J. Richard Hackman et al., "A New Strategy for Job Enrichment," *California Management Review* 17, no. 4 (1975): 57–71.

67. Gerald Ledford, Jr., "Three Case Studies on Skill-Based Pay: An Overview," *Compensation & Benefits Review* (March–April 1991): 11–23. See also, E.C. Dierdorff, et. al., "If You Pay for Skills, Will They Learn? Skill Change and Maintenance Under a Skill-Based Pay System", *Journal of Management* v. 34 no. 4 (August 2008) p. 721–43.

68. Gerald Ledford Jr. and Gary Bergel, "Skill-Based Pay Case No. 1: General Mills," *Compensation & Benefits Review* (March–April 1991): 24–38.

69. Lawrence Zuckerman, "JetBlue, Exception Among Airlines, Is Likely to Post a Profit," *New York Times* (November 7, 2001): C3.

70. Amy Rottier, "The Skies Are JetBlue," *Workforce* 80, no. 9 (September 2001): 22.

71. "JetBlue: Odds Are You Won't Start Two Airlines, Revolutionize Your Industry, or Talk George Soros into Investing in Your Company Anytime Soon," *Fortune Small Business* 11, no. 2 (March 1, 2001): 92.

72. Michelle Maynard, "Southwest, Without the Stunts," *New York Times* (July 7, 2002): BU2.

73. Sally Donnelly, "Blue Skies," *Time* 158 (July 2001): 24–27.

Chapter 11

1. Laird Mealiea and Ramon Baltazar, "A Strategic Guide for Building Effective Teams," *Public Personnel Management* 34, no. 2 (Summer 2005).

2. "Outlook on Teams," *BNA Bulletin to Management* (March 20, 1997): 92–93; Carla Joinson, "Teams at Work," *HR Magazine* (May 1999): 30; http://www.BigAppleCircus.org (accessed March 27, 2006).

3. Jack Osburn et al., *Self-Directed Work Teams: The New American Challenge* (Homewood, IL: Business One Irwin, 1990), 33. See also Bradley Kirkman and Benson Rosen, "Beyond Self-Management: Antecedents and Consequences of Team Empowerment," *Academy of Management Journal* (February 1999): 58–74; and A.J. Fazzari, et. al.," "Partners in Perfection": Human Resources Facilitating Creation and Ongoing Implementation of Self-Managed Manufacturing Teams in a Small

Medium Enterprise", *Human Resource Development Quarterly* v. 20 no. 3 (Fall 2009) p. 353–76.

4. Sandra Robinson and Ann O'Leary-Kelly, "Monkey See, Monkey Do: The Influence of Workgroups on the Antisocial Behavior of Employees," *Academy of Management Journal* 41, no. 6 (1988): 658–72.

5. Ibid., 667.

6. Daniel Feldman, "The Development and Enforcement of Group Norms," *Academy of Management Review* 9, no. 1 (1984): 47–53. See also, R.E. Korte, "How Newcomers Learn the Social Norms of an Organization: A Case Study of the Socialization of Newly Hired Engineers", *Human Resource Development Quarterly* v. 20 no. 3 (Fall 2009) p. 285–306

7. A. P. Hare, *Handbook of Small Group Research* (New York: The Free Press, 1962), 24. See also S. Barr and E. Conlon, "Effects of Distribution of Feedback in Work Groups," *Academy of Management Journal* (June 1994): 641–56.

8. See Stephen Worchel, Wendy Wood, and Jeffrey Simpson, *Group Process and Productivity* (Newbury Park, CA: Sage Publications, 1992), 45–50.

9. F. J. Roethlisberger and William J. Dickson, *Management and the Worker* (New York: John Wiley, 1964).

10. For a discussion of the difficulty of measuring and defining cohesiveness, see Peter Mudrack, "Group Cohesiveness and Productivity: A Closer Look," *Human Relations* 42, no. 9 (1989): 771–85. See also R. Saavedra et al., "Complex Interdependence in Task-Performing Groups," *Journal of Applied Psychology* (February 1993): 61–73.

11. John R. P. French Jr., "The Disruption and Cohesion of Groups," *Journal of Abnormal and Social Psychology* 36 (1941): 361–77. For another perspective, see, M. Van Woerkom, et. al., "The Romance of Learning from Disagreement. The Effect of Cohesiveness and Disagreement on Knowledge Sharing Behavior and Individual Performance Within Teams", *Journal of Business & Psychology* v. 25 no. 1 (March 2010) p. 139–49

12. Hare, op. cit., 244.

13. Robert Blake and Jane Mouton, "Reactions to Inter-Group Competition under Win–Lose Conditions," *Management Science* 7 (1961): 432.

14. Stanley C. Seashore, *Group Cohesiveness in the Industry Work Group* (Ann Arbor, MI: Survey Research Center, University of Michigan, 1954), 90–95. See also Joseph Litterer, *The Analysis of Organizations* (New York: John Wiley, 1965), 91–101; and Daniel Beal et al., "Cohesion and Performance in Groups: A Meta-Analytic Clarification of Construct Relations," *Journal of Applied Psychology* 88, no. 6 (2003): 989–1004.

15. Hare, op. cit., 244.

16. Ibid., 245.

17. Scott Thurm, "Teamwork Raises Everyone's Game," *The Wall Street Journal* (November 7, 2005): B8.

18. These are based on James H. Shonk, *Team-Based Organizations* (Chicago: Irwin, 1997), 27–33, and Leigh Thompson, *Making the Team: A Guide for Managers* (Upper Saddle River, NJ: Pearson, 2008), 116.

19. Susan Cohen and Diane Bailey, "What Makes Teams Work: Group Effectiveness Research from the Shop Floor to the Executive Suite," *Journal of Management* 23, no. 3 (1997): 239–90.

20. Ibid.

21. Ibid.

22. James H. Shonk, *Team-Based Organizations* (Chicago: Irwin, 1997), 27–33.

23. Ibid., 28.

24. John Katzenbach and Douglas Smith, "The Discipline of Teams," *Harvard Business Review* (March–April 1993): 116–18.

25. Everett Adams Jr., "Quality Circle Performance," *Journal of Management* 17, no. 1 (1991): 25–39.

26. Philip Olson, "Choices for Innovation Minded Corporations," *Journal of Business Strategy* (January–February 1990): 86–90.

27. Anthony Townsend, Samuel DiMarie, and Anthony Hendrickson, "Virtual Teams: Technology and the Workplace of the Future," *Academy of Management Executive* 12, no. 3 (1998): 17–29. Christina Gibson and Susan Cohen, *Virtual Teams That Work: Creating Conditions for Virtual Team Effectiveness* (San Francisco: Jossey-Bass, 2004), provides practicing managers with valuable insights into organizing and managing virtual teams. Many companies use international virtual teams to coordinate research and development–type projects. Bjorn Ambos and Bodo Schlemglmich, "The Use of International R&D Teams: An Empirical Investigation of Selected Contingency Factors," *Journal of World Business* 39, no. 1 (February 2004): 37–48.

28. Michael Harvey et al., "Challenges to Staffing Global Virtual Teams," *Human Resource Management Review* 14 (2004): 281.

29. Christa Degnan, "ActiveProject Aids Teamwork," *PC Week* (May 31, 1999): 35.

30. Darleen DeRosa et al., "Trust and Leadership in Virtual Teamwork: A Media Naturalness Perspective," *Human Resource Management* 44, no. 2–3 (Summer/Fall 2004): 219–232.

31. Rochelle Garner, "Round-the-World Teamwork," *Computerworld* (May 1999): 46.

32. Based on information in Bradley Kirkman et al., "Five Challenges to Virtual Team Success: Lessons from Sabre, Inc.," *Academy of Management Executive* 16, no. 3 (2002): 70.

33. This item is based on Bradley Kirkman et al., "The Impact of Team Empowerment on Virtual Team Performance: The Moderating Role of Face-to-Face Interaction," *Academy of Management Journal* 47, no. 2 (2004): 175–92.

34. Osburn et al., op. cit., 8.

35. Charles Fishman, "Engines of Democracy," *Fast Company* (October 1999): 173–202.

36. Tom Peters, *Liberation Management* (New York: Alfred A. Knopf, 1992), 238–39.

37. Osburn et al., op. cit., 22–23.

38. This is based on Philip Hunsaker, *Training in Management Skills* (Upper Saddle River, NJ: Prentice Hall, 2001), 293–96. See also Stacey Furst et al., "Managing the Life Cycle of Virtual Teams," *Academy of Management Executive* 18, no. 2 (2004).

39. Osburn et al., op. cit., 20–27.

40. Osburn et al., op. cit., 20–27.

41. Ibid., 21.

42. Ibid., 22.

43. "Kodak's Team Structure Is Picture Perfect," *Bureau of National Affairs Bulletin to Management* (August 15, 1996): 264.

44. Rojiv Banker, Roger Schroeder, and Kingshuk Sinha, "Impact of Work Teams on Manufacturing Performance: A Longitudinal Field Study," *Academy of Management Journal* 39, no. 4 (1996): 867–88. See also, K.K. Merriman, "On the Folly of Rewarding Team Performance, While Hoping for Teamwork", *Compensation and Benefits Review* v. 41 no. 1 (January/February 2009) p. 61–6.

45. Ralph King Jr., "Levi's Factory Workers Are Assigned to Teams, and Morale Has Taken a Hit," *Wall Street Journal* (May 20, 1998): A1, A6.

46. K. Merriman, "On the Folly of Rewarding Team Performance, While Hoping for Teamwork," *Compensation & Benefits Review* (January/February 2009): 61–66.

47. The following, except as noted, is based on Glenn Varney, *Building Productive Teams: An Action Guide and Resource Book* (San Francisco: Jossey-Bass, 1989), 11–18. See also R.D. Mohr, et. al., "High-Involvement Work Design and Job Satisfaction", *Industrial and Labor Relations Review* v. 61 no. 3 (April 2008) p. 275–96.

48. Vanessa Druskat, "The Antecedents of Team Competence: Toward a Fine-Grained Model of Self-Managing Team Effectiveness," in Margaret Neale and E. Mannix, eds., *Research on Managing Groups and Teams: Groups in Context*, Vol. 2 (Stamford, CT: Jai Press, 1999), 201–31.

49. This section is based on Laird Mealiea and Ramon Baltazar, "Building Effective Teams," *Public Personnel Management* 34, no. 2 (Summer 2005); see also John Katzenbach and Douglas Smith, "The Discipline of Teams," *Harvard Business Review* (March–April 1993): 112–13; R.L. Allen, "Buckingham: Nurture employees' strengths to build successful teams", *Nation's Restaurant News* v. 42 no. 43 (November 3, 2008) p. 30.

50. Mealiea and Baltazar, op. cit.

51. Sal Divita, "Being a Team Player Is Essential to Your Career," *Marketing News* 30, no. 19 (September 9, 1996): 8.

52. Mealiea and Baltazar, op. cit.

53. Philip Hunsaker, *Training in Management Skills* (Upper Saddle River, NJ: Prentice Hall, 2001), 286.

54. From Regina Maruca, "What Makes Teams Work," *Fast Company* (November 2000): 128.

55. "Under the Big Top," *Harvard Business Review* (September–October 1999): 17.

56. Ibid.

57. Ibid.

58. John Day, "Warewithal Online: Assemble Teams Based on Employee Instincts," *HR Magazine* (August 1999): 124–30. See also R.L. Allen, "Buckingham: Nurture employees' strengths to build successful teams", *Nation's Restaurant News* v. 42 no. 43 (November 3, 2008) p. 30.

59. Rensis Likert, *New Patterns of Management* (New York: McGraw-Hill, 1961), 104.

60. Ibid., 9.

61. Ibid., 103.

62. Frederick P. Morgeson, D. Scott DeRue, and Elizabeth P. Karam, "Leadership in Teams: A Functional Approach to Understanding Leadership Structures and Processes," *Journal of Management* 36, no. 1 (January 2010): 5–39.

63. Ibid.

64. Ibid.

65. Ibid.

66. Kimball Fisher, *Leading Self-Directed Work Teams* (New York: McGraw-Hill, 1993), 151–53.

67. Gary Dessler, *Winning Commitment* (New York: McGraw-Hill, 1992), 28.

68. Ibid.

69. Fisher, op. cit.

70. Kets de Vries and F. R. Manfred, "Decoding the Team Conundrum: The Eight Roles Executives Play," *Organizational Dynamics* 36, no. 1 (2007): 28–44.

71. Jay B. Carson, Paul E. Tesluk, and Jennifer A. Marrone, "Shared Leadership in Teams: An Investigation of Antecedent Conditions and Performance," *Academy of Management Journal* 50, no. 5 (October 2007): 1217–34.

72. Ibid.

73. These are based on Fisher, op. cit., 48–56.

74. This is based on Andreas Voigt, Lynda Gratton, and Tamara Erickson, " Bridging Faultlines in Diverse Teams," *MIT Sloan Management Review* (Summer 2007): 22–37.

75. Ibid.

76. Ibid.

77. Michael Carrell, Daniel Jennings, and Christine Heavrin, *Fundamentals of Organizational Behavior* (Upper Saddle River, NJ: Prentice Hall, 1997), 346.

78. For a discussion of these and the following points, see, for example, ibid.

79. F. Liden et al., "Management of Poor Performance: A Comparison of Manager, Group Member, and Group Disciplinary Decisions," *Journal of Applied Psychology* 84, no. 6 (1999) 835–50.

80. Irving Janis, *Groupthink: Psychological Studies of Policy Decisioins and Fiascos*, 2nd ed. (Boston, MA: Houghton Mifflin, 1982). See also James Esser, "Alive and Well After 25 Years: A Review of Group Think Research," *Organizational Behavior and Human Decision Processes* (February/March 1998) 116–42; and P.J. Schoemaker, et. al., "Why We Miss the Signs", *MIT Sloan Management Review* v. 50 no. 2 (Winter 2009) p. 43–4.

81. For an additional perspective on many of these issues, see Randy Hirokawa and Marshall Scott Poole, *Communication and Group Decision Making* (Thousand Oaks, CA: Sage Publications, 1996), 354–64. See also John O. Whitney and E. Kirby Warren, "Action Forums: How General Electric and Other Firms Have Learned to Make Better Decisions," *Columbia Journal of World Business* (Winter 1995): 18–27; Steven G. Rogelberg and Steven Rumery, "Gender Diversity, Team Decision Quality, Time on Task, and Interpersonal Cohesion," *Small Group Research* (February 1996): 79–90.

82. See, for example, Lester Lefton and Laura Valvatne, *Mastering Psychology* (Boston, MA: Allyn & Bacon, 1992): 249.

83. Greenberg and Baron, 393.

84. See Ron Zemke, "In Search of Good Ideas," *Training* (January 1993): 46–52; R. Brent Gallupe, Lana Bastianutti, and William Cooper, "Unblocking Brainstorms," *Journal of Applied Psychology* (January 1991): 137–42; and C. Hollingsworth, "Creative Force", *PM Network* v. 24 no. 11 (November 2010) p. 44–9 .

85. R. B. Gallupe et al., "Electronic Brainstorming and Group Size," *Academy of Management Journal* 35, no. 4 (2000): 350–69.

86. Simon Lam and John Schaubroeck, "Improving Group Decisions by Better Pooling Information: A Comparative Advantage of Group Decision Support Systems," *Journal of Applied Psychology* 85, no. 4 (2000): 565–73.

87. See S. G. Rogelberg, J. L. Barnes-Farrell, and C. A. Lowe, "The Stepladder Technique: An Alternative Group Structure Facilitating Effective Group Decision Making," *Journal of Applied Psychology* 57 (1992): 730–37.

Chapter 12

1. George Miller, *Language and Communication* (New York: McGraw-Hill, 1951), 10, discussed in Gary Hunt, *Communication Skills in the Organization*, 2nd ed. (Upper Saddle River, NJ: Prentice Hall, 1989), 29.

2. This is discussed in and based on Fred Luthans and Janet Larsen, "How Managers Really Communicate," *Human Relations* 39, no. 2 (1986): 162. See also, R. Weiner, "The Seven Rules of Effective Communication", *Public Relations Quarterly* v. 52 no. 2 (2008) p. 9–11

3. Edward Miles et al., "Job Level as a Variable in Predicting the Relationship Between Supervisory Communication anti Job Satisfaction," *Journal of Occupational and Organizational Psychology* 69, no. 3 (September 1996): 277–93.

4. Arthur Bell and Dayle Smith, *Management Communication* (New York: John Wiley, 1999), 19.

5. Daniel Katz and Robert Kahn, *The Social Psychology of Organizations* (New York: John Wiley, 1966).

6. This is based on Bell and Smith, op. cit., 22–24.

7. This section on dealing with communication barriers is based on R. Wayne Pace and Don Faules, *Organizational Communication* (Upper Saddle River, NJ: Prentice Hall, 1989), 150–62, unless otherwise noted. For an example, see S. Kreimer, "Hospitals Grapple with Ways to Overcome Language Barriers", *Hospitals & Health Networks* v. 82 no. 10 (October 2008) p. 21.

8. See, for example, Bell and Smith, op. cit., 36–39.

9. Tom Geddie, "Moving Communication Across Cultures," *Communication World* 16, no. 5 (April–May 1998): 37–41, see also, A.S. Davis, et. al., "Did You Get My E-mail? An Exploratory Look at Intercultural Business Communication by E-mail", *Multinational Business Review* v. 17 no. 1 (Winter 2009) p. 73–98.

10. Pace and Faules, op. cit., 153.

11. Jack Griffin, *How to Say It at Work* (Paramus, NJ: Prentice Hall Press, 1998), 26–28.

12. Ernest Gundling, "How to Communicate Globally," *Training and Development* (June 1999): 28–32.

13. Ibid., 29.

14. Geddie, op. cit., 37–41.

15. See Holly Weeks, "Taking the Stress out of Stressful Conversations," *Harvard Business Review* (July–August 2001): 112–19.

16. Griffin, op. cit., 178.

17. Ibid.

18. Joyce Osland, David Kolb, and Irwin Rubin, eds., *The Organizational Behavior Reader* (Upper Saddle River, NJ: Prentice Hall, 2001), 185–95. The Active Listening Checklist is adapted from Paula J. Caprioni, *The Practical Coach: Management Skills for Everyday Life* (Upper Saddle River, NJ: Prentice Hall, 2001), 86.

19. Caprioni, op. cit., 86.

20. Jay Conger, "The Necessary Art of Persuasion," *Harvard Business Review* (May–June 1998): 85–95, reprinted in Osland, Kolb, and Rubin, op. cit., 468–78.

21. Ibid.

22. Robert Cialdini, "Harnessing the Science of Persuasion," *Harvard Business Review* (October 2001): 72–81; see also, C.L. King, "Beyond Persuasion: The Rhetoric of Negotiation in Business Communication", Journal of Business Communication v. 47 no. 1 (January 2010) p. 69–78.

23. Conger, op. cit., 458.

24. Cialdini, op. cit., 75.

25. James Sebenius, "Six Habits of Merely Effective Negotiators," *Harvard Business Review* (April 2001): 87–95.

26. James C. Freund, *Smart Negotiating* (New York: Simon & Schuster, 1992), 42–46.

27. Ibid., 33.

28. Jitendra Sharma, "Organizational Communications: A Linking Process," *The Personnel Administrator* (July 1979): 35–43. See also Victor Callan, "Subordinate-Manager Communication in Different Sex Dyads: Consequences for Job Satisfaction," *Journal of Occupational and Organizational Psychology* (March 1993): 13–28.

29. William Convoy, *Working Together . . . Communication in a Healthy Organization* (Columbus, OH: Charles Merrill, 1976). See also David Johnson et al., "Differences Between Formal and Informal Communication Channels," *Journal of Business Communication* (April 1994): 111–24.

30. Gary Dessler, *Winning Commitment: How to Build and Keep a Competitive Workforce* (New York: McGraw-Hill, 1993).

31. Pace and Faules, op. cit., 105–6.

32. Earl Plenty and William Machaner, "Stimulating Upward Communication," in *Readings in Organizational Behavior,* ed. Jerry Gray and Frederick Starke (Columbus, OH: Charles Merrill, 1977), 229–40. See also Pace and Faules, op. cit., 153–60.

33. This is based on Tom Peters and Robert Waterman, *In Search of Excellence* (New York: Harper & Row, 1982), 119–218.

34. This is based on David Abel, "New Leader's Style Shakes Up Harvard: Blunt Talk Contrasts with Predecessor's," *Boston Globe* (January 12, 2002): B1.

35. For a review and discussion, see James Smither et al., "An Examination of the Effects of an Upward Feedback Program over Time," *Personnel Psychology* 48, no. 1 (March 1995): 1–34.

36. Ibid., 10–11.

37. Ibid., 27.

38. See, for example, Pace and Faules, op. cit., 99–100.

39. Ibid., 99–100.

40. Kate Leahy, "The 10 Minute Manager's Guide to . . . Communicating with Employees," *Restaurants & Institutions* 116, no. 11 (June 1, 2006): 22–23.

41. R. Aggarwal and B. Simkins, "Open-Book Management—Optimizing Human Capital," *Business Horizons 44*, no. 5 (2001): 5–13. See also Brian Schwartz, "The Open Door Policy," *Business Review Weekly* 27, no. 13 (April 7, 2005): 69.

42. "Employers Profit from Opening the Books," *Bureau of National Affairs Bulletin to Management* (September 5, 1999): 288.

43. Ibid.

44. Keith Davis, "Cut Those Rumors Down to Size," *Supervisory Management* (June 1975): 206.

45. Eugene Walton, "How Efficient Is the Grapevine?" *Personnel* (March/April 1961): 45–49; reprinted in Keith Davis, *Organizational Behavior, A Book of Readings* (New York: McGraw-Hill, 1977). See also, T. Starbucker, "No News Isn't Necessarily Good News", *Conference Board Review* v. 47 no. 3 (Summer 2010) p. 5–6

46. Laura Mansnerus, "Wall Street Lawyers Being Laid Off as Deals Drop," *New York Times* (November 9, 2001): D1.

47. Ted Pollock, "For Improved Teamwork, Keep Them Informed: A Personal File of Stimulating Ideas, Little Known Facts and Daily Problem Solvers," *Supervision* 67, no. 3 (March 2006): 17–19.

48. Ibid.

49. Ibid.

50. Donna Goldwasser, "Me a Trainer?" *Training* (April 2001): 60–66.

51. Ann Pace, "Coaching Gains Ground," *T+D* 62, no. 7 (July 2008): 21.

52. This is based on Richard Luecke, *Coaching and Mentoring* (Boston: Harvard Business School Press, 2004), 8–9.

53. Luecke, op. cit., 9.

54. Gary Yukl, *Leadership in Organizations* (Upper Saddle River, NJ: Prentice Hall, 1998), 164.

55. The following are adapted from Arthur H. Bell and Dayle M. Smith, *Management Communication* (New York: Wiley, 1999), p. 14.

56. Adapted from Arthur H. Bell and Dayle M. Smith, *Management Communication* (New York: Wiley, 1999), p. 14.

57. Paula Caproni, *The Practical Coach* (Upper Saddle River, NJ: Prentice Hall, 2001), 106–8; "In Brief: Office Workers Want Instant E-Mail Responses," *New Media Age* (March 16, 2006): 13.

58. For instance, see Andrea Poe, "Don't Touch That Send Button," *HRMagazine* 46, no. 7 (July 2001): 74–80.

59. Thomas Burton and Rachel Silverman, "Lots of Empty Spaces in Corner Parking Lot Gets CEO Riled Up," *Wall Street Journal* (March 30, 2001): B3.

Chapter 13

1. Peter Glendinning, "Performance Management: Pariah or Messiah," *Public Personnel Management* 31, no. 2 (Summer 2002): 161–78. See also Herman Aguinis, *Performance Management* (Upper Saddle River, NJ: Pearson, 2007), 2.

2. Experts debate the pros and cons of tying appraisals to pay decisions. One side argues that doing so distorts the appraisals. A recent study concludes the opposite. Based on an analysis of surveys from over 24,000 employees in more than 6,000 workplaces in Canada, the researchers concluded: (1) Linking the employees' pay to their performance appraisals contributed to improved pay satisfaction; (2) even when appraisals are *not* directly linked to pay, they apparently contributed to pay satisfaction, "probably through mechanisms related to perceived organizational justice"; and (3) whether or not the employees received performance pay, "individuals who do not receive performance appraisals are significantly less satisfied with their pay." Mary Jo Ducharme et al., "Exploring the Links between Performance Appraisals and Pay Satisfaction," *Compensation and Benefits Review* (September/October 2005): 46–52. See also Robert Morgan, "Making the Most of Performance Management Systems," *Compensation and Benefits Review* (September/October 2006): 22–27.

3. See, for example, Doug Cederblom and Dan Pemerl, "From Performance Appraisal to Performance Management: One Agency's Experience," *Personnel Management* 31, no. 2 (Summer 2002): 131–40.

4. John (Jack) Welch, broadcast interview at Fairfield University, C-SPAN (May 5, 2001).

5. Howard Risher, "Getting Serious about Performance Management," *Compensation and Benefits Review* (November/December 2005): 18–26.

6. Del Jones, "More Firms Cut Workers Ranked at Bottom to Make Way for Talent," *USA Today* (May 30, 2001): B1.

7. Steve Bates, "Forced Ranking," *HR Magazine* (June 2003): 63–68.

8. Steven Cullen et al., "Forced Distribution Rating Systems and the Improvement of Workforce Potential: A Baseline Simulation," *Personnel Psychology* 58 (2005): 1.

9. "Survey Says Problems with Forced Ranking Include Lower Morale and Costly Turnover," *BNA Bulletin to Management* (September 16, 2004): 297.

10. Steve Bates, op. cit., 62.

11. "Straight Talk About Grading Employees on a Curve," *BNA Bulletin to Management* (November 1, 2001): 351; see also, B. Hazels, et. al., "Forced Ranking: A Review:, *Advanced Management Journal* v. 73 no. 2 (Spring 2008) p. 35–9.

12. See, for example, Timothy Keaveny and Anthony McGann, "A Comparison of Behavioral Expectation Scales and Graphic Rating Scales," *Journal of Applied Psychology*, 60 (1975): 695–703. See also John Ivancevich, "A Longitudinal Study of Behavioral Expectation Scales: Attitudes and Performance," *Journal of Applied Psychology* 30, no. 3 (Autumn 1986): 619–28.

13. Based on Donald Schwab, Herbert Heneman III, and Thomas DeCotiis, "Behaviorally Anchored Scales: A Review of the Literature," *Personnel Psychology*, 28 (1975): 549–62. For a discussion, see also N.M. Hauenstein, et. al., "BARS and Those Mysterious, Missing Middle Anchors", *Journal of Business & Psychology* v. 25 no. 4 (December 2010) p. 663–72.

14. Lawrence Fogli, Charles Hullin, and Milton Blood, "Development of First Level Behavioral Job Criteria," *Journal of Applied Psychology* 55 (1971): 3–8. See also Joseph Maiorca, "How to Construct Behaviorally Anchored Rating Scales (BARS) for Employee Evaluations," *Supervision* (August 1997): 15–19.

15. Kevin R. Murphy and Joseph Constans, "Behavioral Anchors as a Source of Bias in Rating," *Journal of Applied Psychology* 72, no. 4 (November 1987): 573–77; Aharon Tziner, "A Comparison of Three Methods of Performance Appraisal with Regard to Goal Properties, Goal Perception, and Ratee Satisfaction," *Group and Organization Management* 25, no. 2 (June 2000): pp. 175–91.

16. http://www.employeeappraiser.com/index.php (accessed January 10, 2008).

17. Vanessa Druskat and Steven Wolf, "Effects and Timing of Developmental Peer Appraisals in Self-Managing Workgroups," *Journal of Applied Psychology* 84, no. 1 (1999): 58–74.

18. R. G. Downey, F. F. Medland, and L. G. Yates, "Evaluation of a Peer Rating System for Predicting Subsequent Promotion of Senior Military Officers," *Journal of Applied Psychology* 61 (April 1976); see also Julie Barclay and Lynn Harland, "Peer Performance Appraisals: The Impact of Rater Competence, Rater Location, and Rating Correctability on Fairness Perceptions," *Group and Organization Management* 20, no. 1 (March 1995): 39–60.

19. Chockalingam Viswesvaran, Denize Ones, and Frank Schmidt, "Comparative Analysis of the Reliability of Job Performance Ratings," *Journal of Applied Psychology* 81, no. 5 (1996) 557–74. See also Kevin Murphy et al., "Raters Who Pursue Different Goals Give Different Ratings," *Journal of Applied Psychology* 89, no. 1 (2004): 158–64.

20. George Thornton III, "Psychometric Properties of Self-Appraisal of Job Performance," *Personnel Psychology* 33 (Summer 1980): 265. See also Cathy Anderson, Jack Warner, and Cassie Spencer, "Inflation Bias in Self-Assessment Evaluations: Implications for Valid Employee Selection," *Journal of Applied Psychology* 69, no. 4 (November 1984): 574–80; See also, M. Audrey Korsgaard et al., "The Effect of Other Orientation on Self–Supervisor Rating Agreement," *Journal of Organizational Behavior* 25, no. 7 (November 2004): 873–91; "Enabling Employee Success", *T+D* v. 63 no. 3 (March 2009) p. 88.

21. Forest Jourden and Chip Heath, "The Evaluation Gap in Performance Perceptions: Illusory Perceptions of Groups and Individuals," *Journal of Applied Psychology* 81, no. 4 (August 1996): 369–79. See also Sheri Ostroff, "Understanding Self-Other Agreement: A Look at Rater and Ratee Characteristics, Context, and Outcomes," *Personnel Psychology* 57, no. 2 (Summer 2004): 333–75.

22. Richard Reilly, James Smither, and Nicholas Vasilopoulos, "A Longitudinal Study of Upward Feedback," *Personnel Psychology* 49 (1996): 599–612.

23. Ibid., 599.

24. The evidence from another study suggests also that "upward and peer 360-degree ratings may be biased by rater affect [whether the rater likes the ratee]; therefore, at this point, these ratings should be used for the sole purpose of providing ratees with developmental feedback." David Antonioni and Heejoon Park, "The Relationship between Rater Affect and Three Sources of 360-Degree Feedback Ratings," *Journal of Management* 27, no. 4 (2001): 479–95.

25. "360-Degree Feedback on the Rise, Survey Finds," *BNA Bulletin to Management* (January 23, 1997): 31. See also T. Maylett, "360-Degree Feedback Revisited: The Transition From Development to Appraisal", *Compensation and Benefits Review* v. 41 no. 5 (September/October 2009) p. 52–9.

26. Carol Hymowitz, "Do 360-Degree Job Reviews by Colleagues Promote Honesty or Insults?" *The Wall Street. Journal* (December 12, 2000): B1.

27. See, for example, Adrienne Fox, "Curing What Ails Performance Reviews," *HR Magazine* (January 2009): 52–55.

28. Andrew Solomonson and Charles Lance, "Examination of the Relationship Between True Halo and Halo Effect in Performance Ratings," *Journal of Applied Psychology* 82, no. 5 (1997): 665–74.

29. Manuel London, Edward Mone, and John C. Scott, "Performance Management and Assessment: Methods for Improved Rater Accuracy and Employee Goal Setting," *Human Resource Management* 43, no. 4 (Winter 2004): 319–36.

30. Ted Turnasella, "Dagwood Bumstead, Will You Ever Get That Raise?" *Compensation and Benefits Review* (September–October 1995): 25–27. See also Solomonson and Lance, "Examination of the Relationship Between True Halo and Halo Effect," 665–74.

31. I. M. Jawahar and Charles Williams, "Where All the Children Are Above Average: The Performance Appraisal Purpose Effect," *Personnel Psychology* 50 (1997): 921.

32. Annette Simmons, "When Performance Reviews Fail," *Training and Development* 57, no. 9 (September 2003): 47–53. See also, D.V. Eremin, et. al., "Systemic bias in federal performance evaluations: Does hierarchy trump a performance management process?", *Public Performance & Management Review* v. 34 no. 1 (September 2010) p. 7–21

33. "Flawed Ranking System Revives Workers' Bias Claim," *BNA Bulletin to Management* (June 28, 2005: 206.

34. Karen Lyness and Madeline Heilman, "When Fit Is Fundamental: Performance Evaluations and Promotions of Upper-Level Female and Male Managers," *Journal of Applied Psychology* 91, no. 4 (2006): 777–75.

35. Madeline Heilman et al., "Penalties for Success: Reactions to Women Who Succeed at Male Gender Type Tasks," *Journal of Applied Psychology* 89, no. 3 (2004): 416–27. Managers may not rate successful female supervisors negatively (for instance, in terms of likeability and boss desirability) when they see the woman as supportive, caring, and sensitive to their needs. Madeline Heilman and Tyler Okimoto, "Why Are Women Penalized for Success at Male Tasks? The Implied Communality Deficit," *Journal of Applied Psychology* 92, no. 1 (2007): 81–92.

36. Jane Halpert, Midge Wilson, and Julia Hickman, "Pregnancy as a Source of Bias in Performance Appraisals," *Journal of Organizational Behavior* 14 (1993): 649–63.

37. Ibid., 655. See also, P. McDonald, et. al., "Expecting the worst: circumstances surrounding pregnancy discrimination at work and progress to formal redress", *Industrial Relations Journal* v. 39 no. 3 (May 2008) p. 229–47

38. Clinton Wingrove, "Developing an Effective Blend of Process and Technology in the New Era of Performance Management," *Compensation and Benefits Review* (January/February 2003): 25–30.

39. Joanne Sammer, "Calibrating Consistency," *HR Magazine* (January 2008): 73–74.

40. Angelo DeNisi and Lawrence Peters, "Organization of Information in Memory and the Performance Appraisal Process: Evidence from the Field," *Journal of Applied Psychology* 81, no. 6 (1996): 717–37.

41. Juan Sanchez and Philip DeLaTorre, "A Second Look at the Relationship Between Rating and Behavioral Accuracy in Performance Appraisal," *Journal of Applied Psychology* 81, no. 1 (1996): 7.

42. Richard Posthuma, "Twenty Best Practices for Just Employee Performance Reviews," *Compensation and Benefits Review* (January/February 2008): 47–54.

43. David Martin et al., "The Legal Ramifications of Performance Appraisal: The Growing Significance," *Public Personnel Management* 29, no. 3 (Fall 2000): 381–83.

44. Jon Werner and Mark Bolino, "Explaining U.S. Courts of Appeals' Decisions Involving Performance Appraisal: Accuracy, Fairness, and Validation," *Personnel Psychology* 50 (1997): 1–24.

45. Wayne Cascio and H. John Bernardin, "Implications of Performance Appraisal Litigation for Personnel Decisions," *Personnel Psychology* (Summer 1981): 211–12; Gerald Barrett and Mary Kernan, "Performance Appraisal and Terminations: A Review of Court Decisions Since *Brito v. Zia* with Implications for Personnel Practices," *Personnel Psychology* 40, no. 3 (Autumn 1987): 489–504; Elaine Pulakos, *Performance Management* (SHRM Foundation, 2004).

46. James Austin, Peter Villanova, and Hugh Hindman, "Legal Requirements and Technical Guidelines Involved in Implementing Performance Appraisal Systems," in Gerald Ferris and M. Ronald Buckley (eds.), *Human Resources Management*, 3rd ed. (Upper Saddle River, NJ: Prentice Hall, 1996), 271–88.

47. Joelle D. Elicker, Paul E. Levy, and Rosalie J. Hall, "The Role of Leader-Member Exchange in the Performance Appraisal Process," *Journal of Management* 32, no. 4 (August 2006): 531–51.

48. Paraphrased from ibid.

49. Ibid.

50. Ibid.

51. Peter Glendinning, "Performance Management: Pariah or Messiah," *Public Personnel Management* 31, no. 2 (Summer 2002): 161–78. See also Herman Aguinis, *Performance Management* (Upper Saddle River, NJ: Pearson, 2007), 2.

52. Howard Risher, "Getting Serious about Performance Management," *Compensation and Benefits Review* (November/December 2005): 19.

53. Wingrove, "Developing an Effective Blend of Process and Technology," 27.

54. http://www.activestrategy.com/events_and_news/press_releases/050108.aspx (accessed March 23, 2009).

Chapter 14

1. http://www.kornferry.com/PressRelease/3440?ckx=1 (accessed May 16, 2009).

2. Bennett Tepper, "Consequences of Abusive Supervision," *Academy of Management Journal* 43, no. 2 (2000): 178–90. See also Samuel Aryee et al., "Antecedents and Outcomes of Abusive Supervision: A Test of a Trickle-Down Model," *Journal of Applied Psychology* 92 no. 1 (2007): 191–201.

3. http://www.mayoclinic.com/health/stress/WL00049 (accessed May 16, 2009).

4. Wendy Boswell and Julie Olson-Buchanan, "Experiencing Mistreatment at Work: The Role of Grievance Filing, Nature of Mistreatment, and Employee Withdrawal," *Academy of Management Journal* 47 no. 1 (2004): 129–39. See also Aryee et al., op. cit.

5. Bennett Tepper et al., "Abusive Supervision and Subordinates' Organization Deviance," *Journal of Applied Psychology* 93, no. 4 (2008): 721–32.

6. G. R. Weaver and L. K. Treviño, "The Role of Human Resources in Ethics/Compliance Management: A Fairness Perspective," *Human Resource Management Review* 11 (2001): 113–34.

7. Michelle Donovan et al., "The Perceptions of Their Interpersonal Treatment Scale: Development and Validation of a Measure of Interpersonal Treatment in the Workplace," *Journal of Applied Psychology* 83, no. 5 (1998): 683–92.

8. Weaver and Treviño, op. cit., 117.

9. Russell Cropanzano and Thomas Wright, "Procedural Justice and Organizational Staffing: A Tale of Two Paradigms," *Human Resource Management Review* 13, no. 1 (2003): 7–40.

10. Suzanne Masterson, "A Trickle-Down Model of Organizational Justice: Relating Employees' and Customers' Perceptions of and Reactions to Fairness," *Journal of Applied Psychology* 86, no. 4 (2001): 594–601.

11. Kenneth Sovereign, *Personnel Law* (Upper Saddle River, NJ: Prentice Hall, 1999), 150.

12. This list is from http://www.legaltarget.com/employee_rights (accessed January 3, 2008).

13. Basically, *common law* refers to legal precedents. Judges' rulings set precedents, which then generally guide future judicial decisions.

14. Sovereign, op. cit., 192.

15. M. Audrey Korsgaard, Loriann Roberson, and R. Douglas Rymph, "What Motivates Fairness? The Role of Subordinate Assertive Behavior on Managers' Interactional Fairness," *Journal of Applied Psychology* 83, no. 5 (1998): 731–44.

16. Bennett Tepper et al., "Procedural Injustice, Victim Precipitation, and Abusive Supervision," *Personnel Psychology* 59,(2006): 11–23.

17. Marshall Schminke et al., "The Effect of Organizational Structure on Perceptions of Procedural Fairness," *Journal of Applied Psychology* 85, no. 2 (2000): 294–304.

18. Rudy Yandrick, "Lurking in the Shadows," *HR Magazine* (October 1999): 61–68. See also Helge Hoel and David Beale, "Workplace Bullying, Psychological Perspectives and Industrial Relations: Towards a Contextualized and Interdisciplinary Approach," *British Journal of Industrial Relations* 44, no. 2 (June 2006): 239–62.

19. W. Chan Kim and Rene Mauborgne, "Fair Process: Managing in the Knowledge Economy," *Harvard Business Review* (July/August 1997): 65–75.

20. Kelly Mollica, "Perceptions of Fairness," *HR Magazine* (June 2004): 169–71.

21. Manuel Velasquez, *Business Ethics: Concepts and Cases* (Upper Saddle River, NJ: Prentice Hall, 1992), 9. See also O. C. Ferrell, John Fraedrich, and Linog Ferrell, *Business Ethics* (Boston: Houghton Mifflin, 2008).

22. The following discussion, except as noted, is based on Velasquez, *Business Ethics*, 9–12.

23. For further discussion of ethics and morality, see Tom Beauchamp and Norman Bowie, *Ethical Theory and Business* (Upper Saddle River, NJ: Prentice Hall, 2001), 1–19.

24. Keith Winstein, "Suit Alleges Pfizer Spun Unfavorable Drug Studies," *The Wall Street Journal* (October 8, 2008): B1.

25. "What Role Should HR Play in Corporate Ethics?" *HR Focus* 81, no. 1 (January 2004): 3. See also Dennis Moberg, "Ethics Blind Spots in Organizations: How Systematic Errors in Person's Perception Undermine Moral Agency," *Organization Studies* 27, no. 3 (2006): 413–28.

26. Kevin Wooten, "Ethical Dilemmas in Human Resource Management: An Application of a Multidimensional Framework, a Unifying Taxonomy, and Applicable Codes," *Human Resource Management Review* 11 (2001): 161. See also Sean Valentine et al., "Employee Job Response as a Function of Ethical Context and Perceived Organization Support," *Journal of Business Research* 59, no. 5 (2006): 582–88.

27. Jennifer Kish-Gephart, David Harrison, and Linda Trevino, "Bad Apples, Bad Cases, and Bad Barrels: Meta-Analytic Evidence About Sources of Unethical Decisions That Work," *Journal of Applied Psychology* 95, no. 1 (2010,): 1–31.

28. Ibid., 21.

29. Vikas Anand et al., "Business as Usual: The Acceptance and Perpetuation of Corruption in Organizations," *Academy of Management Executive* 18, no. 2 (2004): 40–41.

30. "Ethics Policies Are Big with Employers, But Workers See Small Impact on the Workplace," *BNA Bulletin to Management* (June 29, 2000): 201.

31. From Guy Brumback, "Managing Above the Bottom Line of Ethics," *Supervisory Management* (December 1993): 12.

32. Weaver and Treviño, op. cit., 113–34.

33. Ibid., 114.

34. "Former CEO Joins WorldCom's Indicted," *Miami Herald* (March 3, 2004): 4C.

35. See for example, Roberta Johnson, *Whistleblowing: When It Works—and Why* (Boulder, CO: Lynne Rienner, 2003).

36. Dayton Fandray, "The Ethical Company," *Workforce* (December 2000): 74–77.

37. J. Krohe Jr., "The Big Business of Business Ethics," *Across the Board* 34 (May 1997): 23–29; Deborah Wells and Marshall Schminke, "Ethical Development and Human Resources Training: An Integrator Framework," *Human Resource Management Review* 11 (2001): 135–58.

38. Editorial: "Ethical Issues in the Management of Human Resources," *Human Resource Management Review* 11 (2001): 6; See also Joel Lefkowitz, "The Constancy of Ethics Amidst the Changing World of Work," *Human Resource Management Review* 16 (2006): 245–68.

39. William Byham, "Can You Interview for Integrity?" *Across the Board* 41, no. 2 (March/April 2004): 34–38. For a description of how the United States Military Academy uses its student admission and socialization processes to promote character development, see Evan Offstein and Ronald Dufresne, "Building Strong Ethics and Promoting Positive Character Development: The Influence of HRM at the United States Military Academy at West Point," *Human Resource Management* 46, no. 1 (Spring 2007): 95–114.

40. Kathryn Tyler, "Do the Right Thing, Ethics Training Programs Help Employees Deal with Ethical Dilemmas," *HR Magazine* (February 2005): 99–102.

41. Weaver and Treviño, op. cit., 123.

42. M. Ronald Buckley et al., "Ethical Issues in Human Resources Systems," *Human Resource Management*

Review 11, nos. 1, 2 (2001): 11, 29. See also Ann Pomeroy, "The Ethics Squeeze," *HR Magazine* (March 2006): 48–55.

43. Tom Asacker, "Ethics in the Workplace," *Training and Development* (August 2004): 44.

44. Ibid.

45. Michael Burr, "Corporate Governance: Embracing Sarbanes-Oxley," *Public Utilities Fortnightly* (October 15, 2003): 20–22.

46. This list is based on Linda K. Treviño, Gary R. Weaver, and Scott J. Reynolds, "Behavioral Ethics in Organizations: A Review," *Journal of Management* 32, no. 6 (2006): 951–90.

47. R. Bergman, "Identity as Motivation: Toward a Theory of the Moral Self," in D. K. Lapsley and D. Narvaez, (Eds.), *Moral Development, Self and Identity* (Mahwah, NJ: Lawrence Erlbaum), 21–46.

48. M. E. Schweitzer, L. Ordonez, and B. Douma, "Goal Setting as a Motivator of Unethical Behavior," *Academy of Management Journal* 47, no. 3 (2004): 422–32.

49. N. M. Ashkanasy, C. A. Windsor, and L. K. Treviño, "Bad Apples in Bad Barrels Revisited: Cognitive Moral Development, Just World Beliefs, Rewards, and Ethical Decision Making," *Business Ethics Quarterly* 16 (2006): 449–74.

50. Lester Bittel, *What Every Supervisor Should Know* (New York: McGraw-Hill, 1974), 308; and Thomas Salvo, "Practical Tips for Successful Progressive Discipline," *SHRM White Paper* (July 2004): http://www.shrm.org/hrresources/whitepapers_published/CMS_009030.asp (accessed January 5, 2008).

51. David Campbell et al., "Discipline Without Punishment—At Last," *Harvard Business Review* (July/August 1995): 162–78. See also, V. Liberman, "The Perfect Punishment", *Conference Board Review* v. 46 no. 1 (January/February 2009) p. 32–6, 38–9.

52. Robert Grossman, "Executive Discipline," *HR Magazine* 50, no. 8 (August 2005): 46–51; "The Evil Women Thesis," based on Sandva Hartman et al., "Males and Females in a Discipline Situation, Exploratory Research on Competing Hypotheses," *Journal of Managerial Issues* 6, no. 1 (Spring 1994): 57, 64–68; "A Woman's Place," *The Economist* 356, no. 8184 (August 19, 2000): 56.

53. "Employers Turn to Corporate Ombuds to Defuse Internal Ticking Time Bombs," *BNA Bulletin to Management* (August 9, 2005): 249.

54. Dick Grote, "Discipline without Punishment," *Across the Board* 38, no. 5 (September 2001): 52–57.

55. Ibid.

56. Dick Grote, "Attitude Adjustments: To Deal with an Employee's Bad Attitude, Focus on His or Her Specific Behaviors," *HR Magazine* 50, no. 7 (July 2005): 105–107.

57. Niccoló Machiavelli, *The Prince*, trans. W. K. Marriott (London: J. M. Dent & Sons, Ltd., 1958).

58. Gary Yukl, *Leadership and Organizations* (Upper Saddle River, NJ: Prentice Hall, 1998), 200.

59. Milton Zall, "Employee Privacy," *Journal of Property Management* 66, no. 3 (May 2001): 16.

60. Morris Attaway, "Privacy in the Workplace on the Web," *Internal Auditor* 58, no. 1 (February 2001): 30.

61. Declam Leonard and Angela France, "Workplace Monitoring: Balancing Business Interests with Employee Privacy Rights," *Society for Human Resource Management Legal Report* (May–June 2003): 3–6; "Blogs, Networking Sites Drive Workplace Privacy Disputes," *BNA Bulletin to Management* (August 5, 2008): 255.

62. Rita Zeidner, "Keeping E-Mail in Check," *HR Magazine* (June 2007): 70–74.

63. Fredric Leffler and Lauren Palais, "Filter Out Perilous Company E-Mails," *Society for Human Resource Management Legal Report* (August 2008): 3.

64. Bill Roberts, "Stay Ahead of the Technology Use Curve," *HR Magazine* (October 2008): 57–61.

65. "Time Clocks Go High Touch, High Tech to Keep Workers from Gaming the System," *BNA Bulletin to Management* (March 25, 2004): 97.

66. Andrea Poe, "Make Foresight 20/20," *HR Magazine* (February 2000): 74–80.

67. Gundars Kaupin et al., "Recommended Employee Location Monitoring Policies," http://www. SHRM.org (accessed January 2, 2007).

68. "Do You Know Where Your Workers Are? GPS Units Aid Efficiency, Raise Privacy Issues," *BNA Bulletin to Management* (July 22, 2004): 233. See also http://www.WORKRIGHTS.ORG/issue_electronic/NWI_GPS_report.pdf (accessed January 2, 2007).

69. *Vega-Rodriguez v. Puerto Rico Telephone Company*, CA1, #962061, April 8, 1997, discussed in "Video Surveillance Withstands Privacy Challenge," *BNA Bulletin to Management* (April 17, 1997): 121.

70. *Quon v. Arch Wireless Operating Co.*, 529f.3d 892, Ninth Circuit, 2008; "Employers Should

Re-Examine Policies in Light of Ruling," *BNA Bulletin to Management* (August 12, 2008): 263.

71. Kathy Gurchiek, "iPods Can Hit Sour Note in the Office," *HR Magazine* (April 2006).

72. Ibid.

73. Charles Muhl, "The Employment at Will Doctrine: Three Major Exceptions," *Monthly Labor Review* 124, no. 1 (January 2001): 3–11.

74. Michael Orey, "Fear of Firing," *BusinessWeek* (April 23, 2007): 52–54.

75. Robert Lanza and Morton Warren, "United States: Employment at Will Prevails Despite Exceptions to the Rule," *Society for Human Resource Management Legal Report* (October–November 2005): 1–8.

76. Joseph Famularo, *Handbook of Modern Personnel Administration* (New York: McGraw Hill, 1982), 65.3–65.5. See also Carolyn Hirschman, "Off Duty, Out of Work," *HR Magazine* http://www.shrm.org/hrmagazine/articles/0203/0203hirschman.asp (accessed January 1, 2008).

77. Famularo, op. cit., 65.4–64.5.

78. Kenneth Sovereign, *Personnel Law* (Upper Saddle River, NJ: Prentice Hall, 1999); Connie Wanderg et al., "Perceived Fairness of Layoffs Among Individuals Who Have Been Laid Off: A Longitudinal Study," *Personnel Psychology* 2 (1999): 59–84.

79. Wanderg et al., ibid.; Brian Klass and Gregory Dell'omo, "Managerial Use of Dismissal: Organizational Level Determinants," *Personnel Psychology* 50 (1997): 927–53; Nancy Hatch Woodward, "Smoother Separations," *HR Magazine* (June 2007): 94–97.

80. "E-Mail Used for Layoffs, Humiliation," *BNA Bulletin to Management* (October 2, 2007): 315.

81. Jaikumar Vijayan, "Downsizings Leave Firms Vulnerable to Digital Attacks," *Computerworld* 25 (2001): 6–7.

82. Paul Falcon, "Give Employees the (Gentle) Hook," *HR Magazine* (April 2001): 121–28.

83. James Coil III and Charles Rice, "Three Steps to Creating Effective Employee Releases," *Employment Relations Today* (Spring 1994): 91–94; "Fairness to Employees Can Stave Off Litigation," *BNA Bulletin to Management* (November 27, 1999): 377; Richard Bayer, "Termination with Dignity," *Business Horizons* 43, no. 5 (September 2000): 4–10; Betty Sosnin, "Orderly Departures," *HR Magazine* 50, no. 11 (November 2005): 74–78; "Severance Pay: Not Always the Norm," *HR Magazine* (May 2008): 28.

84. See, for example, Richard Hannah, "The Attraction of Severance," *Compensation & Benefits Review* (November/December 2008): 37–44.

85. Jonathon Segal, "Severance Strategies," *HR Magazine* (July 2008): 95–96.

86. "Lawyers Say Reasonable Employer Is Best Defense Against Wrongful Termination Claims," *BNA Bulletin to Management* (November 20, 2007): 379.

87. Based on Coil and Rice, op. cit., 91–94.

88. "One More Heart Risk: Firing Employees," *Miami Herald* (March 20, 1998): C1, C7.

89. Kemba Dunham, "The Kinder Gentler Way to Lay Off Employees—More Human Approach Helps," *Wall Street Journal* (March 13, 2001): B-1.

90. Leon Grunberg, Sarah Moore, and Edward Greenberg, "Managers' Reactions to Implementing Layoffs: Relationship to Health Problems and Withdrawal Behaviors," *Human Resource Management* 45, no. 2 (Summer 2006): 159–78.

91. Adrienne Fox, "Prune Employees Carefully," *HR Magazine* (April 1, 2008).

92. Ibid.

93. "Calling a Layoff a Layoff," *Workforce Management* (April 21, 2008): 41.

94. David Gebler, "Is Your Culture a Risk Factor?" *Business and Society Review* 111, no. 3 (Fall 2006): 337–62.

95. John Cohan, "'I Didn't Know' and 'I Was Only Doing My Job': Has Corporate Governance Careened out of Control? A Case Study of Enron's Information Myopia," *Journal of Business Ethics* 40, no. 3 (October 2002): 275–99.

96. Gebler, op. cit.

97. Ibid.

98. Based on "Theft Is Unethical," *HE Solutions* 34 (October 2002): 66.

99. Bureau of National Affairs, *Bulletin to Management* (September 13, 1985): 3.

Chapter 15

1. Steven Greenhouse, "Board Accuses Starbucks of Trying to Block Union," *The New York Times* (April 3, 2007): B2; http://www.starbucksunion.org/ (accessed March 25, 2009).

2. Much of this chapter is adapted from Gary Dessler, *Human Resource Management* (Upper Saddle River, NJ: Pearson Prentice Hall, 2011), 542–578.

3. http://www.bls.gov/news.release/union2.nr0.htm (accessed April 2, 2009).

4. Ibid.; "Union Membership Rises," *Compensation & Benefits Review* (May/June 2008): 9.

5. Joseph Adler, "The Past as Prologue? A Brief History of the Labor Movement in the United States," *International Personnel Management Association for HR* 35, no. 4 (Winter 2006): 311–29.

6. Stephen Greenhouse, "Most US Union Members Are Working for the Government, New Data Shows," *The New York Time,* (January 23, 2010): B1–B5.

7. Ibid.

8. http://www.bls.gov/news.release/union2.nr0.htm (accessed April 2, 2009).

9. Michael Ash and Jean Seago, "The Effect of Registered Nurses' Unions on Heart Attack Mortality," *Industrial and Labor Relations Review* 57, no. 3 (April 2004): 422–42.

10. Steven Abraham et al., "The Impact of Union Membership on Intent to Leave," *Employee Responsibilities and Rights* 17, no. 4 (2005): 21–23.

11. Paul Monies, "Unions Hit Hard by Job Losses, Right to Work," *The Daily Oklahoman* (via Knight Ridder/Tribune Business News) (February 1, 2005). Now accessible at http://www.accessmylibrary.com/article-1G1-127994772/unions-hithard-job.html (accessed August 11, 2009).

12. Robert Grossman, "Unions Follow Suit," *HR Magazine* (May 2005): 49.

13. Ann Zimmerman, "Pro-Union Butchers at Wal-Mart Win a Union Battle but Lose War," *Wall Street Journal* (April 11, 2000): A14. See also Steven Greenhouse, "Report Assails Wal-Mart over Unions," *The New York Times* (May 1, 2007): C3.

14. Donna Buttigieg et al., "An Event History Analysis of Union Joining and Leaving," *Journal of Applied Psychology* 92, no. 3 (2007): 829–39.

15. Kris Maher, "The New Union Worker," *Wall Street Journal* (September 27, 2005): B1, B11.

16. Arthur Sloane and Fred Whitney, *Labor Relations* (Upper Saddle River, NJ: Prentice Hall, 2007), 335–36.

17. Benjamin Taylor and Fred Witney, *Labor Relations Law* (Upper Saddle River, NJ: Prentice Hall, 1992), 170–71.

18. http://www.dol.gov/whd/state/righttowork.htm (accessed February 13, 2010). Indiana's law applies only to schoolteachers; without Indiana there are 22 right-to-work states.

19. Steven Greenhouse, "Union Rejoining AFL-CIO," *The New York Times* (September 18, 2009): A18.

20. The following material is based on Sloane and Witney, op. cit., 46–124.

21. "Union Membership by State and Industry," *BNA Bulletin to Management* (May 29, 1997): 172–73; "Regional Trends: Union Membership by State and Multiple Jobholding by State," *Monthly Labor Review* 123, no. 9 (September 2000): 40–41.

22. Sloane and Witney, op. cit., 121.

23. Cathie Sheffield-Thompson, "Web Resources and Techniques for Organizing and Membership Development, 2006 Higher Ed State Staff Training," *NEA Research* (December 7–9, 2006), csheffield@nea.org (accessed March 23, 2009).

24. "Some Say Salting Leaves Bitter Taste for Employers," *BNA Bulletin to Management* (March 4, 2004): 79; and http://www.nlrb.gov/global/search/index.aspx?mode=s&qt=salting&col=nlrb&gb=y (accessed January 14, 2008). For a management lawyer's perspective, see http://www.fklaborlaw.com/union_salt-objectives.html (accessed May 25, 2007).

25. Diane Hatch and James Hall, "Salting Cases Clarified by NLRB," *Workforce* (August 2000): 92. For a management lawyer's perspective, see http://www.fklaborlaw.com/union_salt-objectives.html (accessed May 25, 2007).

26. The following are adapted and/or quoted from Kate Bronfenbrenner, "The Role of Union Strategies in NLRB Certification Elections," *Industrial and Labor Relations Review* 50 (January 1997): 195–212.

27. Frederick Sullivan, "Limiting Union Organizing Activity Through Supervisors," *Personnel* 55 (July/August 1978): 55–65. See also Edward Young and William Levy, "Responding to a Union-Organizing Campaign: Do You and Your Supervisors Know the Legal Boundaries in a Union Campaign?" *Franchising World* 39, no. 3 (March 2007): 45–49.

28. See, for example, www.powelltrachtman.com/CM/Publications/pps_unions.ppt (accessed September 30, 2010).

29. Jonathon Segal, "Unshackle Your Supervisors to Stay Union Free," *HR Magazine* (June 1998): 62–65. See also http://www.nlrb.gov/workplace_rights/nlra_violations.aspx (accessed January 14, 2008).

30. Whether employers must give union representatives permission to organize on employer-owned property at shopping malls is a matter of legal debate. The U.S. Supreme Court ruled in *Lechmere, Inc. v. National Labor Relations Board* that employers may bar nonemployees from their property if the nonemployees have reasonable alternative means of communicating their message to the intended audience. However, if the employer lets other organizations like the Salvation Army set up at their workplace, the NLRB may view discriminating against the union organizers as an unfair labor practice. See, for example, "Union Access to Employer's Customers Restricted," *BNA Bulletin to Management* (February 15, 1996): 49; "Workplace Access for Unions Hinges on Legal Issues," *BNA Bulletin to Management* (April 11, 1996): 113.

31. http://www.nlrb.gov/nlrb/shared_files/brochures/basicguide.pdf (accessed January 14, 2011).

32. Michael R. Carrell and Christina Heavrin, *Labor Relations and Collective Bargaining: Cases, Practices, and Law* (Upper Saddle River, NJ: Prentice Hall, 2001), 176–77.

33. John Fossum, *Labor Relations* (Dallas: BPI, 1982), 246–50.

34. *Boulwareism* is the name given to a strategy, now generally held in disfavor, by which the company, based on an exhaustive study of what it thought its employees wanted, made but one offer at the bargaining table and then refused to bargain any further unless convinced by the union on the basis of new facts that its original position was wrong. The NLRB subsequently found that the practice of offering the same settlement to all units, insisting that certain parts of the package could not differ among agreements, and communicating to the employees about how negotiations were going amounted to an illegal pattern. Fossum, op. cit., 267. See also William Cooke, Aneil Mishra, Gretchen Spreitzer, and Mary Tschirhart, "The Determinants of NLRB Decision-Making Revisited," *Industrial and Labor Relations Review* 48, no. 2 (January 1995): 237–57.

35. See, for example, Sloane and Witney, op. cit., 177–218.

36. And with or without reaching a solution, impasses and union-management conflict can leave union members demoralized. See, for example, Jessica Marquez, "Taking Flight," *Workforce Magazine* (June 9, 2008): 1, 18.

37. Fossum, op. cit., 312. See also Thomas Watkins, "Assessing Arbitrator Competence," *Arbitration Journal* 47, no. 2 (June 1992): 43–48.

38. Fossum, op. cit., 317.

39. Mark Fitzgerald, "UAW Lifts Boycott," *Editor and Publisher* (February 26, 2001): 9.

40. For a discussion, see Herbert Northrup, "Union Corporate Campaigns and Inside Games as a Strike Form," *Employee Relations Law Journal* 19, no. 4 (Spring 1994): 507–49.

41. Jessica Materna, "Union Launches Web Site to Air Grievances Against San Francisco Marriott," *San Francisco Business Times* (May 4, 2001): 15.

42. Northrup, op. cit., 513.

43. Ibid., 518.

44. Clifford Koen Jr., Sondra Hartmen, and Dinah Payne, "The NLRB Wields a Rejuvenated Weapon," *Personnel Journal* (December 1996): 85–87.

45. Sloane and Witney, op. cit., 221–27.

46. Carrell and Heavrin, op. cit., 417–18.

47. Reed Richardson, *Collective Bargaining by Objectives* (Upper Saddle River, NJ: Prentice Hall, 1977).

48. Duncan Adams, "Worker Grievances Consume Roanoke, VA Mail Distribution Center," *Knight-Ridder/Tribune Business News* (March 27, 2001): Item 01086009.

49. See M. Gene Newport, *Supervisory Management* (West Group, 1976), p. 273, for an excellent checklist. See also Mark Lurie, "The Eight Essential Steps in Grievance Processing," *Dispute Resolution Journal* 54, no. 4 (November 1999): 61–65.

50. William M. Haraway, III, "Employee Grievance Programs: Understanding the Nexus Between Workplace Justice, Organizational Legitimacy and Successful Organizations," *Public Personnel Management* 34, no. 4 (Winter 2005): 335.

51. Ibid.

52. Jessica Marquez, "NY Unions Cage Inflatable Rat, Try Teamwork," *Workforce Management* (November 3, 2008): 10.

53. See, for example, Jo Blandon et al., "Have Unions Turned the Corner? New Evidence on Recent Trends in Union Recognition in UK Firms," *British Journal of Industrial Relations* 44, no. 2 (June 2006): 169–90.

54. http://www.bls.gov/news.release/union2.nr0.htm (accessed April 2, 2009).

55. Jennifer Schramm, "The Future of Unions," *Society for Human Resource Management, Workplace Visions* 4 (2005): 1–8.

56. Ibid. See also http://www.changetowin.org/about-us.html (accessed February 13, 2010).

57. "The Limits of Solidarity," *The Economist* (September 23, 2006): 34.

58. Chris Maher, "Specter Won't Support Union-Backed Bill," *The Wall Street Journal* (March 20, 2009): A3.

59. "Unions Using Class Actions to Pressure Nonunion Companies," *BNA Bulletin to Management* (August 22, 2006): 271. Some believe that today, "long-term observers see more bark than bite in organized labor's efforts to revitalize." See, for example, Robert Grossman, "We Organized Labor and Code" *HR Magazine* (January 2008): 37–40.

60. Dean Scott, "Unions Still a Potent Force," *Kiplinger Business Forecasts* (March 26, 2003).

61. "Contracts Call for Greater Labor–Management Teamwork," *BNA Bulletin to Management* (April 29, 1999): 133.

62. Steven Greenhouse, "Steelworkers Merge with British Union," *The New York Times* (July 3, 2008): C4.

63. Chris Purcell, "Rhetoric Flying in WGA Talks," *Television Week* 26, no. 30 (July 20, 2007): 3–30; Peter Sanders, "In Hollywood, A Tale of Two Union Leaderships," *The Wall Street Journal* (January 7, 2008): B2.

64. Purcell, op. cit.

65. Ibid.

66. James Hibberd, "Guild Talks Break with No Progress," *Television Week* 26, no. 38 (October 8–15, 2007): 1, 30.

67. Ibid.

68. "DGA Deal Sets the Stage for Writers," *Television Week* 27, no. 3 (January 21, 2008): 3, 33.

69. "WGA, Studios Reach Tentative Agreement," *UPI News Track* (February 3, 2008).

70. Raymond Hilgert and Cyril Ling, *Cases and Experiential Exercises in Management* (Upper Saddle River, NJ: Prentice Hall, 1996), 201–203.

Chapter 16

1. Michael Wilson, "Manslaughter Charge in Trench Collapse," *The New York Times* (June 12, 2008): B1. This chapter is adapted in large part from Gary Dessler, *Human Resource Management* (Upper Saddle River, NJ: Pearson Prentce Hall, 2011), 580–630.

2. For a discussion of specific strategies for reducing fatalities at work, see, for example, Laura Walter, "Facing the Unthinkable: Fatality Prevention in the Workplace," *Occupational Hazards* (January 2008): 32–39.

3. See http://www.bls.gov/iif/oshwc/osh/os/ostb1757.txt (accessed January 19, 2008).

4. "BLS Likely Underestimating Injury and Illness Estimates," *Occupational Hazards* (May 2006): 16; Tahira Probst et al., "Organizational Injury Rate Underreporting: The Moderating Effect of Organizational Safety Climate," *Journal of Applied Psychology* 93, no. 5 (2008): 1147–54.

5. Greg Hom, "Protecting Eyes from High-Tech Hazards," *Occupational Hazards* (March 1999): 53–55; "Workplace Injuries by Industry, 2002," *Safety Compliance Letter* no. 2438 (February 2004): 12; Leigh Strope, "Deaths at Work Rise Slightly to 5,559 in 2003, with Most Occurring in Construction, Transportation," *AP News* (September 22, 2004). See also Katherine Torres, "Stepping into the Kitchen: Protection for Food Workers," *Occupational Hazards* (January 2007): 29–30.

6. "Blame New Computers for Sick Buildings," *USA Today* 129, no. 2672 (May 2001): 8.

7. Michael Pinto, "Why Are Indoor Air Quality Problems So Prevalent Today?" *Occupational Hazards* (January 2001): 37–39, see also, C. Palmeri, "The Dividends From Green Offices", *Business Week* no. 4158 (December 7, 2009) p. 15 .

8. Sandy Moretz, "Safe Havens?" *Occupational Hazards* (November 2000): 45–46.

9. Willie Hammer, *Occupational Safety Management and Engineering* (Upper Saddle River, NJ: Prentice Hall, 1985), 62–63. See also "DuPont's 'STOP' Helps Prevent Workplace Injuries and Incidents," *Asia Africa Intelligence Wire* (May 17, 2004).

10. F. David Pierce, "Safety in the Emerging Leadership Paradigm," *Occupational Hazards* (June 2000): 63–66. See also, for example, Josh Williams, "Optimizing the Safety Culture," *Occupational Hazards* (May 2008): 45–49.

11. Sandy Smith, "Louisiana-Pacific Corp. Builds Safety into Everything It Does," *Occupational Hazards* (November 2007): 41–42.

12. Ibid. In a similar case, in 2008, the owner of a Brooklyn, New York, construction site was arrested for manslaughter when a worker died in a collapsed trench. Michael Wilson, "Manslaughter Charge in Trench Collapse," *The New York Times* (June 12, 2008): B1.

13. "A Safety Committee Man's Guide," Aetna Life and Casualty Insurance Company, Catalog 87684, 17–21.

14. Josh Williams, "Improving Management Support for Safety to Optimize Safety Culture," *Occupational Hazards* 70, no. 6 (June 2008): 71–74.

15. Based on a discussion of the findings in Sandy Smith, "Leadership's Effects on Employee Health, Well-Being," *Occupational Hazards* (September 2008): 18–19.

16. Ibid.

17. Ibid.

18. Ibid.

19. Based on *All About OSHA*, rev. ed. (Washington, DC: U.S. Department of Labor, 1980); http://www.OSHA.gov (accessed January 19, 2008).

20. "Safety Rule on Respiratory Protection Issues," *BNA Bulletin to Management* (January 8, 1998): 1. See also "Staying on Top of OSHA Terms Helps Measure Safety," *Safety and Health* 170, no. 1 (July 2004): 44.

21. "OSHA Hazard Communication Standard Enforcement," *BNA Bulletin to Management* (February 23, 1989): 13. See also William Kincaid, "OSHA vs. Excellence in Safety Management," *Occupational Hazards* (December 2002): 34–36.

22. "What Every Employer Needs to Know About OSHA Record Keeping," U.S. Department of Labor, Bureau of Labor Statistics (Washington, DC), report 412–3, p. 3.

23. "Supreme Court Says OSHA Inspectors Need Warrants," *Engineering News Record* (June 1, 1978): 9–10; W. Scott Railton, "OSHA Gets Tough on Business," *Management Review* 80, no. 12 (December 1991): 28–29; Steve Hollingsworth, "How to Survive an OSHA Inspection," *Occupational Hazards* (March 2004): 31–33.

24. http://osha.gov/as/opa/oshafacts.html (accessed January 19, 2008); Edwin Foulke Jr., "OSHA's Evolving Role in Promoting Occupational Safety and Health," *EHS Today* (November 2008): 44–49. Some believe that under the Democratic administration of President Obama, OSHA may move from voluntary programs back to increased attention on inspections. See, for example, Laura Walter, "Safety Roundtable: The View from the End of an Era," *EHS Today* (December 2008): 30–31.

25. http://www.osha.gov/Publications/osha2098.pdf+OSHA+inspection+priorities&hl=en&ct=clnk&cd=1&gl=us (accessed January 19, 2008).

26. Patricia Poole, "When OSHA Knocks," *Occupational Hazards* (February 2008): 5961.

27. Robert Grossman, "Handling Inspections: Tips from Insiders," *HR Magazine* (October 1999): 41–50; and "OSHA Inspections," OSHA, http://www.osha.gov/Publications/osha2098.pdf (accessed May 26, 2007).

28. These are based on James Nash, "The Top Ten Ways to Get into Trouble with OSHA," *Occupational Hazards* (December 2003): 27 30.

29. Charles Chadd, "Managing OSHA Compliance: The Human Resources Issues," *Employee Relations Law Journal* 20, no. 1 (Summer 1994): 106.

30. Arthur Sapper, "The Oft-Missed Step: Documentation of Safety Discipline," *Occupational Hazards* (January 2006): 59.

31. "A Safety Committee Man's Guide," Aetna Life and Casualty Insurance Company, Catalog 87684. See also Dan Petersen, "The Barriers to Safety Excellence," *Occupational Hazards* (December 2000): 37–39.

32. "Did This Supervisor Do Enough to Protect Trench Workers?" *Safety Compliance Letter* (October 2003): 9.

33. For a discussion of this, see David Hofmann and Adam Stetzer, "A Cross-Level Investigation of Factors Influencing Unsafe Behaviors and Accidents," *Personnel Psychology* 49 (1996): 307–308. See also David Hoffman and Barbara Mark, "An Investigation of the Relationship between Safety Climate and Medication Errors as well as Other Nurse and Patient Outcomes," *Personnel Psychology* 50, no. 9 (2006): 847–69.

34. Jimi Michalscheck, "The Basics of Lock Out/Tag Out Compliance: Creating an Effective Program," *EHS Today* (January 2010): 35–37.

35. Discussed in Douglas Haaland, "Who Is the Safest Bet for the Job? Find Out Why the Guy in the Next Cubicle May Be the Next Accident Waiting to Happen," *Security Management* 49, no. 2 (February 2005): 51–57.

36. "Thai Research Points to Role of Personality in Road Accidents," *Asia and Africa Intelligence Wire*

(February 23, 2005, downloaded May 28, 2005); Donald Bashline et al., "Bad Behavior: Personality Tests Can Help Underwriters Identify High-Risk Drivers," *Best's Review* 105, no. 12 (April 2005): 63–64.

37. Todd Nighswonger, "Threat of Terror Impacts Workplace Safety," *Occupational Hazards* (July 2002): 24–26.

38. Mike Carlson, "Machine Safety Solutions for Protecting Employees and Safeguarding Against Machine Hazards," *EHS Today* (July 2009): 24.

39. Susannah Figura, "Don't Slip Up on Safety," *Occupational Hazards* (November 1996): 29–31. See also Russ Wood, "Defining the Boundaries of Safety," *Occupational Hazards* (January 2001): 41–43.

40. See, for example, Laura Walter, "What's in a Glove?" *Occupational Hazards* (May 2008): 35–36.

41. Donald Groce, "Keep the Gloves On!" *Occupational Hazards* (June 2008): 45–47.

42. You can find videos about new personal protective products at "SafetyLive TV" at http://www.occupationalhazards.com (accessed March 14, 2009).

43. James Zeigler, "Protective Clothing: Exploring the Wearability Issue," *Occupational Hazards* (September 2000): 81–82; Sandy Smith, "Protective Clothing and the Quest for Improved Performance," *Occupational Hazards* (February 2008): 63–66.

44. Laura Walter, "For Clothing: Leaving Hazards in the Dust," *EHS Today* (January 2010): 20–22.

45. "The Complete Guide to Personal Protective Equipment," *Occupational Hazards* (January 1999): 49–60. See also Edwin Zalewski, "Noise Control: It's More Than Just Earplugs: OSHA Requires Employers to Evaluate Engineering and Administrative Controls Before Using Personal Protective Equipment," *Occupational Hazards* 68, no. 9 (September 2006): 48(3). You can find videos about new personal protective products at "SafetyLive TV" at http://www.occupationalhazards.com (accessed March 14, 2009).

46. Sandy Smith, "Protecting Vulnerable Workers," *Occupational Hazards* (April 2004): 25–28. In addition to millions of women in factory jobs, about 10% of the construction industry workforce is female, and there are almost 200,000 women in the U.S. military. Women also represent almost 80% of health-care workers, where puncture and chemical-resistant gloves are particularly

important. David Shutt, "Protecting the Hands of Working Women," EHS Today (October 2009): 29–32.

47. See, for example, Walter, "What's in a Glove?" 35–36.

48. Groce, op. cit., 45–47.

49. Linda Tapp, "We Can Do It: Protecting Women Workers," *Occupational Hazards* (October 2003): 26–28.

50. Katherine Torres, "Don't Lose Sight of the Older Workforce," (Occupational Hazards): (June 2008): 55–59.

51. Ibid.

52. Robert Pater, "Boosting Safety with an Aging Workforce," *Occupational Hazards* (March 2006): 24.

53. Michael Silverstein, "Designing the Age Friendly Workplace," *Occupational Hazards* (December 2007): 29–31.

54. Elizabeth Rogers and William Wiatrowski, "Injuries, Illnesses, and Fatalities among Older Workers," *Monthly Labor Review* 128, no. 10 (October 2005): 24–30.

55. Robert Pater and Ron Bowles, "Directing Attention to Boost Safety Performance," *Occupational Hazards* (March 2007): 4648.

56. Gerald Borofsky, Michelle Bielema, and James Hoffman, "Accidents, Turnover, and Use of a Pre-Employment Screening Interview," *Psychological Reports* (1993): 1067–76.

57. Ibid., p. 1072. See also Keith Rosenblum, "The Companion Solution to Ergonomics: Pretesting for the Job," *Risk Management* 50, no. 11 (November 2003): 26(6).

58. Dan Hartshorn, "The Safety Interview," *Occupational Hazards* (October 1999): 107–11.

59. Laura Walter, "Surfing for Safety," *Occupational Hazards* (July 2008): 23–29.

60. James Nash, "Rewarding the Safety Process," *Occupational Hazards* (March 2000): 29–34.

61. Quoted in Josh Cable, "Seven Suggestions for a Successful Safety Incentives Program," *Occupational Hazards* 67, no. 3 (March 2005): 39–43. See also Jill Bishop, "Create a Safer Work Environment by Bridging the Language and Culture Gap," *EHS Today* (March 2009): 42–44.

62. See, for example, Ron Bruce, "Online from Kazakhstan to California," Occupational Hazards (June 2008): 61–65.

63. Michael Blotzer, "PDA Software Offers Auditing Advances," *Occupational Hazards* (December 2001):

11. See also Eric Anderson, "Automating Health & Safety Processes Creates Value," *Occupational Hazards* (April 2008): 53–63.

64. See, for example, Josh Cable, "Seven Suggestions for a Successful Safety Incentive Program," *Occupational Hazards* 67, no. 3 (March 2005): 39–43.

65. Don Williamson and Jon Kauffman, "From Tragedy to Triumph: Safety Grows Wings at Golden Eagle," *Occupational Hazards* (February 2006): 17–25.

66. James Nash, "Construction Safety: Best Practices in Training Hispanic Workers," *Occupational Hazards* (February 2004): 35–38.

67. Linda Johnson, "Preventing Injuries: The Big Payoff," *Personnel Journal* (April 1994): 61–64; David Webb, "The Bathtub Effect: Why Safety Programs Fail," *Management Review* (February 1994): 51–54. See also http://www.osha.gov/Publications/osha2098.pdf (accessed May 26, 2007).

68. http://www.aihaaps.ca/palm/occhazards.html (accessed April 26, 2009).

69. Blotzer, "PDA Software Offers Auditing Advances," 11.

70. Note that the vast majority of workers' injury related deaths occur not at work, but when the employees are off the job, often at home. More employers, including Johnson & Johnson, are therefore implementing safety campaigns encouraging employees to apply safe practices at home, as well as at work. Katherine Torres, "Safety Hits Home," *Occupational Hazards* (July 2006): 19–23.

71. Michelle Campolieti and Douglas Hyatt, "Further Evidence on the 'Monday Effect' in Workers' Compensation," *Industrial and Labor Relations Review* 59, no. 3 (April 2006): 438–50.

72. See for example, Rob Wilson, "Five Ways to Reduce Workers' Compensation Claims," *Occupational Hazards* (December 2005): 43–46.

73. "Strict Policies Mean Big Cuts in Premiums," *Occupational Hazards* (May 2000): 51.

74. See, for example, *Workers' Compensation Manual for Managers and Supervisors*, 36–39.

75. "Study: No Warm Welcome After Comp Leave," *Occupational Hazards* (February 2001): 57.

76. Ibid., p. 51.

77. http://www.zeraware.com (accessed March 22, 2009).

78. This is based on Paul Puncochar, "The Science and Art to Identifying Workplace Hazards," *Occupational Hazards* (September 2003): 50–54.

79. Recently, the United States has been moving toward adopting the United Nations' globally harmonized system of classification and labeling of chemicals. See Jytte Syska, "GHS: What You Need to Know," *EHS Today* (November 2009): 43.

80. Ibid., 52.

81. Where employees may encounter chemical spills, OSHA standards require that emergency eye washers and showers be available for employees to use. Michael Bolden, "Choosing and Maintaining Emergency Eye Washers/Showers," *EHS Today* (January 2010): 39–41.

82. Sandy Smith, "SARS: What Employers Need to Know," *Occupational Hazards* (July 2003) 33–35.

83. "CDC Recommends and 95 Respirators in Revised H1N1 Flu Guidance for Healthcare Workers," *BNA Bulletin to Management* (October 20, 2009): 329–36; and Pamela Ferrante, "H1N1: Spreading the Message," *EHS Today* (January 2010): 25–27.

84. Based on the report *Workplace Screening & Brief Intervention: What Employees Can and Should Do About Excessive Alcohol Use*, in "Report Says Employee Alcohol Abuse Closely Tied to Companies," *BNA Bulletin to Management* (June 10, 2008): 101.

85. "15% of Workers Drinking, Drunk, or Hungover while at Work, According to New University Study," *BNA Bulletin to Management* (January 24, 2006): 27.

86. "Facing Facts About Workplace Substance Abuse," *Rough Notes* 144, no. 5 (May 2001): 114–18.

87. Todd Nighswonger, "Just Say Yes to Preventing Substance Abuse," *Occupational Hazards* (April 2000): 39–41.

88. See, for example, Kathryn Tyler, "Happiness from a Bottle?" *HR Magazine* (May 2002): 30–37.

89. "New Jersey Union Takes On Mandatory Random Drug Tests," *Record (Hackensack, NJ)*, (January 2, 2008).

90. Frank Lockwood et al., "Drug Testing Programs and Their Impact on Workplace Accidents: A Time Series Analysis," *Journal of Individual Employment Rights* 8, no. 4 (2000): 295–306, and Sally Roberts, "Random Drug Testing Can Help Reduce Accidents for Construction Companies; Drug Abuse Blamed for Heightened Risk in the Workplace," *Business Insurance* 40 (October 23, 2006): 6.

91. William Corinth, "Pre-Employment Drug Testing," *Occupational Hazards* (July 2002): 56.

92. Diane Cadrain, "Are Your Employees' Drug Tests Accurate?" *HR Magazine* (January 2003): pp. 41–45.

93. Salluy Roberts, op. cit., 6.

94. "Alcohol Misuse Prevention Programs: Department of Transportation Final Rules," *BNA Bulletin to Management* (March 24, 1994): 1–8. See also http://www.dol.gov/elaws/drugfree.htm and http://www.dot.gov/ost/dapc/ (both accessed May 26, 2007).

95. "Stress, Depression Cost Employers," *Occupational Hazards* (December 1998): 24. See also Charlene Solomon, "Stressed to the Limit," *Workforce* (September 1999): 48–54; and "To Slash Health-Care Costs, Look to the Company Culture," *Managing Benefits Plans* (December 2004): 1(5).

96. Eric Sundstrom et al., "Office Noise, Satisfaction, and Performance," *Environment and Behavior*, no. 2 (March 1994): 195–222; and "Stress: How to Cope with Life's Challenges," *American Family Physician* 74, no. 8 (October 15, 2006).

97. "Failing to Tackle Stress Could Cost You Dearly," *Personnel Today* (September 12, 2006); "Research Brief: Stress May Accelerate Alzheimer's," *GP* (September 8, 2006): 2.

98. This is quoted from "Drug-Free Workplace: New Federal Requirements," *BNA Bulletin to Management* (February 9, 1989): 1–4. Note that the Drug-Free Workplace Act does not mandate or mention testing employees for illegal drug use. See also http://www.dol.gov/elaws/drugfree.htm, and http://www.dot.gov/ost/dapc/ (this site contains detailed guidelines on urine sampling, who's covered, etc.) (both accessed May 26, 2007).

99. "Few Employers Are Addressing Workplace Stress," *Compensation & Benefits Review* (May/June 2008): 12.

100. See, for example, Elizabeth Bernstein, "When a Coworker Is Stressed Out," *The Wall Street Journal* (August 26, 2008): B1, B2.

101. Karl Albrecht, *Stress and the Manager* (Englewood Cliffs, NJ: Spectrum, 1979). For a discussion of the related symptoms of depression, see James Krohe Jr., "An Epidemic of Depression?" *Across-the-Board* (September 1994): 23–27; and Todd Nighswonger, "Stress Management," *Occupational Hazards* (September 1999): 100.

102. Sabine Sonnentag et al., " 'Did You Have a Nice Evening?' A Day-Level Study on Recovery Experiences, Sleep, and Affect," *Journal of Applied Psychology* 93, no. 3 (2008): 674–84.

103. Catalina Dolar, "Meditation Gives Your Mind Permanent Working Holiday; Relaxation Can Improve Your Business Decisions and Your Overall Health," *Investors Business Daily* (March 24, 2004): 89. See also "Meditation Helps Employees Focus, Relieve Stress," *BNA Bulletin to Management* (February 20, 2007): 63.

104. Madan Mohan Tripathy, "Burnout Stress Syndrome in Managers," *Management and Labor Studies* 27, no. 2 (April 2002): 89–111; Christina Maslach and Michael Leiter, "Early Predictors of Job Burnout and Engagement," *Journal of Applied Psychology* 93, no. 3 (2008): 498–512.

105. Todd Nighswonger, "Depression: The Unseen Safety Risk," *Occupational Hazards* (April 2002): 38–42.

106. Ibid., 40.

107. "Employers Must Move from Awareness to Action in Dealing with Worker Depression," *BNA Bulletin to Management* (April 29, 2004): 137.

108. See, for example, Felix Chima, "Depression and the Workplace: Occupational Social Work Development and Intervention," *Employee Assistance Quarterly* 19, no. 4 (2004): 1–20.

109. Ibid.

110. "Risk of Carpal Tunnel Syndrome Not Linked to Heavy Computer Work, Study Says," *BNA Bulletin to Management* (June 28, 2001): 203.

111. Anne Chambers, "Computervision Syndrome: Relief Is in Sight," *Occupational Hazards* (October 1999): 179–84; and http://www.OSHA.gov/ETOOLS/computerworkstations/index.html (downloaded May 28, 2005).

112. Sondra Lotz Fisher, "Are Your Employees Working Ergosmart?" *Personnel Journal* (December 1996): 91–92. See also http://www.cdc.gov/od/ohs/Ergonomics/compergo.htm (accessed May 26, 2007).

113. Gus Toscano and Janaice Windau, "The Changing Character of Fatal Work Injuries," *Monthly Labor Review* (October 1994): 17. See also Robert Grossman, "Bulletproof Practices," *HR Magazine* (November 2002): 34–42; and Chuck Manilla, "How to Avoid Becoming a Workplace Violence Statistic," *Training & Development* (July 2008): 60–64.

114. Manon Mireille LeBlanc and E. Kevin Kelloway, "Predictors and Outcomes of Workplace Violence and Aggression," *Journal of Applied Psychology* 87, no. 3 (2002): 444–53.

115. Kenneth Diamond, "The Gender-Motivated Violence Act: What Employers Should Know," *Employee Relations Law Journal* 25, no. 4 (Spring 2000): 29–41.

116. Paul Viollis and Doug Kane, "At Risk Terminations: Protecting Employees, Preventing Disaster," *Risk Management Magazine* 52, no. 5 (May 2005): 28–33.

117. "OSHA Addresses Top Homicide Risk," *BNA Bulletin to Management* (May 14, 1998): 148. See also http://www.osha.gov/Publications/osha3148.pdf (accessed May 26, 2007).

118. Jean Thilmany, "In Case of Emergency," *HR Magazine* (November 2007): 79–82; Manilla, op. cit.

119. Scott Douglas and Mark Martinko, "Exploring the Role of Individual Differences in the Prediction of Workplace Aggression," *Journal of Applied Psychology* 86, no. 4 (2001): 554.

120. Dawn Anfuso, "Workplace Violence," *Personnel Journal* (October 1994): 66–77.

121. Feliu, "Workplace Violence and the Duty of Care," 395.

122. Quoted from ibid., p. 395.

123. "Preventing Workplace Violence," *BNA Bulletin to Management* (June 10, 1993): 177. See also Paul Viollis and Doug Kane, "At-Risk Terminations: Protecting Employees, Preventing Disaster," *Risk Management* 52, no. 5 (May 2005): 28(5).

124. Quoted or paraphrased from Younger, "Violence Against Women in the Workplace," 177, and based on recommendations from Chris Hatcher. See also Viollis and Kane, op. cit.

125. Florida recently passed a law giving employees the right to carry guns in cars parked at work. See "Right to Carry Guns in Cars Parked at Work Becomes Loaded Issue in Florida, Elsewhere," *BNA Bulletin to Management* (May 13, 2008): 153.

126. Feliu, "Workplace Violence," 401–402.

127. Donna Rosato, "New Industry Helps Managers Fight Violence," *USA Today* (August 8, 1995): 1.

128. Helen Frank Bensimon, "What to Do About Anger in the Workplace," *Training and Development* 51, no. 9 (September 1997): 28–32. See also Viollis and Kane, op. cit.

129. Shari Caudron, "Target HR," *Workforce* (August 1998): 44–52.

130. Diane Cadrain, "And Stay Out! Using Restraining Orders Can Be an Effective and Proactive Way of Preventing Workplace Violence," *HR Magazine* (August 2002): 83–86.

131. Viollis and Kane, "At-Risk Terminations: Protecting Employees, Preventing Disaster," op. cit., 28–33.

132. Karl Acquino et al., "How Employees Respond to Personal Offense: The Effect of the Blame Attribution, Victim Status, and Offender Status on Revenge and Reconciliation in the Workplace," *Journal of Applied Psychology* 86, no. 1 (2001): 52–59. See also M. Sandy Hershcovis et al., "Predicting Workplace Aggression: A Meta-Analysis," *Journal of Applied Psychology* 92, no. 1 (2007): 228–38.

133. Acquino, op. cit., 57.

134. Eve Tahmincioglu, "Vigilance in the Face of Layoff Rage," *New York Times* (August 1, 2001): C1, C6.

135. This is based on "New Challenges for Health and Safety in the Workplace," *Society for Human Resource Management Workplace Vision*, no. 3 (2003): 2–4. See also "Protecting Chemical Plants from Terrorists: Opposing Views," *Occupational Hazards* (February 2004): 18–20.

136. "Survey Finds Reaction to September 11 Attacks Spurred Companies to Prepare for Disasters," *BNA Bulletin to Management* (November 29, 2005): 377.

137. "Swine Flu Tests Employer Emergency Plan; Experts Urge Communicating Best Practices," *BNA Bulletin to Management* (May 5, 2009): 137–44.

138. Sources of *external* risk include legal/regulatory, political, and business environment (economy, e-business, etc.). *Internal* risks sources include financial, strategic, operational (including safety and security) and integrity (embezzlement, theft, fraud, etc.). William Atkinson, "Enterprise Risk Management at Wal-Mart," http://www.rmmag.com/MGTemplate.cfm?Section=RMMagazine&NavMenuID=128&template=/Magazine/Display Magazines.cfm&MGPreview=1&Volume=50&IssueID=205&AID=2209&ShowArticle=1 (accessed April 1, 2009).

139. Unless otherwise noted, the following is based on Richard Maurer, "Keeping Your Security Program Active," *Occupational Hazards* (March 2003): 49–52.

140. Ibid., 50.

141. Ibid., 50.

142. Della Roberts, "Are You Ready for Biometrics?" *HR Magazine* (March 2003): 95–99.

143. Maurer, "Keeping Your Security Program Alive," 52.

Photo Credits

Chapter 1
Page 1: Andres Rodriguez, Alamy Images Royalty Free; Page 15: Getty Images—Thinkstock; Page 24: Thinkstock

Chapter 2
Page 33: Getty Images—Thinkstock; Page 42: Paul Hakimata, Alamy Images Royalty Free

Chapter 3
Page 65: Jose Pelaez, Alamy Images Royalty Free; Page 67: Bongarts/Getty Images; Page 77: FancyVeerSet15, Alamy Images Royalty Free; Page 87: Getty Images—Thinkstock

Chapter 4
Page 95: Alamy Images Royalty Free; Page 111: Yuri Arcurs, Shutterstock

Chapter 5
Page 123: James Key/REDimages, Alamy Images Royalty Free; Page 128: Mike Powell, Getty Images—Thinkstock; Page 138: Radius Images, Alamy Images Royalty Free; Page 140: Medioimages/Photodisc, Getty Images—Thinkstock

Chapter 6
Page 151: Somos Group 9, Alamy Images Royalty Free; Page 161: Andres Rodriguez, Alamy Images Royalty Free; Page 165: Rayes, Getty Images—Thinkstock

Chapter 7
Page 182: B.A.E. Inc, Alamy Images Royalty Free; Page 192: Vincent Hazat, Alamy Images Royalty Free; Page 195: Digital Vision, Getty Images—Thinkstock

Chapter 8
Page 213: Eric Audras, Alamy Images Royalty Free; Page 223: StockLite, Shutterstock; Page 228: Anna Emilia, Alamy Images Royalty Free

Chapter 9
Page 245: Getty Images—Thinkstock; Page 264: Keith Brofsky, Thinkstock; Page 269: Kablonk RM, Alamy Images Royalty Free; Page 271: Jose Luis Pelaez Inc, Alamy Images Royalty Free

Chapter 10
Page 280: Mel Yates, Alamy Images Royalty Free; Page 299: ImageShop Business D Agency, Alamy Images Royalty Free

Chapter 11
Page 318: Jose Luis Pelaez Inc, Alamy Images Royalty Free; Page 335: Best Pictures, Alamy Images Royalty Free; Page 336: Shoosh, Alamy Images Royalty Free

Chapter 12
Page 348: AVAVA, Shutterstock; Page 354: Hemera Technologies, Thinkstock; Page 366: Eric Audras, Alamy Images Royalty Free

Chapter 13
Page 379: Alamy Images Royalty Free; Page 397: Keith Brofsky, Thinkstock; Page 402: Alamy Images Royalty Free

Chapter 14
Page 414: Adrian Weinbrecht, Alamy Images Royalty Free; Page 427: Stockbyte, Thinkstock; Page 430: FancyVeerSet15, Alamy Images Royalty Free

Chapter 15
Page 448: Ulrich Baumgarten/vario images, Alamy Images Royalty Free; Page 468: Alamy Images Royalty Free

Chapter 16
Page 479: Neal and Molly Jansen, Alamy Images Royalty Free; Page 481: Gaertner, Alamy Images Royalty Free; Page 490: Denkou Business, Alamy Images Royalty Free; Page 495: Brand X Pictures, Thinkstock

Cover
David Madison/Stone/Getty Images

Index

First-line supervisors, 3–4, 6
Fish-bone (causes and effect) diagram, 76, 78
Fisher, Robert, 359
Flat versus tall organizations, 166–167
Forced distribution method, 388, 398
Ford Motor Company, 36, 42, 74, 81–82, 166, 256, 322
FORE (Facts, Opinion, Rules, Experiences), 458
Forecasts and forecasting
    defined, 112
    marketing research, 114
    sales forecasting techniques, 112–113
    supply chain management and, 114
Fortune, 17
Framework Technologies Corp., 324
Freud, Sigmund, 77
Freudenberger, Herbert, 504
Fuel Cell Energy Inc., 4
Functional authority, 162
Functional departmentalization, 154–155
Functional (departmental) strategies, 100

Gantt, Henry, 104
Gantt charts, 104
Gap, the, 18
Gatekeeper, 36
Gates, Henry Louis, Jr., 54
Gender
    career-development issues, 271
    differences in leadership styles, 42
    discipline and, 427
    harassment, 191
    performance appraisal and, 397
    violence in the workplace and, 505
Gender-Motivated Violence Act, 505
Gender-role stereotypes, 22
General Electric (GE), 2, 6, 137, 262, 324–325, 383, 388
General leader, 39, 138
General Mills, 306, 308, 336
General Motors (GM), 102, 156, 157, 262, 263, 354
Generation X, 17
Generation Y (Millennials), 17–18, 38
Genetic Information Non-Discrimination Act of 2008 (GINA), 196, 197
Geographic departmentalization, 154, 156, 157
Geographic scope, 99
Getting to Yes (Fisher, Ury, and Patton), 359
Gladiator, 154
Gladwell, Malcolm, 77
Globalization, 18–19
Goals

See also Plans and planning
    feedback and, 112
    hierarchy of, 98
    importance of, 96
    management by objectives (MBO), 107
    management objectives grid, 107–108
    mission, team, 108–110
    motivational, 110–111, 294, 304
    participative, 111
    SMART, 110, 294, 304, 382
    specifying, 381–382
    support and, 112
    of unions, 450–451
Goal theory of motivation, 291–292, 294
Golden Eagle refinery, 496
Goldman Sachs, 369
Good faith bargaining, 459–460
Google, 108, 233, 248
Graphic rating scale, 383–387, 398
Grievances
    guidelines for handling, 467–468
    procedure for handling, 463–464, 466
    record form for, 465–466
    sources of, 464
Griggs, Wilie, 185–186
Griggs v. *Duke Power Company,* 185–186, 197
Grocery Workers Union, 449
Group cohesiveness, 321–322
Group decision making, 337–339
Group dynamics, 320–322
Group norms, 320
Groupthink, 337–338

Halo effect, 396
Hanks, Tom, 327
Harvard Business Review, 138, 165
Harvard University, 142, 360–361, 430
Hawthorne Studies, 320
Hayward, Tony, 97
Health hazards
    alcohol abuse, 500–501
    asbestos, 500
    burnout, 504
    chemicals, 499
    computer-related problems, 504–505
    depression, 504
    diseases, infectious, 500
    risk management, 508
    security program, 508–509
    stress, 503–504